IMPORTANT

HERE IS YOUR REGISTRATION CODE TO ACCESS MCGRAW-HILL
PREMIUM CONTENT AND MCGRAW-HILL ONLINE RESOURCES

For key premium online resources you need THIS CODE to
gain access. Once the code is entered, you will be able to
use the web resources for the length of your course.

Access is provided only if you have purchased a new book.

If the registration code is missing from this book, the registration
screen on our website, and within your WebCT or Blackboard course
will tell you how to obtain your new code. Your registration code can
be used only once to establish access. It is not transferable.

To gain access to these online resources

1. USE your web browser to go to: **http://www.mhhe.com/quadagno3**

2. CLICK on "First Time User"

3. ENTER the Registration Code printed on the tear-off bookmark on the right

4. After you have entered your registration code, click on "Register"

5. FOLLOW the instructions to setup your personal UserID and Password

6. WRITE your UserID and Password down for future reference. Keep it in a safe place.

If your course is using WebCT or Blackboard, you'll be able to use this code to
access the McGraw-Hill content within your instructor's online course.

To gain access to the McGraw-Hill content in your instructor's WebCT or
Blackboard course simply log into the course with the user ID and Password
provided by your instructor. Enter the registration code exactly as it appears to
the right when prompted by the system. You will only need to use this code the
first time you click on McGraw-Hill content.

These instructions are specifically for student access. Instructors are not
required to register via the above instructions.

The **McGraw-Hill** Companies

Mc Graw Hill Higher Education

0-07-296289-5 T/A QUADAGNO AGING AND THE LIFE COURSE:

AN INTRODUCTION TO SOCIAL GERONTOLOGY, 3/E

Thank you, and welcome to your
McGraw-Hill Online Resources.

REGISTRATION CODE

IGX3-FV3H-8TRX-OTK1-XQ4L

REGISTRATION CODE

The McGraw-Hill Companies
Mc Graw Hill Higher Education

Aging and the Life Course

AN INTRODUCTION TO SOCIAL GERONTOLOGY

Third Edition

Jill Quadagno

Pepper Institute on Aging and Public Policy
Florida State University

Boston   Burr Ridge, IL   Dubuque, IA   Madison, WI   New York
San Francisco   St. Louis   Bangkok   Bogotá   Caracas   Kuala Lumpur
Lisbon   London   Madrid   Mexico City   Milan   Montreal   New Delhi
Santiago   Seoul   Singapore   Sydney   Taipei   Toronto

The McGraw·Hill Companies

Higher Education

AGING AND THE LIFE COURSE: AN INTRODUCTION TO SOCIAL GERONTOLOGY
Published by McGraw-Hill, a business unit of The McGraw-Hill Companies, Inc., 1221 Avenue
of the Americas, New York, NY, 10020. Copyright © 2005, 2002, 1999, by The McGraw-Hill
Companies, Inc. All rights reserved. No part of this publication may be reproduced or distributed
in any form or by any means, or stored in a database or retrieval system, without the prior written
consent of The McGraw-Hill Companies, Inc., including, but not limited to, in any network or
other electronic storage or transmission, or broadcast for distance learning.
Some ancillaries, including electronic and print components, may not be available to customers
outside the United States.

This book is printed on acid-free paper.

3 4 5 6 7 8 9 0 DOC/DOC 0 9 8 7 6 5

ISBN 0-07-287536-4

Publisher: *Phillip A. Butcher*
Senior sponsoring editor: *Carolyn Henderson Meier*
Senior marketing manager: *Daniel M. Loch*
Producer, Media technology: *Jessica Bodie*
Project manager: *Ruth Smith*
Senior production supervisor: *Carol A. Bielski*
Senior designer: *Gino Cieslik*
Associate supplement producer: *Meghan Durko*
Photo research coordinator: *Alexandra Ambrose*
Photo researcher: *Inge King*
Permissions editor: *Marty Granahan*
Cover design: *Gino Cieslik*
Interior design: *Kay Fulton*
Typeface: *10/12 Goudy*
Compositor: *GAC Indianapolis*
Printer: *R.R. Donnelley and Sons Inc.*

Library of Congress Cataloging-in-Publication Data
Quadagno, Jill S.
    Aging and the life course / Jill Quadagno—3rd ed.
        p. cm.
    Includes bibliographical references and index.
    ISBN 0-07-287536-4
    1. Gerontology. I. Title.
    HQ1061.Q33 2005
    305.26—dc22

                                                            2003070601

www.mhhe.com

For Brandon and Francesca

About the Author

Jill Quadagno is Professor of Sociology at Florida State University, where she holds the Mildred and Claude Pepper Eminent Scholar Chair in Social Gerontology. She has been teaching courses on aging for more than 25 years. She received her BA from Pennsylvania State University in 1964, her MA from the University of California at Berkeley in 1966, and her PhD from the University of Kansas in 1976. She also received a Postdoctoral Fellowship from the National Science Foundation to do research at the Cambridge Group for the History of Population and Social Structure in Cambridge, England, in 1979.

In 1992 she received the University Teaching Award from Florida State University and became a Fellow of the Gerontological Society of America. She has also been the recipient of the Distinguished Scholar Award from the Section on Aging of the American Sociological Association and has been awarded a John Simon Guggenheim Fellowship and an American Council of Learned Societies Fellowship. In 1994 she served as Senior Policy Advisor on the President's Bipartisan Commission on Entitlement and Tax Reform. She is the author or co-author of ten books on aging and social policy issues, including *The Transformation of Old Age Security, Social Bonds in Later Life: Aging and Interdependence, States, Labor Markets and the Future of Old Age Policy, From Nursing Homes to Home Care, Ending a Career in the Auto Industry: 30 and Out,* and *The Color of Welfare: How Racism Undermined the War on Poverty.* She served as President of the American Sociological Association from 1997 to 1998. In 2000 she received an Investigator Award in Health Policy Research from the Robert Wood Johnson Foundation to conduct historical research on U.S. health care policy. Her most recent book is *One Nation, Uninsured.* She is also conducting research on assisted living facilities in Florida.

Brief Contents

Contents

Part Two

INTERDISCIPLINARY PERSPECTIVES ON AGING

Part Three
SOCIAL ASPECTS OF AGING

Part Four
MANAGING TRANSITIONS

Part Five
AGING AND SOCIETY

Preface

I taught my first course in Social Gerontology in 1978. Would anyone sign up, I wondered? Why would 18-year-old students be interested in aging? I marched into the classroom and laid out my notes that August day, perspiring from nervousness as much as from the heat. I couldn't help but notice the tall, broad-shouldered guy sitting in the front row. His name, I learned when I called the roll, was Kirby Criswell, an Iowa farm boy transplanted to Kansas to play football. Oh, great luck, I thought, echoing the prejudice college professors sometimes hold against football players. To my surprise, Kirby earned a gentlemanly C+ as well as my abiding affection and respect. I hope his life is going well. He not only laid to rest my stereotype of football players but also taught me why my Social Gerontology classes have filled every semester that I have taught them.

Kirby wrote his required paper on grandparenting, a topic that interested him because of his close relationship to his own grandmother. Much as he loved her, he also witnessed the tensions that arose when she moved in with his parents, into his brother's old bedroom. Aging interested Kirby, as it does most students, because it was so close to his own life. Of course, most college students are not yet worried about growing old themselves. But all young people are members of families, and the dilemmas their parents and grandparents face affect them too. So it's natural that they are drawn to the subject. Then, too, an increasing number of students these days are returning to school after having worked full-time for many years and raised families. These older students have an immediate interest in the topic of aging. The challenge for the instructor is to demonstrate how these personal concerns are linked to larger structural issues, such as how, for example, familial care of the frail elderly is influenced by population aging and by political decisions about the just distribution of societal resources. It was my interest in demonstrating to students how the subject matter of their lives is shaped by larger societal forces that led me to write this text.

Organization

This text is divided into five parts and 17 chapters. The chapters in Part One, "Defining the Field," provide the student with a firm grounding in core methodological and theoretical issues and document key trends in population aging. Part Two, "Interdisciplinary Perspectives on Aging," reflects the fact that social gerontology is an inherently interdisciplinary field. It provides a detailed look at the contributions of history, biology, and psychology to the study of aging.

Part Three, "Social Aspects of Aging," examines changes in social roles, relationships, living arrangements, and health that occur as people age. Although everyone experiences the biological and psychological changes that are inherent in the aging process, the nature of that experience varies widely from person to person. The chapters in Part Four, "Managing Transitions," introduce the social programs that provide income support and health care for the aging and examine key later-life transitions in work, health, and death and dying. Part Five, "Aging and Society," examines aspects of aging at the societal level. The three chapters in this section discuss the economic and political aspects of aging.

Distinctive Chapters

This book includes all the topics typically covered in a social gerontology text and contains three distinctive chapters. One of these is a separate chapter on the life course (Chapter 3, "Life Course Transitions"). I include this topic because of the growing emphasis in the field of social gerontology on the relationship between the quality of life in old age and an individual's cumulative experiences, choices, constraints, and opportunities over the life course.

Another distinctive chapter focuses on the long-term care of the frail elderly (Chapter 10, "Caring for the Frail Elderly"). A substantial body of research on this subject examines the burdens and satisfactions family members experience in caring for their aging kin, the problems associated with nursing home care, and the advantages and disadvantages of various alternative living arrangements. This chapter provides a complete portrait of the range of long-term-care options and of the policy choices facing an aging society. It also includes the fascinating qualitative research on daily life in nursing homes that students find so interesting.

Each semester that I have taught this course, I have found that students were confused by the vast array of social programs for income support, health care, social services, and long-term care in the United States. Most texts scatter explanations of these programs within various chapters. This book includes a separate chapter on the welfare state that explains the differences in how these programs are funded, who is eligible for benefits, what benefits are provided, and the relationship of the programs to each other (Chapter 11, "Old Age and the Welfare State"). It is intended to serve as a ready reference for students as they read about these programs at appropriate points elsewhere in the text.

Pedagogy

Chapter Outline

Each chapter opens with an outline that introduces the student to the topics covered in the chapter.

Looking Ahead Questions

The **Looking Ahead** questions provide students with four or five questions to keep in mind when reading the chapter.

Chapter Opener

Each chapter features a lively introduction to engage students' interest in the subject matter and set the stage for the material that follows.

Key Terms

Key terms and concepts used in the text are highlighted in bold when they are introduced. A list of key terms—with page references—follows at the end of

each chapter. The Glossary at the end of the book provides a definition of each key term used in the text.

Illustrations

Chapters are enlivened by figures, tables, cartoons, and photos that summarize key trends and highlight important issues.

Thematic Boxes

Many instructors have told me they and their students found the boxed discussions timely, informative, and helpful. **An Issue for Public Policy** boxes examine the policy implications of key social issues. **Aging around the World** boxes feature cross-cultural research on aging in other cultures. **Diversity in the Aging Experience** boxes describe variations in how people age in the United States, depending on their gender, race, ethnicity, nationality, and cultural background. Finally, **In Their Own Words** boxes provide first-person accounts of the aging experience.

Looking Back Questions

The questions raised at the beginning of the chapter are answered at the end of the chapter in the **Looking Back** section. These questions and short discussions help students to summarize the main points of each chapter.

Thinking about Aging Questions

A series of thought-provoking questions are designed to stimulate critical thinking and stimulate class discussion.

Exploring the Internet Exercises

The World Wide Web has become an important source of information for students and their instructors. Each chapter concludes with a section called **Exploring the Internet**, which tells students about websites related to the chapter content and provides a series of questions students can answer using materials found on the Internet sites.

This edition has more coverage on geographic, racial, and ethnic diversity in aging. Topics discussed in new boxes include infant and maternal mortality in Afghanistan, life expectancy among the Japanese elderly, elderly Filipino immigrants, and social security systems in Eastern and Central Europe. This edition also provides a lively discussion of current policy issues such as the Enron debacle and its effect on retirement savings, employment problems in the long-term-care industry, voting patterns by age in the 2000 election, and gender differences in access to 401(k) plans. Finally, this edition includes expanded coverage of life course issues including topics such as the effect of childhood obesity on adult health, the effect of parental loss on social networks in later life, and methodological issues in life course research.

Chapter-by-Chapter Changes

The Third Edition has a substantial amount of new text material. All tables, figures, and charts have been updated, and some exciting new topics have been added to every chapter.

Chapter 1 The Field of Social Gerontology
New section on careers in social gerontology
Expanded discussion of successful aging
New discussion of ageism in health care

Chapter 2 Theories of Aging
New research on the activity theory/disengagement theory debate

Chapter 3 Life Course Transitions
New section on methodological issues in life course research
New section on the sequencing of moves in later life
New discussion of the effects of childhood obesity on adult health
New discussion of the effects of childhood parental loss on social networks in later life

Chapter 4 Demography of Aging
New "Aging around the World" box on infant and maternal mortality in Afghanistan
Updated statistics

Chapter 5 Historical Perspectives on Aging
Expanded discussion of living arrangements of the elderly

Chapter 6 Biological Perspectives on Aging
Update on the risks of hormone replacement therapy
Update on driving of older people
New discussion of congestive heart failure

Chapter 7 Psychological Perspectives on Aging
New discussion of depression in the nursing home

New section on learning and information technology
New "In their Own Words" box from novelist Sue Miller's book *The Story of My Father*

Chapter 8 Family Relationships and Support Systems
New section on marital status in later life
Update on Viagra
Expanded discussion of racial and ethnic differences in familial responsibility for the elderly
New section on elder abuse

Chapter 9 Living Arrangements
New section on geographic mobility in later life
Expanded section on assisted living facilities
Updated statistics

Chapter 10 Caring for the Frail Elderly
New section on report cards for measuring the quality of nursing home care
New section on employment problems in the long-term-care industry
New "In Their Own Words" box from John Bailey's *An Elegy for Iris Murdoch*

Chapter 11 Old Age and the Welfare State
New "Aging around the World" box on international variations in health care arrangements for the elderly
Updated statistics

Chapter 12 Work and Retirement
New discussion of phased retirement
Updated statistics on unemployment and labor force participation
New "An Issue for Public Policy" box on extending Medicare to older workers and early retirees

Chapter 13 Health and Health Care
New "In Their Own Words" box on physicians' attitudes toward elderly patients
New "Aging around the World" box on why the Japanese elderly live so long
Expanded section on the risks of smoking

Chapter 14 Dying, Death, and Bereavement
New cross-cultural material on Cambodian and Filipino immigrants
New "In Their Own Words" box on Filipino immigrants to the United States who wish to return home to die
New "An Issue for Public Policy" box on hospice care in nursing homes

Chapter 15 The Economics of Aging

New introduction on Enron and retirement savings
New "Inequality in the Aging Experience" box on the causes of income inequality in later life
New "Aging around the World" box on social security in Central and Eastern Europe
New "Diversity in the Aging Experience" box on sex and 401(k) plans

Chapter 16 Poverty and Inequality

New "In Their Own Words" box on the gendered division of household labor
Updated statistics
New section on income and poverty

Chapter 17 The Politics of Aging

Expanded discussion of the political involvement of the aged
Updated statistics on the 2000 election

Supplements Package

As a full-service publisher of quality educational products, McGraw-Hill does much more than just sell textbooks. The company creates and publishes an extensive array of print, video, and digital supplements for students and instructors. This edition of *Aging and the Life Course* is accompanied by a complete supplements package.

For the Student

- *Making the Grade CD-ROM*—This free electronic study guide packaged with every textbook includes chapter quizzes with feedback indicating why each answer is right or wrong, an Internet guide, a study skills primer, and much more.
- *Online Learning Center Website*—An innovative, text-specific website featuring PowerWeb—online access to articles from the popular and scholarly press, weekly updates, and daily newsfeeds—as well as flash cards that can be used to master vocabulary, quizzes with feedback that students can use to study for exams, and more.

For the Instructor

- *Instructor's Resource CD*—A single CD with an easy-to-use interface providing access to a wide array of important ancillaries:
  - *Instructor's Manual/Testbank*—Includes detailed chapter outlines, key terms, overviews, lecture notes, and a complete testbank.
  - *Computerized Testbank*—Easy-to-use computerized testing program for both Windows and Macintosh computers.
  - *PowerPoint Slides*—Complete, chapter-by-chapter slides shows featuring text, art, and tables.
  - *Online Learning Center Website*—Password-protected access to important instructor support materials and additional resources.
- *Course Management Systems*—Whether you use WebCT, Blackboard, e-College, or another course management system, McGraw-Hill will provide you with a cartridge that enables you either to conduct your course entirely online or to supplement your lectures with online material. If your school does not yet have one of these course management systems, we can provide you with PageOut, an easy-to-use tool that allows you to create your own course Web page and access all material on the Online Learning Center.

Acknowledgments

In the process of writing this text, I have received help from many people. At McGraw-Hill, I am indebted to Patricia Herbst, whose detailed commentary and fine editing vastly improved the book. I also thank Carolyn Henderson Meier, Senior Sociology Editor, Julie Abodeely, Editorial Coordinator, Ruth Smith, Project Manager, and Inge King, who selected excellent photos to complement the text. I also thank Michael Stewart, who helped tremendously with the updating of the Internet materials. For the past three years I have tested the materials in each chapter on the undergraduate students who took my course in Social Gerontology for organization, clarity, and interest. Their comments and ideas have been incorporated into the final version.

Last but not least, I would like to say a special thank you to the following individuals who reviewed the manuscript and whose invaluable suggestions resulted in significant improvements:

Jan AbuShakrah
Portland Community College

Karen Conner
Drake University

Tracy L. Dietz
University of Central Florida

Barbara C. Du Bois
San Diego State University

Jacquelyn A. Feller
University of St. Francis

Susan Schuller Friedman
California State University–Los Angeles

Paige Goodwin
Western Illinois University

Mary Holley
Montclair State University

Rosanne Martorella
William Paterson University

Douglas McConatha
West Chester University

Michael W. Parker
University of Alabama–Birmingham

Lisa Pellerin
Ball State University

Sandra L. Reynolds
University of South Florida

Robert E. L. Roberts
University of California–San Marcos

Jon A. Schlenker
University of Maine at Augusta

Debra Stanley
Miami University

Lynne T. Tomasa
University of Arizona

K. Whisnant Turner
University of North Texas

W. Roy VanOrman
Weber State University

Russell Ward
SUNY–Albany

Shirley A. Waskel
University of Nebraska

Diane Zablotsky
University of North Carolina–Charlotte

Visual Preview

Chapter 3

Life Course Transitions

Chapter Outline

The Life Course Framework
Methodological Issues in Research on the Life Course
  Distinguishing Age, Period, and Cohort Effects
  Cross-sectional Research
  Longitudinal Research
Identifying Life Course Events
  The Timing of Life Course Events
  The Duration of Life Course Events
  In Their Own Words: Time for Myself

The Sequencing of Life Course Events
The Effect of Early Historical Events on Later Life
Course Experiences
Demographic Change and Middle age
Aging around the World: The Effect of Military
Service on Census Veterans of World War II
The Theory of Cumulative Disadvantage
  Gender Inequality over the Life Course
  Racial Inequality over the Life Course
The State and the Life Course
  Diversity in the Aging Experience: Sent Down
  Youth in the Chinese Cultural Revolution

*A*ge norms tell us when we are on time and off time for major life events like getting married, having a child, or retiring.

Looking Ahead

1. How did demographic change create a new phase of the life course called middle age?
2. What are the advantages and disadvantages of cross-sectional and longitudinal research for measuring the course changes?
3. Do people attempt to time the major events in their lives?
4. Can the sequencing of major life events create role conflict?
5. Why do older Americans move over the life course?
6. Can major historical events affect the life course of a whole generation?
7. How can government affect the life course?

t the remarkable age of 50, Betti-Jane Raphael gave birth to her second child. Having a baby at the same time she approached menopause had not been part of her life plan, but she was almost 35 when she met her husband, nearly 40 when she had her first child, a son. Rose was born 10 years

mother at a time when she may need one most. Mostly, however, Betti-Jane is humble for being allowed such blessings at this stage of life (Raphael, 1995).

When people hear of Betti-Jane Raphael's late-life birth, they are surprised and often disappprove.

Three Unique Chapters

Complete coverage of the life course (Chapter 3), long-term care of the frail elderly (Chapter 10), and the welfare state (Chapter 11) help make this the most comprehensive, relevant, and easy to use gerontology book available.

Chapter 10

Caring for the Frail Elderly

Chapter Outline

Family Care
  A Profile of Caregiving
  Gender Differences in Caregiving
  Work and Caregiving
  The Caregiver Burden
  Caregiving and Family Relationships
  In Their Own Words: An Elegy for Iris Murdoch
Home Care
  Home and Community-Based Services
  Diversity in the Aging Experience: Long-Term Care
  of the American Indian Aged

Race, Ethnicity, and Long-Term Care
Private Long-Term Care Insurance
Institutional Care
  The Nursing Home Industry
  Staff Turnover in Long-Term Care
  Access to Nursing Home Care
  An Issue for Public Policy: Staff Levels and Quality
  of Care in Nursing Homes
  Aging around the World: The Rise of Nursing
  Home Chains in Canada
  The Nursing Home as Total Institution

*D*aughters provide most of the care to elderly parents. Here a daughter cares for her mother.

Looking Ahead

1. How does the type of care that family members provide to an elderly relative differ depending on the caregiver's gender?
2. How do the responsibilities of caregiving affect a family member's work and personal life?
3. How does an aged person's need for care affect family relationships?
4. What kind of home and community-based services are available to the frail elderly?
5. Can private long-term-care insurance help families to manage the expense and burden of caregiving?
6. How have government regulations and the rise of for-profit nursing home chains affected the availability and quality of nursing home care?
7. What is life in a nursing home like for the frail elderly?

n Sue Miller's moving novel *The Distinguished Guest*, proud, difficult, and ailing Lily Maynard moves, at the age of 72, into the home of her estranged son, Alan, and his wife, Gaby. The visit revives long-buried family conflicts. Alan has been surprised by his reactions to his mother—surprised and discomfited. He has never pretended to have an intimate or easy relationship with her, but he would have said they had come to some childhraun between themselves.

One night at dinner, tensions boil to the surface when Lily casually remarks, "there's no surer or shorter route to heartbreak than having high expectations for your children" (Miller, 1995:152).

Because of the tensions between Alan and Lily, Gaby has taken on the task of getting her mother-in-law ready for bed each night. "She has surprised herself with the tenderness she sometimes feels for Lily as she performs this service." One evening as Gaby kneels down to untie and remove Lily's shoes,

427

Chapter 11

Old Age and the Welfare State

Chapter Outline

Social Programs of the Welfare State
  Social Assistance
  Social Insurance
  Fiscal Welfare
The Organization of the American Welfare State
  Income Support
  Health Care
  In Their Own Words: Health Care before Medicare
  An Issue for Public Policy: Extending Medicare to
  Older Workers and Early Retirees

Support for the Disabled
Long-Term Care
Social Services
Aging around the World: International Variations
in Health Care Arrangements for the Elderly
Diversity in the Aging Experience: The Use of
Community Long-Term Care Services among
Elderly Korean Americans
The Age versus Need Debate

*M*iss Ida Fuller was the first person to receive Social Security benefits in 1940.

Looking Ahead

1. What kinds of welfare programs are available to aging Americans?
2. What are the government-sponsored sources of income support for the aging?
3. What government health care programs serve the elderly?
4. Which government programs protect the disabled?
5. How is long-term care of the elderly financed in the United States?
6. What social services does the Older Americans Act provide?

ax Cross, age 55, proudly touts his conservative principles. He believes that government is too big and supports politicians who propose cutting wasteful government spending. Yet even while he gripes, his 80-year-old parents receive over $1,600 a month in Social Security benefits, his disabled 49-year-old sister receives Disability Insurance benefits of $1,000 a month, and Max himself gets to deduct more than $20,000 a year off his taxes from the interest payments he makes on the mortgage of his comfortable home in the suburbs and another $10,300 from his contributions to his pension fund.

at the insurance company where he works. When he retires in seven years, he will have ample pension savings and generous Social Security benefits. Like many Americans, Max fails to recognize that he is one of the beneficiaries of big government.

Underlying all public debates about the future of Social Security and Medicare, the quality of health care, and generational equity is the issue of the role of government.

In this chapter, we describe the elaborate network of social programs provided by the government, and we consider their impact on the lives

255

Diversity in the Aging Experience

GENDER AND THE DOUBLE STANDARD OF AGING

The form ageism takes tends to differ by gender. In our society, women are more likely to be evaluated according to their sexual attractiveness, whereas men are more likely to be evaluated by their occupational success. Thus for women, avoiding age discrimination depends on maintaining a youthful appearance. A man with gray hair and wrinkles may be considered distinguished looking, but a woman is simply thought to be old (Gerike, 1990).

In one study of men and women between the ages of 18 to 80, researchers asked respondents whether they had used any cosmetic techniques to conceal their age, such as dying their hair, using wrinkle cream, or having plastic surgery (Harris, 1994). On every measure, women were more likely than men to use such techniques, especially dying their hair (34 percent of women compared to 6 percent of men) and using wrinkle cream (24 percent of women compared to 1 percent of men). Although equal numbers of men and women indicated they used such techniques out of concern for their appearance, women rated looking younger as more important to them, both personally and on the job, than did men. All subjects found signs of aging significantly less attractive in women than in men (Harris, 1994).

In another study, 354 psychotherapists were asked to rate a "mature, healthy, socially competent" individual on the Bem Sex Role Inventory, a scale designed to measure gender stereotypes. Each therapist was given a different description (young, middle-aged, or old; male or female). The results showed the therapists viewed young and middle-aged men and women as assertive and willing to take risks. In rating older subjects, however, the therapists attributed these characteristics only to men. They viewed older women as less assertive and less willing to take risks than men. These stereotypes could have consequences for the course of therapy, for therapists might perceive assertive older women as aberrant or abnormal (Turner and Turner, 1991).

While the double standard of aging is clearly detrimental to older women, stereotypes of men as independent and self-reliant may also harm older men. Aged widowers receive less help and less emotional support from family and friends than do widows, perhaps because of this stereotype (Moyers, 1993).

What Do You Think?

1. Has anyone you know ever resorted to expensive cosmetic treatments such as plastic surgery to conceal the signs of aging? If so, was that person a man or a woman?

2. Over the past few decades, women have made great strides toward equality in educational achievement and career advancement. Why do they still suffer from a double standard as concerns appearance?

Diversity in Aging

Expanded emphasis on geographic, racial, and ethnic diversity underscores important contrasts not only within the United States, but internationally as well.

An Issue for Public Policy

THE MEDICARE HMO CRISIS

A few years ago, HMOs seemed to provide a solution to rising Medicare costs, but recent events cast doubt on that possibility. In 1998 and 1999, HMOs withdrew from Medicare programs in more than 400 towns and cities in 33 states, directly affecting over 734,000 beneficiaries. Then in 2000, HMOs dropped another 900,000 elderly and disabled beneficiaries—nearly one-sixth of all Medicare recipients enrolled in HMO programs.

Why are HMOs dropping their elderly clients? According to representatives of the HMOs, the $6,876 a year the government paid HMOs in 1999 was not enough to cover the expense of treating the elderly. Put more simply, HMOs lose money on Medicare.

Medicare beneficiaries who are dropped by an HMO have the option of enrolling in another managed care plan if one exists in their area, or of turning to a fee-for-service program. For many older people, a fee-for-service program means going up prescription drug benefits and other services that HMOs typically provide (Health Care Financing Administration, 2000a). Prescription drugs can be enormously expensive, averaging $596 a month in 2003. Some older people don't take the medicines their doctors prescribe because they can't afford to pay for them. Currently, nearly 60 percent of Medicare beneficiaries have prescription drug coverage (Kaiser Family Foundation, 2003).

What Do You Think?

1. Do you have an elderly relative who has trouble paying for prescription drugs? If so, has he or she ever gone without medicine or other necessities as a result of the high cost of drugs?

2. If you were a government policymaker, how would you solve the HMO crisis?

could no longer afford to provide health care benefits for its 750 retirees. Retirees and their families were informed that they would lose their coverage on September 1. For decades Pabst had provided fully paid health insurance benefits and prescription drug coverage to former employees like Roman Makarewicz, a 74-year-old retiree, who had worked for Pabst for 42 years. Plagued by high blood pressure, arthritis in his knees so severe that he could hardly walk, Roman would have to pay $112 a month for his medications alone. He felt as though he had been stabbed in the back. Eighty-year-old Leon Rafelitis, who had retired after 34 years with Pabst, also worried about the loss of his wife's prescription drugs. Hopelessly, he asked, "What are you going to do when they start changing the rules? A little guy can't do anything" (Causey, 1996:1).

329

Up-to-the-Minute Coverage

New coverage of ageism in health care, the effects of childhood obesity on adult health, the effects of the Enron debacle on retirement savings, the risks of hormone replacement therapy, assisted living facilities, phased retirement, and much more keeps the book current and meaningful for today's students.

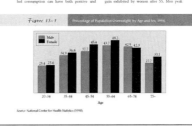

Chapter 13 · Health and Health Care 319

exercise compared to only 138 minutes per week for the control group. Over the eight years of the study, the mortality rate was only 1.5 percent among members of the runners' club, compared to 7 percent among the control group. The gap in disability levels rested at the beginning of the study between the runners' club members and control group continued to widen. Those who no longer belonged to the runners' club but exercised vigorously maintained the same level of fitness as those who continued to run (Fries et al., 1994).

Even moderate exercise can reduce the risk of disease. Scientists monitored a group of men aged 71 to 93 for two years, recording the number of miles they walked each day. They found that men who walked less than a quarter mile a day had a 52 percent increased risk of coronary heart disease compared to men who walked at least one and a half miles a day. The farther the men walked, the less likely they were to develop coronary heart disease (Hakim et al., 1999). The lesson is simple: Leading an active life protects against decline in old age.

The effect of alcohol consumption Alcohol consumption can have both positive and negative effects on health and longevity. Heavy drinkers, defined as people who consume 14 or more drinks per week, are more likely to suffer from cirrhosis of the liver, certain cancers, and hypertension, among other diseases. However, people who drink an occasional glass of wine with dinner actually have a lower risk of mortality than nondrinkers, mainly because moderate alcohol consumption appears to protect against heart disease (Klatsky and Friedman, 1995). In one study, moderate alcohol consumption also decreased the risk of a stroke. Men and women with an average age of 70 who were moderate drinkers or who abstained from alcohol were significantly less likely than heavy drinkers to have a stroke (Sacco et al., 1999).

The effect of diet Being overweight is another factor that increases the risk of disability. People who are obese are at risk of heart disease, diabetes, and joint problems, especially as they get older. Figure 13–1 shows patterns of weight gain over the life course. The percentage of women who are overweight peaks at ages 55 to 64 and then declines. Menopause may be one factor in the weight gain exhibited by women after 55. Men peak

Figure 13–1 Percentage of Population Overweight, by Age and Sex, 1994.

Source: National Center for Health Statistics (1998).

Diversity in the Aging Experience

GENDER AND THE DOUBLE STANDARD OF AGING

In Their Own Words

Living with Osteoporosis

Thematic Box Program

Boxed sections focusing on public policy issues, cross-cultural research, and diversity enhance every chapter and bring material to life, as do unique first-person accounts of the aging experience.

An Issue for Public Policy

WILL THE BABY BOOMERS CONSUME THE FEDERAL BUDGET?

Aging around the World

CROSS-CULTURAL VARIATION IN THE TREATMENT OF THE AGED

Chapter-Opening Previews

Detailed chapter-opening outlines and objectives as well as interesting vignettes draw students in and help them focus on the chapter's most critical concepts.

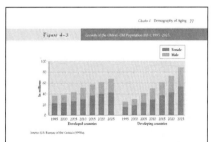

Plentiful Visuals

Updated figures, tables, and charts highlight important concepts, research, and data.

Easy-to-Use Chapter Reviews

Clear, concise chapter summaries, key terms lists, review questions, and Internet activities provide students with essential study materials.

Free *Making the Grade* Electronic Study Guide

A CD-ROM packaged free with every text can help students study for and improve their grades on exams.

- **Chapter-by-Chapter Quizzes**
  Multiple-choice quizzes with feedback explaining why responses are right or wrong help students master material.

- **And More...**
  In addition to 17 separate quizzes, the electronic study guide includes such important resources as an Internet guide, a study skills primer, and more.

Aging and the Life Course — Jill Quadagno — Third Edition
Online Learning Center with POWERWEB
Student Edition

Multiple Choice
(See related pages)

The first practitioners of social gerontology were
- A) sociologists.
- B) developmental psychologists.
- C) psychiatrists.
- D) biologists.

The most controversial aspect of disengagement theory was the idea that disengagement was
- A) unusual.
- B) pathological.
- C) universal.
- D) present in American culture only.

Continuity theory emphasizes that _____ plays a major role in adjustment to aging and that adult development is a continuous process.
- A) personality
- B) health
- C) social status
- D) gender

_____ theory disappeared from the research agenda until recently. Now as older people have become involved in interest groups, questions have arisen about their group identity.
- A) Exchange
- B) Disengagement
- C) Continuity
- D) Subculture

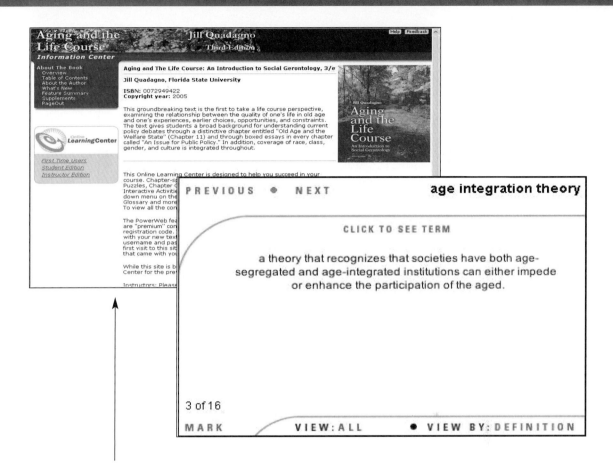

Online Learning Center Website

Unique, book-specific website features online access to a wealth of popular press and scholarly articles, flashcards that can be used to master vocabulary, quizzes, and many other chapter review tools.

DEFINING THE FIELD

ocial gerontology is the study of the social aspects of aging. Among the topics of interest to social gerontologists are family relationships, health, economics, retirement, widowhood, and care of the frail elderly. The chapters in Part One provide a firm grounding in the core issues and key trends in the discipline.

Chapter 1 discusses age discrimination as a historical problem and describes contemporary patterns of ageism. It also describes the range of methodological approaches used in the study of aging.

Chapter 2 introduces the major theories of aging. The chapter illustrates how each theory is influenced by the social, economic, and political context of the particular historical era in which it was formulated.

Chapter 3 discusses the concept of the life course and describes various life course transitions that occur as people move into and out of various roles associated with the family and the workplace.

Chapter 4 introduces the fundamental issues of the demography of aging, the study of the basic population processes of fertility, mortality, and migration. The chapter also describes the aged population in the United States in regard to marital status, income, education, race and ethnicity, and housing and living arrangements.

Chapter 1

The Field of Social Gerontology

This college graduate exemplifies that notion that successful aging involves an active engagement with life.

Looking Ahead

1. What is social gerontology, and how is it related to the broader field of gerontology?
2. How is old age defined, and what difference does the definition make?
3. What is a cohort, and why are social gerontologists interested in cohorts?
4. What is the life course framework, and how is it useful to gerontologists?
5. What is ageism, and how is it perpetuated?

Over the past half century, rapid increases in life expectancy have made the prospect of living to be 100 years old a reality for more and more people. Would you want to live to be 100? Would society be better if everyone lived to be 100? How would you spend those added years beyond age 65?

If you think about these questions for a few minutes, you will probably conclude that a long life is desirable only if it is a good life. A good life, in turn, means having good health and a meaningful and respected place in society (Callahan, 1997). Few people would want to live to be 100 if they were fully dependent on others for their most basic needs. Nor would they wish to live so long if they were alone, with no love or companionship. Freedom from disease and disability, an intact mental capacity, and an active engagement with life are the attributes of **successful aging** (Rowe and Kahn, 1997).

The first part of this chapter defines gerontology and its subfield social gerontology and describes how the focus of the field has shifted from an emphasis on the problems of old age to the promotion of successful aging. We will examine how social gerontologists approach their subject conceptually, including the special challenges of defining old age and determining whether an observed outcome is actually the result of aging processes. And we will consider the methods researchers use to meet those challenges. Next, we will see how research findings can help to dispel misconceptions about aging, which often form the basis for discrimination against older people. The chapter closes with a consideration of the practical contributions of research on aging in a changing political climate.

THE FIELD OF GERONTOLOGY

Defining the Terms

Gerontology is the scientific study of the biological, psychological, and social aspects of aging. The field originated late in the nineteenth century, with the new science of **senescence.** The term *gerontology* was coined in 1904 by the immunologist Elie Metchnikoff. During the 1930s the study of gerontology expanded to include the social as well as the biological aspects of aging (Cole, 1992). In 1938 the first interdisciplinary research in social gerontology (Achenbaum, 1996) was published in the book *Problems of Aging,* edited by Edmund Vincent Cowdry.

Social gerontology is a subfield of gerontology. Social gerontologists are concerned mainly with the social, as opposed to the physical or biological, aspects of aging. Among the topics of interest to social gerontologists are family relationships, health, economics, retirement, widowhood, and care of the frail elderly. Social gerontologists not only draw on research from all the social sciences—sociology, psychology, economics, and political science—they also seek to understand how the biological processes of aging influence the social aspects of aging. The research findings generated by social gerontologists are used in the applied disciplines of social work, public administration, urban and regional planning, and many others to help professionals design and implement programs and policies for aging people in an aging society.

Successful Aging

While early studies tended to focus on the crisis of growing old, social gerontologists now recognize that successful aging depends not just on the prevention of disease and disability, but also on the attainment of peak physical and psychological functioning and participation in rewarding social and productive activities. Instead of taking a negative approach to the problems of aging, social gerontologists are now investigating the factors that create a healthy, fulfilling life in old age (Rowe and Kahn, 1998).

Several factors are associated with successful aging. Successful aging is achieved by setting goals and then working to achieve those goals and by participating in meaningful activities (Holahan and Chapman, 2002). Although one might expect that people in poor health would not score high on measures of well-being, one study of 867 people aged 65 to 99 found that many people with chronic health problems still rated themselves as aging successfully (Strawbridge, Wallhagen, and Cohen, 2002).

Successful aging involves both the individual and society. What should individuals do or avoid doing to age successfully? What social policies and arrangements should society implement to help aging individuals reach their maximum level of functioning? Are certain settings and lifestyles more conducive to healthy aging than others? The "Aging around the World" feature describes some compelling research linking social arrangements on Israeli kibbutz to successful aging.

CONCEPTUAL ISSUES IN RESEARCH ON AGING

In studying aging and the life course, social gerontologists are confronted with the same challenges posed by all social science researchers. They must define the population to be studied, select the appropriate research method (which may be either qualitative or quantitative), determine that their research instruments are accurate, and perform an analysis of the data. Defining the subject matter may seem to be the least complex issue, but we shall see in the following section that old age may be defined in at least four different ways.

Defining Old Age

When is someone old? Although the question sounds simple, definitions of aging and old age vary

Successful Aging on the Israeli Kibbutz

*W*hat is the secret to a long and happy life? The kibbutz communities in Israel seem to have found the answer. In these Jewish communes, organized around the principles of social solidarity, shared values, mutual dependence and joint decision making, all members have equal standing, regardless of their age, strength, position, or status. The kibbutz takes responsibility for their lifelong health, material standard of living, and psychological well-being. Members of the kibbutzim give according to their ability and receive according to their needs.

The kibbutzim were established by young pioneer families shortly after the founding of Israel in 1949. Until the mid-1960s, only a small fraction of the residents reached the age of 65. Since the 1980s, however, the kibbutz population has been aging rapidly. Currently more very old Israelis live in the kibbutzim than in the general population. Despite the challenges of an aging population and the lack of preparedness for them, the kibbutzim have proved to be a good place for Israelis to grow old.

Indeed, the aged who currently reside in the 270 Israeli kibbutzim are living proof that societies can provide social arrangements that promote successful aging. First, residents of the kibbutz have more stability in their lives than most older people. The average elderly resident joined the kibbutz at age 29 or 30 and has lived in the same place for more than 40 years. Few older people ever leave the kibbutz. There they are assured of the security of continuous relationships with family and friends, within a community that they know well and that understands their needs and wishes. More than two-thirds of elderly kibbutz residents have at least one adult son or daughter who lives on the same kibbutz. Most not only share birthdays, holidays, and other symbolic life passages with their children and grandchildren, but see their children and grandchildren on a daily basis.

There is no such thing as compulsory retirement on the kibbutz. As people grow old, they gradually reduce the number of hours they work, but continue to serve as part of the workforce as long as they are physically and mentally able. Fully 79 percent of the men and women aged 65 and older who reside in a kibbutz hold jobs, compared to only 18 percent of Israeli men and 6 percent of Israeli women who live outside the kibbutz.

Nor do older kibbutz residents experience the decline in living standards that frequently accompanies retirement. Kibbutz society fulfills the needs of all members, regardless of their contribution. Even the most feeble member enjoys the same standard of living as the most productive worker.

For all these reasons, life expectancy is considerably higher among the aged on the kibbutz than among the aged in the general population. On average, kibbutz members live three years longer, and enjoy better health and higher life satisfaction, than other Israelis.

What Do You Think?

1. Would you like to live in a kibbutz with your parents and grandparents? Why or why not?
2. What can we in the United States learn from the experience of the kibbutzim?

Source: Leviatan (1999).

widely. In studying older people and individual aging processes, researchers need some marker of age. The choice they make often depends on the nature of the issue under investigation rather than on some abstract conception of old age.

Chronological age   One commonly used marker of old age is **chronological age.** Although often useful for making clear decisions about whom to include as subjects in a study, chronological age can also be an arbitrary marker. For example, in the United States 65 is the age that is most often considered old, because that is when people have become eligible for full Social Security benefits and Medicare. The eligibility age for Social Security benefits will gradually rise to 67. Does this mean old age will then be viewed as beginning at 67? Anyone 50 or older can join the American Association of Retired Persons (AARP), the largest senior citizen organization in the United States. Why isn't 50 considered old?

Chronological age also can be a poor indicator of old age, because some people may be "old" at 50, whereas others may seem "young" at 80. Think of former senator Bob Dole. At age 74 he was the leader of the Senate and a candidate for president in the 1996 election.

Finally, the use of chronological age is problematic because it lumps together people of widely varying generations into a single category. A 65-year-old has as much in common with an 85-year-old in terms of interests and life experiences as the average 20-year-old has in common with a 40-year-old. Why should they both be considered old? Because of these problems, even when chronological age is used as a marker of old age, social gerontologists often divide older people into three subcategories. The **young–old** are people 65 to 74, the **middle–old** are those 75 to 84, and the **oldest–old** are those 85 or older.

Social roles and age   Since chronological age may be an inappropriate indicator of old age for some types of research, social gerontologists sometimes define people as old according to the **social roles** they play. Social roles are sets of expectations or guidelines for people who occupy given positions, such as widow, grandfather, or retiree.

Yet playing a role associated with a social position one typically assumes in old age doesn't mean an individual is old. Some people work at jobs that allow them to retire after a certain number of years of employment. An autoworker, for example, can retire after 30 years. If a young person began working in a factory right out of high school at age 18, he or she would be eligible to retire at 48. Military personnel can retire after 20 years. Widowhood is most likely to occur after age 60, but Jacqueline Kennedy was a widow at 33. The same is true of grandparenting. A woman who had a baby in her teens may become a grandparent in her 30s. But being a grandparent, regardless of one's age, can make a person feel older.

Functional age   A third criterion for determining old age is **functional age.** Definitions of functional age are based on how people look and what they can do. In functional terms, a person becomes old when he or she can no longer perform the major roles of adulthood. Among the Inuit Eskimos, for example, a man becomes old at around 50 when he can no longer hunt during the winter. Women become old about a decade later because the roles they perform are less physically strenuous. Among the Black Carib of Belize, menopause is the marker of old age for women. Thus, a woman may be old at 50, but a man still may be considered middle-aged at 60 (Kerns, 1980).

Functional age also may be measured by such normal physical changes as stiffness of joints, diminished short-term memory, reduced skin elasticity, and diminished aerobic capacity (Schneider, 1983). People not only age in different ways and at different speeds, but different parts of the same person may age at different rates as well. A physically fit marathon runner might have a severe hearing loss. A 54-year-old man might be able to run longer (though probably not faster) than his 23-year-old son.

Finally, functional age may be determined by appearance. Gray hair and wrinkles are physical features we associate with old age. Yet in today's world, hair dye and face-lifts can alter appearances so dramatically that the normal signs of physical aging can be largely obscured. For these reasons, functional criteria may be misleading.

To better classify people by their functional capacities, gerontologists have devised three categories: "well," "somewhat impaired," and "frail." The **well elderly** are people who are healthy and active. They are involved in social and leisure activities and are often employed or busy with volunteer work. They carry out family responsibilities and are fully engaged in the life of the community. The **somewhat impaired elderly** are those in a transitional stage. They are beginning to experience chronic ailments and need some assistance from family or community service agencies. Although they can participate in many aspects of life, they may need support in transportation, shopping, cleaning, or personal care. Finally, there are the **frail elderly.** They show some mental or physical deterioration and depend on others for carrying out their daily activities. They need more care from family members and may be in institutions (Association for Gerontology in Higher Education, 1996).

Subjective age Some of the limitations associated with functional aging can be compensated for easily. A person can make lists of things to do, wear bifocal glasses, and exercise regularly. People who are successful in compensating for functional limitations are able to maintain a **subjective age identity** of themselves as young. This is in keeping with folk wisdom, which says you're as young as you feel. Sometimes a change in chronological age or functional age can alter an individual's subjective age identity. As one woman explained:

When I turned 50, I kept being perplexed because I knew I was 50 and I looked in the mirror and saw somebody with gray hair, but my picture of myself was, I think, more of somebody still getting her training and education. . . . My inner picture is quite different than my chronological age. But I think it's shifting. (Karp, 1991:72)

One study of subjective age identity among older men and women found that two-thirds of those between 60 and 70 defined themselves as "young" or "middle-aged." So did 26 percent of those older than 80! Defining oneself as old may occur gradually as age-linked changes accumulate—reaching 65, retiring, becoming widowed, seeing the gray hair

Navajo elder holding medicine basket containing sacred objects as she greets the morning sun.

and wrinkles spread (Neugarten, 1977). The most important factors in subjective age identity, however, are activity level and health. Older people who do define themselves as old can often pinpoint a particular incident (e.g., a heart attack or a hip fracture after a fall) that made them feel old. The health problems need not be dramatic. Tiring more easily or feeling stiff upon awakening in the morning can make a person recognize that he or she is aging.

Subjective age identity also appears to be influenced by social class. Compared to their wealthier counterparts, people of lower socioeconomic status view the onset of old age as occurring at a younger age. They are more likely to classify themselves as "old" or "elderly" and more likely to feel older than their chronological age. The main reason for these perceptions, however, is that they have more pessimistic feelings about their health (Barrett 2003). Health is the most important factor in determining subjective age identity.

Why is health such an important aspect of subjective age identity? Personal identity is closely linked to body image and appearance, and health can affect both of these. Poor health can also reduce someone's ability to participate in activities he or she enjoys and constrict his or her lifestyle. In fact, being unable to pursue normal interests is a major factor in the shift in age identification.

Regardless of what definition of age a person chooses, tremendous variability exists from individual to individual. The point is not that it is impossible to define old age but rather that the definition social gerontologists use depends on what they want to know.

Once social gerontologists have established how they are going to identify their subject matter, they must then decide how to interpret their research findings. One of the most complex issues they face is distinguishing *age changes* from *age differences*.

Cohorts and Generations

Age changes occur in individuals over time, whereas age differences are ways one age group differs from another. It is often difficult to tell whether an observed outcome is due to an age change in individuals or to an age difference between groups. To help identify age differences, social gerontologists use the concept of a **cohort.** A cohort is the "aggregate of individuals who experienced the same event within the same time interval" (Ryder, 1965:845). Most studies use age cohorts, defined as all individuals born into a population during a specific time period (Uhlenberg and Miner, 1996). But a cohort also can consist of people who enter a particular system at the same time. All college freshmen, for example, regardless of their ages, represent a cohort (Riley, 1995). Youth appears to be an impressionable period of the life course compared to other ages. When older people are asked to recall memorable periods in their lives, they often describe experiences from their adolescence or from early adulthood. What is your most memorable experience? Do you believe that youthful memories are most salient? The process of **cohort aging** "is the continuous advancement of a cohort from one age category to

another over its life span" (Uhlenberg and Miner, 1996:208). When the last member of that birth cohort dies, it is extinguished.

Sometimes the terms *cohort* and **generation** are used interchangeably. Usually, however, social scientists reserve the term *generation* for studies of family processes. In this sense, then, generation refers to kinship linkages. For example, a four-generation study would typically include great-grandparents, grandparents, children, and grandchildren (Bengtson, Rosenthal, and Burton, 1990).

There are many forces that create cohort differences in aging. They include the composition of a cohort as well as the interplay between human lives and large-scale social change. Foremost among these forces is the fact that each cohort lives through its own slice of history.

Historical change   People may be classified as belonging to a cohort according to historical eras. Differences in the year of birth expose people to different historical worlds with varying opportunities and constraints (Elder, 1994). The impact of history on a cohort was captured by the prominent sociologist Everett Hughes (1971), who wrote, "Some people come to the age of work when there is no work, others when there are wars. . . . Such joining of a man's life with events, large and small, are his unique career, and give him many of his personal problems" (p. 48). We call the distinctive experiences that members of a birth cohort share and that shapes them throughout their lives a **cohort effect** (see Chapter 3). For example, people who grew up during the Great Depression of the 1930s may be more cautious about spending money than people who grew up during the 1990s.

We can identify five distinct birth cohorts in the twentieth century. The oldest, born between 1900 and 1926, are called the "swing generation." Next comes the "silent generation," born between 1927 and 1945. The biggest cohort, the "baby boomers," includes all those who were born between 1946 and 1964. They were followed by the "baby bust cohort," born between 1965 and 1976. The most recent cohort is made up of the 72 million "echo boomers." They are the children of the baby boomers who were born between

1977 and 1994. The oldest echo boomers have just recently completed their education and entered the workplace. The youngest are still in grammar school. We have much to learn about how changing historical events will shape these children of the computer age.

How different were the formative years of the silent generation from those of the baby boom generation? John Clausen (1993) described what life was like in the 1920s and 1930s:

Automobiles were just becoming common on the streets. . . . Radios began to appear. . . . Women's hair was bobbed and sexual mores flouted in the flapper age as skirts went up and inhibitions went down. . . . Then came the stock market crash of 1929 and the most prolonged economic depression the country had ever experienced. (p. 9)

The silent generation grew up during the Depression, and those early experiences made an indelible imprint on their lives in the context of lost opportunities for education and employment. Many of the stereotypes we hold about the aged as having little money or being in poor health derive from the real deprivation experienced by the silent generation. Many members of this generation made great sacrifices in World War II. In "In Their Own Words" (see p. 10) a World War II veteran describes how his military training and discipline helped him meet the challenges of civilian life.

As the baby boomers came of age, their lives were forever transformed by the civil rights movement, the women's liberation movement, and the anti–Vietnam War movement, which uprooted traditional social institutions and social norms. Arlene Skolnick (1991) described the 1960s:

[B]etween 1965 and 1975 the land of togetherness became the land of swinging singles, open marriages, creative divorce, encounter groups, alternative lifestyles, women's liberation, the Woodstock nation, and the "greening of America." A land where teenage girls wore girdles even to gym class became a land of miniskirts, bralessness, topless bathing suits, and nude beaches. (p. 4)

Now that the first baby boomers have turned 50, they provide gerontologists with a large sample that can be studied to determine how these early experiences will shape their lives as they grow old.

Compositional differences   Another aspect that distinguishes one cohort from another is its composition and character. Cohorts vary in their racial, gender, and ethnic composition. For example, the cohort born in 1910 consists of many immigrants of Eastern European ancestry, whereas the cohort born in 1970 consists of many immigrants of Hispanic ancestry. Cohorts also differ in demographic factors such as average family size, average age at marriage, and life expectancy.

Size is an especially distinctive characteristic of cohorts. As already noted, the baby boom cohort was much larger than the cohort born during the Great Depression. As the baby boomers grew up, they were confronted with an environment more competitive than the environment their parents encountered—too few places in school, too few entry-level jobs, too few homes to live in. The United States has felt the impact of the baby boomers at every stage of the life course and will continue to do so as they age. As social gerontologist Charles Longino (1994) explained:

Despite their competitive struggle for education, jobs, and housing, boomers have always had political clout. When they turned 18, they got the vote. Boomers stopped the Vietnam War, relaunched the feminist movement, celebrated the first Earth Day, and raised the drinking age before their kids became teenagers. In 2010 the baby boom will demand changes in long-term-care policy. They will want better support in their old age, and they will have it. (p. 42)

Structural changes   People grow old within a cultural context comprised of social institutions, which are sets of roles and rules that define an enduring social unit. Examples of social institutions include the family, the educational system, and the workplace. Institutional change affects the experiences of each cohort in different ways. For example, in the past, older people who could no longer work had to rely on the family, the church, or the local community for support. Then, during the twentieth century, the provision of economic support for the elderly was transformed. Now most older people

In Their Own Words

The Greatest Generation Speaks

*T*om Brokaw, *NBC Nightly News* anchor, calls them "the greatest generation." They are the men and women who came out of the Great Depression, who made lasting sacrifices for the nation in World War II, who built the world we live in today. Philip Cochran, who served as a Marine during the war, recalls his military service with gratitude for the sense of purpose it has instilled in his life:

> Before the war, as the third boy in a family of three boys and three girls, puny and underweight, with two athletically talented older brothers, I had a strong inferiority complex. Indeed, one of my motivations in trying to join the Marine Corps, the rough and tough foot soldiers, was to prove to my Dad that I was as good as my older brothers. Becoming a Marine, graduating tenth in my class at Quantico out of 320, serving the Corps honorably and retiring as a Major gave me a high sense of self-worth . . . [N]ot an ego trip, but just

feeling good about myself, which the Marine Corps gave me, has been a source of strength and well-being throughout my life.

> I returned to civilian life in 1946 with a feeling of great debt for having been spared injury or disabling illness, with a resulting heavy sense of obligation to my family, my community, and my country. Without question this sense of obligation motivated me significantly in striving to repay the debt I believed I owed. As a consequence I have had a lifetime of devotion to community service.

> With all these positive impacts on my life since the war, not for an instant could I think that my service in World War II represented a sacrifice. To the contrary, my life gained so much from these experiences. I returned way ahead of the game, and I'm still ahead. I owe so much to my experiences during the war and to the United States Marine Corp.

Source: Brokaw (1999:171).

receive monthly Social Security benefits, which not only provide greater income stability but also increase their independence.

Throughout the life course, a cohort is linked to other cohorts through bonds of family and kinship, and the institution of the family is one that is experiencing rapid change. The growth of single-parent households, the expansion of female participation in the labor force, and the high incidence of divorce and remarriage all signify complex changes in the structure of household and kinship relations. In the future there will be an increasing number of "blended families," resulting from multiple marriages and the presence of children from previous

relationships. The increase in the number of step- and half-relatives means a dramatic shift in family structure in coming decades.

Such changes in family structure can be either harmful or beneficial to the elderly. Among elderly women who presently are aged 85 to 89, one-quarter are childless and another quarter have only one surviving child. Over the next 20 years, however, the situation will change rapidly. By 2015, more than two-thirds of very old women will have at least two surviving children (Preston, 1992). That means they will likely have stronger family support. On the other hand, because of the trends previously noted, the aged of the twenty-first century will be more likely than the elderly of the twentieth century to have experienced a divorce or to have been single parents. Thus, family support might be more fragile and the sense of filial obligation weaker than in the past (Uhlenberg and Riley, 1995). If a decline in the intensity of kinship relations erodes the capacity of the family to care for older members, then demands on the government are likely to increase.

Multiple forces shape the aging experience, and these forces change across cohorts. Cohort analysis not only strengthens studies of historical change, but also helps us anticipate directions of future change (Riley, Foner, and Waring, 1988). We already know that as the large baby boom cohort grows old, the demand for health care will rise and the cost of Social Security benefits will increase. Other changes that may be even more momentous may be just over the horizon.

AGEISM

Forms of Ageism

The term **ageism** refers to "a systematic stereotyping of and discrimination against people because they are old, just as racism and sexism accomplish this with skin color and gender" (Butler, 1969:243). In an ageist society, "old people are categorized as senile, rigid in thought and manner, old-fashioned in morality and skills" (Butler, 1969:243). People who hold ageist attitudes don't look at the aged as individuals, but instead judge them as members of a social category (Ferraro, 1992:296).

The term *ageism* actually encompasses two distinct concepts: stereotypes and age discrimination. **Stereotypes** are a composite of ideas and beliefs attributed to people as a group or a social category. They may incorporate some characteristics or attributes that accurately describe some people who belong to the group, but they always fail to capture the diverse qualities of all the individuals in the group. Some older people, for example, may be rigid in thought, but many others are open-minded and interested in exploring new ideas.

How predominant are stereotypes about the aged today? In one study researchers interviewed

240 men and women aged 18 to 85, whom they divided into three age groups: young adult, middle-aged, and elderly adult. Many respondents held stereotypical views. When asked how they would describe the typical elderly adult or what they typically thought or read about the elderly, they listed several traits. The researchers sorted the traits into clusters and classified them as either positive or negative. Positive trait clusters included "Golden Ager," someone who is active, adventurous, healthy, and lively; the "Perfect Grandparent," who is intelligent, knowledgeable, wise, and kind; and the "John Wayne conservative," a patriotic, old-fashioned, and conservative individual. Negative trait clusters included the "Shrew/Curmudgeon," who is greedy, selfish, stubborn, and ill-tempered; the "Recluse," a timid, dependent, and forgetful person; and the "Elitist," a demanding, snobbish, prejudiced man or woman. Although young, middle-aged, and elderly respondents held many of the same stereotypes, older people created more groupings of traits and offered more complex views of the elderly than young adults (Hummert, Garstka, Shaner, and Strahm, 1994). They saw older people more realistically, not as stereotypes.

When people act on the basis of negative stereotypes, they are engaging in **age discrimination.** Like discrimination on the basis of race or gender, age discrimination takes many forms (Butler, 1989). One of the most common occurs in the workplace, when employers refuse to hire older workers. Ageism also occurs in health care. There is substantial evidence that the elderly receive differential treatment from physicians compared to younger elder adults (Robb et al., 2002; Williams, 2000). This differential treatment occurs in areas such as physician–patient interactions, less use of screening procedures, and different treatment of various medical problems. For example, patients with cancer of the rectum have the highest chance of survival if they have surgery and receive chemotherapy. Yet one study found that older patients were less likely than young patients to received both treatments (Dharma-Wardene et al., 2002). It may be that doctors fear that their elderly patients are not fit enough to tolerate both treatments or that they are more likely to develop complications. In another study, researchers found that older patients with heart disease were less likely to be referred for further testing, regardless of the severity of their condition (Bond et al., 2003). Similarly, in the British National Health Service, the elderly are excluded from certain health screening programs and surgical procedures (Arber and Ginn, 1991). See "An Issue for Public Policy" for a discussion of the effectiveness of the federal law against age discrimination.

The New Ageism

In recent decades, ageism has taken a new form. The **new ageism** is a tendency to patronize the elderly and be overly solicitous toward them. Well-meaning people may discourage the elderly from taking risks, dissuade them from exercising, and even deny their sexuality. Steve Scrutton (1990:1) describes his own attitude toward his widowed mother:

My father died in 1979, aged 76. After a period of normal grieving, my mother, who was then 74, decided that she wanted to travel. A journey of about 100 miles . . . alone. My first reaction was that she was to do no such thing. I would go to Norwich and bring her myself. My second reaction was to let her do as she wished. . . . This form of patronizing ageism is common where there is genuine care for aging people.

One study of adjustment to life in a nursing home found that the most vulnerable individuals were those who had lost all control over their own lives. A woman in her 80s described her devastating sense of loss after her children sold her home and belongings without consulting her, so she "wouldn't have to worry about it" (Rubin-Terrado, 1994). In the extreme, paternalistic ageism can be as harmful as neglect.

People with ageist attitudes often view women more harshly than they view men. The "Diversity in the Aging Experience" feature discusses the double standard of aging.

Perpetuating Ageism through the Media

Ageist stereotypes are transmitted in a variety of ways—through the family, in the workplace, be-

tween groups of friends. But most importantly, they are perpetuated by the media, including television, the print media, and film.

Television   In our society, television has become the most powerful source of mass communication. A number of studies of the way the elderly are depicted on television have documented enormous improvements over the past two decades. In the 1970s, few older people appeared on TV, and when they did, the images of them were often unflattering. Especially on prime-time shows, "the elderly (were) shown as more comical, stubborn, eccentric, and foolish than other characters" (Davis and Davis, 1986:46). But by the 1990s shows such as *Judging Amy, West Wing,* and *Providence* were portraying older characters in a positive light. In these shows, the older characters were powerful, affluent, healthy, physically and socially active, quick-witted, and admirable (Bell, 1992). They served as positive though somewhat idealized role models.

Less progress has been made in eliminating ageism from TV advertisements. In one study researchers analyzed how people over 50 were portrayed in television commercials by videotaping the three major networks—ABC, NBC, and CBS—in six-hour blocks on a weekday from 3:00 p.m. to 9:00 p.m. They found that only 11.8 percent of the commercials included people aged 50 or over, and that 71 percent of the people over 50 were male. Furthermore, 42.5 percent of the products advertised in commercials that featured over-50 actors were food products, and 25.9 percent were health and hygiene products. The researchers concluded that older people were underrepresented in commercials and excluded entirely from ads for "glamorous" products, such as automobiles, cosmetics and leisure products (Jenkins and Perkins, 1991). These facts might not have great social significance, but the commercials broadcast on television can affect an individual's self-image, making him or her feel older. One man recalled his surprise when he heard an announcer who was selling insurance inquire, "Do you know someone between fifty and eighty years old?" "My God, he's talking about me," this viewer thought with a sense of shock (Karp, 1991, 72).

An Issue for Public Policy

CAN AGE DISCRIMINATION IN EMPLOYMENT BE ELIMINATED?

Until 1967 age discrimination was rampant in the United States. Newspaper employment ads often stated boldly that no one over 45 or 50 need apply. Workers in their 50s and 60s were often forced to retire. But in 1967, after the passage of other civil rights legislation, Congress adopted the Age Discrimination in Employment Act (ADEA). This federal law prohibited employers from firing or demoting workers between the ages of 40 and 65 or reducing their salaries purely on the basis of their age (Clark, 1990). The new law eliminated mandatory retirement for workers under 65. Later amendments extended the protection against mandatory retirement to age 69 and then eliminated the practice altogether in most occupations. Older workers gained further protection in 1990 when Congress passed the Older Workers Benefit Protection Act, which prohibited employers from treating older employees differently from younger ones during layoffs (Israel and McConnell, 1991; Rumack, 1992).

Although the ADEA has prevented employers from firing many older workers, it has had little effect on hiring. Most of the actions taken to enforce the ADEA involve workers who feel they were terminated unfairly. Yet most age discrimination occurs not when workers are leaving the labor force but when they are being hired. The problem is that proving that age discrimination is the reason why someone was denied a job is difficult. Most people have little information about other job applicants and their qualifications (Shaw, 1996). If they don't get a job they applied for, they assume that they did not interview well or that another applicant had better qualifications. Thus, preventing age discrimination against the current workforce solves only one part of the problem. The greater problem is how to convince employers to treat older job applicants fairly.

Recent court decisions have hampered older workers seeking to sue their employers for age discrimination. Judges have raised the burden of proof and limited the use of certain evidence that is often correlated with age. Courts now allow employers to dismiss an employee simply for drawing too high a salary or accumulating too many pension credits. Furthermore, the cost of litigating claims of age discrimination has more than tripled in the last decade, discouraging many employees from filing claims in court. The United States appears to have far to go before age discrimination in employment is eliminated.

What Do You Think?

1. Has anyone in your family ever been discriminated against because of his or her age? If so, what were the circumstances?
2. Why do you think employers discriminate on the basis of age? Might they be overlooking some advantages of hiring older workers?

Diversity in the Aging Experience

GENDER AND THE DOUBLE STANDARD OF AGING

The form ageism takes tends to differ by gender. In our society, women are more likely to be evaluated according to their sexual attractiveness, whereas men are more likely to be evaluated by their occupational success. Thus for women, avoiding age discrimination depends on maintaining a youthful appearance. A man with gray hair and wrinkles may be considered distinguished looking, but a woman is simply thought to be old (Gerike, 1990).

In one study of men and women between the ages of 18 to 80, researchers asked respondents whether they had used any cosmetic techniques to conceal their age, such as dying their hair, using wrinkle cream, or having plastic surgery (Harris, 1994). On every measure, women were more likely than men to use such techniques, especially dying their hair (34 percent of women compared to 6 percent of men) and using wrinkle cream (24 percent of women compared to 1 percent of men). Although equal numbers of men and women indicated they used such techniques out of concern for their appearance, women rated looking younger as more important to them, both personally and on the job, than men. All subjects found signs of aging significantly less attractive in women than in men (Harris, 1994).

In another study, 554 psychotherapists were asked to rate a "mature, healthy, socially competent" individual on the Bem Sex Role Inventory, a scale designed to measure gender stereotypes. Each therapist was given a different description (young, middle-aged, or old; male or female). The results showed the therapists viewed young and middle-aged men and women as assertive and willing to take risks. In rating older subjects, however, the therapists attributed those characteristics only to *men*. They viewed older women as less assertive and less willing to take risks than men. These stereotypes could have consequences for the course of therapy, for therapists might perceive assertive older women as aberrant or abnormal (Turner and Turner, 1991).

While the double standard of aging is clearly detrimental to older women, stereotypes of men as independent and self-reliant may also harm older men. Aged widowers receive less help and less emotional support from family and friends than do widows, perhaps because of this stereotype (Moyers, 1993).

What Do You Think?

1. Has anyone you know ever resorted to expensive cosmetic treatments such as plastic surgery to conceal the signs of aging? If so, was that person a man or a woman?
2. Over the past few decades, women have made great strides toward equality in educational achievement and career advancement. Why do they still suffer from a double standard as concerns appearance?

Print media   Although some studies of the print media have found that the elderly are more likely than other age groups to be portrayed negatively, others have noted an equal number of positive portrayals, particularly in fiction (Vasil and Wass, 1993). In the 1980s and 1990s, a new literary genre, the midlife progress novel, was invented by such writers as Saul Bellow, Margaret Drabble, Anne Tyler, and John Updike. In these novels middle-aged protagonists freed themselves from a preoccupation with lost youthfulness and discovered the benefits of advancing age (Cole, 1992). In Anne Tyler's novel *Breathing Lessons*, for example, Maggie and Ira Moran, married for 28 years, take a journey to attend the funeral of Maggie's girlhood friend. On the way they take several unexpected detours into the lives of old friends and grown children, raising memories of the past. They discover a great deal about marriage, both the expectations and the disappointments, and get the chance to fall in love all over again.

Another common literary theme is intergenerational relationships (Yahnke, 1994). In Philip Roth's autobiographical novel *Patrimony*, a son's sense of obligation to his aging father generates confusion, ambivalence, and even some hostility in him, as he contends with the unanticipated burdens of caregiving. Roth watches as his father, a man of fierce independence, battles with the brain tumor that will gradually kill him.

In contrast to adult fiction, which presents aging and the aged in realistic and often positive ways, children's books consistently portray the elderly in a stereotypical and negative fashion. One study found that the terms "old, little, and ancient" represented 85 percent of all physical descriptions of elderly characters (Vasil and Wass, 1993). It's not surprising, then, that by about age 8, children hold well-defined negative notions of old age and aging. When asked to describe the aged, they commonly used such terms as "tired," "ugly," "ill," "isolated," and "helpless." One study examined whether increased contact improved children's attitudes toward the elderly. The researchers first tested the children in a fourth-grade class in Chattanooga, Tennessee, on their attitudes toward the aged. Then

they organized eight joint activities with elderly people from a local senior center, including a senior's visit to the children's school, a visit by the children to the senior center, a Christmas party, a sharing session, and a farewell party. After participating in these activities the children voiced more positive attitudes toward the elderly. As one child stated, "They seemed scary because they were different, but now I feel they are just like us" (Aday, Sims, and Evans, 1991:381).

Film   The theme of aging as a journey of self-revelation has also been prominent in films such as *A Trip to Bountiful* and *Driving Miss Daisy*. In some other films, older people play the lead roles, and the plot centers on sympathetic characters dealing with the realities of aging or coping with intergenerational relationships. In *Dad*, a middle-aged man who has put all his energies into his career suddenly finds himself responsible for the care of his aging father. As he adjusts his priorities to incorporate his new responsibilities, he is rewarded with the experience of his supposedly dying father suddenly exhibiting renewed energy and interest in life. In another film, *Grumpy Old Men*, Jack Lemmon and Walter Matthau play two feuding neighbors whose long-standing rivalry escalates when they fall in love with the same woman. This comedy debunks stereotypes of the aged as inactive, disengaged, and uninterested in sex. Finally, *Waking Ned Devine*, a film about what happens in an Irish village when one of its inhabitants wins the lottery, is filled with elderly characters who are passionate about life, committed to their community, inventive, resourceful, and ready to do wild and crazy things (Yahnke, 1999).

In sum, despite an increasing number of realistic portrayals of the elderly in books and films, stereotypes of the aging abound in the media as well as in everyday life. Table 1–1 (see p. 16) lists some common myths about the elderly along with the facts. Research by social gerontologists has helped to dispel such myths and stereotypes and replace them with the facts. Research has shown that while some older people are physically frail and economically deprived, many others are in good

Table 1-1	Stereotypes and Facts about Aging

Stereotype	Fact
Most retirees are lonely and depressed.	Most retirees are busy, active, and satisfied with their lives. (Chapter 13)
Most older people are poor.	More than 88 percent of people 65 and older have incomes above the poverty level. (Chapter 15)
The aged are isolated from family members.	The vast majority of older people have regular contact with family members and see at least one child once a week. (Chapter 8)
Most older people are disabled.	Older men and women spend more than 80 percent of their lives free of disability. (Chapter 9)
People become more mellow as they grow old.	Personality is stable. It does not change with age.
Nearly a third of people 65 or older are in nursing homes.	Fewer than 5 percent of people 65 and older are in nursing homes. (Chapter 10)
The aged are politically powerful.	Politicians do take senior citizen organizations into account when considering what policies to support, but these organizations have mainly been effective in preventing major cuts in Social Security benefits. (Chapter 17)
Most Americans retire at 65.	The majority of men and women are out of the labor force by age 62. (Chapter 12)
In the past, older parents commonly lived with their children and grandchildren.	In the United States it has never been common for three generations to live together in a single household. (Chapter 5)
Welfare is for the poor.	The two largest welfare programs in the United States are Social Security and Medicare. Together they account for more than half of all federal social welfare expenditures. (Chapter 11)

health, are economically self-sufficient, and lead active and productive lives (Cook, 1992). The bottom line is that the elderly are as diverse as the rest of the population.

CAREERS IN SOCIAL GERONTOLOGY

More so than most of the social sciences, social gerontology is an applied discipline. Much of the research has direct implications for social policy. One reason for the applied focus is that there exist a myriad of social programs directed primarily or exclusively toward the elderly. These programs—which include Social Security, Medicare, Medic-

aid, the Older Americans Act, congregate meals, subsidized housing, legal assistance, and transportation services—are part of the *welfare state*, a term used by social scientists to describe government programs that provide income, health care, and services. We discuss the welfare state in more detail in Chapter 11. Another reason for the applied focus is that old-age policies and programs constitute over a third of the federal budget (Steckenrider and Parrott, 1998). Many research projects have directly addressed ways to improve the delivery of services to the aged, to evaluate whether programs are working effectively, and to identify unmet needs.

What is fair distribution of resources between generations?

For the past half century, research on aging has been conducted in a political climate that was sympathetic to the needs of older people and that viewed the aged as a deserving clientele of government resources. Programs for the aged were enacted in the context of rapid economic growth and an expanding welfare state. The very success of many programs for older people has raised questions of **generational equity** regarding the fair distribution of societal resources between young and old, and the legitimacy of elderly beneficiaries is now under question (Steckenrider and Parrott, 1998). As the United States enters the new millennium, policy issues concerning the elderly will be at the center of the shifting political spectrum. An older population creates numerous demands for a variety of services, and as America grows old, the demands will increase. The people who provide those services are called *gerontological specialists*. Included in this definition are gerontologists who come from a variety of disciplines concerned with the physical, mental, and social aspects of aging—such as psychology, sociology, and social work—and geriatricians, who come from the fields of medicine, nursing, and rehabilitation.

Careers for Gerontological Specialists

The activities that gerontological specialists perform are diverse but generally fall into seven categories, as shown in Table 1–2.

Some gerontological specialists work directly with older people. They provide care to the frail elderly in hospitals, clinics, nursing homes, adult day care centers, or home care programs. Others provide counseling to older people and their families regarding such issues as caregiving, employment, or mental health. Finally, direct service providers may advise older clients about estate planning and investments.

The second type of work performed by gerontological specialists is program planning and evaluation. These specialists design, implement, and evaluate programs that meet the needs of older people. This work is most often performed by social service agencies funded by the government and in community programs such as senior citizen centers. Many operate through state agencies such as a department of elder affairs, which coordinates and plans these services. Among those offered are transportation, meals delivered in the home, chores for homebound elders, English taught to elderly immigrants, blood pressure checks, and leisure activities such as painting or dancing.

Some cities have begun cooperative programs with police departments to ensure that their elderly residents are safe from crime. In Memphis, Tennessee, Gramma's Day Care recruits and trains older people to work in child care centers. In Maryland, the Self-Esteem through Service Program connects at-risk middle schoolers with isolated elders to provide community service to the homeless (Kingson, Comman, and Leavitt, 1996).

Table 1-2	What Do Gerontological Specialists Do?
Direct service provision	Provide health, legal, psychological, and social services to individuals and their families
Program planning and evaluation	Design, implement, and evaluate programs for older people
Administration	Oversee the operation, staffing, expenditures, and evaluations of agencies and organizations for the elderly
Marketing and product development	Assess the needs of older people and develop and market services and products to meet those needs
Advocacy	Encourage the government and private sector to be responsive to the needs of older people
Education and training	Plan instructional programs for older people or teach courses on aging in universities and colleges
Financial planning	Advise people on the importance of saving and investing to ensure adequate finances in retirement
Research	Conduct basic research on aging processes or applied research on how well various programs meet the needs of the elderly

Gerontological specialists also work as administrators, overseeing the operation, staffing, expenditures, and evaluations of agencies and organizations that serve the needs of the elderly and their families. These managerial activities occur in a variety of settings, including health and social service organizations, corporations, and government agencies.

A fourth category is marketing and product development. Many of these positions are in the private sector where gerontological specialists assess the needs of various groups of older people and develop and market services and products to fill those needs. Among the services offered through private sector agencies are home health care, tours and travel planning, and retirement communities. Those on the marketing end plan advertising campaigns to inform older people of the availability of these new products and services.

Another niche for gerontological specialists is in advocacy. Advocates work as community activists to encourage the government and the private sector to be responsive to the needs of older people. Advocates often work for nonprofit organizations to develop specific programs for

health care, community services, and government policy.

Another niche of growing importance is financial planning. As retirees become more responsible for their own retirement savings, they need advice on how to invest their funds. Financial specialists help people understand the benefits provided by their employers and by Social Security and Medicare. They help them choose among the various options for investing their money and explain the tax consequences of different decisions (Dennis, 2002).

Gerontological specialists are also involved in education and training. Some are active in planning and evaluating instructional programs for older people and their families. Others teach in universities and colleges. There is also a growing need for continuing education for practitioners who work with the aged, and educators often teach noncredit courses and workshops for people who need to keep their knowledge up-to-date.

A final career opportunity for gerontological specialists is as researchers. Some researchers who study aging conduct basic research on the mechanisms of aging; others investigate how well various programs fulfill the needs of the elderly. There is an increasing demand for basic research that will help gerontologists better understand individual aging processes and for applied research that will enable them to design and implement programs to meet the needs of an aging population (Association for Gerontology in Higher Education, 1996).

Expanding Career Opportunities

Some of the fastest-growing occupations are those in which the skills of gerontological specialists will be needed. As the baby boomers move into their 50s, more of them will require the services of financial planners to develop strategies for managing their retirement savings. Financial planners usually have four years of college and some have master's degrees in business or backgrounds in sales or marketing.

Another area in which demand will increase is geriatric social work. The growth of the population of those 85 or older means that more social workers will be needed to help people recovering from illnesses to plan posthospital care and services, to provide counseling in health care settings such as assisted living centers and nursing homes, and to provide grief counseling.

The health care industry, currently the largest industry in the United States, is expected to grow dramatically in the future. The demand for physicians who have specialized knowledge of geriatrics will expand greatly. According to one estimate, every medical school in the country will need to have at least 10 geriatricians on its faculty to meet the need for trained geriatricians (Butler, 2002). Another area in which there will be substantial growth will be in services for people with chronic illnesses. Jobs in this area are likely to be in home care services rather than services provided in a nursing home. Another area of growth will be information technology. People need information about available services and about health and wellness and, thanks to the Internet, many people are educating themselves about wellness and preven-

tion, illnesses and treatment options, care services, and beneficial health behaviors. There will be new jobs in meeting the information need. Finally, there will be more job opportunities to meet end-of-life demands. Employers will be looking for workers who understand pain management, who can design better health care delivery systems and treatment options, and who can manage complex health care systems (Wilber, 2000).

As a more affluent and educated cohort grows old, the demand for leisure activities will increase. The travel and hospitality industries will expand, as will the retirement community industry. Travel agents will see more of their business coming from newly retired baby boomers, and real estate agents will be kept busy selling the homes of retirees who wish to develop leisure-oriented lifestyles.

Becoming a Gerontological Specialist

How does a person become certified as a gerontological specialist? In some professions such as medicine, rehabilitation therapy, and nursing, a certified professional completes a traditional degree program and then takes a course of study to obtain a specialty in aging. Thus, a nursing student would pursue a degree in nursing and then specialize to become a geriatric nurse practitioner. Another option for those who want to work with older people but do not wish to obtain a professional degree in a traditional discipline is to pursue a degree in aging studies or gerontology. An increasing number of universities offer master's and PhD degrees in gerontology.

Presently, more than half of all community colleges, four-year colleges, and universities offer gerontology or geriatrics courses. More than 600 have formal programs of instruction in gerontology. At least 200 schools offer degrees or majors in gerontology, 235 offer credit certificates, and 500 offer gerontology as an area of specialization or a minor (Association for Gerontology in Higher Education, 1996). If you have an interest in aging and the life course, there is a career option for you.

Chapter Resources

LOOKING BACK

1. **What is social gerontology, and how is it related to the broader field of gerontology?** *Gerontology is the study of the biological, psychological, and social aspects of aging. Social gerontology is a subfield of gerontology that focuses on the social as opposed to the physical or biological aspects of aging.*

2. **How is old age defined, and what difference does the definition make?** *There is no single agreed-upon way to define aging and old age. The most commonly used definition in the United States is chronological age, but there are many other ways to determine when someone is considered old. These include taking on a social role such as widow or retiree, functional age, or subjective age identity. The definition that is most useful depends on the purpose. For example, chronological age is often used for defining eligibility for a benefit, such as Social Security, but functional age may be a more useful way to determine who is best suited to perform certain activities.*

3. **What is a cohort, and why are social gerontologists interested in cohorts?** *A cohort is a group of individuals who have experienced the same event in the same time period. The most common way to define cohorts is by year of birth. Cohorts are shaped by historical events, by their size and composition, and by changes that occur in the social institutions around them. Age changes occur in individuals over time; age differences are ways one cohort differs from another. The concept of a cohort is useful for distinguishing age changes from age differences.*

4. **What is the life course framework, and how is it useful to gerontologists?** *The life course framework is an approach to the study of aging that focuses on the interaction between historical events, personal decisions, individual opportunities, and later life outcomes. It combines a concern with individual aging with an awareness of changing age structures. The two core concepts of life course research are transitions and trajectories.*

5. **What is ageism, and how is it perpetuated?** *Ageism is defined as stereotyping and discrimination against people on the basis of age. Stereotypes are a composite of attitudes and beliefs about people as a group. When people act on the basis of these beliefs, they are guilty of age discrimination. Ageism can take many forms. The form ageism takes differs by gender, because there is a double standard concerning aging, whereby men are valued by their accomplishments and women by their appearance. Because of this double standard, women are more likely than men to attempt to conceal their age.*

THINKING ABOUT AGING

1. Are the older members of your family aging successfully? In what ways do they meet or fall short of the criteria for successful aging?

2. Pick someone in your family and define his or her age using each of the four definitions of old age.

3. List the generations in your family, and place each in one of the five cohorts described in this chapter.

4. Suppose a survey of students on your campus shows that many of them hold ageist attitudes. Explain why that could be a problem, and suggest ways to change students' attitudes toward the aging.

5. Select a TV show, book, or movie, and analyze the way aging characters are portrayed in it.

KEY TERMS

age discrimination 11	cohort effect 8
ageism 11	frail elderly 7
chronological age 6	functional age 6
cohort 8	generation 8
cohort aging 8	generational equity 17

EXPLORING THE INTERNET

Note: While all the URLs listed were current as of the printing of this book, these sites often change. Please check our website www.mhhe.com/quadagno *for updates.*

1. The American Geriatrics Society (http://www.americangeriatrics.org) is an organization that works to address the needs of the United States's aging population. In part because the AGS has promoted "health in aging," the White House declared September the Month of Health in Aging.

   Go to the AGS website and click on "AGS Newsroom and Public Policy," then on "AGS Press Releases." Follow the link to the article, "Geriatrics Experts Spotlight Mental Health Treatment for Nursing Home Residents: *Expert Panel Calls for New Standards of Care.*" Read the article, and answer the following questions:

   a. What percentage of current nursing home residents have symptoms of depression?

   b. For what reasons were these new revisions to the standards of care for nursing home residents with depression and behavioral symptoms associated with dementia initiated?

   c. What are some of the AGS and AAGP policy recommendations?

2. One of the leading agencies in the study of aging is the National Institute on Aging (http://www.nia.nih.gov/), whose purpose is to understand the nature of aging and extend the healthy, active period of life.

   On the NIA's home page, click on the News & Events heading, then on Press Releases. Select the subject Aging, general, and browse through the NIA's press releases on that subject. Click on "Well-Being Improves for Most Older People, but Not for All New Federal Report Says—8/10/00." After reading this document, answer the following question:

   a. What does this press release tell us about the number of older Americans in the United States?

   Now click on the Back button to return to Press Releases. Scroll down the page until you see the press release "New Census Report Shows Exponential Growth in Number of Centenarians—6/16/99." Read this document and answer the following questions:

   a. What does this press release tell us about the race/ethnicity, gender, and education of centenarians?

   b. Where do most centenarians live, according to the census?

Chapter 2

Theories of Aging

Chapter Outline

*T*hese women, who are all in their 70s, are competing in the 100-meter dash at the U.S. Senior Games in San Antonio, Texas.

Looking Ahead

1. Who were the first students of social gerontology, and what did they hope to learn?
2. What theories of aging did early gerontologists propose?
3. How did later scholars broaden the scope of the study of aging?
4. What is the relationship between age and social status, and does it vary from one culture to the next?
5. Which theories of aging consider how race, gender, and class affect the social status of the aged?

*C*onsider the following statements about aging:

In every culture and historical period, the society and individual prepare in advance for the ultimate disengagement of death by an inevitable, gradual and mutually satisfying process of social disengagement prior to death. . . . The individual retreats from the social world, which in turn relieves him of normative control. . . . This process is functional for the individual in the sense that it goes with having a high morale, and it is functional for the society in that it retires an age echelon from roles which young people may then fill. (Cumming and Henry, 1961:14)

The decrease in interaction proceeds against the desires of most aging men and women. The older person who ages optimally is the person who stays active and who manages to resist the shrinkage of his social world. He maintains the activities of middle age as long as possible and then finds substitutes for work when he is forced to retire and substitutes for friends and loved ones whom he loses by death. (Havighurst et al., 1968:161)

Although they reach opposite conclusions, both of these statements are theories of optimal aging. Theories are broad explanations that provide a

23

structure for organizing and interpreting a multitude of observable facts and their relationships to one another (Hagestad and Dannefer, 2001). They help to define a research agenda, provide a guide for scientific investigations, and predict what is not yet known or observed (Bengtson, Parrott, and Burgess, 1996).

Theories do not arise in a vacuum. Rather what researchers decide to study and their attitude toward the subject matter are products of the social environment. Theories not only guide scientists in deciding what questions to ask about their universe, they also reflect implicit values about the way things should be. As products of a historical era, they tell us as much about the concerns of the people of that era as they do about the subject matter.

This applies to the two previously quoted statements. The first, drawn from disengagement theory, declares that optimal aging involves withdrawal from the social world. The second, which summarizes the key tenet of activity theory, asserts that the person who ages optimally remains active and involved. Yet as different as they appear, they share certain fundamental properties: The individual is the subject matter, and the issue under investigation is how to age optimally.

Consider now how the following statement differs from the previous two:

> A sociology of age is concerned with two major topics: (1) aging over the life course as a social process and (2) age as a structural feature of changing societies and groups. . . . Aging processes and age structures form a system of interdependent parts that we refer to as an "age stratification system." (Riley, Foner, and Waring, 1988:243)

In age stratification theory, the individual is not the subject matter, the search for optimal aging has been abandoned, and age is defined as an element of social organization.

This chapter traces the historical development of theories of aging. It first discusses the origins of social gerontology as a scientific discipline. Next, micro-level theories, which focus on individual aging processes, are examined. Initially, these theories were motivated by a quest to identify optimal

aging and to understand what constitutes "normal" aging. Among the theories with this as the primary objective were disengagement theory, activity theory, and continuity theory.

As evidence accumulated indicating that there was no one "normal" way to grow old, researchers began to ask instead how the elderly fit into the broader social structure. Theories that provided a bridge between micro-level issues of individual aging and macro issues of social structure included subculture theory, exchange theory, and social constructionism.

It was a natural step from these theories to turn attention to the social system itself. Two macro-level theories of aging—modernization theory and age stratification theory—focused on the relationship between age and social status (Marshall, 1996). What these theories largely ignored, however, was the way that status in old age is also influenced by an individual's race, gender, and social class. The chapter concludes with a discussion of theories of power and inequality, including the political economy approach and feminist theory.

The Origins of Social Gerontology

The first practitioners of social gerontology were developmental psychologists, whose traditional focus on growth and maturation was expanded to include later maturity (Orbach, 1974). Reflecting the discipline's origins in biological concerns, early researchers saw old age as a period of inevitable physical and mental decline. The emphasis on decline in old age grew from an awareness of real physical changes, such as diminished short-term memory or vision losses, as well as increased vulnerability to certain diseases like heart disease, cancer, and stroke (Schneider, 1983). As Orbach (1974) noted, these physical changes were "almost synonymous with aging" (p. 71).

During the Great Depression of the 1930s, interest in this physical decline became coupled with concerns about the well-being of the aged, who suffered disproportionately from poverty and unemployment. Research focused on whether these problems older people faced worsened adjustment to the inevitable biological deterioration.

The economy emerged out of the doldrums during World War II, and at the war's end, the United States embarked upon an era of unprecedented prosperity. Average incomes grew, home ownership expanded rapidly, and spending on consumer goods climbed by more than 200 percent. Reflecting the optimism that accompanied prosperity, the federal government poured money into research focused on pressing social problems (Chafe, 1986).

Research flourished at the University of Chicago under the jurisdiction of the Committee on Human Development, which sponsored a large study on adjustment to aging among white middle-class men and women over 60. The book *Personal Adjustment in Old Age,* published in 1949, presented the results of that study (Cavan et al., 1949). Contrary to expectations, the study suggested that a decline in old age was not inevitable. Rather, poor adjustment was correlated with a lack of activity. People who continued to lead active and productive lives remained well-adjusted in old age.

The discovery that people who were most active scored highest on measures of life satisfaction led to a new quest, namely, to define the boundaries of "normal" aging. During the 1950s, the Committee on Human Development sponsored a series of studies designed to identify how people adjusted to normal aging processes. The **Kansas City Study of Adult Life** coupled the emphasis on adjustment with measures of social role performance across the life span (Cole, 1992).

Central to these studies was the concept of a social role, which refers to the expectations that accompany a given position or status. For example, a person who occupies the position of college professor is expected to give lectures, grade exams, and maintain a professional demeanor. A person who occupies the position of student is expected to come to class on time, take notes, and study. People in a given position may perform the roles that accompany that position well or poorly.

The study of role performance was first applied to age by Fred Cottrell (1942), who examined how well adjusted people were to their age roles and sex roles. The measurement of social role performance later became one central focus of the Kansas City Study of Adult Life, which sought to document patterns of development from middle age through old age. In the first phase of the project, interviews were conducted with 750 residents of Kansas City, Missouri, aged 40 to 70. The results indicated that there was no consistent change in either the competence or quality of role performance in middle age (Orbach, 1974). Rather, people remained fully engaged in their primary occupations and fully absorbed by familial responsibilities (Havighurst, 1957).

One problem with the Kansas City study was that it was incapable of fully answering questions about age-related changes, because no one older than 70 was interviewed and the subjects were interviewed only once. To compensate for these flaws, a second project was launched. In this study, people aged 40 to 85 were interviewed yearly to analyze how personality or internal psychological states changed as they aged. Several measures of personality traits were used, and the results were inconsistent. Some measures showed no consistent age-related changes, whereas other measures showed that people became more disengaged as they grew old. The latter results were interpreted as indicating an "interiorization" of ego functions (Neugarten, 1964). Interiorization meant a withdrawal from involvement in worldly affairs, a decrease in energy available to the ego (the part of the self that organizes the personality and is the site of intelligence), and a decrease in impulse control (Orbach, 1974; Neugarten, 1987). Disengagement theory was derived from these conclusions.

MICRO THEORIES OF AGING

Psychosocial Theories

Disengagement theory   **Disengagement theory** was the first formal theory of aging. It was proposed in 1961 by two prominent University of Chicago researchers, Elaine Cumming and William Henry, who outlined their classic theory in their book *Growing Old: The Process of Disengagement.* Criticizing what they called the "implicit theory" that people can be well adjusted, satisfied, and happy in old age only if they remain active and involved, Cumming and Henry (1961) argued that normal aging involves a natural and inevitable mutual withdrawal or disengagement, "resulting in decreasing interaction between an aging person and others in the social system he belongs to" (p. 14). Because of the inevitability of death, the society and the individual mutually sever their ties in advance so that the death of the individual will not be disruptive to the social system. Either the society or the individual may initiate the disengagement, but once the process is initiated it becomes circular. Lessening social interaction leads to a weakening of the norms of behavior regarding interaction.

A readiness for disengagement occurs when "the individual becomes sharply aware of the shortness of life and the scarcity of time remaining to him, and if he perceives his life space as decreasing" (Cumming and Henry, 1961:215). The individual wants to disengage and does so by reducing the number of roles he or she plays and weakening the intensity of those that remain. Society also offers the individual "permission" to withdraw. When death occurs, both society and the individual are prepared. The process is irreversible, universal, and inevitable.

Disengagement theory shifted the focus away from the individual per se to the relationship between the individual and the social system (Lynott and Passuth Lynott, 1996). It emphasized two ideas that represented classic examples of a broader sociological framework termed *functionalism*. According to functionalist theory, the requirements of the social system are smooth and efficient functioning. In the case of disengagement theory, both the individual and the social system will adjust to prevent death from causing disruption (Parsons, 1951). Many of the criticisms leveled against functionalist theories were also directed toward disengagement theory.

Most controversial about disengagement theory was the idea that disengagement was *universal*, meaning it happens everywhere and in all historical eras; that it was *inevitable*, meaning it must happen sometime to everyone; and that it was *intrinsic*, caused by biological factors rather than social factors (Hochschild, 1975). Critics of disengagement theory amassed a large amount of evidence that contradicted its core premises. One of the largest of these studies was the Duke Geriatric Project involving 250 subjects age 60 and older (Maddox, 1965). Results of the Duke study indicated that older people who measured highest on activity levels scored highest on life satisfaction, not lowest as disengagement theory would predict. The Duke study also demonstrated that regardless of how active people were, if their mental health and physical health were good, they scored high on life satisfaction.

Overall, research indicates that people grow old in many different ways. Culture, social conditions, and personality all contribute to variations in aging. Instead of defining disengagement as a theory of optimal aging, it is more useful to think of it as a process that sometimes, but not inevitably, occurs. The "In Their Own Words" feature presents examples of some older people who are disengaged and of others who have remained fully engaged.

Activity theory   The quest for normal aging continued when Robert Havighurst formalized **activity theory,** what Cumming and Henry had called the "implicit" theory of aging. Havighurst, one of the collaborators on the Kansas City Study of Adult Life, argued that the psychological and social needs of the elderly were no different from those of the middle-aged and that it was neither normal nor natural for older people to become isolated and withdrawn. When they do, it is often due to events beyond their control, such as poor health or the loss of close relatives. The person who aged optimally managed to stay active and resist the shrinkage of his or her social world. That meant maintaining the activities of middle age for as long as possible and then finding substitutes for those that had to be relinquished—substitutes for work, for friends, and for loved ones who died (Havighurst et al., 1968). Successful aging was active aging.

Once activity theory was advanced as an alternative theory of optimal aging, numerous studies were conducted comparing it to disengagement

In Their Own Words

Portraits of Engagement and Disengagement

Social gerontologists Colleen Johnson and Barbara Barer (1992) conducted interviews with 150 of the oldest–old—men and women whose average age was 89. They found that some remained active and engaged; others had become disengaged. Johnson and Barer confirmed certain typical processes that occurred among the disengaged.

One common process among the disengaged was a distancing of themselves from the worries of others. One centenarian said, "I put a frame around my life and only see what I want to see." An elderly man described his reaction to the outside world: "I am like a prize fighter—I step back to lessen the impact of the blows."

Many of the respondents noted a shift in time orientation, accompanied by an awareness that time was finite and that there was no future. One man said, "I used to look back with regret and ahead with trepidation, but now I live day to day." Another declared, "When I was younger, one door closed but another one opened. New individuals always entered my life. Not many doors open at this age, so no one comes in. It's the end and I don't even mind."

The sense of disengagement was not distressing. Rather, many of the disengaged respondents felt a sense of well-being about their remoteness from other people. One elderly woman reported, "I am comfortable being alone. I'm pulling away from everything more and more. I've climbed the mountain and I'm on the other side. My grave is below me." Another woman described her reaction to her son's heart attack: "I worried at first, but I realized I can't do anything about it. I don't take problems seriously anymore" (Johnson and Barer, 1992:359–361). The process of disengagement was not universal. It occurred most often among people who had poor health and a depleted social network; their response was to narrow their social worlds and redefine their optimal level of social integration.

Another researcher, Joel Savishinsky, followed men and women in the midst of the transition to retirement. In his book *Breaking the Watch*, Savishinsky describes some fiercely engaged elders. One was Stefan Nokalsky, who retired from a career in the hotel industry but remained active and engaged in his new vocation with the local school board:

> The fact is, I don't even like the word "retirement." I'm not stopping. I'm changing—pace, direction. I just want to enjoy whatever I'm doing. My parents taught me the hard way... that satisfaction comes from within and not without. Success is in the mind, not someone else or your job telling you you've made it. It's like the way I jog. I like to go alone. Not to be tied to other schedules or pace. Carol calls me The Lone Runner. And I just can't stop to smell the roses, go to matinees, the Farmers' Market, take morning walks. I have this guilt problem, the need to set goals and do useful things. I don't know any better than to want to do an excellent job. . . . Learn a new word every day, do more push-ups, collect coins because some day they'll be worth a lot. . . . I had a son in college who took courses just because they interested him. I never took a damn course unless it led somewhere. (Savishinsky, 2000)

theory. Erdman Palmore tested disengagement theory and activity theory by comparing the process of aging in the United States with that in Japan. Palmore's research, described in his book *The Honorable Elders* (1975), supported activity theory. Japanese society was distinguished by two characteristics: a vertical society and **filial piety.** The idea of a vertical society meant that most Japanese relationships were determined by a delicately graded hierarchy with age superseding all other criteria for ranking. The aged were treated with deference and integrated into the workforce and the family. Filial piety referred to the tradition of respect and duty toward parents and grandparents that had its roots in ancestor worship. Palmore concluded that because of these traditions, the aged in Japan were more active and involved than the aged in other industrialized countries and that higher levels of activity led to better health and more satisfaction in old age.

Another test of activity theory was conducted at Laguna Hill Leisure World, a retirement community in southern California (Lemon, Bengtson, and Peterson, 1972). The study included 411 men and women who ranged in age from their 50s to their 70s. The residents of Leisure World participated in three types of activities: informal, formal, and solitary. Participating in informal activity with friends was associated with higher levels of life satisfaction, but participating in formal activities (e.g., club or church activities) or solitary activities had no effect. A later study of residents of three retirement communities in the Midwest reached similar conclusions (Longino and Kart, 1982). In all three communities, participation in informal activity was the best predictor of life satisfaction. Numerous studies of depression among the elderly also support the basic premises of activity theory. Older people who are engaged in productive activities and have social networks are less likely to be depressed than those who are not engaged (Lennartsson and Silverstein, 2001). In fact, this relationship is so well established that researchers now investigate which aspects of social activity influence depression. What they have discovered is that it is not participation in activities per se that enhances well-being but rather the socializing that accompanies engagement in an activity

(Utz et al., 2002). This research suggests that what matters most is having intimate relations with a network of close friends and relatives.

Social gerontologists no longer view the withdrawal of older people from social roles and social interaction as normal aging. Yet some older people do disengage. The question researchers now ask is, Who withdraws and why?

One answer is that disengagement is associated with changes that make it difficult for people to remain active. Widowhood, poor health, and retirement are all correlated with disengagement and are better predictors of activity level than age (Maddox, 1964; Hochschild, 1975). Poverty can create isolation and lead to involuntary disengagement. Those who are unmarried and childless are especially vulnerable (Ball and Whittington, 1995). Mental deterioration associated with Alzheimer's disease can also lead to disengagement. Those at greatest risk of becoming isolated are the oldest–old, people 85 or older. They have fewer social contacts and fewer social supports than younger people (Antonucci and Akiyama, 1987). Many have lost a spouse or siblings, and some have lost at least one child (Johnson and Barer, 1992).

Despite such potential obstacles to remaining socially active, one study of 150 of the oldest–old found that about half remained engaged (Johnson and Barer, 1992). Those who did were more likely to be married and to have a child living nearby. They also tended to be in better health and more physically fit than those who were disengaged.

By contrast, the disengaged had narrowed their social worlds, both physically and psychologically. Physical disengagement involved simplifying one's social networks, seeing fewer people, and participating in fewer activities. Often the cause of disengagement was physical disability. Psychological disengagement meant distancing oneself from the concerns of others, becoming more introverted, and shifting one's time orientation from the future to the present.

Abandoning the idea of disengagement as a universal and inevitable process has allowed social gerontologists to recognize that aspects of disengagement theory can be useful in helping explain the social and mental lives of some older people.

Disengagement is especially common among residents of nursing homes. One study found that over 50 percent of nursing home residents participated in activities only occasionally or never (Resnick et al., 1997). Some of the disengagement among nursing home residents may be a result of hearing and vision impairments that make communication with others difficult. Depression, a common problem in nursing homes, may also cause elderly nursing home residents to withdraw from interaction (Gilbart and Hirdes, 2000). Moreover, despite many criticisms, the disengagement/activity theory debate has left a legacy of enduring interest among social gerontologists in measuring morale or life satisfaction. Table 2–1 depicts a typical life satisfaction scale.

Although life satisfaction measures have been criticized for measuring only a temporary state of mind rather than a persistent trait or for being biased toward a negative view of the world, social gerontologists remain interested in how various life transitions, such as leaving work or becoming widowed, affect happiness and morale. They are also interested in what sustains people through these transitions. One topic that has been the subject of numerous studies is the relationship between religion and the well-being of the aged. See "Diversity in the Aging Experience" for a discussion of what researchers have discovered about this topic.

Continuity theory **Continuity theory** represents a more formal elaboration of activity theory, using a life course perspective to define normal aging and to distinguish it from pathological aging. First proposed by Robert Atchley, continuity theory draws heavily from the basic dichotomy of internal and external aging processes described in the Kansas City studies. Internal continuity for Atchley (1989) refers to "a remembered inner structure, such as the persistence of a psychic structure of ideas, temperament, affect, experiences, preferences, dispositions, and skills" (p. 184). External continuity is connected to past role performance and can be observed in the continuity in skills, activities, environments, roles, and relationships between middle age and old age.

Continuity theory emphasizes that personality plays a major role in adjustment to aging and that

Table 2-1	A Life Satisfaction Scale			
		Agree	*Disagree*	*Not Sure*
1.	As I grow older, things seem better than I thought they would be.	1	2	3
2.	I have gotten more of the breaks in life than most of the people I know.	1	2	3
3.	This is the dreariest time of my life.	1	2	3
4.	I am just as happy as when I was younger.	1	2	3
5.	These are the best years of my life.	1	2	3
6.	Most of the things I do are boring and monotonous.	1	2	3
7.	The things I do are as interesting to me as they ever were.	1	2	3
8.	As I look back on my life, I am fairly well satisfied.	1	2	3
9.	I have made plans for things I'll be doing a month or a year from now.	1	2	3
10.	When I think back over my life, I didn't get most of the important things I wanted.	1	2	3
11.	Compared to other people, I get down in the dumps too often.	1	2	3
12.	I've gotten pretty much what I expected out of life.	1	2	3
13.	In spite of what some people say, the lot of the average man is getting worse, not better.	1	2	3

Source: Longino and Kart (1982).

Diversity in the Aging Experience

RELIGION AND PERSONAL WELL-BEING

Can religious faith enhance well-being in later life? Most research suggests that the answer to this question is yes. Religious involvement appears to improve health and reduce disability, increase self-esteem, reduce symptoms of depression, and enhance life satisfaction (Levin and Taylor, 1997; McFadden, 1996). One study found that rates of depression were lower among older Catholics and Jews who attended religious services regularly (Kennedy et al., 1996). Another study of Mexican Americans aged 65 to 80 found that those who frequently attended religious services had higher life satisfaction and lower levels of depression than those who did not (Levin, Markides, and Ray, 1996). A recent study of older white and African American adults also found that people who derived a sense of meaning in life from religion had higher self-esteem and life satisfaction and greater sense of optimism than people who are not particularly religious (Krause, 2003).

Religion can support the aged in many ways. Participation in a religious community provides members with a framework for deriving meaning from their experiences, as well as an opportunity to interact with those who share similar values, attitudes, and beliefs. People also receive spiritual support from religion in the form of pastoral care, participation in organized worship and service to others, and prayer. Prayer is the most universal religious activity: 90 percent of Americans say they pray, and 75 percent say that prayer is an important part of their daily lives (Poloma and Gallup, 1991). Older people pray more often than younger people and are more likely to stress the personal significance of prayer (Gallup and Jones, 1989). Prayer may be especially important in helping the aged to adjust to chronic health problems and to face impending death (McFadden, 1996). Indeed, the benefits of personal prayer exceed the benefits of attending religious services (Levin and Taylor, 1997).

Yet one study found no relationship between religion and well-being. In the Ohio Longitudinal Study, 1,100 adults age 50 or older were interviewed first in 1975 and then every few years until the study was completed in 1991. The respondents belonged to more than 30 congregations representing various Catholic, Jewish, and Protestant denominations. Although religion was important to most of the respondents, it had no effect on their health or well-being (Atchley, 1997). Despite these contradictory findings, most research suggests that religious faith does sustain older people through role transitions, the departure of their children from the home, the loss of a spouse or other close relative, and declining health.

What Do You Think?

1. Among your family and friends, do those who are religious seem to have a greater sense of well-being than those who are not? Give some examples.
2. How can those who care for the aging use the results of research on religion and well-being to improve people's health?

adult development is a continuous process. By the time people reach middle age, they have built a life structure that is linked to their past and that becomes the base on which they build their future. Continuity is an adaptive strategy for successful aging. Continuity of personality means that changes can be incorporated that still preserve the unique characteristics of the individual. Continuity of activities allows people to prevent, offset, or minimize the effects of aging. Continuity of relationships preserves an individual's social support system.

The most controversial element of continuity theory is its definition of normal aging. Normal aging, according to Atchley (1989), refers to "usual, commonly encountered patterns of human aging . . . . It can be distinguished from pathological aging by a lack of physical or mental disease" (pp. 183–84). People who age normally can successfully meet their needs for income, housing, health care, nutrition, and so forth. Pathological aging occurs in people who are unable to meet their needs because they are poor or disabled.

The distinction between pathological aging and normal aging has been criticized by Gay Becker (1993), who argued that chronic illness is common in old age and that having a chronic illness "does not preclude the ability to participate in society or in personally and socially meaningful experiences" (p. 149). In her research on male and female stroke victims, Becker found that a serious illness "throws the known self into disarray" (p. 151). Despite the fact that the lives of her subjects were profoundly disrupted by the stroke, many became absorbed in the task of integrating this disruption into their lives. In the process, "a continuous self emerged" (p. 153). In Becker's view it is unnecessary to use a term like *pathological aging*. Rather it is more fruitful and accurate to ask, "What mechanisms do people use to create continuity in the face of disruption?" (p. 157).

Other criticisms of continuity theory have come from feminist theorists (discussed later in the chapter). Feminist theorists contend that because continuity theory defines normal aging around a male model, it turns forms of inequality such as high rates of poverty among older women into indicators of individual pathology. A more accurate depiction would recognize income inequality as a flaw in the social structure (Calasanti, 1996).

Although there are few studies that have formally tested continuity theory, its core premises are similar to some of the theoretical assumptions that inform research on the life course, a subject we explore more fully in Chapter 3.

The Individual and the Social System

The theories discussed in the preceding section were primarily concerned with explaining personal adjustment in old age and in examining the causes of disengagement. The subject of interest was the individual, and the focus, psychosocial, although sociological factors may have been used to explain variations in outcomes. In this section, we discuss theories that emphasize the relationship between the individual and the social system.

Subculture theory   **Subculture theory** shared several traits with activity theory and disengagement theory—a conviction that people lost status in old age, a focus on role changes in later life, and a belief that activity enhanced the lives of the elderly. It differed in that it built on a sociological theory of subcultural development.

Subcultures develop under two sets of circumstances. When people share similar interests, problems, and concerns or have long-standing friendships, they may form a subculture. For example, artists have a common language that identifies styles or approaches that may be unfamiliar to outsiders and a system of ranking based on the prestige of the art show where one's work is exhibited or on membership in certain artists' societies. Subcultures may also develop when groups of people are excluded from full participation in the wider society. African Americans represent an example of a group that has created a separate subculture in response to its exclusion from the broader society (Duster, 1995).

The social gerontologist Arnold Rose applied subculture theory to the study of aging. Rose argued that older people were subject to both conditions. They have a positive affinity for each other based partly on their physical limitations and thus their

These two friends have a good conversation over a cup of coffee.

common interest "in a physically easy and calm existence." They also share "common role changes and . . . common generational experiences in a rapidly changing society" (Rose, 1964:47). Older people are also drawn together because they are excluded by younger people, who tend to evaluate others based on factors such as occupational status or ability in sports. Rose noted that the signs of prestige that accompany old age in many cultures were lacking in the United States, where aging means diminished status. Thus, because the elderly are isolated from young people and share common experiences with other older people, they are likely to form a subculture. Within the subculture of the elderly, high status is conferred on those who have good physical and mental health. As Rose (1964) noted, "Good health is sufficiently rare, and becoming rarer with advancing age . . . that old people . . . exhibit a special admiration for those who remain healthy" (p. 49). High status is also conferred on those who play leadership roles in organizations of the aged.

Although it is true that older people experience common role changes, the idea that the aged form a single subculture has now been discounted. Older people are much more likely to form affiliations on the basis of family ties, racial and ethnic identity, social class, or religious affiliation than on age. Still, the concept of a subculture is useful for understanding the lifestyles of people in age-segregated communities, such as retirement homes, apartment complexes, or nursing homes. For example, in her fascinating participant observation study of 43 older people who lived in Merrill Court, a small apartment building in San Francisco, Arlie Hochschild (1978) found "an unexpected community that involved a subculture with its own customs, gossip and humor" (p. xiv). Hochschild's research confirmed Rose's hypothesis that health and good fortune was a basis for ranking. The widows of Merrill Court created an informal status hierarchy called the "poor dear" system. Those who had lost the fewest loved ones through death, were in good health, and were closest to their children won honor. Those who fell short on these criteria were poor dears, at the bottom of the status hierarchy. Hochschild concluded, "Together the old can establish new and different boundaries" (p. 73).

Subculture theory disappeared from the research agenda until recently. Now as older people have increasingly become involved in interest groups, questions have again arisen about their group identity. Yet as Chapter 17 makes clear, the issue to-day is not whether older people are excluded from society but whether they exert an undue influence on politics.

Exchange theory

Exchange theory is similar to the psychosocial theories previously discussed in its interest in explaining why some older people withdraw from social interaction. Its origins lie in micro-economic theory, however, not in develop-mental psychology. The basic thesis underlying all economic theories is that social interaction be-tween individuals is based on rational calculations and that people seek to maximize their rewards from these exchanges and minimize their costs (Marshall, 1996).

Exchange theorists argue that interaction be-tween the old and the young decreases because older people have fewer resources to bring to the exchange—lower income, poorer health, and less education (Bengtson and Dowd, 1981). Their de-clining resources strain their possibilities for con-tinued interaction with others. As older people confront the cost of increasing dependency, their friends and relatives experience the growing bur-den of support. To balance the exchange equation, the aged begin to disengage (Dowd, 1975). Older people who have the greatest resources and thus can bring more to an exchange with younger peo-ple are most capable of remaining engaged.

A central premise of exchange theory is that re-sources are often unequal and that actors will con-tinue to engage in exchanges only as long as the benefits are greater than the costs (Bengtson, Parrott, and Burgess, 1997). Recent studies have confirmed the usefulness of exchange theory in explaining social support and transfers between generations. For example, one study found that contact between children and parents was greater when parents had a larger amount of inheritable wealth (Bernheim, Shleifer, and Summers, 1985). Other research shows that maintaining an ex-change relationship can be a constant struggle for an elderly person with few resources. For example, Mrs. Lewis needs more help than she can pay for:

She attempts to obligate a large number of people, each of whom can be called upon for small favors.

Her landlady picks her up and takes her grocery shopping each week. A neighbor sends her a plate of hot food several times a week. She can usually locate one of several acquaintances to drive her to cash her SSI check and buy food stamps. (Bould, Sanborn, and Reif, 1989:88)

In exchange for their services, Mrs. Lewis provides her helpers some token payment, such as jars of jelly, leftover desserts, or vegetables from her gar-den. But if she places too many demands on any of these helpers, she risks making them resentful or unresponsive.

There also is a good deal of research that contra-dicts exchange theory. One problem with exchange theory is that it ignores the value of nonrational re-sources, such as love and companionship, which often even out what seems to be an unequal exchange (Passuth and Bengtson, 1988). Another problem is that exchange theory focuses on the immediate inter-actions between older people and other age groups, where the elderly are indeed often at a disadvantage. What it overlooks, however, is that exchanges be-tween generations take place over the life course. To clarify this issue, Bould, Sanborn, and Reif (1989) made a distinction between **immediate exchange strategies** and **deferred exchange strategies.** Mrs. Lewis, described above, adopted an immediate ex-change strategy. The problem is that her ties to her helpers are weak, and she must work constantly to find new helpers. One day her needs may become greater than her ability to maintain a support system. A deferred exchange strategy recognizes the impor-tance of strong ties built up over time. Long-term close relationships with family and friends represent a lifetime of "credit" that is stored up against the more burdensome needs that accompany old age. For ex-ample, Mrs. Davis took care of her grandchildren while her daughter worked, provided financial sup-port, and served as a confidante to all her children. Because she has accumulated "social credits," she has no concerns about having adequate support as she grows old: "I know my family will care for me like they always have" (Bould et al., 1989:89). People redefine the costs and rewards of relationships over a lifetime, and those with strong ties store up social credits that protect them in old age, regardless of their present resources.

Social Constructionism

A long-standing sociological tradition places individual intentions, motivations, and actions at the center of social theory. Social action in this tradition refers to "all human behavior when and insofar as the acting individual attaches a subjective meaning to it" (Weber, 1946:88). Contemporary versions of theories that view human beings as active creators of their own social reality are termed *social constructionist theories*.

Proponents of **social constructionism** do not perceive society as a set of real structures distinct from people. Rather they view humans as active agents who create the society in which they live. The subject matter of social constructionists is the individual's process of interpreting his or her experiences.

Social constructionists who study aging are interested in the "situational, emergent and constitutive features of aging" (Passuth and Bengtson, 1988:345; Lynott and Passuth Lynott, 1996). They study how social meanings of age and self-conceptions of age arise through negotiation and discourse. As Gubrium and Buckholdt (1977) explained, the focus is on human development in which "the meaning of age is presented and negotiated from moment to moment as people participate in sometimes elusive but serious conversation" (p. viii). Consider the following example.

Alzheimer's is a unique disease in the sense that it can proceed with no clinical markers of organic damage. People with Alzheimer's exhibit a variety of behaviors so diverse as to defy classification. Gubrium and Lynott (1983) conducted participant observation research at support groups for caregivers of patients with Alzheimer's disease. They described the support group as a way to transform "the disease's private troubles into public understanding" (p. 350). For example, Harold, a member of the support group, was distraught when his wife, Cynthia, an Alzheimer's victim, accused him of hiding her wedding ring. Yet when the group convinced him that this type of behavior was a typical symptom of the disease, he reinterpreted Cynthia's behavior as being part of Alzheimer's natural progression, rather than continuing to view it as annoying and frightening. As Gubrium and Lynott noted, "each personal elaboration concretized the category used to unify diverse experiences" (p. 367).

The strength of the social constructionist approach is that it reminds the researcher that older people are not passive objects but active subjects who participate in the construction of their social worlds. Yet its emphasis on microsocial processes often neglects the structural features of social life that are imposed by external forces (Passuth and Bengtson, 1988).

MACRO THEORIES OF AGING

The psychosocial theories of aging sought to explain individual patterns of behavior in later life and individual adjustment to the aging process. Subculture theory and exchange theory provided a bridge to macro theories of aging; the emphasis turned from interpersonal processes to questions regarding the status of the aged. The interest in broader structural factors also reflected changing political and economic conditions.

Age and Social Status

Modernization theory   The optimism that characterized the United States in the post–World War II era was shared by social scientists, who believed that if other nations would only follow the American example, they, too, could achieve prosperity and economic growth. This worldview was encapsulated in **modernization theory.** Modernization theorists argued that nations could be placed on a continuum ranging from least developed to most developed, according to such indicators as level of industrialization or degree of urbanization. Those exhibiting certain qualities of social structure were termed *modern*. The presumption behind the theory was that the path to prosperity was similar for all nations. If Western nations infused Third World nations with technology, skills, values, organization, and capital, these undeveloped countries would experience the same trajectory of economic growth (Neysmith, 1991).

The core elements from modernization theory as a theory of socioeconomic development were transmitted largely intact to social gerontology as a theory of aging. Modern societies not only exhibited certain characteristics such as urbanization and industrialization, they also had increased life expectancy and a higher proportion of older people. Social gerontologists now sought to understand how the increase in the proportion of older people affected the status of the aged.

The basic premise of modernization theory was that the aged had been revered in the past and that modernization had caused the status of the aged to decline. The idea that there was once a "golden age of aging" and that societal development led to a reduced status for the aged was not unique to modernization theorists. In 1776, the economist Adam Smith wrote in his famous treatise *The Wealth of Nations* that among the hunting peoples of North America, age was the sole basis for rank, whereas "in opulent and civilized nations" its role was merely residual. More than a century later, the sociologist Emile Durkheim ([1893] 1964) described the importance of the aged in traditional societies, where they served as the living expression of tradition, unique intermediaries between past and present. Social solidarity was maintained by the "authority of age, which gives tradition authority," whereas in civilized society, old men are pitied more than feared.

Modernization theory gave this thesis a contemporary twist by incorporating it into a model of development. The first to link processes of development to the status of the aged was Ernest Burgess, who argued in his book *Aging in Western Societies* (1960) that the changes wrought by the Industrial Revolution had negative consequences for the old. As work moved from the home to the factory, the number of people who were self-employed declined. The aged lost their economic independence and were forced into retirement. Urbanization drew young people from rural areas to cities, destroying the extended family household and isolating the elderly. According to Burgess, the aged became imprisoned in a "roleless role."

Sociologists Donald Cowgill and Lowell Holmes (1972) expanded this theory to include societies ranging from preliterate to modern. Their theory hypothesized that the status of the aged was high in preliterate societies and lower and more ambiguous in modern societies. In a subsequent article, Cowgill (1974) outlined exactly how social changes associated with modernization undermined the position of older people. Four types of social change—health technology, economic technology, urbanization, and mass education—are relevant to Cowgill's model, depicted in Figure 2–1.

First, modernization is accompanied by advances in health technology, such as sophisticated X-ray machines that can recognize cancer in its early stages or blood tests that can identify cholesterol levels. Health technology increases life expectancy, mortality rates decline, and population aging occurs. As lives are prolonged, older workers compete with younger workers for jobs. Retirement becomes necessary to move the elderly out of the labor force. In Cowgill's view, retirement involves the multiple losses of income, psychologically satisfying work, and social status.

The second factor is modern economic technology, which accelerates the pace of retirement because it creates new jobs that older workers lack the training and expertise to handle. Third, Cowgill followed Burgess's argument that urbanization attracted young people to the cities and destroyed the extended family household. As a result, more and more elderly people are found living alone. Finally, the expansion of mass education undermines "the mystique of age" because children now know more than their parents. The honorific position older people held as keepers of communal knowledge disappears. The new elite become the young.

Historians were the first to criticize modernization theory by challenging the idea that a golden age of aging ever existed (Laslett, 1976). In retracing household arrangements in previous centuries, historians discovered that in most European countries and the United States, people rarely lived in extended families with three generations sharing one roof. Indeed, older people were no more likely in the past to be living in their children's home than they are today. When multiple generations did live together, it was usually because grown children could not survive on their own and so moved in with their parents. Nor was retirement a twentieth-century creation. It existed long before industrialization, even in very rural areas. In the past, people

Figure 2-1   Aging and Modernization.

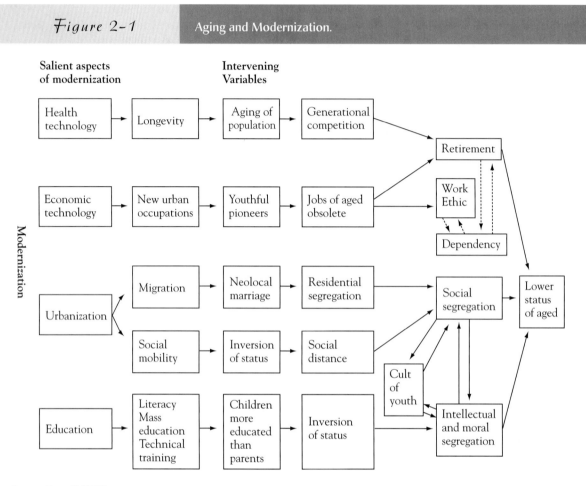

Source: Cowgill (1974).

retired when they had the resources, either land or wealth, to do so. Those without sufficient wealth worked until death. Wealthy older people were also revered, but the aged poor were never held in high esteem (Quadagno, 1982).

The historical and cross-cultural evidence disproves key tenets of modernization theory. Many historians have documented the tremendous diversity in the treatment of the aged in times past, and anthropologists have shown that reverence for the aged varies greatly across cultures. For a description of the treatment of the aged in several preliterate societies, see "Aging around the World."

As social gerontologists began to abandon large-scale concepts of societal development such as modernization theory as a way to explain the status of the aged, a new framework termed **age stratification theory** emerged. Age stratification theory shared with modernization theory a concern for the status of the aged. However, it originated not from population aging but from sociological research on status attainment.

Age stratification theory   Age stratification theory is one of the most influential and enduring gerontological theories (Riley, 1971). In a recent

Aging around the World

CROSS-CULTURAL VARIATION IN THE TREATMENT OF THE AGED

*W*hen the anthropologist Leo Simmons (1945) conducted his classic survey of the treatment of the aged in hundreds of preliterate societies, he discovered great variation among them. Many societies that Simmons studied protected the aged through customs that guaranteed them a special position in the community. Some had elaborate food-sharing privileges that favored the old—long lists of tender morsels forbidden to the young and reserved for the old. In others, elderly men and women who were too feeble to engage in arduous activities shifted to less physically demanding tasks, such as making tools, weapons, pottery, or baskets. Among the Hopi Indians, for example, old men who could no longer follow the flock or work in the field carded wool, knitted, or made sandals. Old women babysat, ground corn, and wove baskets (Simmons, 1945). Knowledge outlasts physical stamina, so those elders who could interpret strange or mysterious phenomena or diagnose and treat illnesses were held in high regard. In some societies, however, older people who became a burden on the group were abandoned and left to die.

Among the tribes of the Amazon rain forest, age is still venerated. The most valuable knowledge is possessed by elderly healers who are called Shamas. In recent decades, logging and oil drilling have destroyed the traditional Amazon tribal communities and brought increased contact with outsiders. A typical lament of the Shamas today is that the young people have no desire to learn about plant and animal life, the seasons and the weather (Dannefer, 2003).

More recent anthropological research suggests that the treatment of the aged often depends on whether they are "intact" or "decrepit," a distinction that corresponds roughly to the "young–old" and the "old–old" (Keith, 1985). The young–old usually play an active role in the political and religious life of the community. Among the Israeli Druze, for example, old people are considered expert in Hindu rituals (Keith, 1990). And among the Kagwahiv, who dwell in the Amazon in Brazil, the elderly are respected for their knowledge and spiritual strength (Gutmann, 1980). But when the old become "overaged," they are sometimes treated with contempt. Among the terms used to describe this phase of life are "the useless state" and the "sleeping period" (Keith, 1985). Perhaps a more accurate way to think about the position of the aged is that their status depends on their ability to control wealth, maintain a position within the family, and perform useful tasks for the community.

What Do You Think?

1. Do the aged members of your family receive special privileges or perform special tasks? If so, describe their roles and prerogatives.
2. In your opinion, do the aged in our society receive sufficient respect? Explain.

memoir, Matilda White Riley, the pioneer of age stratification theory, mused on the debates that dominated social gerontology in the 1960s:

We were sorely puzzled by then-rampant controversies and paradoxes in research on age: the inconsistent relationship between modernization and the status of the elderly;. . . the retirement debate which pitted "disengagement" against "activity," and above all, the wide-spread but false assumption that aging is an exclusively biological process, and that physiological and cognitive declines with advancing age are inevitable and irreversible. A critical social science review of the literature was clearly needed. (Riley and Riley, 1994:217)

To analyze the relationship between age and social structure, Riley (1971) devised a new conceptual framework that she called *age stratification theory.* Age stratification theory has its origin in status attainment research, which like modernization theory, originated in the postwar optimism generated by prosperity and economic growth (Bell, 1973). The underlying image of society in the status attainment literature was that affluent, postwar America was becoming classless as more people were incorporated into an expanding middle layer. As a result of the growth of industry, the spread of egalitarian norms, mass education, urbanization, bureaucratization, and professionalization, economic and political inequality was declining, and social mobility between classes was increasing. The income scale was becoming compressed at both ends of the hierarchy—there were fewer rich and fewer poor (Knottnerus, 1987). Now researchers needed to determine how important ascribed characteristics—one's family of birth, gender, or race, for instance—were compared to achieved characteristics such as education. Because the United States had a fluid class structure, all Americans had virtually unlimited opportunities for upward mobility. The agenda for research was to determine the factors that influenced social mobility (Blau and Duncan, 1967).

Implicit in the status attainment research was a life course perspective, since social mobility occurred across generations. Nearly all of these studies defined social mobility in terms of the transmission of occupational status among men. The focus was on

the degree to which an individual's social standing was associated with the characteristics of his family of origin (Sewell and Hauser, 1975).

Like status attainment theories, age stratification theory began with the underlying proposition that all societies group people into social categories. These groupings provide people with social identities. Age is one principle of ranking, along with wealth, gender, and race. Researchers sought to determine how people moved through the age structure.

The central concept used to examine this issue was that of an **age cohort,** which refers to a group of people who are born at the same time and thus share similar life experiences (see Chapter 1). Aging processes reflect the interplay between two dynamics, as illustrated in Figure 2–2. The first is the changing life course pattern of people in different cohorts; the second, the changing social structures in which these aging processes are experienced. People who are now in their 70s, for example, came of age during the Great Depression (cohort B). Many served in World War II. Few women of that generation worked outside the home, especially when their children were young, and most men expected to work until they were at least 65.

Their children, the baby boom generation, grew up during the 1950s and 1960s (cohort C). They share different experiences and expectations. The majority of women of this age group, even those with young children, are in the labor force. Men are likely to retire quite early, most before they reach 65, and many at 62 or younger. Few are veterans. Each cohort's experience of moving through life's major transitions will differ enormously, because each cohort has been indelibly imprinted by deep historical change. The old age of the baby boomers will only faintly resemble the old age of the Depression generation.

Age stratification theory sets an agenda for research based on four questions:

1. How does an individual's location in the changing age structure of a given society influence his or her behavior and attitudes?
2. How do individuals relate to each other within and between age strata? Is there an inevitable gap between generations?

Figure 2-2   Processes Underlying Age Strata.

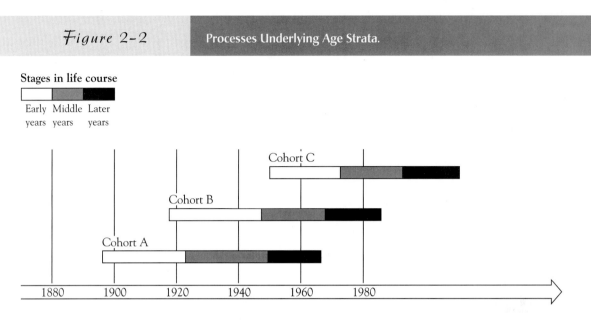

Stages in life course

Early Middle Later
years years years

Source: Riley (1976:191).

3. How do individuals pass through key transitions from infancy to childhood to adolescence to adulthood to old age?
4. What is the impact of the answers to those three questions on the society as a whole?

A large body of research has examined cohort differences in life course experiences. Some studies have analyzed the marked differences between cohorts in education, work history, standard of living, and life expectancy; others considered differences in attitudes and cultural tastes.

One of the more interesting issues is how changes that affect one life transition create a ripple effect in other arenas. For example, compared to women born a century ago, women today begin to menstruate at an earlier age and experience menopause later. Despite the lengthening of the period of fertility, recent cohorts of women spend fewer years in childbearing than their ancestors. They have fewer children than their grandmothers, and they space them more closely together (Riley, 1971). One outcome is that women today have greater choice in planning childbearing. The choice of having children

young, at 22 or 23, instead of later, say at 35, shapes the rest of the individual's life course. Such life course events as career trajectory, age of grandparenting, timing of retirement, and ability to provide care for aging parents all are affected by the timing of childbearing. Biological change has immense repercussions across many aspects of the life course, but its effect depends on a variety of social influences.

Even though Riley's original model included both individual life course rhythms and large-scale structural change as components of age stratification, most research derived from this model has ignored the latter emphasis. This is partly because the concept of social structure is broad and includes many possible definitions. At the most general level, social structure refers to the "idea of pattern or constraint underlying the behavior and interactions of individuals and groups" (Dowd, 1987:319). In the age stratification model, structure has a more precise meaning. It refers to a set of positions and relationships among positions with rewards allocated for performance of various roles (Marshall, 1996). For example, people who perform the roles associated with being a physician are accorded greater prestige and monetary rewards than people who perform the roles associated with being a secretary.

One criticism of age stratification theory is that defining structure as relationships among positions ignores power relationships that determine how statuses and roles are allocated. Just a generation ago, medical schools had quotas on the number of women they would admit. Thus, few women had an opportunity to occupy the status of physician. Age may be a pivotal source of social identity, but often it has less impact on one's life chances than other dimensions of stratification (Dowd, 1987). Within age cohorts, race, gender, and social class create wide variation in opportunity (Hogan and Astone, 1986).

Age integration theory

Age integration theory draws on a core premise of age stratification theory, the idea that society is stratified on the basis of age. Age stratification can create age-segregated institutions, in which age acts as a barrier to entrance, exit, or participation. But society also has age-integrated institutions, which are characterized by an absence of age-related criteria (Uhlenberg, 2000:261).

Most people are involved in both age-segregated and age-integrated institutions. Think about whom you see on a typical day. As a student, you attend classes that are largely age-segregated. If you live in a dormitory, most of the people around you are probably about the same age as you. Schools, sports teams, and nursing homes are just a few examples of institutions that consist primarily of people in a single age group. By contrast, workplaces usually include people from many age groups. Families are the most age-integrated institutions of all. Attend any family event and you will be likely to see people of all ages, from a newborn baby to an elderly grandparent.

In practice, there is no such thing as a completely age-segregated society. A totally age-integrated society is equally unlikely. Some societies are more age-integrated than others, and within any given society, the degree of age integration may vary over time.

The concept of age integration applies not just to social institutions but also to periods in the life course. In an age-segregated life course, education

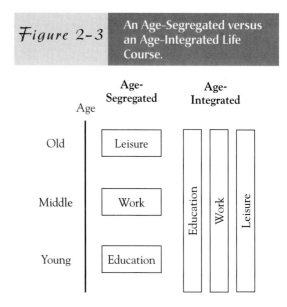

Figure 2–3   An Age-Segregated versus an Age-Integrated Life Course.

Source: Riley and Riley, 2000:267.

is reserved for young people, work for people in their middle years, and leisure for the retired. In an age-integrated life course, people of all ages have an opportunity to pursue education, work, and leisure. Figure 2–3 illustrates the difference between an age-segregated and an age-integrated life course. When outdated social structures prevent people of certain ages from participating fully in society, the society is said to suffer from *structural lag*.

None of these theories can explain why people within age cohorts age so differently. As a result, social gerontologists have become interested in the underpinnings of power differences. Their interest stems not only from gaps in the macro theories but also from larger social changes.

Theories of Power and Inequality

In the early 1970s, the United States was still at war with communism. The war in Vietnam created moral and political turmoil on college campuses across the country, and an array of social movements proposed a new form of personal politics. Civil rights, black power, antiwar, feminist, gay–lesbian, and environmental activists had complex and differing agendas but "shared a concern to set politics in a

Civil rights leader Martin Luther King Jr. at the March on Washington, 1963.

vital relation to the personal" (Lemert, 1995:3). In a sense, sociology was in the streets with those who challenged the social order. In the next decade, it moved from the streets to the classroom, as the ideals of practical politics became translated into radical social theories. As social scientists reflected critically on the relationships between "personal troubles" and public issues of social structure, theories derived from a political economy perspective and from feminism sought to link the micro with the macro.

Political economy theories The political economy perspective is not so much a formal theory as it is a framework for examining the larger social context of problems associated with old age (Passuth and Bengtson, 1988). **Political economy theories** highlight the structural influences on aging and emphasize the relevance of social struggles embedded in power relationships for understanding how the aged

are defined and treated (Estes, Linkins, and Binney, 1996). This focus is distinct from psychologically oriented theories, which view aging as a process of adjustment to changes in physical health and social roles. The political economy approach understands the nature of old age to be socially constructed and to be created through power struggles.

Proponents of the political economy approach share with modernization theorists an interest in explaining the status of the aged. They differ in emphasizing how, in a capitalist economy, political and economic forces distribute societal resources in ways that maintain or increase inequality on the basis of class, race, or gender. As Estes (1991) explained, "the political economy of aging offers a theoretical and empirical perspective on the socioeconomic determinants of the experience of aging and old age and on the policy interventions that emerge in the context of capitalist society"

(p. 19). The challenge for social gerontology is not simply to understand how people interpret their private troubles but rather to consider also how these private troubles become public issues generating societal responses (Estes et al., 1984).

A core supposition of the political economy approach is that public policies for income, health, long-term care, and social services are an outcome of the social struggles and dominant power relations of the era. Sometimes social programs that appear to benefit the people in reality benefit capitalist interests more, an outcome that occurs because business interests often exert undue influence in shaping the policy agenda (Estes, 1979; Quadagno, 1988a). Consider, for example, the drug industry's opposition to a proposal in 2003 to include prescription drugs under Medicare. The big drug companies have persistently opposed including this plan for fear that government payment for prescription drugs could lead to government regulation of drug prices (Quadagno, 2003). Another current policy issue concerns the regulation of long-term-care insurance. For a discussions of some of the problems that have been reported within this recently developed type of insurance, see "An Issue for Public Policy."

A problem with the political economy framework is that older people clearly benefit from many social programs. Social Security has provided a stable source of income for nearly all retired people, and its provisions for automatic cost-of-living increases guarantee that inflation will not erode the value of those benefits. The Older Americans Act provides funds for nutrition sites, meals-on-wheels, and many other programs that improve the quality of life for the elderly. Thus, the issue is not so much whether social welfare programs provide support for the elderly—they do—but rather to determine how and why support is distributed unequally. In Chapter 16, we examine how government policies that purportedly benefit the elderly also contribute to inequality for women and minorities.

The political economy approach has shifted the focus of gerontological research from the individual's ability to adapt to aging to broader social processes that determine how resources are distributed. In this sense, it responds to concerns that age stratification theory ignores power relations. Yet in

abandoning questions about life satisfaction and morale, political economy theorists often ignore entirely individual actors and their motivations, perceptions, and activities. For these reasons, it has been criticized for being too negative and for viewing older people as too passive (Bengtson, Parrott, and Burgess, 1996).

Feminist theories **Feminist theories** of aging are less a formal body of theory than an approach that reflects a commitment to use theory in certain ways. The central purpose of feminist theory is to illuminate the gendered nature of society. A theory can be classified as feminist if gender relations are the main subject matter, if notions of masculinity and femininity are seen as socially constructed, and if emphasis is placed on the different ways aging is experienced by men and women (Arber and Ginn, 1991). As Orloff (1993) explained:

by "feminist," we refer to analyses that take gender relations into account as both causes and effects of various social, political, economic and cultural processes and institutions. . . . By "gender relations," we mean the set of mutually constitutive structures and practices which produce gender differentiation, gender inequalities, and gender hierarchy in a given society. (p. 2)

Among the questions feminist theorists ask are the following: Why do women remain more poorly paid than men? What effect do women's familial responsibilities have on their employment? Why are poverty rates higher among women than men at all stages of the life course?

Feminist theorists criticize research on aging on several grounds. One is that researchers have created separate models of aging by relating certain topics to males and others to females. Widowhood and family life have generally been seen as being about women, for example, while retirement has been seen as being about men (Calasanti and Zajicek, 1993). Thus, until the 1980s, nearly all retirement research involved only male subjects. The neglect of women in retirement studies is partly because women's involvement with retirement is a relatively recent phenomenon, at least for a large share of women. In the past, most women had intermittent patterns of labor force participation and

THE REGULATION OF LONG-TERM-CARE INSURANCE

*P*rivate long-term-care insurance was almost nonexistent until the mid-1980s when the private insurance industry discovered this potentially lucrative, new market. By 1987, 72 companies offered a long-term-care product. As the insurance industry began covering long-term-care policies, numerous abuses surfaced. Investigators for a House subcommittee sent seven senior citizens to spy on insurance agents who sold these policies and discovered that agents exaggerated what the policies covered, sold people duplicate policies, delayed paying covered expenses, and disqualified policyholders when they filed for benefits (U.S. House of Representatives, 1989). Most policies provided little protection against the cost of nursing home care. Few were indexed to keep up with inflation. Most required a prior hospitalization, many would pay only for skilled care and not for custodial care, and more than half excluded admissions for Alzheimer's disease, the main cause of nursing home admission. Some insurance companies paid a commission of as much as 60 percent of first year's premiums, giving agents an incentive to churn clients. For example, Mrs. S purchased similar Medigap policies from three different agents. Mrs. M's agent sold her a Medigap policy, then changed companies four months later and sold her a new policy. An 86-year-old Wisconsin woman bought 19 different policies from six agents representing nine companies (U.S. House of Representatives, 1991).

The insurance industry fiercely resisted any efforts by the federal government to regulate long-term-care insurance, preferring to leave regulation to state insurance departments. Some states did enact minimum standards to reduce the potential for abuse but left numerous loopholes that allowed insurers to ignore the standard. Finally, in 1991 Congress enacted legislation that allowed insurers to offer only nine policy choices and that placed limits on the kind of sales tactics that could be used (Light, 1992).

By the end of 2001, 8.26 million long-term-care insurance policies were in effect. Most policies pay for services received in a nursing home, in an assisted living facility, or at home. Nearly all policies sold today meet federal standards. However, problems still remain. Some people drop their policies when their premiums increase, just at the point when they are most likely to need coverage. Not all policies include protection against inflation. Since many people purchase long-term-care insurance many years before they ever need services, it is critical that the value of their policies increase on a yearly basis. Otherwise, they will find that their insurance covers only a small fraction of the services they need (Kassner, 2003).

What Do You Think?

1. Who do you think should pay the cost of nursing home care?
2. Has anyone in your family purchased a long-term-care insurance policy? If so, what is the monthly cost?

| 2-2 | A Summary of Theories of Aging |

Micro Theories	Macro Theories

Micro Theories

Disengagement theory—Normal aging involves a natural and inevitable withdrawal from society.

Activity theory—The elderly are no different from the middle-aged, and it is neither natural nor inevitable to withdraw.

Continuity theory—Normal aging involves a continuity in personality structure and in patterns of social interaction.

Subculture theory—Older people are likely to form a subculture based on their common interests and their common experiences of exclusion from the wider society.

Exchange theory—Interaction between young and old declines because the elderly have fewer resources to bring to an exchange relationship.

Social constructionism—Human beings are active creators of their own reality, and social meanings of age arise through negotiation and discourse.

Macro Theories

Modernization theory—Although the aged were revered in the past, modernization has caused the status of the aged to decline.

Age stratification theory—All societies group people into age categories, and age represents a powerful source of social stratification.

Age integration theory—Although age is one criterion for organizing social institutions, levels of age segregation and integration vary both across social institutions and over the life course.

Political economy theories—Inequality in old age is caused by political and economic forces and especially by the distribution of societal resources through the welfare state.

Feminist theories—Men and women experience aging differently not because of basic biological differences but because of the organization of social structure and gendered social definitions of reality.

---

thus did not experience an abrupt transition from work to retirement. Another reason is that researchers presumed that men's identity was obtained through work and women's identity came from their family roles. Thus, retirement was perceived to be a more difficult experience for men (Carp, 2001).

Another criticism is that research that is technically gender neutral—that is, women are included as subjects—is often based on a conceptual model derived from men's experiences. Such research often treats women as if they were men, measuring women against the masculine model. For example, research on adjustment to retirement measures women's adjustment in terms of how similar it is to that of men (Calasanti and Slevin, 2001). Yet women have more intermittent patterns of labor force participation than men, are employed in different sectors of the labor market and in different occupations within those sectors, and are less likely than men to find intrinsic rewards in work. One might expect, then, that the predictors of life satisfaction typically applied to a

male model of employment would be inadequate for measuring women's adjustment to retirement (Calasanti, 1996).

A third criticism is that arguments about how social programs produce inequality emphasize class effects but ignore gender effects. A large body of feminist research suggests that social welfare programs reproduce male domination by creating economic inequality between men and women. Feminist theorists contend that in all welfare programs where benefits are linked to wages, women fare worse than men (Harrington Meyer, 1990). For example, Sweden is generally considered to have the most generous old-age provisions among nations. Sweden has two types of pension payments, a flat benefit (termed ATP) that all citizens receive and a social insurance pension (similar to the U.S. Social Security program) calculated on prior earnings (Sainsbury, 1996). Women receive similar benefits to men under the ATP pension; but on average they receive significantly lower benefits than men under the social insurance system because of fewer years in the labor force and lower wages (Sainsbury, 1996).

Despite gender inequality in benefit levels, social insurance systems such as Social Security have done much to eliminate poverty in old age. The dilemma for feminist analysis, like class analysis, has been to decide whether the social welfare programs are friend or foe.

Theories of aging, like all scientific theories, have been influenced by broader historical trends. These trends have helped to establish the core research agenda and have influenced the method to be used in pursuing it. The major turning points in the history of theories of aging have been the Depression of the 1930s, the post–World War II era of economic growth, and the social movements of the 1960s. As events have moved certain issues, such as inequality, to center stage, other issues, such as adjustment and morale, have exited the limelight. To summarize, we can see that these theories can be broadly characterized as micro or macro, and that as we move forward in history, an emphasis on processes over the life course becomes more salient. Table 2–2 summarizes the main aging theories.

Each set of theories has left behind a legacy of useful information about the aged and about processes of aging. In subsequent chapters, we will draw on these theories to help us understand the broader themes underlying specific research findings and to identify how they have informed public policy debates.

Chapter Resources

LOOKING BACK

1. **Who were the first students of social gerontology, and what did they hope to learn?** *Social gerontology originated as a distinct field of study during the Depression. Its first practitioners were developmental psychologists who had traditionally studied growth and maturation. They viewed the basic task of research as documenting the inevitable decline that occurred in old age. Then during the 1940s researchers became interested in "normal" processes of aging. The basic premise underlying this research was that growing old meant surrendering the social relationships and social roles typical of adulthood: thus, retirement, widowhood, the loss of distant goals and plans, and the growing dependence of the elderly on others for support, advice, and management of daily activities.*

2. **What theories of aging did early gerontologists propose?** *Disengagement theory was the first formal theory of aging. It was based on the premise that normal aging involved a natural and inevitable withdrawal of the individual from society. Life satisfaction was highest among those who successfully disengaged. Subsequent research found that some people did disengage but that disengagement was neither universal nor inevitable.*

   Activity theory became an explicit theory of aging in response to disengagement theory, but its core premise—that successful aging was active aging—was implicit in most prior aging research. Activity theory asserts that older people have the same psychological and social needs as younger people and that it is neither normal nor natural for people to disengage.

3. **How did later scholars broaden the scope of the study of aging?** *Scholars broadened the scope of the study of aging to include how social forces and large-scale societal processes influenced individual aging processes. For example, subculture theorists argued that the aged are* likely to form a subculture because they share physical limitations and role losses. Another explicitly social theory of aging is age integration theory, which recognizes that societies use chronological age as a criterion for entrance, exit, or participation.

4. **What is the relationship between age and social status, and does it vary from one culture to the next?** *Modernization theory attempts to understand the relationship between age and social status. Its basic premise is that older people were revered in the past and in preliterate societies and that their status declines with economic development. Yet historical evidence indicates that a "golden age of aging" never existed, while cross-cultural evidence suggests there is great variation in how older people are treated in preliterate societies.*

5. **Which theories of aging consider how race, gender, and class affect the social status of the aged?** *Political economy theory is concerned with explaining how and why social resources are unequally distributed. A central focus of research stemming from the political economy tradition is on how public policies reproduce existing forms of inequality. Feminist theory also attempts to illuminate the gendered nature of society. Feminists criticize traditional research for creating separate models of aging for men and women, for using "male models" to interpret women's experiences, and for failing to recognize how various social welfare programs reproduce gender inequality.*

THINKING ABOUT AGING

1. What is the benefit of having a theory of aging? Do gerontologists really need theories?

2. What type of professional might find micro theories of aging particularly useful? Who might prefer to use macro theories?

3. What might be the professional drawbacks of depending on a single theory of aging?

4. If you were an aged person, which theories of aging would you think were most pertinent to your own life circumstances? Which theories might you disagree with?

5. What is the single most useful or important insight you have gained from reading this chapter?

KEY TERMS

age integration theory 40

activity theory 26

age cohort 38

age stratification theory 36

continuity theory 29

deferred exchange strategies 33

disengagement theory 25

exchange theory 33

feminist theories 42

filial piety 28

immediate exchange strategies 33

Kansas City Study of Adult Life 25

modernization theory 34

political economy theories 41

social constructionism 34

subculture theory 31

EXPLORING THE INTERNET

Note: While all the URLs listed were current as of the printing of this book, these sites often change. Please check our website www.mhhe.com/quadagno for updates.

1. Infoaging.org is a website dedicated to providing information about current research and useful day-to-day knowledge we all need to live healthier, longer lives. Go to the website (www.infoaging.org) and link to News. On the left, link to the section, "Learn: Find out more about healthy aging" by clicking on the yellow "Go" button. Link to the "Healthy Aging Center," click on the exercise link, then on the link asking how exercise is related to aging and answer the following questions:

   a. What are some of the benefits of exercising for the elderly?

   b. What percentage of adults age 85 and older need assistance with their daily living activities?

   Now go to the link on exercise and heart disease on the right and answer the following questions:

   a. What kinds of heart disease risk factors can we eliminate or modify to improve our health?

   b. Which of these, as research suggests, can impact our health the most?

2. Go to the infoaging.org website and link to the section on finding out more about healthy aging. Next, click on "disease center," then "Alzheimer's disease," and answer the following questions:

   a. How do they define Alzheimer's?

   b. Approximately how many people does it affect and how much does it cost?

   c. What are the four stages of Alzheimer's disease?

Life Course Transitions

A ge norms tell us when we are on time and off time for major life events like getting married, having a child, or retiring.

Looking Ahead

1. How did demographic change create a new phase of the life course called middle age?
2. What are the advantages and disadvantages of cross-sections and longitudinal research for measuring life course changes?
3. Do people attempt to time the major events in their lives?
4. Can the sequencing of major life events create role conflict?
5. Why do older Americans move over the life course?
6. Can major historical events affect the life course of a whole generation?
7. How can government affect the life course?

A t the remarkable age of 50, Bette-Jane Raphael gave birth to her second child. Having a baby at the same time she approached menopause had not been part of her life plan, but she was almost 35 when she met her husband, nearly 40 when she had her first child, a son. Rose was born 10 years later. Bette-Jane worries that Rose, when she reaches her teenage years, may be embarrassed by having a wrinkled and gray-haired mother. And Bette-Jane fears dying and leaving Rose without a mother at a time when she may need one most. Mostly, however, Bette-Jane is humble for being allowed such blessings at this stage of life (Raphael, 1995).

When people hear of Bette-Jane Raphael's late-life birth, they are surprised and often disapprove. The disapproval reflects the uneasy sense that she has violated societal expectations about the proper timing for such an event. Social gerontologists refer to these expectations as age norms. **Age norms** are informal rules that specify age-appropriate roles and behavior and, in so doing, provide a road map for traversing the course of life. These rules often remain unspoken until they are violated, and then we recognize that they exist.

Age norms help to determine when people marry, how many children they have, and how they balance work and leisure. Yet life's road map is constantly being redrawn because of changes in demography, the economy, and government policy. These deep transformations reorganize social life and alter individual patterns of growth and development. Social gerontologists who study this road map adopt what is called the **life course** approach. The life course approach recognizes that developmental changes based on biological processes mold human behavior from birth until death, but that human development is also influenced by an array of psychological, social, historical, and economic factors (Featherman, 1983).

In the first section of this chapter we consider how the timing, duration, and order of life's major events are shaped by demographic change and individual experiences and opportunities as well as large-scale social, economic, and political events, such as wars, periods of depression or prosperity, and government policy changes. Then we learn about the causes of inequality in later life. Finally, we discuss the role government policy plays in shaping the way people move through the life course.

THE LIFE COURSE FRAMEWORK

The **life course framework** is an approach to the study of aging that emphasizes the interaction of historical events, individual decisions and opportunities, and the effect of early life experiences in determining later life outcomes (Elder, 1994). In making major decisions, such as when to have a child, people usually consider immediate issues such as their current finances or educational plans. They are less likely to consider how the decisions they make when they are young will influence the rest of their lives. Take the decision to have a child. What are the advantages of having a child early in life, at age 23 or 24, compared to later, at

age 35 or 37? Over the short term, early childbearing may delay the purchase of a house, because saving money is difficult when a couple has a child to support. A woman may also find that her career advancement is delayed. By the age of 45, however, the child will be grown, and the couple will have many more years to work and save before retirement. By contrast, a couple who waits to have children will have ample time to establish themselves in a career, buy a home, and become financially secure. Yet their children may not be independent until they have reached age 60! At a time when this couple should be saving for retirement, they will be paying for college.

These examples illustrate the lifelong consequences of some important individual decisions. The life course of individuals is shaped partially by such decisions made early in life and partially by events that are beyond a person's control.

As people age, they move through different social roles that provide them with different identities—student, husband or wife, worker, parent. Sociologists call these role changes **transitions.** The concept of transitions refers to the role changes individuals make, as they leave school, take a job, get married, have children, or retire. Transitions are age-graded in the sense that there are certain expectations for when the transition from one role to another should take place (Streib and Bourg, 1984). For example, there are societal expectations regarding when people should marry, when they should bear their first children, and when adult children should leave home. Yet traditional expectations are constantly being altered, as people delay marriage, divorce, or live 30 years past retirement. People also experience **countertransitions,** which are produced by others' role changes. When you marry, your mother automatically becomes a mother-in-law. When you have a child, your father automatically becomes a grandfather. Should your spouse die, you will become a widow or widower. Although you yourself did not change, someone related to you did, and that change produced your countertransition. Finally, a series of transitions is called a **trajectory.** In the past, gerontologists viewed trajectories as relatively stable and as having a clear order. The work trajectory, for example, was characterized in terms of three stages: preparation for work (education), work, and retirement. Now researchers recognize that there are multiple pathways in the ordering and timing of life events. For example, there have been distinct gender differences in employment trajectories, with women having more disorderly work careers than men as they move in and out of the labor force to care for children and aging parents. The work trajectories of women have had a negative impact on their income security in old age, because interrupted work histories mean lower Social Security benefits and less access to private pensions (O'Rand, 1996b). Recently, however, the number of years a man has worked for the same employer has declined, and the male work trajectory has become more disorderly even as women's work careers have become more continuous. In the future, the gender difference in income security in old age that is characteristic of the aged today may disappear, because the work trajectories of men and women are becoming more similar. Social gerontologists now recognize multiple pathways in the ordering and timing of life events.

The intellectual origins of the sociological approach to the life course lie in several traditions that cross disciplinary boundaries. The idea that age may be used as a criterion for organizing social relations was elaborated by social theorists such as Sorokin (1941), Parsons (1942), and Eisenstadt (1956), who attempted to understand "why and when age is used by society as a means for sorting people into positions and as a device for allocating goods and services" (Featherman, 1983:9). Age stratification theory, discussed in Chapter 2, represented an effort to integrate these ideas into a formal statement (Riley and Foner, 1968). Three aspects of age stratification theory are relevant to the study of the life course. First, age is one of the bases for regulating social interaction and for ascribing status; second, the timing of the entry into and exit from social positions has age-related consequences; and third, the pattern of biological aging and the sequence of age-related roles are altered by historical events (e.g., improvements in health care, new technologies).

Another influence on the life course approach is the anthropological study of age grading. **Age grades** are ways of using age as a social category to group people by status. Every society has generational principles for organizing the life course. In age-graded systems, males are ranked in hierarchical order according to their age group. Each group has a different role or grade, such as warrior for young men or elder for old men (Fry, 1999). The Arusha of Kenya recognize six grades: youth, junior warrior, senior warrior, junior elder, senior elder, and retired elder. Other societies have only two or three. Interestingly, most societies have more clearly marked age grades for males than for females. Keith (1982) speculated that it may be because women are more tightly integrated into familial roles than men and that these kinship ties create vertical bonds between generations rather than horizontal bonds of age.

METHODOLOGICAL ISSUES IN RESEARCH ON THE LIFE COURSE

Distinguishing Age, Period, and Cohort Effects

A central methodological issue in life course research is how to distinguish between age effects, period effects, and cohort effects. An **age effect** is a change that occurs as a result of advancing age. The basic assumption in measuring age effects is that changes due to aging reflect biological and physiological developments that are independent of specific times, places, or events. The clearest example of an age effect is declining health. For instance, aging is accompanied by an increasing risk of high blood pressure.

A **period effect** is the impact of a historical event on the entire society. For example, in 1963, when police in Birmingham, Alabama, turned fire hoses on black children who were demonstrating peacefully for the integration of lunch counters, buses, and stores, public opinion across the nation swung in favor of civil rights (Schuman et al., 1997). At the individual level, this type of change is called "attitude conversion." Have you experienced memorable events that created a period effect?

A **cohort effect** is the social change that occurs as one cohort replaces another. For example, when members of an older cohort who hold one set of attitudes die, they are replaced by younger people who hold different attitudes. The attitudes of the population as a whole will shift as a result of this cohort replacement. For instance, southerners who were raised during an era when racial segregation was legal hold more conservative racial attitudes than their grandchildren, who grew up after segregation was outlawed (Schuman et al., 1997). A remarkable change occurring in the age of expected retirement is the result of a cohort effect. As Figure 3–1 shows, people born between 1965 and 1978 expect to retire much earlier than people born between 1923 and 1945.

Although the concepts of age, period, and cohort effects sound simple, they can be quite difficult to measure. For example, older people are more likely to vote than younger people. Is this disparity in voting patterns caused by an age effect, meaning that people become better citizens as they grow old? Or is it caused by a cohort effect? The people who are currently old may always have voted in large numbers. We explain this problem in more detail below. Social gerontologists frequently use *cross-sectional research* to distinguish age, period, and cohort effects, but *longitudinal research* is a better approach.

Cross-sectional Research

Research comparing people of different age cohorts at a single point in time is called **cross-sectional research.** Researchers conducting a cross-sectional study ask the same information of people in several age groups. For example, they might ask 20-year-olds, 40-year-olds, and 60-year-olds, "Would you say you are a liberal or a conservative?" The results of that comparison would help to answer the question, Are older people more politically conservative than younger people? Many surveys of political beliefs do find that political conservatism is higher among older age groups. Because of these findings, some researchers have mistakenly concluded that people become more conservative in their political beliefs as they grow older—that is, that an aging effect is occurring. Yet research also suggests that it's likely that many older people were conservative earlier in life and remained so as they aged. What was being observed, then, was a cohort effect, not an age effect (Campbell and Alwin, 1996).

Let's consider another example of a cohort effect that appears to be an age effect. Early research on cognitive ability suggested that intelligence declined with age. The correct interpretation of age differences on intelligence tests, however, is that

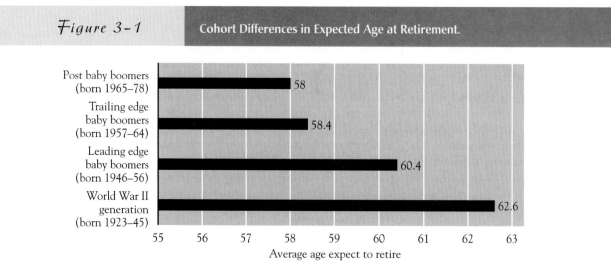

Figure 3-1   **Cohort Differences in Expected Age at Retirement.**

Source: Moen, Plassman, and Sweet (2001).

members of younger cohorts are better educated than their predecessors, which largely accounts for their higher test scores (Riley, 1995). What these tests were measuring, then, were cohort differences in level of education rather than an effect of aging on intelligence. The mistaken conclusions were drawn because cross-sectional data were used. These examples illustrate how easy it is to confound a cohort effect with an aging effect.

Differences between age groups that appear to be age effects also may result from period effects. History creates a period effect when change is relatively uniform across successive birth cohorts (Wasserman, 1989; Elder, 1994). The Great Depression, World War II, the assassination of President Kennedy, the civil rights movement, and the Vietnam War were grand events that distinguished the lives of those who lived through them from people born later.

In judging the importance of a historical event, however, it's important to recognize that the impact of an event is likely to affect each age cohort differently. For example, African Americans who were elderly during the civil rights movement had little opportunity to benefit from expanded opportunities for jobs and education that flowed from passage of the Civil Rights Act of 1964. By contrast, those who were still young at that time were more likely to attend college and enter occupations that had previously been closed to them.

Although cross-sectional studies are not ideal for distinguishing age, period, and cohort effects, they are often the most feasible method for studying aging. They are less costly than longitudinal studies, and they allow researchers to draw conclusions about cohort effects that cannot be gained through the study of a single age group.

Longitudinal Research

Some of the complex methodological issues involved in distinguishing between age effects, cohort effects, and period effects can be sorted out through **longitudinal research.** In contrast to cross-sectional studies that compare subjects from different cohorts, longitudinal studies follow the same group of people over time.

The Health and Retirement Survey is one example of this research design. In this survey, 13,000 individuals born between 1931 and 1941 were first interviewed in 1991 and will continue to be interviewed in successive waves. Analysis of data from the first wave has been published, and some interesting findings have come to light. For example, the first wave of the survey showed that Hispanics of preretirement age have very low levels of health insurance coverage. Subsequent waves will be able to document the effect on their health in old age (Angel and Angel, 1996). The survey's results also provide the first indication of how the rising divorce rate will affect the income security of the aged in the future. Among the respondents, one-third of all households with a married couple had a previous marriage that ended in divorce or widowhood. These couples have lower income and assets than couples in first marriages (Holden, Kuo, and Hsiang-Hui, 1996). When subsequent installments of the survey are ready for analysis, they will provide longitudinal data highlighting the long-term effects of these trends.

One of the most prominent examples of longitudinal research is the Longitudinal Study of Generations conducted by the social gerontologist Vern Bengtson and his colleagues (1996) at the University of Southern California. This study began in 1971 when 300 three-generation families were selected to participate in a survey of how values, attitudes, and traits were transmitted from one generation to another and how they changed in one generation over time. These same families were followed for a quarter of a century, with new surveys being collected every three years. One of the important findings disputed the myth that there has been a gradual weakening of family ties. Rather, the researchers showed that family solidarity remained continuous over the life course. However, they also found considerable variation in forms of family solidarity, with daughters having more contact with aging parents than sons, with widowhood increasing parent–child contact, and with working-class children having more contact with parents than middle-class children (Bengtson, Rosenthal, and Burton, 1990).

The results of this research, now extended to four generations, have been reported to government panels making policy decisions about the family. The findings have been used as a basis for designing intergenerational programs that bring young and old together and by family practitioners involved in counseling or in establishing support groups (Bengtson, Parrott, and Burgess, 1996).

Another major longitudinal study is the Baltimore Longitudinal Study of Aging (BLSA), launched in 1958. More than 1,100 volunteers have participated in this study, the first to track how healthy people grow old. The results of the BLSA have challenged a number of stereotypes about old age. One major finding is that personality doesn't change after age 30; a cranky 40-year-old will be a cranky 80-year-old (Ruth and Coleman, 1996). Another important finding is that only 10 percent of people older than 65 ever develop dementia but that those who do develop it show subtle changes in memory 10 to 20 years earlier (Gatz, Kasl-Godby, and Karel, 1996).

An ambitious new longitudinal study is currently under way called AHEAD (Asset and Health Dynamics among the Oldest Old). AHEAD is an investigation of people aged 70 and older who were born in 1923 or earlier. It includes questions on health, cognitive functioning, income, and exchanges between family members. Data collection began in 1993 and will continue every other year. In 1998, when the original AHEAD respondents were 75 years old, a new cohort of people born between 1924 and 1930 was added (Soldo et al., 1997). Sociologists have already learned from this study that black respondents are less likely than white respondents to receive assistance or to use informal sources of home care (Norgard and Rodgers, 1997); that disability is associated with increased risk of depression (Stump et al., 1997); and that many parents provide financial assistance to their children in exchange for caregiving (McGarry and Schoeni, 1997). We will learn much more in the future, as new data from this study are analyzed.

Longitudinal studies are better than cross-sectional studies for distinguishing age effects from cohort effects because they follow a particular group of people over time. They not only provide data about differences between age cohorts, they also make it possible to make inferences about age change within each cohort and the effect of living through a period across cohorts. We will feature results from longitudinal studies in several chapters in this book.

There are also disadvantages associated with longitudinal studies. By their very nature, they are costly because they follow subjects for years or even decades. They also have biases because subjects are lost over time as people drop out, move away, or die. Those who are left at the end of a longitudinal study may differ in some significant ways from those no longer a part of the sample. For example, numerous studies indicate that people of lower socioeconomic status have poorer health than more affluent people but that these health differences decline with advancing age. The problem is that people in the poorest health may die sooner, leaving a sturdier population of survivors (Ross and Wu, 1996).

Now that we have described some basic concepts and methodological issues in the life course approach, let's examine research findings on the social, economic, and demographic factors that influence the *timing, duration,* and *sequencing* of life course transitions (Rossi, 1980).

IDENTIFYING LIFE COURSE EVENTS

The Timing of Life Course Events

Age norms   Timing refers to the idea that there are appropriate ages for making various life course transitions (Elder, 1985). In the 1960s, a team of researchers led by Bernice Neugarten asked a representative sample of middle-class, middle-aged men and women aged 40 to 70 to indicate the appropriate age for various life events and behaviors. They concluded that the life course was regulated by age norms, defined earlier in the chapter as informal rules that specify age-appropriate roles and behavior (Neugarten, Moore, and Lowe, 1965). The researchers argued that age norms were deeply imbedded in the cultural fabric of adult life and formed a pervasive system that tell us when we are "on time" or "off time" for life events.

Commonplace remarks often reflect an implicit awareness of age norms: "She had her children late." "He's too old to be working so hard." "She's too young to wear makeup." "He's too old to be living at home with his parents." Age norms define

In the later stage of middle age, parents relinquish responsibility for their adult children.

everything we mean when we say, "Act your age." They act as prods or brakes on behavior, sometimes hastening an event, at other times delaying it. In combination, age norms form a prescriptive time-table, called a **social clock,** that orders major life events. The social clock not only influences when people marry, have children, and retire, it also may affect how they feel about entering a new life phase. For example, when grandchildren arrive "too early," women lack preparation for the role, have little peer support, and often reject the idea of becoming a grandmother (Hagestad, 1988).

Are people really aware that their social clocks are ticking? Neugarten and her colleagues discovered that they were. In their research, conducted in the early 1960s, they asked people about the proper timing for one group of events related to the family life course and for a second set related to the occupational life course. They found that their subjects could identify clear expectations about the timing of events that initiated the transition to adulthood—finishing school, marrying, and, for males, beginning work. Neugarten and her associates concluded that men and women recognized that a social clock was ticking and were aware of whether they were on time or off time for major life events.

Many of Neugarten's measures now seem biased in ways that no longer reflect societal norms. This is especially true in regard to gender issues. Neugarten's research was based on the implicit assumption that men were the breadwinners and women the family caregivers. Middle-aged men were seen to be in the prime of life, and middle age was seen to be the time when men accomplished the most, held their top jobs, and assumed the greatest responsibility. The accomplishments of women came earlier in the course of raising their families. With more than 70 percent of women currently in the labor force, these implicit assumptions no longer hold. More recent research reflects the influence of large-scale changes in the family and the labor force.

Age timetables   Settersten and Hagestad (1996a, 1996b) attempted to replicate Neugarten's research on age norms. They interviewed a random sample of 319 adults in the Chicago metropolitan area and asked a series of questions about 11 life course transitions. In the family sphere, the events included leaving home, returning home, getting married, becoming a parent, completing childbearing, and becoming a grandparent. In the sphere of education and work, the events began with leaving school and ended with retirement. Settersten and Hagestad found that a high proportion of their respondents could identify an age deadline for most events. Table 3–1 shows the average age deadline for these life course transitions. Differences in the expected timing of events compared to Neugarten's results reflect demographic and social change. For example, in Neugarten's study, most people agreed that the best age for a woman to marry was between 19 and 24.

This consensus reflected actual marriage patterns, for in the 1950s half of all women were married by the age of 21. Between the mid-1950s and 1993, the median age at first marriage rose by four years (Cherlin, 1996). Settersten and Hagestad's results reflect this rise in the age of marriage.

The concept of age norms implies that sanctions are attached to behavior and that people who are off time for various life events will experience disapproval or even stronger sanctions. However, Settersten and Hagestad found that although consensus existed on the timing of life events, most people believed that there were no consequences for missing cultural age deadlines. Perhaps the influence of cultural age deadlines is less important than researchers in the past presumed, or perhaps the concept of age norms itself is a product of a historical era and thus increasingly irrelevant. Because the expected timing of important life events is looser and more flexible than it may have been in the past, Settersten and Hagestad preferred the term **age timetables** rather than age norms.

One 80-year-old grandmother rejected suggestions about what she should be doing "at her age," asserting that this is her time to do what she wants (see "In Their Own Words").

The Duration of Life Course Events

Duration refers to the number of years spent in each phase of the life course (Hagestad, 1990). The duration of life events is continually being transformed.

One distinctive change in the duration of a life course phase is the extension of adolescence. Historically, adolescence ended when young people left the family home. Until about 1980, grown children were expected to become independent and not return home as permanent residents, regardless of whether they were single or married. In the past two decades, young people have remained longer in the parental home or left and then returned, creating a **crowded nest** (Schnaiberg and Goldenberg, 1989). In 1992, 60 percent of young men aged 18 to 24 and 48 percent of women of that age were still living at home with their parents. Even among men 25 to 34, 15 percent were

Table 3-1	Age Timetables for Major Life Events	

	Average Age Deadlines	
	Male	*Female*
Family events		
Leaving home	21.7	21.9
Returning home	27.2	28.2
Marriage	27.9	25.9
Parenthood	29.9	28.8
Completing childbearing	44.2	39.1
Grandparenthood	52.3	50.9
Work and educational events		
Exit full-time schooling	26.4	25.5
Enter full-time work	22.8	21.7
Settle on career/job	29.0	28.9
Peak of work career	41.7	39.8
Retirement	61.3	59.3

Source: Settersten and Hagestad (1996a, 1996b).

In Their Own Words

Time for Myself

$\mathcal{A}$ grandmother in her 80s finds she is savoring new experiences.

On my 80th birthday, my family and friends gave me a lovely party. They congratulated me and said with straight faces that I looked 60. I thanked them, but thought to myself, I was no beauty at 60, why would I want to look like that now?

Moreover, why should I want to be young now? As my grandchildren say, "Been there, done that." Yet I am being hit from all sides with things I must do, foods I must eat, ways I must think to stay forever young. I get exhausted just thinking about it. . . . Think positive, be upbeat, they say, and this bunch of vitamins will help. (Even though, after spending your money, you may be told that the rules have changed and you took the wrong ones.)

Working out in a gym is a must. I tried it once and was told by a gorgeous 30-year-old woman that my posture was lousy (I knew that) and that a woman my age should be careful on the machines. I was careful not to go back.

There are other ways to search for youth after the age of 70. You can spend lots of money and many hours in a beauty salon changing the color of your hair, and even get lured into wearing short skirts and hobble on high heels to look youthful. You can hand your retirement money over to a plastic surgeon for a few tucks around the eyes or the chin or both. Or buy some magic wrinkle cream that will supposedly erase those wrinkles. Not me. I am rather fond of my wrinkles.

They get me a seat on the bus and a discount at the movies.

I want my old age to be different from my youth, not just a continuation of it. Old age is a new experience. I've never been here before. I have never had the luxury of not having to do anything. No commitment, no demand on my time.

I rather fancy my days, languid stretches of time out of a Gothic southern novel. In the morning I can snuggle back under my luscious down comforter and get up when I please. . . . I might answer some letters, pay bills, glance at catalogues or write—at the typewriter. No computer here. A sandwich, a cup of tea, a siesta, then a long walk along a nearby lake might round out my day until dinner.

Uneventful? Yes. But taken, in the context of a life that always had a time schedule, always an unending list of things to do, my day is a gift from the gods. Each age has been different and I have enjoyed them all. I am not going to waste this age by trying to skip it.

My life now is my dessert, the whipped cream of leisure I was longing for. It probably sounds empty to many, and not useful, but I am tired of being useful. This is my time to enjoy the quietness of just being, of stopping to look and feel and think, of indulging myself. Time for myself at last.

Source: Colman (1998:84).

still living with parents (U.S. Bureau of the Census, 1993b:60). This trend led Hartung and Sweeney (1991) to suggest that a new age definition of young adulthood has developed. Instead of children setting out to make their way in the world, the parental home now serves as a base of operations during the phase that precedes marriage (DaVanzo and Goldscheider, 1990).

Why won't the "baby birds" leave the nest? One reason is that low wages for young workers and high costs of housing have made it difficult for young people to establish independent households or at least to maintain lifestyles to which they are accustomed. In addition, divorced adult children often return home, many times with children of their own (Goldscheider and DaVanzo, 1985).

Another change in the duration of a life course phase has been the extension of old age. The increase in life expectancy that has occurred in the past half century among people older than 65, especially among those older than 85, means that the period of old age may last as long as 30 or 40 years. Most people live long enough to become grandparents and to play an active role in their grandchildren's lives. Many people who are themselves elderly may have children who are old (Uhlenberg, 1996b).

The Sequencing of Life Course Events

The idea of sequencing presumes that transitions should be made in a particular order (Rindfuss, Swicegood, and Rosenfeld, 1987). The implication is of orderliness and irreversibility. How orderly is the life course? In some cases, sequencing is quite apparent. Today it is rare to find an overlap between parenthood and grandparenthood. The two

roles are clearly sequenced, although that was not true in the past (Hagestad, 1988). But, as we have noted elsewhere, the average number of years people can expect to have both parents alive has tripled in the past century. Thus, middle-aged adults are now more likely to have simultaneous obligations to children and to parents (Watkins, Menken, and Bongaarts, 1987).

Disorder in the sequencing of life events may have negative consequences for later life transitions. For example, interrupted schooling and early parenthood are both associated with lower income later in life (Rindfuss, Swicegood, and Rosenfeld, 1987). The overlapping of life events may also create role conflicts. Middle-aged people who have both dependent children and aging parents often are described as the "sandwich generation." When parenting, employment, and parent care coincide, the strains can be enormous.

Yet how typical is this situation? A large majority of men and women in their early 40s do have at least one living parent, as do 60 percent of people in their late 50s (Bengtson, Rosenthal, and Burton, 1996). But one study of Canadian women found that only 16 percent who had a living parent helped the parent monthly or more often with housework, transportation, financial support, or home maintenance (Rosenthal, Matthews, and Marshall, 1989). Further, as Table 3–2 shows, the

The proverbial "empty nest" has become the "crowded nest" as more young adults return to the parental home.

Table 3-2	Women with Parents Aged 65 or Older and Children Younger than 18 in Household	
Women's Ages	Parents Age 65+	Children Younger than 18 in Household
40–44	97%	17%
45–49	92	18
50–54	78	4
55–59	60	2
60–64	35	1
65–74	14	<1

Source: Boyd and Treas (1989).

likelihood of having child rearing and parent care overlap is relatively small. Fewer than 17 percent of 40- to 45-year-olds have children under 18 still living at home. To estimate the extent of multiple role conflicts in middle age, Spitze and Logan (1990a) interviewed 1,200 women aged 40 and over in a three-county area in New York. They found that only 36 percent of those aged 40 to 44 and 27 percent of those aged 45 to 49 had living parents, a child in the household, *and* a job. The midlife squeeze may be even more prevalent than these figures suggest, for two reasons. One is the trend toward the crowded nest, which increases the chance of having active parenting and care of an elderly parent overlap. The other is the increase in the number of well-educated women who delay childbearing (Boyd and Treas, 1989).

Social scientists have also discovered a sequencing in the order of later life moves (Bean et al., 1994). The first move occurs among young retirees seeking a comfortable lifestyle. These migrants are more likely than nonmigrants to be married, to have higher incomes and educational levels, and to be healthy (Biggar, 1980; Longino, 1990). A second move occurs 20 or more years later, when older people develop chronic disabilities, experience a serious illness, or become widowed. In this case, the move is motivated by a desire to be closer to children. Some older people move into a child's home; others choose a location nearer their children. Finally,

physical incapacity may force a third move to a nursing home or assisted living facility (Longino et al., 1991). This last move is usually local rather than long-distance. Despite the popular image of the young–old as a population in flux, the oldest–old are most likely to have changed residences in the past five years. Among people over 85, widowhood, disability, and institutionalization prompt frequent moves (Bould, Sanborn, and Reif, 1989).

The relevance of the life course perspective in analyzing the social impact of later-life moves is obvious. An influx of young–old retirees creates economic benefits for a community (Fuguitt and Beale, 1993). Newcomers expand the tax base and create jobs for businesses oriented to their needs. By contrast, regions left with a disproportionate number of frail and poor elderly experience heavy demands on local resources and a drain on state budgets (Longino, 1990).

The Effect of Early Historical Events on Later Life Course Experiences

Inherent in the life course approach is the notion that early experiences reverberate across the whole life course. These cumulative effects have been difficult to document, because few studies are conducted over a sufficiently long time span. A few pioneering studies have been able to overcome this problem to some extent.

Glen Elder's (1974) research on how events experienced early in life influence later life transitions and outcomes has become a model for the life course approach. His book *Children of the Great Depression* reported the results of his work on two cohorts of children. The first, born in the early 1920s, were adolescents during the Depression; the second, born in 1928–29, experienced the Depression as young children. Elder found that the younger children were more adversely affected by the Depression than the older children. These results illustrate one principle of life course research: It's not just living through a major historical event such as the Depression that matters but the age at which one experiences that event.

In a later study, Shanahan, Elder, and Miech (1997) analyzed how the Depression influenced career success for two groups of men who participated in the Stanford-Terman Study of Gifted Children.

All the men came from privileged backgrounds. One group of men, those born between 1904 and 1910, were just beginning their careers when the Depression struck. These men could take refuge from a contracting labor market in colleges and universities. They graduated college and received advanced degrees. When the hard times ended, they launched careers, only to have their chance for job mobility interrupted by World War II. At the war's end, they returned home to find that career opportunities had passed them by. In contrast, men born slightly later, between 1911 and 1917, completed their education after the Depression had ended and began their careers in the postwar period of economic prosperity and expanding opportunity. By middle age, the later-born men had as much career success as the earlier-born men, even though they had less education. This study illustrates another important principle of the life course approach: History and social context place structural limitations on achievement. "Aging around the World," which describes how German soldiers fared after World War II, illustrates the same principle.

Another study of women who were in their 30s during the Depression found that many married late and postponed motherhood (Hofferth, 1984). These decisions had lifelong consequences. When they reached retirement age, women who postponed their first birth until age 30 or later were financially more secure than women who had their first child sooner. Family size also influenced income security over the life course. Women who had one or two children were better off financially than those who had larger families. Thus, late childbearing (after age 29) and small family size were associated with a higher standard of living later in life.

The quality of family relationships in childhood also has an effect on mental health in adulthood. Adults with divorced parents compared with adults of parents who remained married report greater unhappiness, less satisfaction with life, and more symptoms of anxiety and depression. Parental conflict and divorce erodes ties between parents and children in later life and leads to greater conflict among siblings as adults (Amato and Sobolewski, 2001; Panish and Stryker, 2001). These results occur in studies of people not only in the United States but also in Great Britain, Canada, and Australia.

Early life patterns have an effect on health in later life as well. A number of studies have found that children who are overweight are much more likely than slim children to be obese as adults. Being overweight at age 15 and 16 is a strong predictor of adult obesity. Genetic factors may be responsible, but it is also possible that obesity is a learned behavior caused by parental eating habits. These results suggest that weight reduction interventions for children are needed to break the chain of risk and improve health over the entire life course (Ferraro, Thorpe, and Wilkinson, 2003).

Finally, some research suggests that childhood traumas influence subsequent life course patterns. One study of women who had been sexually abused as children found that they were more sexually active in adolescence and adulthood than other women. They had sex at earlier ages, had more sexual partners, were more likely to have a sexually transmitted disease and forced sex, and were more likely to become parents in their teens (Browning and Laumann, 1997). Another study examined the effect of the early loss of both parents on elderly African Americans. The researchers interviewed 109 men and women aged 85 and older and found that those whose parents had died or deserted the family were less integrated into family and friendship networks in late life. One example is Mrs. Long, who never knew either parent:

My mother died when I was very small. I got shuffled from one family member to another. I went to live with my mother's sister, and then she died, so I got sent to my father's mother. She died, and I don't remember after that. I just kept getting sent from one family member to another.

Now at 86 Mrs. Long lives alone. Her days consist of meals, medicine, and television. No one calls on her birthday (Johnson and Barer, 2002:114). These findings indicate that problematic transitions at one point in time may have long-term consequences.

Demographic Change and Middleage

The life course "begins and ends with demographic events—birth and death," and demographic change creates variations in the experiences of

Aging around the World

THE EFFECT OF MILITARY SERVICE ON GERMAN VETERANS OF WORLD WAR II

*H*ave you served in the military? Have any of your friends? Military service is becoming an increasingly rare phase in the life course of American men. In the United States, approximately 80 percent of men born in the 1920s served in the military, compared to only 10 percent of men born in the 1960s (Putnam, 2000).

How does military service influence the life course of soldiers? One answer to this question is provided by a study of German veterans of World War II. The war had a devastating effect on the German people, a large proportion of whom served in the army. Many soldiers lost their lives, leaving behind massive numbers of widows and orphans. Allied forces occupied the war-ruined country, which soon fell into a deep economic crisis. Many Germans became refugees (Mayer, 1988).

German veterans who survived the war resumed their lives in the midst of turmoil. Yet surprisingly, one researcher found that the war did not have its most adverse effects on men who had served in the army (born from 1920 to 1925) or on those who had served the longest (Mayer, 1988). Rather, it had the greatest effect on those men who entered the labor market for the first time soon after the war ended (those born between 1926 and 1932). Maas and Settersten (1999) used the Berlin Aging Study (BASE), a random sample of West Berliners born between 1887 and 1922, to trace the consequences of military service on these men's lives. Compared to those who did not serve in the military, veterans did experience an immediate negative impact on their careers. Men who had served as soldiers were more likely than nonsoldiers to be unemployed at the end of the war, and less likely to enjoy upward mobility. The longer they had served in the military, the more negative the effect. But the negative effect of military service was not long-lasting. By 1955, as the German economy began to recover, veterans were indistinguishable from other civilians. Most of those who had been downwardly mobile immediately after the war recovered their class positions. Researchers concluded that while military service does have a short-term effect on men's lives, over the entire life course the effect is negligible.

What Do You Think?

1. Do you know anyone whose life course was changed because of military service? If so, explain the circumstances.
2. Can you guess why German veterans were eventually able to overcome the negative effects of their military service? Does military service have long-term benefits?

different cohorts (Uhlenberg, 1996c:226). One effect of demographic change has been the creation of a new phase of the life course—middle age. Until recently, middle age was indistinct from the rest of adult life. In the nineteenth century, women had their first children when they were in their twenties and continued having children until they were nearly 40. Because women bore many children, the years from 40 to 60 were consumed by childrearing tasks. For nineteenth-century women, 90 percent of their married lives were spent in child rearing. Not until the average couple reached 60 were their children fully launched. It was not uncommon for people to become grandparents while they were still caring for dependent children. Given low life expectancy, a married couple could then expect to survive together for only two years after age 60 before one of them became widowed.

By the 1970s, the average couple had their first child by their mid-20s and had a total of two children spaced two years apart. Only 40 percent of married life was spent in child rearing. By the time husband and wife reached their mid-40s, their children had left home. This left a period of 20 years or more with a couple alone together, not yet old, in an **empty nest.** Thus, changing patterns of childbearing, along with increasing life expectancy, created middle age as a separate phase of the life course.

When Bernice Neugarten (1968) interviewed 100 men and women between the ages of 45 and 60, she discovered that they saw middle age as a distinct period that differed qualitatively from other life periods. Her subjects felt an increasing sense of distance from the young as they recognized the vast differences in life experiences between the two cohorts. For example, one 48-year-old man who was interviewed in 1965 noted that he had graduated from college in the middle of the Depression. "Today's young people are different," he explained. "They've grown up in an age of affluence." Another man noted that the young people in his office had never seen a Shirley Temple film or an Our Gang comedy: "Then it struck me with a blow that I was older than they. I had never been so conscious of it before" (Neugarten, 1968:94).

These middle-aged adults identified more now with their parents' generation. As one woman explained, "My parents, even though they are much older, can understand what we are going through, just as I now understand what they went through" (Neugarten, 1968:95). Increasing age also brought an awareness that time is finite. "There is now the realization that death is very real. Those things don't quite penetrate when you're in your twenties, and you think that life is all ahead of you. Now you know that death will come to you too" (Neugarten, 1968:97).

While middle age was once defined as a separate phase of the life course, following marriage and parenthood, sociologists are now witnessing a restructuring of the middle adult years. During the early phase of middle age, beginning around age 35, adults typically carry a full set of social and personal responsibilities. Their children are reaching school age, adolescence, or early adulthood. Mothers are returning to the labor force or shifting from part-time to full-time work. For some, careers are peaking. In the later stage of middle age, adults gradually relinquish responsibilities as their adult children leave home. Some people choose to retire early, but others continue their careers into old age (Moen and Wethington, 1999). Increasingly, late middle age includes caregiving for aging parents, a result of declining mortality among the very old. Although adult children have always provided care for aging parents, only recently has this phase become commonplace and anticipated. The prospect of the caregiver burden looms large, because a growing number of middle-aged people have living parents but fewer siblings to help provide care (Uhlenberg, 1996b).

THE THEORY OF CUMULATIVE DISADVANTAGE

Over the life course, there is increasing diversity between members of a cohort, which creates greater inequality. Inequality among people 65 or older is the highest of all age groups (O'Rand, 1996a). A central concern of life course research is to explain why inequality increases with age. The **theory of cumulative disadvantage** highlights the influences of earlier life experiences on the quality of life in old age.

Those who are advantaged early in life have more opportunity to obtain an education, get a good job, earn a high salary, and save for retirement. Inequality in later life is a product of the interaction between institutional arrangements, individual actions, and access to opportunity. Among the questions raised by the theory of cumulative disadvantage are these: What facilitates the increase in inequality over time? Why have federal programs done little to reduce inequality among the elderly? We attempt to answer these questions in Chapter 16. Here we briefly discuss the implications of the theory of cumulative disadvantage for gender and racial inequality in old age.

Gender Inequality over the Life Course

There is extensive research showing how traditional gender roles affect the social and economic status of women. Performing household work and caring for children or parents disadvantages women in the labor market. Women who have dependent children or parents under their care often sacrifice higher earnings or prospects for advancement in exchange for flexible schedules and ease of exit and reentry into the labor force. Women who take time out to provide family care and then return to the labor force are often treated as newcomers and paid low wages. For example, women who planned their labor force participation around family goals take jobs that provide greater flexibility, but these are also more likely to be dead-end jobs that lack opportunities for upward mobility (O'Rand, 1990). Consequently, years after their child rearing is completed, these women's wages are substantially lower than those of men with the same qualifications (Hogan and Astone, 1986). Moreover, gender differences in income extend into retirement, for women are penalized for their intermittent work histories in the amount of income they receive from Social Security, private pension plans, and individual retirement accounts (Harrington Meyer, 1990). As younger women "follow the male life course model . . . with such continuous work, they are more likely to improve their financial prospects in retirement" (Kohli et al., 1991:29).

Racial Inequality over the Life Course

In the case of African American men and women who entered the labor market before passage of the Civil Rights Act of 1965, restricted opportunity in the form of low wages, high rates of unemployment, and more part-time employment had life course consequences (Fillenbaum, George, and Palmore, 1985; Palmore et al., 1985). Irregular work histories and lower-paying jobs result in lower Social Security payments and less income from private pensions (Farley and Allen, 1987). By contrast, African American men and women who entered the labor market after passage of the Civil Rights Act were paid more equitably and had more job opportunities than those who had entered the labor market earlier (Farley, 1984). Yet, as discussed in Chapter 16, pension coverage among minorities has actually been declining, both because of continuing racial discrimination in employment and because of changes in the labor market. The historical legacy of racial discrimination is still operating even when barriers to opportunity are formally eliminated. Income inequality by race should decline among the elderly in the future if cohort differences in life course employment opportunities are realized.

THE STATE AND THE LIFE COURSE

Some of the life course uncertainties related to economic risks have been alleviated by the state. In sociological theory, *state* is a global term that defines the complex functions and components of government, including its executive, legislative, and judicial branches, the military, and public health and welfare institutions (Estes, 1996). The modern nation-state evolved from the attempts of rulers to consolidate and enlarge a territory and to establish central authority in a struggle against external and internal powers. It consists of a rational-legal constitution, rational law, and a bureaucracy acting according to impartial laws and regulations (Mayer and Muller, 1986).

As the state has assumed functions that were previously performed by the family, the church,

A teacher reads Quotations from Chairman Mao to students in China, 1969.

and private charities, it has altered the nature of the life course (Mayer and Schoepflin, 1989). The most notable effect has been to standardize life course transitions by specifying certain ages for particular rights, responsibilities, and public benefits (O'Rand, 1990; Kohli, 1986). The outcome has been a periodization of life defined by distinct breaking points (Mayer and Muller, 1986). Three types of state intervention can affect the individual life course: (1) regulations and laws (i.e., the age at which students can leave school); (2) social programs (i.e, income support programs such as Social Security, which prevent sudden, steep income

losses); and (3) services provided to people of a given age (i.e., the Older Americans Act).

The state has had the greatest impact on two phases of the life course: adolescence and old age (Dannefer, 1984; Kohli, 1985). For example, the transition from adolescence to adulthood is now defined by regulations regarding the age for voting, for obtaining a driver's license, for purchasing and consuming alcoholic beverages, and for marrying without parental consent. Similarly, the transition to old age is marked primarily by eligibility for Social Security benefits. These benefits make older people less dependent on others for economic

Diversity in the Aging Experience

SENT-DOWN YOUTH IN THE CHINESE CULTURAL REVOLUTION

In 1968, when college students in the United States were engaged in antiwar protests, young people in China were in turmoil as well. The radical Red Guard rebellion had closed government offices and paralyzed schools. High school students waited to graduate and receive job assignments from the government. Instead, the Chinese communist leader Mao Zedong issued his revolutionary send-down policy: "It is necessary for the educated youth to go to the countryside and be reeducated by the poor peasants," he proclaimed (Zhou and Hou, 1999). Over 17 million urban youths were forced to relocate to rural areas. Though some volunteered, most had no choice. One sent-down youth recalled:

> When Chairman Mao's instruction was announced, my father "voluntarily" applied for going to rural areas on behalf of his three children. . . . When he came home that day, he held the three of us in his arms and cried: "It is not that I don't want to keep you in the city. But I dare not do so." I can never forget my father's eyes that day, filled with torture, fear, sadness, and guilt. . . . Sending his three children to rural areas did not save my father's soul. Instead he put upon himself an enormous psychological burden. He died of lung infection in the winter of 1971. (Zhou and Hou, 1999:16)

(continued)

security and more capable of making plans to retire based on stable expectations of income (Mayer and Muller, 1986). By defining the end of adolescence and the beginning of old age, the state has established predictable life course markers.

One of the most extreme examples of state intervention in the life course occurred in China during the Cultural Revolution, when Communist leaders instituted a harsh "send-down" policy. During a 12-year period beginning in 1967, more than 17 million urban Chinese youths were forced to relocate to impoverished rural areas. The "Diversity in the Aging Experience" feature describes the effect of being "sent down" on the life course of these youths.

One question now being raised concerns whether the division of the life course into three stages is still functional. Not only are people living longer, they are also healthier than in the past. Most older people have no serious disabilities, and many remain active well into their 80s (Manton, and Stallard, 1996). At the same time, the American workforce has suffered periodically from over- and undersupplies of professionals and skilled labor. Demographic changes may further decrease the supply of young workers in the future (Featherman, 1983). Why, then, can't older people learn new skills so that they can continue to contribute to society? Today, there are serious proposals to reduce age differentiation and spread education, work, and leisure over the entire life course.

For many youths, the send-down experience was a traumatic event. Most urban youths had never lived in a rural area, and most were sent far from home. Many were allowed to visit their families for only a few weeks every three years. For more than 12 hours a day, seven days a week, they worked in the fields. Some were stationed in the country for about five years, others for as long as 12 years. After Chairman Mao died in 1979, triggering riots and protests by the sent-down youth, government leaders ended the program.

How did being sent down influence these young people in later life? A follow-up study of sent-down youth conducted in 1993 and 1994 found that the experience had a significant effect on them (Zhou and Hou, 1999). For those young people who had stayed in rural areas for a long time, marriage and childbearing were significantly delayed. When they finally returned to the city, they started out on the lower rungs of the occupational ladder. Yet there were some positive consequences. Compared to youths who had never left the cities, sent-down youth were more likely to obtain a college education; among young women, those who were sent down had higher incomes. The hardship of their rural experience may have fostered perseverance and risk taking, making them more capable of taking advantage of opportunities. Another possibility is that the sent-down youth were more likely to graduate college because they were well-connected politically and thus likely came from more prosperous backgrounds to begin with. This study confirms the decisive role the state can play in restructuring the individual life course.

What Do You Think?

1. Do you know anyone who has left a comfortable home to live and work in an underdeveloped area? If so, how did the experience change that person's life course?
2. Compare the experience of the sent-down Chinese youth to that of the German veterans of World War II (see "Aging Around the World"). Are there any similarities between their experiences? What general conclusion might you draw from the life course of these two groups?

Over the past decade, research incorporating the life course perspective has emphasized that aging is a dynamic process that must be studied in a historical and social context and that age, period, and cohort effects shape the aging experience for individuals and social groups (Bengtson et al., 1997). Although much of the research on the life course emphasizes modal patterns, large numbers of people do not fit these patterns. Rather, the path through life is quite heterogeneous, challenging the idea that there is an "institutionalized" life course (O'Rand, 1996a). There is also much to be learned about how the life course stages described by psychologists interact with wider structural changes. Given our recognition that stages are constantly being transformed, a more useful approach may be to emphasize the transitions that link life phases to diverse trajectories.

Chapter Resources

LOOKING BACK

1. **How did demographic change create a new phase of the life course called middle age?** *Changing demographic trends have altered the nature of the life course for each new cohort. Until recently middle age did not exist as a separate phase of the life course. It was created by declining fertility and rising life expectancy, which provided a married couple 20 or more years alone together after their children had left home.*

2. **What are the advantages and disadvantages of cross-sectional and longitudinal research for measuring life course changes?** *In cross-sectional research, comparisons are made between people of different age cohorts at one point in time. Cross-sectional studies are useful for examining age differences in attitudes and behaviors, but they cannot measure age changes. Longitudinal research, which follows the same individuals over time, is better suited for distinguishing between age, period, and cohort effects.*

3. **Do people attempt to time the major events in their lives?** *The timing of life course transitions is regulated by age norms, which define age-appropriate roles and behavior. Research shows that people have clear expectations about the timing of various life course events and know when they are "on time" or "off time." However, recent studies suggest that the term "age timetable" may be more appropriate than "age norm," since there are few negative sanctions attached to being off time for life course transitions.*

4. **Can the sequencing of major life events create role conflict?** *The concept of sequencing presumes that transitions should be made in a particular order. Some life events are clearly sequenced, such as parenting and grandparenting, while others overlap. Overlapping events can create role conflict. The idea of a midlife squeeze caused by role conflicts stemming from role overlap has received much attention. Yet only a relatively small percentage of middle-aged adults simultaneously have all children under 18, paid employment, and responsibilities for an aging parent.*

5. **Why do older Americans move over the life course?** *Young retirees tend to gravitate to warmer climes in search of a more carefree lifestyle. Later in retirement, after an illness or the death of a spouse, many Americans make a second move to be closer to their children. Those who live longest may make a third move, to a nursing home or assisted living facility.*

6. **Can major historical events affect the life course of a whole generation?** *Although there is insufficient longitudinal data to test all the ideas researchers have about the long-term consequences of early life experiences, some research has been able to overcome these limitations. Studies show that the impact of early experiences such as living through an economic depression can influence the life course of an entire generation. However, the consequences vary depending on the individual's age at the time the event occurred and on what decisions were made about how to deal with that event.*

7. **How can government policy affect the life course?** *When government policy gives people at specific ages particular rights, responsibilities, and public benefits, such as Social Security, it helps to standardize the life course. Currently, there are three clearly demarcated stages in the life course—education, work, and leisure. As society and the economy grow more complex, the challenge now is to explore ways policies can be restructured to allow more flexibility over the life course.*

THINKING ABOUT AGING

1. What are the practical implications of the life course approach to social gerontology?

2. Analyze the timing, duration, and sequencing of your parents' life course. Was it typical for their generation?

3. What was the major historical event of your parents' life course? How did it affect their lives?

4. If government officials want to promote social equality, at what stage of the life course should they intervene? Explain.

5. If you were a government policy maker, would you use the power of the state to alter the course of adolescence? If so, how?

KEY TERMS

age effect 51

age grades 51

age norms 49

age timetables 56

cohort effect 51

countertransitions 50

cross-sectional research 52

crowded nest 56

empty nest 62

life course 50

life course framework 50

longitudinal research 53

period effect 51

social clock 55

theory of cumulative disadvantage 62

trajectory 50

transitions 50

EXPLORING THE INTERNET

Note: While all the URLs listed were current as of the printing of this book, these sites often change.

Please check our website www.mhhe.com/quadagno for updates.

1. Go to the website (http://www.aifs.org.au/) and link to Research Program, then Previous Research, then Research Projects and Publications 1996–1998. Read the article, "Life Course of Australian Families" and answer the following questions:

   a. What was the purpose of the longitudinal study described in this article?
   b. How were the data obtained?
   c. What were some of the research issues addressed in this study?
   d. Why do you think studies that examine changes in the life course are important?

2. Most people expect that by the time they retire, they will no longer have young children in their homes. Yet today, more grandparents are raising their grandchildren than ever before. To see suggestions about this trend from the American Association of Retired Persons, go to http://www.aarp.org/confacts/programs/grandraising.html and answer the following questions:

   a. What percent of children under 18 live in a grandparent-headed household?
   b. Name a few organizations that can assist with legal issues.
   c. How can grandparents raising grandchildren inquire about financial assistance?

Chapter 4

Demography of Aging

The echo boomers helped create the world of dot.com businesses. David Hargis, a promotions manager at Listen.com, spends much of his day on the computer.

Looking Ahead

1. How is a population's age structure related to its stage of economic development?
2. What is the relative life expectancy of men versus women, and how is it related to the sex ratio?
3. In the United States, how have fertility, mortality, and migration rates changed over the past century, and what has been the effect on the nation's population?
4. How has life expectancy in the United States changed over the past century, and does it differ from one group to the next?

eaned on video games, day care, CDs, and hip hop, the **echo boomers** are the generation of Americans born between 1977 and 1994. They can teach their parents the fine points of surfing the Web, have no problem accepting women as leaders, and know firsthand about family breakups and the tragedies of drugs and guns. Ideally suited to carry America forward into a wired world, the echo boomers are nearly as large a generation as their parents', the 75 million **baby boomers** born between 1946 and 1964. At 72 million strong, the echo boomers are more racially and ethnically diverse than the baby boomers. Only 66 percent of the echo boomers are white, 15 percent are African American, and 14 percent are Hispanic. Among baby boomers, 75 percent are white, 11 per cent are African American, and 9 percent are Hispanic.

As the echo boomers enter the labor force, their parents will enter old age. The oldest of the baby boomers are now in their late-50s; many will retire in the next decade, creating the largest cohort of senior citizens in U.S. history. Each new cohort makes its mark as its size and composition changes the nature of the world around it. Cohort size is determined by basic population processes—fertility (the number of births), mortality (the number of deaths), and migration (the arrival of new members from other countries). These processes are the subject matter of **demography;** in combination they determine a population's **age structure,** or the proportion of people in various age cohorts. Every birth, every death, every move from one region or country to another, reflects the decisions people have made, the crises they have faced, the plans and dreams they have for the future. Together, these individual decisions and experiences create a population with identifiable characteristics. Demographers study these population characteristics to make population projections for the future, to determine the effects of public policies, to anticipate policy-related political, economic, and social changes, and to expose social problems that might be resolved by informed planning.

This chapter begins with a brief description of the sources of demographic data. A discussion of the process of **population aging**—a gradual increase in the proportion of older people to younger people—follows. We pay particular attention to the phenomenon of the demographic transition, illustrated by international trends in age structure. On an individual level, we define two basic measures of individual aging: life span and life expectancy. Next, we focus on how declines in fertility and in mortality coupled with changing patterns of migration have altered the nation's population profile. The chapter concludes with a description of the diverse characteristics of older Americans—their marital status, income and poverty levels, education, and geographic mobility.

SOURCES OF POPULATION DATA

Demographic analysis is based on census counts taken by public or private agencies. In the United States the Bureau of the Census is the central clearinghouse for all national population data. The Census Bureau makes national counts of the population every 10 years and obtains information from each household on births, deaths, country of origin of the residents, health, living arrangements, occupation, and income.

Using the data gathered, the Census Bureau prepares reports and documents that are released to the public. Though the Bureau constantly monitors the accuracy of its data and makes monumental efforts to cross-check its records, errors inevitably arise from the undercounting of people who are difficult to reach and from the failure of some people to respond and of others to respond accurately to census takers. Since policy decisions are made on the basis of census numbers, such errors can affect which groups receive funding and how much they receive. Thus, constituents struggle constantly over the definition of racial and ethnic groups and whether counts are accurate.

These problems are magnified when the United Nations confronts the task of compiling world population data. Age, in particular, is one of the most difficult measures on which to obtain precise data. One problem is that different countries use different methods of calculating age. In China, the traditional practice was to calculate that a child was one year old at birth, whereas in the West, the age of a newborn is set at zero. Among populations with low literacy rates, formal birth records are not kept, making age impossible to determine accurately. In some countries, census counts may lag 10 or 20 years behind the present.

The best-known case of age exaggeration was reported in the Caucasus region of Georgia, one of the states of the former Soviet Union. In 1959, scientists claimed they had discovered 500 people who were between 120 and 165 years of age. As Western newspapers picked up the tale of the long-lived Georgians, even more old people were discovered. In 1966, *Life* magazine published a story about 165-year-old Shirali Mislimov, and soon scientists from all over the world were vying to discover the secret of these long-lived people.

What they found was that the Georgians' claims of long life were greatly exaggerated. Why would people lie about their age? One reason was that in Georgia, extremely old people enjoyed the highest level of social authority and the greatest honor. The older the person, the greater was the esteem conferred on him or her. Another explanation was that men who had not wanted to serve in the czar's army during World War I had claimed to be older than they really were to avoid the draft. Some young men had used their fathers' identities to support this fiction. When the war ended, many continued the ruse for fear of punishment. The lack of written birth records allowed people to pretend they were older than they really were; there was no basis on which to challenge their claims (Hayflick, 1996).

In an attempt to deal with such problems, the United Nations has developed a code for indicating its confidence in international demographic data. While the quality code draws attention to the problem, it of course does not eliminate it. Thus, comparisons of international population trends must be made with caution.

INDIVIDUAL AGING PROCESSES

There are two ways we measure individual aging—life span and life expectancy. Gender differences in life expectancy affect the sex ratio.

Life Span

One measure of individual age is the **life span,** defined as the greatest number of years any member of a species has been known to survive. By this definition, our closest companion, the dog, has a life span of 16 years, which then varies by breeds. Although the common belief is that elephants live for 100 years or more, they do not; the maximum life span of an elephant is 69. Humans, in fact, are the longest-lived animals (Hayflick, 1996). The human life span appears to be about 120 years, although there are a few recorded cases of people living to be much older.

Most scientists believe that the human life span has not changed since prehistoric times. What has happened over the past century in developed countries is that human life expectancy has moved closer to the human life span. As modern medicine allows people to live longer, we will see more centenarians, 100-year-olds like Joseph Goldstein, who tells his life story in "In Their Own Words."

Life Expectancy

Life expectancy is the average number of years people in a given population can expect to live or, more precisely, the mean age at death. This concept is a measure of the combined outcome of many births and deaths. Life expectancy is calculated by taking the sum of the ages at death of all individuals in a given population and dividing it by the number of people in that population.

Except in a handful of nations, life expectancy worldwide is higher for females than for males. In developed countries such as Japan, France, England, and Sweden, women can expect to live six to eight years longer than men. In developing countries such as Egypt, South Africa, and India, women outlive men by three to five years (Kinsella and Gist, 1998). Scientists cannot fully explain the gender difference in life expectancy, which arises from a complex interaction among biological, social, and behavioral factors. One reason why women live longer is that men are more likely to smoke and consume alcohol and to engage in dangerous work. But although one might expect that young women's increased use of alcohol and tobacco and their rising labor force participation rate might reduce the gender gap in life expectancy, so far no clear pattern of change has emerged in developed countries.

The Sex Ratio

The **sex ratio** is defined as the number of males to every 100 females. It is affected both by the number of males relative to females at birth and by different survival rates for males and females. For every 106 male babies that are born, there are only 100 females. No one knows why more males are born than females. Perhaps it is nature's way of adjusting for the greater risk of death and injury men will face from birth on. After birth, death rates are persistently higher among males, beginning in infancy and continuing into old age. As a result, the sex ratio declines progressively over the life course from a small excess of young boys over girls to a massive deficit of men in extreme old age. In most nations elderly women greatly outnumber elderly men.

POPULATION AGING

A population ages because of an increase in the proportion of older people in a society. A population's age structure can change through three fundamental demographic processes: fertility, mortality, and migration. The **fertility rate** is a measure of the incidence of births or the inflow of new lives into a population. At any given time the number of older people in a population is a direct result of the number of babies born 65 or more years earlier. Generally, changes in the number of births play the most important role in determining a country's age structure (Hobbs & Damon, 1996). **Mortality rates,** the second process that influences age structure, reflect the incidence of death in a population. **Migration,** the third process, is the movement of people

In Their Own Words

Joseph Goldstein, 100

My parents came over in the 1880s from Lithuania. When my father acquired enough money to buy my mother a passage, they got married in this country on Yom Kippur. They fasted after their wedding ceremony because that firmed the whole marriage up. I was the third child and the first son to be born in a family with eight siblings.

I grew up in a North Boston neighborhood that was full of tough kids. The gangs waited for me—the Little Lord Fauntleroy—going to school with curls and starched jumpers [shirts] with lace on the collar. My earliest recollection was hearing somebody shout, "Kill the Jews."

In the West End we played games in the street. There were no autos—only horses. We played kick the wicket. You put a section of hose pipe over the curbstone at an angle and kicked it, ran as if you were playing baseball—to first, second, home. In the summer, we went to the Charles River to skinny-dip inside a mud scow.

We moved to Dorchester, another section of Boston, in 1908. It was the move Jews made when they moved up another rung on the ladder, just like when the Irish moved to South Boston. There were gangs, too, at Dorchester High School. I was a member of the track team, though, and I remember hearing the captain of the team telling a couple of his lieutenants, "Leave Goldie alone; he's a good kid, and he's winning us points in meets."

I did pretty well at school, so I got into Harvard when I was 18. I lived at home and got there by taking two streetcars and an elevated train. There weren't too many Jewish students.

The First World War came just at the end of college, and I enlisted immediately. There was no discrimination in the Army. I had rank and that made a difference. Oh, there would be snide remarks behind my back, but nothing big. The Army recognized that there were different religions. Your dog tags had a J if you were a Jew, C for Catholic. We went across in a British troop ship, dodging German U-boats, and it wasn't long before we got into combat. I bit on my pipe so hard once, because I was scared, that I bit off everything but the stem in my mouth. You just never forget the fear.

When I came back I was only a hero to my girl, Anna Stern. We got married pretty quickly after that. I believe in a Hebrew proverb that asks, "Who is rich?" The story is that a rabbi asked that question centuries ago of his students, and it took them a long time to figure out that the answer is: "He who is content with what God has provided in his life." Well, I had a wonderful life with this woman for 71 years. We never had a fight. Why? I gave in.

Source: U.S. News and World Report, Aug. 28, 1995:62, 88.

across borders. Migration typically exerts the least influence on age structure.

One way to display the age structure of a population is to construct a **population pyramid,** a bar chart that reflects the distribution of a population by age and sex. When a population is "young," it exhibits the classic triangular shape seen in Figure 4–1a: wide at the bottom, where fertility is high, and narrower at

| Figure 4-1 | Population Pyramids for Three Countries in Asia, 1998. |

Bangladesh: Young **South Korea: Middle-Aged** **Japan: Old**

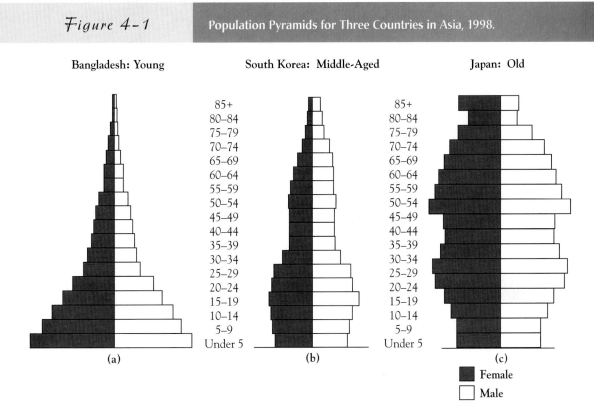

(a)   (b)   (c)

■ Female
□ Male

Source: U.S. Bureau of the Census (1998a).

the top, where death takes its toll. Bangladesh is an example of a "young" nation. A population becomes "middle-aged" when fertility declines along with infant and child mortality. As fewer children are born and more of them survive, the bottom of the triangle is squared off (see Figure 4–1b). South Korea is an example of a "middle-aged" nation. A population becomes "old" when mortality is reduced at all ages, but especially among the elderly. Japan is an example of an "old" nation whose population has a rectangular shape (see Figure 4–1c).

The Demographic Transition

In all developed nations, the three-stage shift from high mortality and fertility rates to low mortality and fertility rates occurs through a socioeconomic process called the **demographic transition** (Myers, 1990). As countries industrialize, accompanying changes in fertility and mortality produce changes in population structure. At the end of this process, a country's population is both older and larger (Grigsby, 1991). Let's take a closer look at this process.

In the first stage of the demographic transition, the economy is agricultural, women marry young and have many children, and infants commonly die from acute and infectious diseases. Because birth rates and death rates are both high (see Figure 4–2), few people reach adulthood, and even fewer survive to old age. The population pyramid forms a perfect triangle.

The second stage of the demographic transition is characterized by declining death rates and

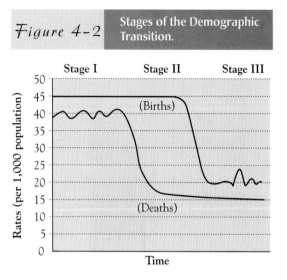

Figure 4-2 Stages of the Demographic Transition.

In the first stage of the demographic transition, birth and death rates are both high. In the second stage, the birth rate remains high while the death rate declines, leading to rapid population growth. In the third stage, the birth rate declines and population growth decreases.

population growth. Initially, the control of infectious and parasitic diseases produces modest declines in mortality among infants and young children (Martin and Kinsella, 1994). As more babies survive into adulthood, the age structure grows younger, and the bottom of the age pyramid expands (U.S. Bureau of the Census, 1988). When these children reach childbearing age, significant population growth occurs. Through improved sanitary measures and health care, life expectancy increases, mortality among the old begins to drop, and the proportion of older people in the population grows.

In the third stage, the population as a whole begins to age, and more deaths are caused by chronic ailments than by acute illness. Populations that have entered this stage become more rectangular in shape. When birth and death rates are both low, the demographic transition is complete. At that point a nation can be characterized as "old," demographically speaking. (This process is described more fully in Chapter 2, in the discussion of modernization theory.)

International Variations in Population Aging

In 1990 the world held 325 million people over age 65; by 2025 that number will more than double to 822 million (Preston and Martin, 1994). Most of the world's population is aging, and in the future, most of the growth in the number of elderly will take place in developing countries, more than half of it in Asia (World Bank, 1994).

According to statistics, most of Africa and parts of Asia and Latin America are still in the first stage of the demographic transition with high levels of fertility, young population profiles, and low life expectancy. In Africa life expectancy in 2000 was only 46 (World Bank, 2003). At the opposite end of the spectrum, European countries have had low fertility and mortality rates for decades and now have high proportions of elderly. In 1990 nearly 18 percent of the Swedish population was over 65. In Great Britain, people over 65 made up nearly 16 percent of the population; in Germany, the figure was 15 percent (Organization for Economic Cooperation and Development, 1994).

These disparities in population structure will not persist for long, however, for the pace of demographic change is picking up. In the industrialized world, population aging took a century or more. Belgium took more than 100 years to double the share of population over age 60 from 9 to 18 percent; France needed 140 years. In developing countries the pace of change will be more rapid, as modern health technology increases life expectancy among the aged. Many of these countries will triple or quadruple the number of older people in just three decades. China will double the percentage of people over 60, from 9 to 18 percent, in just 34 years; Venezuela will do the same in 22 years (World Bank, 1994).

Not only are populations aging around the world, the older population is itself aging. Worldwide, the fastest-growing segment of the older population is the oldest–old, people aged 80 and older. As Figure 4–3 shows, the number of oldest–old is growing most rapidly in the developing countries (Velkoff and Lawson, 1998).

The challenge posed by rapid population aging is daunting. Developing countries can benefit from

Figure 4-3   Growth of the Oldest–Old Population (80+), 1995–2025.

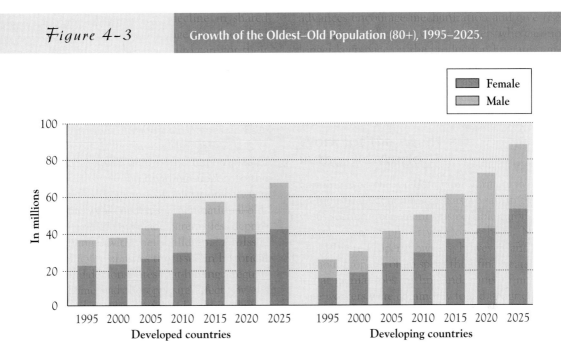

Source: U.S. Bureau of the Census (1998a).

recent advances in medical technology and will learn from other nations how to provide health and income security to the elderly. Yet most developing countries will have fewer resources to meet these needs because they will reach "old" demographic profiles at lower levels of per capita income than the industrial nations. Furthermore, solutions that have been feasible in European nations may not work well in countries with different cultural traditions. For these reasons, population aging poses formidable challenges for developing nations in the twenty-first century

Afghanistan has one of the world's youngest population structures. The "Aging around the World" feature discusses some of the problems facing Afghanistan today as it attempts to reduce its high rates of ingant and maternal mortality.

Dependency Ratios

Another way to measure population aging is through dependency ratios, which indicate the burden of supporting an aging population. The ratio of old people to adults, called the **elderly dependency ratio,** is calculated as the number of persons aged 65 and older per 100 persons of working age (18 to 64 years old). It provides a rough estimate of the proportion of workers to retirees. From a demographic perspective, however, a nation's ability to support its oldest members depends not only on the ratio of workers to retirees, but also on the number of persons under age 18 relative to those of working age. The **child dependency ratio** indicates the number of persons under age 18 relative to those of working age. The combined ratio of children and older people to workers is called the **total dependency ratio.**

Of course, some people under age 15 and some over age 65 do work, and some people of working age do not. In some Western countries, most people leave the labor force at age 60. In less developed nations, children as young as 10 may work 12 hours a day. Thus, dependency ratios are more useful as illustrative devices than as analytic tools; age-specific labor force participation rates are more helpful (Martin and Kinsella, 1994).

Aging around the World

INFANT AND MATERNAL MORTALITY IN AFGHANISTAN

Afghanistan has the highest rate of maternal mortality anywhere. Nationally, the ratio is more than 2,000 maternal deaths for every 100,000 live births. Millions of women in Afghanistan live in a continual cycle of pregnancy and birth throughout their adult lives. In fact, nearly half of the deaths of Afghan women aged 15 to 49 are the result of complications during pregnancy and childbirth. Afghanistan ranks fourth in the world in infant mortality and deaths of children under age 5. Many women give birth to 10 or 15 children but lose many babies in childbirth or in the first year of life. The World Bank has made efforts to provide information on family planning, but many women hesitate to take it because of opposition from their husbands.

The reasons for these startling statistics include poor nutrition, which leads to stunted growth and increases the chances of a difficult birth, teenage marriages, and women's low social status. These problems are made worse by a lack of skilled medical care, especially in the many remote villages, where there are few trained medical personnel, and by cultural traditions that forbid women from seeing a male physician. As a result, Afghanistan has one of the "youngest" population profiles in the world (World Bank, 2003).

What Do You Think?

1. Does the United States have a responsibility to help reduce infant and maternal mortality in Afghanistan?
2. How have the problems Afghanistan is facing been solved by other countries?

Afghan women and children waiting to enter a health clinic in Kabul.

POPULATION TRENDS IN THE UNITED STATES

The Changing Age Structure

The population of the United States aged throughout the twentieth century. As Figure 4–4 shows, in 1900 just 4.1 percent of all Americans were over 65; by 2000 that figure was 12.4 percent. Even more amazing, between 1950 and 2000, the proportion of people aged 85 and over grew from 590,000 to 4.2 million, an increase of more than 300 percent!

By 2030, when the baby boomers have become old, more than 20 percent of Americans, or one out of every five, will be over 65. And by 2040 the 85 and older population will quadruple in size to nearly 14 million (Hobbs and Damon, 1996). For a discussion of the policy implications of the aging of the baby boomers, see "An Issue for Public Policy."

Fertility

The baby boom was created by an upsurge in fertility during the postwar era. As the U.S. economy prospered and average wages rose, more families could afford the accoutrements of a middle-class lifestyle: a single-family home, a car (or two), and a washer and dryer. Rising real wages contributed to the optimistic expectation that each generation would improve its living standard (Levy and Michel, 1991). No wonder that fertility began to climb in 1946, peaking in 1958 at a whopping average of 3.17 children per woman. Women who reached childbearing age during the 1950s hold the record as the most fertile of the twentieth century. Three-quarters of them gave birth to their first child before they reached their mid-20s, and ultimately 93 percent became mothers.

But then, between 1971 and 1980, the fertility rate dropped dramatically, reaching an all-time

---

Figure 4-4   Percentage of Total Population Age 65 and Older, 1900–2000.

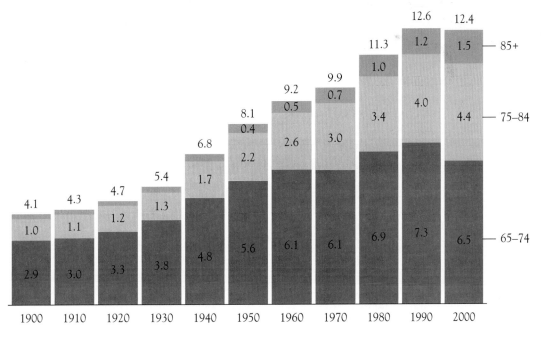

Source: Hobbs and Stoops (2002:59).

WILL THE BABY BOOMERS CONSUME THE FEDERAL BUDGET?

*L*ike the proverbial python that swallowed the pig, the United States has had to make way for the baby boom generation at every stage of the life course. When the baby boomers entered kindergarten, trailers littered the playgrounds of suburban grade schools, serving as temporary classrooms for millions of 5-year-olds. When the boomers graduated from high school, college enrollments surged. Not only did more young people enter college, but more members of this generation sought an advanced education than had men and women in earlier generations. Almost twice as many boomers went to college as did members of their parents' generation (U.S. Bureau of the Census, 1994a). And in the 1970s, when the baby boomers started buying homes, housing prices skyrocketed in response to increasing demand. Between 1970 and 1980 the median price of a new home in the United States doubled from $26,600 to $47,200 (Siegel, 1993).

The oldest baby boomers are now in their late-50s. They are the leading edge of a tidal wave of senior citizens. Some people fear that such an increase in the number and proportion of older people will transform the United States into a nation devoted to care of the aged instead of to

low of 1.7 children per woman. Several factors contributed to this reduced fertility. One was the birth control pill, which became available in the early 1960s. For the first time in history, women had a reliable way to control the number of babies they had and when they had them. Another was an increase in educational opportunities for women. When the first wave of baby boomers reached college age in 1965, women of that generation entered college in record numbers. Nearly twice as many female baby boomers graduated from college as women in the cohort that preceded them. For many of these women, attending college meant delaying marriage—30 percent of them were still single in their mid-twenties (U.S.

Bureau of the Census, 1994a). Significantly, delaying marriage not only delays childbearing; it also decreases lifetime fertility. Finally, female labor force participation expanded rapidly in the 1960s. As women became more highly educated, they sought work outside the home in increasing numbers.

Although baby boom women had fewer children than their parents' generation, the number of babies born to their generation increased simply because there were so many boomers. Almost as many children were born between 1977 and 1994 as during the baby boom years. Figure 4–5 shows the number of live births that created these two cohorts, the baby boom and the echo boom.

economic growth and innovation. The boomers, they warn, will overload health and retirement systems and consume most of the federal budget. The only solution, they claim, is to drastically cut Social Security, Medicare, and other programs for the aged. Are these fears realistic, and are large cuts in social programs the only solution to an aging population?

First of all, we must recognize that population projections are just that—estimates of what will happen in the future. These figures are based on predictions about future birth and death rates, economic growth, unemployment, immigration, and numerous other factors—predictions that may or may not be accurate. The Census Bureau has released high, medium, and low projections for the size of the U.S. population in the year 2040. These projections vary by as much as 170 million people! Economic growth is especially difficult to predict. Projections made in 1960 could not possibly have predicted the fax machines, personal computers, and cell phones that Americans enjoy today, to say nothing of the steady increase in female labor force participation, the economic boom of the 1990s, or the spurt in productivity caused by the Internet.

Finally, today's elderly are healthier, wealthier, and better educated than any older generation in history. The baby boomers will be even more so: They will be better prepared to provide for themselves than their parents or grandparents were. Although no one should presume that the future will take care of itself, dismantling the social programs that have improved the health and income security of so many older Americans would be equally unwise.

What Do You Think?

1. Are you, your parents, or grandparents part of the baby boom generation? If so, are you worried about the future of retirement programs such as Medicare and Social Security?
2. Is growth in the number of elderly people always inconsistent with economic growth? In what ways might an aging population encourage economic growth?

The effect of these fertility trends on the age structure of the United States is shown in Figure 4–6. The pyramid for 1950 is still triangular with a distinct pinch in the lower middle from ages 15 to 24 due to the exceptionally low birth rate during the Depression years. The baby boom bulge that is just beginning appears at the very bottom among children under age 5. In 2000 the baby boomers are middle-aged, and the echo boomers are in their teens and early 20s.

By 2010 the baby boomers will be aged 46 to 64, and the echo boomers will be aged 15 to 35. By 2050 many of the baby boomers will have died; those who are still alive will be very old, in their late 80s and 90s. The echo boomers will be growing old as well.

Mortality

Over the past century, the United States has witnessed a dramatic improvement in mortality rates. In 1900, the chance of surviving to old age was shockingly low. Approximately 20 percent of white children and 33 percent of nonwhite children died before their fifth birthday (Hobbs and Damon, 1996). Fewer than two-thirds (63 percent) of white females and only 32 percent of nonwhite females would live to 60. Among white males, just over half (55 percent) would live to 60, as would only 28 percent of nonwhite males (Serow, Sly, and Wrigley, 1990). By 1990, infants had a much better chance of living to old age. Whites still had an

Figure 4-5   Number of Live Births in the United States, 1945–1995.

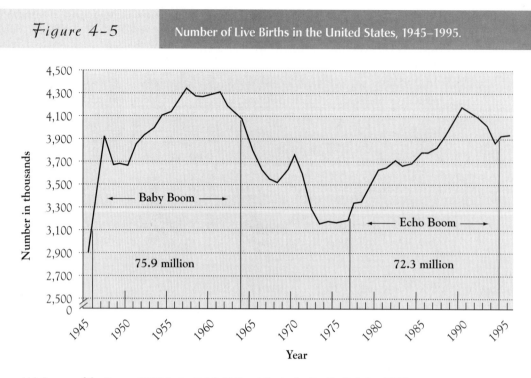

Source: U.S. Bureau of the Census (1975, Series B-14); National Center for Health Statistics (1998).

Figure 4-6   U.S. Population by Age and Sex, 1950 and 2000.

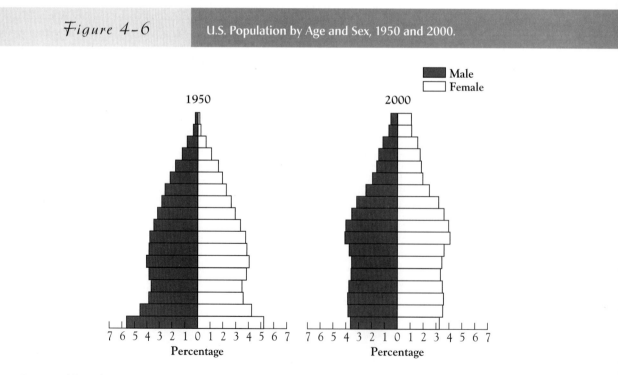

Source: Hobbs and Stoops (2002:54).

advantage over nonwhites, but the racial gap had narrowed. Ninety-three percent of white females and 88 percent of white males would reach 60, but so would 91 percent of nonwhite females and 83 percent of nonwhite males (Serow et al., 1990).

The greatest declines in mortality occurred during two periods, the 1940s and the 1970s. In the 1940s medical advances led to major gains against infant and child mortality and maternal mortality. Then, beginning in the late 1960s, the death rate from heart disease began to fall, largely because of better prevention and treatment: Fewer people smoked, and new medications helped to control hypertension (high blood pressure). This progress against heart disease stands out as the most important reason for the reduction in the mortality rate in the past quarter century. Its impact was greatest among older people, especially older men (Treas, 1995a).

Ironically, deaths from cancer have actually increased among the elderly. One possible explanation is that declining mortality from heart disease has allowed more people to live long enough to die from cancer. The trend is more positive than it might at first appear to be, however, for the overall increase in cancer deaths masks declines in deaths from specific forms of cancer. Cervical cancer has dropped because more women routinely obtain pap smears. Among men, deaths from lung cancer have declined because of the decline in smoking. But deaths from lung cancer are rising among older women because more women have smoked or are still smoking than was the case in earlier generations.

Despite advances in prevention and treatment, heart disease remains the leading cause of death among people over 65, as Table 4–1 shows. Heart disease and cancer are responsible for two-thirds of all deaths among people 65 to 84. Among those over 85, heart disease ranks first, followed by cerebrovascular disease (stroke) and then cancer.

The racial differences in mortality rates just noted are reflected in racial differences in the risk of disease. For example, for all three of the leading causes of death, mortality among African Americans is higher consistently than it is for whites: 5 percent higher for heart disease, 17 percent higher for cancer, and 24 percent higher for strokes (Gibson, 1994a). What explains these racial differences?

Table 4-1	Leading Causes of Death in the United States, Age 65 and Older, 2000	
Cause	Number of Deaths	Mortality Rate
All causes	1,799,825	5,175.4
Diseases of the heart	593,707	1,707.2
Malignant neoplasms (cancer)	392,366	1,128.2
Cerebrovascular diseases	148,045	425.7
Chronic lower respiratory disease	106,375	305.9
Influenza and pneumonia	58,557	168.4
Diabetes mellitus	52,414	150.7
Alzheimer's disease	48,993	140.9
Nephritis and nephritic syndrome	31,225	89.8

Source: National Center for Health Statistics (2002).

Although hereditary components of some diseases may explain part of the difference, the primary cause is socioeconomic status (SES). SES is usually measured by income, occupation, and education, but because most older people are retired and because income drops across the board in retirement, education is used often as the sole SES measure for the elderly. As such, it becomes a proxy for a variety of social, economic, and lifestyle factors. For example, the decline in mortality from heart disease varies significantly with level of education (Preston and Taubman, 1994). For information about some of the ways race and gender affect life expectancy, see "Diversity in the Aging Experience."

SES affects health in several ways. People with higher incomes are more likely than the poor to have health insurance and good health care. They are also more likely to live in less polluted areas and to have better access to public services (Preston and Taubman, 1994). Women in higher-income groups are also more likely to have mammograms, which means they receive earlier diagnosis and treatment for breast cancer (Blustein, 1995). SES also affects lifestyle. Middle-class people are more likely than the poor to exercise regularly, control their weight,

Diversity in the Aging Experience

RACE AND GENDER DIFFERENCES IN LIFE EXPECTANCY

*S*hould your gender or race determine how long you live? Although Americans saw tremendous improvements in their life expectancy over the twentieth century, not everyone benefited equally. The general trends tend to obscure major differences by sex and by race.

In general, women can expect to live six years longer than the average man. Such has not always been the case. At the beginning of the twentieth century, women had only a slight advantage over men in life expectancy, for many women died giving birth. Then in the 1940s, deaths from childbirth declined and the life expectancy differential began to widen. Women added years more rapidly than men until the 1980s, when medical science made significant progress against heart disease. Since then, male life expectancy has improved dramatically, and the gender gap has begun to close. By 1996 life expectancy at birth was 79.1 years for women and 73.1 years for men.

Precisely why do women live longer than men? Among the possible explanations are that men tend to engage in more dangerous occupations than women and are more likely to smoke and abuse alcohol. Women are more likely to seek regular medical care than men. The most likely answer is some combination of hereditary and environmental factors.

Race, too, continues to influence life expectancy. Throughout the twentieth century, black life expectancy trailed white life expectancy. But from 1972 to 1985 the racial gap in life expectancy narrowed. At least four factors contributed to this trend. First, racial differences in smoking declined. Second, black people experienced a huge reduction in the prevalence of hypertension, especially among men. Third, with the passage of the Medicare and Medicaid programs in 1965 (see Chapter 11), African Americans gained greater access to health care. Finally, racial differences in income narrowed during these years (Preston and Taubman, 1994).

But in the 1990s the racial gap in life expectancy began to widen again, especially among men (Farley, 1996). AIDS and deaths from violence increased the racial differential in the 1990s (Hobbs and Damon, 1996). White men can now expect to live more than eight years longer than black men, and white women more than six years longer than black women.

What Do You Think?

1. Which side of the gender and racial gaps are you on? Do you think other factors, such as your lifestyle, will affect your own life expectancy?
2. What can be done to narrow the gender and racial gaps in life expectancy?

and eat breakfast, and they are less likely to smoke or drink excessively. (The reasons for such differences in health behavior are discussed in more detail in Chapter 13.) Because African Americans as a group have lower incomes and fewer years of schooling than whites, their mortality rates are higher.

Most of the racial differences in mortality between African Americans and whites occur among those under 65. Black infants die at more than twice the rate of white and Hispanic infants (Treas, 1995a). Homicide ends the lives of many young black men. In 1990 death rates from homicide were 69.2 per 100,000 among black men compared to 9.0 per 100,000 for white men. Among black women, homicide deaths were 13.5 per 100,000 compared to 2.8 per 100,000 for white women (U.S. Bureau of the Census, 1993a).

Among the very old, the advantages associated with being white disappear. An intriguing phenomenon, one not fully understood, is what is called **race crossover.** After age 85, the mortality rate for African Americans falls *below* that of whites. Demographers cannot fully explain why, but some argue that African Americans who have survived the environmental stresses of their younger years may have a survival advantage that destines them to live an especially long life (Siegel, 1993).

In sum, the second half of the twentieth century witnessed a significant decline in mortality, especially among the old. As a result, more people are living to advanced old age, and the elderly have become the fastest-growing segment of the population. This significant population aging cannot be ignored. Necessary adaptations can be made with the aid of long-range planning. Population aging should be viewed as an outcome of the desirable demographic processes associated with economic development, which nonetheless require some adjustment in social institutions (Grigsby, 1991).

Migration

The Statue of Liberty has long been a beacon drawing immigrants to the shores of the United States. The biggest wave of immigrants arrived in the late nineteenth and early twentieth centuries, when thousands of Italians and East Europeans crossed the Atlantic Ocean. By 1910 more than 15 percent of the U.S. population was foreign born (U.S. Bureau of the Census, 1975). More recent immigrants trace their ancestry to Asia and Latin America. Of the half-million people who immigrate to the United States annually, well over half are Hispanic and Asian (Bagby, 1994).

Most immigrants are relatively young. Seventy-seven percent of all Hispanic immigrants who arrived in the United States between 1970 and 1980 were under 35 (Siegel, 1993). When large numbers of young people migrate to a country, its age structure appears to become younger. Unless immigration continues in a steady stream, however, the "younging" effect is short-lived. Immigrants who stay eventually grow old and add to the ranks of the elderly (Treas, 1995a).

Most older people find moving to another country difficult; they have deep roots in their homeland. Not surprisingly, only 10 percent of recent immigrants have been over age 65. Of these, nearly one-fourth were refugees. In 1990, after the end of communism, 17.5 percent of older immigrants came from the former Soviet Union. Another large group of elderly came from the Philippines and China; smaller numbers came from India and Mexico (Treas, 1995a). According to estimates by the Census Bureau, about 8 percent of the total growth of the elderly population in the United States from 1992 to 2000 was due to international migration (Hobbs and Damon, 1996).

Because of higher immigration and birth rates, the Hispanic, African American, and Asian populations are increasing more rapidly than the white population of the United States. By 2050 the non-Hispanic white population is projected to decline from 85 percent of people 65 and older to only 67 percent. Thus, the elderly population of the future will be considerably more racially and ethnically diverse than the elderly population of today (see Figure 4–7).

What are the consequences of age differences in population diversity? One observer suggests they are likely "to provoke more us-against-them" attitudes (MacManus, 1996:176). Younger people may come to resent paying taxes to support a predominantly white older population. A more optimistic

Friends and family members surround a Cuban birthday girl dressed in white during the celebration of her quinceanera, the coming-of-age party given for a girl when she reaches age 15.

scenario is that young Americans of all racial and ethnic backgrounds will recognize the value of a social contract that benefits everyone, across the generations.

Dependency Ratio

The fact that the large cohort of the baby boom was followed by a small cohort of the baby bust means that the elderly dependency ratio will rise from 20 per 100 in 1990 to 36 per 100 by 2030. In the year 2000 there were more than five workers for each person over 65; by 2030, there will be fewer than three (Friedland and Summer, 1999). In that year the total dependency ratio will be no higher than it was in 1970, but the composition of dependents will be different (see Table 4–2) (Easterlin, 1996). The total dependency ratio was

82 in 1960, but most of the dependents in that year were children. In the twenty-first century, many more dependents will be old.

What are the consequences of an older population? Some people worry that an aging population will increase the burden on the younger population, especially in health care costs and income support. Certainly, demand will increase for health care and housing that caters to the aged' special needs, and there will be fewer workers to pay Social Security taxes. But though many older people may not be working, they will still be paying taxes. Those who do not work will also contribute to the economy by consuming goods and services they finance out of their own savings. Many older people will also serve as volunteers, helping their families and communities by providing social services free of charge.

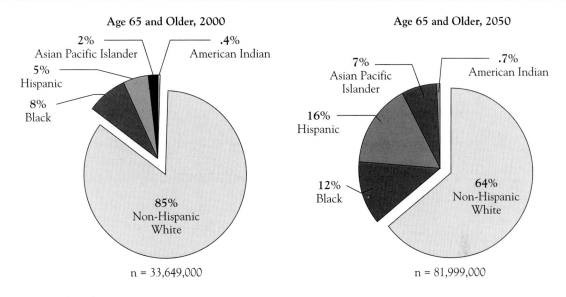

Figure 4-7

Racial and Ethnic Composition of the 65 and Older Population in the United States, 2000 and 2050.

Note: n = total number.
Source: Hobbs and Stoops (2002).

Table 4-2

Dependency Ratios for Child and Older Populations in the United States, 1900–2050

Year	Child Dependency Ratio	Old-Age Dependency Ratio	Total Dependency Ratio
1900	73	7	80
1910	66	8	74
1920	64	8	72
1930	59	9	68
1940	49	11	60
1950	51	13	64
1960	65	17	82
1970	61	18	79
1980	46	19	65
1990	42	20	62
2000	42	21	63
2010	39	22	61
2020	40	27	67
2030	42	36	78
2040	42	37	79
2050	42	36	78

Source: U.S. Bureau of the Census (1975; 1993c, P25–1104, table 2).

Table 4-3	U.S. Life Expectancy at Birth and Age 65 by Sex, 1900–2000 (in years)					
	At Birth			**At Age 65**		
Year	*Total*	*Male*	*Female*	*Total*	*Male*	*Female*
1900	47.3	46.3	48.3	11.9	11.5	12.2
1950	68.2	65.6	71.1	13.9	12.8	15.0
1960	69.7	66.6	73.1	14.3	12.8	15.8
1970	70.8	67.1	74.7	15.2	13.1	17.0
1980	73.7	70.0	77.4	16.4	14.1	18.3
1990	75.4	71.8	78.8	17.2	15.1	18.9
2000	77.2	74.4	79.7	17.8	16.0	19.2

Source: National Center for Health Statistics (2002).

Life Expectancy

Because of the decline in death rates that occurred in the twentieth century, Americans have experienced an enormous increase in life expectancy. As Table 4–3 shows, between 1900 and 2000, overall life expectancy at birth increased nearly 30 years, from 47.3 to 76.1. The statistic 47.3 does not mean that in 1900 people typically lived to be 47. Rather, it is an average. In 1900 many infants and children died in the first five years of life. If a person survived to age 20, then he or she might easily live to 65.

Not only has the chance of living to old age improved, so has the chance of living beyond age 65. By 1997, the average 65-year-old man could expect to live another 15 years; the average woman, an extra 19 years (National Center for Health Statistics, 1998). Despite these gains, significant racial and ethnic disparities in life expectancy remain, as Figure 4–8 shows.

Increasing life expectancy and a reduction in mortality rates for even the oldest–old have important implications for income security and health care. At issue is whether the retirement programs presently in place will remain financially sound, and whether health practices will improve the quality of life in old age or merely increase the number of years people live.

The U.S. Sex Ratio

During the twentieth century, there was a significant decline in the sex ratio among people 85 and older, from around 80 until the mid-1940s to only 41 by 2000. This lopsided ratio was a result of the greater increase in female life expectancy compared to male life expectancy. The high proportion of women among the oldest–old has important social consequences. It means that the majority of older women are single—and single women have the highest poverty rates among the aged. It also means that while most men will have a resident caretaker when they become ill or disabled, many women will be institutionalized.

The expected increase in the number of older Americans has immense implications for the quality of life in the twenty-first century. One of the most pressing issues is health care, for aging is usually

Figure 4-8 Life Expectancy at Birth by Sex and Race.

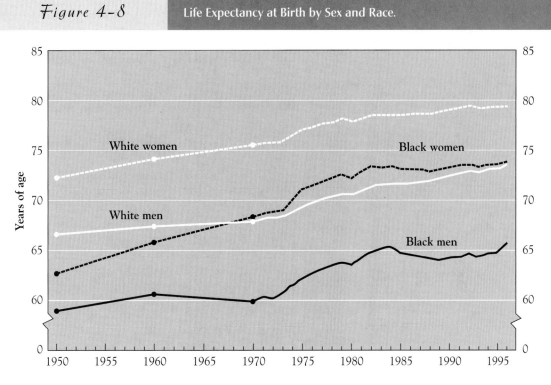

Source: National Center for Health Statistics (2002).

accompanied by declining health. Who will provide health care for the more than 75 million baby boomers, and who will pay for it? Another issue is economic security. Now that people are living well beyond age 65, policymakers are beginning to wonder whether they should be encouraged to retire later. Will Americans reevaluate policies that have encouraged early retirement and add incentives to continue working? These are issues we will address in Chapter 12.

Chapter Resources

LOOKING BACK

1. **How is a population's age structure related to its stage of economic development?** *The population age structure indicates the relative proportions of older, middle-aged, and younger people within a population; it is often illustrated by a population pyramid. Populations can be classified as predominately young, middle-aged, or old, depending on the age structure that results from fertility and mortality rates. A population ages through a process known as the demographic transition, in which economic development causes a fall in both fertility and mortality rates. Developed countries such as the United States, Sweden, and Germany have relatively old populations, whereas developing nations in Africa and parts of Asia have relatively young populations. An important aspect of the population age structure is the total dependency ratio, the combined ratio of children and old people to people of working age.*

2. **What is the relative life expectancy of men versus women, and how is it related to the sex ratio?** *Life expectancy is the average number of years people in a given population can expect to live or, more precisely, the mean age at death. In most nations, women live longer than men—six to eight years longer in developed countries, three to five years longer in developing countries. The sex ratio is the number of males to every 100 females. At birth males outnumber females about 106 to 100, but because women live longer than men, the sex ratio declines with age until elderly women greatly outnumber elderly men.*

3. **In the United States, how have fertility, mortality, and migration rates changed over the past century, and what has been the effect on the nation's population?** *In the United States after World War II, rising fertility rates created a baby boom. Fertility began to decline in the 1960s with the introduction of the birth control pill and increased levels of education and employment among women. It reached a historic low in the early 1970s, creating what demographers call a baby bust. The twentieth century also brought dramatic declines in mortality rates. Medical advances against infant and childhood diseases began the trend; later, improved treatments for heart disease lowered mortality rates among older people. The result has been population aging and an evening out of the population pyramid.*

   Two waves of migration to the United States occurred during the twentieth century: the first, around the beginning of the century, from Italy and central Europe, and the second toward the end of the century, from Latin America and Asia. Because most of these immigrants were young, they changed the nation's age structure, increasing the proportion of younger people to older Americans. Overall, the nation's total dependency ratio has been falling since World War II. The composition of the dependent portion of the population is also changing: Once the majority of dependents were children, but soon, when immigrants and baby boomers retire, the majority of dependents will be elderly.

4. **How has life expectancy in the United States changed over the past century, and does it differ from one group to the next?** *Over the past 100 years, life expectancy in the United States increased from about 47 years to over 75. Life expectancy varies significantly with both race and gender. On average, whites live longer than African Americans, and women live longer than men. Because women's life expectancy has increased faster than men's, the sex ratio has declined, from 101.1 to 100 in 1910 to only 65 to 100 in 1990.*

THINKING ABOUT AGING

1. Social Security has been called the third rail of American politics, meaning that to touch it (change the program in any way) is to die

(lose office). Given the rising number of re-tirees and the declining number of workers, do you think the program should be revised? If so, how?

2. The proportion of working-age Americans to retired Americans has been dropping for several decades as the result of declining fer-tility and mortality rates. Should the gov-ernment encourage couples to have more children? Why or why not?

3. Demographers recognize the contributions immigrants make to a developed nation's population structure. Yet many Americans feel threatened by immigrants. What can be done to improve the immigrant's public image?

4. Poverty rates among older women, espe-cially minority women, are very high. What kind of measures might help to reduce poverty among the elderly?

5. From the point of view of the elderly, what might be the advantages and disadvantages of living in a state with a large elderly popu-lation? From the point of view of younger generations?

KEY TERMS

age structure 71

baby boomers 71

child dependency ratio 77

demographic transition 75

demography 71

echo boomers 71

elderly dependency ratio 77

fertility rate 73

life expectancy 73

life span 73

migration 73

mortality rate 73

population aging 72

population pyramid 74

race crossover 85

sex ratio 73

total dependency ratio 77

EXPLORING THE INTERNET

Note: While all the URLs listed were current as of the printing of this book, these sites often change. Please check our website www.mhhe.com/quadagno for updates.

1. The Administration on Aging (http://www.aoa.dhhs.gov/) provides statistical information on older persons, including their life expectancy and self-reported health status. Go to the website and link to Professionals, then Statistics, then to "Older Americans 2000: Key Indicators of Well-Being." Under Indicators, link to Health Status, read about life expectancy and self-related health status. Answer the following questions:

   a. In your own words, explain the concept of life expectancy.
   b. What is the life expectancy of Americans at ages 65 and 85?
   c. How are differences in life expectancy con-nected to one's race?
   d. How do older Americans rate their health?
   e. What are the gender and racial differences in self-rated health status?

2. The U.S. Census Bureau web page (http://www.census.gov/) also provides informa-tion on aging. Go to the website and link to Poverty; under How the Census Bureau Mea-sures Poverty, select Poverty Thresholds.

   a. Explain who is included in the official poverty data. Poverty is not defined for certain people. Who are they?
   b. What is the current poverty threshold for persons age 65 and over?

Now link to Current Population Survey (CPS). Select and read "Poverty in the U.S.: 1999."

   a. In general, what does this press release say about poverty in the United States?
   b. What does this press release say about poverty among persons aged 65 and over?

INTERDISCIPLINARY PERSPECTIVES ON AGING

ocial gerontology is an inherently interdisciplinary field, and every chapter in this book includes insights from a variety of disciplines. The focus is primarily on social science research, but the fields of history, biology, and psychology have advanced our understanding of aging. Part Two provides a detailed look at the contributions of these three disciplines to our broader knowledge of aging.

Chapter 5 describes historical perspectives on aging, which have been informed by a quest to understand the influence of social change on the elderly. Among the subjects explored are changes in attitudes toward the aged in family life and in work, the nature of retirement, and the care of the frail elderly. Social processes of aging are affected by biological changes that occur as people grow old.

Chapter 6 first examines some prominent theories of biological aging and then describes age-related changes in various body systems as well as illnesses that sometimes accompany these changes.

Chapter 7 provides an overview of psychological research on aging. It examines age-related changes in intelligence, learning, and memory and the effect of aging and of certain diseases, such as Alzheimer's disease, on mental health. The chapter also discusses personality traits and the effect of aging on personality. It concludes by explaining stage theories of human development.

Chapter 5

Historical Perspectives on Aging

In Iran, elderly religious leaders are venerated.

Looking Ahead

1. How have attitudes toward the aged changed over time?
2. Did elderly people live with their children in the past?
3. How did the rise of cities affect the way older people and their families lived?
4. Have older people always been able to retire?
5. How did society care for the frail elderly in the past?

Once upon a time, there was a golden age of aging. The old were few but held great power and authority in the community and in the family. The extended family household, which was the site of production and education, was dominated by older family members. The skills needed to pursue a craft were passed from the older to the younger generation. Because few people were literate, community traditions were orally transmitted by the elderly. The position of the aged in society could best be summarized by a single word: **veneration.**

Then a revolutionary process called modernization shattered this traditional society. As urbanization drew young people to the cities, the extended family household was destroyed. As industrialization moved work from the household to the factory, parents lost the ability to teach their skills to their children. As mass education increased rates of literacy, the aged were no longer the repositories of wisdom and family tradition. The veneration of the aged was replaced by a cult of youth. Isolated from their families and pushed out of the labor force, the aged were forced to spend their final days in institutions (Cowgill, 1974). This view, which reflects the basic tenets of modernization theory (described in Chapter 2), presents a compelling tale. But is it true?

In this chapter, we weigh the evidence historians have gathered about a so-called golden age of aging. In exploring these issues, we demonstrate how various social forces, such as cultural beliefs and ideals, and social, economic, and technological changes have influenced the way the elderly have been perceived and treated across different cultures and in different historical eras. This chapter neither can nor should cover every time period or major event in history. That would be an impossible task. Rather, its objective is to provide a broad historical sweep of key influences on age relations. Throughout the chapter, we use modernization theory as a framework for organizing the questions we ask about how sociohistorical forces have shaped our perception and treatment of older people today. Important historical events are listed in Table 5–1.

WERE THE AGED VENERATED IN PREINDUSTRIAL SOCIETY?

Veneration in Non-Western Cultures

The idea of veneration was borrowed by modernization theorists from non-Western traditional cultures, where the elderly are often accorded great respect and esteem. Among the Kirghiz, for example, a small community of 2,000 people who live in the high valleys of Afghanistan, the household head, called *oey bashi*, is the most senior male or, in the absence of a male, the most senior female. The oey bashi exercises complete authority over the household and represents its social relations with the community (Shahrani, 1981).

Traditional Chinese culture also places a high value on old age. The veneration of the old is linked to Confucian values emphasizing that the parent should treat the child with *zi*, or nurturance, and the child should treat the parent with *xiao*, meaning filial piety or absolute obedience. To be *xiao* means showing one's parents respect at all times, performing acts of ancestor worship when they die, and generating grandsons to carry on the family name. *Xiao* extends beyond respect for one's own parents to include deference to all elderly people. It is accompanied by many symbolic and conventional gestures such as speaking politely, deferring in conversation to those older than oneself, and never ridiculing or insulting the aged. It would be a shameful breach of *xiao* to neglect the needs for

Table 5-1	Important Events in History
1607	Jamestown founded
1619	First Africans arrive in Virginia
1620	First Pilgrims land on Cape Cod
1630	Massachusetts Bay colony founded
1640	Great migration to New England ends
1664	First almshouse built in Boston
1670s	Imports of African slaves to southern colonies increase dramatically
1776-83	Revolutionary War
1790	Industrial Revolution begins in England
1808	African slave trade closes
1820	Median age of U.S. population is 16.7 years
1820-60	Wave of immigration to the United States
1860	Frontier reaches the West Coast
1860-65	Civil War
1873-78	Depression
1880	First big cities reach over 100,000 residents
1880	More than 5 million workers employed in manufacturing
1900	Median age of U.S. population reaches 22.9 years
1908	British national Old Age Pension enacted
1920	Majority of U.S. population lives in cities
1914-20	World War I
1929	Stock market crash ushers in Great Depression
1935	Congress passes Social Security Act
1940-45	World War II
1965	Congress passes Civil Rights Act
1965	Congress enacts Medicare and Medicaid
1973	Energy crisis and end of postwar economic boom
1995	Median age of U.S. population reaches 34.3 years
2006	First wave of baby boomers reach age 60

clothing, food, or medical care of the elderly or to put them in a nursing home. Although women always have lower status than men, the position of a woman in Chinese culture improves as she ages, and a few old women become genuinely powerful (Amoss and Harrell, 1981).

Policies adopted by the communist regime that rose to power in China in 1949 plus the impact of modernization and population aging have gradually shifted responsibility for the aged from the family to the government. The policy of one child per family has reduced the number of kin available to provide care to the elderly. The government now provides pensions and health insurance, and the number of nursing homes has been growing rapidly (Olson, 1988).

The question asked by modernization theorists is whether practices common in traditional non-Western cultures were ever found in Western societies in the preindustrial past and, if so, whether modernization and industrialization destroyed the tradition of veneration for the elderly. A cursory glance through Western history indicates that people have always held negative views of the aged. In his *Rhetoric*, Aristotle accused the aged of being cowardly, selfish, timorous, fearful, small-minded, ill-humored, and avaricious (Scrutton, 1990). In Shakespeare's *As You Like It*, the melancholy character Jacques describes old age as "second childness and mere oblivion, sans teeth, sans eyes, sans taste, sans everything" (*As You Like It*, 3.7). The prejudice persisted in modern times. For instance, the physician Sigmund Freud (1905:149) wrote that "psychiatry (was) not possible near or above the age of 50; the elasticity of the mental processes on which the treatment depends is as a rule lacking—old people are not educable."

Most historians believe that the elderly were venerated in the colonial period of American history. They disagree on whether this unusual tradition of respect in Western history extended to all elderly people or to just a few privileged older men.

Veneration of the Aged in Colonial Times, 1620–1770

Beginning in the 1620s, thousands of dissenters from the Church of England embarked on a journey to the new land to escape religious persecution. These Pilgrims wanted to abolish the church hierarchy and "purify" it from corrupt influences; hence they were called Puritans. Instead of a church subordinated to the interests of the state, they wanted a church free from political interference.

Puritan ideals and religious beliefs Puritans were the followers of John Calvin, a Swiss cleric who stressed the omnipotence of God and the ordinance of predestination, the belief that one's fate was determined before birth and that Christians could do nothing to alter their destiny. Members of the elect were saved, regardless of their actions, and those who were damned could not change their fate no matter how many good deeds they performed. There was an incentive to be philanthropic, however, for although doing good works could not earn an individual a place in heaven, holding high status in the community was seen as an indication of salvation.

The Puritan ideal was to establish a commonwealth in the true sense of the word, a community in which each person put the good of the whole ahead of his or her personal needs. The ideal was expressed in the doctrine of the covenant, which communicated the Puritans' belief that God had made a covenant with each of them when he chose them for this special mission in America. In turn, they entered into covenants with each other to work toward their goals. Despite the concern with community, however, differences in status were an inevitable part of colonial society (Norton et al., 1982).

In this hierarchical society, the elderly occupied a position at the pinnacle. Elders were guides and leaders in all matters. Veneration of the elderly was anchored in the Puritans' strong religious beliefs, which viewed life as proceeding through a series of developmental stages with spiritual development peaking in old age. Thus, the aged were uniquely qualified to serve as moral exemplars for the young. Veneration signified respect, honor, obligation, deference, and something even more profound—a feeling of religious awe and reverence that approached a form of worship. As Cotton Mather, the most prominent member of a family of distinguished ministers, wrote, "These two qualities go together, the ancient and the honorable" (cited in Fischer, 1977:29). Because there was no fixed age of retirement, older men continued practicing the ministry well into their 70s and 80s.

Many cultural practices symbolized the ideal of veneration. In the meetinghouses and churches of colonial New England, the places of honor in the center pews in front of the minister were reserved for the elderly. Forms of dress also flattered older people. As David Hackett Fischer (1977:87), the renowned historian of age, wrote:

During the eighteenth century clothes were cunningly tailored in such a way that the shoulders were made narrow and rounded, the hips and waist were actually broadened, and the backs of the coats were designed to make the spine appear to be bent by the weight of years. Only one part of the body was revealed—the lower leg, which is perhaps, an old man's last anatomical advantage. (p. 87)

Hair was hidden beneath a wig and powdered white. In family portraits, the father stood above his family with his wife seated below him and the children placed below the wife, an arrangement that reflected the hierarchical relationships between the sexes as well as the generations.

Although colonial society was a **gerontocracy,** a community ruled by the aged, not all elderly people held power and prestige. Veneration was reserved for older men but rarely granted to women, immigrants, or slaves, who nonetheless sometimes found respect and esteem within familial or interpersonal relationships.

The status of aged women

Provisions of English and colonial laws kept women in a subservient position to their husbands. Under common law doctrine, a married woman became one person with her husband. She could not make contracts, buy or sell property, or draft a will. Any property she owned before marriage became her husband's after the wedding. Any wages she earned legally belonged to him. Only widows or single women could run businesses of their own (Norton et al., 1982). The women who held high status were married to esteemed men.

In colonial New England, a woman often entered into a new set of relationships with her family and community when she became a widow. Her past status had rested on her position as wife of the household head, and her security depended on her husband's wealth (Haber, 1983). Although legal statute and tradition guaranteed widows one-third of their husbands' property, many had little actual control because their property was still part of their sons' inheritance. Moreover, widows sometimes inherited their husbands' debts as well as their estates. Restricted by financial pressures and a lack of management skills, many widows remained dependent on others for support (Premo, 1990). The low status of older women is indicated by evidence showing that some children placed their aged mothers in the homes of others as boarders (Haber, 1983).

Given the precarious position of many older women, it is not surprising that perceptions of them were often negative (Blom, 1991). Terms such as *hag* and *old maid* were commonplace. Sometimes widows were even viewed as sorcerers and witches. Yet counterpoised against such negative images were visions of beloved grandmothers and strong and determined older women (Roebuck, 1983).

The status of aged slaves

Before the American Revolution of 1776, slavery was practiced in both North and South, though slave-based agriculture was not profitable. When the Revolutionary War ended in 1783, slavery was abolished in the northern states, and the African slave trade was closed in 1808. Yet England's burgeoning textile industry fueled the demand for cotton grown in America; and between 1800 and 1860, the South emerged as the most vigorous slave economy in the world. Although two-thirds of southern families owned no slaves and 80 percent of slaveowners owned fewer than 20 slaves, the large slaveholding plantations dominated the South's economy and its politics. Ownership of slaves enabled plantation owners to produce cotton and other crops on a large scale. Slaveholding was the main determinant of a family's social position.

To slaveowners, slaves were investments and commodities, not human beings. Their devaluation as humans was reflected in the Constitution, which counted slaves as three-fifths of one person for purposes of determining the apportionment of

In Their Own Words

The Grandmother of Frederick Douglass, a Former Slave

*I*f any one thing in my experience, more than other, served to deepen my conviction of the infernal character of slavery, and to fill me with unutterable loathing of slave holders, it was their base ingratitude to my poor old grandmother. She had served my old master faithfully from youth to old age. She had been the source of all his wealth; she had peopled his plantation with slaves; she had become a great-grandmother in his service. She had rocked him in infancy, attended him in childhood, served him through life, and at his death wiped from his icy brow the cold death-sweat, and closed his eyes forever. She was nevertheless a slave—a slave for life—a slave in the hands of strangers; and in their hands she saw her children, her grandchildren, and her great-grandchildren, divided, like so many sheep, without being gratified with the small privilege of a single word, as to their or her own destiny. And, to cap the climax of their base ingratitude and fiendish barbarity, my grandmother, who was now very old, . . . having seen the beginning and the end of all of them, and her present owners finding she was of old age, and complete helplessness fast stealing over her once active limbs, they took her to the woods, built her a little hut, put up a little mud-chimney, and then made her welcome to the privilege of supporting herself there in perfect loneliness; thus turning her out to die!

Source: Douglass (1960:76–77).

congressional representatives. Because slaves were valued for their labor, their price declined as they grew older. Indicators of slaves' monetary value are found in records of sales and in inventories of slaveholders that assess property values for tax purposes. The records show that the most valuable slaves were males between the ages of 18 and 30. The value of slaves gradually declined as they grew older and became negative after 75. The prices and tax values of female slaves were similar to those of males, although the peak values occurred at younger ages and were lower overall by 20 to 40 percent (Fogel and Engerman, 1974).

Although the laws of most southern states made slaveowners responsible for the support and protection of their charges, some unscrupulous planters freed their aged slaves so that they would not have to provide food, housing, clothing, and medical care. To prevent this practice, a law passed in 1782 forbade the emancipation of slaves above age 45 so they would not become a burden on the community (Savitt, 1978). The "In Their Own Words" feature contains an excerpt from the autobiography of the former slave Frederick Douglass, who described how his elderly grandmother was turned out into the woods by her master.

Although aged slaves were of little value to their masters, they were revered within the slave community. In West Africa, the homeland of many American slaves, elders frequently occupied a position of honor and authority in the household and in the community. There are parallels in the African American slave experience. Statements concerning the respect and deference accorded elders are common in the slave narratives, a collection of oral histories gathered from former slaves during the 1930s (Barber, 1983).

Within the family, the oldest person was considered the household head, a position that was accorded deep respect. Because many married couples were separated by death or sale, single grandparents commonly moved into the cabin of a married child after they became too old to work (Webber, 1978). When they became incapacitated, they were cared for by their children. Older people also played a dominant role in the religious life of the slave community. The minister was usually an older man, and church elders wielded control of religious affairs. Older women were the senior practitioners and teachers of conjuring, sign reading, and herbal medicine (Armstrong, 1931). To some extent, then, the veneration accorded the aged in the slave community compensated for the loss of value in the wider society. However, older slaves were categorically deprived of most sanctions of power and authority by the institution of slavery, which was geared to level all status differences between people except for their productive capacity (Barber, 1983:314).

The Decline of Veneration of the Aged, 1770–1860

Historians generally agree that the veneration of the aged gradually disappeared as a societal value. According to Fischer (1977), this occurred over a relatively brief period, between 1770 and 1820, when the social position of the elderly declined precipitously. No longer were the aged revered. In churches, for example, wealth replaced age as the criterion for assigning seats. Some churches sold the best seats at an auction to the highest bidder. After 1770, legislatures began requiring public officials to retire from office at a set age, usually 60 or 70. In that same period, clothing styles changed. Instead of flattering the aged, they were designed to make the old look younger. In family portraits, all generations were now placed at the same level. Rather than being venerated, the old were described in pejorative terms. *Gaffer*, once a term of endearment, now expressed a sense of contempt

for old men. *Fogy*, which originally referred to a wounded veteran, became a term of disrespect.

Fischer contends that attitudes toward the aged became increasingly negative throughout the nineteenth century, permeating nearly every aspect of American life. Social commentators began to speak of the uselessness of old men and promoted the idea that people made their greatest contributions to society when they were young. Why, they asked, should unproductive people absorb an employer's resources? It was this attitude that helped stimulate the growth of retirement. As rates of retirement increased, poverty among the aged rose, confirming the negative stereotypes.

The cause of this transformation, in Fischer's view, was the influence of the ideals of equality and liberty, which were transported to the United States after the French Revolution in 1789. The ideal of equality destroyed the hierarchical conception of the world on which the authority of age had rested. The growth of the ideal of individual liberty undermined the communal values of Puritanism. As society became more individualistic, the ties of obligation between members of a community weakened.

An equally plausible explanation for the transformation in age relations is that the American Revolution against British rule instituted a new value system that promoted loyalty to the nation over the local community and rejected ideals of hierarchy based on monarchy or aristocracy in favor of government based on the will of the people. According to some historians, it was this value system, not one imported from France, that destroyed the traditional status hierarchy that revered age and replaced it with a more egalitarian ethos.

Thus, Fischer agrees with modernization theorists that a turning point had occurred in the status of the aged. Where he differs is in his interpretation of the cause. The decline in the status of the aged could not have been caused by industrialization or modernization, because these events occurred much later in the nineteenth century, after the demise of the veneration of age. In Fischer's view, they were secondary in importance to the ideals of equality and liberty. What mattered was a change in *ideals*, not a change in material life.

Most slave families lived in crude and crowded quarters, but the five generations pictured here drew their strength from close family ties. Older slaves held a position of honor and authority in the household and in the community of other slaves.

Another historian, W. Andrew Achenbaum (1978), conducted his own study of the history of aging. Like Fischer, Achenbaum believed that veneration had declined, but his evidence indicated that the transition in age relations began much later, around 1865, after the Civil War. From the end of the Revolutionary War until the late nineteenth century, according to Achenbaum, the old had a useful role to play in building a new nation. At the beginning of the nineteenth century, America was still undeveloped. The federal government could barely muster the military force needed to defend its borders. The land was still untamed, more than two-thirds of the people lived within 50 miles of the eastern shore, and most people eked out a living on small farms.

In a world filled with disease, sickness, and injury, it was believed that the frequency with which people survived to old age "provided a valid measure of the impact of the civil and natural environment on human health" (Achenbaum, 1978:12). The aged not only provided insights about the secrets of longevity but were living proof that certain virtues of temperance, moderation, industry, and exercise helped to prolong life. Old age was attained through righteous living, and the stature gained from years of experience made the elderly ideally qualified moral exemplars. According to Achenbaum, Americans believed that one's moral facilities improved with age and that older people could instill integrity and honesty in the young. Imbued with the wisdom of advanced age, the elderly could help direct and safeguard the moral development of the young nation.

From Veneration to Degradation in the Post–Civil War Period, 1860–1920

It was not until after the Civil War, according to Achenbaum (1978), that "Americans began to challenge nearly every favorable belief about the usefulness and merits of age that had been set forth" (p. 39). After the Civil War, the aged were more often seen as ugly and disease ridden. By the outbreak of World War I in 1914, "most Americans were affirming the obsolescence of old age."

Achenbaum tested three hypotheses derived from modernization theory to explain why ideas about the aged changed. First, he asked whether an increase in the proportion of older people may have caused Americans to view old age in a more negative way. He concluded that demographic change could not have been responsible for the change in public opinion because population aging was slow and undetectable until after 1920, when attitudes toward the aged had already become negative. Second, he asked whether increasing rates of retirement might have made people view the aged as less useful. However, retirement rates didn't accelerate significantly until after 1930, long after unfavorable notions about the aged were already commonplace. Thus, they could not have caused a decline in veneration. Finally, Achenbaum asked whether increased dependency among the aged could have caused a dramatic reevaluation of their status. Again, his answer was *no*, because there was no evidence that aged dependency rose in the nineteenth century. As late as 1920, only 2 percent of people over 65 were in institutions (Haber and Gratton, 1994).

More important than these changes in social and economic conditions were advancements in scientific knowledge, which undermined the view that older people possessed the secret to promoting longevity. Scientists now played a greater role in advancing the principles conducive to increasing longevity. The advice of experts replaced the wisdom of experience. Finally, Achenbaum (1978) concluded that changes in popular conceptions of the aged were unrelated to observable shifts in older Americans' actual position in society; rather, ideas about the worth and functions of the elderly had a life of their own, the effect of "the interplay of broad intellectual trends" (p. 86).

Romanticizing the World We Have Lost

Fischer and Achenbaum agreed that the aged were venerated in the past and that their status declined in modern society. Where they disagreed was over the timing and causes of the transition. Other scholars, however, have challenged the view that a golden age of aging ever existed. These historians argue that wealth and control of property have always been more important than age in determining one's status in life. For example, in his study of the Plymouth colony, John Demos (1978) noted that the old often commanded respect, but that old age per se did not invariably bring honor; indeed, the elderly were often depicted in negative terms, as "touchy, peevish, . . . hard to please . . . and full of complaints" (p. 223). When the old commanded respect, it was not because they were revered; it was because they controlled property and other valued resources.

Research on other preindustrial cultures also casts doubt on the thesis that the elderly were universally venerated in traditional society. In exploring views about the aged in France, for example, Peter Stearns (1977) found outright disdain, which persisted well into the contemporary era. From the eighteenth century to the period between the two World Wars, the French outlook toward old age remained unchanged.

The British historian Keith Thomas (1976) also rejected the view that there was once a golden age of aging. Most seventeenth- and eighteenth-century writers took it for granted that "old age was a wretched time of physical deterioration," and most portrayed the aged as peevish, forgetful, covetous, garrulous, and dirty (Thomas, 1976:244). Thomas concluded that there is no reason to romanticize the past. Once health and mind started to decay, wealth was the only basis for respect. Thus, although there was indeed once an ideal of old age that fit the definition of veneration, in practice this ideal was reserved for some select elites.

Historians are often interested in culture, so it is not surprising that the first generation of historians who studied aging and society focused on the history of ideas about the aged. Using modernization theory as a starting point, they explored the transformation of cultural beliefs over two centuries. But modernization theory is not primarily about *ideas* but rather about changes in material conditions. The period from 1860 to 1920 was one of rapid change as the population base shifted from farms to cities and as the nature of work changed from farming and small craft production to mass production in factories. In more recent research, historians and sociologists have analyzed how these far-reaching economic and demographic changes affected retirement, family life, and old-age dependency. Precise historical analyses not only challenge some of the myths about the past, they also elucidate the complex nature of the relationships among social, economic, and demographic variables.

The Aged as a Social Problem, 1920–1970

For much of the twentieth century, the predominant stereotype of the aged was that they were poor, frail, and deserted by their children. The poem "Over the Hill to the Poorhouse," which became popular in the 1920s, told of upstanding elderly people, abandoned by their children and too infirm to work, who sought final refuge in the poorhouse (Haber, 1994). Beginning in the Depression years of the 1930s, the aged were increasingly viewed as a social problem. Many older workers were thrown out of work, so poverty rates among the elderly were high. They remained high until the mid-1960s: poverty rates among people 65 and older during this period were more than 35 percent higher than for any other age group. The main goal of public policy in this era, not only in the United States but in many European countries, was to provide citizens income security in their old age (Walker, 1999).

The Tyranny of the Aged

In the past few decades a new stereotype has replaced the older view of the aged. They are now often seen as a prosperous, selfish, and politically powerful group that is gobbling up scarce societal resources (Binstock, 1996). In 1992, for example, a cover story in *Fortune* magazine proclaimed "The tyranny of America's old . . . is one of the crucial issues facing U.S. society" (Smith, 1992). Similarly, an article in the *New Republic* magazine characterized older people as "an unproductive section of the population, one that does not even promise (as children do) one day to be productive" (Fairlie, 1988:19).

One of the reasons for these changing stereotypes is the dramatic improvements that have taken place in the economic status of the aged. Between 1960 and 1996, the proportion of people over 65 with incomes below the poverty level dropped from nearly 40 percent to just over 12 percent. Another factor in the change in attitudes has been the debates about how future generations will pay for the health care and income security of an aging population (Binstock, 1996). Regardless of the cause, these stereotypes are as inaccurate as those that portrayed the elderly as poor, frail, and incompetent.

We now turn to the arguments social scientists have made about how modernization has affected the aged in the family, the workplace, and the nursing home. Each section weighs the evidence to determine whether it is true that modernization was harmful to the elderly.

Did Modernization Undermine the Extended Family?

A core premise of modernization theory is that industrialization destroyed the economic basis of the extended family by removing production from the home. Because family members no longer worked together farming or in some household endeavor, the **extended family household** was replaced by the **nuclear family household,** composed solely of parents and children. Factory production accelerated the process of urbanization, and as younger people moved to cities, aged parents were left behind, isolated in rural areas (Cowgill, 1974).

We now know that this argument contains many misconceptions about family life in the past. Perhaps the primary flaw is that the extended family household was only one of many types in preindustrial society (Shorter, 1975). Household composition

Aging around the World

INHERITANCE PATTERNS AND HOUSEHOLD STRUCTURE IN THE OLD WORLD

The idea of a golden age of aging when the elderly found sanctuary in the bosom of the extended family was first challenged by the British historian Peter Laslett (1976). Laslett used census records to reconstruct households in preindustrial England, and his data showed that, from as far back as the Middle Ages, nuclear family households predominated. Older people were not much more likely in the past than they are today to be living in the homes of married children. Under the demographic conditions of the times, the average family contained many children, many more than in the present. Women continued to bear children until they reached menopause. At age 60, a typical couple still had dependent children at home, and it was not uncommon for an elderly couple to have children and grandchildren of the same age. Because life expectancy was considerably lower than it is today, an older couple rarely survived long after their last child left home. Therefore, the only reason the aged in the past were more likely to be living with children than they are today is because they were still actively involved in parenting.

Nonetheless, Laslett did find some extended family households that included aging parents and married children. Under what conditions did this occur?

Preindustrial societies were based on agricultural production, and parents had control of the family farm. Inheritance patterns often determined household structure. One inheritance pattern is called **primogeniture.** Under primogeniture, a father passes his property on to one child, usually the eldest son. It was often the custom that a son could not marry until his father had died or retired and had given him control of the farm (Schlumbohm, 1996). When the father retired, his son and wife might move into the parental home, where the two generations would live together until the parents died.

Joint living was not always the custom. In some regions, the parents would build a retirement cottage on the land or designate a portion of the property on which the son could build his own home. Turning over the property to a son entailed some risk, for it meant the parents were now at their children's mercy for care in their old age. Parents did not depend solely on the goodwill of their children when relinquishing control of the family farm but wrote elaborate **retirement contracts** providing detailed instructions regarding their rights and their children's responsibilities (Howell, 1976; Sabean, 1976). In some cases, a retiring farmer would make a contract with his son that provided for a monthly income for him and his wife in exchange for the land (Guinnane, 1996). In other cases, retirement contracts spelled out exactly what food and goods the parents would receive and how the property would be divided. For example, one contract from Denmark in 1785 read:

> Our son-in-law Peder will pay to us for the farm Gentofte once and for all 100 rigsdaler. We reserve the use of the old large house and Peder will build a new one for himself. In addition he will yearly pay us a

pension of 20 rigsdaler, 3 barrels of good rye flour, 3 barrels of malt brewed into good quality beer, 1 barrel of unmilled rye, 1 barrel of barley, 1 barrel of oats, 4 geese with their goslings well fatted, 4 sheep with their lambs fed winter and summer, 2 fresh swine yearly and 1 barrel of good butter, 2 pots of milk daily when the cows are milking and 8 loads of peat-turf. Care and maintenance with woolens, linens and cleanliness. (quoted in Gaunt, 1979)

Although tying the transmission of property to parental obligations provided security for the aged, it also created tensions between generations. An Austrian folk song from the early eighteenth century expresses a son's frustration at having to wait for his father's retirement to marry:

Father, when ya gonna gimme the farm,
Father, when ya gonna sign it away?
My girl's been growing' every day,
And Single no longer wants to stay.
Father, when ya gonna gimme the farm,
Father, when ya gonna gimme the house?
When ya gonna retire to your room out of the way,
And dig up your potatoes all day?
(quoted in Berkner, 1972:403)

Indeed, some evidence suggests that young women intentionally became pregnant in an effort to force their future fathers-in-law to turn over property.

In Sweden, Germany, and the Netherlands, many cases of elder abuse by children were reported after parents retired and gave up their property. There are numerous folktales describing fighting between parents and children, even murder. An anonymous writer in the *Westfalisches Anzieger* in 1798 proposed establishing a Court for Morality to adjudicate conflicts between peasant parents and children (Gaunt, 1979).

Even in an agricultural society, not all people were landowners. Those with no property to transmit to their children had no bargaining power. For example, in late-eighteenth-century Switzerland, *rastgaben* was a practice in which children inherited property in exchange for providing a retirement allowance for their parents. In this region, landless laborers received no allowances from children (Braun, 1966). Similarly, in Austria, where extended family households were common, nuclear family households predominated among the poor and landless (Berkner, 1972). These cases provide excellent empirical support for exchange theory, described in Chapter 2, which emphasizes the importance of an even balance of resources between generations as protection for the frail elderly.

Thus, extended family households in Europe did exist in preindustrial society, not as the normative pattern but as a phase of the life course tied to inheritance patterns (Hareven and Plakans, 1987; Plakans, 1996). The control parents exerted over property protected them in old age but sometimes at the expense of familial harmony.

What Do You Think?

1. Has the handing down of a farm or business from one generation to the next created friction in your family? If so, what was the major issue?
2. What do you think of the idea of a retirement contract between parents and their children? Could it be adapted to modern life? Should it be?

ranged from the simple, nuclear family in England, the Netherlands, Sweden, Denmark, and northern France to complex stem households consisting of parents, adult siblings, and their families in Austria, Germany, and Japan (Wrigley, 1977; Alter, Cliggett, and Urbiel, 1996; Schlumbohm, 1996). The question, then, is not about what destroyed the extended family but rather what determines the type of household that is formed. The answer lies both in demographic patterns and in cultural traditions.

"Aging around the World" explores familial traditions in seventeenth- and eighteenth-century Europe.

Inheritance Patterns and Household Structure

Colonial families, 1620–1770

The Puritans brought their Old World traditions with them, and some survived relatively intact in the new land. In colonial New England, sons waited to marry until their fathers made them economically independent. Sometimes a son was deeded land outright; in other instances, he had to wait until his father died to take over the family farm (Greven, 1970). **Deeds of gift** were often used like retirement contracts, specifying obligations owed to parents, including money payments. Both deeds and wills carefully provided for widows, obligating children to provide lodging, food, and income to their mother. Widowed men, too, sometimes made formal arrangements for their own care following the death of their wives, promising bequests on their deaths in exchange for maintenance in old age (Shammus, Salmon, and Dahlin, 1987). Sometimes children challenged probate proceedings, arguing for reimbursement for food and care rendered parents earlier.

As in the Old World, extended households were rare; the typical household was nuclear in arrangement (Ruggles, 1987). Older couples enjoyed living near children but preferred to remain independent (Demos, 1978). Custom dictated that one child remain with an aging parent. In return for a homestead or a larger portion of the estate, that child—usually a daughter—would

care for her aging parents (Haber and Gratton, 1994).

Aging on the frontier, 1800–1920

In 1800, the edge of the frontier began in western New York and traversed down through Kentucky and Tennessee. By 1860, the frontier had reached the West Coast. Some of the settlers were easterners seeking land, for northeastern farmers had already cultivated as much land as they could. As the sons and daughters of farmers gave up farming or went west, the legal boundaries of the nation grew.

A wave of immigration, which began in the 1840s and peaked in the 1880s, further expanded frontier settlement. Most of the immigrants were Protestants and Catholics from Germany, Scandinavia, Ireland, and England. Although the majority settled in the major cities, many German, Dutch, and Scandinavian farmers were lured to the Midwest by recruiters hired by state governments and land developers. Some, like the Amish and Mennonites, included entire religious communities who fled religious persecution in their native land. These immigrant farmers purchased large tracks of land in the Midwest and established close-knit communities that adapted their cultural traditions to their new life. See "Diversity in the Aging Experience" for more information about the traditions of the Mennonites.

Urbanization and Household Structure

Industrialization is a complex process that defies precise definition. Its predominant characteristics include production by machine rather than by hand; involvement of an increasing proportion of the workforce in manufacturing rather than in agriculture; the concentration of production in large factories; a rapid increase in population; and an increase in the size of cities (urbanization).

According to modernization theory, urbanization destroys extended family households and isolates the aged as children leave rural areas. Historical studies of these processes suggest that the effect of industrialization on the family life of the aged is more complex than modernization theory indicates.

Diversity in the Aging Experience

THE MENNONITES ON THE FRONTIER

A colony of Russian Mennonites emigrated to the plains of Kansas in 1874 to escape forced military service. There they established the Alexanderwohl community and reconstructed their traditional way of life (Rempel, 1973–74). Among the immigrants was the family of Cornelius and Helena Richert Voth, who were married in 1853, 21 years before the mass emigration. Between 1855 and 1874, the Voths had 11 children. Two died in infancy and one at the age of 20. On the open Kansas plains, the Voths became successful farmers and wealthy landowners. Their experiences serve as a case study of inheritance patterns, household structure, and intergenerational relations in mid-nineteenth-century America.

Over their life course, Cornelius and Helena helped their children establish their own farms by deeding parcels of the familial homestead or by funding their emigration to other states like Arizona where land was plentiful and cheap. As the parents aged, their children and grandchildren provided an extensive social support system. All the daughters married in their early 20s except Suzanna, their youngest child, who remained at home with her parents through her thirty-first year. When in 1901 their daughter-in-law died in childbirth, Suzanna left her parents' home to care for her brother's children. In the absence of Suzanna, the Voth's children and grandchildren who lived on nearby farms pitched in to help. In a letter to Suzanna, Mother Voth expressed her loneliness but also spoke of the extensive support their children and grandchildren provided:

> I was so sad when you had left, I had to cry almost all the time, especially the first few days. It's better now. . . . Greta was here the first week, Liese the next. . . . Greta finished my dress, also sewed the hat. . . . Liese went home yesterday. Today we're alone. I think little Lena will come tomorrow, she can already help a lot. . . . As far as the milking is concerned, I'll be able to do that. (Quadagno and Janzen, 1987:42)

When Mother Voth became ill a few weeks later, their son Peter temporarily stayed with his parents, but a short time later their daughter and her husband sold their own farm and moved in with the elderly couple. This arrangement was temporary until the Voths could build their own retirement house on the family homestead and turn the main property over to Helena and Peter.

In the absence of their daughter Suzanna, the Voths were able to mobilize support from other children and grandchildren to help them function. The children were a crucial resource for the parents in their old age, and the transfer of land provided the resources for a comfortable retirement and for generational continuity.

What Do You Think?

1. Does anyone in your family play Suzanna's role—that of an unmarried caretaker for elderly parents? If so, does that person expect to inherit the parents' home when they die?
2. The Voths lived on the American frontier. What might their retirement have been like if they had stayed in Russia?

107

Urbanization and household structure in the old world

England was the first country to industrialize, beginning around 1790, and much of our knowledge of industrialization's impact comes from research by British historians. Michael Anderson (1972) compared rural and urban regions of Lancashire, England, in 1851 to test hypotheses about the living arrangements of the elderly. If modernization theory is accurate, then more older people should be living with children in rural areas than in cities. Contrary to expectations, however, Anderson found that older people in the cities were more likely to be living with married children than those residing on farms and that few old people in either region were living alone.

Why were the elderly less likely to be living with their children in rural areas? One reason is that family farms had continually been divided among heirs, and by the nineteenth century the family estate was often too small to support more than one generation. As children grew up, they were forced to move off the farm to find employment. Another reason is that in urban, industrial areas wives of factory workers often worked outside the home. Older parents were taken in because they provided care for young children (Litchfield, 1978). Finally, housing shortages in urban areas may have forced two generations to live together.

Urbanization and household structure in the United States, 1860–1900

Research on the United States supports the conclusion that urbanization may draw families closer together, not destroy familial bonds. The United States was primarily rural until relatively late in the nineteenth century. In 1860, rural residents far outnumbered urban dwellers, and it was not until the 1880s that large, urban areas such as New York, Boston, Washington, Chicago, and St. Louis had populations of over 100,000. Along with population growth came overcrowding and housing shortages, especially in immigrant communities where large families lived packed into small tenements.

Family historians Howard Chudacoff and Tamara Hareven (1978) used census records to reconstruct households in eight communities in Essex County, Massachusetts, for two periods—1860 and 1880. In 1860, the economy was prospering. Young adults typically left home, found jobs, and established independent households. Then a severe depression that lasted from 1873 to 1878 wracked the nation. In 1880, few young adults were living on their own. A lack of job opportunities combined with a housing shortage meant that adult children were forced to live with their parents. Many families also took in boarders to make ends meet. Thus, during hard times, the homes of older family members became a haven for many kin as well as nonrelatives, as kin and strangers pooled their resources to survive.

Chudacoff and Hareven conclude that instead of isolating the aged, urbanization and the pressures of a weak economy enhanced familial ties. Rather than parents being burdens on their children, the two generations were involved in a mutually beneficial exchange. Aged parents shared their homes and in return their children ran errands, did household chores, and provided company.

Throughout most of U.S. history, elderly couples and aging widows attempted to maintain an independent household for as long as possible, moving in with children only when all other options failed. Nonetheless, old people experienced less social segregation than they do today. Although few lived with their adult children, they often resided nearby and provided each other with mutual support and aid. In cases of illness or poverty, the elderly were supported by their children or other relatives. Institutions like nursing homes were a last resort (Hareven, 2001).

Independent living arrangements in the twentieth century

In 1910 over half of married women over 65 and three-quarters of widows with living children resided with at least one child (Elman and Uhlenberg, 1995). The children who cared for their elderly parents in their own homes were among the more affluent members of society. Farmers, professionals, and business owners were much more likely to have a parent living with them than ordinary laborers. Only the wealthier families could afford to support someone who was not bringing in income (Costa, 1998).

Since the early 1900s, however, the percentage of older people who live with family members has fallen steadily. By 1990 only 3 percent of older Americans were living with an adult child

(Costa, 1998). Why did this decline in shared households occur? Was it a change in values? Did children no longer feel obligated to care for their aged parents? A more likely explanation is that the creation of Social Security allowed the aged to continue to live independently by providing them with a secure income. Indeed, the majority of older people prefer to live in their own homes and see family members frequently, as visitors.

Some people argue that as the importance of the government's role in providing support to the aged has increased, the sense of obligation between generations has weakened. If so, then national old-age pensions would have made parents less dependent on exchanges with their children. "An Issue for Public Policy" examines this issue in historical perspective and demonstrates that having a regular source of income had the opposite effect. By enhancing the independence of the elderly, it allowed familial ties to be based on choice, companionship, and affection.

In summary, historical evidence demonstrates that the extended family household, at least in Western countries, was only rarely the predominant household type. Extended family households were typically formed at the point in the life course when parents retired and passed their property on to their children. Parents who had no property typically lived alone. Extended family households were also formed when a crisis such as a weak economy or a lack of housing forced two generations to share a home. At other times independent living was preferred.

DID INDUSTRIALIZATION PUSH OLDER WORKERS OUT OF THE LABOR FORCE?

Modernization theory is based on large-scale quantitative studies comparing rates of retirement across nations. These studies suggest that a decline in agriculture and skilled craft production is associated with increased retirement and unemployment among the aged (Palmore and Manton, 1974; Pampel and Weiss, 1983). A decline of farming eliminates the main source of employment for people in rural areas. Skilled craftsmen lose autonomy in the workplace as technological

advances encourage mechanization and give rise to factory production. Older workers who can no longer keep pace on the production line are summarily fired. Historical evidence indicates that there is much truth to these assertions but also that work in preindustrial society is sometimes romanticized.

Work for the Aged in the Old World

Farming was the predominant form of work in preindustrial economies, and as we saw in the previous section, retirement was possible through the transmission of property to one's heirs. Not all people were property owners, however, and those without property often spent their final years working at menial jobs. In England, gangs of migrant-type workers were commonly found in agricultural districts. These gangs often included old men and women (Quadagno, 1982). Old women also sometimes cared for young children and infants whose mothers had gone to work in the fields. Generally, the work of the aged was marginal and sporadic, as the following account illustrates:

An old lady still living in the village used to scare crows for the whole of the harvest holidays: she was paid six shillings. She was given a wooden clapper and had to keep making noise with it: if she once stopped and the clapper was silent, the man who hired her would look out of his house to see what she was doing. (quoted in Quadagno, 1982:63)

Work for the Aged in Colonial New England, 1620–1770

In colonial New England, a pattern of partial or gradual retirement predominated among the landless. Men who had worked as farm laborers in their youth and early adult years took odd jobs in old age mowing grass or hauling grist to the local mill (Demos, 1978). Older women went to work when they became widowed or when their husbands were ailing or unemployed. Usually their "low levels of skill and sporadic employment experience restricted them to unskilled, irregular, and low-paying jobs" (Tilly and Scott, 1978:128). Widows commonly took in boarders, managed stores and taverns, or

An Issue for Public Policy

DOES STATE SUPPORT FOR THE AGED UNDERMINE FAMILIAL OBLIGATIONS?

*P*art of the golden age myth asserts that state support of the aged became necessary because of a decline in familial support. As evidence, proponents of this view have pointed to the increase in institutions for the elderly and the increase in the proportion of older people living alone. For example, Paillat (1977) argued that the demographic increase in the proportion of the aged undermined the family network, "which offered help and assistance during many centuries, [and which] does not—or cannot—play its role as completely and efficiently as before" (p. 64). In his view, the traditional solidarity between generations was replaced by bureaucratic structures. Halper (1978) agreed. He tied this loss specifically to the pension system:

> The adoption of Social Security, for instance, was greeted as a great boon to the elderly, and yet it is obvious by now that its blessings have been very mixed. For the assertion of a governmental responsibility to provide for the aged would seem to have permitted the loosening of the bonds of family responsibility thereby making it easier for persons to neglect their debts to their elderly relatives. It is not quite so hard to shunt them aside, after all, when one believes that the government will take care of them. (p. 324)

Were national old-age pensions instituted because familial support of the aged had broken down? Is there evidence that such pensions have destroyed family ties?

One researcher examined the household structure of the aged in Ireland before and after the British Old Age Pension of 1908 was passed (Guinnane, 1996). In theory a pension could have one of two effects. It could provide additional resources so that an elderly individual could live independently. Or a pension might make caring for an elderly relative a less onerous burden for

worked as midwives (Premo, 1990). Others held jobs as domestics and washerwomen (Chudacoff and Hareven, 1978).

To summarize, agricultural production provided relative security in old age only for those who were landowners and allowed farmers to plan an orderly withdrawal from the labor force. The landless held a marginal position in the labor force, had few resources for their old age, and continued working not by choice but because they had no other source of income.

The Decline of Skilled Craft Labor, 1860–1920

In 1800, manufacturing was relatively unimportant to the economy, and the production of goods took place in small workshops and homes where family members. An aged person who could contribute a few shillings a week to household expenses might be readily taken in by kin.

Several features of the prepension period are notable, the most important being that few aged people lived alone. Living with children was common, whether or not the children were married. Older people who had no children typically lived with other family members—nieces, nephews, or siblings. Single older people lived with persons who were nonkin. It was a practice in rural areas of Ireland to provide support for all the needy aged:

> Take the case of an old person living with relations on a farm or with a stranger on a farm—because the Irish people are tremendous charitable in their way, and I find many old people living with absolute strangers. (quoted in Guinnane, 1996:107)

What, then, was the effect of the British Old Age Pension on living arrangements of the aged? After 1908, older people were more likely to have unmarried children living with them and less likely to have married children in their homes. One effect of the pension, then, was that it provided resources for older parents so that they could continue to provide for their single children. Married children were most likely to be living with aged parents in those cases where the parents had given them the farm in exchange for support. For many, however, the pension allowed elderly parents to maintain an independent residence rather than having to share a household. Another effect of the pension was an increase in the number of older widows who remained household heads living with their unmarried children, while the proportion of widows living with married children decreased. The pension allowed a widow to maintain her home without turning her resources over to her children. Guinnane concluded that the pension had no effect on the tendency for the aged to live with relatives but that the composition of these arrangements changed to reflect the increased economic security of the parental generation. The evidence contradicts the hypothesis that government support for the aged undermines familial obligations.

What Do You Think?

1. Did the creation of the Social Security system change the living arrangements in your family? Compare your parents', grandparents', and great-grandparents' living arrangements in their old age.
2. Does the existence of Social Security benefits strengthen or weaken family ties in the United States?

apprentices were taught the trade by master craftsmen. Tailors, shoemakers, and blacksmiths made articles by hand according to the needs of their customers. Most continued to work in old age. Retirement was uncommon (Hill, 1994).

From as early as the 1820s, skilled craft workers in such trades as woodworking, shoemaking, and tailoring had established unions organized by occupation. Through the unions, workers sought to protect themselves against competition from inferior workmen by regulating apprenticeships and establishing minimum wages.

By the 1840s, machinery had begun to replace the traditional tools, and some work was contracted out by middlemen. But as late as 1850, fewer than 1.5 million workers were employed in manufacturing. The mass production of goods was stimulated by technological advances that

Skilled craftsman teach apprentices to make and repair shoes, 1899.

made it possible to produce hundreds of articles a day, and by increased consumer demand that accompanied rapid population growth. By 1880, nearly 5 million workers were employed in manufacturing, and most goods were no longer produced by skilled craft workers in the home but rather by semiskilled employees in factories. As factory work replaced craft production, workers lost control over the production process. No longer could the worker decide when to begin and end the day, when to rest, and what tools and techniques to use. The pace of work was rapid. A shoemaker who had made one pair of shoes a week as a skilled craftsman might make 2,400 pairs a day in a factory. Older workers often had difficulty keeping up, and employers viewed them as undesirable employees because they were at greater risk of injury or illness (Achenbaum, 1978; Haber, 1983).

As the skilled craftsmen found their livelihood threatened, their unions became increasingly concerned with protecting their members against the risks of unemployment, illness, or old age. They established provident funds paid from dues that members could draw on in times of need. Many funds also paid benefits to widows of deceased workers. The first union pension was instituted by the Granite Cutters International Association in 1905. The International Typographical Union followed suit in 1907 (Quadagno, 1988a).

As the skilled crafts declined, the union membership grew older. Fewer young workers were supporting more retirees, and the pension funds were rapidly depleted. By the 1920s, unions that had regularly paid pensions to retirees were forced to take harsh measures. Several unions stopped paying pensions entirely. Others dropped widows' benefits (Quadagno, 1988a). As it became apparent that the unions could not fund these benefits on their own, the skilled craft workers began a campaign for a national old-age pension.

Although interest in a national pension was expressed as early as 1912, it was not until the Great Depression of the 1930s, when many unions' pension funds were depleted and unemployment among workers over 45 was widespread, that such legislation was enacted. In 1934, President Franklin Roosevelt appointed a Committee on Economic Security to plan a national old-age pension (Kingson and Berkowitz, 1993). As the committee members investigated the obstacles facing older workers, they found that, especially in the heavy-manufacturing industries, older workers were unable to keep pace with the demands of machines. Not only were older workers at greater risk than younger workers of becoming unemployed, their spells of unemployment were longer. The Depression only worsened their problems (Committee on Economic Security, 1937). The committee concluded that after long years of productive labor, workers had earned the right to rest.

In summary, historical evidence shows that retirement is not a creation of modern, industrial society. Contrary to the portrait depicted by modernization theory, the ability to retire was associated with the ownership of property. Older people who lacked property lived a harsh existence and worked until they died. Those in skilled craft unions had pooled their resources to allow their members to retire, but in the long run these pensions funded out of workers' dues were unsustainable. Clearly then, retirement was not just associated with factory production. Retirement in the early twentieth century did differ from retirement today in one key respect. It involved a gradual withdrawal from the labor force rather than an abrupt departure (Hareven, 2001). Being able to retire with dignity is one of the great boons of modern society.

Retirement as a Tool of Labor Market Management, 1920–70

More important than industrialization in drawing workers out of the labor force was the creation of public and private pensions, which provided workers with enough income to retire from their jobs. In 1935 Congress passed the Social Security Act, which created a program that provided retirement benefits to workers at age 65. To ensure that older workers did indeed retire, a strict "earnings test" was added to the act. Anyone under age 70 who earned more than $15 a month forfeited all his or her Social Security benefits (Graebner, 1980). Since 1935 the Social Security Act has been amended several times to extend benefits to dependents and the disabled, and to allow workers the option of retiring before age 65 (Kingson and Berkowitz, 1993).

Though some employers had provided private pensions for their workers since the nineteenth century, employer-based pensions did not become widespread until after 1948, when the National Labor Relations Board ruled that trade unions could include pensions in their collective bargaining agreements. Immediately, the large industrial unions began demanding pensions as part of the wage package (Quadagno, 1988a). In 1949 Ford Motor Company agreed to provide company-financed pensions of $100 a month to retired workers who were at least 65 years old and who had worked at Ford for 30 years. The concept soon spread to other industries, and by the late 1950s, over half of all unionized workers were covered by pension plans. Employer-based pensions boosted workers' retirement income, easing their withdrawal from the labor force.

In the 1960s some manufacturing firms added **early retirement incentive programs (ERIPs)** for workers under age 65. The trade unions supported early retirement as a protection for older workers who had lost their jobs but were too young to qualify for regular retirement benefits. Changes in technology had rendered many older workers' jobs obsolete (Gordus, 1980). When obsolescent plants closed or relocated, these workers faced the difficult choice between moving away from their homes or trying to find new jobs with old skills. The first early retirement provisions were added to a collective bargaining agreement between the United Auto Workers and the Big Three—General Motors, Chrysler, and Ford—in 1964. The new provisions allowed autoworkers who had at least 10 years of service to retire at age 60, and those with at least 30 years of service to retire at age 55. Other companies followed suit, instituting an era of expanding private sector pensions.

The combination of income from increasingly generous Social Security benefits and private pensions allowed workers to retire at a younger age and enjoy a secure old age. But the trend began to reverse in the 1970s and 1980s. Chapter 12 will cover current trends in retirement.

IS INSTITUTIONAL CARE A PRODUCT OF MODERN SOCIETY?

According to modernization theory, the ultimate consequence of the breakdown of the family and the increase in retirement is the abandonment of the aged in institutions. Yet the historical evidence suggests that institutional care is not a product of modern, industrial society and that there have always been vulnerable elderly who became wards of the community.

Boarding the Frail Elderly in the Colonial Era, 1620–1770

The Puritan settlers in New England brought with them from the mother country a concept of poor relief borrowed from the **Elizabethan poor laws.** The Elizabethan poor law of 1601 established a system of local government and local responsibility for the poor. Each parish appointed overseers who levied taxes on property and used the funds to provide relief to the poor. Of primary importance was the division between neighbors and strangers. Responsibility extended to family and community and ended there. Both English and American poor laws required communities to assist their permanent residents. Others who were needy were shipped to their community of origin. Thus, the laws reflected an era during which most people clearly belonged to some community, but an era in which the boundaries between family and community were blurred (Katz, 1989).

A second distinction was made between the "deserving" and "undeserving" poor. The poor laws were designed to restrict aid to those truly in need—the lame, the impotent, the old, the blind, and the widowed—while excluding the able-bodied poor, who were presumed capable of working. Colonial settlers unanimously agreed that there was a need to help the deserving poor but withheld their support from the able-bodied.

During the first decades of the colonies, needy individuals received assistance from their local communities, a reflection of the Puritans' ideology concerning the responsibilities of members of a commonwealth. By law, parents and grandparents were required to support the young, and adult children were responsible for their parents. Those with no kin had to appeal to the public authorities for charity. There are many tales in colonial documents of elderly people who became wards of the town. For example, in 1660 Mr. Burrowes, a resident of Providence, requested help from local relief authorities because of "age and weakness." He turned over all his property and possessions to the town treasury and was placed in the home of a local family. A similar fate awaited the widow Baldwin when the citizens of Hadley voted to move her from house to house "to such as are able to receive her" and "let her remain a fortnight in each family" (Quadagno, 1988a:25).

In 1664 the first **almshouse,** an institution for the poor, was built in Boston. Over the next several decades, other almshouses dotted the countryside (Haber and Gratton, 1994). But institutional care of the poor was rare. As long as aged and disabled members of local communities made up most of the poor, town councils were willing to provide **out-relief** (direct grants of aid) or board them in the homes of local residents.

The Rise of the Almshouse, 1770–1850

Between 1820 and 1860, more than 5 million immigrants entered the United States. Although they came from all over the world, the majority were Irish and German. By 1850, the population of many cities was one-third foreign-born. Periodic economic depressions in the late eighteenth century set large numbers of wage laborers adrift across the countryside in search of employment. Many were immigrants. When they were unable to find work, these unemployed men applied for poor relief, causing native citizens to view this new type of pauper with alarm. The poor were now strangers, and pauperism became defined as a pressing social problem (Clement, 1985). Around 1820, among the cities on the eastern seaboard, a campaign was waged to eliminate out-relief and require paupers to enter almshouses. The intent of this policy was to discourage people from applying for aid. Between 1820 and 1840, 144 new almshouses were erected in Massachusetts alone. As a result of this early version of the war on welfare, the proportion of paupers receiving out-relief declined, and the number of paupers in almshouses rose (Rothman, 1971).

Public officials deemed the aged among the deserving poor, and they were treated less harshly than the able-bodied poor. Many more elderly, a high proportion of whom were women, received out-relief in their homes. In Charleston, South Carolina, for example, the city relief roster indicated that aged women accounted for 30 percent of paupers awarded out-relief. Only in rare instances were the aged forced to end their days in an almshouse (Haber and Gratton, 1989).

The Growth of Specialized Institutions for the Aged, 1850–1920

As the population continued to grow, it became apparent that pauperism was largely a consequence of unemployment and that all the unemployed could not be contained in almshouses. Inspections of almshouses revealed that conditions were grossly inadequate, and the almshouse experiment was deemed a failure. In the second half of the nineteenth century, charity experts began categorizing the poor and moving people into specialized institutions. Those judged to be lunatics were confined to asylums for the insane. Destitute children were placed in orphanages. Homes for the deaf and blind were established (Rosenberg, 1987). As other categories of paupers were moved into specialized institutions, the almshouses increasingly became de facto old-age homes for the impoverished elderly. By the end of the nineteenth

century, one-third of almshouse residents were aged; by 1923, 67 percent were (Haber and Gratton, 1994). Still, only 10 percent of native-born elderly over age 80 and 13 percent of foreign-born lived with strangers or in institutions. The vast majority were cared for by family members (Achenbaum, 1978).

As the almshouses lost their punitive function for the undeserving poor, there was growing public dissatisfaction with the treatment of the nation's impoverished elderly. Many who spent their final years in an almshouse were "respectable" widows. The threat of the almshouse became a vivid symbol in the campaign for a national old age pension (Quadagno, 1988a).

The Growth of the Nursing Home Industry, 1920–70

The conversion of almshouses into old-age homes culminated in the modern nursing home industry. Most nursing homes were private profit-making facilities that provided housing and medical care for those who could afford it. Some nursing homes were nonprofit facilities that were maintained by religious or fraternal organizations.

Beginning in the 1940s, some states began to provide funds to cover medical care for the aged poor who were living in county homes (Costa, 1998). Then in 1950 amendments to the Social Security Act permitted state welfare departments to negotiate with private nursing homes for the care of the aged. The nursing home industry expanded rapidly in the 1950s, largely because the federal government began subsidizing the construction of nursing homes and some nursing home care for the aged poor. The Hill-Burton Act (1956) provided public funds for the construction of nonprofit nursing homes, while the Federal Housing Administration offered federally insured loans for the construction of for-profit nursing homes. In the same year Congress earmarked more federal funds for nursing home care for the aged poor.

In 1960 Congress passed the Kerr-Mills Act, which paid the costs of nursing home care for elderly people who could not afford to pay their own expenses. The problem with Kerr-Mills, however, was that the payments the government provided were usually only enough to cover poor-quality custodial care, not skilled nursing care.

The nursing home industry expanded again after the Medicaid program was enacted in 1965. A health insurance program for the poor, Medicaid paid the full cost of nursing home care. In the same decade the deinstitutionalization of residents in mental hospitals further increased the demand for nursing home care. By the early 1970s, more than 1 million older people were residing in nursing homes (Uhlenberg, 1997). The nursing home industry today is a billion-dollar business, a subject we discuss in more detail in Chapter 10.

MODERNIZATION THEORY AND HISTORICAL EVIDENCE

As the preceding discussion makes clear, the argument that industrialization isolated older people from family members and increased their risk of ending their lives alone vastly oversimplifies the historical record. Throughout history there have always been vulnerable older people who have become charges of the community. The form of support they have received has varied from boarding in the homes of neighbors to life in an almshouse to specialized homes for the elderly. Moreover, as Chapter 8 shows, the argument that the aged are neglected or repudiated by their children in modern industrial society is not valid. Study after study has shown that this view of modern society is inaccurate, that children perform a variety of personal and protective services for their aged parents, and that these relationships are reciprocal. Today, most of the aged remain firmly embedded in a kin network, just as they did in the past.

Modernization is an abstract concept that summarizes a complex series of events that occurred over more than 150 years in Western societies. There is abundant evidence to challenge many of the hypotheses derived from this viewpoint. Veneration may have existed as a cultural ideal, but in practice it was reserved for a few elites. The extended family household was never universal but typically was formed during the phase of the life course when property was transmitted between generations. The shift of work from the household to the factory is not synonymous with the breakdown of the family. Retirement is not solely the creation of modern society, although the large-scale national pension systems that characterize late-twentieth-century nations are. There have always been vulnerable older people forced to rely on the community for support in their declining years.

Identifying the flaws in modernization theory does not mean that it is entirely without merit. The government has come to play a more extensive role in the provision of economic support in old age than in the past. Rising rates of retirement among older workers is a distinctive and notable trend. Older people are more likely to be living alone today than they were in the past. Nonetheless, it is misguided to view these trends solely as products of modernization or industrialization. Much work remains to be done before we can fully understand the impact of sociohistorical forces or views of aging on such matters as retirement, family life, and long-term care. Those subjects are explored in the other chapters in this text.

Chapter Resources

LOOKING BACK

1. **How have attitudes toward the aged changed over time?** *In non-Western cultures the elderly are often accorded great respect and esteem. Were the aged venerated in the past in Europe and the United States? Some historians have used evidence about cultural practices toward old people elsewhere to argue that the aged in the European Old World and in the New World were held in high esteem. Others contend that veneration was merely a cultural ideal that was rarely practiced. Evidence for the colonial period in North America suggests that the ideal of veneration did exist but did not extend to aged women, immigrants, or members of minority groups.*

   For much of the twentieth century the aged were viewed as isolated, frail, and poor. Recently older people have been depicted as prosperous, selfish, and politically powerful. Such stereotypes are not completely accurate.

2. **Did elderly people live with their children in the past?** *Extended family households consisting of two generations of married couples were most common during one phase of the life course, not as the preferred living arrangement. Typically, such households were formed when the parents retired and passed their farms on to their children.*

3. **How did the rise of cities affect the way older people and their families lived?** *According to modernization theory, urbanization leaves the aged isolated in rural areas. This generalization is not entirely accurate, however, for in certain periods overcrowding in cities forced families to live together in family households. This arrangement was most likely during bad economic times. If young adults had trouble finding good jobs, they would continue living with their parents.*

4. **Have older people always been able to retire?** *Retirement is not a new phenomenon. In the past, retirement was associated with the ownership of land. Farmers would retire by giving their property to their children in exchange for care in old age. People who owned no property could not afford to retire and often worked at marginal jobs in old age. Skilled craft workers also pooled their funds to provide retirement pensions for union members.*

5. **How did society care for the frail elderly in the past?** *Although the family has been the primary haven for the aged, there have always been vulnerable older people who turned to the community for care in old age. In the colonial period, care was often provided in the homes of local families. As pauperism became associated with unemployed transients, almshouses replaced other forms of public welfare. The almshouse experiment proved to be a failure, and almshouses became de facto old-age institutions. Since the 1940s there has been a growth in nursing homes; but even so, fewer than 5 percent of people aged 65 or older are residents of nursing homes.*

THINKING ABOUT AGING

1. Is the Puritan idea of the deserving poor still with us? Explain.
2. In the United States today, does an aged person's gender make a significant difference in his or her status?
3. In your judgment, what is the appropriate way for younger generations to treat the aged? Explain the basis for your answer.
4. On the whole, are present-day ways of caring for the aged a step forward? Why or why not?
5. Of all the historical periods discussed in this chapter, which do you think was the best for the aged? Why?

KEY TERMS

almshouse 114

deed of gift 106

early retirement incentive programs (ERIPs) 113

Elizabethan poor laws 114

extended family household 103

gerontocracy 98

industrialization 106

nuclear family
household 103

out-relief 114

primogeniture 104

retirement contract 104

veneration 95

EXPLORING THE INTERNET

Note: While all the URLs listed were current as of the printing of this book, these sites often change. Please check our website www.mhhe.com/quadagno for updates.

1. David Hackett Fischer, a well-known social historian, is the author of *Growing Old in America* (1977). In this book, Fischer discusses the traditional veneration of the aged and how Americans' attitudes toward the aged have changed over time.

    Go to the website (http://www.unt.edu/natla/), type "changing attitudes" in the search bar, and click on the third link to select and read the article titled "Changing Attitudes," which discusses Fischer's work. After reading the article, answer the following questions:

    a. Americans' new attitudes toward age and the aged have been manifested in several ways. What are three of those ways?
    b. What is gerontophobia?
    c. What happened when the old system of family responsibility for the aged began to break down?

2. Alan Pope of Duquesne University wrote an article about changing attitudes toward the elderly that was published in the *Janus Head Journal*. Go to (http://www.janushead.org/), type "attitudes toward elderly" in the search bar, and link to JanusHead/Alan Pope/Elderly in Modern Society. Read the following sections in Pope's article: "Introduction," "The Elderly as a Cultural Figure," and "Historical Development of the Elderly." Then answer these questions:

    a. Explain what the author means when he writes, "One way that people hide from the reality of ageism is to cast as benevolent those very ways in which elderly individuals are dissociated from society."
    b. Pope claims that when the term "Elders" was replaced with "the elderly," society ceased to venerate the aged. Explain why he makes this claim.
    c. How are the elderly viewed in both modernization and egalitarian theory?

Chapter 6

Biological Perspectives on Aging

*I*n this YMCA senior fitness class, women work with exercise balls.

Looking Ahead

1. How do environmental hazards, developmental processes, and genetic tendencies contribute to the aging process?
2. What is the difference between normal aging and pathological aging?
3. How does aging change a person's physical appearance and mental functioning?
4. How does aging affect a person's sensory organs?
5. What effects does aging have on the bones, joints, and muscles?
6. How does aging change a person's sexual capacity?
7. What effects does aging have on the heart and blood vessels?

They call her Grambo. She holds 75 American and world records in endurance events such as 100-mile runs and 24-hour ultramarathons. Her best effort in a six-day run is 373 miles. In a typical training week, she jogs up and down the equivalent of four Mount Everests. Who is this biological wonder? An Olympic champion? No, it's Helen Klein, grandmother of nine, great-grandmother of three, who turned 78 in 2000 (Konik, 1995).

Helen feels no aches and pains; she has no arthritis. She attributes her amazing fitness to good genes and good diet. An atypical 78-year-old, Helen exemplifies optimal biological aging. Her remarkable fitness provides support for the argument that behavioral and social factors can reduce the risk of illness and death in old age and even reverse the aging process. At the other end of the spectrum are people like Reverend Scott, who at

121

age 71 is crippled by severe rheumatoid arthritis. Unable to work or drive a car, he maneuvers around his house in a battery-powered wheelchair (Ball and Whittington, 1995). His condition would appear to support an opposing view, that aging is inevitably characterized by an increased likelihood of disease and dependence (Kaplan and Strawbridge, 1994).

If we think of Helen Klein and Reverend Scott as falling on opposite ends of a continuum representing physical well-being in old age, we would find that, contrary to popular belief, most older people fit somewhere in the middle of the spectrum. They are neither running marathons nor wheelchair bound, and only a small fraction of their life before death entails illness and disability (Verbrugge, 1994). Genetic, biological, and behavioral factors, as well as social factors such as socioeconomic status, gender, and race all influence how long people remain free of disease and dysfunction and how successful they are in slowing down the aging process.

People differ not only in how they age but also in how they react to the changes taking place in their bodies. Some accept the changes gracefully. They view their wrinkles and gray hair as symbols of a life well lived. Others are devastated by the first gray hairs or the first tiny wrinkles that appear at the corners of their eyes. They may go to great lengths to hide these telltale signs of aging, by using creams and lotions that promise to provide a youthful appearance or by taking more aggressive measures, such as undergoing cosmetic surgery to eliminate sagging chins and bags under the eyes. People who are more concerned with physical health than with appearance may take megadoses of vitamins and herbs, convinced that such a regimen can slow or reverse the aging process. They are also likely to exercise regularly. Yet the proverbial fountain of youth remains elusive.

Many theories attempt to answer the question, Why do we age? This chapter describes the more commonly proposed theories of aging and examines the normal processes of biological aging in selected systems of the body. It also examines the difference between normal aging and pathology, for as each body system ages, some pathological conditions occur. In this chapter we also consider the causes of

age-related illness and explore preventative measures for improving health and functioning in later life. Throughout the chapter we consider the relationship between biological aging and its social consequences.

THEORIES OF BIOLOGICAL AGING

A century before the Pilgrims arrived in the New World, the Spanish explorer Juan Ponce de León landed on the shores of North America intent on finding "the river, whose water rejuvenated the aged" (Achenbaum, 1996:4). Although Ponce de León never found the fountain of youth, interest in increasing longevity remains. For centuries, philosophers and scientists have searched for a central mechanism that causes aging. The new explorers are armed not with ships and soldiers but with the tools of science. Like the explorers who preceded them, gerontologists are interested in understanding why people grow old and what can be done to reduce illness and disability in old age. The result of a better understanding of aging is a broader range of treatments and strategies for improving the quality of life of elderly people (Cristofalo, 1996).

Most scientists now agree that aging probably does not have a single cause. The aging process occurs in part because of environmental factors and in part because of some genetically programmed purposeful process in which vulnerability to the environment increases over time as the body advances through a natural developmental process from adulthood to death. In this section, we focus first on the environmental theories of aging and then turn to a discussion of the developmental and genetic theories of aging.

Environmental Theories of Aging

Environmental theories of aging view senescence as the result of random damage (Cristofalo et al., 1999).

Wear and tear theory   An early theory of aging, first proposed in 1882 by the German biologist August Wiesmann, is the **wear and tear theory.** According to this theory, the body is analogous to a machine, like an old car or truck, that simply wears out (Cristofalo, 1988). However, the wear and tear theory is difficult to test. Because we don't know what constitutes normal wear and tear, we can't predict the breakdown of various body systems (Hayflick, 1996). Another problem is that the idea of wear and tear implies that a more active organism should age more quickly. Yet the opposite is true in humans. Research clearly shows that low levels of physical activity are associated with an increased risk of death (Kaplan and Strawbridge, 1994). For these reasons, the wear and tear theory is now largely discredited.

Somatic mutation theory Over a lifetime, a person's body is exposed to many external insults from air pollution, chemicals in food and water, and radiation. According to the **somatic mutation theory of aging,** these insults cause mutations (genetic damage) to somatic (body) cells. Genetic damage, in turn, can cause aging of cells and tissues (Cristofalo, 1996). Consider, for example, the exposure of the skin to sunlight. Over the years, the sun not only ages the skin but, if sun exposure is excessive, also increases the risk of skin cancer by causing normal cells to mutate.

The somatic mutation theory of aging may explain variations between body systems in the process of aging. As we learn more about how environmental stressors affect the body, we will be better able to explain differences between body systems in the rate of aging. As a general theory of aging, however, the somatic mutation theory fails to explain basic processes of normal change.

Developmental/Genetic Theories of Aging

Developmental/genetic theories of aging emphasize programmed processes that cause an organism to age (Cristofalo et al., 1999).

The immune function theory The basic function of the immune system is surveillance. It is the body's army, constantly on alert, programmed before birth to recognize and destroy invaders. The invaders are foreign proteinlike materials called antigens, such as viruses, bacteria, or precancerous cells, that the immune system recognizes as nonself. The immune system creates antibodies to destroy antigens.

The **immune function theory of aging** is based on two scientific discoveries. The first is that protective immune reactions decline with age, as the body becomes less capable of producing sufficient quantities and kinds of antibodies (Miller, 1990). For example, one hypothesis proposes that rates of cancer are higher in older people because precancerous cells that are recognized and destroyed in younger individuals may slip past the immune system's surveillance mechanism in older individuals.

The second discovery that lends support to the immune system theory is that the aging immune system mistakenly produces antibodies against normal body proteins, leading to a loss of self-recognition. In other words, the immune system loses some of its ability to distinguish between self and nonself and instead attacks the proteins produced by the body as if they were invaders. Rheumatoid arthritis (discussed later in this chapter) is one example of what can happen when the immune system no longer recognizes self and begins to attack tissue in the joints of the body.

Although a decline in immune system functioning causes disease, there is no evidence to suggest that a less efficient immune system causes normal aging (Hayflick, 1996). Thus, the immune function theory suffers from the same limitation as the somatic mutation theory. It is unable to account for the mechanism of biological aging. Further research is necessary before we can confirm or disprove the immune system theory of aging.

Cross-linkage theory Our cells are composed mostly of protein. One of the most common proteins, found in tendons, ligaments, bone, cartilage, and skin, is collagen. Collagen is the glue that binds cells together by cross-links, which can be likened to the rungs of a ladder that connect the two side boards. In young people, the molecules that make up the collagen protein are held together by only a few cross-links. As we age, cross-links become more numerous, resulting in tissue that is stiffer and less flexible (Hayflick, 1996).

According to the **cross-linkage theory of aging,** the accumulation of cross-linked collagen is responsible for such changes as the loss of elasticity of the skin, hardening of the arteries of the circulatory system, and stiffness of joints throughout the body (Goldstein, Gallo, and Reichel, 1989; Spence, 1995). Although cross-linking is one of many biochemical changes that occur over time, there is no reason to think it is the most important cause of aging.

Free radical theory

One of the most popular theories of aging is the **free radical theory.** A molecule is a group of atoms that are chemically linked. Free radicals are unstable molecules that are produced when the body transforms food into chemical energy. This transformation occurs at the level of the individual cell. Free radicals also may be generated in the body through the influence of cigarette smoke, drugs, and radiation (Goldstein et al., 1989). They are a by-product of normal cells.

When free radicals try to unite with other molecules that may be in the vicinity, they can damage the cell or cause cell mutation. According to this theory of aging, free radicals contribute to the aging process by forming age pigment and by producing cross-links. Free radicals have also been implicated in various cancers and in Alzheimer's disease (Hayflick, 1996).

The body has its own natural defense in the form of chemical inhibitors called antioxidants, which suppress the formation of free radicals and reduce the cellular damage they cause. Among the antioxidants that suppress free radicals are vitamins E and C and betacarotene (related to vitamin A). Some animal studies have shown that when rats or mice are fed antioxidants, their life spans are lengthened (Hayflick, 1996). The question for humans is whether increasing the dietary intake of antioxidants can increase longevity.

The free radical theory combines an explanation of developmental change with environmental factors. Although it is useful for understanding why some individuals are at greater risk of certain diseases than others and for describing part of the aging process, it is not, in itself, a general theory of biological aging.

Genetic control theory

In Chapter 4, we defined the life span as the greatest number of years a member of a species has been known to live. In humans that appears to be about 120 years. One of the oldest living humans whose longevity has been confirmed by birth records is a Danish immigrant called CM, who was 114 years old in 1996. CM was born in the village of Skaarup, Denmark, in 1882, immigrated to the United States in 1930, married briefly during the 1920s, then divorced and worked at a factory for 21 years. He retired in 1950 at the age of 68 and then lived in Texas until 1978, when at the age of 96 he moved to San Rafael, California, to live in a retirement community, where he was still living when he was discovered by social scientists at the University of California at Berkeley (Wilmoth et al., 1996).

Was CM biologically programmed for such exceptional longevity? No one knows for sure, but the variation in life span among different species does suggest that life span may be programmed into the genes. Studies of human twins also support the idea of genetic programming. Identical twins, who share the same genetic makeup, have similar life spans and tend to die of similar causes. Fraternal twins, who are no more alike in their genetic makeup than any other siblings, do not (Goldstein, 1971; Goldstein et al., 1989).

Where might the genetic control for aging reside? The **genetic control theory of aging** proposes that it is programmed into each cell of our bodies. Fascinating experiments using cell cultures support this idea. In these experiments, cells are taken from human embryos as well as from people of various ages and grown in cultures in a laboratory. The cells from an embryo will divide approximately 50 times before dying, but similar cells from an adult will divide only 20 times. Despite such evidence supporting the theory that the genetic information in our cells provides a blueprint for the entire aging process, other factors also seem to be at work. Many complex changes that precede cell death cannot be explained solely by genetics (Cristofalo, 1996).

The search for an explanation for biological aging has long preoccupied scientists, perhaps because humans wish to discover the secret to a long life. The prominent biologist Leonard Hayflick (1996) argued that instead of asking why we age, scientists should ask, Why do we live as long as we do? (p. 260). Answering that question would help us understand how we might intervene in the aging process to minimize the portion of life compromised by physical disabilities and, in so doing, improve the quality of life in old age.

THE AGING BODY

Biological aging refers to the structural and functional changes that occur in an organism over time. It is a period in the life history of an organism that begins at maturity when development is complete and lasts for the rest of the life span (Cristofalo, 1996). Although everyone has a commonsense notion of what aging is, in practice it is difficult to distinguish between disease and processes of normal aging. According to Miller (1994:3), "Aging is a process that converts healthy adults into frail ones, with diminished reserve in most physiological systems and exponentially increasing vulnerability to most diseases and death." Yet normal processes of biological aging are rarely lethal on their own. What creates an increased risk of death and disability is the onset of aging-dependent diseases, including cancer, diabetes, heart disease, osteoporosis, and Alzheimer's disease (Solomon, 1999). This increased vulnerability to stress and the increased probability of death is called **senescence**.

A good example of increasing vulnerability is the reaction of the aging body to a fall. An 18-year-old boy who slips and falls on ice will react quickly, putting out his hand to break the fall. He might fracture his wrist and have to wear a cast for six weeks but then will resume his life as if nothing had happened. An 85-year-old woman who takes a similar fall has a good chance of fracturing a hip. She would probably spend time in a hospital and then more time in a convalescent home. Often, a broken hip will mean the end of independent living forever. In the worst cases it can mean death, for if people are inactive for an extended period, their lungs fill with fluid. Death from pneumonia may follow. It is this enhanced susceptibility to risk from minor mishaps or health problems that makes vulnerability a part of aging (Masoro, 1991).

Another aspect of aging is increasing limitations in the ability to physically perform the normal activities of daily living because of physical impairments and disease. For some people these limitations become chronic; for others they appear episodically. Often medical interventions can slow the progression of age-related diseases by blunting their symptoms and restoring functioning. Then people may be able to return to work, participate in sports, and enjoy simple pleasures like attending the theater or working in the garden. Sometimes, however, medical interventions fail. When chronic conditions like arthritis, heart disease, or osteoporosis make it difficult for people to go about their daily activities, we say that they are disabled (Verbrugge, 1994).

Although disability is a distressing outcome of some aging processes, most people spend very few

© Lynn Johnston, "For Better or For Worse." Lynn Johnston Productions, Inc. Distributed by United Feature Syndicate, Inc. Reprinted with permission.

of their years disabled. The measure of the number of years a person can expect to live without a disability is called **active life expectancy.** Recent statistics show that men have an active life expectancy of 60 years, which is 84 percent of their whole life expectancy. Women can expect 58 years of disability-free life, which constitutes 82 percent of their lifetime (Kinsella and Gist, 1998). Women have fewer years of active life expectancy because they are more likely than men to live past 85, when the risk of becoming disabled from chronic ailments increases rapidly and they are more prone to disabling conditions like arthritis and osteoporosis.

Race and ethnicity are also related to active life expectancy, because minorities are less likely to have health insurance, more likely to be employed at jobs where there is greater risk of injury, and more likely to engage in behaviors like smoking that increase the likelihood of disability. We discuss this topic in more detail in Chapter 13. A 20-year-old white, non-Hispanic male can expect 14.5 percent of his predicted future years to be inactive due to disability. By contrast, an African American 20-year-old will have 18.6 percent of those years inactive, and a Native American, 24.8 percent (Hayward, Friedman, and Chen, 1996). Thus, active life expectancy varies by gender, ethnicity, and race. Finally, active life expectancy varies from one nation to the next. See "Aging around the World" for a comparison of the active life expectancies in several Pacific, European, and North American nations.

Some of the bodily changes that occur with age decrease active life expectancy; others have few or no health consequences. Let's take a closer look at some of these changes.

Aging of the Exterior Body: Skin and Hair

Wrinkles and sagging skin   The skin serves as the body's first line of defense. It protects against water loss, regulates heating and cooling, and contains receptors that monitor pain and pressure. One of the most obvious signs of aging is the change in skin texture that we know as wrinkling.

Some wrinkling is related to use. Common facial expressions such as smiling and frowning hasten the appearance of wrinkles at the corners of the eyes (crow's-feet), forehead, and mouth (Hayflick, 1996). Most wrinkling, however, is caused by biological change that occurs as we age because the deeper layers of the skin lose their elasticity. As elasticity is lost, wrinkles appear in the smooth skin around the eyes and at the corners of the mouth; the chin sags. Hard areas of salt deposits further reduce the flexibility of the deeper skin layers.

The natural process of skin aging has no health consequences. No one dies of skin failure, although many people try to hide the aging process through the use of creams, surgical face-lifts, and collagen implants. The attempt to retain a youthful appearance that is so pervasive in our society reflects negative stereotypes and attitudes about aging (Gerike, 1990). It also reflects age discrimination in the workplace, which pushes people to maintain a youthful appearance.

Hair   Another common sign of aging is gray hair. In the hair roots, cells called melanocytes produce chemical proteins that determine the coloring of hair and skin. With age, the melanocytes weaken and their pigment-producing mechanism begins to cease functioning. The graying of hair is caused by a decrease in the number of active pigment-producing cells (Spence, 1995). When the melanocytes stop working completely, the hair turns white. There is great variation in how rapidly graying occurs. Some people may turn gray in their 40s; others still have their natural hair color at 70.

Hair loss may also accompany aging, especially in men. It occurs through the interaction of genes with the male hormone testosterone. Men who have a genetic predisposition for baldness may show the classic signs of male pattern baldness as young as 20. In these men, testosterone acts with the genes to promote baldness. Men who lack this genetic predisposition may still have a full head of hair in their 80s.

Hair also grows as we age, but it seems to grow in all the wrong places. In men, the hair of the scalp grows more slowly, but hair in the nostrils,

Aging around the World

INTERNATIONAL VARIATIONS IN ACTIVE LIFE EXPECTANCY

*A*lthough nearly everyone wishes to live as long as possible, most people believe that active life expectancy is more important than just living more years. Average life expectancy varies dramatically across nations, so it is not surprising that active life expectancy is also influenced by where you live. Active life expectancy is highest in Switzerland, where men can expect to live 79 years free of disability and women 76 years (see Figure 6–1). It is much lower for both men and women in Australia and Canada. The United States is somewhere in the middle. In most countries, women have lower active life expectancy than men.

Making comparisons across nations is still difficult, because active life expectancy is not an exact concept. It is measured by an individual's ability to complete **activities of daily living (ADLs)** such as bathing, eating, getting in and out of bed, and toileting. There are no standard measures of how well people perform these functions, but researchers are working to develop some.

What Do You Think?

1. What is the active life expectancy of people in your own family? How does it compare to the average active life expectancy in the nation where you live?
2. Can you think of any reasons for the differences in active life expectancy shown in Figure 6–1?

---

ears, and eyebrows grows more rapidly. In women, hair growth may occur above the upper lip, as a result of the decrease in the hormone estrogen that accompanies menopause. Although excess hair growth has no effect on health, many people find it unattractive and become self-conscious about their appearance. Fortunately, electrolysis is a simple procedure that eliminates unwanted hair.

Skin discoloration The superficial layers of the skin also show signs of aging in the form of darkened spots and other skin changes. **Lentigo** is the discoloration or spotting that commonly appears on the face, back of hands, and forearms of people older than 50. Lentigo is caused by accumulation of the pigment melanin, a dark pigment that determines skin color or complexion. If you look at the backs of the hands of very old people, you will often see purple bruises, called **senile purpura.** These are sites where fragile blood vessels have ruptured. Lentigo spots and senile purpura are cosmetic changes and pose no danger, but they may make people self-conscious.

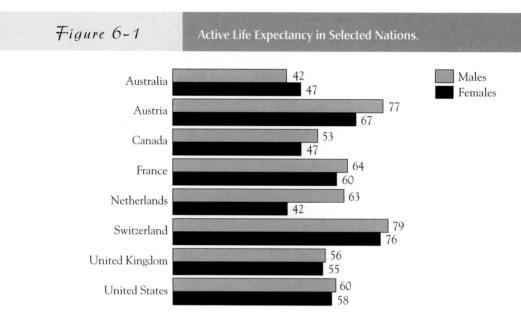

Figure 6-1　**Active Life Expectancy in Selected Nations.**

Source: Kinsella and Gist (1998:5); Verbrugge (1994).

Age-related illness: skin cancer

As noted earlier, skin cancer is common in people who have been exposed to the sun without using protective sunscreens. The risk of skin cancer increases with age because sun damage accumulates. A common type of skin cancer is **basal cell carcinoma.** Although this cancer rarely spreads to other parts of the body, it must be removed before it destroys surrounding tissues. A more dangerous skin cancer is **malignant melanoma.** Melanomas can metastasize, sending cancerous cells to other parts of the body, including the bones, the brain, and other organs. The best preventative measure for skin cancer is to protect the skin from the sun.

Aging of the Nervous System

The nervous system coordinates all other body systems. It is responsible for such important functions as sleep patterns, mood, intelligence, and memory. In this chapter, we introduce basic processes of aging in the nervous system; in Chapter 7, we describe in more detail the consequences of these changes for the sensory organs and cognitive functioning.

Changes in brain functioning

The nervous system can be divided into two parts: the **central nervous system (CNS),** which consists of the brain and spinal cord, and the **peripheral nervous system (PNS),** which consists of all other parts of the nervous system, including the spinal nerves that arise from the spinal cord (see Figure 6–2). The basic units of the nervous system are **neurons,** or brain cells, which carry information throughout the body in the form of electrical signals. Peripheral nerves called **sensory nerves** carry incoming messages from the environment to the CNS. This information comes from the skin as well as from sensory structures such as the eyes, ears, and nose. Peripheral nerves called **motor nerves** carry outgoing information from the CNS to muscles and glands throughout the body. Each brain area is responsible for specific capacities, functions, and traits such as personality, intelligence, and verbal ability. The brain also contains areas that interpret and comprehend experiences and areas that receive sensory information from structures such as the eyes and ears.

As people grow older, neurons die and are not replaced. Because this cell loss is not uniform, its effect depends on where it occurs in the nervous system.

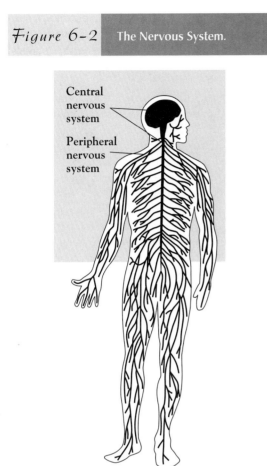

$\mathcal{F}igure$ 6-2   The Nervous System.

Central nervous system

Peripheral nervous system

Some areas of the brain lose few cells, whereas other areas, such as those that control voluntary movements, may lose up to 30 to 40 percent. The loss of these cells accounts for the decreased flexibility, slowness of movement, and stooped, shuffling gait seen in many elderly people (Selkoe, 1992).

Balance and falls   A brain structure known as the **cerebellum** is involved in body movements and, to some degree, balance. This area is located at the back and base of the brain and is essential in the fine-tuning of voluntary and involuntary muscular movements. Damage to this area produces disruptions in balance and muscular movements. The cerebellum losses approximately 25 percent of its cells with aging. The loss of balance and coordination with age,

which is one consequence of this loss of cells in some individuals, can cause a shuffling gait.

A change in gait is not harmful by itself, but it may limit an individual's activity. Restrictions in activity, in turn, may cause further declines in physical functioning and increase the risk of a fall. Falls occur among 25 percent of people 65 or older and are the leading cause of hip fractures (Ulfarsson and Robinson, 1994). About 40 percent of people older than 80 living independently fall at least once per year (Simoneau and Leibowitz, 1996). Falls in nursing homes and skilled care facilities show the same trend, with 45 percent of all residents falling at least once per year and women falling more often than men (Simoneau and Leibowitz, 1996).

Hip fractures are one of the most common consequences of falls in the elderly, and their incidence increases with age. Approximately 10 percent of all falls in individuals older than 85 result in hip fractures (Prudham and Evans, 1981). A hip fracture can involve a lengthy hospital stay and often time in a convalescent type home for physical therapy and recovery.

An elderly person who has fallen becomes more fearful of falling again. The term **postfall syndrome** has been used to describe the fear of falling in the elderly who have had a prior fall (Murphy and Isaacs, 1982). Many older people who have fallen give up activities that put them at risk for falling. They stay home on days when it is snowing or when ice is on the ground. The elderly are often seen holding on to solid objects in an attempt to stabilize their standing or walking. Although therapeutic exercise programs have been found·to reduce the incidence of falls in the elderly, falling remains a major problem that reduces active life expectancy (Myers, Young, and Langlois, 1996).

Changes in sleep patterns   The nervous system also regulates sleep. The normal process of sleeping involves two systems that act in opposition to each other: the arousal system and the sleep-producing system. These systems, located deep in an area of the brain called the brain stem, are set by the day–night cycle of light and dark. During the daylight hours, the arousal system is activated and the sleep-producing system is inhibited. At night, the sleep-producing system takes over and the arousal system is depressed.

There are two basic types of sleep: slow wave, or nonrapid eye movement, sleep and rapid eye movement sleep (REM). Slow wave sleep has four stages progressing from light (stage 1) to deep sleep (stage 4). In slow wave sleep the body is relaxed, brain wave activity is reduced, and heart rate, rate and depth of breathing, and blood pressure drop. Dreaming occurs during REM sleep. Over the course of the night, the body alternates between slow wave sleep and REM sleep, with REM sleep occurring approximately four to six times per night (Kelly, 1991a).

As people grow old, the normal sleep pattern changes (Kelly, 1991b). In the young adult, REM sleep takes up about 20 to 25 percent of sleep time. In older people, REM sleep decreases. Older people also sleep less each night, awaken more frequently after falling asleep, and spend less time in deep sleep. By age 70, few people experience stage 4 deep sleep at all (Goldman and Cote, 1991; Kelly, 1991b). The elderly also have more difficulty regaining their normal sleep pattern if they have jet lag (Kelly, 1991b). Because they sleep less and sleep more fitfully, the elderly are prone to chronic insomnia, which is the inability to obtain the amount or quality of sleep necessary to function effectively during the daylight hours (Kelly, 1991a).

Aging of the Sensory Organs

Our sensory organs supply information about our environment. Changes in our sensory capacities to see, hear, touch, taste, and smell have a profound effect not only on our interaction with our physical world but also on our social relationships.

We gather information about our environment through our senses of vision, hearing, smell, and taste. Our eyes convert light rays into nerve impulses that lead to vision; our ears transform sound waves into impulses that produce sounds and hearing; gaseous molecules stimulate our noses and create smells; and taste buds on the tongue convert dissolved food particles into nerve impulses and create taste sensations. From the moment we first smell the aroma of freshly brewed coffee in the morning until we turn out the light after reading a chapter or two

of a good novel, our senses provide pleasure, stimulation, and knowledge of the world around us.

As people grow older, they experience some loss of sensitivity in their sensory abilities (Kline and Scialfa, 1996). These changes are gradual and almost imperceptible from the mid-20s until age 50 and then become more apparent. Of course, there are exceptions. Ten percent of 80-year-olds still have 20–20 vision, like Harry Porter, who at age 89 had logged more than 17,000 hours of flying time and was still an active pilot (Perlmutter and Hall, 1992). But the majority of people first become aware of sensory change by the time they reach their mid-40s. The first indication is often difficulty reading fine print. Have you ever seen someone holding a book at arm's length? That's a symptom of **presbyopia,** an inability to focus on near objects. Presbyopia is easily treated with bifocal glasses. The upper part of the bifocal lens corrects distance vision, which we need for driving or viewing a movie; the lower portion helps the eye to focus on close objects like words in a book or newspaper.

Most middle-aged adults adjust with little difficulty to incremental sensory losses that are easily corrected. More problematic is severe sensory deprivation, which curtails our knowledge of and interaction with the environment. Large declines in vision or hearing make it difficult to manage daily activities and interfere with the ability to communicate with others.

Vision   From the moment we wake up and look at the alarm clock until we go to sleep for the night, we depend on our vision to negotiate our way through the day. Although even some children need corrective lenses to see clearly, most age-related changes in vision have their onset in young adulthood. So many people now wear contact lenses that we forget how common the need for vision correction is. People generally adapt readily to modest vision changes. Fifteen percent of individuals 45 to 64, 17 percent of those aged 65 to 74, and 26 percent of those 75 or older report some vision loss (Lighthouse Research Institute, 1995). As people reach middle age, vision impairments, defined as severe vision loss, increase. Most visually impaired older people have some degree of partial vision as opposed to being totally blind. Severe vision loss is a serious matter, for it can constrict an individual's activities, lower self-esteem, and lead to a loss of independence. Along with osteoporosis and cardiovascular disease, vision impairment is one of the leading causes of disability for people 65 or older (Reinhardt, 1996).

What causes vision problems? As we age, changes in various parts of the eye reduce the ability to receive visual stimulation. The vitreous humor, which is the fluid-filled chamber behind the lens, becomes more opaque in part because of prolonged exposure to sunlight (Schein et al., 1994). The pupil, which allows varying amounts of light to enter the eye, decreases in size and responds more slowly to light. Although the pupil continues to constrict when light is increased and widen as light is reduced, the difference in size in the light-adapted pupil and the dark-adapted pupil diminishes. The lens, which changes shape to focus onto the retina, thickens. As the lens thickens, it becomes less flexible or elastic (Kline and Scialfa, 1996).

As a result of these changes, older people need more light to perceive depth and to see clearly. Diminishing depth perception can be dangerous, because it can cause an individual to trip over things or miss his or her footing on steps or curbs. One study of people between the ages of 62 and 97 found that poor vision was more important than age in limiting activities. Sixty percent of visually impaired women and men gave up activities such as gardening, cooking, sewing, knitting, and writing, whereas those with few vision problems remained active (Heinemann et al., 1988). Another study found that older people who reported a significant decline in vision were more likely than others to need help with shopping and bill paying and were less likely to leave their homes (Branch, Horowitz, and Carr, 1989).

Many older people stop driving at night, because they can't see well at dusk and their eyes adjust poorly to the glare of oncoming cars. But most older people are reluctant to relinquish their driver's licenses, because it means a loss of independence. Many older people who have vision or other health-related problems that interfere with their driving police themselves by driving slowly or by driving only at certain times of the day (Kosnik,

What an individual with normal vision sees.

What an individual with a cataract sees.

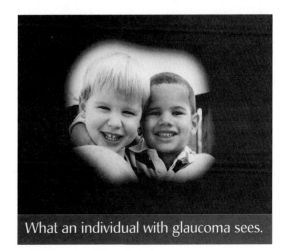

What an individual with glaucoma sees.

An Issue for Public Policy

SHOULD THE DRIVING OF OLDER PEOPLE BE RESTRICTED?

For most older people, mobility is crucial to maintaining independence. The ability to drive helps older individuals stay connected to family, friends, and the community and has a positive influence on their physical and mental health (Coughlin, 2001). Older individuals who do not have ready access to transportation often use words like "handicapped" or "disabled" to describe their loss of ability to go get a haircut, see a friend, or go to the grocery store (Coughlin, 2001). In the past, people could stay mobile by using public transportation or by walking, but now most Americans depend on their cars for transportation. Presently, nearly 90 percent of people aged 65 or older have held driver's licenses for most of their lives, and older people make 90 percent of their trips in private vehicles (American Association of Retired Persons, 1995).

Most older people are safe drivers, but as a group the oldest drivers pose a risk to themselves and to public safety. The rate of crashes per mile driven begins to rise at age 70 and increases substantially among people 85 or older. Older people have the most accidents making left turns against oncoming traffic (Bruce, 1994). Drivers 85 or over are more than 10 times as likely to die in a crash as are drivers aged 40 to 49, although the drivers with the highest rate of fatal accidents are males aged 16 to 19 (Massie, Campbell, and Williams, 1995; American Association of Retired Persons, 1996a).

Sekuler, and Kline, 1990). Others do not restrict their driving in any way. States vary in the extent to which they regulate driving among older people. See "An Issue for Public Policy" for arguments for and against limiting driving among older people.

Visual disorders such as glaucoma and cataracts are not a part of normal aging, although they become increasingly common with advancing age. A **cataract** is caused when the lens of the eye becomes cloudy and light cannot penetrate. In the past, cataracts could severely impair vision. Now most cataracts can be removed surgically. Laser surgery, the newest development, takes less than 15 minutes and requires minimal recuperation time. The lens may be replaced by an artificial lens, or the person may wear a contact lens or special glasses.

Glaucoma is a serious condition that can lead to blindness. Glaucoma occurs when fluid cannot leave the anterior cavity of the eye through the normal channels. Pressure builds up within the eye, gradually destroying vision. About 3 percent of people 65 or older have glaucoma (Perlmutter and Hall, 1992). Glaucoma can be treated with eyedrops or laser surgery if it is detected in time. However, some people don't see a doctor until the condition is so far advanced that it is untreatable.

These results are consistently found in both international studies and those conducted in the United States. One study of fatal traffic accidents in Finland revealed that rates of at-fault collisions and single car accidents increased significantly among drivers aged 65 or older, especially women. The authors concluded that declines in health and cognitive ability caused the age effect but that women had more accidents than men because they had had less driving experience (Hakamies-Blomqvist, 1994).

Because older drivers may pose a risk to themselves and others, some politicians have proposed ending driving privileges at some set age—say, 75 or 85. Opponents of this proposal contend that older people regulate themselves by limiting their driving to essential trips, by driving only during the day, by driving only in familiar neighborhoods, and by driving carefully (Marottoli et al., 1993). For example, drivers aged 30 to 39 drive an average of 11,808 miles per year, compared to only 3,055 miles for drivers 75 or older (Insurance Institute for Highway Safety, 1992). And the vast majority of older drivers are safe and careful in their driving habits.

Various public policy measures can be taken to increase the safety of older people and other drivers while maintaining their mobility. One solution is to improve public transportation in suburban and rural areas so that older people would not be dependent on others for transportation if they stopped driving. Another solution is to screen people of all ages, not just the aged, as part of the driver licensing and testing process to identify those who are at high risk of being involved in accidents. At the present time 33 states do not require any testing as people age (Coley, 2001). The number is likely to change as proponents and opponents argue their cases in the states. Then special licenses could be issued that tailor driving restrictions (like not driving at night) to an individual's needs and capabilities.

What Do You Think?

1. Are you worried about an elderly relative's driving? If so, do you know how to deal with the problem?
2. Do you favor age-related restrictions on or testing of drivers? What about improved public transportation for the aged?

People can adapt successfully to a moderate degree of vision loss if they modify their environment and learn compensatory skills. Such simple items as telephones with large dial numbers or books with large print can improve the quality of life for the elderly. Social support is also a critical factor in reducing stress and improving morale among the visually impaired. Visually impaired elderly people who have a network of family members and friends are more likely to seek and complete rehabilitation and to experience higher life satisfaction and less depression than those who are socially isolated (Reinhardt, 1996).

Hearing   Like vision, hearing is most acute when we are in our 20s. As we age, our ability to receive and interpret sound declines. Hearing loss begins in some people as young as 25 and accelerates after 50. Men are especially susceptible to hearing loss (Kline and Scialfa, 1996). One longitudinal study of men and women aged 50 to 102 found that only 12.1 percent of women but 23.6 percent of men had moderate or severe hearing loss, and that hearing loss increased with advancing age. Nearly one-third of the oldest men in the study, those aged 80 or older, reported moderate or severe hearing loss (Strawbridge et al., 2000). The normal loss of hearing with age is termed **presbycusis.** It can occur at different rates in each ear and is first noticeable when people cannot hear high-pitched sounds. Because women's voices are softer and higher in pitch, they are often harder to hear (Spence, 1995).

The loss or decline of hearing has many social consequences. In the longitudinal study just mentioned, people who had trouble hearing also had problems with morale and social functioning. They were more likely than people with good hearing to have difficulty paying attention, to say they didn't enjoy their free time, and to feel disappointed with their accomplishments. They were also more likely to feel lonely and left out, even when they were part of a group (Strawbridge et al., 2000). Family members and friends may become frustrated when trying to communicate with a hearing-impaired older relative. They may exclude the individual from the conversation or talk around him or her. The older person may then withdraw from social interaction and stop initiating conversations. Thus, a hearing loss can lead to social isolation, even in someone who is otherwise in good health.

The problem of hearing loss has been partially solved by high-technology hearing aids, which amplify sounds and greatly improve hearing. However, many older adults refuse to use hearing aids, and even the most technologically advanced hearing aids do little for people with severe hearing loss.

Smell and taste

Smell and taste are closely related. We eat, smell, and taste our food simultaneously. Remember the last time you had a bad cold and stuffy nose? Your food probably did not taste as good as when you were healthy. That's because you couldn't smell what you were eating. With age there is a loss in ability to detect odors (Hayflick, 1996). Being unable to smell perfume or flowers or the scent of a freshly powdered baby reduces the quality of life. And being unable to smell leaking gas or burning food could be dangerous.

The loss of taste is caused by degeneration of the taste buds or by a change in the way the brain perceives the information from the taste buds (Hayflick, 1996). Although not life threatening, such changes can lead to poor nutrition. If food doesn't taste as good, people may lose their appetite and risk becoming malnourished. Many older people compensate for the loss of taste by eating more highly seasoned foods. Using large amounts of salt can pose other health risks, however, for salt contributes to high blood pressure.

Touch and temperature

The sense of touch also diminishes with age, especially touch on the skin of the fingertips, which becomes less sensitive. There is also a decreased sensitivity to pain, although since pain is measured by self-reports, it is difficult to conduct scientific tests.

As people grow old, their bodies also lose some ability to regulate heating and cooling. People who visit relatives in nursing homes frequently complain of overheated rooms, but the warmer room temperatures are comfortable to the elderly residents. Older people have problems staying warm because of the loss of the layer of fatty tissue beneath the skin that helps insulate the body. Blood circulation also decreases in older people. Because of these changes, the elderly tolerate the cold poorly and feel more comfortable in rooms that seem overheated to younger people (Hayflick, 1996).

The inability of the elderly to cool down occurs as the sweat glands in the skin decrease or become nonfunctional. The remaining sweat glands gradually lose their ability to produce sweat (Hayflick, 1996). Because older people sweat less, they have more difficulty maintaining normal body temperature in hot weather, putting them at risk of hypothermia. They also suffer easily from heat exhaustion or heat stroke. The failure to maintain a relatively constant body temperature can put the elderly at risk of death when a heat wave or cold spell occurs; fatal conditions can develop in just a few hours. Low-income elderly are particularly susceptible to death from excessive heat or cold, because they often live in poorly insulated dwellings and may try to save money by turning down the heat. Older women are most likely to die from excessive heat, whereas older men are disproportionately likely to die from excessive cold, most likely because they are homeless (Macey and Schneider, 1993).

Aging of the Skeletal System: Bones, Cartilage, and Connective Tissues

The skeletal system, which consists of bones, cartilage, and various types of connective tissue, performs many important functions. It provides a structural framework for the body, protects vital structures such as the heart and lungs, provides attachment sites for muscles, and acts as a lever that helps the muscles produce movements. The skeletal system also stores calcium and other essential minerals and is the site where blood cells are manufactured. As people age, their skeletal systems undergo various changes, which affect their activities of daily living and their overall health.

Bone degeneration   Bone is a dynamic tissue made up of calcium and protein. When calcium is needed by the body, old bone is removed; then new bone is formed as calcium is added back. From childhood to adulthood, bone is made faster than it is broken down, and the bones become larger and denser. Peak bone mass occurs around age 30. As people age, the process begins to reverse. Bone is broken down faster than it is made, resulting in bone loss. Some bone loss after age 35 is normal in both men and women and causes no problems. Severe bone depletion is termed **osteoporosis.**

Age-related illness: osteoporosis   When a person has osteoporosis, the outside walls of the bone become thinner and the inner part becomes spongy. In the later stages of osteoporosis, symptoms include a loss of height, back pain, and a curving of the upper back or spine. The permanent curving of the spine, sometimes called a dowager's hump, occurs as the spinal bones weaken and slowly collapse under the weight of the upper bones (see Figure 6–3).

The physical consequences of osteoporosis can have a devastating impact on a person's psychological and social well-being. Patients with severe osteoporosis often feel a sense of hopelessness, suffer a loss of self-esteem, and become depressed. They may curtail their activities for fear of falling. Working women may have to quit their jobs because they are unable to lift, carry, or bend. They may also experience a loss of familial roles. For example,

Figure 6-3	**The Progression of Osteoporosis.**

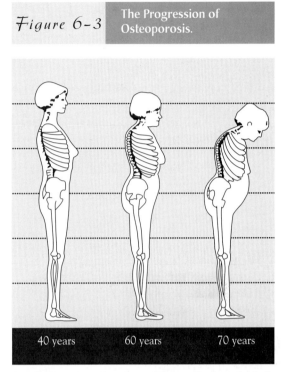

40 years   60 years   70 years

As spinal bones weaken, they collapse under the weight of the upper body.

grandmothers who cannot carry their grandchildren for fear of fractures may be denied an important means of bonding. Wives may be unable to do simple household chores (Gold and Drezner, 1995). The "In Their Own Words" feature presents a woman's description of the unpleasant consequences of living with osteoporosis.

In 1995, more than 24 million Americans were afflicted with osteoporosis. Osteoporosis accounts for 500,000 vertebral fractures and 300,000 hip fractures annually (Gold et al., 1993). Although both men and women may develop osteoporosis, women have a much greater risk (Nguyen et al., 1994). One reason is that their bones are smaller and lighter than men's to begin with. Another is that women lose bone mass faster than men, especially after menopause. The hormone estrogen, which is produced in a woman's ovaries, appears to protect against bone loss. After menopause, the ovaries stop producing

Living with Osteoporosis

$\mathcal{A}$ 74-year-old woman describes the difficulty of living with osteoporosis:

I think it all started 20 years ago, although I didn't know it at the time. I had aches and pains in my spine and joints and was diagnosed as having arthritis. I wasn't told anything about needing extra calcium or estrogen. Nothing was mentioned about osteoporosis. I took prednisone for many years. It was the only thing that made the pain bearable. Only within the last few years have I discovered that prednisone is a bone thinner, and that you're not supposed to be on it as long as I was.

Over the years my spine became very curved. I had terrible pains and was in and out of the hospital. My X-rays showed that I had multiple spinal fractures. "That can't be possible," I told the doctor. "I didn't have any accidental falls." That's when it was explained to me that I had

osteoporosis. My bones had become so thin that they fractured by themselves.

Within the last two years I lost seven inches of height—I'm now in constant pain, mainly in my shoulder blades, collarbone, and lower back. I used to like to dance. Now I have trouble even walking to the corner. I can't stand straight. I can't bend. I'm so hunched over that I can't even reach to the shelves to get the dishes. If I exert myself just the least, I get terribly short of breath. My husband has to help me with everything.

I'm now taking calcium pills and estrogen. I wish I knew more about these things when I was younger. Maybe my condition wouldn't have progressed to this point. Now it's too late. I'm told I just have to live with it.

Source: Trien (1986:238–39)

---

estrogen; thus, menopause increases the risk of osteoporosis. Although osteoporosis does occur in men, it is less severe than in women because men continue to produce androgens (male hormones) well into old age.

Several studies have found different rates of osteoporosis and bone loss among women of different racial and ethnic groups. Because they often are smaller boned, white and Asian women older than 40 have fracture rates one and a half times greater than black women (Farmer et al., 1984). Diet is also a factor. A study comparing Japanese women born in the United States (second generation) with those born in Japan (first generation) found that both groups were at high risk for osteoporosis because of

their small stature and inadequate consumption of calcium; but the risk was higher for second-generation women. First-generation women consumed more calcium-rich foods from a typical Japanese diet, including tofu, other bean products, whole dried fish, and fish bones, whereas second-generation Japanese women adopted American habits and consumed significantly less dietary calcium (Matsumoto et al., 1996). This study is important because it illustrates how both lifestyle and genetic disposition can increase the risk of osteoporosis. Other risk factors for osteoporosis include age of onset of menopause, smoking, alcohol intake, and exposure to sunlight. Table 6–1 poses a series of questions that can help you evaluate your risk of osteoporosis.

Table 6-1	Evaluate Your Risk of Osteoporosis

These questions will help you evaluate your risk of osteoporosis. The more frequently you answer *yes,* the greater your risk.

1. Do you have a small, thin frame and/or are you Caucasian or Asian?
2. Have you or a member of your immediate family broken a bone as an adult?
3. Are you a postmenopausal woman?
4. Have you had an early or surgically induced menopause?
5. Have you been taking high doses of thyroid medication or high or prolonged doses of cortisone like drugs for asthma, arthritis, or other diseases?
6. Is your diet low in dairy products and other sources of calcium?
7. Are you physically inactive?
8. Do you smoke cigarettes or drink alcohol in excess?

Source: National Osteoporosis Foundation (1996).

The best protection against osteoporosis is prevention. Women who consume an adequate amount of calcium are less likely to have hip fractures and postmenopausal bone loss than those whose calcium intake is inadequate (Matsumoto et al., 1996). Bones also stay stronger with regular exercise. Because bone loss occurs any time muscles are not used, active people have higher bone density. A number of studies have found that exercise increases bone density in older women. In one study, 39 women between the ages of 50 and 70 were involved in a program of high-intensity strength training two days a week using five different exercises. The results showed that strength training provided numerous health benefits, including increases in bone density, muscle mass, muscle strength, and balance (Nelson et al., 1994).

As previously noted, decreased estrogen is one of the main causes of osteoporosis. Although **hormone replacement therapy (HRT)** does reduce the risk of bone fractures, it is no longer recommended therapy. A clinical trial comparing one group of postmenopausal women who were taking HRT and with another group of postmenopausal women who were taking a placebo (sugar pill) found that women taking HRT had an increased risk of heart disease, stroke, and blood clots in the lungs (Kuller, 2003). Although the HRT group had fewer cases of hip fractures and colon cancer, the risks outweigh the benefits. Other medications exist to combat osteoporosis, and many women are now using them instead of HRT. These drugs include Fosamax, Actonel, Evista, and Miacalcin (a nasal spray). Each works by a different mechanism, but the end result is to inhibit bone loss (*Physician's Desk Reference,* 2003).

Age-related illness: rheumatism and arthritis

The most cited reason for disability in older people is **arthritis** (Verbrugge, 1994). Arthritis is a chronic disease that afflicts more than one-third of men and one-half of women older than 65 (Hayflick, 1996). The term is used to describe joint inflammation and its consequences of pain, swelling, and deformity. The causes of arthritis include overuse, trauma from injury, bacterial or viral infections, and the immune system attacking the tissues in the joint.

The most common type of arthritis is degenerative joint disease, which results from wear and tear at the joint surfaces where bones join other bones.

The cartilage, a thin layer of connective tissue covering the ends of the bones in the joint, degenerates with age. When the ends of the bone are no longer protected by the cartilage, they rub against each other, causing pain, swelling, and discomfort.

Rheumatoid arthritis involves the inflammation of the synovial membranes, which line the joint capsule and the cartilage that covers the bones. It is caused by the immune system attacking the synovial membrane. In the most advanced stages of rheumatoid arthritis, the bones in the joint degenerate and the delicate synovial membranes thicken from scarring, resulting in severe deformity of the joints, particularly the wrist, fingers, and feet. This type of arthritis can occur at any age and is more common in women than men.

Mild arthritis can be managed with medication called ibuprofen, but severe arthritis may drastically curtail an individual's activities and reduce the quality of life. It not only translates into economic effects such as higher medical costs and lost wages, but also has social consequences such as an inability to play sports or difficulty in performing housekeeping activities (Callahan, Rao, and Boutaugh, 1996).

If a joint degenerates to a point where the pain and disability seriously compromise daily activities, it can be replaced with a prosthesis. A prosthesis is an artificial joint constructed of high-technology materials. Deformed joints in the hand and fingers are replaced with plastic joints, which are functional and cosmetically pleasing. The larger joints such as those of the knee and the hip are replaced using stronger materials like steel or Teflon. These artificial joints can last as long as 10 or 15 years but then must be replaced. Long-wearing artificial joints are more expensive than those that last just a few years, and as pressure increases to reduce health care costs, physicians are now forced to consider the potential life expectancy of a patient in choosing an artificial joint.

Aging of the Muscular System: Muscle Mass and Strength

The muscles of the body come in all shapes and sizes, ranging from the massive muscles on the front of the thigh to the tiny muscles of the eyelid. All muscles have the ability to contract, producing voluntary movements, that is, movements under an individual's control. The skeletal system and skeletal muscles work together to produce movement. For most muscles to exert an action, they must cross a joint (where two bones join each other). A muscle attached to a single bone cannot produce movement.

As people age, they experience a gradual loss of muscle strength and aerobic capacity beginning around age 30 but typically not becoming noticeable until after age 50. Between the ages of 30 and 80, an individual may lose 30 percent of muscle mass (Spence, 1995). Muscle atrophy can also occur because of disuse, even in younger individuals. For example, a person who is immobilized from knee surgery for six weeks will lose 40 to 60 percent of the muscle mass in the large muscles on the front of the thigh. Extensive physical therapy is then needed to bring the muscles back to normal functioning. Because older people are more likely to have ailments that reduce their activity levels, they are more susceptible to muscle atrophy.

Although the loss of muscular mass and strength is not life threatening, it can make daily activities more difficult and reduce levels of overall physical activity, which in turn may cause other health problems. The loss of muscle mass and endurance can be greatly reduced by high-intensity resistance (strength) exercise (Topp et al., 1993). Several studies have reported substantial increases in maximum muscle strength and muscle size in healthy middle-aged and older people (50 to 75 years old) and in the frail elderly (80 to 100 years old) with strength training (Fielding, 1995). Even low-intensity aerobic exercise among wheelchair-bound people has been shown to have beneficial effects (Mills, 1994).

Aging of the Reproductive System

The term **climacteric** is used to describe the syndrome of changes, both physical and behavioral, that occurs in the reproductive system during middle age (Byer and Shainberg, 1994).

The aging female   In women the climacteric is referred to as **menopause,** the permanent cessation of the menstrual cycle. It occurs when the

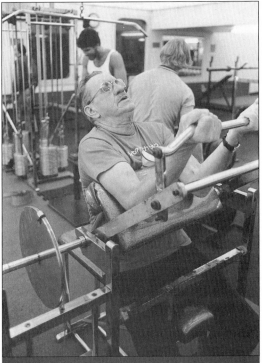

The loss of muscle mass and endurance can be reduced by exercise. Here a 74-year-old man works out on the arm machine of his local health club.

flow of the menstrual cycle begins to change. Others don't experience their first hot flash until after they have had their final menstrual period. Most women report that while hot flashes are bothersome, they cause little disruption to one's daily life. Other menopausal symptoms include irritability, volatile mood swings, fatigue, and anxiety.

Until recently, commonly prescribed treatment to eliminate the physical symptoms of menopause was HRT. HRT eliminates hot flashes and allows the vaginal walls to remain supple and moist, making sexual intercourse more comfortable for women who might otherwise experience pain during vaginal penetration (Walling, Anderson, and Johnson, 1990). However, HRT has also been shown to increase a woman's risk of heart disease, blood clots, and stroke. The transformation of opinion regarding the use of HRT for relieving menopausal symptoms is the subject of "Diversity in the Aging Experience."

The aging male Is there a male menopause? The answer is *no*. Though testosterone levels begin to decline when men reach 50 or 60, they have no clear effect on fertility in healthy older males (McKinlay and Feldman, 1994). Men may father children well into their 70s and 80s. While male sexual responsiveness does begin to change in middle age, this period is not equivalent to female menopause, which involves a complete cessation of reproductive activity. In the male climacteric, the frequency of sexual activity gradually declines, but sexual interest and enjoyment usually do not.

Other biological changes may have a greater effect on sexual functioning than declining testosterone levels. Typically, older men take longer to achieve an erection than younger men. The older man's erect penis is usually softer, and an older man may have incomplete erections. These normal changes can make older men feel sexually inadequate, causing them to reduce or cease sexual activity altogether for fear of disappointing their sex partners (Leiblum, 1990).

Age-related illness: erectile dysfunction
A common problem in older men is **erectile dysfunction,** better known as impotence. Specifically,

ovaries stop functioning, leading to (1) the end of the monthly menstrual flow; (2) the cessation of ovulation (the release of eggs from the ovaries on a monthly basis; and (3) a decline in the production of the female hormones estrogen and progesterone. As estrogen levels decline, the walls of the vagina become thinner, and the amount of natural vaginal lubrication is reduced. The result is that the vagina takes longer to lubricate in response to sexual stimulation. These changes can make sexual intercourse painful. Menopause is considered complete when a women goes one full year without a menstrual cycle. In the United States women usually experience menopause around age 50.

As menstrual periods cease, 75 to 85 percent of women experience hot flashes, the classic sign of menopause. Some women may get hot flashes during the premenopausal years when the length and

Diversity in the Aging Experience

WOMEN'S HEALTH AND HORMONE REPLACEMENT THERAPY

In the summer of 2002, a major clinical trial of the effect of hormone replacement therapy (HRT) on women's health was abruptly halted when early evidence indicated that continued use increased the risk of heart disease, stroke, and breast cancer. Before the results were released, physicians routinely prescribed HRT for the relief of menopausal symptoms and to prevent bone loss. Many physicians also believed HRT protected women against heart attacks and helped prevent dementia. Although there was some evidence that HRT did increase the risk of blood clots and breast cancer, no conclusive evidence was available. In the clinical trial, which had been going on for slightly more than five years, one group of postmenopausal women was given HRT while another group took a placebo (sugar pill). To the great surprise of the researchers, the women taking HRT had a significantly higher incidence of heart disease, stroke, and blood clots than the placebo group (Kuller, 2003). Then another study published the following year showed that women taking HRT actually had an increased risk for dementia (Shumaker et al., 2003). The only good news was that the HRT group had fewer cases of hip fractures and colon cancer. Since the risks clearly outweighed the benefits, the study was ended. Most physicians have stopped prescribing HRT, except for short-term relief of menopausal symptoms.

What has yet to be explained is why so many women were prescribed HRT for long-term use when there was no conclusive evidence that it could improve their health. How could the physicians and the pharmaceutical industry be so wrong in their claims for HRT? According to Pearson et al. (2002), "The widespread popularity of hormone replacement therapy in the United States is a triumph of marketing over science and advertising over common sense." One thing seems clear. Scientifically designed studies employing control and placebo groups must be used to test the efficacy and safeness of new drugs. The pharmaceutical industry with its obvious conflicts of interest must not do all of the testing or provide the funding for testing.

What Do You Think?

1. Have any women in your family taken hormone replacement therapy? If so, how have they reacted to news that it may be unsafe?
2. Should the government outlaw hormone replacement therapy?

erectile dysfunction refers to the inability to maintain an erection sufficient for penetration or sexual intercourse (Masters and Johnson, 1970). After age 50, rates of erectile dysfunction increase dramatically, and by age 65, approximately 25 percent of all men are impotent (Walsh and Worthington, 1995).

What causes erectile dysfunction? In many cases erectile dysfunction is caused by ordinary stress and anxiety. Erectile dysfunction may also be physiological in origin; approximately 20 percent of all cases of erectile dysfunction can be traced to physical or biological causes (Walsh and Worthington, 1995; Masters and Johnson, 1970). Among the physical causes are vascular diseases that interfere with blood flow to the penis (obstruction of the arteries), neurologic disorders such as Parkinson's disease, and chronic diseases such as arthritis, heart disease, and endocrine disorders. Erectile dysfunction is also a common problem for men who have had surgery for prostate cancer.

To determine if erectile dysfunction is psychological or physiological in origin, a physician will try to find out if a man has nocturnal erections while sleeping. The occurrence of nocturnal erections during dream states (the dreams do not have to be of a sexual nature) indicates that a man is physiologically capable of having an erection. In these cases, the erectile dysfunction has a psychological cause.

A major breakthrough in the treatment of erectile dysfunction occurred in 1998 with the introduction of the drug Viagra. Viagra improves erectile function in the majority of men who take it, and many men regain full sexual functioning (Licht, 1999).

Aging of the Cardiovascular System: Heart and Blood Vessels

The cardiovascular system consists of the heart and all of the blood vessels of the body. The function of the cardiovascular system is to provide oxygen and nutrients to all the cells and to carry waste products away from the cells. The blood vessels that carry blood rich in oxygen away from the heart are called arteries; those that carry oxygen-poor blood back to the heart are called veins.

The heart   The heart is the pump that moves the blood around the body. It also moves blood to the lungs, where the blood picks up oxygen and gives up carbon dioxide. The heart has its own supply of arteries and veins to nourish its muscle cells. Unlike most other muscles, heart muscle can contract on its own. The conduction system, which is responsible for controlling the rate of the heartbeat, contains a pacemaker that fires and causes the heart to contract.

There are a number of age-related changes that occur in the heart, including some muscle atrophy and a reduction in the amount of blood pumped with each contraction. There is also an increase in nonconducting cells, including connective tissue and fat, which make the heartbeat more irregular. A routine medical procedure to regulate the heartbeat in older people is the surgical implantation of an artificial pacemaker, which stimulates the heart muscle on a set program, eliminating the problem of irregularity.

Blood vessel changes   One of the key changes that occurs with aging is the loss of elasticity of the blood vessels. A normal artery—and to a lesser degree, a vein—is elastic. When squeezed it will feel spongy to the touch because of a muscular layer that contains elastic fibers. The pressure that blood exerts on the arteries is called blood pressure. With age, the blood vessels become less pliable because of the loss of elastic fibers, and blood pressure increases.

Age-related illness: hypertension and heart attacks   In a person with normal blood pressure, the heart contracts with just enough force to move blood through the arteries and around the body. In a person whose arteries are less pliable, the heart must work harder to push the blood through the arteries. This condition is called high blood pressure, or **hypertension.** People can have hypertension for many years before it is discovered because it has few if any symptoms. Over time, however, the extra work done by the heart of an individual with high blood pressure will take its toll in the form of a heart attack or ruptured blood vessel.

The arteries that carry blood to the muscle cells of the heart are called the coronary arteries. In older people, hypertension is made worse by the accumulation of fatty deposits called plaque, which narrow the arteries. Plaque formation has been linked to diet, particularly food rich in saturated fats such as red meats, whole milk, cheese, ice cream, and many baked goods. This narrowing, along with the loss of elasticity, can block the arteries, reduce blood flow, and cause a heart attack. Autopsies performed on men who died in their 60s showed that 60 percent had major blockage of the blood vessels supplying the heart.

There are several medical techniques to correct this problem. The most invasive procedure involves replacing the blocked arteries using blood vessels from other parts of the body, usually a vein from the leg. In this surgical procedure, called **coronary bypass surgery,** the surgeon opens the chest and uses the vein to bypass the blocked portions of the coronary arteries. If two arteries are bypassed, the procedure is called a double bypass; if four are bypassed, it is termed a quadruple bypass. A less invasive approach to open up blocked coronary arteries is called balloon angioplasty. In this procedure a device termed a catheter is inserted into an artery in the neck region. A small balloon is then inserted into the blocked artery, which presses the plaque against the artery wall and opens the artery.

Hypertension leading to a heart attack is called **hypertensive cardiovascular disease.** Hypertensive cardiovascular disease results from an intricate process of biological and behavioral factors. Having a genetic predisposition is one factor, for heart disease does run in families. Environmental factors also play a role. Among the environmental factors associated with increased risk of hypertensive cardiovascular disease are occupational stress, smoking, obesity, lack of exercise, and low socioeconomic status.

One study of the prevalence of **angina,** which is chest pain that may precede a heart attack, was conducted on male and female Swedish twins. Because some were reared in the same home and others had been separated at birth, it was possible to separate genetic from environmental risk factors.

Genetic factors played only a small role in the risk of having angina-like chest pain. Of the subjects who were younger than 65 and still working, several psychosocial factors were associated with increased risk of angina, but the profiles differed by gender. In women, the factors associated with angina were smoking, obesity, and exhibiting what is known as type A behavior, defined as a personality type that is tense or hyper. In men, the factors associated with angina were work pressure, being in physically demanding work, smoking, and having a low level of emotional well-being (Knox, 1996).

A condition known as **congestive heart failure** occurs when the heart is unable to pump enough blood to meet the needs of the body. The risk of congestive heart failure increases with advancing age (Spence, 1995). Damage after a heart attack, valve damage, or chronic hypertension put stress on the heart, forcing it to work harder to provide blood to all the cells of the body. When a person has congestive heart failure, fluid accumulates in the lungs and ankles. This medical condition is treated with various drugs including those that promote urination to rid the body of excess fluid.

Many studies have shown that exercise can reduce the risk of heart disease. Older people who exercise regularly have a lower resting heart rate and lower blood pressure (Limacher, 1994). Exercise can also help control plaque formation, but it can't eliminate the consequences of a high-fat diet.

In the past, many older people became disabled from the bodily changes that occur with normal aging. People who are now reaching old age are in better health and have higher levels of fitness than was true of earlier generations. Advances in medical technology along with improvements in diet and exercise levels mean that many of these age-related problems can be corrected or eliminated. As a result, rates of physical disability in old age have been declining. Scientists now know that the secret to maintaining vitality in old age is not likely to be found by bathing in vital spring water, as Ponce de León believed, but rather in a complex mix of biological, psychological, and social factors.

Chapter Resources

LOOKING BACK

1. **How do environmental hazards, developmental processes, and genetic tendencies contribute to the aging process?** *Most scientists agree that aging is probably caused by a combination of environmental, developmental, and genetic factors, but they disagree on which factors may be most important. Two theories, the wear and tear theory and the somatic mutation theory, emphasize the role of the environment. The wear and tear theory, which is based on the idea that the body is like a machine that simply wears out, is now largely discounted. The somatic mutation theory holds that environmental insults cause genetic damage, which hastens aging.*

    Several other theories highlight the role of developmental processes and genetic programming. The immune function theory of aging emphasizes the gradual breakdown of the immune system as the central cause of aging. Another theory, the cross-linkage theory of aging, is based on the idea that the gradual accumulation of cross-linked collagen causes a number of bodily changes associated with aging, such as hardening of the arteries and stiffness of joints. A third theory emphasizes the role of free radicals, unstable molecules that are implicated in a number of diseases. Finally, according to genetic control theory, our life span is programmed into our genes.

2. **What is the difference between normal aging and pathological aging?** *Biological aging refers to the structural and functional changes that occur in an organism over time, beginning at maturity and lasting until death. This normal process of aging is rarely lethal on its own. Instead, aging-dependent diseases, including cancer, diabetes, heart disease, osteoporosis, and Alzheimer's disease, increase a person's vulnerability to stress and the probability of death. This increased vulnerability is called senescence. While disability rates increase as people age, most people spend most of their lives free of disability.*

3. **How does aging change a person's physical appearance and mental functioning?** *As we age, a number of changes occur in the skin. Some, such as wrinkles, sagging chins, and age spots, have no health consequences. The risk of skin cancer also increases with age, because of the cumulative effects of a lifetime of exposure to the sun. Age-related changes in the nervous system, which coordinates all other body systems, can affect walking, sleep patterns, learning, and memory. As people age, they spend more time in the lighter stages of sleep and awaken more often during the night. Because of changing sleep patterns, older people are more prone to chronic insomnia. They are also more likely to fall.*

4. **How does aging affect a person's sensory organs?** *As people age, they lose sensitivity to perceptual experiences associated with vision, hearing, taste and smell, and touch. Older people need more light to see clearly and may have trouble seeing in the dark. They also may have presbyopia, which refers to an inability to focus on near objects. Two visual disorders that become increasingly common with advancing years are cataracts and glaucoma. Both can be prevented or cured with proper medical treatment. As people age, their ability to receive and interpret sound declines. The loss of hearing can lead an otherwise healthy individual to become socially isolated from family and friends. Taste and smell being closely related, as people lose their ability to smell distinct odors, their sense of taste also suffers. A loss of taste in turn affects eating habits. People who can't taste their food may eat less and become malnourished. Finally, the sense of touch, especially in the fingertips, diminishes with age as does the ability of the body to regulate heating and cooling. As a result, older people are more affected by heat waves or cold spells. Since most of these changes occur gradually, most older people adjust to them by making incremental changes in their lifestyles.*

5. **What effects does aging have on the bones, joints, and muscles?** *Bone depletion is a natural part of aging that begins as young as age 30.*

One of the more serious consequences of bone loss is osteroporosis. Those at greatest risk of osteoporosis are small-boned postmenopausal women. New treatments for osteoporosis promise to increase bone density and improve the quality of life for older women.

In both women and men, the most common cause of disability in later life is arthritis, a disease of the joints. Mild arthritis causes pain and discomfort; severe forms, like rheumatoid arthritis, can be crippling. The development of artificial joints has restored freedom of movement to severely arthritic persons.

Finally, as people age, their muscles atrophy and their strength declines. Studies show that strength training and other forms of exercise can dramatically reduce the loss of muscle strength in the aged.

6. **How does aging change a person's sexual capacity?** Menopause signals the end of a woman's fertility. The physical changes associated with menopause include hot flashes and the loss of natural vaginal lubrication. Hormone replacement therapy can relieve these menopausal symptoms, but is associated with a slightly increased risk of breast cancer.

There is no male equivalent to menopause, although male hormone levels do decline with age. One problem some older men experience is erectile dysfunction, or impotence. While some cases of erectile dysfunction have a physical cause, more often the cause is psychological.

7. **What effects does aging have on the heart and blood vessels?** High blood pressure, or hypertension, occurs when a person's arteries become less pliable with age or are blocked by accumulations of plaque. If the coronary artery becomes blocked, a heart attack will ensue. A number of medical procedures can reduce the risk of heart attacks. Balloon angioplasty is a technique that is used to open blocked arteries. In coronary bypass surgery, blocked arteries are replaced with blood vessels taken from other parts of the body. Finally, artificial pacemakers can be inserted in the chest to steady an irregular heartbeat.

THINKING ABOUT AGING

1. Some scientists believe that the human life span can be extended far beyond its current limits. What do you think of this idea? Do the theories of aging you have read about in this chapter seem to support it?

2. In the United States, the cosmetic surgery business is in the midst of a boom. Many patients who request this type of surgery are motivated by a wish to regain their once youthful appearance. Why do you think Americans are so concerned with the outward signs of aging, most of which are relatively harmless? Is this a positive or a negative social trend?

3. Aging can affect mental functions such as learning and memory. But is the image of the forgetful older person a reality or a false stereotype? Is there anything people can do to maintain their mental functions as they age?

4. Doctors advise people that to reduce their risk of osteoporosis later in life, they should build up their bones as much as possible before they reach maturity. Do you and your classmates do anything special to strengthen your bones, such as exercising or eating calcium-rich foods? If not, why not?

5. Scientists say that most cases of erectile dysfunction are psychological rather than physical in origin. Yet sales of the new drug Viagra are booming. What do these two facts suggest to you about sexuality in our society? About attitudes toward aging? Are all the people who take Viagra elderly?

KEY TERMS

active life
expectancy 126

activities of daily living
(ADLs) 127

angina 142

arthritis 137

basal cell
carcinoma 128

cataract 132

central nervous
system (CNS) 128

cerebellum 129

EXPLORING THE INTERNET

Note: While all the URLs listed were current as of the printing of this book, these sites often change. Please check our website www.mhhe.com/quadagno for updates.

1. The National Center for Health Statistics (http://www.cdc.gov/nchs/) is the U.S. government's principal vital and health statistics agency. Go to the center's website and link to Fast Facts A TO Z. Select arthritis and answer the following questions:

   a. How many Americans have arthritis?
   b. How many Americans over the age of 45 have arthritis?
   c. In what region of the country is arthritis most prevalent?

2. The National Institute on Aging (http://www.nia.nih.gov/) is one of the leading agencies that studies aging, including diseases that affect the elderly. Go to its website then select Osteoporosis—The bone thief—age page—health information. Read the first three paragraphs of the document and answer the following questions:

   a. Why is osteoporosis called the "silent disease"?
   b. What does the inside of a normal bone look like? What does a bone with osteoporosis look like?
   c. What are the causes of osteoporosis?
   d. How many men and women over age 50 will sustain an osteoporosis-related fracture at some time in their lives?
   e. Why are men at lower risk for osteoporosis than women?

Chapter 7

Psychological Perspectives on Aging

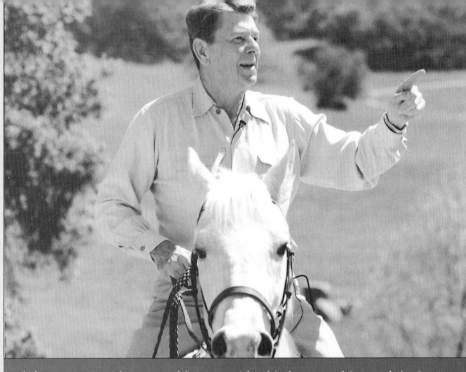

*F*ormer President Ronald Regan rides his horse at his ranch in Santa Barbara, California.

Looking Ahead

1. What effect does aging have on creativity, wisdom, and intelligence?
2. How does aging change a person's ability to learn and remember?
3. What mental disorders are more common among the aged than among the young?
4. How does a person's personality affect his or her ability to cope with changes that come with age?
5. What stages of development do adults go through, and how do older men and women differ in their development?

*I*n a poignant, handwritten, public letter, former president Ronald Reagan announced in November 1994 that he had entered the early stages of Alzheimer's disease, an incurable brain disorder that destroys memory and ends in death. Reagan wrote,

> My fellow Americans, I have recently been told that I am one of the millions of Americans who will be afflicted with Alzheimer's disease. . . . At this moment I feel just fine. I intend to live the remainder of the years God gives me on this earth doing the things I have always done. I will continue to share life's journey with my beloved Nancy and my family. I plan to enjoy the great outdoors and stay in touch with my friends and supporters. . . . I now begin the journey that will lead me into the sunset of my life. I know that for America there will always be a bright dawn ahead.

President Reagan's announcement was greeted with sorrow by people from all along the political spectrum. That a former president could succumb to Alzheimer's disorder was a vivid reminder that aging pays no heed to power and privilege. The intense public reaction not only reflected the sympathy most Americans felt for Reagan as a human being but the fears many people have about losing the essential elements of memory and personality that make each of us a unique individual.

These issues are the subject matter of psychology, the scientific study of behavior and mental processes. Psychology is a discipline that focuses on the individual. Social gerontologists who study psychology attempt to explain processes of development and change that affect people over the life course as well as individual differences in the level and type of change. This chapter begins with a discussion of the psychological elements of personality, individual identity, intelligence, and memory that comprise the basic elements of the self. Then we explore how psychological functioning changes with advancing age and consider various adaptations that individuals make to these changes. The last section of this chapter reviews stage theories and research on adult development.

Throughout the chapter, we emphasize that there is often a wider range of individual differences within a group such as the aged than between groups in various aspects of psychological functioning. Among the factors that create variation in psychological functioning are a person's health, psychosocial history, aspects of individual identity such as race or gender, and environmental influences such as social class, level of education, and social support system.

AGING AND COGNITIVE CHANGE

The mind not only coordinates bodily functions but determines who we are as individuals. As far back as the ancient Greeks, people have been curious about how the mind operates, because behavior, at least voluntary action, is the result of mental processes. **Cognitive psychology** is the study of mental processes. Psychologists have conducted extensive research on how mental processes change over the life course. Social gerontologists are concerned with identifying and understanding patterns of change in mental processes associated with age.

In this section, we report results of research on changes in intellectual functioning over the life course. Age-related changes in psychological functioning can affect an individual's ability to lead a normal life, so we also look at how cognitive changes influence social interactions, work performance, and interpersonal relationships.

Creativity and Wisdom

In 1994, the art world was consumed by a contentious debate over the most recent paintings of 90-year-old artist Willem de Kooning (1904–97). As a young man, de Kooning had established a reputation as one of the leading twentieth-century artists for his complex, richly detailed abstract compositions of the female figure. His latest paintings, done when he was in his 80s, consisted of simple, rhythmic strokes that one art critic called "ribbons of color" (Sylvester and Schiff, 1994:201). Were de Kooning's spare new creations an indication of a "serene simplicity" and "new sense of rigor" as his admirers claimed, or did they reflect, as his critics contended, a loss of his creative powers and advancing senility? In fact, there was no way to adjudicate that debate, for **creativity** is the most elusive mental process to define and measure. Much lies in the eye of the beholder.

Because the most notable contributions of many scientists, artists, and authors have been made before the age of 40, some researchers believe that creativity peaks early. After all, Einstein won the Nobel Prize for his contribution to quantum theory when he was only 26. But novelist John Updike wrote his prize-winning book *Rabbit at Rest* when he was in his 60s, and Grandma Moses was still painting at 100 (Moody, 1994). Although evidence suggests that people of any age can make creative contributions in science, the arts, and literature, people nearing the end of a creative career typically produce half as much as they did in their late 30s or early 40s (Simonton, 1990). Sometimes, though, a loss of quantitative productivity can be offset by gains in quality. That is an issue contributing to the controversy surrounding de Kooning.

Whereas creativity is a measure of divergent thinking, meaning the production of alternative solutions to a problem or situation, expert knowledge that people acquire in the fundamental pragmatics of life is what most people think of as **wisdom** (Baltes and Smith, 1990; Baltes, Smith, and Staudinger, 1992). Wisdom is not simply another form of intellectual knowledge; rather, it is the rediscovery of old truths through a deeper, more profound understanding of phenomena and events. More precisely, wisdom is an ability to grasp paradoxes, reconcile contradictions, and accept compromises. Because wise people weigh the consequences of their actions on themselves and others, wisdom is suited to practical decision making. As Ardelt (1997) explained, "Wise people do not necessarily know more facts than other individuals, but they comprehend the deeper meaning of the generally known facts for themselves and others" (p. P16). Older people have been shown to evaluate a stranger's personality and judge character more accurately than younger individuals (Helmuth, 2003). For example, when given a list of behaviors of fictional people, older people overlook distracting but relatively unimportant actions and focus on those behaviors that are more diagnostic of character (Hess and Auman, 2001).

Wisdom helps people adapt to aging. Although stressful life events such as a health problem are responsible for differences in well-being among the elderly, older people do not react to identical situations in the same way. What may be unbearable for one person might be tolerable or beneficial for another. Research suggests that wisdom does not alter the challenges facing an older person but that one who has this elusive characteristic is likely to be more satisfied with life (Ardelt, 1997).

Intelligence

Creativity and wisdom are components of intelligence. Researchers believe that the quality we refer to as **intelligence** is the product of two fundamental types of skills: fluid intelligence and crystallized intelligence.

Fluid intelligence **Fluid intelligence** refers to the capacity to process novel information. It is the ability to apply mental power to situations that require little or no prior knowledge. It is largely uninfluenced by prior learning. In this sense, it is partly synonymous with creativity. Fluid intelligence is required to identify relationships and to draw inferences on the basis of that understanding. Being able to figure out the rules governing a number series is an example of fluid intelligence.

Psychologists measure fluid intelligence along two broad dimensions, verbal and performance intelligence. On tests, the verbal component focuses on learned knowledge, including comprehension, arithmetic, and vocabulary; the performance component measures puzzle-solving ability involving blocks or pictures.

Early psychological research consistently found age-related declines in verbal and performance intelligence among people older than 60, a finding so persistent it was called the **classic aging pattern** (Moody, 1994). However, recent results from the Seattle Longitudinal Study conducted by psychologist K. Warner Schaie and his colleagues challenge the idea that intelligence inevitably declines with age. Schaie collected data on more than 5,000 individuals aged 25 to 88 during six waves beginning in 1956, with the last tests conducted in 1991. Although Schaie's research confirmed in a general way the classic aging pattern, his results show a more complex picture of cognitive change. Schaie measured intelligence in terms of the primary mental abilities of verbal meaning, spatial orientation, inductive reasoning, and number and word fluency. These abilities have been established as accounting for the major share of individual differences in cognitive ability among children and adolescents (Schaie, 1994). His research focused on four questions:

1. Does intelligence change uniformly through adulthood or are there different life course patterns?
2. At what age do noticeable declines in ability occur?
3. What accounts for the vast individual differences in age-related change in adulthood?
4. Can intellectual decline be reversed by educational training?

On average, the subjects in the Seattle Longitudinal Study showed a gain in all components of

Figure 7-1   Longitudinal Change in Primary Abilities.

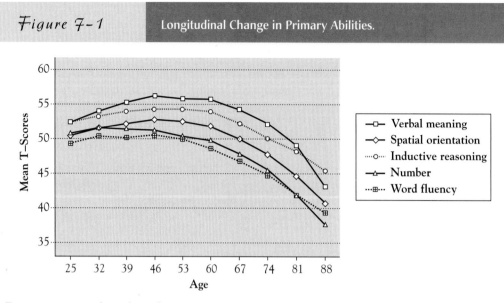

Note: From seven-year within-subject data.
Source: Schaie (1994:306).

intelligence until they reached their late 30s or early 40s. The period of gain was followed by a period of stability until the early 60s, when most subjects showed a modest decline in some abilities. Then, around age 70 the decline in measures of intelligence increased (see Figure 7–1). Although all of Schaie's subjects had declined on at least one of five mental abilities by age 60, none had declined on all five, even by age 88. Schaie also conducted a cohort analysis of intelligence scores and found that the gap in test scores between young and old has been declining. Schaie concluded that significant intellectual decline occurs only late in life, that there is great variation in the type and level of change between individuals and between cohorts, and that many people maintain high levels of intellectual functioning on many measures in advanced old age (Schaie, 1996). Other research by the psychologist Timothy Salthouse has confirmed the age-related decline in fluid intelligence. Salthouse cautions, however, that many older adults perform above the average level of young adults, and that many young

adults perform below the level for older adults (Salthouse, 1999).

Schaie sought to explain these individual differences. Why, he asked, did some people maintain high levels of cognitive functioning while others showed significant decline? One factor was the absence of cardiovascular and other chronic diseases. Healthier people maintained higher levels of intellectual functioning than those who were ill. In the very old, for example, nearly one-half of the differences in intelligence are related to visual and hearing deficits (Lindenberger and Baltes, 1994).

Socioeconomic status was also associated with variation in intellectual change. People of high socioeconomic status were better able to maintain their intellectual abilities than those of low socioeconomic status, due to favorable environmental circumstances such as above-average education, interesting work, and above-average income that provided them with access to intellectually stimulating activities such as reading, travel, attending cultural events, and participating in professional associations.

Aging around the World

A Swedish Study of the Heritability of Intelligence

Are environmental factors more important than genetic factors in explaining differences in cognitive abilities over time? That's the question Swedish researchers sought to answer through a study of 240 sets of identical twins with an average age of 83. Identical twins make ideal subjects in studies of the relative importance of nature versus nurture because they have the same genes. Yet over a lifetime, twins are likely to be exposed to many different influences that could affect their cognitive abilities. Where they live, their level of education, their socioeconomic status, their nutritional habits, their jobs, their health and their exposure to stress—all could affect their intelligence. Amazingly, tests of the twins' cognitive ability showed that genetic factors accounted for 55 percent of their individual differences (McClearn et al., 1997). Nature turned out to be more important than the researchers had anticipated. Nevertheless, the results mean that nearly half of intelligence is determined by environmental factors.

What Do You Think?

1. Do your brothers, sisters, or cousins differ much in their cognitive abilities? If so, how do you explain the differences? Do you think they are mainly genetic or environmental? If environmental, what would you guess is the single most important factor?
2. What is the significance of the findings of the Swedish twin study for gerontologists?

One of the most positive findings to come out of the Seattle Longitudinal Study was that training could reduce or reverse declines in intellectual functioning. Two-thirds of the subjects who received training on spatial orientation and inductive reasoning showed significant improvement, and seven years later they still maintained the advantage over those who received no training.

Other research suggests that there is a strong genetic influence (heritability) on intelligence that remains stable over the life course. The "Aging around the World" feature describes the results of a Swedish study of the heritability of intelligence.

Crystallized intelligence Although research does show some decline in fluid intelligence in old age, there is little or no decline in crystallized intelligence. **Crystallized intelligence** is based on the information, skills, and strategies that people have learned through experience. It reflects accumulated past experience and socialization. Defining a word draws on crystallized intelligence. Whereas fluid

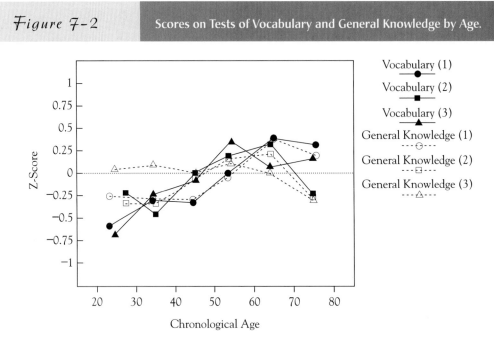

Figure 7-2   Scores on Tests of Vocabulary and General Knowledge by Age.

Source: Salthouse (1999).

intelligence denotes a capacity for abstract creativity, crystallized intelligence refers to the acquisition of practical expertise in everyday life. Figure 7–2 shows the results of multiple-choice measures of vocabulary and general knowledge tests given to subjects in Salthouse's laboratory. Note that on most measures, adults remain stable or improve with advancing age (Salthouse, 1999).

Some studies have found that as people grow older, they demonstrate increasing competence in solving problems in their chosen fields and in their ability to handle daily challenges. In one study, for example, researchers constructed an inventory of problematic situations in managing a home, resolving conflicts with family and friends, and dealing with technical information (Cornelius and Caspi, 1987). A group of judges then rated the effectiveness of responses of young, middle-aged, and older adults. The results suggested that everyday problem-solving capability improved into late adulthood.

Everyday problem solving cannot be studied as an isolated act of pure cognition in a laboratory or test-taking situation. Problem solving in the real world is largely defined by the goals of daily living that allow the elderly to maintain an independent lifestyle (Willis, 1996). What older people fear most is being unable to care for themselves and becoming institutionalized. The Seattle Longitudinal Study found that training in the laboratory not only improved test scores but also had practical value. People who received training showed improved ability to perform instrumental tasks of daily living (Willis and Schaie, 1986).

Learning and Memory

Have you ever tried to introduce a friend to another person and found, to your embarrassment, that you could not remember her name? This rather common occurrence, known as the tip-of-the-tongue phenomenon, reflects a problem in retrieving information from memory. As people get older, such annoying minor lapses in memory become more frequent. These lapses reflect normal age-related changes in cognitive functioning.

In most individuals these memory lapses are not symptoms of Alzheimer's or any other disease. They are simply part of normal aging processes that have a minimal effect on functioning. Although forgetfulness can be frightening, most people find ways to compensate. They may make lists of things to do, keep keys and glasses in the same place when they aren't using them, and attempt to memorize the name of a new acquaintance by associating the name with a physical feature. All these techniques help improve memory and avoid the tip-of-the-tongue phenomenon. Some people use age as an excuse to manage conversations when they experience a memory lapse. Older people who forget a friend's phone number or where they put a shopping list may say things like "Getting old does that to your memory." Others may try to put the blame elsewhere, perhaps saying, "I've never been able to remember phone numbers" or "There is so much going on it's impossible to remember anything" (Ryan et al., 2002). These techniques help keep them from feeling embarrassed about temporary forgetfulness. In the following section we first describe age-related changes in memory and then describe differences between short-term and long-term memory.

Age-related changes   Learning and memory are important and intimately related components of cognition. **Learning** is the process of acquiring knowledge and skills; **memory** is the retention or storage of that knowledge. During a stage of memory termed **encoding,** information that is learned is placed into memory and stored for later use.

One of the most common ways of measuring changes in learning rates has been through studies of changes in **eye blink classical conditioning (EBCC).** EBCC is the reflex that makes us blink when air is blown into the eye. In classical conditioning, a puff of air aimed at the eye is preceded by a noise tone. At first, subjects blink only in response to the air puffs. Eventually, however, the sound of the tone alone will elicit the eye blink.

Recent studies have adopted EBCC for studying age-related changes in learning and memory, and results suggest that conditioned response declines with age. A 20-year-old might only have to hear

the tone a few times to learn that it will be followed by a puff of air. The blinking reflex will occur automatically on hearing the tone after just a few trials. A 60-year-old will take much longer to associate the two events (Ferrante and Woodruff-Pak, 1995).

Early studies also suggested that patients with Alzheimer's disease lost the ability to exhibit an EBCC response (Solomon et al., 1991). However, these studies tested subjects only over a single conditioning session. More recent research shows that after a four-day trial, Alzheimer's patients respond as well as matched control subjects (Solomon et al., 1995). This suggests that reaction time can be increased with practice.

Why do learning rates seem to decline with age? Portions of an area of the brain known as the hippocampus lose neurons at a fairly predictable rate. This critical area is involved in learning and memory. After age 50, an individual loses approximately 2 percent of the neurons in the hippocampus a year (Selkoe, 1992). Some psychologists theorize that the loss of neurons explains why it takes some older people longer to learn a task than younger people (Hayflick, 1996; Goldman and Cote, 1991). But what appears to be a decline in learning rates may simply indicate a desire on the part of the elderly to be careful and accurate.

Research also suggests that older people have greater difficulty storing learned material than young adults and that it takes older people longer to search their memories and retrieve information (Papalia, Camp, and Feldman, 1996). Some studies also find that older people are less efficient than younger people at encoding new information. Overall, however, research on encoding has found no consistent age-related differences, and psychologists now believe that there is not a linear relationship between age and encoding ability (Craik and Jennings, 1992). Recently it was shown that the testing conditions that are used to probe age-related changes in memory can have a significant effect on the results (Helmuth, 2003). Hasher tested 20-year-olds in the late afternoon and 60- to 70-year-olds in the morning and found age differences on basic memory tests were cut in half (Hasher, 2002). It was concluded that older people were "morning people" and college-age students were "afternoon people" in terms of this test-taking task. To comprehend why some memory processes work less efficiently in older people, we must understand the structure of memory—where information is kept and how it is handled.

Short-term and long-term memory

Think about all the sights and sounds you experience in a single day. You take notes in class. You receive an assignment from your teacher. You read information in a textbook. You try a new recipe for dinner. You watch a rerun of *Seinfeld*. You agree to meet your friends at a basketball game at a certain time and place. How does your mind keep track of all this information? It does so by processing it in two different but related storehouses. The first storehouse is working memory, or **short-term memory.** Short-term memory is a "limited capacity system that keeps

memory in consciousness" (Perlmutter and Hall, 1992:222). It lasts only a few seconds. Consider, for example, what can happen when an operator gives us a phone number, and we try to dial it accurately seconds later. If we are interrupted while dialing, we will probably forget the number before we can finish dialing it.

Long-term memory is the permanent storage site for past experiences. It involves our ability to recall distant people and events, such as those from our childhood, as well as various skills we have learned, such as reading and driving. Our stored memories allow us to remember places, events, and individuals from our past. They also help us make meaningful connections between the past and the present. We need our long-term memory to negotiate our day-to-day activities. We call on these memories for such simple tasks as shopping, finding our way around town, and recognizing acquaintances.

Residents on this housing complex for older adults learn how to send messages on the Internet.

Long-term memory does not seem to be affected by age. An 80-year-old is able to retain information placed in long-term storage as well as a 20-year-old. That's not the case for short-term memory. Numerous studies have shown that the capacity of working memory to store information declines with advancing age (Smith, 1996). One common way researchers assess how age influences short-term memory is to ask people to repeat longer and longer sequences of digits. Although the digit span, that is, the number of digits a person can recall in the correct order, is only slightly affected by age, older adults do more poorly than younger people when asked to repeat the digit span backward (Craik and Jennings, 1992). Some evidence suggests that age differences in short-term memory are caused by older adults' reduced capacity to perform a cognitive task while trying to remember some of the information for a later task (Smith, 1996). Substantial age differences appear when older people are asked to manipulate information in short-term memory or solve additional problems (Hultsch and Dixon, 1990).

Short-term memory also seems to slow down with age. Older people can retrieve as many items from short-term memory as younger people, but it takes them longer to do so. Much of the difference reflects differences in perceptual speed. Although older people whose response rate is slower perform more poorly on measures of short-term memory than younger people, age differences nearly disappear when perceptual speed is controlled (Smith, 1996). Thus, declines in working memory and speed are important in accounting for age differences in memory performance. Yet what matters most in performing daily activities and maintaining an independent lifestyle is the ability to use problem-solving skills. In this regard, most older people have few difficulties unless poor health undermines their sense of self-reliance.

Learning and Information Technology

The Internet has revolutionized the world. Children as young as age 2 play computer games, college students get class assignments and communicate with their teachers by e-mail, and workers in many industries and occupations spend much of their day on the computer. The Internet can be an important source of information, enhance communication with family and friends, and even help with routine tasks such as banking and shopping (Czaja and Lee, 2001).

Currently, only 17 percent of people over age 50 use the Internet; the percentage is twice as high among younger people. Why are older people less computer-savvy? So far there has been little research on how age-related behavioral changes influence the ability of older people to learn computer skills. One reason older people use computers less is that they have had less exposure to the new technology and feel less confident about their ability to use computers. It may also be more difficult for them to learn to use the computer. One study found that although older people are able to use the computer and can learn a variety of skills, they do take longer to complete training. Compared to younger computer users, they make more errors, need more practice, require more help, and have more problems remembering when and where they have searched for information (Czaja and Lee, 2001). Older people also have more trouble working the mouse to point, double click, and drag. These problems are largely due to declines in motor control and manual dexterity rather than to any decline in learning ability. Another study compared 12 younger people (aged 22 to 39) with 19 older people (aged 59 to 80) on four tasks. Older adults had more difficulty performing the tasks initially but improved with practice (Sit and Fisk, 1999).

MENTAL DISORDERS

There are many disorders in brain functioning that can cause problems in old age. The section that follows describes three of the more common problems: dementias, Parkinson's disease, and depression.

Dementias

Dementias are mental disorders caused by severe organic deterioration of the brain. They affect memory, cognitive functions, and personality to a degree sufficient to interfere with normal activities and social functioning (American Psychiatric

© Lynn Johnston, "For Better or For Worse." Lynn Johnston Productions, Inc. Distributed by United Feature Syndicate, Inc. Reprinted with permission.

Table 7-1	Rates of All Cases of Dementia and Alzheimer's Disease, Expressed as the Percentage of the Disorders in Each Age Group Represented						

	Age Group						
	60–64	*65–69*	*70–74*	*75–79*	*80–84*	*85–89*	*90–94*
Dementia	0.6%	1.4%	2.6%	4.7%	8.7%	15.8%	29.0%
Alzheimer's	0.2	0.4	0.9	2.1	4.7	10.8	24.8

Source: Ritchie, Kildea, and Robine (1992).

Association, 1994). Symptoms of dementia include impairment of memory, intellect, judgment, and orientation and excessive or shallow emotions (Butler and Lewis, 1986; Katzman, 1986). The two most common forms of dementia are Alzheimer's disease and vascular dementia.

Although dementias are uncommon even late in life, they are most often found in the elderly (Gatz, Kasl-Godby and Karel, 1996). One study in Great Britain found that the rate of dementia rises from about 2 percent among people 75 or older to about 8.5 percent among people 85 to 89 (Paykel, 1994). As Table 7–1 shows, rates of dementias and Alzheimer's almost double every five years. Most research shows no clear gender differences in susceptibility until after 85, when women are at greater risk (Miech et al., 2002).

Alzheimer's disease   **Alzheimer's disease** is a common type of dementia. The onset of Alzheimer's disease is often slow and involves subtle changes.

One of the early signs of Alzheimer's, which also occurs in many aging individuals without this disorder, is the loss of short-term memory. However, Alzheimer's patients forget permanently, whereas aging adults with normal memory loss may forget only temporarily. For example, a normal individual may forget where she put her keys but then trace back her steps and remember she left them on her desk. An Alzheimer's patient will never find his keys.

Other signs of Alzheimer's are repetition and confusion. Alzheimer's patients may ask the same question over and over or confuse day and night. They may do things that are dangerous, like leaving a pot of food cooking on a stove or wandering outside and getting lost. Memory loss slowly progresses until the individual is unable to perform daily activities such as dressing and bathing.

Alzheimer's patients may also exhibit dramatic personality changes. People who were once outgoing and personable may become withdrawn and verbally or physically aggressive. These changes are particularly disturbing to their caregivers and can place great stress on family relationships, a subject we discuss in more detail in Chapter 14. Most Alzheimer's patients are cared for at home until they reach advanced stages when they lose bodily functions and require skilled nursing care. Eventually the disease causes their death.

The daily fluctuation in the level of functioning of people with Alzheimer's disease is often confusing to family members and professional caregivers. Johnson and Johnson (2000) conceptualize Alzheimer's disease as a "trip back in time." Their "trip back in time" model explains why a person with Alzheimer's disease can discuss in detail something that happened 40 years ago but may be unable to recall what they had for lunch or the current year. It also helps explain why people who suffer from Alzheimer's disease might not recognize their reflection in a mirror—in their minds they are not elderly.

The exact cause of Alzheimer's disease is unknown, but there are many theories, which fit into two general categories: genetic predisposition and environmental influences such as nutrition, disease, or stress (Gatz, Kasl-Godby and Karel, 1996). Support for the view that people are genetically predisposed comes from research showing that a family history of Alzheimer's increases one's risk. One study of 8,000 twins who were World War II veterans and ranged in age from 65 to 75 found a low prevalence of Alzheimer's overall, less than 1 percent (Breiter et al., 1990). Among the veterans who were fraternal twins, there were no cases where both twins were diagnosed with Alzheimer's disease. This is what one would expect, because the genetic background of fraternal twins is no more alike than that of any other siblings. The story was quite different for identical twins, who do share the same genetic material. Among the veterans who were identical twins, 35 percent of those who had Alzheimer's also had a twin who was afflicted with the disease. This study strongly supports the theory that a tendency to Alzheimer's is inherited. At the same time, it suggests a strong environmental component, since 65 percent of the identical twins who had Alzheimer's had twins who did not. Researchers continue to search for a specific gene associated with Alzheimer's.

Other studies supporting a genetic theory have found that Cherokee Indians who are of pure ancestry have a lower risk of Alzheimer's disease than those of mixed ancestry. But additional evidence for an environmental component comes from findings that Japanese men who emigrated to the United States have higher rates of Alzheimer's than those who remained in Japan (Rosenberg and Richter, 1996).

At present there is no cure for Alzheimer's disease, and the downward progression of failing memory may be rapid. Cognex was the first drug approved for the treatment of Alzheimer's disease. It was promoted as a treatment that would stabilize the progression of Alzheimer's for people who were in the early stages of the disease. The problem was that Cognex had to be taken four times a day and monitored through regular blood tests. Over time its effect on memory has proved to be modest and transient. In February 1997, the FDA approved a new drug, Aricept. Aricept is also designed to stabilize people in the early or intermediate stages of Alzheimer's, but it has few side effects, is taken only once a day, and does not require blood tests. "An Issue for Public Policy" discusses current research on Alzheimer's disease and explains why it is important for the government to fund research that can provide unbiased information on various strategies and drugs.

Reality orientation (RO) is a form of therapy often used in nursing homes with Alzheimer's patients. Staff continuously remind patients of their names, the date, and current events (Smyer, Zarit, and Qualls, 1990). RO helps people maintain connection with the world in the short term but has no effect on the long-term progression of the disease. "In Their Own Words" has a story by Sue Miller about the final months of her father's life.

Vascular dementia   A **stroke** is a rupture or obstruction of a blood vessel to the brain that damages brain tissue. **Aphasia,** damage to the speech and language centers in the brain, is one of the consequences of a stroke. Aphasia occurs when the brain is deprived of oxygen. An individual suffering from aphasia may be unable to produce meaningful speech or to understand spoken or written language. Other consequences of a stroke include memory deficits, emotional liability, and depression.

An Issue for Public Policy

WHY THE GOVERNMENT SUPPORTS RESEARCH ON ALZHEIMER'S DISEASE

*R*apid advances in knowledge about Alzheimer's disease have led to the development of many new drugs and treatment strategies, but these new strategies have to be proved effective and safe before they can be adopted for widespread use. Clinical trials, which are studies involving human subjects to scientifically test how well a treatment works, have become increasingly important in Alzheimer's disease research. Currently, the National Institute on Health is supporting clinical trials of a variety of treatments for Alzheimer's disease. During the first phase of a clinical trial, researchers give the treatment to a small number of volunteers and examine its effect on the body, its safety, and its effects at various doses. This phase usually lasts only a few months. If the results show that the treatment appears safe, then it is tested on larger numbers of people over longer periods of time. In these trials, the researcher attempts to discover whether the treatment is safe and effective and what side effects it might have.

Trials are currently being conducted on the causes of early memory loss, treatments for behavioral symptoms, vitamin therapy, and the use of anti-inflammatory drugs to delay symptoms. Government-funded studies are important because they are conducted by researchers who use solid research methods and have no financial interests in the results.

What Do You Think?

1. Has anyone in your family had Alzheimer's disease? If so, has this person taken medications to alleviate symptoms?
2. Do you think the government is too cautious in insisting that drugs be thoroughly tested before they are sold to the public?

An estimated 53 percent of stroke patients eventually develop **vascular dementia.** This disease results from the cumulative effect of a number of small strokes, which eventually impair brain functioning. Symptoms of vascular dementia include blackouts, heart problems, kidney failure, and hypertension (Emery and Oxman, 1994).

The major risk factor for vascular dementia is high blood pressure. Eighty percent of vascular dementia patients have a history of high blood pressure. Other risk factors are diabetes, obesity, and smoking. As is the case with Alzheimer's, there is no cure and the damage is irreversible.

In Their Own Words

The Story of My Father

*I*n the fall of 1988 the novelist Sue Miller found herself caring for her father, a retired professor from Princeton Theological Seminary, as he slipped into the grasp of Alzheimer's disease. Here she describes some of her haunting memories from his final months of life:

> On a June morning in 1986, I was sleeping late in the bright sunshine pouring into my bedroom. . . . There was a touch on my shoulder and I opened my eyes. My husband was bending over me. His lower face was covered in shaving foam. There were one or two broad dark stripes in the white on his cheek, marking the path of the razor where he'd started to shave and had been interrupted. . . . He looked strange—partly on that account, of course, but partly because there was fear in his face. He was speaking to me in a deliberately controlled voice, slowly and carefully, but what he was saying made no sense. The police and my father. The police had him. My father. He was somewhere in western Massachusetts. . . they'd picked him up between three and four in the morning in semirural territory when he'd knocked on someone's door, announcing he was lost. . . .
>
> My father was a small man, trim and neat. He had a gentle, nearly apologetic voice. He cleared his throat often, a tic and also a response to chronic dryness. He often had trouble being forceful or direct. I couldn't imagine him—so modest as to be almost comical sometimes, so much wishing not to be trouble for anyone—doing what the police described: stumbling around the countryside trying to wake someone, ringing doorbells in the middle of the night. Bothering people. Not my father.
>
> From the time my father arrived back east permanently to live near me in a continuing care retirement community in suburban Boston, he was hallucinatory. . . . Sometimes the hallucinations seemed painful. One of his recurring ideas, for instance, came because he missed his library, all those books he'd left behind in Denver. Within a few months of his arrival at Sutton Hill, he became convinced someone had stolen them from him, that they were locked somewhere in the basement of the building. . . . Tentatively I'd say I didn't *think* they were stolen. . . . But this cut no ice with him. . . . Most often, though, the hallucinations I had to accept as part of his reality were pleasant ones. . . . my mother came to see him, as did his parents. He reported lively visits from friends. . . . He always had a lot of reading to do now to get ready for one thing or another—though in reality, of course, he couldn't read at all any longer.

Source: Miller, 2003:10, 12–3, 121–23, 128–29.

Parkinson's Disease

Parkinson's disease is a chronic brain disorder that may occur as early as age 30 but is more commonly diagnosed among people aged 60 or older. As with Alzheimer's, it develops slowly. Characteristic signs of Parkinson's disease are a slowing of movement, a stooped posture with the head forward, elbows flexed, a shuffling gait, slurred speech, and a noticeable tremor. Between 40 to 60 percent of people with Parkinson's disease also show mental impairment involving a loss of memory, an inability to concentrate, and a deep depression (Bootzin and Acocella, 1988).

Because no diagnostic test exists for Parkinson's disease, clinical knowledge and skill are key to making an early, accurate diagnosis. Recent studies have shown a lower incidence of trembling in patients who began therapy early with a drug called L-dopa. A combination of medication and rehabilitative therapy can often help patients achieve adequate control of motor symptoms and maintain a high quality of independent living (Marjama-Lyons and Koller, 2001).

Depression

Is it depressing to grow old? The answer partly depends on how depression is defined. According to current psychiatric philosophy, depression is more than a fleeting sense of sorrow or despondency that we all feel on occasion (Perlmutter and Hall, 1992). Rather, **clinical depression** is a set of symptoms that include (1) depressed mood, (2) loss of interest in pleasurable activities, (3) loss of appetite, (4) sleep disturbance, (5) fatigue, (6) feelings of worthlessness and guilt, (7) difficulties in thinking and concentration, (8) psychomotor disturbances, and (9) suicidal notions for at least a two-week period (American Psychiatric Association, 1994). To be diagnosed with major clinical depression, an individual must report five of those symptoms, and the five must include the first two symptoms listed.

For the population of the United States as a whole, the rate of clinical depression is approximately 8 to 12 percent for men and 18 to 23 percent for women, and the likelihood of qualifying for a psychiatric diagnosis of clinical depression declines with age (Skodol and Spitzer, 1983; Gatz and Hurwicz, 1990; Blazer et al., 1991). However, current psychiatric diagnoses of major clinical depression exclude much of the sadness and malaise caused by illness, grief, poverty, restricted activity, and physical disability.

When depression is measured more broadly to include such feelings and behaviors as an inability to get going, feeling sad, having trouble sleeping, feeling lonely, being unable to shake the blues, and having trouble concentrating, the results differ dramatically, as Figure 7–3 shows. Depression is rela-

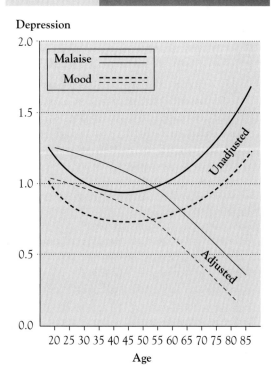

Depression

Source: Mirowsky and Ross (1992:199).

tively high among people younger than 30, falls in middle age, and rises among people older than 60. People 80 or older report the most depression, followed by those 70 to 79 (Mirowsky and Ross, 1992). What accounts for the rise in old age?

Factors other than an association between age and depression per se may be involved. Mirowsky and Ross (1992) contended that depression may appear to increase with age because cognitive decline produces symptoms similar to those of depression or because women average higher levels of depression than men but live longer. Another explanation is that depression is associated not with age per se but rather with changes in social status and an increase in other stressful events that often occur in later life. Many studies have noted that the link between physical illness and depression and advancing age is associated with increased chronic disease, disability, physical and mental dysfunction, and restricted activity (Revicki and Mitchell, 1990; Bazargan and Hamm-Baugh, 1995).

Particular life course events can also cause fluctuations in emotional well-being. People in their 20s enter adulthood with low earnings and little personal wealth. As people approach middle age, their career patterns are more stable and they have higher earnings and greater wealth. They are also more likely than younger people to be married and lead a more routine, orderly life (Umberson, 1987). All these factors are associated with high levels of life satisfaction and well-being. Around age 60, income begins to decline as people retire from the labor force and the likelihood of being widowed increases. Thus, much of the depression that occurs among the aged may not be due to aging per se; rather, it may be a consequence of having low income, being single, and being detached from social networks and stable employment (Mirowsky and Ross, 1992).

Rates of depression are especially high among nursing home residents, ranging anywhere from 25 to 50 percent. Depression is three to five times higher among nursing home residents than among older people who live in the community (Minicuce et al., 2002). There are many reasons why nursing home residents are likely to be depressed. Most have moderate to severe health problems that limit their daily activities, many have lost close relatives and friends, and some experience pain on a daily basis (Finne-Soveri, 1998). Not all nursing home residents are depressed. What distinguishes residents who are depressed from those who are not is social engagement. Residents who remain socially engaged have fewer feelings of sadness and anger, less tearfulness and sighing, and fewer thoughts of death (Gilbart and Hirdes, 2000). Having friends in a nursing home is particularly important for the elderly. One study found that residents who made new friends were less likely to be depressed or feel lonely than residents whose only social contacts were with relatives or friends outside the institution (Fressman and Lester, 2000).

"Diversity in the Aging Experience" describes gender differences in rates of depression and discusses some possible causes.

PERSONALITY AND ADAPTATION

We have seen in the previous sections that multiple changes occur as a result of normal aging. How an individual adapts to these changes is greatly influenced by his or her personality. Personality is a social construct that defines who we are and how we react to our environment. In this section, we explore the research on personality continuity and examine how personality styles affect the ability of older people to adjust to changes in sensory capacity and cognition.

In the broadest sense, personality includes all facets of who we are and how we react to events and situations in our environment. It is often measured according to attributes called **personality traits,** which are enduring dispositions toward thoughts, feelings, and behavior, both inherited and learned.

According to **trait theory,** everyone has most personality traits to some degree, but everyone also has a core group of traits that define his or her personality. These defining traits can be organized into five major factors: neuroticism, extroversion, openness, agreeableness, and conscientiousness (Costa and McCrae, 1989). For example, people who are high on neuroticism tend to be worrying, self-pitying, self-conscious, emotional, and vulnerable. They complain about their health, report sexual and financial problems, and are dissatisfied with life. People who are high on extroversion value power and humanitarian concerns, are usually happy, and show high levels of well-being. People who are high on openness have eventful lives, change jobs often, and score low on economic values (McCrae and Costa, 1984).

An individual's self-perception is also central to his or her individual personality. The organized and integrated perception of self, known as the **self-concept,** consists of such aspects as self-esteem, self-image, beliefs, and personality traits (Perlmutter and Hall, 1992). It includes the ideas and images people have of themselves and the stories they tell about themselves. A person's answer to the question "Who am I?" provides some clues to that person's self-concept. Some people describe themselves in terms of their attributes, such as their physical appearance (tall, short, pretty, athletic), family roles (son,

Diversity in the Aging Experience

GENDER DIFFERENCES IN DEPRESSION

*W*hy do women have higher rates of depression than men? At all ages women report more distress and higher levels of depressive symptoms than men, and men report more symptoms reflecting personality disorders (Feinson, 1991). In part, women may report feeling more depressed because of tensions arising from combining work and family responsibilities. On average, even women who work full-time do more housework than their husbands, and they carry primary responsibility for child care and parent care. One study of 144 married women aged 54 to 74 found that wives whose husbands shared household responsibilities reported a higher level of marital quality and less depression than those who did all the work themselves (Pina and Bengtson, 1995).

The gender gap in rates of depression increases with age. As Figure 7–4 shows, women of all ages report higher levels of depression than men, and among the oldest–old, the gap grows significantly. The causes of the increasing gender gap are multiple, including the loss of a support network–such as a spouse, siblings, and friends–declining health, and decreased income (Mirowsky, 1996). These losses have less effect on men because they are more likely than women to remarry after becoming widowed and they have lower rates of disability.

The presence of a social support network can help alleviate the symptoms of depression. Elderly people who see children and grandchildren regularly, have a network of friends, and participate in organizations maintain higher levels of well-being than people who have little social interaction (Lennartsson and Silverstein, 2001).

What Do You Think?

1. Do you know an older person who suffers from depression? If so, what personal circumstances do you think might be contributing to the disorder? Do any of those circumstances have to do with the person's gender?
2. Besides the measures recommended here, what other remedies might help an elderly person who is depressed?

mother, granddaughter, brother), or personality traits (outgoing, shy, independent). Others emphasize what they do rather than who they are: "I've just been divorced," "I work for a computer company," "I love to go kayaking" (Herzog and Markus, 1999).

How enduring are these traits? Think about your high school classmates. What will they be like when they are middle-aged? Does the life of the party remain extroverted and popular? Is the shy, thoughtful student still quiet and introverted at 50?

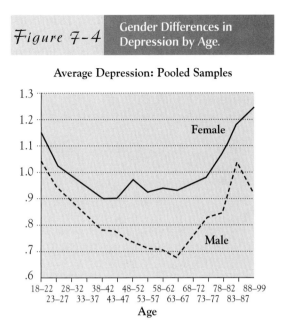

| *Figure 7-4* | Gender Differences in Depression by Age. |

Average Depression: Pooled Samples

Source: Mirowsky (1992:376).

These questions are the subject of numerous psychological studies regarding the stability of personality traits over the life course.

Personality and Aging

In her stirring book *If I Had My Life to Live Over, I Would Pick More Daisies,* Nadine Stair expressed a desire to change her basic temperament:

I'd dare to make more mistakes next time. I would be sillier than I have been this trip. I would take more chances. I would climb more mountains and swim more rivers. I would eat more ice cream and less beans. . . . You see, I'm one of those people who live sensibly and sanely hour after hour, day after day. . . . I'm one of those people who never goes anywhere without a thermometer, a hot water bottle, a raincoat and a parachute. . . . If I had my life to live over, I would start barefoot earlier in the spring and stay that way later in the fall. . . . I would pick more daisies. (Quoted in Stoller and Gibson, 1997:95)

But would she be able to pick more daisies? Or leave her raincoat and hot-water bottle at home?

Being flexible and easygoing rather than resistant to new experiences appears to be largely determined by **temperament,** "a person's characteristic, biologically based emotional style of approaching and reacting to people and situations" (Papalia, Camp, and Feldman, 1996:409). Although our belief systems and values may change, our basic temperament is relatively enduring (Costa and McCrae, 1988; Schaie and Willis, 1991; Birren and Schroots, 1996). Longitudinal data from the Baltimore Longitudinal Study of Aging (see Chapter 1) suggest that personality is stable after age 30.

Nevertheless, although personality has a great deal of continuity, it is also constantly evolving. One cross-sectional study of men and women between the ages of 27 and 52 found that at the younger ages women were more emotionally dependent and concerned with promoting interpersonal relations, whereas men emphasized competence (Wink and Helson, 1993). Among older subjects, these gender differences disappeared. Indeed, older women expressed somewhat greater self-confidence than older men. However, these differences may not reflect changes in core personality traits but rather changes in roles and responsibilities.

Personality and Coping

Most people have an intuitive sense that personality affects an individual's ability to deal with life's ups and downs. Personality theorists who have studied aging have focused on two questions. First, how does an aging individual cope with life events typically encountered in old age? Second, how can an aging individual develop and maintain a positive self-image despite obstacles like illness that may accompany aging (Ruth and Coleman, 1996).

Coping refers to a state of compatibility between the individual and the environment that allows a person to maintain a sense of well-being or satisfaction with quality of life (George, 1980). Coping strategies may be active, confrontational, and purposeful, or they may be passive, emphasizing avoidance, minimization of threat, or resignation. **Adaptation** refers to a range of behaviors an individual uses to meet demands, such as developing habits to confront problems, and to manage frustration and anxiety (Ruth and Coleman, 1996).

In a classic study of coping styles, Bernice Neugarten and her associates concluded that individuals develop and refine a repertoire of strategies that are compatible with their personalities and lifestyles (Neugarten, Havighurst, and Tobin, 1968). The research team developed a four-category typology of personality structure. Each core personality type developed a different coping strategy to deal with aging. Those who fell into the "integrated" category were well-functioning people with a complex inner life and intact cognitive abilities. A second type were the "armored" or "defended." These were the striving, achievement-oriented personalities who had a need to maintain tight control over their impulses and who maintained high life satisfaction by staying active. These are individuals likely to say "I'll work till I drop." Individuals labeled "passive-dependent" could remain content as long as they had another person to rely on. Finally, the "unintegrated" showed a disorganized pattern of aging. They had gross defects in psychological functions, often lost control of emotions, and exhibited a deterioration in thought processes.

More recent research confirms that personality disposition plays a significant role in coping effectiveness (George, 1980). High levels of anxiety hinder an individual's ability to cope with a stressful situation by interfering with the appraisal of alternative courses of action and by reducing the ability to implement behavioral goals. Openness to experience, by contrast, indicates flexibility toward one's environment, which facilitates coping. Poor impulse control often precludes well-planned action based on adequate information about a range of behavioral alternatives. An individual who denies or represses threat is unable to gather information needed to formulate a constructive plan of action.

Research has shown that three adaptive skills are especially helpful in coping with stressful life situations (Kahana and Kahana, 1996). The first is being able to marshal social support. As we have seen, there is substantial evidence that a social support system provides a buffer against stress. Second, a person who is able to compensate for losses in social roles by substituting new roles will feel less

lonely, remain more active and involved in relationships, and find greater meaning in life. Finally, being able to modify one's environment either architecturally or by moving to a more suitable home can reduce stress and enhance life satisfaction and emotional well-being.

Coping styles are not solely related to personality. Social factors such as financial well-being, health, social support, and education can also facilitate coping and alleviate stress. For example, education teaches skills that can be used in confronting stressful situations and enhances problem-solving skills. Research confirms that people with high levels of education are less likely to ignore problems and more likely to use problem-focused coping rather than avoidance (Holahan and Moos, 1987).

As people grow older, they experience changes in sensory capacities and cognitive abilities. Individual personality traits have a great deal of influence on how people adjust to these changes. Equally important in determining adjustment and ultimately well-being in old age are social factors such as having a social support system and adequate resources.

STAGE THEORIES OF ADULT DEVELOPMENT

Psychologists have long been intrigued by the question of whether human psychological development, like physical development, proceeds according to an orderly progression. Many major life events take place in middle age; the opportunities and choices made during this time have enormous consequences for the quality of life in old age. In the section that follows we will examine some prominent psychological perspectives on the stages of adult development.

Erikson's Theory of Identity Development

One of the first individuals to analyze adult development systematically was Erik Erikson (1902–94). Erikson referred to his theory as a theory of ego development, meaning that he intended to trace the

This infant is in Erikson's first stage of psychosocial development. Her intense interest in the cat shows she is becoming aware of her external environment.

development of the conscious self (the ego) over the life course. Erikson presumed that there was a pattern inherent in all human development, one that proceeded in stages. Each developmental stage had its time of ascendancy, which was defined by a pair of opposing possibilities or dilemmas. One possibility described the optimum outcome of the dilemma; the other, the negative, or less healthy, outcome. To successfully resolve the dilemma posed at a given stage and move on to the next developmental stage, a person needed to master certain developmental tasks (Erikson, 1959). If a person did not master a task appropriate to a particular stage, development in subsequent stages would be impaired, as unresolved conflicts from earlier stages were perpetuated. At every stage the individual would incorporate earlier themes in the process of confronting the central developmental task (Erikson, 1964).

According to Erikson's theory, humans experience eight stages of psychosocial development from infancy to old age (see Table 7–2). The first six stages unfold during the years between birth and young adulthood. Not until the seventh stage does a person enter the broad span of mature adulthood, from age 26 to 50. In this stage, the opposing possibilities are "generativity" and "stagnation." Mature adulthood requires that each individual find some way to satisfy the need to be generative and to turn outward toward others. Generativity can be expressed by bearing and rearing children, by guiding or mentoring younger adults, or by contributing to society through productive or creative activity. If the individual does not somehow nurture and guide members of the younger generation, he or she becomes self-indulgent, leading to a sense of frustration and a lack of fulfillment, and ultimately to stagnation (Erikson, Erikson, and Kivnick, 1986).

Table 7-2	Erikson's Stages of Psychosocial Development

Opposing Possibilities	*Developmental Tasks*
1. Basic trust versus mistrust	Birth to 12 months—Baby develops sense of whether world is good or bad
2. Autonomy versus shame	18 months to 2 years—Child develops balance of independence over doubt
3. Initiative versus guilt	3 to 6 years—Child begins to try out new things and is not overwhelmed by failure
4. Industry versus inferiority	6 years to puberty—Child must learn basic skills of the culture or develop a sense of incompetence
5. Identity versus identity confusion	Puberty to young adulthood—Adolescent must gain a sense of self or experience confusion about roles
6. Intimacy versus isolation	Young adulthood—individual attempts to make commitments to others or suffers from isolation and self-absorption
7. Generativity versus stagnation	Middle adulthood—Mature adult is concerned with guiding the next generation or feels a lack of fulfillment
8. Integrity versus despair	Old age—Individual must integrate caring for others with the need to accept care and the possibility of death

Source: Papalia and Olds (1998:76).

In the eighth and final stage of life, which culminates in a person's 70s and 80s, the opposing possibilities are "integrity" and "despair." Old age imposes its own challenges, as the certainty of death gives experiences a new meaning. The challenge of this stage is to draw on a life path that is nearly complete, to place oneself in perspective among generations still living, and to accept one's place in an infinite historical progression. A person who feels his or her life has been appropriate and meaningful achieves integrity. But someone who feels that his or her life has been unfulfilling, that the time remaining is too short, and that death is to be feared falls into despair.

Table 7–2 lists the eight stages of human development according to Erikson's theory. His model has had a formative influence on theories of adult development; nearly all subsequent theorists have paid homage to him in some way. However, the span of years between ages 26 and 50 is a long one; researchers have since identified several developmental stages within this quarter-century span.

Transitions through Adulthood

In 1978 the psychologist Daniel Levinson published *The Seasons of a Man's Life,* in which he reported the results of a series of in-depth interviews he had conducted with 40 men between the ages of 35 and 45. Nearly two decades later, he published *The Seasons of a Woman's Life* (1996), based on interviews with 45 women. Levinson's research was motivated by three questions that reflected Erikson's influence. The first question was, Is there a human life cycle—an underlying order or sequence of seasons through which the human life must pass? Second, Is there an adult development process that resembles the child development process? And third—a question Levinson raised only in his research on women's lives—What is the significance of gender in adult development?

Levinson discovered that men and women shared a developmental pattern that could be divided into a sequence of eras, each with a distinctive bio-psychosocial character and each centered on a certain developmental task. The eras were connected by cross-era transitions, which terminated one era and initiated the next. Figure 7–5 illustrates Levinson's conceptual model of adult development.

Men's transition through adulthood The era of **early adulthood,** which lasts from ages 17 to 45, begins with the **early adult transition,** a time when childhood draws to a close. The developmental task of this era is to begin forming an adult identity and ultimately to separate from one's family by moving out of the home, becoming financially independent, and taking on new roles. Most of the men in Levinson's study managed to separate from their families of origin without conflict, but

nonetheless created considerable distance from their parents. Eight experienced major conflicts with their parents, usually their fathers, which lasted for several years. In one case the rift between father and son became permanent.

As the men entered the **age 30 transition,** they had an opportunity to work on the flaws and limitations of their first adult choices to create a more satisfactory life. Some made a smooth transition, but others experienced wrenching conflicts as they tried to decide who they were and what they wanted out of life. In this phase many of the men moved, changed occupations, or got divorced.

In their early forties, most of the men went through a **midlife transition.** As they sought an answer to the question "What have I done with my

| *Figure 7-5* | Developmental Periods in the Eras of Early and Middle Adulthood. |

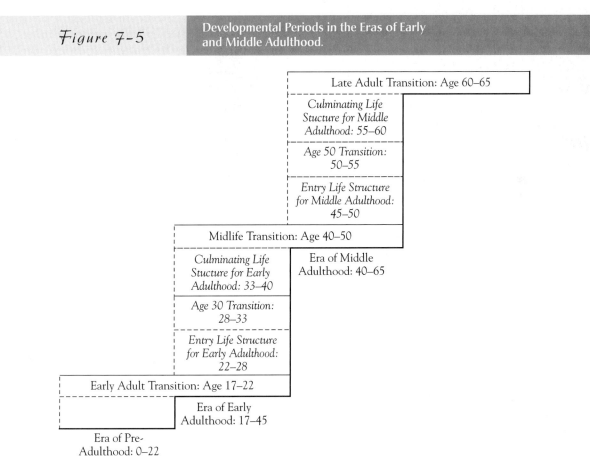

Source: Levinson (1996).

life," they struggled both within themselves and with the external world. Convinced they could not continue in their past patterns, they questioned every aspect of their lives. Some who had been achievement oriented in the past wanted a more sensual, carefree, even nomadic life. Others had to come to grips with the fact that however successful they were, they would never fulfill all their dreams. Even those who had achieved great success were likely to ask themselves "Where do I go from here?" Often they took several years to forge a new path or modify the old one.

One of Levinson's important discoveries was that men who had made work and career their overwhelming priority shifted gears in midlife and invested more in family and private concerns. Other studies have confirmed this finding (Vaillant, 1977). In her award-winning book *Men and Women of the Corporation*, Rosabeth Moss Kanter (1977) noted a shift in priorities, especially among men who had failed to make a rapid climb up the corporate ladder. After spending the early years of their marriages as passive spectators, many of these middle-aged men made a deeper commitment to fatherhood. Unfortunately, their transformation often occurred when their children were nearly grown, and only in the aftermath of dashed dreams, a life-threatening experience, or a reassessment of their earlier life choices (Rossi, 1980).

The third era in adult development, **middle adulthood,** lasts from about age 40 to 65. Levinson's characterization of the tasks in this era reflects Erikson's legacy, specifically the notion of generativity:

Most of us during our forties and fifties become "senior members" in our own particular world. We are responsible not only for our own work and perhaps the work of others but also for the development of the current generation of young adults. . . . It is possible in this era to become more maturely creative, more responsible for self and others, more universal in outlook, more capable of intimacy than ever before. (Levinson, 1996:20)

Unfortunately, middle adulthood can also be a period of progressive decline, of a growing emptiness and loss of vitality.

Women in the midlife transition   Although Levinson later concluded that women and men followed a similar path of adult development, he also discovered some profound gender differences. Among the 45 women in Levinson's study, some began adulthood as traditional homemakers and embraced the ideal of the "Traditional Marriage Enterprise"; others pursued competitive careers in business; and still others sought to balance homemaking with careers.

The traditional homemakers began their adult lives expecting to participate in a Traditional Marriage Enterprise, a life that promised comfort, security, and the satisfaction of being a good wife and mother. Along with these benefits, however, came the cost of being an appendage to their husbands, subordinate to him in the home and the larger social world. Even though these traditional homemakers spent their lives caring for others, they had difficulty becoming fully independent adults, for independence clashed with a basic precept of a traditional marriage, letting a man take care of them.

As the traditional homemakers reached midlife, they became less tolerant of marital problems and more demanding in their expectations. Middle age brought both a sense of loss stemming from the departure of their children and a sense of liberation. Freed from much that had been burdensome to them, they became free to make changes in their lives. Although they had attempted to make their families the central component of their lives in early adulthood, by midlife most had concluded that the attempt had failed. By the completion of the study, only one traditional homemaker was still maintaining a traditional lifestyle, committed to her first marriage and not working outside the home. The others in the group wanted a different kind of marriage and family life.

Both groups of career women attempted with varying degrees of success to balance their occupations with their family lives. In early adulthood they struggled with the issue of how they could meet the demands of family life while still remaining engaged in their careers. Half the women who worked in the business world resolved the dilemma initially by not marrying. Those who did marry espoused an egalitarian ideal of marriage in which husband and wife would share the burden—an ideal they rarely realized. They tried to combine full-time work with marriage and a family, all three of which were central to their lives.

The Myth of the Successful Career Woman—the heroic woman who could have it all—was real and challenging to these women. But as early adulthood ended, the career women began to question their neo-traditional marriages, acknowledging that in reality they were almost totally responsible for household tasks. And though the businesswomen and academic women were all benefitting from the opportunities for personal growth their busy lives provided, they struggled with essential questions of who they were and what they wanted. By middle age many had concluded that the price of "having it all" was too high.

None of Levinson's subjects were over 45, so he could only speculate about what might happen next. Other research on middle-aged women has noted a resurgence of energy and self-assertion after 45 (Rubin, 1979). In her book *Secret Paths*, psychologist Terry Apter (1995) reported the results of her interviews with 80 women between the ages of 40 and 55. Many of the themes she developed were similar to Levinson's. Apter found that her subjects faced rapid social change. Many had been raised in traditional households, where they were taught

they would grow up to be wives and mothers. In Apter's words, "their place of work would be the home; and their goals would be to produce and maintain a family" (Apter, 1995:17). As these women reached adulthood, they encountered new opportunities for careers, but were constrained by the vast amount of child care and domestic work that remained largely their responsibility.

Apter identified four types of women in midlife: *traditional, innovative, expansive,* and what she called *protestors.* Each type approached midlife with a distinct orientation; each faced a different crisis; and each resolved that crisis by defining a new self. Table 7–3 summarizes Apter's four types of women in midlife.

The first type, **traditional women,** continued to fulfill conventional social expectations and defined themselves in terms of their family roles. Being wives and mothers was crucial to their identity, more important than their own needs. As they approached midlife, however, many traditional women became increasingly frustrated by the demands of others and angry at their inability to express their own desires. The departure of their children from home often forced them to face these internal conflicts. Women who successfully resolved this crisis learned to limit their responses to their families' demands and define their own needs. As they resolved their midlife crisis, they embraced their newfound freedom.

Table 7-3	Four Types of Women in Midlife

Type	*Characteristics*
Traditional	Role of wife/mother crucial to identity; needs of family have priority; ambition channeled into domestic activity
Innovative	Strong career ambitions; guards against distractions; works hard to minimize traditional feminine roles
Expansive	Actions guided by others' expectations; familiar patterns and relationships sought for safety; challenges avoided because of lack of confidence
Protestors	Early maturity due to traumatic experience; needed to be responsible and dependable; suppressed desires and ambitions lurked in background

Source: Apter (1995).

Innovative women were pioneers in a man's world. Having modeled their careers on men's, they routinely worked 60 to 80 hours a week. Many had achieved career success while struggling to raise families without compromising their ambitions. At midlife they began to question the value of these long-held ambitions, and to wonder if they had paid sufficient attention to their families and their personal lives. Confronted with persistent inequality in the workplace, they also became unwilling to follow male rules.

Many of the innovative women resolved the contradictory pressures of career and personal life by rethinking their career goals. When 44-year-old Lynn Fairn was offered a partnership in a law firm, she turned it down, explaining:

I work fifty hours a week as it is, and now I'm facing an eighty-hour week. . . . That is not for me. . . . though I wanted it once—the partnership, the

This working mother is happy to hear about her son's day at school.

responsibilities, the involvement, the work—the money!—I now want other things more. (Apter, 1995:138–39).

Successful resolution of this crisis occurred among those innovative women who were able to pursue their goals on their own terms. They did not abandon their careers, but rather made compromises that allowed them more time for leisure, friendships, and family.

Expansive women sought fundamental change in their lives. Self-described as "late starters," many were limited by lack of education or training. Although expansive women were similar in many ways to traditional women, they differed in seeking a radical break with the past. Impatience with the status quo was a sure sign of an approaching crisis. A divorce was often the catalyst that helped a woman recognize her anger at the constraints imposed by others or her frustration with her lack of skills. The challenge these women faced was to overcome the limits of their past and to form new goals in midlife. Those who met the challenge were thrilled by the experience of development and change.

Finally, **protestors** had faced responsibilities that constrained their early adulthood. Some had become pregnant as teenagers or married early, taking on obligations beyond their years. Others had been forced to care for siblings after the loss of a parent. Now in midlife, they were waging a war against age as they sought ways to develop the spontaneity they had not enjoyed earlier. Those who passed through this transition successfully were able to resurrect their suppressed desires and goals and refashion them to fit their present lives.

An Evaluation of Stage Theories

Both Levinson and Apter proposed that adult development occurred in predictable stages and followed identifiable patterns. One problem with their research is that both made broad generalizations about universal developmental processes based on only a small number of subjects. Levinson's male subjects were all white and middle- or upper-middle class; poor or working-class men might follow a different life path. Both Levinson's and Apter's conclusions may reflect a cohort effect rather than a developmental path. Although their results may explain how one generation of women has adapted to the expansion in female employment opportunities and the lack of clear role models for combining work and family, the next generation of women is likely to face a different set of developmental issues. Demographic trends such as highly educated women delaying childbearing and adult children returning to their parents' home are likely to alter this new generation's passage through middle age (Hagestad, 1988). Finally, stage theories cannot explain why developmental changes occur or what their impact on the life course is likely to be.

For these reasons, social gerontologists are critical of stage theories, which rely on an implicitly biological model of development and basically ignore historical and environmental factors (Dannefer, 1984). Research suggests that individuals do not move through a fixed linear and irreversible sequence of different stages toward some ultimate end. Instead, people may experience both gains and losses as they move through the life course with no inevitable relationship between early experience and later functioning. Stage theories fail to take account of the multiple contexts in which people live their lives and the way that these social contexts constrain or promote developmental opportunities (Settersten, 1999). Traditionally, sociologists have analyzed the life course as a social phenomenon that reflects the intersection of social and historical factors with personal biography. In doing so, they build on the insights of stage theorists, but they incorporate demographic, social, and economic factors as well (George, 1993). We take this approach in Chapter 3.

Chapter Resources

LOOKING BACK

1. **What effect does aging have on creativity, wisdom, and intelligence?** *Creativity has no clear association with aging. Although some great scientists and artists have made their most significant contributions when they were in their 20s, others have made creative contributions when they were in their 60s, 70s, or even older. Wisdom is a difficult concept to measure. Since it involves a profound understanding of the world, it is likely to increase with age.*

    Psychologists describe two types of intelligence: fluid intelligence and crystallized intelligence. Fluid intelligence involves reasoning, memory, and information-processing skills. Crystallized intelligence refers to the information, skills, and strategies learned through experience. Although some older people experience a slight loss of fluid intelligence, aging appears to have no effect on crystallized intelligence.

2. **How does aging change a person's ability to learn and remember?** *Learning is the process of acquiring knowledge and skills. Studies of eye blink classical conditioning show that learning ability slows down as people grow older. Memory is the retention or storage of knowledge. Memory includes both short-term memory, quickly committing a phone number to memory, for instance, in order to dial it, and long-term memory, which is the storehouse of past experience. Short-term memory is more dramatically affected by age than long-term memory.*

3. **What mental disorders are more common among the aged than among the young?** *Dementias are mental disorders that affect memory, cognitive functioning, and personality. One common form of dementia that is most likely to occur in old age is Alzheimer's disease. Symptoms of Alzheimer's disease include memory loss, personality change, and loss of control of bodily functions. Older people are also more prone to strokes than younger people. A stroke*

    can damage speech and language centers in the brain, causing aphasia, which means a language deficit. A person with aphasia may be unable to produce meaningful speech and be unable to understand written or spoken language. More than half of all stroke patients develop vascular dementia, which impairs brain functioning.

    Parkinson's disease is a chronic brain disorder that becomes more common in old age. Symptoms include a slowing of movement, a stooped posture, a shuffling gait, and slurred speech. The drug L-dopa can control some of the symptoms but it does not cure the disease. Clinical depression is more common among young people, but the elderly are more likely to exhibit depressive symptoms. Depression in old age is linked to stressors such as the loss of a loved one, chronic illness, or financial problems.

4. **How does a person's personality affect his or her ability to cope with changes that come with age?** *Personality influences the way an individual adapts to the changes associated with normal aging. Personality traits are relatively enduring dispositions toward thoughts, feelings, and behavior. The most unchanging component of personality is temperament, an individual's characteristic style of reacting to people and situations. Although personality tends to be stable, gender differences that are quite distinct among young people tend to disappear as people grow older.*

5. **What stages of development do adults go through, and how do older men and women differ in their development?** *One of the first theories of adult development was proposed by the psychologist Erik Erikson. Erikson suggested that there were eight stages of ego development, beginning with infancy and ending with old age. Each stage has its own developmental tasks and its own competing tensions. In middle age people enter the seventh stage, in which the opposing possibilities are generativity and stagnation. The major task is to establish and guide the next generation. In old age, the*

eighth and final stage of life, the opposing tensions are between ego integrity and despair. The central task is to integrate the painful conditions of old age into a new form of psychosocial strength.

Psychologist Daniel Levinson studied men and women in midlife to learn if there was an underlying order to adult development. He discovered that people did pass through a series of developmental stages that could be divided into a sequence of eras, each with a distinctive bio-psychosocial character and each with explicit developmental tasks. Psychologist Terry Apter conducted research on middle-aged women and found four types—traditional, innovative, expansive, and protestors. Each type approached midlife with a distinct orientation, and each resolved the crisis of midlife by defining a new self.

THINKING ABOUT AGING

1. Does our society take advantage of the wisdom and experience of older people? How might the aged be encouraged to share their wisdom with younger generations?

2. What stereotypes of the aged might be founded in the symptoms of age-related mental disorders? What do these stereotypes say about our society?

3. You are a professional gerontologist who has been asked to help a local social agency address the high incidence of depression among aging women. What suggestions would you make?

4. Contrast the experiences of two older people you know: one who copes well with the challenges of aging and one who doesn't. How might their personalities affect their ability to cope?

5. Could failure to resolve a conflict that is central to adult development affect a person's ability to cope in old age? If you were a researcher in the sociology of aging, how would you find out?

KEY TERMS

adaptation 163
age 30 transition 167
Alzheimer's disease 156
aphasia 157
classic aging pattern 149
clinical depression 160
cognitive psychology 148
coping 163
creativity 148
crystallized intelligence 151
dementia 155
early adulthood 167
early adult transition 167
encoding 153
expansive women 170
eye blink classical conditioning (EBCC) 153

fluid intelligence 149
innovative women 170
intelligence 149
learning 153
long-term memory 154
memory 153
middle adulthood 168
midlife transition 167
Parkinson's disease 159
personality traits 161
protestors 170
reality orientation (RO) 157
self-concept 161
short-term memory 154
stroke 157
temperament 163
traditional women 169
trait theory 161
vascular dementia 158
wisdom 149

EXPLORING THE INTERNET

Note: While all the URLs listed were current as of the printing of this book, these sites often change. Please check our website www.mhhe.com/quadagno for updates.

1. The Alzheimer's Association (http://www.alz.org) is the nation's largest voluntary health organization committed to finding a cure for Alzheimer's and helping people who are afflicted with the disease. Go to the website and link to "About Alzheimer's," then to "Statistics" and answer the following questions:

   a. How many persons over age 85 have Alzheimer's disease?

   b. How many Americans have Alzheimer's disease?

c. How many persons worldwide does the Alzheimer's Association estimate will develop the disease by 2025?

d. What are the warning signs of Alzheimer's disease?

e. How does Alzheimer's disease progress?

2. The American Association for Geriatric Psychiatry (http://www.aagpgpa.org/default.asp) is a national association dedicated to promoting the mental health and well-being of older people and improving the care of those with late-life mental disorders.

Go to the AAGP website and click on the heading Patients and Caregivers. Next, click on Depression Fact Sheet. After reading the article "Late Life Depression—a Fact Sheet," answer the following questions:

a. How many out of every 100 adults over age 65 in the United States are affected by depression?

b. Depression is particularly common in elderly patients with which diseases?

c. List at least six symptoms of depression in older adults.

d. Depression among older adults is often mistaken for what disease?

e. How is grief distinguished from depression?

f. What are some common treatments for depression among the elderly?

Part Three

SOCIAL ASPECTS OF AGING

eople age in a social context. The next three chapters examine the social context of aging.

People move through the life course surrounded by a social support system that consists of the network of relatives, friends, and organizations that provide emotional support and help in managing activities of daily living.

Chapter 8 begins with an analysis of research on the social support system, then turns to a more detailed discussion of the family in later life.

Chapter 9 examines the living arrangements of older people. It describes variations in household structure and the advantages and disadvantages of aging in place. It also discusses research on alternative living arrangements for people who need assistance with the tasks of daily living or who choose various social settings in which to grow old.

As people age, many of them need help managing their daily activities.

Chapter 10 explores issues of long-term care, the range of services designed to help people with chronic conditions who cannot function independently. The chapter first examines family care, then long-term care in a variety of living situations using various social services. The long-term-care option of last resort is the nursing home. The chapter concludes by discussing the organization of the nursing home industry and describing daily life in a nursing home.

Chapter 8

Family Relationships and Social Support Systems

*F*amilies are an important source of social support across the entire life course.

Looking Ahead

1. What is a social support system, and what effect do gender and family structure have on it?
2. How do older Americans compare to other Americans in marital status?
3. How does marital satisfaction change over the life course?
4. How do sibling relationships change in later life?
5. What factors influence parent–child relationships in later life, and what effect does divorce have on these relationships?
6. What factors influence the grandparent–grandchild relationship in later life, and what effect does divorce have on this relationship?
7. What kinds of social support do older gay men and women depend on?
8. Is friendship a good source of support in later life?

Brad Troxel, the father of two children, had never married his children's mother, Tommie Granville. He lived at home with his own parents, Jennifer and Gary Troxel. In 1993 Brad committed suicide. Afterward Tommie let the Troxels visit their two grandchildren one afternoon a month but refused their requests for more frequent visits. Worried they would lose touch with their grandchildren, the Troxels took their case to court, backed by a Washington state law that allowed them to petition for visiting rights. They won the right to see their grandchildren one weekend a month and one week during the summer.

With her new husband, Tommie appealed the ruling. On June 6, 2000, the U.S. Supreme Court struck down the Washington law, ruling that "parents had a fundamental right to make decisions regarding the care, custody, and control of their children." The Troxels lost their generous visitation privileges and now hope that Tommie will let them see their grandchildren one afternoon a month.

The case of *Troxel v. Granville* raises fundamental issues about families, issues that anyone who belongs to a family understands. Families are the source of strong emotional bonds but also the source of deep interpersonal conflict. Although the social changes that have taken place over the past century have transformed family life, the family remains the core element of an individual's social support system.

In this chapter we will first define the concept of social support, emphasizing that social support systems are never one-sided but are reciprocal in nature. These relationships may involve either immediate exchanges of various kinds of assistance or long-term exchanges over the entire life course. We will examine how social and demographic changes have altered the typical family structure by creating family support systems of four or even five generations. Finally, we will consider the various types of interpersonal relationships and patterns of exchange older people engage in, from the marital relationship to parent–child, sibling, and grandparent relationships. The chapter closes with an examination of the family support systems of older gay men and women and a brief note on the importance of friendship to all seniors.

THE SOCIAL SUPPORT SYSTEM

Defining the Concept of Social Support

Whom do you see on a daily, weekly, or monthly basis? Whom would you call if you were sick? How about when you have the blues? Your answers to these questions provide a description of what social gerontologists call a **social support system.** Your family members are almost certainly a part of your support system, but so too are your friends and perhaps the organizations to which you belong. The social support system is defined as the network of relatives, friends, and organizations that provides both emotional support, such as making the individual feel loved or comforted, and instrumental support, which refers to help in managing activities of daily living. Support networks can be described by the characteristics of the people with whom an individual has ties. Such characteristics may include age, sex, number of years known, relationship, and geographical proximity. The term *support function* refers to what network members actually do (Antonucci, 1990). Often, researchers make a distinction between the quality of support as measured by an individual's satisfaction with his or her relationships and the quantity, or number, of relationships the individual reports.

Researchers identify support networks by making grids of these relationships, tracking whom people see, the frequency of the contact, and who is involved in helping exchanges. Studies employing such grids find that most older people are firmly embedded in an extensive social support network and that there tends to be a division of labor within the support network, with family providing more instrumental support and friends more emotional support (Bengtson, Parrott, and Burgess, 1996).

Although grids are useful for tapping the immediate structure of a social support system, such systems involve exchanges over a lifetime. The simplest way to understand this idea is to think of a **support bank.** Deposits are made early in the life course in anticipation of future needs, or withdrawals (Antonucci, 1985). The few longitudinal studies of support networks suggest that they remain stable in the quality of interaction with family and friends, although participation in organizations, except church-related ones, declines with age (Antonucci, 1990). This is not to suggest that support networks never change. Marriage, divorce, and remarriage add and subtract people as do education, geographical moves, and new jobs. Robert Kahn and Toni Antonucci (1980) coined the term **convoy model of social relations** to describe how social support systems operate over the life course. The term *convoy*

is used to evoke the image of a protective layer, in this case, of family and friends, who surround the individual and help in the successful negotiation of life's challenges. Each person can be thought of as moving through life surrounded by a group of people to whom he or she is related through the exchange of social support. Convoys are thought to be dynamic and lifelong in nature, that is, changing in some ways but remaining stable in others, across time and situations. (Antonucci and Akiyama, 1987:519)

The convoy model emphasizes that social relationships are dynamic and continuous, as people move into and out of them.

Gender Differences in Social Support Systems

Over the life course, women are more likely than men to maintain social networks. It is often the woman in a family who writes the holiday greeting cards, remembers the birthday of family members, and plans social events. As one might expect, then, women have more people in their support networks than men, more frequent contact with network members, and more complex relationships with these individuals.

The social involvement of women can be an advantage in old age, for they are likely to have more resources on which to draw. Being extensively involved in intimate networks also has its drawbacks. There often is friction in social networks and conflict between network members. Women are more likely than men to be negatively affected by family tensions and by the stressful life events that occur among people who are close to them (Antonucci, 1990).

Changing Family Structure and Social Support Systems

The core societal institution is the family, consisting of positions such as spouse, parent, child, and stepmother and of roles that prescribe how individuals who hold those positions should act. A traditional two-parent family composed of husband, wife, and child is called a **nuclear family.** The **extended family** includes the network of familial relationships—grandparents, aunts, uncles, cousins, nieces, and nephews—outside the nuclear family.

Needless to say, the structure of a person's family affects the structure of that person's social support systems. Older people today are part of a revolution in the demography of family life. Individuals are now aging in families that are different, both quantitatively and qualitatively, from those of their grandparents (Bengtson et al., 1996). Some observers pessimistically view the modern family as Parsons did, "stripped down to its bare essentials—just two adults and two main functions: childbearing and the provision of affection and companionship to its members" (Popenoe, 1993:540). From a generational perspective, however, family life has not become simpler; it has become more complex than it was in earlier times.

Declining mortality has created an unprecedented potential for people at all stages of the life course to experience complex kin relationships and to be part of an intricate web of intergenerational family ties (Bengtson et al., 1990; Burton, 1993). Think about these statistics: In 1900, only 21 percent of people had at least one living grandparent when they reached age 30; 76 percent did by 2000. Over that same period, the chance of having neither parent still living at age 60 declined from 92 to 56 percent. Older people today are also more likely than older people in the past to have a living sibling and to have their children survive them. And older women now have a much better chance of having a surviving husband than they did in the past. In 1900, only 33 percent of women had a husband alive at age 70; by 2000, 61 percent did. Although declining death rates have increased the potential number of years that men and women can live in uninterrupted marriages, increasing divorce rates have had the opposite effect. Divorce ended only 10 percent of marriages contracted at the beginning of the twentieth century, compared to 50 percent of those contracted at the century's end (Uhlenberg, 1996b).

These trends are indicative of what social gerontologists call the **verticalization** of the family system, a term that refers to the increase in links (vertical ties) between preceding and subsequent generations. People now are more likely than ever to grow older in four- or even five-generation families, a phenomenon sometimes described as the **bean pole family structure.** The family looks like a bean pole because

Table 8-1	Marital Status of the U.S. Population Age 65 and Older, by Gender and Race/Ethnicity, 2000					
	Men			Women		
	White	*Black*	*Hispanic*[b]	*White*	*Black*	*Hispanic*[b]
Total (1,000s)[a]	12,335	1,095	720	16,545	1,659	1,032
Percent of total						
Never married	3.8%	9.1%	3.8%	3.5%	5.9%	5.6%
Married, spouse present	74.3	53.9	67.5	42.9	25.0	38.0
Married, spouse absent	1.1	2.5	2.4	1.4	1.8	2.5
Widowed	13.9	21.0	15.0	44.4	54.6	39.4
Divorced	6.0	8.4	8.4	7.1	8.9	11.1

[a]Noninstitutionalized population.

[b]Persons of Hispanic origin may be of any race.

Source: U.S. Bureau of the Census (2002b).

of an increase in the numbers of **generations** in a family alive at the same time—grandparents, parents, children, grandchildren, great-grandchildren, and even great-great-grandchildren. This type of family structure contrasts to one characterized by horizontal links between individuals of a single generation (Hagestad, 1988). Smaller family size has decreased the number of people within a given generation. Instead of having four or five siblings, the average person now has only one (Bengtson et al., 1990; George and Gold, 1991).

These demographic changes mean that people will spend more years than ever before occupying intergenerational roles. Declining mortality means that the lives of parents and their children may overlap by more than 50 years. Indeed, the number of years people will spend as adult children to parents 65 or older will approach the number of years they will spend with children younger than 18 (Bengtson et al., 1990). The grandparent–grandchild relationship may now extend over 40 years.

Marital Status in Later Life

Given the sex ratio in the United States, one would expect that few older women are married, and indeed that is the case. In 2000, only 52 percent of women aged 65 to 74 were married, and only 26 percent of women aged 75 to 84. By contrast, 77 percent of men aged 65 to 74 were married, as were 71 percent of

men aged 75 to 84. For men, marriage rates remain remarkably stable, even in advanced old age (U.S. Bureau of the Census, 2000).

Aside from the fact that most women outlive their husbands, there are other reasons older men are more likely to be married. Widowed men are seven times more likely to remarry than widowed women, in part because of the shortage of available men. But there is also a double standard for an appropriate marriage partner. At all ages, women marry men older than themselves, but men seldom marry older women.

There are also substantial racial and ethnic differences in marital status in old age, as Table 8–1 shows. Older African American women are less likely to be married than either white or Hispanic women, partly because of higher divorce rates but also because of higher mortality rates among black men. About the same proportion of white and Hispanic women are widows, but elderly Hispanic women are slightly more likely than white women never to have married.

THE LATER STAGES OF MARRIAGE

The marital bond is the most intimate and complex social relationship that can develop between two people. Despite the high probability of failure, most people marry at some time in their lives. Marriage provides companionship, affection, and sexual gratification. It also forges an economic relationship that depends increasingly on the joint contributions of husband and wife. People marry not only for love but because they recognize it provides many benefits. Married people report greater well-being than unmarried people, and they enjoy better health and lower mortality (Taylor, Keith, and Tucker, 1993).

The Family Life Cycle

Over the life course, the nuclear family takes different forms, and marital satisfaction varies at different stages. Family sociologists use the concept of a **family life cycle** to describe the evolution of the nuclear family. As originally described by Duvall (1962), the family life cycle begins at stage 1 when a couple marries. Stages 2 through 6 reflect the phases of childbearing and child rearing, beginning with the birth of the first child and ending when the children begin leaving home. The last two stages are reserved for middle age and old age. Stage 7 is the empty nest, or postparental, stage; stage 8 is that of aging families, when one or both spouses have retired.

Duvall's model no longer accurately reflects the typical life course of a nuclear family. One problem is that his model presumes that the nuclear family is the main family form and that it endures over the entire life course. Yet about half of contemporary marriages will end in divorce. Among those who become divorced, more than three-fourths will remarry. The recycling of adults through marital relationships and the accumulation of children exposed to divorce and long periods of single-parent life or second or multiple families means that this ideal-typical model of a family life cycle applies only to a minority of families (Featherman, 1983).

Another problem is that this eight-stage model ignores the way increases in life expectancy, decreases in family size, and early retirement have added more stages to the later years. To more accurately reflect contemporary family life, Duvall's model needs to be amended to include the new stages of marriage. These include (1) postchildbearing, preretirement, or middle age; (2) post–child rearing, early

retirement, the young–old; and (3) post–child rearing, late retirement, the old–old (Swenson, Esker, and Kohlkepp, 1984). Although much of the research on marital relationships covers the early years of marriage, these three later stages can consume 30 to 40 years of adult life.

Given that a typical couple can now expect to live so many years in the post–child-rearing phases, understanding what happens in later stages becomes especially important for evaluating the quality of marital relationships. What is marriage like when the children have left home? Are people happy in these later stages of married life? Research on marital satisfaction suggests that for many couples the postparental years are, indeed, fulfilling and satisfying.

Marital Satisfaction over the Life Course

Research has persistently shown that marital satisfaction follows a U-shaped pattern over the life course. Levels of marital satisfaction are high in the early years, decline precipitously during the child-rearing years, and then begin to rise, peaking in the retirement years.

What accounts for these patterns? The initial decline in marital satisfaction is associated with the arrival of children. The first years of parenting are demanding and difficult, so a couple has less time for other satisfying activities (Cherlin, 1996). But why does marital satisfaction dip even further during the middle years? One theory blames the decline on role conflict, an inability to meet competing demands of two or more roles. Role conflict diminishes marital quality as demands of multiple roles make work and parenting responsibilities burdensome and give married couples less time for each other (Huyck, 1995).

Role conflict is not the only explanation for the decline in marital satisfaction that occurs in middle age. A restlessness in the marital relationship seems fairly common among people who have long marriages. Today, some people pay attention to marital problems that had been previously ignored, and marital difficulties that at one time were hidden by the demands of daily life now surface (Levinson, 1996). Some couples find that the

These newlyweds dance at their wedding.

departure of children forces them to confront the problematic aspects of their marriage, and those who have stayed together for the sake of the children may divorce. Overall, however, the risk of divorce is highest in the early years of marriage and declines steadily. Seventy-four percent of all divorces occur before age 40, whereas only 1.3 percent occur after age 65 (Johnson, 1993). Couples who are still married by the time they reach 65 are the survivors. These couples typically rate their marriage as highly satisfying. They report fewer marital problems, fewer arguments, and more positive interactions than younger couples.

Because of divorce, death, or late age at marriage, fewer than 3 percent of all marriages last 50 years. Long-married couples tend to be very happy with their marriages. The celebration of 50 years of marriage signifies a remarkable accomplishment, given the risk of becoming divorced or widowed. Earlier role strains and interpersonal conflicts have been resolved. Older couples tend to agree on basic values and goals, the division of household tasks, and family relationships, and they perceive themselves as compatible. They also share a great deal of intimacy. In one study of couples married 45 to 55 years, more than 80 percent said that they confided

In Their Own Words

Marriages That Last a Lifetime

Mrs. PA: I think we did remarkably well. For two people who were married so young and no money, and neither one of us with a college degree . . . we put three kids through college . . . that's a big accomplishment. We've paid off the house. It's a tiny house, but it's ours. And so we did very well.

Mr. WT: As you grow older, and you dispense with your responsibilities, the load gets lighter. We don't worry about our children any more. . . . The last ten to fifteen years have been the best years of our marriage, because all the problems disappeared along the way. . . . We're enjoying life together now.

Mr. AL: The feelings become deeper . . . because we went through a great deal of experiences together. . . . The bond has gotten stronger over the years, by having mutual experiences that you can recall.

Source: Alford-Cooper (1998:160, 163)

---

in their mates most of the time, that they kissed their spouse every day or almost every day, and that they laughed together frequently. Ninety-eight percent liked their spouse as a person, and 94 percent rated their spouse as their best friend (Lauer, Lauer, and Kerr, 1995). Of course, not all long-term marriages are satisfying. Some people will remain in a marriage that has lost its vitality because of convenience, because they do not want to face the financial or emotional consequences of divorce, or simply because the marriage is comfortable, like an old pair of slippers.

Some people have marriages that last a lifetime because they find the key to a successful marriage. Others stay married out of a sense of duty and commitment. The Long Island Long-Term Marriage Survey consisted of interviews with 576 couples who had been married 50 years or more. The survey included questions on overall marital happiness, marital intimacy, attitudes toward marriage, methods of dealing with conflict, and happiest and unhappiest times. A smaller number of couples participated in in-depth interviews lasting two to three hours (Alford-Cooper, 1998).

What are the secrets to a successful marriage? The happiest couples are those who share their lives and have compatible interests and values. Other factors that are important include agreement about life's goals, an ability to laugh together, and an ability to resolve conflicts. In the "In Their Own Words" feature, some of the people from the Long Island Long-Term Marriage Survey describe the satisfactions they derive from their marriage.

Long-term marriages that are satisfying provide an important source of social support for older people. Comparisons between married and unmarried people show that marriage has a positive effect on well-being. Both married men and women have better mental health than divorced, widowed, or single men and women. Indeed, marital happiness is the best predictor of overall well-being (Keith, 1989).

That half of all marriages now end in divorce may reflect an erosion of marital quality. Such social forces as the decline in male earning power, the increase in employment among mothers of young children, and the decline of traditional gender roles all may strain marital relations. One study measured changes in marital quality among two cohorts of Canadian couples: One group was aged 20 to 35 in 1980, and a second group was aged 20 to 35 in 1992 (Rogers and Amato, 1997). The researchers found that members of the younger cohort reported more marital conflict, less marital interaction, and more problems in their marriages than members of the older cohort. Despite the decline in marital quality, however, there were no cohort differences in marital satisfaction, and, indeed, the commitment to the ideal of a lifetime marriage was stronger in the younger cohort than in the older one. Combined with previous research on life course patterns of marital satisfaction, these results suggest that if young couples can withstand the role strains of these demanding years, they will find sustenance in their marriages in old age.

Marriage and Sexual Activity

Surveys of sexual behavior have consistently found that the frequency of sexual activity declines with age for both men and women, although men report less decline. The decline occurs in both sexual intercourse and other sexual behaviors, such as oral sex, as well as in the frequency of masturbation and of sexual thoughts (Kingsberg, 2002). In the classic Kinsey study done in the late 1940s, college-age individuals reported having sex about 2.5 times per week, and individuals aged 55 and older reported having sex slightly less than once per week (Kinsey, Pomeroy, and Martin, 1948). A more recent large study reached similar conclusions. College-age individuals reported having sex about two to three times a week, and among people aged 55 to 59 (the oldest age group included in the survey), only 11 percent reported engaging in sexual activity that often (Lauman et al., 1994). But despite the decline in reported activity, a second finding stands out: Both men and women continue to find satisfaction and enjoyment in sexual activity as they get older. Indeed, several studies have found no age differences in sexual satisfaction and enjoyment (Johannes and Avis, 1997).

Among long-married couples, one cause of a decline in sexual activity is monotony, or **psychologic fatigue,** as sexual activity becomes patterned and routine (Walz and Blum, 1987). Changes in physical appearance may also cause people to lose interest in sex. Research shows that males place more importance than females on the physical appearance of their partners. One study of middle-aged couples found that men who believed their spouses were declining in physical attractiveness were more likely than other men to report sexual problems in their marriages (Margolin and White, 1987:26).

Some older women experience decreased interest in sex following menopause (Kingsberg, 2002). During menopause, which occurs in most women at age 50, the ovaries stop producing the hormone estrogen. Declining estrogen levels cause vaginal dryness and a shrinking of the vagina, which can make sexual intercourse painful. Some women find relief by using vaginal creams containing estrogen (Kingsberg, 2002).

Sexual dysfunctions that can occur in later life may also reduce sexual activities in older couples. In the Massachusetts Male Aging Study, 40 percent of men aged 60 to 69 and 67 percent of men aged 70 and older experienced mild to severe erectile dysfunction (an erection insufficient for intercourse) (Feldman et al., 1994). The much-publicized drug Viagra is used to treat erectile dysfunction in men of all ages. Viagra works by increasing blood flow to the penis and has helped many couples that had stopped having sexual intercourse to become sexually active again. However, Viagra can have a negative effect on an older couple's sexual equilibrium if the woman does not wish to resume having sex (Kingsberg, 2002).

Despite some problems with sexual boredom, only a minority of married couples report sexual problems (Margolin and White, 1987). Most married couples remain sexually active and express continued interest in and enjoyment of sexual intimacy (Marsiglio and Donnelly, 1991). In fact, the vast majority of married men and women continue to have sexual intercourse well into their 70s. Continued sexual activity, in turn, is associated with marital satisfaction. One study of 244 married couples over the age of 65 found that couples who reported remaining sexually active said they had happy marriages (Ade-Ridder, 1990).

A recent study conducted at UCLA helps to explain these statistics. The researchers interviewed 1,216 older people, ranging in age from 70 to 94. Among women, the most important predictor of sexual activity was marital status: 42 percent of the married women were sexually active, compared to only 2.7 percent of the unmarried women. Marital status was less a predictor of sexual activity for men; 47 percent of the married men reported sexual activity, and 31 percent of the unmarried men (Mathias et al., 1997).

Among very old men and women, the nature of sexual activity changes. One study of healthy 80- to 102-year-olds found that the most common sexual activity was touching and caressing; the second most common was masturbation; and the least common, sexual intercourse (Bretschneider and McCoy, 1988). The following case study illustrates how the frail elderly modify their sexual behavior to accommodate changes in their health and functioning.

Mr. N was deaf, blind, and unable to talk due to a recent laryngotomy. He was quite dependent on Mrs. N who had severe arthritis and had had a mastectomy years ago. . . . They slept in twin beds and indicated they no longer engaged in intercourse. Yet they had a nightly ritual in which Mr. N helped his wife bathe and then gave her a massage in bed, which they described with some embarrassment and blushing. (Rose and Soares, 1993:170)

Although Mr. and Mrs. N no longer engaged in sexual intercourse, their relationship remained sensual.

Gender and Marriage

Among today's older couples, men were socialized early on to be responsible primarily for their wives' material and financial security, and women were expected to be the family caretakers and to be attentive and physically and emotionally responsive to their husbands' needs throughout marriage. Among couples in old age, the division of household tasks and the emotional aspects of the marital bond reflect this socialization. Timothy Brubaker (1985) interviewed 32 golden anniversary couples, who had been married an average of 56 years. He found that although some household tasks were shared, most conformed to a traditional division of labor. The husbands were primarily responsible for the yardwork, car maintenance, and house repairs; the wives cooked the meals, washed the dishes, did the laundry, and wrote letters to friends and family members. Only if the wife became ill was the husband willing to do the tasks considered "women's work." As one husband explained:

I include the basement as my territory along with the outside—there's always repairing and stuff to be done. She has her place and I kinda got mine. . . . I see these guys doing the dishes, doing half the cooking, changing diapers, and stuff like that. It don't seem to me like that's the thing for them to be doing. . . . I was raised that that is the woman's job. If there's illness or something, then that's different. (Brubaker, 1985:36)

Another study found a similar division by gender in the emotional aspects of long-term marriages. Quirouette and Gold (1995) interviewed 120 men and women who had been married over 35 years. They found that a wife's sense of well-being was closely tied to certain characteristics of her husband but not vice versa. The most important factor in a wife's well-being was her husband's perception of the marriage. Wives whose husbands were satisfied with their marriage had a greater sense of well-being than wives whose husbands were dissatisfied with the marriage. A wife's sense of well-being was also influenced by her husband's personality traits. Women married to pleasant, energetic, and enthusiastic men were happier than those married to men with low energy and enthusiasm for life. A husband's health was also a significant predictor of his wife's well-being. Interestingly enough, a husband's sense of well-being was not affected by his wife's happiness, personality traits, or health; rather, it was influenced most strongly by his *own* health (Quirouette and Gold, 1995). Thus, the traditional division of labor that characterized these marriages earlier in life was reflected in the emotional benefits that marriage conferred in old age.

One explanation for these results is that men derive more benefits from marriage than women. Studies consistently find that men report higher levels of marital satisfaction than women and that men receive more emotional support from the marital bond. In one study, husbands who said they had a confidant overwhelmingly confided in their wives, whereas fewer than half of the wives confided in their husbands. Women were more likely to mention friends or their children (Clausen, 1993).

Retirement Satisfaction and Marriage

When one or both members of a couple retire, they often renegotiate the division of labor in and around the home. The way in which housework is divided affects a woman's satisfaction with retirement. Both employed and retired women expect their husbands to do more around the house after the husbands retire. Yet retirement often does not bring great changes in domestic arrangements. Wives who continue to work full-time after their husbands retire are most likely to be dissatisfied with a husband who won't help with housework. Wives who are not employed full-time expect less from their husbands and are therefore more satisfied regardless of how much help they get from their husbands (Pina and Bengtson, 1995). Wives and husbands who time their retirements to coincide and then share household chores have the highest level of well-being.

PARENT–CHILD RELATIONSHIPS

Next to the marital tie, there is no more important familial relationship than that between parent and child. Parents and children now spend decades of life together. A growing number share more than a half century, and for the majority of those years the children will be adults and parents themselves. Four-generation families have three tiers of parent–child relationships and two generations that are simultaneously parent and child (Hagestad, 1987).

The parent–child relationship is unique. It is permanent and involuntary. You can choose your wife, but you can't choose your mother. Nor can you divorce your parents, although you can become estranged from them. Positive parent–child relationships increase psychological and physical well-being. Older parents who have close relationships with their adult children are less likely than those who don't to be depressed or lonely. They have higher morale and higher life satisfaction (Dean, Kolodny, and Wood, 1990).

Yet conflict between parents and their adult children is pervasive, a natural part of family interactions. One study found that parents and children quarreled over six basic issues. A frequent complaint was that communication was strained or nonexistent. As an adult daughter explained while complaining about her father's lack of honesty with her:

My dad (63) divorced his second wife and pretended to still be married to her for six months until he told us. Weird! He told us 15 years after the fact that he'd had a drinking problem and gone to AA. I don't understand why he keeps personal things so private. (Clarke et al., 1999:265)

Another source of conflict was differences in lifestyles and personal habits. One father complained about his son's frequent use of credit cards, another of his daughter's failure to save for a rainy day. Parents and their adult children also disagreed over child-rearing practices, religion, politics, and work habits. Despite tension and disagreements, however, family members also reported frequent contact and a great deal of affection and support.

Social Interaction and Exchange

Societal norms strongly encourage continued social interaction between parents and children. Numerous studies of the family in later life demonstrate that adult children remain very involved with their aging parents, with most maintaining regular and frequent contact (Umberson, 1992). However, the amount of social support families provide varies. According to the **theory of intergenerational solidarity,** families adjust their living arrangements over time to reflect the changing needs and resources of different generations. Early in the life course, the economic needs of adult children determine their proximity to their parents.

This Hispanic couple wash windows together outside their home in south Florida.

Later in the life course, the parents' economic and health needs more strongly influence how close the children live to them (Spitze and Logan, 1990b; Silverstein and Litwak, 1993).

Researchers have identified three phases in this life course pattern. Children live with or near their parents before they reach age 25. Then there is a period of separation, as children marry and move away in pursuit of education and employment. Healthy elders may also retire and move away from the children. In later life, however, when these aging parents become ill or disabled, they move closer to the children. Thus, families reconstitute themselves in later life, not necessarily in the same household, but through close contact and frequent visits (Silverstein, 1995).

Intergenerational living arrangements are influenced by a family's social class. Children from middle-class families are more likely than others to move away from home for education and employment. When parents in middle-class families become ill or lose a spouse, however, they may move to be near

Table 8-2	Life Course Patterns of Help between Parents and Adult Children							

	Respondent (Parent) Age							
	40–44	*45–49*	*50–54*	*55–59*	*60–64*	*65–69*	*70–74*	*75+*
Help to parent								
Housekeeping	0%	2%	2%	3%	2%	1%	3%	7%
Shop, errands	0	4	4	7	3	7	6	29
Repairs, yard	11	0	9	7	15	9	9	8
Any type of help	11	4	13	13	18	14	16	38
Mean hours/week	.19	.40	.38	.61	1.13	.57	.35	1.69
Help to child								
Housekeeping	19%	26%	17%	8%	11%	15%	19%	9%
Shop, errands	26	25	22	18	19	12	23	5
Repairs, yard	4	13	10	17	12	9	10	2
Babysitting	22	26	43	35	36	25	16	3
Any type of help	52	55	60	54	50	40	48	16
Mean hours/week	1.74	1.91	2.44	2.14	2.66	1.15	1.30	.29
N	24	53	95	96	126	110	69	95

Source: Spitze and Logan (1992:302).

their children. But even then, parents in middle-class families rely more on friends and purchased services than do working-class parents. Children from working-class families are more likely than middle-class children to take jobs near home and remain close to their parents, though recent changes in the labor market, such as the decline in well-paid factory jobs, may be changing this pattern. Thus, working-class parents may have a smaller local support network when they grow older, and fewer resources to fall back on, than affluent parents (Greenwell and Bengtson, 1997).

Intergenerational solidarity has six components: (1) the frequency of interaction, (2) the amount of interaction, (3) the amount of positive sentiment about family members, (4) the level of agreement about values and beliefs, (5) the degree to which services are exchanged, and (6) the amount of geographical proximity (Roberts, Richards, and Bengtson, 1991). Some families are high on all six components; others are low. But no matter what the culture, families the world over provide mutual support

from one generation to the next. "Aging around the World" describes intergenerational solidarity in France.

The exchange of services between generations also varies over the life course, with a gradual shift from parents as givers to parents as receivers. For most of their lives, parents give substantially more help to children than vice versa (Lewis, 1990). As Table 8–2 shows, help to adult children peaks when the parents are in their early 50s, when 60 percent provide some kind of help. It remains high (48 percent) until parents are in their early 70s. Not until their parents are 75 or over do adult children give more help than they receive (Spitze and Logan, 1992). Are there racial and ethnic differences in the sense of responsibility children have for their aging parents and grandparents? "Diversity in the Aging Experience" examines this question.

The statistics on helping patterns don't fully explain the complex family dynamics that come into play as parents age. Some parent–child conflict is natural and inevitable. Yet unless these conflicts are

Aging around the World

INTERGENERATIONAL SOLIDARITY IN FRANCE

The concept of intergenerational solidarity appears to be a universal element of family life. The French social scientist Claudine Attias-Donfut (2000) interviewed families of three generations—grandparents, parents, and children. The grandparents had retired and were beginning to experience health problems; the parents were still active in the workforce. Some members of the youngest generation were in school; others were working at a first job.

Attias-Donfut noted numerous exchanges between generations, some upward from children to parents, but most downward from parents to children. Financial assistance involved mostly downward transfers: Over a third of the grandparents gave money to their adult children, and nearly as many gave money to their grandchildren. Parents also gave money to their children.

Services were exchanged widely, both upward and downward. Most of the parent generation (89 percent) provided some help to the grandparents, and about half (49 percent) also gave their children some type of help. Children also provided various services to their parents, and sometimes to their grandparents.

Although the nature of family life in France is changing, the family remains an enduring institution. Experts think the increase in life expectancy will prolong the duration of exchanges between generations and increase the opportunities family members have to help each other.

French families, like families around the world, engage in numerous exchanges of help and support across the generations.

What Do You Think?

1. Do the members of your family extend financial assistance to one another or exchange their services in other ways? If so, does the assistance flow mainly from grandparents to parents, from parents to grandparents, or in both directions?
2. Would you expect intergenerational solidarity to vary much from one culture to another? Why or why not?

Diversity in the Aging Experience

RACIAL AND ETHNIC VARIATIONS IN FILIAL RESPONSIBILITY

*A*pproximately 40 to 50 percent of adult children see their aging parents at least once a week (Rossi and Rossi, 1990). This figure is higher among elders who are members of ethnic and racial minorities. Because of higher fertility, extended family living arrangements, and the incorporation of nonblood relatives (fictive kin) into definitions of family, African American, Asian American, Mexican American, and Native American elderly people have a potentially larger support network than white Americans. For example, one study reported that 90 percent of African American children said they helped their parents, and one-third said they frequently helped them (Chatters and Taylor, 1993).

There is also evidence that racial and ethnic differences exist in parents' expectations of younger family members. Two recent studies comparing black, white, and Hispanic attitudes found that the black and Hispanic elderly expected more help from their children than did the white elderly (Lee, Peek, and Coward, 1998; Burr and Mutchler, 1999).

What Do You Think?

1. Why do you think attitudes toward helping elderly relatives vary among people of different racial and ethnic groups?
2. What is your racial or ethnic background? Does your culture have specific norms about helping elderly family members?

severe, they tend to dissipate as children become adults. When children leave home, establish their own households, and have children of their own, they find it easier to identify with their parents. In particular, the birth of a child strengthens the mother–daughter bond (Rossi and Rossi, 1990). Differences become muted, and there is more tolerance for the differences that remain (Suitor et al., 1995). One 63-year-old son described his relationship with his 89-year-old father:

My Dad let me know on the day he moved here that there wasn't much likelihood that our relationship would improve. It's gotten worse in a way, because I was unaware of the reservoir of his negative feelings until he repeatedly confronted me with a litany of complaints about my long-standing lack of concern. . . . With all that, I do find pleasure in visiting, eating lunch together, talking politics, and in knowing that he's nearby, and that I can help him should he need it. . . . I talk to him every day on the phone. He's now part of my basic network and is both a source of pleasure and frustration. (Moss and Moss, 1992:265)

Not all familial conflicts are peacefully resolved. The level of intergenerational solidarity at any time is related to family interaction patterns established earlier, which persist over time and are often revived in new or uncertain situations. In one study of 451 families, married adult children were asked to describe their relationships with their parents when they were children (Whitbeck, Hoyt, and Huck, 1994). Children who recalled a high level of parental rejection now felt less concerned about staying in touch with aging parents and with monitoring their parents' well-being. Being concerned about parents' welfare, in turn, was a strong predictor of the amount of support children, especially daughters, were willing to provide to their elderly parents.

Parent–child relationships often suffer when children fail to pursue the normative course of adult development. Hagestad (1986) found that mothers hoped their children would "grow up, establish themselves as functioning adults, and become important supports" (p. 685). When children failed to become independent at the expected time, mothers felt a sense of failure and strain. The relationship of an adult son with his parents often becomes strained if he loses his job. He has failed to meet their expectations. Indeed, when generations share a household, unemployment is one of the best predictors of conflict with parents (Aquilino and Supple, 1991).

Sometimes family tensions can result in abuse of a frail, older person. The terms *elder abuse* and *neglect* encompass a variety of different behaviors directed toward the elderly. In the simplest sense, elder abuse consists of acts of commission and omission that cause unnecessary suffering (Wolf, 1998). Most researchers, legal experts, and members of the helping professions include the following behaviors as constituting elder abuse: neglect, financial exploitation, and physical, emotional, and sexual abuse (Choi and Mayer, 2000; Reay and Browne, 2001; Gordon and Brill, 2001). It is estimated that somewhere between 1 and 11 percent of the population over the age of 65 have been the

victims of some type of elder abuse or neglect (Comijs et al., 1998). No one really knows the actual incidence of elder abuse because much is likely to go unreported (Bolland and Maxwell, 1990; Branch, 2002). Elder abuse can be found in family situations as well as institutional settings such as nursing homes.

Why would anyone want to abuse or neglect an elderly parent, grandparent, or spouse? According to one widely accepted theory, the "stressed caregiver hypothesis," the abuser is most likely to be an overworked and underappreciated family member who has major responsibility for the care of an older person. The pressure and stress associated with daily caregiving responsibilities can cause that person to lose control. Another theory, the "learned violence hypothesis," proposes that the abuser might have been a victim of abuse in the past and now becomes the abuser. Finally, the "dependency hypothesis" suggests that abuse occurs when the victim is mentally and physically incapacitated and increasingly vulnerable and dependent on a caregiver and the caregiver takes advantage of this dependence and abuses the victim (Gordon and Brill, 2001).

Those who are most at risk of abuse are elderly women who are cognitively or physically impaired and who live with their abusers (Wilber and Nielsen, 2002). Certain personality traits of the victim have also been associated with elder abuse. A victim who reacts aggressively to daily frustrations is more likely to be verbally abused by a caregiver (Comijs et al., 1999). Physical abusers of the elderly are more likely to be consumers of excessive amounts of alcohol and to have experienced past childhood abuse by their fathers (Reay and Browne, 2001).

The Effect of Divorce

By 2010, the proportion of people 65 or older who have been divorced is expected to reach 50 percent. The increase in the divorce rate means that many more people will reach old age with no spouse for help and support. The role of children thus will be even more important in the future.

Although people generally agree that children have a responsibility to help elderly parents who cannot manage on their own, divorce complicates the issue. Divorce not only dissolves the marital relationship, but it severs other family ties, such as those between in-laws. Divorce may also change the nature of the parent–child relationship, especially if one parent gets full-time custody of the children. When divorced people remarry, new step-relationships are created, which complicate the issue of children's obligations to their parents: Are children responsible for an aging parent if they didn't grow up with that parent? Should children help their aging stepparents?

A number of studies have shown that parental divorce changes the relationship between adult children and their parents. Ganong and Coleman (1998) interviewed 208 women and 83 men who lived in eight midwestern communities. They asked these subjects to respond to a series of vignettes regarding a woman's obligations to assist a divorced parent and a stepparent. For example, one vignette involved Sally, the adult daughter of divorced parents. The subjects were asked what assistance, if any, Sally should provide to her nonresidential father and her stepfather. Ganong and Coleman found that their subjects agreed that adult children should help elderly divorced parents but disagreed about what kind of help they should provide. Subjects also felt that the extent of an adult child's responsibility to a parent or stepparent should depend on the amount of contact the child had had with the parent over the years.

Overall, children whose parents have divorced have less of a sense of obligation to parents than children from intact families (Silverstein and Bengtson, 1997). The consequences of divorce on social support in old age are particularly negative for fathers. One study, which examined older men's contact with adult children, found that about 90 percent of married men had weekly contact with their children but only 50 percent of divorced fathers saw their children that often. About 10 percent of divorced fathers had no contact with their children (Cooney and Uhlenberg, 1990). Similarly, Webster and Herzog (1995) found that children from two-parent families saw their parents more often and reported more positive relationships than children whose parents had divorced. However, they also discovered a large gender difference, with divorced fathers having much less contact with adult children than divorced mothers. Adult children of divorced parents reported feeling less loved and less listened to as children by their fathers than children from intact families. The authors concluded that "the effect of parental divorce on frequency of contact cannot be explained away by accounting for memories of childhood family problems. . . . Divorce, regardless of the family problems that follow or precede it, reduces the frequency with which fathers and adult children communicate" (Webster and Herzog, 1995:31).

The Effect of Remarriage

Among people 65 or older, only a small fraction (2 percent) of widows and a somewhat larger number (20 percent) of widowers remarry. The most common reason for remarrying among the widowed is companionship. More commonly, remarriages follow a divorce (Bengtson et al., 1990; Cherlin, 1996). Remarriages are somewhat more likely to end in divorce than first marriages. Remarriage creates multiple ties across households and generations that may include children from current and previous marriages, parents and stepparents, and grandparents and stepgrandparents.

Most stepparents report that they are happy with their new roles, but ratings of people in stepfamily households are consistently less positive than those in two-parent biological households (Furstenberg, 1987). Studies also show that the well-being of children in stepfamily households is lower than in two-parent, biological families and that stepchildren leave home earlier (Goldscheider and Goldscheider, 1993). These findings suggest that the ties between parents and children in stepfamilies may be weaker when the parents are old and thus that their social support system may also be weaker.

THE UNMARRIED ELDERLY

Although most older people live near at least one child, some older people lack a family support network (Suitor et al., 1995). Sometimes their children have moved away; others have no children or have never married. In the United States, approximately 5 percent of men and women remain single all their lives. The small amount of research on the single elderly suggests that ties to members of the kinship group are very important, especially for women. Unmarried women have close relationships with their own aged parents and with uncles, aunts, siblings, cousins, nieces, and nephews (Bengtson et al., 1990).

The circumstances of the unmarried elderly tend to vary cross-culturally. In the United States, nearly two-thirds of single, childless elderly people belong to a social support network. In Canada, however, only one-quarter of the childless elderly participate in an exchange network that provides instrumental support; even fewer receive emotional support. Indeed, 75 percent of unmarried, childless Canadians age 65 or over receive no emotional support from family or friends (Wu and Pollard, 1998).

As we noted earlier, the family is the main provider of instrumental support. When single people grow old, their support network has fewer individuals willing to provide this type of help compared to married people. Siblings in the support network may be struggling with their own health problems, or they may be responding to the needs of their children and grandchildren. Nieces or nephews may provide some help but not at the levels provided by children (Keith, 1989). On the positive side, people who have been single all their lives are often self-reliant, independent, and used to living alone.

SIBLING RELATIONSHIPS IN LATER LIFE

Siblings relationships are unique. Siblings share a family history, they have a relationship that can last a lifetime, and they are members of the same generation. Older adults often mention the importance of their brothers and sisters, and as people age, the sibling bond becomes even more important. Siblings often provide support to each other and are a source of psychological well-being in old age (Scott, 1990).

Sometimes siblings become closer when they have to plan care for an aging parent. Siblings may also care for each other as they grow older, although more likely, they provide only emotional support. In one study of Canadians aged 55 and older, the majority of respondents felt that their siblings would help them in a crisis, although only 25 percent had actually received such help (Connidis, 1994). Illness often reconstitutes the sibling social support network. One widow explained how her sisters pitched in when her husband became sick:

When my husband became very ill, I just couldn't do everything for him. . . . My sisters came over to stay with him when I needed to get out, to help me bathe him and change his sheets. Without them, he would have had to go to a nursing home. (Gold, 1996:241)

The nature of the sibling relationship is partly determined by the size and gender composition of the sibling group. A brother whose siblings include a sister is more likely to be close to his siblings than one who has only brothers (Matthews, 1994). The bond between sisters is closest, and sisters are most likely to take care of each other. For example, Mary, a 75-year-old widow, left her children in the East when her husband died and returned to her Ohio hometown to be near her two sisters. The three sold their own homes, bought a home together, and pooled their possessions and other resources. When one of the sisters became ill, they hired an aide to provide some daily care. And because all the sisters pitched in, no single individual had to bear a large burden (Moyer, 1993).

The nature of sibling relationships also changes over the life course. Sibling ties may be strong among children, then become weaker as jobs, marriage, and parenting make demands on time and energy. During these middle years, siblings may live far apart and have little in common in terms of values and interests. Later-life events such as the departure of children from the home, retirement, and widowhood often bring siblings closer together (Bedford, 1995). One man remarked about his relationship to his sister:

It helped our relationship when her children were out of the house and married. I don't think she didn't care about me during the earlier part of our adult lives—I think she just didn't have time! (Gold, 1996:237)

Past tensions and family feuds can keep siblings apart. If parents have kept their children in emotional bondage by withholding approval and love, children compete for affection and become alienated from each other. In such families, adult siblings may be unable to reconcile until one or both parents die (Moyer, 1993). Instead, they continue to replay earlier sibling rivalries in their old age.

GRANDPARENTHOOD

There have always been grandparents, but as we saw in Chapter 3, grandparenting is relatively new as a distinct phase of the life course. In the nineteenth century, grandparenthood was rare. Few people lived long enough to spend many years as grandparents, and most still had dependent children at home if they did. Presently, one-half of Americans become grandparents by age 50; three-fourths of people age 65 or older are grandparents (Hogan, Eggebeen, and Snaith, 1996; Szinovacz, 1998).

Styles of Grandparenting

In a survey of 510 grandparents, Andrew Cherlin and Frank Furstenberg (1992) identified three styles of grandparenting: **remote, companionate,** and **involved.** Grandparents with remote relationships saw their grandchildren so infrequently that their relationship was mainly ritualistic and symbolic. Most simply lived too far away and thus were unable to play a role in their grandchildren's lives. Divorce often was a factor, especially for the grandparents on the father's side. When a former daughter-in-law moved away, it was often difficult for the grandparents to keep in touch with the children.

Grandparents who maintained a companionate relationship with their grandchildren focused on emotionally satisfying, leisure-time activities and reported an easygoing, friendly style of interaction. These grandparents felt they already had raised a family and were now prepared to leave the tough

work of parenting to their children. Their attitude toward their grandchildren was to love them and then send them home. Another feature of the companionate style was a "norm of noninterference." Grandparents emphasized that they had no right to tell their married children what to do. Because of this norm, they had little sense of authority over their grandchildren and were powerless to demand more access to them.

Involved grandparents took an active role in rearing their grandchildren, frequently behaving more like parents than grandparents. They were in almost daily contact with their grandchildren, often because they were living with them. Involved grandparents usually became surrogate parents after a disruptive event such as a divorce, a death in the family, or an out-of-wedlock birth. Some were raising their grandchildren themselves.

Grandparents Raising Grandchildren

Over the past three decades there has been a small but distinct increase in the number of young children being raised by their grandparents, from 3.2 percent in 1970 to 5.5 percent in 1997 (Szinovacz, DeViney, and Atkinson, 1999). Just over two-thirds of custodial grandparents are white; 29 percent are African American, 10 percent Hispanic, 2 percent Asian American, and 1 percent Native American (Burnette, 1999). These statistics have stimulated interest in why grandparents choose to raise their grandchildren and how well they cope with the task.

Among many Native American tribes, it is customary for grandparents to rear their first and second grandchildren for several years. As one Lakota Sioux grandmother explained, "The grandparents always took . . . at least the first grandchild to raise. . . . They think that they're more mature and have had more experience" (Yee, 1994:197). A contemporary version of this tradition occurs among grandparents whose children have moved off reservations to urban areas. Many keep their grandchildren during the summer holidays, teaching them their cultural heritage so they will know Indian traditions. The grandchildren actively participate in the ceremonial life of the reservation, dance in full regalia at powwows, and become immersed in reservation life. In this way, the native traditions are passed on to a new generation (Yee, 1994).

More often grandparents come to raise their grandchildren under difficult, and sometimes tragic, circumstances. Grandparents become surrogate parents during family crises resulting from divorce, drug abuse, alcoholism, teenage pregnancy, or parental abuse or abandonment of the children (Hayslip et al., 1998). In a study of 398 white and 319 black custodial grandmothers, Rachel Pruchno found the primary reason they began caring for their grandchildren was drug or alcohol addiction by the parents. As one grandmother explained:

I guess the final straw where someone said yes, these children need help was on a Friday, our daughter had checked herself into a drug and alcohol rehab center and so the children were left in the care of their father and he went out drinking on Saturday night and left the children alone and he went out drinking again Sunday and left the children at which time he had been picked up by the police. (Pruchno, 1999:215)

The grandmother's task was made more difficult because many of the grandchildren in Pruchno's study exhibited a wide range of behavioral problems. They had sudden mood swings, were often nervous and argumentative, stubborn, or disobedient. Many had been diagnosed as hyperactive and were experiencing difficulty in school.

Not surprisingly, most researchers have found that custodial grandparents experience a decline in well-being when they begin caring for their grandchildren (Burnette, 1999). Linda Burton and Cynthia deVries interviewed African American grandmothers, grandfathers, and great-grandmothers with full-time responsibility for their grandchildren. Many said that they worried about keeping up with their young grandchildren, both physically and intellectually. For example, Harold, a 68-year-old grandfather, was frustrated by his inability to help his granddaughter with her math homework: "I don't know nothing about this new arithmetic. I can't help her at all. I am too embarrassed to go to her teacher and tell her I can't help" (Burton and

deVries, 1993:105). These surrogate parents were also concerned about their ability to balance their new child-rearing responsibilities with their jobs and other responsibilities.

One of the greatest challenges grandparents can experience is caring for more than one generation simultaneously. Sarah was a 63-year-old great-grandmother living with her 35-year-old daughter, her daughter's four children and three of her brother's children. Two of Sarah's teenage granddaughters were pregnant. Not only did Sarah care for this large household, she also traveled frequently to a nearby state to help her other daughter and granddaughter. As Sarah told the interviewer, "Can you believe I do all this? I can't even believe it myself. All these people depend on me" (Burton and deVries, 1993:103–4).

Despite these challenges, many grandparents say they don't regret their decision to raise their grandchildren, and feel grateful for the companionship and love the children bring into their lives (Hayslip et al., 1998). As one 80-year-old great-grandmother explained, "I don't know what I would do without my granddaughter. She is my best friend. With her here with me, even though she did have a baby, I feel like I will never be alone" (Burton and deVries, 1993:107).

The Quality of the Grandparent–Grandchild Relationship

The quality of the grandparent–grandchild relationship is mediated by the parents' relationship to their own parents. When parents and grandparents are close, the children see their grandparents more often and feel greater emotional closeness to them than when there is distance (Kivett, 1985). Middle-aged parents who interact regularly with their own parents provide role models for their children. Spending time with the grandparent generation establishes family norms of reciprocity and strengthens links between generations (Hodgson, 1992). In fact, when family ties are strong, grandmothers' feelings for their granddaughters are often indistinguishable from their feelings for their daughters (Thompson and Walker, 1987).

These links across generations not only reflect present relationships but also past experiences. A team of researchers evaluated the quality of the childhood relationship between parents and grandparents by asking their respondents whether they felt their parents had really cared for them (Whitbeck, Hoyt, and Huck, 1993). They found that when the parents viewed the grandparent generation as uncaring, the quality of relationships was poorer across all three generations. Grandchildren whose parents had poor relationships with their own parents saw their grandparents less often and rated the quality of the relationship lower than those whose parents recalled caring relationships.

Studies based on recalled memories of early life experiences are potentially compromised by the possibility that people who are presently emotionally distant from their parents may reinterpret their childhood memories. However, longitudinal studies suggest that relationships do reflect continuity over time. Whitbeck, Hoyt, and Huck (1993) concluded that "perceptions about early family relationships provide a blueprint for later family relationships across generations" (p. 1033).

The Grandparent Career

As with other family relationships, there is a life course pattern to grandparent–grandchild relationships, called a **grandparent career** (Cherlin and Furstenberg, 1992). Grandparents see their grandchildren often when they are very young, and they find this period of grandparenting most satisfying. Then, as grandchildren grow up, the frequency of contact declines as teenage grandchildren develop relationships outside the family. As they become young adults, they begin to establish families of their own and choose occupations. Their grandparents remain important in their lives, however, for college students report they enjoy being with their grandparents and feel that their grandparents have had a large influence in shaping their values, their personal identities, and their religious beliefs (Roberto and Stroes, 1992).

When grandchildren reach adulthood, the relationship between grandparents and grandchildren becomes closer. Contact is frequent, and both generations place great value on the relationship. Hodgson (1992) interviewed a national sample of over 200 adult grandchildren. Only 1.5 percent had no contact with their grandparents. The majority were in touch with their grandparents through visits or phone conversations several times a month, and 40 percent had weekly contact. As might be expected, young men and women who lived near their grandparents saw them more frequently. Physical proximity also increased the sense of emotional closeness they felt toward their grandparents.

Hodgson found that grandchildren felt closer to their grandmothers, especially on the maternal side, than to their grandfathers. This finding is consistent with other studies, which find that women derive more satisfaction from grandparenting than men (Thomas, 1986). But many grandfathers also express high satisfaction with the grandparenting role, particularly men who have been involved in their grandchildren's care.

One way to think of the grandparent–grandchild relationship is as one element in the convoy of social support that occurs in lifelong social networks (Kahn and Antonucci, 1980). As grandchildren grow up, they become part of their grandparents' support system, giving and receiving emotional and instrumental support (Langer, 1990).

Grandparenting after Divorce

There is a good deal of research on how divorce affects parents and children, but much less is known about the impact of divorce on other kinship relations. One study identified three patterns that occurred in the relationship between parents and their divorcing children (Johnson, 1993). One pattern was an increase in the bond between parents, the adult child, and grandchildren. This pattern occurred most often between a daughter and her parents and resulted from the economic and practical assistance provided by the parents. Children who relied heavily on their parents paid a price, however, for they lost much of their independence. Parental intervention in divorce also meant that the shield of privacy that surrounds marriage was lowered. When parents helped their adult children, they felt justified in commenting on child-rearing practices or dating patterns, topics that grandparents normally feel are taboo. This arrangement was usually temporary. As the divorced children reestablished stability in their lives, they reasserted their independence.

In a second pattern, the divorced children struck out alone and retained a separate, private life. The intergenerational bond was characterized by intimacy at a distance. Finally, in a third pattern, there was a blurring of relatives by blood, marriage, divorce, and remarriage. Relationships with relatives of divorce were maintained while new relationships were formed with remarriage. Grandchildren provided the link in families where sons and daughters-in-law remained close after a divorce. A former daughter-in-law might no longer be a son's wife, but she remained the mother of one's grandchild. Thus, ties to former daughters-in-law were most commonly maintained among paternal grandparents. Maternal grandparents automatically would have greater access to a grandchild because their daughter typically would have custody. As a result, they saw less of their former sons-in-law.

As we saw earlier, although divorce is often viewed as a severing of family ties, it can also multiply them (Johnson, 1993). With the divorce and remarriage of children, new in-laws are accumulated. Grandparents who maintain contact with a former daughter-in-law may find themselves part of an extended kin network that includes her new spouse if she remarries and new children and stepchildren. In general, however, relations with maternal grandparents become closer after a divorce and relationships with paternal grandparents suffer. Parents mediate the relationship between grandchildren and grandparents, and parental custody patterns determine the amount of contact between grandchildren and grandparents.

The role played by parents in mediating the grandparent–grandchild relationship becomes less important among older grandchildren. Cooney and Smith (1996) interviewed 485 grandchildren between the ages of 18 and 23. Half had experienced a parental divorce in the past 15 months; the other half were from intact families. They found that there were no differences between the two groups in how close the grandchildren felt toward their grandparents or in how often they saw them. In fact, young adults from divorced families were more likely to initiate visits with their grandparents than were those from intact families. In adulthood, then, parents no longer mediate relationships between grandparents and grandchildren. Grandchildren manage their relationships on their own, and parental divorce has less effect than it does on young children. Indeed, the authors concluded that "the strength and stability of relations with their grandparents may be particularly beneficial to young adults' adjustment" (Cooney and Smith, 1996:95). For a discussion of the legal issues that arise when grandparents seek to maintain contact with grandchildren after a divorce, see "An Issue for Public Policy."

Demographic change and rising divorce rates have transformed family structure, but the family remains the core societal institution. Indeed, the strength of familial ties is most visible in old age. Although some older people do become isolated from family members, most are firmly embedded in an extended kin network. And the elderly are active members of these extended kin networks, giving more help than they receive until they are very infirm. Only then does the aid flow in the other direction.

THE FAMILIES OF OLDER GAY MEN AND WOMEN

Gay men and lesbians have many different types of family relationships that provide support as they grow old. Some are involved in long-term relationships with a partner or companion (Peplau, 1991). Many couples have exchanged vows in private ceremonies and consider themselves married. In 2003 Canada legalized gay marriages, and in 2004 Massachusetts made gay marriages legal. Many states grant same-sex couples the same

An Issue for Public Policy

SHOULD GRANDPARENTS HAVE VISITATION RIGHTS AFTER A DIVORCE?

*U*ntil the 1970s, grandparents had almost no rights to visit their grandchildren except with the consent of the child's parents. Then, during the late 1970s and 1980s, legislation was enacted in all 50 states granting grandparents the right to petition the court for legally enforced visitation privileges with their grandchildren. Moreover, in 1983 the House of Representatives recommended that the states develop a uniform statute ensuring grandparents' visitation rights (Thompson et al., 1989).

The increase in the divorce rate, which skyrocketed in the 1970s, was one factor in stimulating legislation protecting grandparents' rights to see their grandchildren. Another factor was the increasing political clout of senior citizen organizations that took on grandparents' rights as an issue. And in general, the laws were passed quickly because "in many states lawmakers could see no harm in simply giving grandparents the right to petition to see their grandchildren when the child would benefit from the continuing contact" (Thompson et al., 1989).

Although most people immediately sympathize with the pain experienced by grandparents who are cut off from their grandchildren when their children divorce, determining what is in the best interest of the grandchildren in these situations is a complex issue. In the past, the denial of independent visitation rights to grandparents was justified on the grounds that it would undermine parental authority. In cases that come before the courts, battles over visitation may involve the child

rights, benefits, and protections as married couples, allowing them to enter into what the state called civil unions. One national study found that 60 percent of gay and bisexual men and 64 percent of lesbian and bisexual women said they were in a relationship. It is easy to find gay men who have lived together openly as couples for 40 years (Kimmel, 1992). However, no good statistics exist on the prevalence of long-term same-sex marriages. Gay marriage is a politically controversial issue that is unlikely to be resolved soon.

Some gay men and women become alienated from their families of origin if their relatives disapprove of their sexual identity. In such cases, they may have little contact with family members. Aware that they cannot count on their own families for support, they plan for aging by creating a support system. They typically live within a network of friends, significant others, and selected biological family members, which may offer the kind of mutual support a family system can provide.

198

in intergenerational conflict between his/her parents and grandparents. Children may become caught in conflicts of loyalty between their parents and their grandparents, and if visitation is granted, the conflicts may continue. Children who are already experiencing distress because their parents are divorcing may thus become mired in further legal conflict.

Relatively few states permit grandparents to petition for visitation under any circumstances. Usually petitions are allowed only in connection with certain triggering conditions: when the child's natural family has been disrupted through death or divorce; when a parent is declared unfit; or when the grandparent has had custody of the child in the past. If family relations are harmonious, then grandparents have no need to petition the courts. Thus, virtually all cases of petition reach the courts over the objections of the child's custodial parent. The benefit of visitation to the child must then be weighed against the harm that may come from placing a child in the center of familial conflict (Myers and Perrin, 1993). This is a judgment that the court is often poorly prepared to make. Because legislative guidelines on these issues are vague, judges often rely instead on their own intuitive assessments of the family. The result is unreliable decisions made on a case-by-case basis.

Granting grandparents the right to petition the courts also raises questions about how deeply the legal system should intervene in the family. The threat of a lawsuit alters the leverage in family disputes in favor of grandparents over parents. Parents who are in the midst of a divorce or who have suffered the loss of a spouse through death are financially and emotionally vulnerable and less prepared to take on a court battle. The more fundamental issue, however, is whether family relationships should be determined by the legal system or remain a private matter. The June 6, 2000, U.S. Supreme Court decision giving parents the right to make decisions regarding the care and custody of their children is likely to reduce the number of petitions filed by grandparents.

What Do You Think?

1. In your family, has the death, divorce, or remarriage of a parent separated the grandparents from their grandchildren? If so, how did the grandparents handle the situation?
2. Should the legal system intrude into family relationships? If so, under what conditions?

Not all gay men and women are alienated from family. Often they have special roles in their families of origin. They might be the caretaker for an aging parent because they are unmarried and geographically mobile. They may also have more disposable income to help with the care of an aging parent because they have no financial responsibilities for children. And they might provide counseling and emotional support (Kimmel, 1992).

FRIENDS AND SOCIAL SUPPORT SYSTEMS

Friendships are especially meaningful in old age. They form a central part of an individual's social support network. Yet unlike family interactions that may involve daily needs and routine tasks, friendships are dictated by pleasure. The unique quality of friendships allows people to transcend

Some gay women establish long-term relationships with a partner or companion.

mundane daily realities. Although people consistently list family members as close and intimate members of their network, they name friends as people they most enjoy spending time with. They also say that they are most likely to engage in leisure activities with friends and that friends have the greatest impact on their well-being. Friends are important for an individual's morale, for providing affection and emotional support, and for being there to help out spontaneously when needs arise (Antonucci and Ayikama, 1995).

Patterns of Friendship

Having a close friend significantly adds to life satisfaction for both men and women. What do friends do for each other? In one study people who were 85 or older described their friendship patterns. Table 8–3 reports the results of this study. It shows that more than half of the women and 38 percent of the

men had a close friend, even though many had lost a friend recently. A common refrain was, "I am outliving all my friends." Many of the men and women had made new friends recently, often through contacts at churches or senior centers. Most had weekly contact with their friends (Johnson and Barer, 1997).

Friends occasionally provide instrumental help in performing basic tasks of daily living such as providing transportation or shopping. Men were more likely than women to share a laugh with friends; women were more likely than men to confide in their friends. Another study of 60 women over age 65 found that they viewed the exchange of companionship as one of the basic functions of interaction with friends. Close friends were listeners, people who confided in one another. As one woman noted, "I think you need family *and* friends (Armstrong and Goldsteen, 1990). The giving and receiving of love and affirmation is one of the most

Table 8-3	Friendship Patterns by Gender		
	Men (n = 26)	*Women (n = 85)*	*Total (n = 111)*
Friendship involvement			
A close friend	38%	57%	53%
Weekly contact	77	78	78
Satisfied with friends	54	43	45
Lost friend, past year	59	42	47
New friend 65+	54	68	64
New friend 85+	31	49	45
Source			
Neighborhood	31	65	57
Associations	77	58	63
Family	8	20	15
Work	31	10	15
Functions of friendships			
Confide in	—	15	12
Share a laugh	54	42	45
Household help	4	5	5
Transportation	8	14	13
Caregiver	—	4	3
Potential caregiver	8	—	3

Source: Johnson and Barer (1997:105).

important components of friendship, and it is something that can be maintained even among the most severely disabled individuals, as the following story makes clear:

Mrs. White was 78 when she became friends with Mrs. Smith. When Mrs. Smith's husband died two years later, she and Mrs. Smith became best friends and confidants. . . . If one feels lonely, she calls up the other to join her for lunch or dinner. This is possible because they are neighbors, and even though Mrs. White has very poor vision, she can still walk over to Mrs. Smith's house. . . . They share many meals and laughter. (Bould, Sanborn, and Reif, 1989)

Research suggests that friendships change over the life course. Although some studies find that people have fewer friends when they are old, the nature of those relationships may be more intimate.

In some cases, people maintain the same friendship for decades. Francis (1990) recorded the life history narratives of five women who began work at the Metropolitan Housing Authority during the 1930s and remained friends over a lifetime. Their shared experiences and the common frame of reference that resulted created a bond of shared understanding and affirmation. In midlife all were involved with work and family responsibilities, leaving little time for leisurely friendship activities. Despite the constraints of busy lives, they helped each other through such crises as illness, the loss of a spouse, and divorce. At the time of the interviews, all were retired and could now enjoy their lifelong friendships more fully. They socialized at a group dinner every few weeks and spoke to each other frequently on the phone. Through their lifelong friendship, they saw their own biographies reflected. As they reminisced about their common experiences, they valued the assurance that their friendships were based on complete acceptance of who they were.

Widowhood frequently changes the composition of the friendship network. Widows often report feeling uncomfortable socializing with couples and instead create a new group of friends consisting of other single women (Van den Hoonaard, 1994).

Dating in Later Life

Men and women may also establish intimate relationships in later life. This is more difficult for women because of the shortage of older men. Even so, many older people do date after widowhood or divorce. Kris Bulcroft and Richard Bulcroft (1985) interviewed men and women over age 60 who belonged to a singles club. Unlike young adults who most often meet a dating partner through a friend, most of their subjects met through that club or another organization, such as the American Legion. Both men and women initially felt awkward returning to dating, and the setting of a club may have made reentry to the dating scene more comfortable.

Many of the behaviors that older people described on a date reflected the historical traditions of their age cohort. Men were expected to pick up their date, to drive, and to pay the expenses, except in long-term dating relationships, in which the Dutch treat arrangement was more common. Asking for a date was a male prerogative. None of the men had ever been asked for a date, and none of the women had ever asked a man for a date.

While most of the subjects hoped that dating would lead to marriage, they also stressed the pragmatic side of the dating relationship. Both men and women enjoyed the companionship, and women were also likely to stress the romantic aspects of dating.

It should be readily apparent that the family is the core of the social support system. Families provide emotional support and instrumental help in managing activities of daily living. They protect the elderly from social isolation and help them adapt to the challenges of old age associated with retirement, health crises, and widowhood.

Chapter Resources

LOOKING BACK

1. **What is a social support system, and what effect do gender and family structure have on it?** *A social support system is the network of relatives and friends who provide emotional and instrumental support. Support systems create a convoy, which follows people over the life course. Women have more extensive social support networks than men and thus have more of the benefits they provide but also more of the strains. Some older people lack a family support network, either because their children have moved away or because they have no children or have never married. Among the never married elderly, other kin often play the role typically reserved for children. The increase in life expectancy over the past century has created a bean pole family structure, expanding the potential social support system of aging people to include four or even five generations.*

2. **How do older Americans compare to other Americans in marital status?** *Elderly women are significantly more likely than younger women to be single, simply because they live longer than men. And because they tend to marry older men, they are not likely to remarry after being widowed.*

3. **How does marital satisfaction change over the life course?** *Studies of marital satisfaction over the life course consistently show a decline during the child-rearing years. In part, the decline during the child-rearing years is caused by role strain. As the children leave home, marital satisfaction rises, peaking in the retirement years. The later-life satisfaction peak may also be a function of divorce—that is, those who remain married are the survivors. Still, the research is consistent enough to suggest that marriage is very satisfying for most people in old age.*

4. **How do sibling relationships change in later life?** *There is a life course pattern to sibling relationships. Many siblings feel close as young children, then drift apart to attend to the needs of their own families. As siblings grow older, they often become close once again. Siblings mostly provide emotional support but some, especially sisters, also care for each other in old age.*

5. **What factors influence parent–child relationships in later life, and what effect does divorce have on these relationships?** *Relationships established earlier in life affect the quality of interaction between parents and children in later life. Children who recall their childhood in a positive way are more concerned about their aging parents than those who perceived parental rejection. People who have been divorced have less contact with their adult children and report less positive interaction than those who remain married. Losing touch with children after a divorce is especially a problem for men.*

6. **What factors influence the grandparent–grandchild relationship in later life, and what effect does divorce have on this relationship?** *The relationship between parents and their children is often passed on to the grandchildren. When parents and grandparents are close, the grandchildren see their grandparents more often and feel closer to them. When parents divorce, the grandparent–grandchild relationship is affected. The paternal grandparents are most likely to lose contact with their grandchildren. Divorce does not necessarily mean a severing of familial ties, however, for some parents remain close to their former daughters-in-law. With the divorce and remarriage of parents, family ties may multiply.*

7. **What kinds of social support do older gay men and women depend on?** *Some gay men and women become alienated from their families if family members disapprove of their lifestyles. They may plan for aging by creating a support system of friends and significant others. However, many gay men and women play special roles in their own families, as caretakers of aging parents.*

8. **Is friendship a good source of support in later life?** *Friends form a special part of an individual's support network. Whereas family relationships are dictated by obligations and responsibilities, friendships are voluntary, pleasurable, and the primary source of companionship.*

THINKING ABOUT AGING

1. On balance, should the trend toward verticalization of the family system have a positive or negative effect on the aged? Explain your reasoning.

2. Studies have shown that men derive greater emotional support from their marriages than do women. As gender roles change over time, would you expect the gender difference in perceived emotional support to change? Why or why not?

3. When couples divorce, they must decide who will be responsible for the care of their children. Should they also agree on who will care for their parents, if the need arises?

4. Should aging grandparents who are raising their grandchildren receive some help from social welfare agencies? If so, what kind of help would be appropriate?

5. What happens to the aged when the social support system breaks down?

6. What can be done to strengthen the social support systems of elderly people who are slowly becoming isolated?

KEY TERMS

bean pole family structure 179

companionate grandparenting 194

convoy model of social relations 178

extended family 179

family life cycle 181

generations 180

grandparent career 196

intergenerational solidarity 188

involved grandparenting 194

nuclear family 179

psychologic fatigue 184

remote grandparenting 194

social support system 178

support bank 178

theory of intergenerational solidarity 186

verticalization 179

EXPLORING THE INTERNET

Note: While all the URLs listed were current as of the printing of this book, these sites often change. Please check our website www.mhhe.com/quadagno for updates.

1. CNN offers a great deal of information on many topics in *World Report Magazine*. Go to (http://www-cgi.cnn.com/WORLD/world.report/index8.23.html) and read the article titled "Global Graying Leads to Social Strains" by Kevin Grieves. Then answer the following questions:

   a. Where in the world is the number of elderly people increasing most rapidly?
   b. What is the United Nations doing to bolster social support for senior citizens in the developing world?
   c. What action is the Filipino government considering to ease the plight of elderly Filipinos?

2. The Grandparenting Foundation (http://www.grandparenting.org/) is a nonprofit organization whose mission is to raise grandparent consciousness. The foundation also provides information on state laws and grandparent visitation rights.

   Go to the foundation's website. On the left side of the home page under shortcuts, click on "GP Visitation & Laws" and scroll down the page until you see Grandparent Visitation Statutes. Answer the following questions:

   a. What are the seven criteria that are important in considering grandparent visitation rights?

   Scroll down the page further until you see the state in which you live.

   b. Which of the seven criteria apply to grandparent visitation rights in your state?

   Continue scrolling down the page until you see the Visitation Rights Enforcement Act.

   c. When was this act signed into law?
   d. What rights does the act guarantee to grandparents?

Living Arrangements

This couple shops for ice cream at their neighborhood grocery store.

Looking Ahead

1. How do an extended family's living arrangements change in response to the changing needs of different generations?
2. With whom do most older people live?
3. What kind of housing do older people have, and what housing problems do they face?
4. What are the benefits and drawbacks of shared housing, board and care homes, and assisted living facilities?
5. What is a continuing care retirement community, and what is life in such a community like for an older person?

dward "O" is an elderly tenant of a rundown hotel in a deteriorating Chicago neighborhood. A World War II veteran, he has worked at various jobs, from shipping clerk to salesman. His life has been a constant struggle for financial survival. Once married, Edward divorced in 1973 and now has no contact with anyone in his family. Recently, after struggling with a bone disease, he was admitted to a veteran's hospital, where both his legs were amputated. He now spends his days sitting in the hotel lobby or, on

nice days, on the sidewalk outside, watching people go by (Rollinson, 1990). He is afraid that he will soon be unable to manage on his own, because he has no way to get help. (See the "Diversity in the Aging Experiences" feature later in this chapter.)

Marge and Ben Sayer live in a sunny two-bedroom condominium in a retirement community. Marge is taking a course in financial management; Ben sings in a men's chorus. They eat their meals with friends they have made in the community, and they play cards with them in the evenings. If either should develop a health problem, they will probably be able to remain where they are. The community has nurses on call, and assisted living arrangements are available for people who need help.

As those two stories show, the living arrangements of older adults are critically important to their quality of life and well-being and often determine whether they are able to remain independent. The aged's arrangements are not stable but shift in response to their changing needs (Wilmoth, 1998). Older people who live alone are more likely to fear an emergency than those who live in a planned community, and they are at higher risk of placement in a nursing home. In the first part of this chapter, we will explore the issues confronting older people who remain in their own homes and communities. Then we will consider the alternative living arrangements available to those who wish to live in a communal setting with others of their age group.

HOUSEHOLD STRUCTURE

When her husband died, Ida Harper, age 71, moved from the small town in upstate New York where she had lived all her life to Atlanta, Georgia. Although she left behind a network of siblings, nieces, nephews, and cousins, the move brought her closer to her daughter and grandchildren, whom she sees now on a weekly basis. Because Ida's eyesight is poor, she no longer drives, but she has no transportation problems. Her daughter takes her to the doctor's office, to church, and on errands. Ida's social life, however, is centered not on her daughter but on her close friend Nancy, a widow who lives two apartments away. Every Monday, Ida and Nancy go grocery shopping and then have lunch together at a restaurant.

Ida Harper's living arrangements are typical of those of many older Americans. Sociologists who have studied the topic have found that the aged maintain close ties with younger generations, even though they may not live with them.

Ida Harper's life is a good illustration of the **theory of intergenerational solidarity,** which states that over time, a family will adjust its living arrangements to reflect the changing needs and resources of different generations. Early in the life course, the economic needs of adult children determine their relative proximity to their parents. Later in the life course, the parents' economic and health needs influence how close their children live to them (Spitze and Logan, 1990b; Silverstein and Litwak, 1993). Researchers have identified three phases in the parent–child life course in terms of proximity of living arrangements. Children live with or near their parents before they reach age 25. Then there is a period of separation; children marry or move away in pursuit of education and employment. Healthy elders may also move away from their children to a retirement destination. In later life, however, when aging parents become ill or disabled, they move nearer to their children. Thus, families reconstitute themselves in later life, not necessarily in intergenerational households but through close contact and frequent visits (Silverstein, 1995).

These shifting living arrangements are influenced by social class in a variety of ways. If economic conditions are good, children from working-class families are more likely than middle-class children to take jobs near home and remain close to their parents in young adulthood. Middle-class children, by contrast, often move far from their parents, for educational or employment reasons. But when middle-class parents face a health crisis, they may move near their children. Even then, however, they rely less on their children and more on friends and on purchased services than do working-class parents. As high-paid factory jobs become scarcer, it may become more difficult for children from working-class families to remain in their hometowns. Then, compared to more affluent elders, working-class parents may have smaller support networks at home and less ability to move to be near their children (Greenwell and Bengtson, 1997). Although the proportion of older people who live with their children increases with age, it never gets very high (Treas, 1995a).

Older Americans' living arrangements are also influenced by their gender and by race and ethnicity. Older women are much more likely than older men to live alone. The great majority of men 65 and older (72 percent) live with their wives; only 40 percent of women live with their husbands (see Figure 9–1).

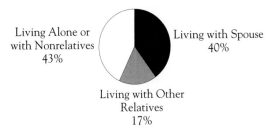

Figure 9-1 Gender Differences in Older Americans' Living Arrangements.

Living Arrangements of Males 65 Years and Over, 1995

Living Alone or with Nonrelatives 20%

Living with Other Relatives 8%

Living with Spouse 72%

Living Arrangements of Females 65 Years and Over, 1995

Living Alone or with Nonrelatives 43%

Living with Spouse 40%

Living with Other Relatives 17%

Source: U.S. Department of Housing and Urban Development (1999).

In contrast to the United States, where three-generation households are uncommon, cultural values in many other countries dictate the formation of intergenerational households. For a description of how the living arrangements of the elderly vary from one country to the next, see "Aging around the World."

Table 9–1 shows older Americans' living arrangements by race, ethnic origin, and gender. Older white women are most likely to live alone; older white men are most likely to live with a spouse. In general, women are more likely than men to live with other relatives, an arrangement that is most common among Hispanics. Forty-six percent of Hispanic and 41 percent of black women over age 75 live with a relative.

What explains these racial and ethnic differences in living arrangements? Interpreting the patterns among Hispanic Americans is difficult because the label "Hispanic" covers people of widely different backgrounds. Among those who are labeled "Hispanic" are Mexican Americans, who constitute 60 percent of those of Spanish descent; Puerto Ricans, 12 percent; and Cuban Americans, 5 percent. The high percentage of Mexican Americans who live with children or other relatives reflects a cultural tradition of extended kin relationships. In Mexico, the fundamental family unit is not the nuclear family of parents and children, but what

Table 9-1 U.S. Household Composition by Race, Ethnic Origin, and Gender among Persons 65 and Older

	Whites Living:			African Americans Living:			Hispanics Living:		
	Alone	*With Spouse*	*With Other Relatives*	*Alone*	*With Spouse*	*With Other Relatives*	*Alone*	*With Spouse*	*With Other Relatives*
Male									
65–74	11%	80%	6%	29%	57%	8%	10%	75%	11%
75+	20	69	7	34	43	18	13	67	18
Female									
65–74	35	53	12	40	29	30	23	46	30
75+	52	24	19	42	12	41	31	20	45

Source: U.S. Bureau of the Census (2002a).

Aging around the World

LIVING ARRANGEMENTS OF THE AGED IN OTHER CULTURES

In the United States older people rarely live with their adult children, but in many other cultures children are expected to care for their aged parents. In Muslim countries most aging parents live with their children. For example, in Kuwait 89 percent of women and 94 percent of

In some countries, most elderly people live with their children.

men live in households with at least one son or daughter (Shah et al., 2003). In Africa it is common for adult children and grandchildren to move into their elderly parents' household, but in Asia it is more common for elderly parents to move into the homes of their children (Bongaarts and Zimmer, 2002).

What explains these differences in living arrangements across cultures? Modernization theory (described in Chapter 2) links the extended family household to low levels of economic development. In traditional societies, the elderly live with their children in large extended family units for economic reasons. But with modernization, children move to urban areas, leaving older people behind in isolated rural areas (Burgess, 1960). Yet modernization theory cannot explain why extended family households were never common in the United States or England, or why families in Italy, which is fully modernized, maintain a strong tradition of intergenerational living (Laslett, 1976). Clearly, economic development alone cannot explain preferred living arrangements.

Another theory links intergenerational living arrangements to inheritance patterns. In some cultures, the **stem family** pattern of inheritance predominates. Under this system, parents live with a married child, usually the oldest son, who then inherits their property when they die. The stem family system was once common in Japan, but changes in inheritance laws, as well as broader social changes wrought by industrialization and urbanization, have undermined the tradition. In 1960 about 80 percent of Japanese over 65 lived with their children; by 1990 only 60 percent did—a figure that is still high by U.S. standards but has been declining steadily (Morioka, 1996). In Korea too, traditional living arrangements are eroding: the percentage of aged Koreans who live with a son declined from 77 percent in 1984 to 50 percent 10 years later. Although most elderly Koreans still expect to live with a son, their adult children do not expect to live with their children when they grow old (Kim and Rhee, 2000).

Although cultural values influence elders' living arrangements, large-scale social change caused by war or migration can erode these traditions. Vietnamese culture, for example, is influenced by Confucianism, which places strong emphasis on respect for elders. After the Vietnam War ended, many middle-aged and elderly Vietnamese migrated to the United States with their families or joined relatives through a family reunification program. In the United States, they found that the large, extended family system that had provided a clear role for them in Vietnam had broken down. Playing the traditional role of elder—that of offering advice and wisdom to younger relatives—was difficult for them when their counsel was based on cultural values foreign to their new homeland. As their children learned new skills, obtained an education, and got good jobs, many elderly Vietnamese remained at home, with no clear position in the family and little opportunity to participate in the labor force. Instead, the traditional roles were reversed, as they came to depend on their children and grandchildren for cultural guidance (Yee, 1994). Similar problems have been reported among Russian Jewish immigrants (Thomas, Sokolovsky, and Feinberg, 1996:65).

What Do You Think?

1. Did immigration to the United States erode the status and role of elders in your family? If so, describe the change in your relatives' worlds.
2. Why do you think urbanization and industrialization have encouraged different generations to live separately?

sociologists call a "grandfamily"—an extended family unit of grandparents, adult children and spouses, and grandchildren (Cherlin, 1996). In the United States, these three-generational links remain a feature of Mexican American family life.

For African Americans, racial differences in living arrangements are partly a function of demography: There are more single people (divorced, widowed, never married) among the African American elderly than among the white elderly (Haines, 1996). Racial differences in living arrangements also stem from cultural practices. Among poor black families, social support often comes from an extended kin network—an alliance of individuals who are linked socially and economically through the regular exchange of goods and services (Queen, Habenstein, and Quadagno, 1985).

Some older Americans continue to live in the homes they occupied in their younger years; others move long distances to enjoy better weather or be nearer family. In the next section we examine the reasons why some people leave their homes and communities while others age in place.

To Move or To Stay?

Geographic Mobility

Each year thousands of retirees migrate to the Sun Belt states of Florida, Arizona, Nevada, New Mexico, and North Carolina. Between 1970 and 1985 these five states witnessed a 75 percent increase in the proportion of residents over age 65 (Siegel, 1993). The movement of older people to the Sun Belt, called a **migratory stream,** is diffuse in origin. Those who enter the stream come from many states, cities, and towns. Their destinations, however, are highly specific: places with a warm climate and reasonably priced retirement housing (Longino, 1990).

Other states, such as those in the declining industrial area called the Rust Belt (Michigan, Ohio, and Illinois) and the farming regions of the Corn Belt and Great Plains, also have a high proportion of older people, but for a different reason. Lack of job opportunities has chased younger people away (Bean et al., 1994) from these states, aging their populations. The term used to describe the natural aging of an area's population, which is often accompanied by the out-migration of young adults, is *aging in place* (Golant and LaGreca, 1994).

A net increase in elderly migration and in aging in place will increase the proportion of older people in a region. In 2000, nine states had more than 1 million elderly: California, Florida, New York, Pennsylvania, Texas, Illinois, Ohio, Michigan, and New Jersey (see Figure 9–2). In some of these states, a high percentage of the population is over 65. In Florida, people over 65 are 18.4 percent of the population. In Iowa, fewer than one-half million older people make up 15.4 percent of the population (U.S. Bureau of the Census, 2002b). The former pattern is created by a migratory stream, the latter by aging in place.

Aging in Place

Aging in place is "an accommodation between an aging individual and his or her environment over time, with the physical location of the individual being the only constant" (Lawton, 1990:287). Most older people prefer to remain in their own neighborhoods (American Association of Retired Persons, 1990). Overall, older people are less likely to move to a new home or community than younger people. The majority choose not to move but to age in place—a choice that is sometimes a problem. Aging in place can mean occupying deteriorating housing that is poorly designed to meet the needs of those with limited physical mobility. To a large extent, then, aging in place results from continued home ownership among the elderly.

Home Ownership

The majority of older people want to stay in their own home's and communities, where they have friendships and support networks. Approximately 95 percent of people over age 65 reside in a community setting, most in their own homes. Indeed, rates of home ownership among the aged are at a historic high. In 2002, 81 percent of Americans aged 65 and older were home owners (see Figure 9–3) (U.S. Bureau of the Census, 2003). Most older home owners (72 percent) occupy single-family homes; only 6 percent live in mobile homes (Hobbs and Damon, 1996:4–26). Rates of home ownership are lower among single women who live alone, no doubt a reflection of the sale of a home at widowhood.

Figure 9-2   Percentage of the Population Age 65 and Older, by State, 2000.

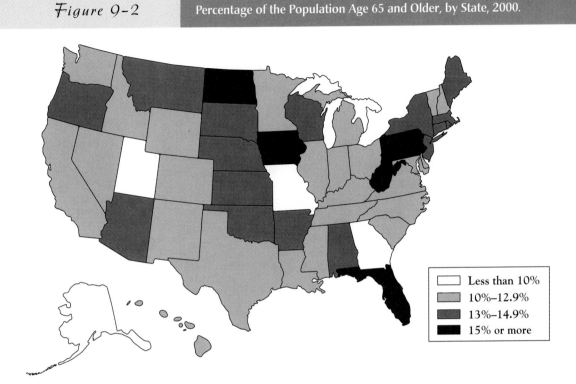

Less than 10%
10%–12.9%
13%–14.9%
15% or more

Source: U.S. Bureau of the Census (2002b).

Figure 9-3   Home Ownership Rates by Age of Householder, 2002.

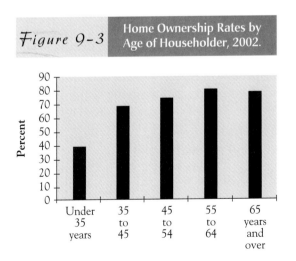

Source: U.S. Bureau of the Census (2003).

The high rates of home ownership among older people obscure significant differences among certain subgroups. Etta and Henry Jones live in south-central Los Angeles in a predominantly black neighborhood. They purchased their modest three-bedroom home with the equity from their first home. From their combined 80 years of steady work, the couple can anticipate a stable income, pensions, health insurance, and sufficient assets when they retire. Indeed, thanks to good timing in the housing market and modest but regular savings, at age 62 they have compiled a net worth of nearly half a million dollars. Yet if they had lived in a white neighborhood where housing prices have skyrocketed, their assets would now be worth millions (Oliver and Shapiro, 1995). Although 79 percent of older whites are home owners, older African Americans and Hispanics have much lower rates of home ownership: 64 percent and 59 percent, respectively (Golant, 1996). Some of the

| Figure 9-4 | Elderly Home Ownership by Selected Characteristics, 1995. |

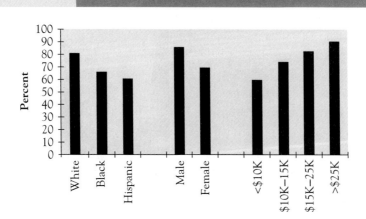

Source: U.S. Department of Housing and Urban Development (1999).

disparity is due to racial discrimination in housing, which has prevented members of minority groups from purchasing homes (see Chapter 17). Members of minority groups are also more likely than whites to have low incomes, and home ownership is linked to income. As Figure 9–4 shows, in 1995 only 61 percent of older people with incomes below $10,000 owned their own homes, compared to 91 percent of those with incomes above $25,000. While households with incomes above $25,000 are not necessarily affluent, 61 percent is still high compared to the percentage of low-income people in other age groups who are home owners (U.S. Department of Housing and Urban Development, 1999). The good news is that home ownership has been growing rapidly among racial and ethnic minorities, a trend that is likely to reduce inequality in the future (U.S. Bureau of the Census, 2003).

Although the majority of older people live in high-quality housing that they can afford, millions live in substandard housing. What should be done to ensure that all older people live in safe, affordable housing?

Housing Quality

The ability of the frail elderly to remain in their own homes depends in part on the quality of their housing. As a general rule, the housing of elderly

Americans is basically sound; only 3 percent of housing units occupied by an older American have severe physical problems, and only 5 percent have moderate problems (Hobbs and Damon, 1996). The vast majority of homes occupied by the elderly have complete kitchens and baths, and most have a washing machine, a telephone, and air conditioning.

Still, a home can be a financial burden. Since homes owned by the elderly are typically old, they often need costly repairs. Some are located in aging neighborhoods that are no longer safe or convenient. Many also have architectural barriers, such as steep stairs or deep bathtubs. More than a million older people could benefit from modifications to their homes that would promote self-care and safe, independent living (Struyk and Katsura, 1987). "An Issue for Public Policy" discusses some ways to help older people remain in their own homes.

Housing problems of the aged   Not surprisingly, poor-quality housing is concentrated among the poorest elderly—those who live in rural areas, belong to a minority group, or live alone (Pynoos and Redfoot, 1995). Poor-quality housing is a problem especially for people who occupy rental properties. Among older renters, nearly 6 percent of whites, 16.6 percent of Hispanics, and 21.2 percent of African Americans live in inadequate housing (Golant and LaGreca, 1994). In some inner-city neighborhoods,

An Issue for Public Policy

IMPROVING THE HOUSING OF OLDER AMERICANS

Almost two-thirds of older Americans with physical limitations live alone. Often, these frail elderly can remain in their own homes if minor modifications are made. One inexpensive improvement that can reduce the risk of a fall is a grab bar or handrail in the shower or bathtub. Wide doorways that can accommodate a wheelchair can also make daily life easier, as can ramps, stair lifts, and push bars on doors. As Figure 9–5 shows, only a small percentage of the elderly have these modifications in their homes.

Traditionally, efforts to help low-income people modify their homes have taken the form of government grants and loans. Another approach is to allow older people to tap the equity in their homes to finance health and safety improvements. Equity loans work like a **reverse mortgage**; they allow people with paid-up mortgages on their homes to sell their homes back to the bank in exchange for a monthly payment (Rasmussen, Megbolugbe, and Morgan, 1995). The extra income can then be used to pay for home improvements.

What Do You Think?

1. Have your elderly relatives' homes been modified to accommodate their changing needs? If so, describe the modifications. How effective are they, and how much did they cost?
2. If you were a government policy maker, what steps would you take to help the aged remain in their own homes?

the movement of young working-class families to the suburbs has left dense pockets of poverty populated mainly by the elderly (Wilson, 1996). An aged African American woman who lived on the south side of Chicago for more than 40 years described to William Julius Wilson how her neighborhood had changed in that time:

I've been here since March 23, 1953. When I moved in, the neighborhood was intact. It was intact with homes, beautiful homes, mini mansions, with stores, laundromats, with cleaners. . . . We had drugstores. We had hotels. We had doctors over on Thirty-Ninth Street. We had doctors' offices in the neighborhood. We had the middle class and upper middle class. It has gone from affluent to where it is today. And I would like to see it come back, that we can have some of the things we had. Since I came in young, and I'm a senior citizen now, I would like to see some of the things come back so

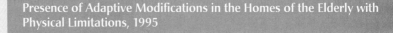

Figure 9-5   **Presence of Adaptive Modifications in the Homes of the Elderly with Physical Limitations, 1995**

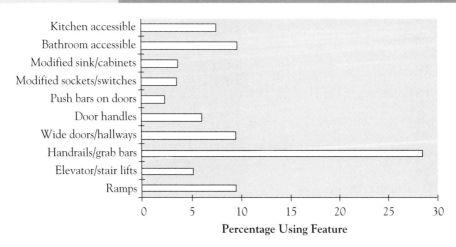

Source: U.S. Department of Housing and Urban Development (1999).

I can enjoy them like we did when we first came in. (Wilson, 1996:3)

A deteriorating living environment can have a negative effect on the physical and mental health of elderly residents, for several reasons (Krause, 1996). Many studies have shown that sanitation in dilapidated buildings is often inadequate, and contributes to the spread of diseases. Poor upkeep of stairs, halls, and elevators can also increase the risk of falls. Thus elderly people who live in rundown buildings tend to become physically and socially isolated (Krause, 1998).

At the very bottom of the rental market are **single room occupancy hotels,** commonly known as **SROs.** Also described as "flophouses" (Eckert, 1980), these apartment dwellings or old hotels are usually located in dilapidated and deteriorating inner-city areas. A typical SRO unit is a single, sparsely furnished room with limited cooking space; bathrooms are communal. "Diversity in the Aging Experience" describes life in an SRO in Chicago.

The homeless aged   Early studies of the homeless population in the United States focused on male alcoholics living in cheap hotels like SROs. Today, a growing number of homeless people live in shelters or on the streets. The Bowery, a

Older people who live in deteriorating neighborhoods tend to be more physically and socially isolated and to be at greater risk of having poor health.

Diversity in the Aging Experience

LIFE IN A SINGLE ROOM OCCUPANCY HOTEL

In a deteriorating Chicago neighborhood, the buildings are rundown, the sidewalks poorly maintained, and the gutters filled with broken beer and liquor bottles. The single-family homes in this part of the city have been converted into rooming houses, or SROs. There are 19 of them in the neighborhood, renting rooms by the week or the month. Their tenants are drifters, drug addicts, and the aged poor, who for various reasons have few family contacts or resources. The mean age of the elderly who reside here is 70. Most are extremely poor, with no savings and little education.

The rooms they inhabit are small, sparsely furnished, dark, dirty, and bug-infested—an unsuitable environment for aged people who may need help with daily activities. Although all have heaters, few have fans, which makes the rooms, many of whose windows are stuck shut with old paint, unbearably hot in the summer. Because most of the rooms have no stoves, the elderly residents cook on hot plates. Torn carpeting in the hallways poses a hazard to tenants with canes and wheelchairs. The elevators often do not work, forcing many residents to remain in their rooms.

Although the lobbies are cold, rundown, and dark, many aged residents can be found seated there on dilapidated couches, watching the activity around the front desk. Even in this bleak and inhospitable environment, friendships and social support systems develop. Some tenants sit outside on nice days, where friends and neighbors stop to talk. But most of the social ties formed in these communities are fleeting and ephemeral, and the dangers elderly residents face are numerous.

What Do You Think?

1. Do you know anyone who lives in an SRO? If so, describe the conditions in the building.
2. Should society allow the aged—or anyone—to live in substandard conditions like the ones described here? What steps might government officials take to improve the living conditions in SROs?

Source: Rollinson (1990).

16-block area in lower Manhattan, once contained numerous flophouses and missions, just a few of which remain. On any given night, each flophouse shelters anywhere from 34 to 500 men or more in 4-foot by 7-foot cubicles with a bed, locker, and night table. Other men sleep in "ticket hotels," large dormitories that are dimly lit, dirty, and crowded (Cohen et al., 1997).

Because homeless men and women look and act like people who are 10 or 15 years older, studies of the homeless usually count anyone who is 50 or older as "elderly." Estimates of the proportion of the homeless in the United States who are "elderly" range from 15 to 28 percent of those who live in shelters and as high as 50 percent of those who live on the street and stay occasionally in flophouses. In one study of homeless men and women in St. Louis, approximately 13 percent of the men and 3 percent of the women were found to be age 50 or older (DeMallie, North, and Smith, 1997). Substance abuse was a significant problem among the homeless of all ages. Older homeless people were more likely than others to be alcoholics; younger homeless people were more likely to be drug abusers. The researchers concluded that homelessness is a severe outcome of alcohol and drug disorders combined with other social problems. Though many older homeless people needed treatment for psychiatric disorders and substance abuse, as well as basic medical care, most were not receiving any services.

ALTERNATIVE LIVING ARRANGEMENTS

There are an increasing number of housing options for older people who may not be able to remain in their own houses because they need some help with activities of daily living or who are perfectly capable of living on their own but want the security of knowing that help is available if they need it. This section describes some of these alternative living arrangements.

Some older people move out of their homes when they retire. No longer constrained by their jobs, they want to live in a place with good weather and recreational facilities (Litwak and Longino, 1987). Others decide to move when they find daily life difficult to manage on their own.

Supportive housing is the general term for a variety of group housing options that offer elders assistance with daily living. Such facilities are designed to help residents stay in one place and delay or avoid the need for institutional care. Shared housing, board and care homes, assisted living, and continuing care retirement communities are all supportive housing arrangements. The services they offer residents vary widely (Blanchette, 1997).

Shared Housing

The **shared housing** movement began in 1953 with a Hartford, Connecticut, program called Project Homeshare. Over the next decade a number of shared housing programs were established around the country; by the 1980s, more than 400 were operating. Group homes are one type of shared housing arrangement in which residents have private rooms but share a common living space. These residences range from charming Victorian mansions to modern facilities built expressly for the purpose. Although most are exclusively for the elderly, some accept students, displaced homemakers, and working couples (Jaffe, 1989). Most group homes are sponsored by nonprofit agencies that own, lease, and manage the dwellings.

Another type of shared housing is the match-up program, in which a public agency recruits, screens, and matches home owners with suitable home sharers. This arrangement is particularly attractive to the elderly because it allows them to remain in their own homes (Jaffe, 1989). In a typical match-up, an older person shares his or her home with a home seeker, who receives the use of a private room and access to the kitchen and other common rooms.

Income, security, companionship, and service are among the reasons older people sign up for home-sharing arrangements (Jaffe, 1989). One study described three types of home sharers. First were active, healthy older people who wanted someone in their homes who would perform occasional services, such as snow shoveling. Typically, these home sharers charged reduced rent in exchange for such services. Second were elderly people with chronic diseases who needed help with cooking, shopping, and other routine errands. In these arrangements, home sharers offered free room and board in exchange for the boarders' help. Third were physically or mentally frail elderly who offered not only free room and board, but a monthly salary (Jaffe and Howe, 1988).

Although home sharing has been promoted as a solution to the long-term-care needs of the frail elderly, it has never fulfilled expectations. Many older home sharers wait until their health has seriously deteriorated to apply for live-in help. They then have trouble finding someone who is willing to provide the extensive care they need. Often the matches that are made are short-lived: The vast majority last less than three months, and only rarely does one last as long as a year (Jaffe and Howe, 1988). As funding sources for these programs have declined, the number of programs has leveled off; many have been discontinued (Liebig, 1998).

Board and Care Homes

Board and care homes provide meals, assistance with daily activities, and a supportive living environment to people who cannot survive on their own. These facilities range from small, unlicensed rooms in a residential setting to hotel-like arrangements housing 200 or more residents (Moon, 1989). They should not be confused with nursing homes. Though residents of board and care homes often need help with dressing, eating, toileting, bathing, and monitoring of medications, they do not need extensive medical care (McCoy and Conley, 1990).

The past two decades have seen a rapid increase in the number of board and care homes, for several reasons. One is the growing population of the old–old, who often need some help with daily activities. Another is the deinstitutionalization of people with mental illnesses, a process that began in the 1950s, when the treatment of mental patients was shifted from hospitals to community settings (Gronfein, 1985). Many formerly hospitalized mental patients have ended up in board and care homes when they have grown older. Finally, board and care homes have become an alternative living arrangement for people with developmental disabilities and low-income people with no other alternatives (Ruchlin and Morris, 1987).

Most board and care facilities are formerly private residences that now function as "mom and pop" operations with three or four clients. The typical board and care operator is a woman in her early 50s with a high school education or less and a low median annual income (Flint and Applebaum, 1993). A major source of funding for these residences is Supplemental Security Income (SSI), the federal income program for the aged, the blind, and the disabled poor (see Chapter 11). At about one-third the cost of a nursing home, board and care homes provide an alternative for people with limited resources (Moon, 1989).

Most residents of board and care homes are widowed white females. About half have been institutionalized in a facility for the mentally ill or mentally retarded. One study of these homes found that 88 percent of the residents were unmarried and 61 percent had no children. More than one-fourth of the residents had no close kin, one-third had only one regular caller or visitor, and one-fourth had no visitors at all (Morgan, Eckert, and Lyon, 1993). Another study found that 40 percent of residents had less than an eighth-grade education and their median income was below poverty level (Eckert and Lyon, 1991). In general, then, the residents of board and care homes are poor, socially isolated, and powerless.

A national survey of 205 board and care facilities paints a bleak picture of daily life there. Most of the residents spend their time in bed, watching television, or sitting and doing nothing (Dittmar, 1989). Many lack adequate care and conceal abuse (Tichenor, 1995). The most notorious case happened in the home of Dorothea Puente, a California operator who was accused of killing nine residents and burying their bodies in her garden (Tichenor, 1995). Other cases, while less dramatic, are equally disturbing. When the House Subcommittee on Health and Long Term Care held hearings on the quality of care in board and care homes in 1989, hundreds of abuses were exposed (U.S. House of Representatives, 1989a):

A grand jury in Brooklyn, New York, found that a board and care home operator had indiscriminately tranquilized residents to keep them quiet. (p. 61)

A network of at least seven personal care homes in Pittsburgh was accused of physically abusing elderly residents and draining them of their assets. One owner absorbed more than $65,000 belonging to a couple in their eighties and abused the husband while he was in her care. (p. 24)

In a Massachusetts rest home, patient areas were filthy, cluttered with trash, and reeking of urine.

Outdated medications with expiration dates as early as 1969 were still in use in the 1980s. (p. 20)

Although the federal Health Care Financing Administration enforces national standards for nursing homes, there are no national regulations for board and care homes. As a result, regulations vary widely from state to state. For example, in the 1980s fire alarms were found in 100 percent of facilities in Washington but only 21.9 percent of facilities in Texas (Dittmar, 1989). The first attempt to regulate board and care homes was the **Keys Amendment** to the Social Security Act (1976), which required states to establish and enforce standards for homes serving residents who receive SSI. The Older Americans Act of 1981 extended nursing home ombudsman programs (see Chapter 10) to board and care homes. As a result, the 1980s saw increased local and state regulation of these homes (Flint and Applebaum, 1993). But though regulation has expanded, it is still inadequate. Responsibility is divided among a number of different agencies, and followup varies tremendously from one state to the next.

Assisted Living

The most significant trend in housing for the elderly is the growth of **assisted living facilities (ALFs).** Much of the growth has occurred to meet the demand for an intermediate level of care—higher than the care typically provided at home but less than the care provided in a nursing home. Substantial overlap in the characteristics of some ALF residents and nursing home residents suggests that ALFs could effectively meet the care needs of at least some frail elders residing in nursing homes (Pruchno and Rose, 2000).

A key component of the ALF philosophy is the idea of aging in place. Assisted living residents and their families choose ALFs in the hope they will not have to make another move (Gorshe, 2000). To help their residents achieve this goal, most ALFs provide meals, personal care, limited medical assistance, housekeeping, utilities, social activities, transportation, and security. Many ALFs separate personal care from the basic package of services, charging residents who need personal care an additional sum. ALFs have a variety of options to retain residents who need services not provided by the facility. They can hire skilled nurses to provide care (a common option following surgery) or bring in outside home care services (Gorshe, 2000). Ideally, a facility adjusts its services and level of care to meet residents' changing needs, avoiding the discharge of a resident needing additional care to a nursing home (Chapin and Dobbs-Kepper, 2001).

However, a number of studies have found that an assisted living facility is not a permanent home but

Jennie Fuller in her senior housing apartment at Gateway Village, Salisbury, Maryland.

rather is another step along the continuum of long-term care. One national study found that residents stay in ALFs for an average of only 30.8 months. Researchers in Kansas investigated ALF admission, retention, and discharge policies. Chapin and Dobbs-Kepper (2001) found that the primary reason for discharge from Kansas ALFs was that residents' health care needs became too great. Residents were also likely to be discharged if they exhibited behavior problems or had a tendency to wander. Another study found that among ALF residents suffering from dementia, 48 percent were discharged within 25 months and 77 percent of discharge locations were nursing homes. Researchers found that most ALF transfers of residents with dementia were caused by depression, falling, or wandering (Kopetz et al., 2000). Thus, these studies suggest, an assisted living facility typically provides an intermediate level of care that follows home care and precedes nursing home admission.

There are currently between 30,000 and 65,000 ALFs in the United States. The majority of residents are female (74 percent) and white (97 percent). Residents tend to be more satisfied with small facilities with fewer than 30 residents than with large facilities with several hundred residents. They also are more likely to be satisfied with non-profit facilities than with for-profits. Because many nonprofits are sponsored by religious or fraternal organizations, residents may have ties to other residents before they move in. Nonprofits may also have more of an ethos of service (Sikorska, 1999).

Continuing Care Retirement Communities

About 8 percent of older people reside in a planned retirement community (Pynoos and Golant, 1996). Many of these are **continuing care retirement communities (CCRCs),** which grew out of the life care concept developed by religious groups for the care of aging lay people and clergy. Today a typical CCRC provides a continuum of housing arrangements and services, from independent living to assisted living and skilled nursing care. Most CCRCs ask residents to pay an up-front fee and a continuing monthly fee, which includes rent, utilities, one meal

a day, access to a health clinic, and transportation. A typical apartment in a CCRC consists of a single room with a bathroom and efficiency kitchen, though some of the newer, more expensive developments offer one and two bedroom apartments. Many communities also include on-site recreational facilities and social activities (Netting and Wilson, 1994).

A new type of CCRC, called an **independent living community,** offers many of the same amenities provided in other long-term care communities, together with activities geared toward a younger, healthier clientele. In addition to staples such as bingo, bridge, and shuffleboard, these communities offer spas, exercise rooms, tai chi classes, yoga, book clubs, educational seminars, and trips to the theater or symphony (McKinnon, 2000).

A move to a retirement community is a big step that starts with an often difficult decision and involves adjustment to new and usually more modest living quarters.

The decision to move   Some people are attracted to CCRCs because they know their needs will be met if they require intensive medical care. As their health declines, they can move from an independent unit to a unit that offers more services without leaving the community. Others choose CCRCs because they have come to feel isolated in their own homes. Many older people who live in single-family homes find managing and maintaining their homes to be quite difficult. The major precipitating events preceding a move into a CCRC include the feeling of being overwhelmed by housework and gardening, decreased ability to get around the neighborhood, or a catastrophe such as the death of one's spouse. Lack of transportation to the store or doctor's office is also a major problem for many older people (Young, 1998). Most often older people make the decision to move after discussing the issue with family and friends, though sometimes they are forced to do so by their families. In "In Their Own Words," two older women describe how they made the move to a retirement community.

Adjustment to the move   A move can be a stressful event at any time in the life course. It involves not only the loss of a home but also the loss of friends, community, and familiar surroundings.

In Their Own Words

Making the Move

An 81-year-old woman moved into a retirement community after consulting with her family, who helped her to find the right place and make the transition:

> I was having quite a time getting things together and then my sight failed. And here I was, and even cooking got to be hard to see where to turn on the heat and I couldn't shop unless I had a companion. So I thought to myself, life's too short to be frustrated every time you turn around. So I thought about it for six months and then started getting my stuff distributed. And then I called my family, and I said I have to do something. And my darling grandson found me this place and between them they all fixed it up pretty.

A 72-year-old woman who had been hospitalized for depression had a more difficult time with the move, which she felt she was forced to make:

> When you are depressed and can't face decisions, he, my son, was in a rather difficult position in some ways too because he felt that I should not live alone in that house. I mean, I don't want to draw any judgments on my son because I don't think he would have done it without feeling. They wanted to clear the house and get it rented and get me placed. In certain senses I feel put here.

Source: Young, (1998:157)

For elderly people who move from a house to a CCRC, a move usually means reduced living space, which forces them to give up many of the possessions they have accumulated throughout their lives. Sorting through these possessions is a physically taxing, emotionally exhausting, and time-consuming task. An 82-year-old woman who was preparing to move explains how hard it was to give up her life's possessions:

I finally arrived at the point . . . not to look too long at anything, to just let it go. . . . I had our wedding gift dishes in the basement, never been opened since we had lived in that house. Beautiful stuff . . . And I had saved all my grocery sacks and papers. . . . And of course all the jars. I used to can my own food. I had so many things in boxes. From umpteen years. (Young, 1998:157)

Some people adjust poorly to the move. Johnson and Barer conducted a study of the oldest–old—people

aged 85 or older—many of whom lived in some type of congregate housing. One retired Navy man explained his dissatisfaction with his new residence: "Before I came here, I was busy all the time. Now here I have nothing really to live for, because there is nothing to do" (Johnson and Barer, 1997:50). But most older people adjust quickly, make new friends, and find renewed satisfaction in life.

Friendship networks in CCRCs A variety of structured and unstructured activities provide opportunities for residents of CCRCs to form friendship networks. Meal time is the best opportunity to meet other residents. In Johnson and Barer's study, people formed close friendships with those they met at meals: "A group of us have formed a breakfast club, one man and three women. It's so much fun. We sit together at breakfast every morning. We live for that hour. It's wonderful. It makes the day begin very happy even though we go our own way afterwards" (Johnson and Barer, 1997:50). Similarly, in Perkinson and Rockemann's study of Riverdale Village in southeastern Pennsylvania, the evening meal was an important social event at which some residents took advantage of the opportunity to make new friends:

We always eat with different people. We do what we call "Riverdale Roulette" in the dining room. And you go in and you either start a table or finish a table. And that way you get to meet a lot of people. (Perkinson and Rockemann, 1996:166)

Others sat with the same people every night:

My husband and I eat with four other women. We've kind of settled into eating, a routine kind of eating at a six-top table in the Chesapeake Room every night, which I guess limits friendship because you're not sitting with other couples all the time. (Perkinson and Rockemann, 1996:166)

Friendships are frequently determined by marital status. Single women tend to become friends with other single women, and married couples with other married couples. At Riverdale Village, there was a distinct social division between the two groups. As one woman explained:

You find that here, a lot of couples stick together and a lot of single ladies stick together. I guess that's

normal. . . . I am friendly with some ladies that are still with a spouse, but the rest of them tend to keep together, which is fine. They have more in common. (Perkinson and Rockemann, 1996:167)

By helping to solve the problem of loneliness in old age and providing services that many older people need, CCRCs reduce the risk of institutionalization (Sloan, Shayne, and Conover, 1995). The main problem with CCRCs is that fewer than half of older people can find one they can afford. For the majority of older people, the entry fees and monthly maintenance costs are far too expensive. In a relatively inexpensive CCRC, the entry fee can range from $25,000 to $35,000 and the monthly maintenance fee $1,500 to $2,500. Many are considerably more costly, with entry fees as high as $500,000 and maintenance fees of $3,500 to $5,000 a month. Thus, economic resources have a major effect on the quality of life in old age.

As the proportion of people 85 or older continues to grow, the most important health care issue will be the providing of long-term care. In Chapter 10, we discuss the various ways, the long-term care needs of the frail elderly who have multiple chronic ailments are met.

Chapter Resources

LOOKING BACK

1. **How do an extended family's living arrangements change in response to the changing needs of different generations?** *As children grow up, they often move away from parents to establish their own family. Parents, too, may move away from children to a retirement home. As parents grow ill or disabled, they move closer to their children once again.*

2. **With whom do most older people live?** *Most older people prefer independent living, and most live in their own homes. High rates of home ownership among the elderly obscure differences by race and ethnic origin. African American and Hispanic elderly are less likely to own their own homes than whites. Gender also influences living arrangements. The majority of older men live with a spouse, but older women are more likely to live alone.*

   Although in the United States adult children do not typically live with their parents, most maintain regular and frequent contact with them. These relationships are important for the parents' physical and mental health. Parents who have close relationships with their children are less likely to be depressed or lonely. However, in many other countries children are expected to care for their aging parents, and cultural patterns dictate intergenerational households.

3. **What kind of housing do older people have, and what housing problems do they face?** *Although most older people live in sound and affordable housing, some reside in old homes that need repair or that have environmental barriers that make them unsafe. A deteriorating living environment can have a negative effect on physical and mental health.*

4. **What are the benefits and drawbacks of shared housing, board and care homes, and assisted living facilities?** *The concept of supportive housing refers to a range of alternative living arrangements that combine housing with long-term-care services. Supportive housing arrangements vary considerably in quality and affordability. Shared housing is an arrangement that pairs older people in various settings with others who need housing. Board and care homes provide a supportive living environment for people who cannot live on their own. Board and care residents are often poor and sometimes have developmental disabilities or psychological problems. Assisted living facilities provide many of the same services as board and care homes, but they cater to a more affluent clientele. They provide small apartments that include private baths, recreational facilities, and individualized care.*

5. **What is a continuing care retirement community, and what is life in such a community like for an older person?** *Continuing care retirement communities provide a continuum of housing alternatives ranging from independent living to nursing home care. People move into CCRCs to maintain their independence. Research shows that most residents of most CCRCs adjust quickly and remain healthier than counterparts who remain in the community.*

THINKING ABOUT AGING

1. Would families be better off if several generations lived together? List the benefits and drawbacks of such an arrangement for each generation.

2. Is it healthy for the aged to live alone? What health problems might be worsened by living alone?

3. Besides modifications to the home, what other measures might help elders who are aging in place?

4. Does the government have a moral obligation to prevent homelessness among the aged?

5. Many older people wait too long to adjust their living arrangements to their deteriorating health. What might be done to help them plan ahead?

KEY TERMS

aging in place 212

assisted living facility (ALF) 220

board and care home 219

continuing care retirement community (CCRC) 221

independent living community 221

Keys Amendment 220

migratory stream 212

reverse mortgage 215

shared housing 218

single room occupancy hotel (SRO) 216

stem family 211

supportive housing 218

theory of intergenerational solidarity 208

EXPLORING THE INTERNET

Note: While all the URLs listed were current as of the printing of this book, these sites often change. Please check our website www.mhhe.com/quadagno for updates.

1. Census data provide a great deal of information about people's living arrangements. BC Stats is the central statistical agency for the Canadian province of British Columbia (http://www.bcstats.gov.bc.ca/). Go to the agency's website and link to Census, then 1991 Census. Select "Living Arrangements of Seniors" and "Senior in Care" and answer the following questions:

   a. What percentage of seniors in British Columbia lived with their families in 1991?

   b. How many women aged 75 and older lived alone?

   c. In 1991, what percentage of females aged 75 and over were living with relatives? How did that percentage compare to the same figure in the 1980 census?

   d. In 1991, how many of every thousand older British Columbians were institutionalized? In 1980?

   e. How does the agency explain the decline in the institutionalization of seniors from 1980 to 1991?

2. The Administration on Aging (http://www.aoa.dhhs.gov/) is a site designed for older Americans and their families, as well as anyone who is interested in the elderly. Go to the organization's website and click on Professionals and then Statistics. Link to "A Profile of Older Americans: 2002" and read about living arrangements. After looking at the pie charts, answer the following questions:

   a. Where did the majority of noninstitutionalized older persons live in 2000?

   b. How many noninstitutionalized older persons lived alone in 2000?

   c. What percentage of men aged 65 and older lived with a spouse in 2000?

   d. What percentage of older women lived with relatives in 2000?

Chapter 10

Caring for the Frail Elderly

*D*aughters provide most of the care to elderly parents. Here a daughter cares for her mother.

Looking Ahead

1. How does the type of care that family members provide to an elderly relative differ depending on the caregiver's gender?
2. How do the responsibilities of caregiving affect a family member's work and personal life?
3. How does an aged person's need for care affect family relationships?
4. What kind of home and community-based services are available to the frail elderly?
5. Can private long-term-care insurance help families to manage the expense and burden of caregiving?
6. How have government regulations and the rise of for-profit nursing home chains affected the availability and quality of nursing home care?
7. What is life in a nursing home like for the frail elderly?

In Sue Miller's moving novel *The Distinguished Guest*, proud, difficult, and ailing Lily Maynard moves, at the age of 72, into the home of her estranged son, Alan, and his wife, Gaby. The visit revives long-buried family conflicts. Alan has been "surprised by his reactions to his mother—surprised and discomfited. He has never pretended to have an intimate or easy relationship with her, but before this visit, he would have said they had come to a kind of peaceful equilibrium between themselves."

One night at dinner, tensions boil to the surface when Lily cruelly remarks, "there's no surer or shorter route to heartbreak than having high expectations for your children" (Miller, 1995:150).

Because of the tensions between Alan and Lily, Gaby has taken on the task of getting her mother-in-law ready for bed each night. "She has surprised herself with the tenderness she sometimes feels for Lily as she performs this service." One evening as Gaby knelt down to untie and remove Lily's shoes, "she had a sense, suddenly, of doing something holy, something that made her feel, in some deep way, *of use*. Holding the shapeless foot in its thick stocking on her lap, she had felt tears of compassion and love spring to her eyes" (p. 33).

Like all great fiction, Sue Miller's book is compelling in its ability to elucidate common human themes—the effect of early family relationships on later life transitions, the transfer of caregiving responsibilities to female family members, the bonds that develop between women in these relationships. Ultimately, the family bears the burden and reaps the rewards of providing care to the frail elderly. In this chapter we review research on the family care of the frail elderly. We describe how caregiving responsibilities are distributed among family members, theorize about why much of the care is provided by women, and examine how caregiving burdens affect all familial relationships.

Family care is sometimes supplemented by formal services, which often make it possible for a person with a disability to remain in his or her own home. When home care becomes unmanageable, elderly people move into nursing homes. Although some nursing homes provide high-quality care, many are profit-oriented businesses that have incentives to reduce costs, often at the expense of quality. The third section of this chapter examines the organization of the nursing home industry and describes daily life in a nursing home for the people who reside there.

This chapter is organized around a model that implies that care of the frail elderly exists on a continuum from least formal (family care) to most formal (nursing home care). It's important to recognize, however, that family members rarely relinquish their responsibilities for their elderly kin and that the family plays a role in the provision of care, regardless of the setting.

FAMILY CARE

A Profile of Caregiving

It may seem ironic that living independently into advanced old age often means learning to accept help, although Erikson (1950) recognized this as life's final developmental task (see Chapter 7). In the United States, about 12 million people need some assistance with daily living (General Accounting Office, 1995). Although only 9 percent of people aged 65 to 69 need help in performing activities of daily living, 43 percent of those older than 85 need such help (Uhlenberg, 1996a). Many need help with such basic functions as eating, bathing, dressing, getting to and from the bathroom, getting in and out of bed, and walking (National Center for Health Statistics, 1994a). As noted in Chapter 6, these are called **activities of daily living (ADLs).** A typical questionnaire used to measure ADLs is shown in Table 10–1. Some people who have no limitations in ADLs still cannot manage to live independently because they are unable to perform **instrumental activities of daily living (IADLs),** such as keeping track of money, doing light housework, taking medicine, and running errands.

The term **long-term care** refers to a range of services designed to help people with chronic conditions compensate for limitations in their ability to function independently (General Accounting Office, 1995). Typically, long-term care involves not high-tech medical care but rather help with ADLs and IADLs.

Most long-term care of the frail elderly is provided by their families, especially by their children. Figure 10–1 shows the extent of care provided to the frail elderly by family members. Children are most likely to provide care to their aging parents, followed by a spouse. Even grandchildren provide some care. It is notable that Hispanic elderly are significantly more likely to be cared for by their children than are either black or white elderly, which suggests that Hispanics are reluctant to allow outsiders to provide care to aging parents or to place them in a nursing home (Angel, 2001). This is true all over the world. Table 10–2 contains comparative statistics on what children do for their aged parents in five countries: the United States, the United Kingdom, Japan, West Germany, and Canada. Support from children is most extensive in Japan because of the tradition of filial responsibility described in Chapter 8; but in all of these countries, between 75 and 89 percent of aged parents receive some help from their children (Rein and Salzman, 1995).

Table 10-1	11 Self-Report, ADL Items and 4 Response Categories of Groningen Activity Restriction Scale

ADL items

1. Can you, fully independently, dress yourself?
2. Can you, fully independently, get in and out of bed?
3. Can you, fully independently, stand up from sitting in a chair?
4. Can you, fully independently, wash your face and hands?
5. Can you, fully independently, wash and dry your whole body?
6. Can you, fully independently, get on and off the toilet?
7. Can you, fully independently, feed yourself?
8. Can you, fully independently, get around in the house (if necessary with a cane)?
9. Can you, fully independently, go up and down the stairs?
10. Can you, fully independently, walk outdoors (if necessary with a cane)?
11. Can you, fully independently, take care of your feet and toenails?

Response categories

1. Yes, I can do it fully independently without any difficulty.
2. Yes, I can do it fully independently but with some difficulty.
3. Yes, I can do it fully independently but with great difficulty.
4. No, I cannot do it fully independently, I can only do it with someone's help.

Figure 10-1	Who Provides Care for the Frail Elderly?

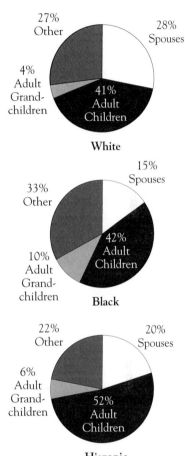

Source: Angel (2001:11).

Although caregivers for most aged parents are their adult children, spouses also provide a good deal of the care. In one national survey, 23 percent of primary caregivers were wives and 13 percent, husbands (Stone, Cafferata, and Sangl, 1987). The data suggest that marriage provides protection against the likelihood of being institutionalized. Only 25 percent of people who were married at the time of their death had spent some time in a nursing home, compared to 40 percent of those who were widowed, divorced, or separated (California Department of Aging, 1994).

As a phase of the life course, caregiving lasts five to seven years, longer than the average person spends obtaining a college degree (Azarnoff and Scharlach, 1988). The average caregiver spends 6 to 10 hours a week helping an elderly relative, but some caregivers spend as many as 35 hours a week. Most caregivers

Table 10-2	What Children Give Their Aged Parents				

	Percentage of Aged Receiving Any Help from Children				
	United States	*United Kingdom*	*Japan*	*West Germany*	*Canada*
Help when sick	65%	74%	79%	85%	70%
Help with care of house	36	57	67	57	47
Money	20	29	47	23	18
Transportation	39	55	67	70	48
Any family help	75	81	87	89	78

Source: Rein and Salzman (1995).

provide emotional support and companionship. Many also help with instrumental tasks of daily living—grocery shopping, transportation, home maintenance, managing finances. A smaller percentage perform personal care by bathing, feeding, dressing, doing laundry, or preparing meals for their elderly relative (Azarnoff and Scharlach, 1988; Lechner, 1991). The majority of caregivers rate their own health as excellent or good, but nearly 40 percent rate it as fair or poor. Thus, a substantial number of caregivers of ill and disabled elderly people are struggling with their own health problems.

Gender Differences in Caregiving

Nearly all studies of caregiving have found that women usually are the **primary caregivers** of ill and disabled family members. Among children who care for their elderly parents, 80 to 90 percent are daughters (Mellor, 2000). Although the primary caregiver tends to be the daughter who has fewest competing obligations—usually one who is not working or is unmarried—many daughters take on the caregiving role regardless of their other responsibilities (Abel, 1986; Brody, 1990). Daughters who provide care for elderly parents do not give up their other obligations; they give up their free time.

When sons provide care, they tend to perform different tasks than female caregivers. The division of labor among caregivers tends to replicate the general division of labor between males and females. Daughters are more likely to provide hands-on care such as feeding, dressing, bathing, or cleaning up after a bowel accident; sons are more likely to do household chores, arrange transportation and social services, and provide help with house repairs, yardwork, and financial management (Chang and White-Means, 1991; Stoller, 1994).

Relatively little is known about the experiences of caregiving sons. In one study (Harris, 2000) researchers interviewed 30 men who cared for their elderly parents. Subjects represented a range of ages and backgrounds, from a 32-year-old white stockbroker who had been caring for his mother at home for 10 years to a 71-year-old African American real estate broker whose mother had just entered a nursing home. One-third of the sons participating in the study were caring for their fathers, two-thirds for their mothers. The men expressed a sense of obligation to their parents, a willingness to take charge, and emotions ranging from love, compassion, and sadness to anger, resentment, and guilt.

There are also gender differences in the amount of care provided (Allen, 1994). As Figure 10-2 shows, daughters, sisters, and daughters-in-law consistently provide more hours of care than their male counterparts. Sons devote less time to caregiving and rely more on help from their spouses (Horwitz, 1985; Mellor, 2000).

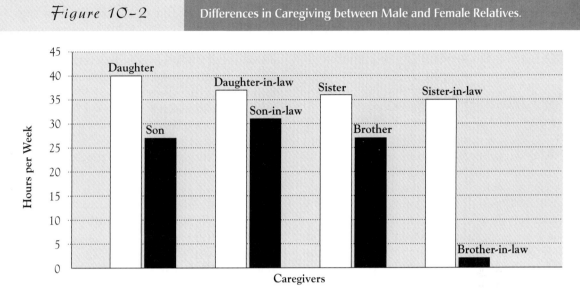

Figure 10-2   Differences in Caregiving between Male and Female Relatives.

Source: Chang and White-Means (1991).

Men and women *feel* equally obligated to care for their parents. Wolfson and colleagues (1993) "found no difference between sons and daughters in their expressed sense of moral obligation to provide . . . financial, emotional and physical (care) nor were there any differences in their perceived ability to provide care" (p. 321). Why, then, do women shoulder a disproportionate share of the burden? One reason is that caregiving reflects a broader gendered division of labor. Men have been socialized to be family breadwinners. Their heavy investment in work has precluded their assuming caregiving responsibilities at any stage of the life course. Many middle-aged women have had tenuous ties to the labor force, moving in and out of employment or working part-time as they raised families. Because their primary responsibility has been for unpaid domestic labor, they are seen as natural caregivers (Stoller, 1994). On a more pragmatic note, since women typically earn less than men, it is often easier on the family budget for the wife to reduce her hours of employment or quit work altogether in order to take on caregiving responsibilities (Moen, Robison, and Fields, 1994).

Men and women also respond differently to caregiving. Although both sons and daughters experience emotional strain from conflicts between caregiving and their other responsibilities, daughters perceive higher levels of stress and less satisfaction with life than sons. Gender differences in the caregiving experience may reflect that daughters perform more intimate tasks for their elderly parents than sons do or that they spend many more hours providing care. It may also be that women's identities and satisfaction are more tied up in the caregiving role. For example, daughters are more likely than sons to find caregiving stressful if their relationship with an elderly parent is strained (Chang and White-Means, 1991; Mui, 1992).

The gender gap in caregiving disappears when husbands and wives care for each other. Husbands and wives provide many more hours of care than children. Although more wives care for their husbands than vice versa, when men are their wives' caregivers, they spend slightly more hours per week in caregiving than do women (Chang and White-Means, 1991). One study of elderly men, aged 68 to 88, caring for wives who had Alzheimer's disease found that they were deeply committed to providing care. As one man explained, "This is part of life, and she would have done the same thing for me. . . . I will never abandon her" (Harris, 1993:554).

Work and Caregiving

The traditional assumption that women are available to provide care because they are unencumbered by work is becoming increasingly outmoded. Although two-thirds of caregivers are no longer working, about one-third are employed full-time or part-time (Anastas, Gibeau, and Larson, 1990). Since 1970, there has been a substantial increase in paid employment among women. Presently, over 60 percent of married women aged 40 to 54 are in the labor force (Boyd and Treas, 1989). The ongoing revolution in women's roles places their previously taken-for-granted responsibilities for caregiving in the spotlight. What is the effect of women's employment on caregiving? Does paid employment reduce the amount of caregiving provided by women? Or does caregiving force women to reduce their time at work or to disengage from the labor force altogether?

A partial answer is provided by the Women's Roles and Well-Being Project, a two-wave study of wives and mothers from a midsize community in upstate New York (Robison, Moen, and Dempster-McClain, 1995). The first wave was conducted in 1956 when a random sample of 427 wives and mothers aged 23 to 50 was interviewed. Twenty years later, 293 of these same women were interviewed again. The researchers found that full-time employment did not preclude a woman from becoming a caregiver. For example, one woman in the study worked full-time as a secretary for an aircraft manufacturing company while caring for her elderly aunt. A 43-year-old grade school teacher cared for her father-in-law in her home for seven years until he moved into a nursing home. Many women simply added the unpaid work of caregiving to their other responsibilities.

Not surprisingly, caregivers experience greater stress on the job and more work–family conflicts than noncaregivers. In a survey of 635 employees

at a large state university, Goldsmith and Goldsmith (1995) found that more than two-thirds of caregivers felt fatigued at work and at home, and nearly three-fourths reported conflicts between family demands and job demands. High levels of job stress and work–family conflicts were most common among caregivers whose relatives had the greatest needs for personal care and highest levels of impairment. Most pressured were female caregivers who also had dependent children at home, those members of the sandwich generation described in Chapter 3 (Gottlieb, Kelloway, and Fraboni, 1994).

Employed caregivers compensate for the additional responsibilities in several ways. In one study, 21 percent worked fewer hours, 29.4 percent rearranged their schedules, and 18.6 percent took time off without pay (Scharlach, 1994). Those who took time off the job for caregiving worked overtime or weekends, took work home, or received help from co-workers. Others simply fell behind.

Employers often recognize that caregiving affects the job performance of caregivers. In 1989, *Fortune* magazine and John Hancock Financial Services conducted a survey of 1,000 senior executives to determine how caregiving affected workers at their firms. Sixty percent of the executives mentioned specific problems stemming from employees' caregiving responsibilities. Among the problems noted most often were employee stress (45 percent), unscheduled days off (38 percent), late arrivals and early departures (37 percent), above-average telephone use (32 percent), and absenteeism (30 percent) (Goldsmith and Goldsmith, 1995).

Some employers have introduced special programs to reduce stress and turnover and ease the burden for their workers. Employees commonly wish for flexible working hours, and some firms provide this option. Other firms have adopted information and referral services, lunchtime seminars, special insurance programs that cover elder care costs, and counselors who lead weekly support groups (Azarnoff and Scharlach, 1988). These options are not commonly available, however, and most employed caregivers struggle on their own to meet multiple demands on their time and energy.

Because of these strains, some caregivers quit their jobs (Stone et al., 1987; Stone and Kemper, 1990). Estimates of how many quit range from as low as 9 percent to as high as 33 percent. In one large study of employees, 20 percent reported some caregiving responsibilities (Scharlach and Boyd, 1989). One-quarter of the caregivers answered that quitting their jobs for caregiving was somewhat or extremely likely. Of those who considered quitting work, three-quarters were women. Those most likely to quit work are older, in their late 50s and early 60s, and thus closer to retirement age than their younger colleagues. Some research has shown that the need to care for a parent or spouse is a major factor in the timing of a woman's retirement decision (Stoller, 1994). But it may be that such women had simply reached retirement age and were ready to retire anyway (Moen et al., 1994).

The disincentives to work related to caregiving responsibilities need to be explored further in light of ongoing efforts by policymakers to encourage later retirement. The Family and Medical Leave Act of 1993 relieves the job strain to some extent. It allows employees to take up to 12 weeks of paid or unpaid leave (at the discretion of the employer) for family-related reasons, including caring for a parent with a serious health condition. The act is definitely a help for working caregivers, but it does not fully solve the dilemma associated with family care of elderly parents. One problem is that it applies only to firms that employ at least 50 people, so all small businesses are exempt. Another problem is that many employees cannot afford to take unpaid leave. Still, this legislation does give workers the right to take leaves of absence without the risk of losing their jobs.

The Caregiver Burden

Caregivers of the frail elderly experience many costs. There are emotional strains, there is the loss of a familiar lifestyle that comes with greater confinement, and there are disrupted plans. The woes of many caregivers are compounded by the financial worry associated with having to pay for home care services, health care, and nursing home care. Yet there are also positive aspects associated with caregiving;

many caregivers derive satisfaction from fulfilling the needs of a loved one. However, most research has concentrated on the psychological costs of caregiving, not on the rewards.

Researchers distinguish between **caregiver burden** and **caregiver stress:** Burden typically refers to management of the tasks; stress refers to the strain felt by the caregiver. The degree of stress felt by a caregiver depends partly on the coping skills she or he may have developed to deal with other life events and partly on the kind of social support available (Pearlin et al., 1996). One study of caregivers found that 88 percent had helpers who provided hands-on help (Penrod et al., 1995). Although relatives are the most important source of support for caregivers, friends frequently help out as well. And some caregivers have professional help from home care workers.

Contrary to what one might expect, women who are not employed outside the home report the greatest levels of stress. Stoller and Pugliesi (1989) explained that caregiving, like housework, isolates the individual from normal daily contacts. Isolation may lead to depression and anxiety, which in turn increase the stress. Homebound caregivers also complain that "there are no boundaries in time, no sense of completion, and no time off. Unlike most workers, caregivers are free from supervision, but there are also no rewards available as incentives for good performance" (p. 232). Thus, women who do not work outside the home may have fewer outlets for the release of tension, whereas employed caregivers may have a heavier burden but feel less stress because work provides satisfaction and stimulation (Scharlach, 1994).

One of the most disturbing possible outcomes of caregiver stress is abuse of the care recipient. Vinton (1992) examined elder abuse reports from the state of Wisconsin over a two-year period. Of 362 reported cases of abuse, 27 percent were by primary caregivers. Among victims 85 and older, 55 percent of the abusers were primary caregivers. Compared to abuse cases involving younger people, caregiver abuse was less likely to involve beatings and more likely to involve neglect. More than half of the elderly victims were quite frail, and a third suffered from Alzheimer's disease.

What can be done for caregivers who often spend hours alone with an ailing loved one? Caregiver support groups have had some success in reducing stress. These groups provide an outlet that allows caregivers to vent their frustrations and to spend time in a supportive environment (Greene and Monahan, 1989). Individual and family counseling can also relieve distress (Whitlach, Zarit, and von Eye, 1991). Counseling can improve coping skills, reduce feelings of guilt and inadequacy, and help caregivers plan for their elder's future (Smith, Smith, and Toseland, 1992). Yet many caregivers do not have access to support groups and counseling. Further, most counseling is short-term, whereas caregivers are dealing with long-term chronic situations that usually get worse, not better, with time.

Caregiving and Family Relationships

The first generation of research on caregiving focused on the primary caregiver in isolation from other family members. Recently, however, there has been a shift in emphasis to a consideration of the entire family system (Beach, 1997). New research suggests that caregiving not only affects the emotional well-being of the caregiver but reverberates across other family relationships. A caregiver may experience a wrenching loss as an aging parent or spouse seemingly becomes a different person (Abel, 1986). Siblings may quarrel over the division of caregiving tasks. And marriages may be strained by the loss of time couples have for each other when one spouse cares for an aging relative. Nevertheless, caregiving can also be a positive influence on the family relationship by bringing kin together to accomplish a shared goal, by making family members appreciate the contributions each makes to the family unit, and by reestablishing connections that may have been weakened over the years.

The effect on parent–child relationships
The relationship between the caregiver and an elderly parent can take many forms. One study of 29 mothers and daughters found three patterns (Walker and Allen, 1991). One type was characterized by *mutuality*, with both mother and daughter

describing a rewarding relationship characterized by joint activities and minimal conflicts. For example, one housebound mother with a degenerative bone disease reported:

Every day I wait for my daughter to come. She don't have to come every day, but she just does it on her own. It might not be for a long time if she's got other things to do, but she always comes. We're just like sisters.

Her daughter agreed: "My mother is my best friend. We're closer now than we've ever been" (Walker and Allen, 1991:391).

Other mothers and daughters had relationships the researchers described as *ambivalent*. There were rewards but also costs, and the relationships were sometimes tense. Finally, a third type of relationship is *conflicted*. Here there are few rewards and frequent costs. As one daughter said, "My mother is very self-oriented; very possessive of my time. She's generous and compassionate to others, but not to me" (p. 393).

Adult children, especially daughters, are most likely to feel stress when the parent is demanding, critical, and unappreciative of their efforts. Children are particularly distressed when they feel that no matter what they do, it will never be enough (Townsend and Noelker, 1987). Stress increases if **role reversal** occurs. Suddenly, the parent who has always been there as a guide becomes the dependent one. One study of caregivers and their aging parents found children, but not parents, very aware of this role reversal. As one daughter noted, "I think now the roles have been reversed. I think she's the child and I'm the parent" (Fischer, 1985:107). Yet parents sometimes refused to recognize that their child was now in charge. One son told the interviewer, "My mom does not accept the fact, hey, we might know what might be good for her now as compared to when we were growing up . . . so she has trouble, I think accepting that, and that creates conflicts because we're looking out for her better and she doesn't accept that fact" (p. 108).

The effect on sibling relationships
Caregiving also can generate tension between primary caregivers and their siblings. Primary caregivers often report that siblings do not carry their share of

the burden and that their efforts are unappreciated (Townsend and Noelker, 1987). One study found that the greatest source of stress for women caring for a parent with Alzheimer's was their siblings (Suitor and Pillemer, 1993). As one woman said about her brother who refused to help care for their mother, "I'm hurting about it. I don't feel his views have any place. He won't take her out anywhere. He says he has a family now, but my mother is still his mother too" (Strawbridge and Wallhagen, 1991:775). Different types of sibling conflict create different responses by caregivers. Disagreements over how to care for a parent may lead to depression. Disagreements over whether siblings are taking their fair share of responsibility more often generate anger (Semple, 1992).

Although sibling conflicts can be detrimental to the caregiver's mental health, increase her or his perceived sense of burden, and generate resentment or hostility toward the absent siblings, caregiving can also have positive effects on sibling relationships. In one study of 100 adult caregivers caring for frail elderly parents, 60 percent reported that caregiving had not created conflict but rather had increased closeness between siblings. As one caregiver explained, "We learned more about the particular skills each of us has and came to appreciate each other more" (Strawbridge and Wallhagen, 1991:776).

The effect on marital relationships

Marriage can also be affected by caregiving responsibilities. On the negative side, caregiving can reduce the time husbands and wives have for each other. Women may be too worn out from performing caregiving duties to spend quality time with their husbands and may worry about whether caregiving demands are harming their marriage. On the positive side, many caregivers feel "that the esteem and effectiveness they gained through caregiving [is] beneficial for their marital relationship" (Stephens and Franks, 1995:14).

The most stressful caregiving situation occurs when one partner has Alzheimer's disease. What happens to love when the person you loved experiences a dramatic change in personality? That was the question Wright (1991) asked two groups of married couples. One group consisted of 30 couples where one had been diagnosed with Alzheimer's disease. The comparison group consisted of 17 healthy couples. The healthy couples experienced shared meaning in all dimensions of their marriage, but that bond had disappeared in the Alzheimer's cases. Even in the early stages of the disease, Alzheimer's took its toll. Many caregivers stated that they were exhausted from a spouse's repeated questioning about simple things (what time it is, what to wear) and that the afflicted spouse's clinging and demanding behavior made them seek companionship elsewhere. Thus, caregiving for an ill mate can dramatically alter the marital relationship. Iris Murdoch, a prolific English novelist, poet, and philosopher, was diagnosed with Alzheimer's disease when she was in her late 70s. In *Elegy for Iris*, her husband, John Bailey, a well-known literary figure in his own right, described his sense of loss as Iris's illness undermined but did not destroy their treasured relationship (see "In Their Own Words").

The effect on grandchildren

When adult children care for their aged parents, their own children often become part of the caregiving nexus. Among the problems that arise are stress between grandparent and grandchild, the disruption of the teen's social life, and resentment of their mother's caregiver burden (Brody, 1989). Children may have to compete with their grandparents for their parents' attention. They may also be forced to make financial sacrifices or endure a more crowded household. Despite such potential strains, several studies have found that family caregiving may also have positive consequences for grandchildren.

In one recent study, 20 adolescent grandchildren of Alzheimer's patients were interviewed in depth regarding their feelings about their relationships to their grandparent and their feelings toward other family members (Beach, 1997). Most grandchildren felt the caregiving situation had had a positive influence on family relationships. What they especially appreciated was that caregiving gave them more time to spend with their siblings, especially older siblings who no longer lived at home. Another positive effect of caregiving was

In Their Own Words

An Elegy for Iris Murdoch

$\mathcal{M}$oving from stage to stage. How many are there? How many will there be? I used to dread Iris's moment of wakening, because the situation seemed to strike her in full force, at least for a minute or two. Reassuring noises, so far as possible, and then she would go back to sleep, and I would sit beside her, reading and typing. . . . Lying beside me, she is like an athlete who had passed on the torch to a back-up member of the relay. I couldn't do what she had done, but I was doing something. . . .

The exasperation of being followed about the house now by Iris is as strong and genuine as is my absolute need for it. Were she to avoid me to "tactfully" leave me alone, I would pursue her anxiously, if not quite so obsessively, as she now pursues me. I don't feel any particular pleasure or emotion when I return to the car after ten minutes of shopping. But I remember it if I wake up in the night, and then I reach out to her.

Source: Bailey (1999:237–38).

---

that it made the young people more empathetic toward other adults and their grandparents. One teenage boy explained:

I'm less (likely) to look negatively at someone who's had a stroke or something. . . . It doesn't really phase me anymore. I don't think of them as being different. I'm more interested in looking out for them. (Beach, 1997:235)

The adolescents repeatedly described feeling closer to their mothers, who were nearly always the primary caregivers. They felt rewarded when their mothers praised them for the help they provided, and they learned to appreciate and respect their mothers. Finally, the adolescents carefully selected friends whom they knew would be sensitive to their situation and felt that they had achieved a high level of intimacy with these chosen friends.

People who are now in their 60s, 70s, and 80s are the parents of the baby boomers. Only 10 percent had no children. This demographic fact bodes well for the future of caregiving. But an increased number of marriages have ended in divorce for this cohort. Although little research has been conducted on the caregiving patterns of children of divorced parents, one might infer that children who have had little contact with a parent will feel less sense of responsibility to care for that parent (Himes, 1992). Still to be determined is whether large family size will compensate for a higher divorce rate in terms of the availability of care.

HOME CARE

Home and Community-Based Services

Many frail elderly who might otherwise have to enter institutions are able to remain in their own homes if they have access to **home and community-based services (HCBS).** The most common home and community-based services are (1) personal care, such as bathing, dressing, feeding, and grooming, (2) housekeeping, including meal preparation and planning, grocery shopping, transportation to medical services, and bill paying, and (3) case management.

Meals-on-wheels is one of the most important services the elderly receive under the Older Americans Act. People receive a hot meal and a friendly visitor.

Case management is usually provided by a social worker who assists frail elderly people and their families in obtaining the medical, social, and personal services they need (General Accounting Office, 1995). In many communities, other services may be available. They include respite care, which provides temporary relief to caregivers; adult day care that provides recreation, social stimulation, and sometimes some medical or rehabilitative care; and hospice service, which is support for people with terminal illnesses (see Chapter 14). Home health care, such as visiting nurses, is also a commonly provided long-term-care service.

The increasing demand for an expanding array of options for HCBS raises complex issues about the cost, distribution, and quality of care (Zedlewski and McBride, 1992). Much of the interest in expanding home and community-based services comes from a desire to reduce nursing home costs. Yet policymakers fear that if paid home and community-based care services are expanded, family and friends will stop providing care and costs will increase instead. Are these concerns realistic?

Most research shows that families do not withdraw support when home and community-based services are provided but rather that the disabled elderly receive more care (Wiener and Hanley, 1992). However, there is no evidence that home and community-based services reduce costs or nursing home use (Wiener and Illston, 1996). The reason is that many disabled older people desire such services but are managing without them. If access to home and community-based services were expanded, it would fill the unmet demand in the community rather than serve as a substitute for nursing home care. Costs would then rise because the severely disabled elderly would still enter nursing homes and more people would receive services (Liu, Manton, and Liu, 1985; Rivlin and Wiener, 1988; Liu, McBride, and Coughlin, 1990).

Quality is another important issue. Evidence suggests that home and community-based services are not always adequate. Many workers who provide these services have little training and receive low wages. Among home health aides, for example, the "typical aide is female, representative of a racial or

Diversity in the Aging Experience

LONG-TERM CARE OF THE AMERICAN INDIAN AGED

The American Indian aged represent 300 recognized tribes, 200 Alaskan Native villages, and several hundred other groups that are not officially recognized. Together, they speak 150 different languages. Thus, it is difficult to speak of "the American Indian experience." As a general rule, though, the concept of formal long-term care is foreign to American Indians, who believe that families and tribal members should care for each other. An Odawa Indian explained this tradition:

> It's such a norm to take care of the family ... it's not a burden ... something you know is just part of you. For example, we were talking to an elder who is at least 60 and he said he was going to take food to his mother and every other day he checks on her. ... There is that constant closeness and we always try and check up on them too and see how they're doing and so we know where they are. (Chapleski, 1997:385)

Given this attitude, the use of formal services by an aged tribal member represents a failure of family care. As one Michigan Ojibwa explained:

> Well, in general, long-term care is not the ideal situation according to the way an Indian community is supposed to work because the fact that we have long-term care means that the family's not able to perform or unwilling to perform that role. (Chapleski, 1997:377)

ethnic minority, middle-aged, poorly educated and trained, and the primary wage earner of a household" (Wiener and Hanley, 1992:84). Low wages and poor working conditions create high turnover among home health aides. Although some aides provide excellent care, older people frequently have an unfamiliar and unreliable individual providing help.

Presently, there is little regulation of home and community-based services, and although they are presumed to be superior to nursing home care, there is no hard evidence to back up that assumption. What evidence we do have suggests that the quality of care can be compromised by an effort to reduce costs. What can be done? One solution is to employ better-trained people to perform these services.

Another solution is to pay better wages to those who are presently employed in these positions. Recent efforts to monitor the quality of home care suggest that services are improving. More than 90 percent of the respondents to one survey said their home care workers performed the job properly and were kind and courteous (Coleman, 2000).

Race, Ethnicity, and Long-Term Care

Although in general, the minority elderly are in poorer health than the white elderly, they are actually less likely than others to receive home and community-based services or even to enter nursing

Not surprisingly, tribal members who live in urban areas seldom use formal services. But when home and community-based services are provided on a reservation, and are run in ways that reflect tribal values, elders are more likely to take advantage of them. Elders simply are more comfortable when service providers are members of the tribe and traditional foods and healers are offered. In one study, reservation dwellers were 4.1 times more likely than urban dwellers to use home care services, 3.8 times more likely to use a home health aide, and 5.5 times more likely to accept a home visit (Chapleski, 1997).

Nationwide, 24 tribes run their own nursing homes on their reservations. In Wisconsin, the Menominee refused reimbursement from Medicare or Medicaid so they could practice traditional medicine and allow residents to control their own care (Chapleski, 1997). (The federal government's strict standards do not permit payment to traditional healers.) In one study, 70 percent of Indians listed a nursing home as their least preferred option for care, stating that they would go farther from home to be with other American Indians. Indeed, some urban-dwelling elders are moving back to reservations so they can spend their last years in the tribal community.

What Do You Think?

1. What is your family's attitude toward formal long-term-care services such as meals-on-wheels, visiting nurses, and home health aides? Do you think your family's cultural background affects their attitude?
2. Should federal standards for Medicare and Medicaid reimbursement be relaxed to accommodate traditional healing practices?

homes. Some people argue that cultural preferences are the reason for these differences. For example, language barriers or unfamiliar food may discourage the Hispanic elderly from using long-term-care services. That certainly is the case among the Native American aged (see "Diversity in the Aging Experience"). Among some minority groups, cultural norms concerning the responsibility of children for their aged parents may also have an effect (Angel and Angel, 1997).

Lack of access is another reason why members of minority groups receive nursing home care less frequently than whites. Minority neighborhoods have fewer nursing homes than white neighborhoods, and minority elderly may not be willing to move to a nursing home that is far from their families (Keith and Long, 1997). Government policy has also had an adverse effect. Later in this chapter we will see how recent changes in Medicaid reimbursement policies have affected access to nursing homes among the minority elderly.

Private Long-Term-Care Insurance

Today, neither Medicare nor Medicaid pays much for home care services. Although in the future the federal government is likely to continue to dominate the financing of long-term care, even more responsibility will probably fall on the private sector. What are the alternatives?

One option is private financing through long-term-care insurance (Hudson, 1996). Close to 4 million private long-term-care policies were in effect in 1997, compared to just 2 million in 1991 (Kingson and Berkowitz, 1993; Wiener, Tilly, and Goldenson, 2000). The attraction of long-term-care insurance is that it pays not only for nursing home care but also for alternative services in the home. Most people would like to have a choice between home care and nursing home care.

Although private insurance represents a potential solution for some people, it also poses challenges. Premiums are costly because most people wait until they are in their 70s or 80s to purchase insurance. If people purchased these policies when they were younger, the yearly cost would be considerably less. Another problem is that people with health problems are often turned down by private insurers. Finally, a high proportion of policyholders allow their policies to lapse. One analysis suggests that 50 percent of people who purchase long-term-care insurance stop paying the premiums within five years, risking thousands of dollars in lost payments (U.S. House of Representatives, 1993).

In the year 2000 only 2.5 percent of long-term-care expenditures in the United States were paid by private insurance policies. This percentage is bound to increase as more Americans learn that neither the states nor the federal government pays for most long-term-care services. More employers are now including long-term-care insurance in their employee benefits. In 1996 the federal government began allowing tax payers to take a deduction for their long-term-care insurance costs; several states have offered similar incentives, including Maine, Maryland, and Oregon (Wiener et al., 2000). Although these government policies have not yet had a major impact, more middle-aged people are becoming aware of the need for protection against long-term-care costs.

INSTITUTIONAL CARE

The **nursing home** is the long-term-care option of last resort. Presently, about 7 percent of older people living in the community enter a nursing home in any two-year period (Cowart and Quadagno, 1995). More than 40 percent of Americans who turned 65 in 1990 will spend some time in a nursing home (Foner, 1994). Most are severely disabled, but 29 percent of nursing home residents have no limitations in activities of daily living. Some have mental impairments, but others simply lack a support system that would allow them to remain at home (Hardwick et al., 1994).

The Nursing Home Industry

The increasing demand for nursing home care has created explosive growth in the nursing home industry. In 1954 there were only 260,000 nursing home beds in 9,000 nursing homes in the entire country. By 1999 that number had soared to more than 1.6 million in nearly 17,000 nursing homes (Health Care Financing Administration, 2000b). Part of the increase in nursing homes is due to the growth of the aged population, especially of those older than 85 who have multiple chronic ailments and the greatest need for intensive medical care. Federal subsidies and loans for nursing home construction in the 1950s and 1960s have also stimulated their growth, as has the Medicaid program, which paid for more than 60 percent of nursing home costs in 2000. (Health Care Financing Administration, 2000b).

Although many nursing homes provide adequate and, in some cases, exceptional care, poor-quality care is a continuing problem. A report by the General Accounting Office (1995) found that one-third of the nation's nursing homes were operating at a substandard level. Among the problems documented were untrained staff, poor health care, unsanitary conditions, poor food, and unenforced safety regulations. In no other segment of the health care industry is such poor-quality care provided. Continually, investigations find inadequate care and evidence of abuse and neglect of residents (Harrington, 1991).

Staff Turnover in Long-Term Care

Formal long-term care for frail elderly people traditionally has been provided in nursing homes by nursing assistants, but in the past decade care provided in assisted living facilities or in an individual's own home has increased significantly (Street et al., 2003). Over 90 percent of the providers of this care are women between the ages of 22 and 45 (Van Kleunen and Wilner, 2000). They are disproportionately women of color; approximately 35 percent are black and 10 percent are Hispanic (Stone and Wiener, 2001). One-fifth of employed African American women work in the health care industry, many in direct care jobs (Himmelstein, Lewontin, and Woolhandler, 1996). In general, training for nursing assistant jobs is brief, between 75 and 100 hours, and many direct care workers receive no training at all (Stone and Wiener, 2001).

The starting salary for nursing assistants is usually the minimum wage, and they receive few fringe benefits such as health insurance or pensions. Care is needed on a 24-hour basis, so many of these aides work nights, weekends, and holidays. The work frequently requires aides to manually lift patients, which often results in back injuries. Each year, nursing assistants are more likely than miners, construction workers, or steel mill operatives to be injured on the job. In most cases, opportunities for advancement and participation in the planning of care for residents are few, and management–employee relationships are poor (Gregory, 2001). All these conditions create high levels of stress and burnout. Not surprisingly, turnover among workers in these jobs is high, occasionally exceeding 100 percent each year (Stone and Wiener, 2001). High turnover, in turn, leads to poor care, placing the most vulnerable population group at risk of bedsores, falls, and inadequate diet. "An Issue for Public Policy" discusses the results of recent government reports on the quality of nursing home care.

Many of the quality problems arise because the nursing home industry has more for-profit ownership than any other segment of the health system. In 1998, 70 percent of all nursing homes were profit-making ventures, 25 percent were nonprofit, and 5 percent were government owned. A growing number of nursing homes are part of multinational chains, which operate facilities both in the United States and in foreign countries. In Canada nearly half of the small "mom and pop" nursing homes have been replaced by nursing home chains. "Aging around the World" discusses some of the causes of

the growth of chains, and the consequences for the quality of care in nursing homes. Not surprisingly, research consistently shows that the highest quality of care is provided in homes run by nonprofit organizations, especially those that are attached to a religious group (Minkler, 1989).

Access to Nursing Home Care

In 2003 the average yearly cost of nursing home care in the United States exceeded $56,000. That is substantially more than the cost of tuition, room, and board at even the most exclusive private college. Medicare pays only a small fraction of these costs. Only when an older person is released from a hospital to a skilled nursing facility will the government pay for nursing home care (Mellor, 2000), and even then only for the first 20 days (see Chapter 11). Medicaid pays nearly 40 percent of all nursing home costs.

Because states set different income limits to determine eligibility for Medicaid, determining whether elderly people are being denied care is difficult. In Illinois, for example, policymakers concerned about the rising costs of Medicaid froze nursing homes' reimbursement rates for a three-year period. Even though the cost of care continued to rise, the amount of money the nursing homes received from Medicaid did not. As a result, many nursing homes began to limit the number of Medicaid patients they would accept. Some stopped taking Medicaid patients entirely and instead admitted only private patients who could pay the full cost of care. As one nursing home administrator explained:

Many people want to live here because this is a nice nursing home. Yet we routinely turn people away. . . . We refuse admission if someone is on Medicaid even if we have empty beds. It is a calculated risk. We would rather have the bed empty. We give preferred admissions to private payers. I have to admit that . . . we keep two waiting lists. (Harrington Meyer and Kesterke-Storbakken, 2000)

Another problem is that Medicare currently pays almost three times as much as Medicaid for patient care in many states. As a result, nursing homes have attempted to increase the number of residents

An Issue for Public Policy

STAFF LEVELS AND QUALITY OF CARE IN NURSING HOMES

Compared to the horrendous conditions reported in the 1950s and 1960s, the quality of nursing home care in the United States has improved in recent years. Yet problems remain. One recent government report found that residents of some nursing homes still suffer from severe bedsores, malnutrition, and abnormal weight loss. Some patients have had to be hospitalized for life-threatening infections, dehydration, and congestive heart failure. The main cause of these problems is insufficient staff (Health Care Financing Administration, 2000).

Why is adequate staffing so important? Forty-seven percent of nursing home patients need some help eating; 21 percent cannot feed themselves at all. In homes that are understaffed, aides push patients to eat quickly, forcing huge spoonfuls of food into their mouths and causing them to choke. After patients have eaten part of their meals, the aides move on to other patients. Thus, nursing homes with low staffing levels tend to have large numbers of patients with nutrition problems. They are also more likely than others to have patients with bedsores (Harrington et al., 2003). To prevent bedsores, which can easily become infected and damage underlying muscle and bone, bedridden patients need to be turned or moved every two hours.

Federal standards require that nursing home patients receive an average of two hours of care each day from nursing assistants and 12 minutes a day from nurses. These are minimum standards, not optimal levels of care. Currently, only 46 percent of nursing homes provide this level of care; one-fourth have deficiencies that could actually harm patients or even cause injury or death. Because 95 percent of nursing homes receive federal funds through Medicare or Medicaid, they must comply with these regulations or lose their funding. Yet representatives of the nursing home industry say they cannot afford to hire additional staff unless the government increases the amount paid per resident. Since 1998, several nursing home chains have filed for bankruptcy protection, including Sun Healthcare, Vencor, Integrated Health Services, and Mariner Post-Acute Network. So the dilemma remains: How will society pay for care and ensure that nursing home residents are protected?

What Do You Think?

1. Have you visited a nursing home recently? If so, did you notice any problems with the quality of care the residents were receiving?
2. What can government officials do to help nursing home operators meet federal quality-of-care standards?

THE RISE OF NURSING HOME CHAINS IN CANADA

Thirty years ago only 7 percent of the nursing homes in Ontario, Canada, were operated by chains; today 43 percent are chain-operated. Why are the small "mom and pop" nursing homes being replaced by chains? One reason is increased government standards and regulations, which have been difficult for small homes to follow. Regulations forbid nursing homes to charge more than the government fee schedule. While the rules help to hold costs down, they also penalize small homes, which cannot absorb new costs as easily as homes owned by a large chain. To cut costs, some nursing home chains have a policy of accepting only the least problematic (and thus least costly) residents. Thus some very ill elderly have had a difficult time finding a place to live. Other chains have reduced costs by lowering the wages they pay employees. Finally, chains offer more services than "mom and pop" homes can afford. They are slowly driving the smaller homes out of business.

The closure of the independent homes has created a nursing home shortage in Canada. Nursing home beds are now in demand regardless of the quality of care offered. Concern about the quality of care in for-profit homes has galvanized some organizations to work on behalf of the aged. In 1987 the Canadian Parliament passed legislation that established a resident's bill of rights and created residents' councils to monitor care; it also required the Ministry of Health to hold a public hearing before granting or renewing a nursing home license. Although these measures have improved the quality of nursing home care in Canada, quality of care and access to care remain problematic for those who need a supportive living environment.

What Do You Think?

1. Has a large nursing home or hospital chain moved into your community recently? If so, what concerns did community members raise?
2. Should government regulations be revised to allow smaller nursing homes to survive? What might be a better way for policymakers to address the need for nursing home care?

Source: Baum (1999).

whose care is paid by Medicare, leaving fewer beds available for Medicaid patients (Street et al., 2003).

As a result of such policies, Medicaid recipients are denied access to many nursing homes. They wait longer to gain admission to a nursing home and end up in less desirable homes. Many of those who experience these difficulties are racial and ethnic minorities. Yet all racial groups are likely to be affected, given the high cost of care.

Paying for nursing home care through Medicaid imposes many hardships on the aged and their families. Medicaid is intended for the needy, yet few middle-class families can afford to pay the costs of nursing home care. Consequently, many people who enter a nursing home as private-pay patients rapidly deplete their income and assets and thus become poor through a process known as *spending down*. Many people with meager incomes are ineligible for Medicaid because their assets exceed the cutoff for Medicaid eligibility. Because the rules governing eligibility are complex and vary from state to state, most people don't know whether they will be eligible until a health crisis forces them to apply for support. Then they are ill prepared to deal with the consequences (Quadagno, Harrington Meyer, and Turner, 1991).

Because members of racial and ethnic minorities have higher poverty rates than whites, they are more readily accepted for Medicaid on admission to a nursing home. Using data from the 1985 National Nursing Home Survey, Harrington Meyer (1994) found that 56.2 percent of all African American and Hispanic nursing home residents were eligible for Medicaid at the time of their admission, compared to only 32.7 percent of whites. In fact, 33 percent of the Hispanic elderly received Medicaid in 1990 (Lacayo, 1993). White men and women are more likely to enter nursing homes as private-paying patients and then convert to Medicaid when they have spent down their assets (Harrington Meyer, 1994).

The Nursing Home as Total Institution

A nursing home is what the sociologist Erving Goffman (1961) called a **total institution.** The central features of total institutions are the breakdown of the normal barriers that separate the main spheres of life—sleep, work, and play—and the handling of many human needs by a bureaucratic organization. Bureaucratic management involves the care and movement of people in blocks so that they can be supervised by personnel whose chief activity is surveillance.

Total institutions can be roughly grouped into five categories (Goffman, 1961). One type is designed to serve as a retreat from the world, such as a monastery or convent. Another type is organized to protect the community from people who are considered dangerous. Prisons, POW camps, and concentration camps are examples of this type. A third kind of total institution is established to pursue some worklike task, such as an army barrack or boarding school. Fourth are institutions designed to care for people who are incapable of looking after themselves and are perceived to be a threat to the community. Among this type are mental hospitals and TB sanitariums. Those in the fifth category are established to care for people who are both incapable and harmless; nursing homes are the primary example of this type of total institution.

Adjusting to a nursing home   People who have lived independently in a community find the transition to institutional life difficult. Several participant-observation studies of life in a nursing home provide an insider's view of how people make the adjustment.

Sociologist Jaber Gubrium spent several months as a participant observer in a large nursing home he called Murray Manor. In his book *Living and Dying at Murray Manor*, Gubrium (1975) recounted heartbreaking tales of people who sold or gave away their lifelong possessions and moved to a nursing home. For the residents of Murray Manor, the move meant severing ties with people, objects, and familiar places. People sometimes wept recalling some cherished piece of furniture or a comforting daily routine. The most wrenching loss was the loss of independence to make even simple decisions for oneself about indulging in small pleasures—the walk to the neighborhood donut shop for a cup of coffee and a chat with the proprietor, or the ability to choose lasagna instead of meatloaf for dinner. As one resident explained:

It isn't home here. I woulda' liked to have stayed with the children. We had a cat and I miss that cat quite a bit. I miss my little radio and the window I had where you could see the dog in the yard next door. Sometimes I really miss that nice little carpet I had next to my bed. I was used to that. (Gubrium, 1975:87)

Older Hispanics or other immigrants who enter nursing homes face unique obstacles in adjusting to institutionalization, including language and cultural differences. Recently, some nursing homes have become more sensitive to the cultural needs of residents and have begun providing food and activities that reflect different ethnic backgrounds (Yeo, 1993). Most, however, are too busy providing basic care.

Daily life in a nursing home

Perhaps the most difficult aspect of life in a total institution is the monotonous daily routine. The routine results from pressure on nursing home aides to meet the basic needs of the residents. Residents must be fed, dressed, bathed, and prepared for bed. The nursing home itself must also be kept clean and orderly. Gubrium referred to this daily routine as "bed-and-body work."

Daily life begins with the awakening of residents to prepare them for breakfast. This sounds like a simple job, but many residents require extensive help in getting up, toileting, and going to the dining hall. Since the night shift ends at 7:30 A.M., nursing assistants must begin awakening the most difficult residents as early as 5:30 A.M. Incontinent patients must be changed and their beds remade if they are wet or dirty. When the patients are dressed and ready, those who are able to walk go to the dining hall on their own. The others must be taken in their wheelchairs. Patients awakened last are the "feeders," those who have their meals in bed and must be fed by aides. Aides constantly feel rushed and often complain that there isn't sufficient time to do everything (Gubrium, 1975).

The bureaucratic requirements of nursing home care reward nursing assistants who are efficient, orderly, and neat. When anthropologist Nancy Foner (1994) conducted research at Crescent Nursing Home, a large and well-run facility in New York City, she found that the most favored aide was Mrs. Jones. A fast worker, she finished her bed-and-body work early and always got her paperwork done on time. Yet she was curt, sometimes even cruel to patients, especially those who ate slowly or needed extra help and thus delayed her schedule. By contrast, the most gentle and considerate aide, Ana Rivera, was constantly criticized by her supervisor because she spent too much time on "emotional work" with residents and was constantly behind on her schedule. Ana gently urged patients who refused to eat and encouraged them when they took a bite, "Good, eat, eat, it's good for you." When a new rehabilitation aide mistakenly put Mrs. Calhoun into restraints, she went out of control, screaming and shaking. "Ana gently removed the restraint and stroked Mrs. Calhoun's head for several minutes as she calmed down" (Foner, 1994:62). It wasn't only Ana's slowness that got her into trouble; her supervisor felt she was undermining the bureaucratic order. By placing the residents' needs first, she was challenging the standards of efficiency.

Another participant-observation study of nursing homes was conducted by sociologist Timothy Diamond, who worked as a nursing assistant in three Chicago-area nursing homes. Diamond experienced the constraints faced by staff and residents firsthand. In his book *Making Gray Gold: Narratives of Nursing Home Care,* Diamond (1992) demonstrated how poorly paid nursing assistants struggled to reconcile the care they wanted to give with the care they were required to give. They were forced to adhere to the shower schedule long after the hot water had run out, to deny food between meals to hungry residents, and to dispense sedatives but not aspirin if it was not on a resident's chart.

Diamond discussed the effects of the mind-numbing routine on the patients and on the poorly paid, overworked staff of nursing aides who served their needs. Every day after breakfast the residents who were not bedridden congregated in the dayroom. Diamond observed that there was a notable absence of conversation, even though 30 or 40 people may have been in the same room. Rather they sat in their assigned places, some slumped over in sleep.

One morning Diamond was assigned to give Hazel Morris her shower. An active woman, Hazel

Daily life in a nursing home can be monotonous. Mealtimes help break the routine and provide residents an opportunity to socialize.

roamed all over the floor in her tennis shoes, wandering from her room to the dayroom and up and down the halls. He felt awkward showering a woman and felt that their gender difference permeated their interaction. As Diamond recalled:

> As I blushingly proceeded to help Mrs. Morris, she seemed to sense my embarrassment and attended to it gracefully with questions like "You're new here, aren't you? How do you like the place? Don't worry, you'll get used to it." (p. 86)

Although it was not planned that a man should give women showers, neither was it planned that a man should not give them. What mattered was strictly adhering to the set shower schedule.

Diamond learned from the inside out how nursing homes operate as industrial enterprises. His book shows how the goals of profit-oriented owners and budget-strained state and federal administrators outweigh the personal needs of residents. His study also reveals how the mental and physical health of residents and workers alike is compromised by an industry and a government determined to minimize long-term-care costs.

Patient abuse   Patient abuse in nursing homes is a continuing concern. It may involve verbal or physical abuse. Abuse typically does not stem from intentional cruelty but rather from instances in which overworked, underpaid aides, who provide all of the hands-on care, become frustrated or simply make mistakes (Foner, 1994).

High turnover and high absenteeism among nursing home staff create situations that provoke abuse. Absenteeism means that the staff present have to take on work in addition to their regular tasks. Turnover means that there are often new workers who are unfamiliar with nursing home routines and thus more prone to error. Turnover also means that many nursing homes fail to perform adequate background checks on their prospective employees, because they are constantly hiring new workers. The following instance of a serious scalding that led to the death of an elderly nursing home resident shows how overworked staff can inadvertently place a patient at risk (Stannard, 1973).

The scalding involved a complicated situation. On that day, the man who worked in the laundry did not come to work. As a result, the evening shift was short of linens, towels, clothes, and diapers for the incontinent patients. That night the evening shift was also short of help. When putting Mr. Jones to bed, a nursing assistant found that the elderly patient had soiled himself and the bed. The aide undressed Mr. Jones and put him in the bathtub. He then discovered there were no towels and asked the janitor to watch Mr. Jones while he went to the basement laundry room. Instead of watching Mr. Jones, the busy janitor took out a load of garbage. When the orderly returned, he found Mr. Jones sitting alone in a steaming tub with the faucet running. Panicking, he took Mr. Jones out of the tub, wrapped him in a clean sheet and put him in bed. An hour later when a nurse checked on Mr. Jones, she found him lying in bed "with the skin and tissue on his legs and lower trunk coming off in hunks" (Stannard, 1973:240). No one knew for sure what happened, but it seemed likely that Mr. Jones, in his mental confusion, was attracted by the shiny faucet and turned on the water. Then in his pain and confusion he was unable to turn it off.

Such gross neglect is rare. Aides do sometimes use restraints to control patients, pinch them, or slap them (Foner, 1994). More often, however, the abuse is more subtle and psychological in nature. Foner reported that numerous instances of verbal abuse occurred at Crescent Nursing Home. Yet in most cases, the mistreatment of patients was not deliberate cruelty by the aides but rather stemmed from the abstract and impersonal application of bureaucratic rules to helpless human beings.

The federal government as well as states have established increasingly vigilant rules in an attempt to protect patients. The greatest protection against abuse in nursing homes is the presence of an **ombudsman program.** Ombudsmen may be paid employees of the state or they may be volunteers. Serving as watchdogs, ombudsmen monitor the quality of care in nursing homes by investigating complaints by families and residents against facilities, reporting complaints to other regulatory agencies, gathering information, and meeting with those involved in disputes. Research has shown that the presence of an ombudsman significantly improves the quality of nursing home care (Cherry, 1993).

Families of the institutionalized elderly

Caregiver stress often does not end after an aging parent or spouse is admitted to a nursing home. Indeed, sometimes it increases. Some of the added stress is caused by factors unrelated to the nursing home itself, such as traveling to and from the nursing home for visits, giving up other activities to visit, or paying the extra expenses not covered by the basic nursing home fees. Constant conflict with the staff adds to the stress, as caregivers who formerly attended to every need of their loved ones now find they are at the mercy of strangers. Whether the needs are met is a constant worry.

Nursing assistants provide technical care, but their hectic schedules often prevent them from performing the personal care that could make a resident comfortable. Foner (1994) found that families continually complained about the staff's failure to attend to specific requests. For example, Mrs. Bernard told the crowd at a meeting between staff and family members, "I left a laundry bag to put dirty laundry in every day. I explained it to the aides and left a big sign. What do you think? I come and the laundry is not in the bag" (p. 117).

More serious complaints concerned the failure of nursing assistants to follow doctor's orders: not putting on special stockings a doctor had requested for one patient with circulation problems; using the wrong size of incontinence briefs, which caused a rash; not paying sufficient attention to the patient's eating habits.

Highest levels of stress and depression occur among caregivers of patients with severe behavioral problems and memory loss. Because their relatives are problem patients, these caregivers undoubtedly experience more stress in their interactions with staff and less confidence in the quality of care their relatives receive (Stephens, Ogrocki, and Kinney, 1991).

In an effort to improve relationships between nursing home staff and the family members of residents, a group of researchers at Cornell University developed a series of workshops that focused on improving listening skills and enhancing communication. The researchers found that family members who participated in the workshops had greater empathy with the staff, staff members who participated had more positive feelings about their jobs, and reports of conflict declined (Pillemer et al., 2003).

Until recently, family members have had to rely on their intuition in deciding which nursing home is likely to offer the best care for a frail relative. Then some researchers developed a report card to help families pick a nursing home. The report card includes information on a variety of factors that might affect the quality of care, including the number of deficiencies and complaints and the turnover rates among employees (Harrington et al., 2003). As report cards become more widely used, they will help improve care because families will avoid nursing homes with many indicators of poor quality.

The long-term-care system in the United States consists of family care, home care, and nursing home care. At each level of care there are unmet needs. Often, families struggle for years to maintain their disabled elderly in the home, a struggle complicated by a shortage of services. Supportive housing arrangements provide a promising solution to the nation's future long-term-care needs if they can be regulated and made affordable for the average person. Placement in a nursing home is usually the last resort, for good reason, because high-quality nursing home care is a scarce commodity. The struggle to find an adequate solution to the nation's long-term-care needs is likely to become more pressing as the population ages. The central issues will focus on who will provide the care, who will pay for the care, and who will monitor the quality of care.

Chapter Resources

LOOKING BACK

1. **How does the type of care that family members provide to an elderly relative differ depending on the caregiver's gender?** *Although men and women both feel a sense of obligation to provide care to their aging parents, women are more likely to be the primary caregivers to the frail elderly and to provide the greatest amount of care. Men and women also tend to perform different tasks. Daughters typically provide hands-on care such as feeding, dressing, or bathing. Sons are more likely to help with household chores, financial management, and yardwork.*

2. **How do the responsibilities of caregiving affect a family member's work and personal life?** *Although the majority of caregivers are not in the labor force, approximately one-third are employed. Caregiving affects work in several ways. Even if employed caregivers continue working full-time, caregiving responsibilities may force them to work fewer hours, rearrange schedules, and take time off. Some caregivers quit work or retire earlier than planned if their caregiving responsibilities create conflicts with their ability to perform their jobs. The psychological toll that caregiving takes on caregivers is measured in terms of stress and burden. Surprisingly, although women employed outside the home seemingly have a higher burden than nonemployed women, they report less stress. It may be that satisfaction from work and contact with the outside world reduces stress, despite greater responsibilities from dual roles.*

3. **How does an aged person's need for care affect family relationships?** *Caregiving may strain family relationships, but it may also enhance them. A child may be disturbed by personality changes in an aging parent or by the role reversal that may occur when the parent becomes dependent. Siblings may quarrel over the division of caregiving tasks. Marriages may be strained when spouses have less time for each other because of caregiving burdens. When the burden is shared equally, however, family members may appreciate each other and feel that familial ties have been strengthened.*

4. **What kind of home and community-based services are available to the frail elderly?** *Home and community-based services help the frail elderly remain in their own homes. Among the services most commonly provided are personal care, housekeeping, and case management. Some communities also provide respite care for caregivers, adult day care, medical or rehabilitative care, and hospice services.*

5. **Can private long-term-care insurance help families to manage the expense and burden of caregiving?** *Although currently only 2.5 percent of long-term-care costs in the United States are paid by private insurance, this percentage is increasing as people learn that the government does not pay for most services. Yet there are many problems to be resolved before long-term-care insurance fills the long-term-care needs for most Americans. One problem is that many older people cannot afford to pay the premiums for long-term-care insurance. Many let their policies lapse and lose thousands of dollars in payments. Another problem is that private insurers often turn down people who need insurance the most, those with major health problems.*

6. **How have government regulations and the rise of for-profit nursing home chains affected the availability and quality of nursing home care?** *A growing number of nursing homes are owned by for-profit multinational chains that operate facilities in the United States and in other countries. These chains are businesses that are responsible to shareholders to show a profit. Research shows that the best care is provided by nonprofit homes, especially those that are attached to a religious group.*

7. **What is life in a nursing home like for the frail elderly?** *People dread the thought of moving to a nursing home, and the adjustment to institutional life is difficult. The monotonous daily routine demanded by bureaucratic procedures*

reduces the quality of life for residents and places pressure on the aides who provide care. Residents are often denied the small pleasures that make life worthwhile by aides who are required to maintain a dehumanizing schedule. Patient abuse is a continuing concern in nursing homes. Although physical abuse is rare, psychological abuse is unfortunately more common. Not so much intentional, abuse results from the frustrations of overworked and underpaid aides.

THINKING ABOUT AGING

1. What kind of social support would be helpful to stressed-out sandwich-generation caregivers?

2. As a concerned citizen or social worker, how would you argue for greater government support of home-based services to the elderly?

3. Should long-term-care insurance be available to everyone, regardless of health?

4. Federal standards for nursing home care often conflict with federal reimbursement limits. What is the source of this conflict, and how might it be resolved?

5. Many people fear ending their lives in a nursing home. In your view, what is the worst aspect of life in a total institution? If you were a nursing home operator, how would you address it?

KEY TERMS

activities of daily living (ADLs) 228

caregiver burden 233

caregiver stress 233

home and community-based services (HCBS) 236

instrumental activities of daily living (IADLs) 228

long-term care 228

nursing home 240

ombudsman program 247

primary caregiver 230   total institution 244

role reversal 234

EXPLORING THE INTERNET

Note: While all the URLs listed were current as of the printing of this book, these sites often change. Please check our website www.mhhe.com/quadagno for updates.

1. Caregiving has become an important aspect of aging in our society. To learn more about caregiving, go to the website for the Administration on Aging (http://www.aoa.dhhs.gov). From the main page, link to "Pressroom," and then "Fact Sheets." Scroll down and link to the PDF article, "Family Caregiving." Answer the following questions:

    a. How many individuals are informal caregivers, providing unpaid help to older persons living in the community?
    b. The National Family Caregiver Support Program promotes five basic services for family caregivers. What are they?
    c. Who is eligible to take part in the program?

2. The Center of Medicare and Medicaid Services is a government organization providing information and quality service for beneficiaries and providers. Link to their website (www.cms.hhs.gov), link to "Public Affairs" and then "Press Releases." Scroll down to the July 31, 2003 article, "Medicare increases nursing home payment rates," and answer the following questions:

    a. How much is the increase estimated to be, and where will it go?
    b. What is SNF PPS, and when was its inception?
    c. The increase is based on the daily needs of Medicare patients. What are some of these daily needs?

MANAGING TRANSITIONS

ll individuals experience the biological and psychological changes of aging, but the nature of that experience varies enormously from person to person. The four chapters in Part Four explore how society meets the health care needs of the aged.

Chapter 11 provides an overview of the basic social programs for the elderly, which in combination are defined as the welfare state. The chapter describes who pays for each program, who receives benefits, and what benefits are provided. The chapter concludes with a discussion of a controversy over whether benefits should be provided on the basis of age or need.

Chapter 12 analyzes changing patterns of labor force participation among older men and women in the transition from work to retirement. It documents the increase in early retirement that occurred in the second half of the twentieth century, and it explores labor market trends and changes in public policy as causes. It demonstrates that the nature of the transition to retirement and individuals' ultimate satisfaction with that experience are the result of numerous earlier life course choices and opportunities. Finally, the chapter describes activities and contributions of the aged after retirement.

Chapter 13 considers whether the increase in life expectancy means more years of poor health or more good, active years. Part of the answer depends on an individual's race, gender, and social class, all of which influence lifestyle practices such as smoking, drinking, and exercise as well as access to health care. The chapter concludes by considering the key health policy issues related to population aging that face the United States and other nations.

Although death is an individual experience, the process of dying is socially conditioned.

Chapter 14 first describes cross-cultural and historical practices regarding dying and death. It considers some timely debates over the right to die. Finally, it analyzes research on widowhood and grief, looking at death from the perspective of those who are left behind.

Old Age and the Welfare State

*M*iss Ida Fuller was the first person to receive Social Security benefits in 1940.

Looking Ahead

1. What kinds of welfare programs are available to aging Americans?
2. What are the government-sponsored sources of income support for the aging?
3. What government health care programs serve the elderly?
4. Which government programs protect the disabled?
5. How is long-term care of the elderly financed in the United States?
6. What social services does the Older Americans Act provide?

ax Cross, age 58, proudly touts his conservative principles. He believes that government is too big and supports politicians who propose cutting wasteful government spending. Yet even while he gripes, his 80-year-old parents receive over $1,400 a month in Social Security benefits, his disabled 49-year-old sister receives Disability Insurance benefits of $1,000 a month, and Max himself gets to deduct more than $20,000 a year off his taxes from the interest payments he makes on the mortgage of his comfortable home in the suburbs and another $10,500 from his contributions to his pension fund

at the insurance company where he works. When he retires in seven years, he will have ample pension savings and generous Social Security benefits. Like many Americans, Max fails to recognize that he is one of the beneficiaries of big government.

Underlying all public debates about the future of Social Security and Medicare, the quality of health care, and generational equity is the issue of the role of government.

In this chapter, we describe the elaborate network of social programs provided by the government, and we consider their impact on the lives of the elderly, their families, and the larger society. The first section of the chapter delineates the underlying principles on which these programs are based, highlighting the role of cultural beliefs and values in influencing the direction of the programs. It also looks at how social welfare programs in the United States compare to those in other Western industrialized nations. The second section of the chapter describes major provisions of the core programs of the American welfare state. The chapter concludes with a discussion of current debates about the equitable allocation of national resources, specifically, whether benefits should be distributed on the basis of age or need.

SOCIAL PROGRAMS OF THE WELFARE STATE

Social scientists, use the term *welfare* broadly to refer to all programs that protect people from the risks of loss of income due to unemployment, disability, divorce, poor health, or retirement. Thus, welfare means not only cash assistance to the poor but any social program that enhances well-being and provides financial security. The term **welfare state** refers to all the government programs that serve these objectives. Although these programs may appear to provide individual benefits only, they do much more. For example, the welfare state influences employment patterns in a variety of ways. Of course, Social Security benefits provide income to retirees, but they also help manage an orderly exit of older workers from the labor force. Medicare not only provides the elderly with health insurance but also creates employment opportunities for a vast industry of health care providers.

The welfare state also influences family relationships. Income from Social Security provides the elderly with an independent income so their children do not have to support them. Public housing for the aged means that fewer three-generation households are formed. And long-term-care services enable some of the frail elderly to live independently in the community rather than with relatives or in a nursing home.

As these examples make clear, the social programs of the welfare state not only provide income and social services but also organize social relations. In this respect, welfare states are "key institutions in the structuring of class and the social order" (Esping-Anderson, 1990:55). They are sets of rules and policies that redistribute resources across social classes and generations. The rules establish levels and forms of taxation and eligibility criteria and formulas for determining benefits. Thus, the welfare state does not merely seek to lessen social inequality but is, in itself, a system of stratification. What this means is that it contributes to the ranking of individuals in a social hierarchy (Smelser, 1988).

Welfare programs can be classified into three types: *social assistance, social insurance,* and *fiscal welfare*. Each has its own set of rules regarding who pays for the benefit, who is eligible to receive it, and how much beneficiaries receive. Moreover, each type of program reflects a particular set of values and attitudes toward the needy.

Social Assistance

Social assistance programs provide minimal benefits for the very needy. They are based on a set of values that presume people suffer from a lack of medical care, food, housing, and income because they do not live as they should (Marmor, Mashaw, and Harvey, 1990). Welfare programs based on a social assistance model contain eligibility criteria—that is, rules for receiving benefits—that are designed to encourage the able-bodied to work, families to take responsibility for the care of the young, the old, and the disabled, and individuals to prepare for their own future. These eligibility criteria determine who can apply for benefits, such as widows, the sick, the disabled, or the aged, and what conditions these individuals must meet to receive benefits. Typically, the most important condition is being very poor, but other conditions such as being widowed, deserted, or old have also been applied.

Social assistance benefits derive from the sixteenth century British system of poor relief. The early poor-law philosophy emphasized that the nonworking poor should not be treated better than the lowest-wage earners (Myles, 1989). Social assistance (i.e., welfare benefits) is still accompanied by moral judgments designed to teach civic lessons about the importance of self-sufficiency. One distinguishing feature of social assistance programs is that applicants are subject to a **means test** to prove they are worthy of support. Means tests are often considered demeaning because individuals' income, assets, and behavior are examined and judged by a caseworker. Even very poor people may be denied benefits because they are viewed as thriftless or immoral. Because means-tested benefits are quite low and often stigmatizing, they compel all but the most desperate to participate in the labor market.

Social assistance benefits are typically paid for through income taxes. These are **progressive taxes,** meaning that the higher one's income, the higher the tax rate.

Advocates of means testing claim that allocating benefits on the basis of need encourages people to work and efficiently distributes scarce resources. Critics claim that means testing not only stigmatizes those who receive the benefits but is also politically divisive. They note that any program in which gains for some result in losses for others arouses opposition. Middle-class people, for example, often resent paying taxes for programs that help the poor and seemingly give members of the middle class nothing in return. When people believe that outcomes are profoundly inequitable, resentment may turn into open hostility, triggering a backlash against both the program and its beneficiaries.

Social Insurance

The principles underlying **social insurance** programs differ from those of social assistance. The basic purpose of social insurance is to provide economic security over the life course and to prevent people from falling into destitution, not to rescue them after they have already fallen. The central concept of social insurance is an earned entitlement (Marmor et al., 1990). Social insurance is based on two principles that distinguish it from social assistance: (1) the notion that people contribute to a common pool and (2) the view that people share common risks—the risk of unemployment, disability, or loss of wages in retirement. Making contributions gives workers an earned right to benefits. Pooling the risks means that the costs for one family or individual do not become overwhelming but are shared across an entire population. Social insurance benefits provide income and health care benefits to workers who make contributions over their working life and who earn the right to receive benefits automatically when they reach the age of eligibility. With such programs, age, not need, determines who receives benefits.

Social insurance benefits are paid for through **payroll taxes,** which are considered contributions. The present rate of the payroll tax is 15.2 percent. Half is paid by the worker and half by the employer. Self-employed people pay the full 15.2 percent.

Social insurance benefits promote equality in principle: All workers are endowed with equal rights to benefits, regardless of whether they are poor. In practice, however, social insurance reduces inequality in old age but does not eliminate it, because benefit levels are tied to previous earnings. Those who earn less money over the course of their working lives receive lower benefits when they retire.

Fiscal Welfare

At first glance, the public expenditures of the welfare state appear to be distinct from private benefits, such as pensions paid to former workers by their employers. But a third category of benefits, referred to as **fiscal welfare,** consists of indirect payments to individuals through the tax system. Fiscal welfare blurs the public–private dichotomy because benefits are provided through the private sector but are subsidized by the tax system (Shalev, 1996).

In the United States, fiscal welfare is called **tax expenditures.** Tax expenditures are special income tax provisions implemented through the tax code. In other words, they are tax breaks. What makes them similar to spending programs is that they are designed to accomplish some social or economic goal. For example, if the government wants to subsidize wages for low-income workers, it could try to accomplish this goal in several ways. It might set a minimum wage that businesses must pay; it might provide direct wage subsidies to workers in the form of food stamps;

or it might reduce income taxes for low-income workers and even give a tax refund to those who owe no taxes. In fact, the U.S. government does all three, but only the last is a tax expenditure. The Earned Income Tax Credit not only refunds taxes paid by low-income families, it also provides them an income supplement. Tax expenditures are part of the "hidden welfare state" (Howard, 1993).

Other tax expenditures include employee contributions to employer-provided pensions, personal savings for retirement, employer-provided health insurance, and home mortgage interest. These programs represent an indirect approach to achieving public objectives such as encouraging savings for retirement, expanding health insurance coverage, and encouraging home ownership.

Tax expenditures are inherently unequal in their impact. One reason is that they allow individuals receiving the same income to pay taxes at different rates. For example, workers who contribute to an employer-provided pension fund pay less in taxes than workers who make no pension contributions. Similarly, individuals who receive health insurance through their employers pay lower taxes than those who have no health insurance. Home owners can deduct the interest they pay on their mortgage, whereas renters with similar incomes aren't eligible for this deduction. Mainly, however, tax expenditures promote inequality because middle- and upper-middle-class Americans are the primary beneficiaries; the working class and the poor receive little or no benefit from them because they are more likely to rent than to own their own homes and less likely to have jobs that provide benefits. In 1996, for example, a $1,000 deduction for home mortgage interest was worth $396 to a taxpayer in the highest bracket but only $150 to a home-owning family of four earning $40,000 (Office of Management and Budget, 1996).

Public scrutiny about how to fairly distribute resources has focused primarily on direct public benefits, especially Social Security and Medicare (see Chapter 17), and on payroll taxes, which have increased about 3 percent per decade since 1935. We will examine these debates in greater detail in Chapters 13 and 15. Largely ignored in these controversies have been tax expenditures. In the twenty-first century, all types of social programs must be considered in devising an equitable solution to rising public budgets.

THE ORGANIZATION OF THE AMERICAN WELFARE STATE

Franklin Delano Roosevelt took office in 1933 with a mandate to inaugurate a new era in government intervention. Until he became president, the United States had no national social welfare programs, and only scattered, meagerly funded state-level programs for old age pensions, mothers' pensions, and workers' compensation.

The cornerstone of Roosevelt's New Deal, the **Social Security Act of 1935,** marked the initiation of the American welfare state. It created two programs for the elderly: **Social Security** for retired workers and **Old Age Assistance** for the aged poor. From 1935 to the 1970s, the welfare state expanded to include benefits for spouses and widows (1937), public housing projects to house the poor (1937), **Disability Insurance** to provide income for workers of all ages who were unable to work (1956), and in 1965 two new health insurance programs, **Medicare** and **Medicaid,** and a piece of legislation known as the **Older Americans Act,** which established a network of social services for the aged. Although these social programs supported a variety of people ranging from single mothers to the unemployed, the vast majority of expenditures were allocated to older people. Consequently, researchers have sometimes called this array of social programs the "welfare state of the elderly" (Myles and Teichroew, 1991).

Although the welfare state of the elderly appears complex in terms of benefits and eligibility criteria, most programs fall into one of the three categories previously described: social assistance, social insurance, or fiscal welfare. Table 11–1 categorizes the core programs of the American welfare state and delineates the basic features of each.

Income Support

Social security system   In the nineteenth century, formal retirement from the labor force was reserved for a privileged few. Most people continued to

The first national welfare programs were legislated in 1935 when President Franklin Delano Roosevelt signed the Social Security Act into law.

work throughout their adult lives, and employers sometimes shifted their older employees to less arduous work rather than give them a pension. The family was a major source of support for most elderly people. Charity payments provided a safety net for those who lacked other support; for the truly destitute, poor relief, or "welfare," was the measure of last resort.

During the Great Depression of the 1930s, unemployment was a major social problem. The risk of unemployment was especially high among older workers (Quadagno, 1988a). The Social Security Act of 1935 created Social Security, the nation's first program of social insurance, which was established to provide a minimum level of financial support but not to be the sole source of income for retirees. Benefits were to be paid out of contributions that workers and their employers made into a trust fund. At 65, workers would be eligible automatically for benefits that were linked to prior earnings and length of work history. Social Security

thus intervened directly in the labor market to achieve the social goals of retiring older workers and creating jobs for younger workers. To ensure that older workers did indeed retire, a strict **earnings test** was added. Anyone under age 70 who earned more than $15 a month forfeited all his or her Social Security benefits (Graebner, 1980). In 2000 the earnings test was eliminated for workers aged 65 to 69. Workers in this age group may earn as much as they can and keep all their Social Security benefits.

Since 1935, the Social Security Act has been amended several times. In 1939 a spouse benefit and a widow's benefit were added. Initially, only wives and widows of retired male workers were eligible, but today both men and women are eligible for these benefits. The spouse benefit is currently 50 percent of the worker's benefit; the widow's benefit is equal to 100 percent of the worker's benefit (see Chapter 16). Later amendments to the Social Security Act

Table 11-1	Organization of the American Welfare State	
Type of Program	**Funding Source**	**Who Benefits**
Social assistance		
Medicaid	Income tax	Health insurance for aged, blind, and disabled poor
SSI	Income tax	Income for aged, blind, and disabled poor; may also receive Medicaid
Social insurance		
Social Security	Payroll tax paid by workers and employers	Income for workers at age 62 or later or dependents
Medicare	Payroll tax paid by workers and employers	Health insurance for Social Security recipients and for spouse at age 65
Disability Insurance	Payroll tax paid by workers and employers	Income for any disabled worker who has contributed to Social Security; also eligible for Medicare
Fiscal welfare		
Tax expenditures for pensions	Tax break for employees	Firms that contribute to pension funds; workers who contribute to pension funds or retirement savings accounts
Health Insurance deductions	Tax break for employees	Workers who have employer health insurance
Home mortgage interest	Tax break for home owners	Home owners

provided benefits for the disabled and allowed workers to retire at age 62 with a reduced benefit.

In 2000 more than 44 million Americans received Social Security benefits. As Figure 11–1 shows, Social Security has evolved into the most important source of income for people 65 and older. Nearly 40 percent of the income of older people comes from Social Security. Almost two-thirds of the elderly rely on Social Security for over half their income. Some persons rely on Social Security for their entire income. Those totally dependent on Social Security include 18 percent of elderly white women, 38 percent of elderly blacks, and 38 percent of elderly Hispanics (Hungerford et al., 2003). Without Social Security, nearly 40 percent of the elderly would have incomes below the poverty level (see Figure 11–2). These benefits do even more to reduce poverty among the single elderly and the black and Hispanic elderly.

Social Security benefits provide income for many types of people. In 1998 only 43 percent of Social Security benefits went to retired workers. As Figure 11–3 shows, 16 percent of the benefits went to the disabled, 13 percent to widows, widowers, and parents, 20 percent to children, and 8 percent to wives and husbands of retired workers (Social Security Administration, 1999).

Because Social Security is a social insurance program, all who contribute receive benefits as a right. Benefit levels are determined by a formula that reflects the length of time worked and the amount of wages earned. As a result, people who have low earnings while they are working ultimately receive lower benefits than high earners when they retire.

The term **replacement rate** refers to the amount of preretirement pay that is replaced by the Social Security retirement benefit. For example, a worker who earned an average of $35,000 yearly and who

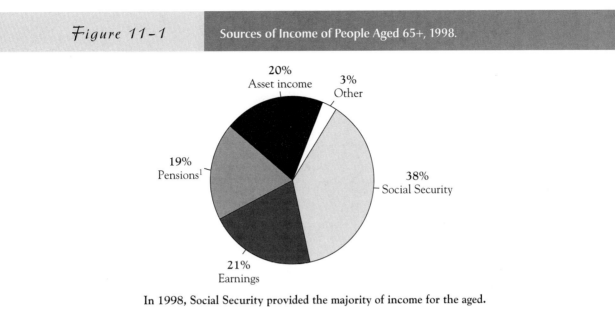

Figure 11-1 · Sources of Income of People Aged 65+, 1998.

- 20% Asset income
- 3% Other
- 38% Social Security
- 21% Earnings
- 19% Pensions[1]

In 1998, Social Security provided the majority of income for the aged.

[1]Includes private pensions and annuities, government pensions, Railroad Retirement, and IRA, Keogh, and 401(k) payments.
Source: Social Security Administration (1999).

retired at age 65 would receive a benefit that was 37 percent of his or her final pay, or $13,000 a year. To compensate for the inequity stemming from the labor market, Social Security provides higher replacement rates to low earners. People with higher lifetime earnings have lower replacement rates. For example, a high-wage earner has a replacement rate of just 28 percent whereas a low-wage worker has a replacement rate of 78 percent (Koitz, 1996a). Giving low-wage workers higher replacement rates eases the effect of market inequity to some extent, but it doesn't eliminate inequality. Although replacement rates are higher for the poor, actual benefits remain lower than those of wealthier individuals. Table 11–2 shows average Social Security benefits for low earners, average earners, and high earners for 2001 and projected benefits for 2030. In 2001 low earners received $7,661 yearly while high earners received $16,419.

Benefit levels are also determined by age at retirement. Workers who retire at age 62 receive benefits that are reduced by 20 percent of what they would have received at 65. For example, an individual who earned average wages would receive

Table 11-2 · Estimated Annual Benefits to Workers Who Retire at Age 65, by Earnings Level

Year	Low Earner	Average Earner	High Earner
2001	$7,661	$12,642	$16,419
2030	$9,598	$15,843	$20,936

Source: Social Security Administration (2003).

$899 a month at age 62 compared to $1,124 at age 65. The percentage will gradually rise to 30 percent. By 2030, a worker who retires at age 62 will receive only 70 percent of the full retirement benefit, and workers who want to receive the maximum amount will have to wait until they reach age 67.

In 2004, the average monthly Social Security benefit was $922. Benefits varied greatly by race and gender. Women and minorities received lower benefits on average than white males. The reasons for these disparities will be examined more fully in Chapter 16.

Figure 11-2   Social Security's Role in Reducing Poverty, 1998.

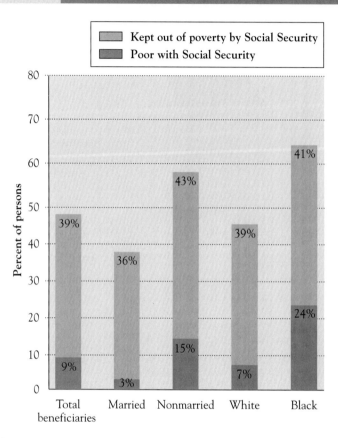

Source: Social Security Administration (1999).

Supplemental security income   As noted,
the Social Security Act also created a program of
social assistance for the aged poor who had not
earned the right to Social Security benefits. It was
called Old Age Assistance and was jointly funded
and administered by the states and the federal
government. Because states had a good deal of lee-
way in setting benefit levels, there was significant
variation across states. When the program was
enacted in 1935, benefits were as low as $7 a
month in Mississippi, compared to $27 in Massa-
chusetts or $30 in California (Quadagno, 1988a).
In 1972, Old Age Assistance became a fully federal
program when Congress converted it to **Supplemental Security Income (SSI).**

SSI is a means-tested social assistance program
for the aged, blind, and disabled poor, but as a program of social assistance, it includes several features
that make it inadequate for protecting the poorest
elderly. One problem is that the federal minimum
benefit is set below the poverty level. In 2004, the
benefit was $564 for a single individual and $846
for a couple (Social Security Administration,
2003). Some states add a supplement to these federal minimums, which amount to only 75 percent
of poverty-level income for an individual and
89 percent for a couple. Thus, even those who receive the benefit remain poor. Another problem is
that SSI payments are reduced by one-third if the
recipient lives with a relative. This penalizes elderly

Figure 11-3   Social Security Benefits by Type of Recipient, December 1998.

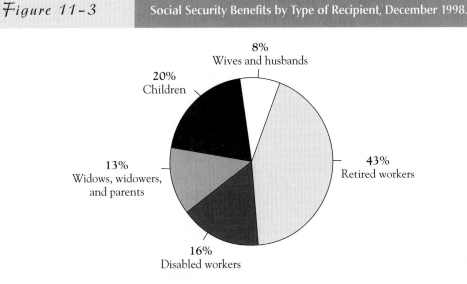

Source: Social Security Administration (1999).

women, who are more likely than men to move in with relatives because of limited income, failing health, or both. A further problem is that anywhere from 30 to 50 percent of those who are eligible do not apply for benefits because they don't know the benefits are available or because of the social stigma attached to them (Bould et al., 1989). Many older people are unwilling to endure the humiliating scrutiny of a means test. Although SSI benefits were very low in the 1990s, Congress became concerned about reports that elderly immigrants were abusing the program.

When Congress enacted welfare reform under the Personal Responsibility and Work Opportunity Reconciliation Act of 1996, it made legal immigrants ineligible for welfare programs, including SSI. In 1997 it modified the legislation to exclude only those elderly legal immigrants who arrived in the United States after August 22, 1996. Thus, legal immigrants who arrived before that time remain eligible for benefits. What caused Congress to act to prevent legal immigrants from receiving SSI?

People who support restricting public aid argue that many immigrant families brought their aged relatives to the United States to shift the burden

of their support to the state and federal governments. They believe that immigrants who live in this country for more than five years should show their commitment to it by becoming citizens. Critics note that, like citizens, legal immigrants must pay taxes and register for the Selective Service (Congressional Budget Office, 1995b) and therefore should not be denied the benefits accorded citizens.

In fact, the idea that SSI serves as a magnet that attracts poor elderly immigrants is a myth. Most of the growth in the SSI caseload represents immigrants who have lived in the United States for at least 10 years. Only a small proportion of SSI cases involve recent immigrants (Van Hook and Bean, 1999).

What would be the likely consequences of restricting eligibility for SSI to citizens? Demographer Judith Treas (1995b) estimates that in California, home to nearly half the nation's alien SSI recipients, two-thirds of those who lost their benefits would have no other means of cash support. Of those who would have lost their benefits under the initial legislation, 36 percent could not work because they were disabled, 41 percent had less than four years of schooling, and 75 percent could not speak English well, if at all. Compounding the problem is the fact that many older immigrants are not permitted to work in the United States.

Undoubtedly, families would provide some support to their aging kin; they are already required to do so by law. However, not all legal aliens have relatives nearby, and among those who do, family members are often poor themselves. Thus, the loss of SSI benefits could mean that many legal immigrants would lose any independent source of income. Instead of contributing to their family's household, many would become a financial burden on their children and grandchildren.

Finally, in many states the law obligates county governments to care for the poor. Thus, provisions barring recent legal aliens from SSI are likely to be shifted to lower levels of government—to the states and counties—moving responsibility for elderly immigrants to the units of government least able to absorb the cost.

Tax expenditures for pensions

Tax expenditures for employer pensions have played an important role in expanding private pension programs. As early as the 1930s, the tax code encouraged firms to introduce pension plans for their employees by allowing them to accumulate contributions to these plans tax free. Amendments to the tax code in the 1940s increased the tax advantage on money paid into pension funds and on interest generated by those funds (Quadagno and Hardy, 1996).

The amount of tax expenditures for pensions is a considerable sum that rivals public spending through Social Security. In the U.S. tax code, tax expenditures for private pensions represent the single-largest deduction. The tax relief granted to individuals for pension savings was $82 billion in 1995, an amount that was one-quarter of all direct outlays for Social Security and that exceeded direct expenditures for SSI by three times (U.S House of Representatives, 1995).

The United States is not the only country that encourages private sector provision through tax expenditures. In Canada and Great Britain, personal and occupational pensions receive similar treatment. In 1989, the Canadian government spent a total of $11.9 billion to subsidize private pension savings, approximately one-third the cost of all direct public expenditures on pensions (Street, 1996). Similarly, in Great Britain the amount of tax forgone to subsidize private pension schemes amounted to one-third the cost of current public pensions (Wilkinson, 1993). Whereas the United States is similar to Canada and Great Britain in encouraging private sector provisions through tax expenditures, it differs from these countries in its use of tax expenditures for health insurance.

Health Care

Like the programs for income in retirement, the programs for health care are divided among the categories of social insurance, social assistance, and fiscal welfare.

Medicare

Congress enacted Medicare in 1965 as a national health insurance program for all people 65 or older who are eligible for Social Security. It is a social insurance program granted as an automatic right to all qualified workers and their spouses. The battle for Medicare began in 1950; after a struggle of 15 years, Congress finally passed the legislation. Who would oppose Medicare? Many physicians opposed it because they were afraid that if the government paid for health care, federal officials might lower their fees or interfere in their medical practices. The insurance industry also opposed Medicare, because insurers feared government competition.

Yet insuring the elderly was a costly enterprise, and by the early 1960s, private insurance clearly was not meeting the need. One physician and Medicare supporter, Dr. Caldwell Esselstyn, who ran a clinic for the elderly and the poor from 1946 to 1964, recalled how older people would avoid going to a doctor even when they were seriously ill, because they could not pay the doctor's fees. These people's only option was medicine provided through the local welfare system. In the "In Their Own Words" feature, Dr. Esselstyn recalls some of the difficulties older people faced as a result of their inability to pay for health care.

Medicare focuses primarily on acute care and pays little for preventive care or long-term care, subjects we consider in more detail in Chapters 10 and 13. The program has two parts. **Medicare Part A**

In Their Own Words

Health Care before Medicare

All along the way, we were faced with this problem of trying to provide medical care of high quality to people who certainly were in need, to people who really were entitled, according to all of the eligibility tests, to welfare, but who were reluctant to lose the old family homestead and who were reluctant to turn to their children and become a burden on their children. . . . There are some real hair-raising stories that can be told about the people that just kept putting off and putting off. These were people in their 70s and 80s. . . . I can think of a call one time we got from my next door neighbor. They said that Mother was hemorrhaging from a rupture. . . . When I got there here was Grandma in the middle of the kitchen. It was a single room house with outdoor toilet facilities and here was Grandma in the middle of a pool of blood. . . . It turned out that she had an umbilical hernia, . . . which had become punctured and hung out maybe 18 inches, about a week before. Here it was ten days later.

Well, these are the kinds of things which I think people who have been in the practice of medicine are fully aware of. I think of an old man who came in with a so-called basal cell epithelioma on the side of his face, which involved his ear. . . . Again, here was something which had gone on and on, and the man was reluctant to do anything about it, because it would involve his children.

Source: Esselstyn (1965:3–4).

---

is hospital insurance paid for through payroll taxes. It covers hospitalization for up to 90 days for a "spell of illness" plus a one-time supply of 60 "lifetime reserve days" that can be used to extend the covered period. The first 60 days of a spell of illness are fully covered by Medicare after the individual has made a co-payment. After the 60 days are up, the individual has to pay $194 per day. For example, in 2003 a Medicare recipient had to pay the first $840 of a hospital stay as a co-payment, then $194 per day for days 60 through 90 of a hospital stay. The limitation on payments for a lengthy hospital stay is designed to discourage the use of hospitals for recovery. People who need extensive care to recuperate from surgery or illness are sent to a nursing home.

Medicare Part B is an optional program that pays for 80 percent of the cost of physician office visits. Over 98 percent of all Medicare beneficiaries

elect Part B. A Medicare beneficiary who has Part B coverage must pay the first $100 each year on allowable charges plus 20 percent for each physician visit and any additional amount beyond that covered by Medicare that the physician is allowed to charge (Moon, 1993).

Part B entails two financing mechanisms. The first is a premium paid by beneficiaries, which in 2003 was $49.50 a month. Premiums pay about 25 percent of the actual cost of the program. The rest is funded from income taxes. In the 1997 federal budget agreement, Congress raised the premiums so that older people pay a higher percentage of the cost of the program.

There is no doubt that Medicare has been an enormous boon for the aged. Before Congress passed Medicare, few older people had health insurance. Yet even with Medicare, many health

Seventy-seven-year-old Myrtle Gosse pays the pharmacist for her order. New prescription drug coverage under Medicare will help alleviate some of the burden on the elderly.

care needs remain uncovered. Medicare does not pay for any of the following: routine physical exams, routine eye exams and glasses, hearing aids, routine foot care and orthopedic shoes, most immunizations, and services considered not "medically necessary." In 2003 a new prescription drug benefit was added to medicare. This benefit will help to alleviate some of the burden of health care expenses, which are especially heavy for the poor. In 2000 elderly people with income below the poverty level spent 35 percent of their income on health care (American Association of Retired Persons, 2000). Another problem is that Medicare does not cover people who retire before they reach 65. People aged 55 to 64 who are unemployed, retired, or employed in jobs that do not provide health insurance can find it very difficult to obtain health insurance at an affordable price. For a discussion of a proposal to allow older peo-

ple to buy in to Medicare, see "An Issue for Public Policy" on page 267.

Because so many expenses are not covered by Medicare, many older people purchase **Medigap policies** from private insurance companies. Nearly three-fourths of people 65 or older have some form of Medigap coverage. Medigap premiums can be as high as $3,000 a year, depending on age and health, so it is not surprising that poor people are less likely to have these policies. One study found that only 41 percent of elderly with incomes below the poverty level had Medigap policies, compared to 78 percent of those with average incomes (Commonwealth Fund, 1987). Medigap coverage also varies by race, especially among the poor. The study cited previously found that 48 percent of poor whites had Medigap policies, compared to only 17 percent of poor nonwhites. Among the poor, the racial disparity may

An Issue for Public Policy

EXTENDING MEDICARE TO OLDER WORKERS AND EARLY RETIREES

Medicare provides health insurance for Social Security beneficiaries aged 65 or older, and Medicaid provides health insurance for the very poor. All other Americans must obtain their health insurance in the private market. Private insurance companies prefer to provide coverage to younger, healthy individuals who will be unlikely to need many health care services and who therefore are the most profitable customers. Because of this preference, people aged 55 to 64, a group called the "near-elderly," can be at risk of losing their health insurance if they lose their jobs or become divorced or widowed. One analysis of the Health and Retirement Survey of individuals born between 1931 and 1941 found that 78.3 percent of married individuals had health insurance, compared to 59.9 percent of divorced persons and 54.8 percent of widowed persons (Johnson and Crystal, 1997).

Over the past 15 years, states and the federal government have enacted a number of reforms to prevent insurance companies from refusing to provide coverage to older or unhealthier high-risk people (Pollitz, 2001). One reform, called COBRA, requires insurance companies to offer temporary coverage to people who retire early, become divorced or widowed, or become unemployed. Another reform, called HIPAA, prohibits insurance companies from using an individual's health to determine eligibility for coverage. The problem is that neither COBRA nor HIPPA regulates costs. Many older people who lose their jobs or become divorced or widowed find that private health insurance can be extremely expensive.

One plan to solve their problem would allow people aged 55 to 64 to buy into Medicare. Although this plan would help the near-elderly who may find it difficult to purchase a policy in the private insurance market, it would significantly raise the cost of the Medicare program. Congress considered this idea in 2000 but failed to act. The issue is unlikely to be resolved in the near future but will certainly be raised again.

What Do You Think?

1. Do you have health insurance? Does everyone in your family have health insurance?
2. What are some consequences of being uninsured?

be due to discrimination by insurers. Whatever the reason, the discrepancy illustrates the inequity that arises in access to benefits in the private sector.

Medicaid   In the same year that Congress enacted Medicare, it also established Medicaid, a social assistance program of health insurance for the aged, blind, and disabled poor. In contrast to Medicare recipients, only those with very low incomes are eligible for Medicaid. Medicaid pays for a variety of health care services, including acute care services, hospitalization, diagnostic testing and treatment, physician visits, and prescription drugs. Medicaid also pays many of the costs Medicare does not cover as well as paying for nursing home care.

Although Medicaid has provided health insurance to people who otherwise would have none, only those with incomes well below poverty level are eligible. As a result, fewer than one-third of all poor older people receive Medicaid (U.S. Bureau of the Census, 1990b, table 148:98).

Another limitation is that Medicaid reimburses physicians for their costs at rates lower than the fees they charge their private-pay patients and prevents them from billing their patients for any uncovered portion of the bill. Because of these provisions, many physicians refuse to see Medicaid patients. Just 6 percent of all physicians see one-third of all Medicaid patients (Harrington Meyer, 1991). A pressing public policy issue is whether the government should equalize payments to physicians across public and private sector programs in order to eliminate the incentives to avoid Medicaid patients.

Tax expenditures for health insurance
The United States is the only Western nation that lacks national health insurance for all citizens. Instead, it has used the tax code to encourage employers to provide health insurance. The tax code allows employers to deduct expenditures for the health insurance they provide. Instead of giving an employee a higher salary to defray the cost of health insurance premiums, the employer pays the premiums, which are not counted as wages for tax purposes (U.S. House of Representatives, 1994). In 1997, employer-paid health insurance premiums cost nearly $57 billion in lost tax revenues (Office of Management and Budget, 1996).

The result of these tax provisions has been an increase in inequality in the distribution of tax benefits. The tax expenditure for health insurance means that individuals who earn the same yearly income may pay different taxes depending on whether their employer provides health insurance.

Support for the Disabled

Disability insurance   Retirement is not the only major change that workers may confront as they grow older. People sometimes become disabled before they reach retirement age. Consider the case of Estelle Guitierrez, who had worked on the assembly line of a canning factory for 31 years. At the age of 52, she developed a heart condition that made it impossible for her to stand eight hours a day on her feet. Because she was no longer able to do her job, Estelle was eligible for Disability Insurance (DI) benefits. Although she was only 52, she received the same amount she would have received in Social Security benefits had she been 65.

Disability Insurance is part of the Social Security system. It insures workers against the loss of income should they become physically or mentally disabled. For purposes of Disability Insurance, a person is disabled if he or she is unable to engage in any "substantial gainful activity" because of a physical or mental impairment expected to cause death or to last at least 12 months. The definition of substantial gainful employment is quite imprecise. Some people with severe disabilities nonetheless work full-time. Others who may be less physically disabled remain unemployed because they can't find a suitable job. People who are temporarily disabled (i.e., for less than six months) are ineligible for benefits.

Physicians are involved in determining whether an applicant for DI meets the criteria for benefits. The problem is, determining disability requires knowing not only what the individual's impairment is but what abilities his or her job requires. Confounding the problem is the fact that many people have no clear organic impairment. Complaints such as lower back pain, chronic fatigue syndrome, whiplash, repetitive strain injury, and chest pain may not involve detectable damage (Loeser and Sullivan, 1997). Furthermore, some people with a given impairment, such as repetitive strain injury, may be able to work but others may not, depending on their tolerance for pain and the type of work they do. Because disability is a flexible concept, disability rates fluctuate over time. Between 1990 and 1993, when the U.S. economy was in recession, the number of DI recipients increased 24 percent (Koitz, 1994b), suggesting that people who might otherwise have continued working applied for DI benefits after losing their jobs. Plant closings, downsizings, mergers, or other economic changes that place the jobs of older workers at risk will expand the DI rolls.

Benefits are paid to the disabled worker and to his or her children under age 18, to the aged spouse, or to a spouse of any age who is caring for an eligible child (U.S. House of Representatives, 1993). Once an individual is awarded disability benefits, he or she may continue to receive them until (1) death, (2) conversion to regular Social Security benefits at age 65, or (3) medical recovery or return to work. After 24 months of being disabled, an individual is also eligible for Medicare. Although workers of all ages are eligible for DI benefits, more than 60 percent of those who receive them are older than 45. Thus, the DI program operates as a de facto retirement system.

SSI disability Some people with disabilities have never worked for wages or have not worked long enough to qualify for Disability Insurance. For example, Michael Cancion was a 19-year-old college sophomore when he suffered a spinal cord injury in an auto accident that left him paralyzed from the waist down. Because he had worked only a few part-time jobs before his accident, he was ineligible for Disability Insurance. Michael's support comes from Supplemental Security Income. Receipt of SSI benefits also means he is eligible for Medicaid (Koitz, 1994b).

Work disincentives Most people who enter the disability programs never leave, although surveys show that two-thirds of working-age persons with disabilities want to work. One reason people remain on disability is that they fear losing their jobs. They also fear that they may not earn enough to survive.

These fears are realistic, for disabled people do have unstable employment and often work in jobs that pay only minimum wages (National Academy of Social Insurance, 1994). Many can't risk giving up disability benefits to take a job and then find they are out of work six months later. The DI program itself does little to help people with disabilities find employment. In 1993, only 12 percent of the people with disability claims were referred for vocational rehabilitation; of those, only 4 percent got jobs (National Academy of Social Insurance, 1994).

Fear of losing health insurance also keeps disabled workers from seeking work. Disability Insurance recipients receive free health care through Medicare while on the rolls, but they must pay their full share of the costs when they work. Since so many disabled people work at low wages, they usually can't afford the Medicare premiums.

As with the Disability Insurance program, the fear of losing health insurance prevents many SSI beneficiaries from seeking work. Although SSI is run by the federal government, Medicaid is a joint federal–state program. That means that the rules about Medicaid eligibility vary enormously from state to state. In some states, SSI recipients risk losing all health insurance when they find a job. Many SSI recipients state that the fear of losing Medicaid is greater than the fear of losing the cash benefits (National Academy of Social Insurance, 1994).

Long-Term Care

Most Americans 65 or older are physically active and able to care for themselves. With advancing age, however, the prevalence of disability rises steeply to 58 percent among people 85 and older (Rivlin and Wiener, 1988). Those with multiple disabilities need long-term care. **Long-term care** refers to the range of services and supportive living environments that help the elderly and disabled live independently. It also refers to institutional care for those who need more extensive help. Ideally, long-term care services should track clients over time and include an array of health, mental health, and social services that fulfill a range of needs. Because the United States has no national long-term-care program, this ideal has not even been partially realized. Instead, limited services are available; service provision is fragmented, divided among several programs, and underfunded; and many needs remain unfulfilled.

Medicare's long-term-care benefits   Medicare pays a tiny, though rapidly growing, proportion of long-term-care expenditures. One type of long-term-care service is home health care. Medicare provides for a limited amount of home health care, but there are strict rules about who can receive such services. They must be provided by a physician with the expectation that the patient can be rehabilitated. Care for chronic illnesses such as arthritis and Parkinson's disease, in which the goal is to slow the pace of deterioration, is excluded. Patients who need home care must be confined to their homes, and their mobility must be considerably impaired. Otherwise, they are expected to go to an outpatient facility for treatment (Schaffer, 1993). People who show no improvement lose their benefits. Medicare does not pay for general household maintenance such as laundry, grocery shopping, or other home care services that help people manage their daily lives.

The objective of paying for rehabilitation for those who can get well but not for those who cannot recover is to save money. In the long run, however, the costs of such an approach may be greater. For example, a person suffering from a degenerative disease such as multiple sclerosis might stay mobile and active much longer with regular physical therapy. Without therapy, that person might become wheelchair-bound and need more intensive personal care.

Medicaid's long-term-care benefits   The main source of public funding for long-term care is Medicaid. Although Medicaid does pay for the costs of long-term custodial care in a nursing home, these benefits are provided only to low-income aged who sufficiently spend down their assets to qualify (Grogan and Patashnik, 2003). In 2000 the Medicaid program spent more than $31 billion on nursing home care and $4.9 billion on home and community-based services (Rich, 2002). Most older people would prefer to receive services in their own home rather than go to a nursing home, and in the past decade, there has been a shift toward services. As Figure 11–4 shows, however, the vast majority of Medicaid dollars are spent on institutional care.

The Medicaid payment system also fosters inequality in the treatment people receive. Many nursing homes have separate wings for Medicaid

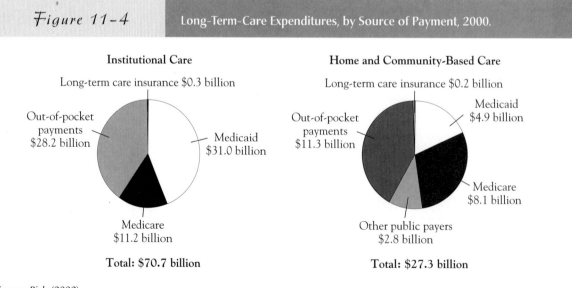

Figure 11–4   Long-Term-Care Expenditures, by Source of Payment, 2000.

Institutional Care

Long-term care insurance $0.3 billion

Out-of-pocket payments $28.2 billion

Medicaid $31.0 billion

Medicare $11.2 billion

Total: $70.7 billion

Home and Community-Based Care

Long-term care insurance $0.2 billion

Medicaid $4.9 billion

Out-of-pocket payments $11.3 billion

Medicare $8.1 billion

Other public payers $2.8 billion

Total: $27.3 billion

Source: Rich (2002).

and private-pay residents. In the Medicaid wing "as many as four residents share a room and bath in surroundings that are relentlessly functional—metal beds, plastic utensils, linoleum floors." In the non-Medicaid wing, by contrast, "the halls are carpeted and the dining room tables may gleam with real china and glassware; each resident has a room and bath to herself" (Margolis, 1990:167).

In 1981, in response to concerns that Medicaid was encouraging unnecessary institutionalization, Congress allowed states to apply for waivers so they could experiment with innovative ways to provide services. The **Home and Community-Based Waiver Services Program (HCBS)** allows states to provide the poor and the disabled with a variety of services, including homemaker services, respite care, day care, meals-on-wheels, physical therapy, and help with chores (Neuschler, 1987). As a result, nationwide HCBS expenditures are expanding. In just two years, from 1991 to 1993, total spending for Medicaid HCBS services increased by 20.4 percent from $4.8 billion to $5.7 billion. By 2003 all 50 states had waivers that provided HCBS services to the poor and disabled (CMS, 2003).

Efforts to increase home care and reduce institutionalization have begun to pay off. Compared to six other countries, the United States is second only to Canada in providing access to home care services (see Figure 11–5). France and Japan provide the least, most likely because of cultural values that emphasize family care.

Figure 11-5 **Access to Home Care for People Aged 65 and Older in Seven Countries.**

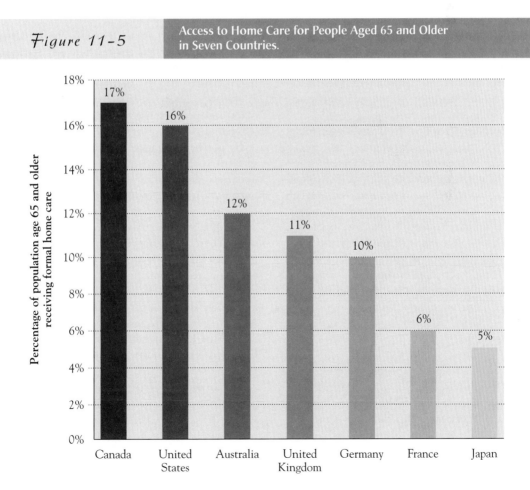

Source: Organization for Economic Cooperation and Development (1998).

Private long-term-care insurance   A growing option for the payment of long-term-care services is private insurance. Long-term-care insurance policies cover everything from home and community-based care to nursing home care. The cost varies according to the type of policy purchased, the age of the person at the time it is purchased, and the person's health.

Although private long-term-care policies have been available since the early 1980s, as of 1992 only about 3 million policies were in effect (Cowart and Quadagno, 1995). Until 1997 there were no tax incentives to purchase long-term-care as there are for regular health insurance. The 1997 federal budget agreement added some tax incentives for long-term-care insurance that may encourage more people to purchase policies. Another problem has been a lack of regulation to ensure that the plans are financially stable and pay the promised benefits. People lose confidence when they see examples of fraud, overcharging, and failure to provide promised services. A final impediment is that people with serious health problems are rarely accepted for long-term care coverage.

As people age, their health care needs generally increase. Whether, and under what circumstances, these needs are met, however, is as varied as are health policies throughout the world. Elderly people in most developed countries have substantial access to high-quality Western medicine whenever need arises. In other countries, availability of and access to even basic medical services for elderly people (or for individuals of any age) is far less predictable. For a description of the various arrangements for health care for the elderly around the world, see "Aging around the World."

Social Services

Medical services help keep people healthy; nonmedical services allow people to remain independent, living in their own homes. In the United States, social services are divided between those available to all elderly through the Older Americans Act (OAA) and those available only to the elderly poor through Medicaid waiver programs, as described above.

The older americans act   Passed in 1965, the Older Americans Act, provides a number of services intended to enhance independent living, including congregate meals (group meals at a chosen site such as a senior center), personal care and nursing services, day care, chore services, and meals-on-wheels (Ozcan and Cotter, 1994). Although these services are supposed to be available to all older people, there has never been sufficient funding to fully implement the Older Americans Act. Thus, although communities may have an infrastructure in place, many people who need the services are unable to obtain them. Long waiting lists for services are common.

The OAA also provided funding for **senior centers,** community-based facilities that provide meals and social activities. Most communities now have senior centers. Indeed, senior centers are the most widely used service created by the Older Americans Act. People are drawn to senior centers because of their meal programs and their health maintenance services (Ferraro and Cobb, 1987). People who attend senior centers are somewhat older and poorer on average than nonattenders (Miner, Logan, and Spitze, 1993).

Senior centers have the potential to provide services to groups that have traditionally been underserved (Ralston, 1991). Yet some of these organizations have only minimally attempted to reach minority audiences (Krout, Cutler, and Coward, 1990). Some early research on the use of senior centers demonstrated that low-income, minority, elderly people often failed to use the senior centers in their communities. Among the barriers to service use were lack of transportation, lack of knowledge about the centers, and lack of culturally sensitive programs to serve people of diverse racial and ethnic backgrounds. To correct this problem, the OAA was amended several times to emphasize targeting services to people in greatest social and economic need. As a result, a number of innovative programs were designed to enhance access to services to this underserved population. Included were better transportation, neighborhood satellite clinics, culturally sensitive programs, and the delivery of services to the home (Baker and Pallett-Hehn, 1995). Although presently there is higher attendance at

Aging around the World

INTERNATIONAL VARIATIONS IN HEALTH CARE ARRANGEMENTS FOR THE ELDERLY

In most Western nations, basic coverage of health care services for the aged is inseparable from the health care benefits available to the population as a whole. In Great Britain, the National Health Service (NHS) administers health services funded by compulsory contributions to a national insurance fund (Ruggie, 1996). In Canada, the federal government provides revenues to the provincial health ministries, which have responsibility for health care services (Maioni, 1998). In Norway, as in Denmark, Sweden, and Finland, health care is a public responsibility that is financed by individual taxes and payments from employers (Elstad, 1997). Unlike the United States, in none of these countries is health care for older people distinguishable from care provided to other population groups.

Many countries also provide special care for the frail elderly, often in combination with other social services. In the United Kingdom and Australia, long-term care has shifted away from nursing homes and residential care as the main environments and toward community care models designed to allow elders to remain in their own homes as long as possible (Bernard and Phillips, 2000; Howe, 2000). Germany and Japan now have the two most progressive and innovative models of long-term-care insurance anywhere. In Germany the elderly qualify for support based on physical need and may receive either cash or services (Lassey and Lassey, 2001). The program also supports home and community-based services, and the majority of beneficiaries receive long-term-care services outside of nursing homes (Cuellar and Wiener, 2000). In 2000, Japan implemented a mandatory long-term-care insurance system that covers both care in a nursing home and care in an individual's own home (Campbell and Ikegami, 2000).

Most countries also have begun to recognize the importance of informal caregivers in their visions of long-term care and have begun to implement services to support caregivers. Indeed, Germany's system pays cash benefits to informal caregivers as a way to encourage family caregiving (Schunk and Estes, 2001). Australia and Denmark pay family caregivers directly in order to compensate (though inadequately) for lost employment earnings. Australia, Great Britain, and Germany offer respite services to informal caregivers (Merlis, 2000). International policies and programs designed to meet the coming challenges of population aging must inevitably be evaluated in terms of their impact on the economy as well as a larger issues of social justice and the well-being of the aged.

What Do You Think?

1. Who should be responsible for the long term care to the frail elderly?
2. Do you have any relatives who need long term care?

Senior centers attempt to reach out to provide services to the minority elderly.

senior centers among African Americans than there used to be, little data is available about center usage among Asian, Hispanic, and Native American elderly. "Diversity in the Aging Experience" discusses the problem of providing access to services to elderly Korean Americans.

Concern that the Older Americans Act was duplicating services provided under the Medicaid waiver program has led to efforts to coordinate services between the two programs. Now an older person who is eligible for HCBS services under a Medicaid waiver program may have those services provided by funding available through the OAA (Hudson, 1996). Because of scarce resources, there has also been an increasing emphasis on targeting OAA services to the poor. Thus, the lines of demarcation between the two programs have become blurred.

Housing   Housing policy in the United States today consists of three components. The first is the tax expenditure component of housing policy, a mortgage-guarantee program that allows home owners to deduct mortgage interest from taxable income. Home mortgage interest deductions cost $43 billion in 1997 (Office of Management and Budget, 1996). The second component of housing policy is a modest subsidy program, which increases the housing supply for the poor by encouraging developers to construct low-income housing and by subsidizing rents for poor people (Liebig, 1998). The subsidy program began in 1974 when the federal government sought to expand the supply of low-income housing through a provision known as Section 8. Section 8 encouraged nonprofit sponsors to develop rental units and provide rental assistance for low-income households. Since that time, more than 300,000 rental units have been built for ambulatory, moderate, and low-income elders. Among households receiving federal rent subsidies, nearly one-fourth are elderly. There is also a small public housing program for the poor. A disproportionate share of this benefit also goes to the elderly. In 1995, 45 percent of the nation's public housing units were occupied by older people (Liebig, 1998).

Because housing is a core component of independent living, an ideal housing policy would provide a continuum of services ranging from programs for people who are largely independent to institutional care for those fully disabled. Although an objective of the Older Americans Act was to provide suitable housing for all older people, the prospects for achieving this have become more remote every year. In practice, only the people at either end of the spectrum are supported.

During the 1980s, there was growing recognition that suitable housing for the aged encompassed more than bricks and mortar. Several demonstration programs were launched to combine housing with a package of services and to renovate older units so that people could age in their own homes. Yet these programs were quite limited in scope, and in general, the 1980s was a period of cutbacks in federal housing support. Between 1981 and 1985, federal funds for subsidized housing were slashed from $26.1 billion to only $2.1 billion (Slessarev, 1988:358). Because of limited funding, waiting lists for public housing are long. The average wait is over a year, and some people have to wait more than four or five years, a considerable amount of time for the elderly (Bould, Sanborn, and Reif, 1989).

As housing funds have declined, the elderly have been forced to compete with other groups for scarce resources. The group least able to afford independent housing is the disabled, who, as noted, have difficulty finding and keeping stable employment. To cushion the impact of the decline in housing support, Congress introduced measures that blended eligibility criteria. Eligibility for government-subsidized housing became based on a combination of age, economic need, and disability.

To some extent, the states have filled the gap created when the federal government reduced its level of funding. Since 1980, more than 100 new programs have been created in 40 states. Many of these programs have focused on developing supportive housing, which includes a range of services such as meals, laundry, and personal care to semi-independent, low-income elders who require some assistance with daily activities but do not need nursing home care (Pynoos and Parrott, 1996). Although the states have been innovative, state budgets are inadequate to meet growing needs.

Because social services are not coordinated well with each other and housing is so limited and unconnected to the services that do exist, older people have many unmet needs. The following account illustrates a typical situation facing an individual needing assistance with activities of daily living.

Mr. Thomas, age 86, needs long-term care. He has an advanced case of Parkinson's disease and cannot get out of bed or even turn over. His wife turns him over with the help of a mechanical lift, but she cannot do this more than twice a day. Consequently, he gets bedsores. These severe health problems do not qualify him for home health care assistance from Medicare. When Mr. Thomas gets pneumonia, however, he can be admitted to the hospital, and Medicare will cover his bills. Following the hospitalization, he will qualify for home health care for three weeks. After that, any help he receives must be paid for out-of-pocket because the couple's income is too high for them to qualify for Medicaid. There are no other available services in their community (Bould et al., 1989).

The provision of long-term care in housing and social services is an issue that will become even more compelling in the twenty-first century. Although the United States is poorly prepared, Denmark provides a model for optimal long-term-care planning.

Denmark has been a pioneer in designing and implementing a long-term-care program that promotes home care and reduces institutionalization. Unlike many countries, which provide social welfare mostly in the form of cash benefits, Denmark provides extensive social services, especially for children and the elderly. In Denmark public policy supports "the old people's possibilities of staying in

Diversity in the Aging Experience

THE USE OF COMMUNITY LONG-TERM-CARE SERVICES AMONG ELDERLY KOREAN AMERICANS

*H*ow do you think you would feel if, at age 65 or 70, you packed up all your worldly belongings and moved to another country where you did not speak the language? That is the way many elderly Korean Americans feel today. Korean Americans are one of the fastest-growing ethnic groups in the United States. Unlike Asian American groups who have a long immigration history (Chinese, Japanese, and Filipinos), Koreans did not begin to immigrate to the United States in large numbers until the mid-1970s, and many Koreans brought their aging parents with them.

These elderly immigrants face not only a language barrier but a social service system designed for people of a very different culture. Not surprisingly, the Korean American aged are much less likely than other Americans to use the services available to them under the Older Americans Act, even though many of them could benefit from those services. Compared to whites, aged Korean Americans are much less likely to go to a senior center, receive transportation services or

independent homes as long as possible" and maintains "the elderly in an active daily life to prevent them from being placed in nursing homes or other institutions" (Plovsing, 1992:14).

To achieve this goal, planners have developed well-coordinated medical, social, and community care services for the elderly. Since 1989 all elderly Danes have been entitled to public services, including free home help, district nursing, day care centers, technical aids, and meals-on-wheels. Of these services, permanent home help with cleaning, shopping, cooking, and personal hygiene is the most common and most important. Combined with district nursing, home help provides full service, round-the-clock care. Children commonly help their parents through short-term crises and assist them in mobilizing public services, but the goal

is to allow the elderly and their children to live independently.

When the frail elderly cannot remain at home, they receive high-quality care in a nursing home. The nursing home package includes a private room and bath, skilled nursing care, occupational therapy, and hair dressing. Since 1987 the Danish government has banned the building of new nursing homes and encouraged the construction of special apartments for the old, with baths and kitchens designed specifically for the disabled. The idea is to allow the aged and disabled to live in independent dwellings in the community (Plovsing, 1992).

Denmark has developed what appears to be an ideal model for providing secure and comfortable accommodations and long-term-care to the frail elderly. While the Danes, like most Europeans, meals-on-wheels, or employ a home health aide. Yet they are more likely than others to be in poor health and have extremely low incomes (Moon, Lubben, and Villa, 1998).

A stated objective of the Older Americans Act is to provide services to minority groups and the socially disadvantaged. Why do the service needs of aged Korean Americans remain unfulfilled? One reason is lack of awareness of available services: Many Korean Americans have never heard of these services. Once they become aware that services are available, they are more likely to use them (Moon, Lubben, and Villa, 1998). Korean Americans also fail to use some services because they are culturally inappropriate. Consider mental health services. In Asian culture, mental illness is considered a "loss of face" for the family. The traditional Asian family believes that the mentally ill should be cared for within the family, out of public view. Thus, the lack of use of mental health services by Korean Americans may represent a desire to keep the problem of mental illness private. Similarly, Korean Americans may be uninterested in meals-on-wheels because the program does not feature Korean food (Cho, 1998).

Some policymakers charge that the Older Americans Act has failed to serve the needy elderly because resources are inadequate and outreach programs have not increased public awareness of services. But even if more resources are poured into services, many eligible and needy older people may never receive them unless they are designed to meet people's cultural preferences.

What Do You Think?

1. Do any of your elderly relatives fail to take advantage of community services because the programs are culturally inappropriate for them? If so, explain.
2. How can those who deliver community services to the aged reach out to members of minority groups? Be specific.

are now confronting rising public expenses as the result of population aging, they have been able to maintain these Cadillac-style benefits because of a healthy economy and low unemployment rates. Health care expenditures are quite low—only 6.7 percent of total domestic expenditures (Organization for Economic Cooperation and Development, 1994). Although some cutbacks may be required in the future, for the present Denmark's elder care system illustrates what can be accomplished with broad public support for optimal care for the elderly.

As the specter of population aging has fueled debates in the United States about whether to cut Social Security and Medicare, questions have been raised about whether present eligibility criteria, which favor age over economic need, are the most

appropriate. In the next section, we discuss the debate over age versus need.

THE AGE VERSUS NEED DEBATE

From the 1930s until the 1980s, the aged, many of whom were poor, were seen as deserving recipients of social benefits in this country. Age became the major criterion for determining eligibility for more than 134 programs for income support, health, and social services (Binstock, 1994a). As the economic status and health of older people improved, the public consensus that age should be the sole basis for determining eligibility for social benefits began to erode. The suggestion that eligibility for programs and services be based on need rather than age was first proposed by the social gerontologist Bernice Neugarten (1979). According to Neugarten, age had become increasingly irrelevant as a predictor of lifestyle, and programs designed around this criterion were falling short of the mark.

The debate over age versus need has remained the subject of controversy for the past two decades. There are a number of arguments in favor of eliminating age as a criterion for public policy. Proponents of a need-based policy contend that age-based policies aggravate intergenerational tensions. They contend that promoting programs for one age group not only appears selective and biased but also stigmatizes an entire group of people as poor, frail, lonely, or depressed (Skinner, 1997).

Need-based programs, they argue, would reflect a more caring and ethical response to the nation's most disadvantaged citizens and reduce generational inequity in the distribution of societal resources.

In contrast, those who favor age targeting point with pride to the success of Social Security and Medicare. They argue that these programs enjoy strong public support because people do not have to undergo means testing to prove their eligibility (Kutza, 1997). They also note how successful these programs have been in reducing poverty and improving access to health care. Increasingly, changes in public policy have blurred the boundaries between age and need. That may be the trend of the future.

Chapter Resources

LOOKING BACK

1. **What kinds of welfare programs are available to aging Americans?** *There are three types of welfare programs. Social assistance is a minimal means-tested benefit for the poor, paid for by income taxes. Social insurance provides benefits as an automatic right to all who have contributed. Payment comes from payroll taxes. Fiscal welfare operates through the tax system. It uses tax incentives to encourage savings for retirement, expand health insurance access, and encourage home ownership.*

2. **What are the government-sponsored sources of income support for the aging?** *Social Security provides more than 40 percent of the income of older people. Individuals who contribute to the system by paying payroll taxes during their working years automatically receive benefits when they reach the age of eligibility. Supplemental Security Income is a joint federal– state program for the aged, blind, and disabled poor. Benefits are quite low, below the poverty level in most states, and many who are eligible fail to apply for such assistance because of the social stigma attached to means testing.*

3. **What government health care programs serve the elderly?** *Medicare is a program of national health insurance for people over age 65 who are eligible for Social Security. It covers many of the costs of a hospital stay (Part A) and physician office visits (Part B). Although Medicare is an important program for the aged, older people still pay a large and increasing share of their income for health care. Medicaid is a program of health insurance for the aged, blind, and disabled poor. It pays for a range of health care services as well as a large share of the cost of nursing home care.*

4. **Which government programs protect the disabled?** *Two programs provide income for disabled people: Disability Insurance, which is one of the benefits of Social Security, and SSI, which provides a minimal income for those who*

have not contributed to Social Security. Both programs contain work disincentives, since beneficiaries stand to lose health insurance coverage if they return to work.*

5. **How is long-term care of the elderly financed in the United States?** *Long-term care refers to the range of supportive services and living environments that help the elderly continue to live independent lives for as long as possible and that provide institutional care when independent living is no longer feasible. In the United States long-term-care benefits are provided by a complex array of programs including Medicare, Medicaid, and services under the auspices of the Older Americans Act. Medicaid is the main source of public funding for long-term-care. To discourage institutional care, during the past decade states have been allowed to use a portion of their Medicaid dollars for waiver programs to provide services in the home. Among the services offered are homemaker services, adult day care, meals-on-wheels, physical therapy, and help with chores.*

6. **What social services does the Older Americans Act provide?** *The Older Americans Act also provides funds for a number of services including congregate meals, day care, and meals-on-wheels. Many of these services overlap with those provided by Medicaid waiver programs. Although services through the OAA were originally supposed to be available to all elderly regardless of income, scarce resources have meant that these services increasingly have been targeted to the elderly poor and to minorities.*

THINKING ABOUT AGING

1. How would you reply to Max Cross, the conservative who benefits from government welfare programs but complains that they are wasteful? (See the opening page of this chapter.) Do you agree or disagree with him?

2. Should government welfare programs reinforce social class divisions, or should they serve as social equalizers? Justify your position.

3. Should Americans be concerned that U.S. welfare programs give far less support to the aging than similar programs in European countries?

4. Should Medicare cover the cost of prescription drugs to the elderly? What about other expensive services such as home care?

5. Should the United States have a universal system of health care coverage that would treat all Americans, young or old, rich or poor, equally?

KEY TERMS

Disability Insurance 258

earnings test 259

fiscal welfare 257

Home and Community-Based Waiver Services Program (HCBS) 271

long-term care 269

means test 257

Medicaid 258

Medicare 258

Medicare Part A 264

Medicare Part B 265

Medigap policy 266

Old Age Assistance 258

Older Americans Act 258

payroll taxes 257

progressive taxes 257

replacement rate 260

senior centers 272

social assistance 256

social insurance 257

Social Security 258

Social Security Act of 1935 258

Supplemental Security Income (SSI) 262

tax expenditures 257

welfare state 256

EXPLORING THE INTERNET

Note: While all the URLs listed were current as of the printing of this book, these sites often change. Please check our website www.mhhe.com/quadagno for updates.

1. The Center for Medicare and Medicaid Services is a government organization providing information and quality service for beneficiaries and providers. Link to their website (www.cms.hhs.gov), click on "Statistics and Data" on the left toolbar, and then "2002 Data Compendium." Scroll down, link to Part IV on population, and answer the following questions:

   a. In 2001, what percent of Medicare recipients are aged 65 or older?
   b. What percent are covered by Parts A and B?
   c. Did male and female beneficiaries see similar rate changes between 1966 and 2001?

2. To learn more about Supplemental Security Income (SSI), go to the AARP's home page (www.aarp.org), link to "Money and Work," and then "low income help." Scroll down to the section on SSI, click on "Get the Facts on this Program," and answer the following questions:

   a. What are the eligibility requirements?
   b. What are the income limits?
   c. What are the limits on how much a qualified applicant can receive?

Chapter 12

Work and Retirement

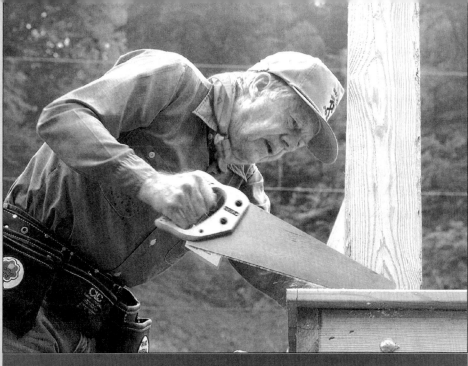

*F*ormer President Jimmy Carter has led a full and busy life since he left office at the age of 56. Here he volunteers for Habitat for Humanity, an organization that builds homes for the poor.

Looking Ahead

1. How has the percentage of Americans who work changed over time, and how do workers' gender, age, and racial or ethnic group affect their employment rate?
2. What are the employment prospects for older workers, and how are they affected by age discrimination?
3. What economic forces cause workers to withdraw from the labor force?
4. How do individuals decide when to retire?
5. What personal factors are associated with an individual's relative satisfaction in retirement?

*F*ormer President Jimmy Carter experienced an abrupt and involuntary retirement when he lost the 1980 presidential election to Ronald Reagan. Because he did not expect to lose, all his future plans centered around what he hoped to achieve in his second term in office. Suddenly, he was out of a job at age 56, one of the youngest ex-presidents in U.S. history. What would the former Navy submariner, nuclear engineer, farmer, and politician do with the next 30 or 40 years of his life? Carter found the answer to that question in humanitarian activities. Now, at age 75, his schedule is so packed

that his staff can hardly keep up with him. He lectures around the world on everything from politics to health care, builds houses for Habitat for Humanity, and works to promote world peace.

Like Jimmy Carter, 69-year-old Irene Shapiro also has a busy life. She goes to the gym four or five times a week, and belongs to a computer club, a women's club, and a singles club. She is also captain of the speed-walkers club, which won a silver medal last year in the senior quarter-mile relay. Yet her route to retirement was quite different from that of the former president. Irene didn't start

283

working until her youngest son was 11. She then went to work full-time in a pediatrician's office, until 1996, when she cut down to twice, then once a week. Finally, Irene stopped working altogether.

Although some people work until they are 65 and then retire completely, Jimmy Carter and Irene Shapiro illustrate the experiences of an increasing number of Americans. Some people make a gradual transition to retirement, reducing their hours or changing to less stressful jobs. Others find themselves forced out at an early age, with no warning. In this chapter we will examine these diverse paths to retirement. We look at how people make the transition from work to retirement. We learn about the increase in early retirement that occurred from 1960 to the 1980s, and about the recent halt in the trend. Finally, we will learn about the experience of being retired, and what factors contribute to a person's satisfaction in retirement.

PATTERNS OF WORK IN LATER LIFE

The Transition from Work to Retirement

The first generation of social gerontologists who studied retirement viewed it as a single event that followed a period of employment. The implicit model was that the life course could be divided into three phases: education, work, and retirement. Increasingly, it has become clear that the long-standing definition of retirement as an abrupt departure from a lifetime career is inadequate in view of a job market in which more and more people change jobs frequently. For the parents of the baby boomers, for example, those who were aged 58 to 63 in 1969, 55 percent of men and 28 percent of women held a job that lasted 20 or more years. Among that same cohort, 31 percent of men and 11 percent of women held a job that lasted 30 or more years (Salisbury, 1994). Job length peaked in 1983 and has been declining ever since (Farber, 1996). The decline in lifetime employment with a single firm makes it difficult to define retirement as leaving one's "main work."

Another problem with the traditional view of retirement is that many Americans do not leave the labor force completely when they leave their full-time jobs (Quinn, Burkhauser, and Myers, 1990). They may take temporary jobs or leave but then reenter the labor force several times. In one survey, only half of men who left their full-time career jobs also left the labor force (Quinn et al., 1990). One-quarter reduced their hours to part-time on the same job, and the other quarter switched to different jobs. Another study found that about one-fourth of men aged 60 to 65 returned to work after retiring (Ruhm, 1989). As Figure 12–1 shows, the proportion of part-time workers increases with age. Among workers aged 60 to 69, 61 percent work full-time, but among workers 70 or older, 72 percent work part-time. A more accurate way to describe the transition to retirement is to say that it may be *crisp*, meaning that a shift from the role of worker to that of retiree occurs at a precise point in time. Or it may be *blurred*, meaning that the role transition is gradual, with two roles sometimes overlapping (Mutchler et al., 1997).

How, then, do we define retirement? One yardstick might be current employment. One might argue that when an older person has zero hours worked in a given year and is no longer looking for work, then he or she is retired. Although this definition may be useful for identifying those who are fully retired, it groups all people who have any hours of work as not retired. This would exclude many part-time older workers who consider themselves retired (Ekerdt and DeViney, 1990). Another definition might be people who have reduced their work effort. But many people who work 20 or 30 hours a week don't consider themselves retired and might plan to work many more years at this level (Ekerdt and DeViney, 1990).

Receiving a pension presents another possible way of singling out the retired, except this tells us nothing about the work experience of the individual. People who have served in the military, for example, might retire at age 40, receive a full military pension, and then work full-time at another job for 25 more years.

Perhaps, then, it might be best to let people define for themselves when they have retired. If so, what do they mean when they say they are retired?

Figure 12-1	Work Status of Older U.S. Workers, by Age.

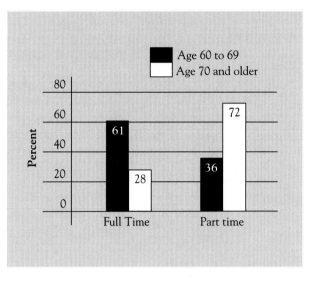

Source: National Academy on an Aging Society (2000).

Are they confirming a role exit, moving from work to leisure? Or does being a retiree mean assuming a new social identity? Research suggests that individuals' past work history influences whether they define themselves as retired. People who have worked continuously, with few interruptions, are more likely to say they are retired than those who have been employed intermittently. Members of the latter group may feel they are only temporarily not working (Szinovacz and DeViney, 1999). Social gerontologists now recognize that there are many pathways to retirement and that different definitions reflect different patterns of withdrawal from the labor force.

Trends in Labor Force Participation

When we say people are "in the labor force," we mean they are either working or looking for work. Some people remain in the labor force until they are quite advanced in years, while others leave the labor force at a relatively young age. The following section will briefly outline trends in labor force participation among older workers. In subsequent sections we will analyze the causal forces behind these trends.

Labor force participation of men   Nearly all men who are in their 30s and early 40s are in the labor force. We expect men to work, and most do. A few men drop out of the labor force when they are in their late 40s or early 50s, primarily because of health problems, but most men continue to work into their early 50s. These trends have been relatively stable for at least a half century.

More variable is the rate of labor force participation among older men. As Figure 12–2 shows, the period 1965 to 1995 brought only a slight decline in labor force participation among men aged 50 to 54, but a more substantial decline among men aged 55 to 59. Then between 1995 and 2000 the trend turned upward for men in their early 50s. A similar pattern appeared for men aged 60 to 64, except that the decline in participation was much steeper. Seventy-nine percent of these men were working in 1965, but only 52 percent of them by 1995. Between 1995 and 2000, however, labor force participation among men aged 60 to 64 began

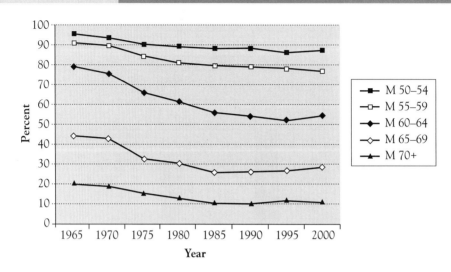

Figure 12-2   **U.S. Labor Force Participation Rates, Men by Age, 1965–2000.**

Source: U.S. Bureau of Labor Statistics (2000).

to rise; it stands now at 56 percent. Labor force participation has also increased slightly among men aged 65 to 69.

Labor force participation of women

The work histories of women are quite different from those of men. Since 1965 there has been a sharp increase in labor force participation among women aged 50 to 59, and a more modest increase among women in their 60s (see Figure 12–3). What explains this trend, which runs counter to the trend for men?

One factor has been a dramatic increase in the labor force participation of married women. Single women have always had high rates of labor force participation, but in 1960 only 36.2 percent of married women aged 35 to 44 were in the labor force. By 1998, however, 76 percent of married women in this age group were employed (U.S. Bureau of the Census, 1998b). Even more spectacular has been the increase in labor force participation among women with young children. Between 1970 and 1998, the proportion of married women with young children who took jobs outside the home doubled (U.S. Bureau of the Census, 1998b).

Women have been drawn into the labor force by a number of economic and legal changes. One was passage of the Civil Rights Act of 1965, which outlawed discrimination on the basis of sex (Oppenheimer, 1970). Another was the expansion of the service sector of the economy, a traditional source of employment for women (Farley, 1996). A third was a decline in the wages men earned, which meant that many families needed two incomes to maintain a middle-class lifestyle.

Although more middle-aged women are working today than in the past, some women in their late 50s and early 60s are retiring. But their decision to withdraw from the labor force tends to be obscured by the increased labor force participation of other women (Pampel, 1986; Hayward, Crimmins, and Wray, 1994).

Racial and ethnic differences in labor force participation

Over the life course, there are racial and ethnic differences in employment histories, which translate into different patterns of labor force participation in later life. In every age group, unemployment rates are higher for black and Hispanic men and women than they are for

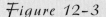

Figure 12-3

U.S. Labor Force Participation Rates, Women by Age, 1965–2000.

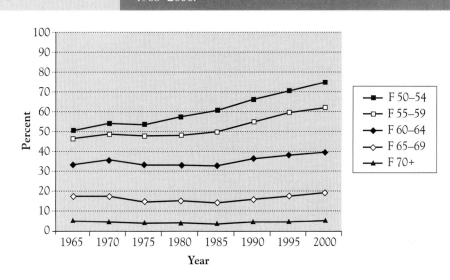

Legend:
- F 50–54
- F 55–59
- F 60–64
- F 65–69
- F 70+

Source: U.S. Bureau of Labor Statistics (2000).

Table 12-1

Employment Status of U.S. Residents Aged 51 to 55, by Sex, Race, and Ethnic Origin

	Men			Women		
Employment Status	*White*	*Black*	*Hispanic*	*White*	*Black*	*Hispanic*
Employed	79.7%	64.9%	71.2%	67.8%	65.6%	57.6%
Unemployed/laid off	4.5	8.3	9.8	3.8	5.2	9.3
Retired	9.7	10.6	5.7	7.7	7.4	3.1
Out of labor force	6.1	16.3	13.2	20.6	21.8	30.1

Source: Flippen and Tienda (2000).

whites. Unemployment rates are highest among black men until age 54, when they are exceeded by Hispanic men. Black women have the highest unemployment rates until age 44, when they, too, are exceeded by Hispanic women. The causes are complex and interactive. They include a history of overt racial discrimination in employment by employers and trade unions as well as underfunding of schools in minority neighborhoods, which results in black and Hispanic workers bringing fewer skills to the job market (Tigges and Tootle, 1993).

An early history of unstable employment translates into greater risk of job loss later in life. Table 12–1 reports racial and ethnic differences in employment among men and women aged 51 to 55 who participated in a longitudinal study called the Health and Retirement Survey. Among men, whites were most likely to be employed, while blacks were most likely to be out of the labor force entirely. Hispanic women were less likely to be employed than either black or white women, and more likely to be unemployed or out of the labor

Diversity in the Aging Experience

WORK EXPERIENCES OF MEXICAN AMERICAN FARMWORKERS

Today, many elderly Hispanics are Mexican Americans who came to the United States under the bracero agreement of 1942. Under this program, temporary Mexican farmworkers—called *braceros*—were brought to the United States to reduce the labor shortage caused by World War II. The program lasted for 22 years, and many of the supposedly temporary workers stayed in the United States after it ended.

Most braceros worked in factories and on ranches and farms, often at the dirtiest, lowest-paying jobs. Many were not covered by Social Security or private pensions (Flippen and Tienda, 2000). Plagued by periodic unemployment throughout their lives, these laborers must now cope with their lack of retirement income by working into old age (Markides and Mindel, 1987). Worse, because many older Hispanics are ineligible for Social Security, they are also ineligible for Medicare. In 1990 only 49 percent of Hispanics aged 65 and older were covered by Medicare. Indeed, Hispanics are less likely than the general population to have health insurance of any kind. They are also in poorer health and experience more days bedridden, more days of restricted activity, and greater disability in performing the activities of daily living than others their age (Espino, 1993).

What Do You Think?

1. Do you know an older person who is ineligible for Social Security and Medicare benefits? If so, what is or was the person's occupation, and what is his or her racial or ethnic group?
2. Why do you think certain occupations have not always been covered by the Social Security Act?

force (Flippen and Tienda, 2000). The "Diversity in the Aging Experience" feature explains how older Hispanics' current patterns of labor force participation have been shaped by their previous employment experiences.

Much of the decline in work among black men reflects higher rates of disability (Hayward, Friedman, and Chen, 1996). Among men aged 45 to 64, blacks are two and a half times as likely as whites to suffer from hypertension, circulatory problems, diabetes, and nervous disorders. They are also more likely to work in physically strenuous blue-collar jobs, where chronic health problems cannot be as easily accommodated as in white-collar jobs (Daly and Bound, 1996). Thus, a substantial part of the race difference in labor force participation among older men is due to race differences in capacity to work (Bound, Schoenbaum, and Waidmann, 1995).

The patterns for women are different from those of men. At all ages, Hispanic females have the lowest rates of labor force participation. From age 50 to 74 (except 55 to 59), white females have higher rates of labor force participation than black females, but in very old age (75 or older), black females work more. These statistics may underestimate the employment of older black women, because many work in the underground economy as domestic servants. In 1940, there was only *one* job open to most African American women—70 percent were household servants (Taueber and Allen, 1990). Undoubtedly, many older black women continue to work in these same jobs, but their employment does not appear in any official reports. Although domestic servants have been covered by Social Security since 1954, many work in private homes for employers who don't pay Social Security taxes for them. Some domestic servants have worked for 30 or 40 years without receiving Social Security credit. Thus, the higher rates of labor force participation among black women 65 or older reflect their lack of retirement income (Perkins, 1993).

Younger black women will enter old age at a distinct advantage compared to their mothers or grandmothers. They will have had more education and will have worked more continuously over their entire lives. In 2001 only 12 percent of African American women were employed in domestic service, but nearly 33 percent of Hispanic women were employed in these jobs (Kajakazi, 2002). The advantages of having worked in better-paying jobs that include eligibility for Social Security will make it easier for black women to retire.

Employment Prospects for Older Workers

Older men and women can remain in the labor force only if employers are willing to hire them. Although age discrimination has been illegal since 1967, older workers are still at a disadvantage when looking for work. The prosperous economy of the 1990s alleviated their difficulties but did not eliminate them.

The effects of age discrimination The American public first became aware of age discrimination in 1965, when the Department of Labor issued a report showing that more than half of all jobs were closed to applicants over age 55. In that year help-wanted ads often read "No one over 55 need apply," and about 25 percent of all jobs were closed even to people as young as 45. In response to these statistics, Congress passed the **Age Discrimination in Employment Act of 1967 (ADEA),** which banned discrimination against workers aged 40 to 65 (see Chapter 1) and forbade employers to fire, demote, or reduce the salaries of older workers without good cause (Bessey and Ananda, 1991). But a number of loopholes in the law allow employers to jettison older workers without running afoul of the law. During a merger or downsizing, for instance, which typically requires massive layoffs, a company might shed workers of all ages and then selectively rehire only younger workers. So while the ADEA has provided some protection to older workers against being unfairly fired, it has not eliminated discrimination in hiring.

Why are some employers biased against older workers? One reason is that older workers generally earn higher salaries, and companies are always looking for ways to reduce costs. Older workers (those over 55) are also thought to be less productive than younger workers. One international survey of 773 corporate executives found that most believed workers reach their peak performance in their 40s, and then begin to decline in their 50s (Global Aging Report, 1998a). But though workers in physically demanding jobs do experience an age-related decline in productivity, white-collar workers do not. In the past, older workers have also been perceived as slow, undependable, incapable of adapting to change and accident-prone, though there is some evidence those attitudes are changing (Stearns and Stearns, 1995). Indeed, many studies show that older workers often are more reliable than younger workers, call in sick less often and display more loyalty to their employers (Barth, McNaught, and Rizzi, 1995).

When older workers lose their jobs, they pay a high cost. They take longer than other workers to find a new job and are more likely to take a pay cut when they do (Farber, 1993; Ruhm 1989). In 1990, for example, nearly 80 percent of younger

These Mexican farmworkers weed in the onion fields in Syracuse, New York.

Table 12-2	U.S. Unemployment Rates by Age and Sex, 2002	
Age	*Male*	*Female*
16–19	17.6%	14.5%
20–24	9.3	8.5
25–44	4.7	5.1
45–64	3.2	2.9
65 and over	4.3	3.7

Source: U.S. Bureau of Labor Statistics (2003).

displaced workers found new jobs, compared to fewer than 50 percent of workers aged 55 to 64 (Applebaum and Gregory, 1990). About one-third of the older displaced workers eventually abandoned their job search and retired (Useem, 1993). Table 12–2 shows U.S. unemployment rates for 2002 by age and sex. Notice that unemployment rates were highest among younger workers and then dropped off continually, for both men and women, until age 65, when they rose slightly. Unemployment rates were low among older workers not because they found new jobs but because they stopped looking for work. When discouraged workers—those who have given up looking for work—are included among the unemployed, unemployment rates among older men and women rise dramatically (Schulz, 1995).

Perhaps the greatest cost of job loss in later life is the loss of health insurance. Medicare coverage doesn't begin until age 65, so workers who lose their jobs before that age risk being uninsured. Nearly three-quarters of all insured Americans obtain their health insurance through their employers (Fronstin, 1999). Unemployed workers who must purchase their own insurance find that their insurance costs skyrocket, because employers can take advantage of cheaper group rates. Those who can get health insurance are lucky, however, because unemployed people who have a health problem are at risk of being uninsurable in the private market. Commercial insurance companies simply don't want to insure people who are likely to get sick.

To help unemployed or displaced workers keep their health insurance, Congress passed the Consolidated Omnibus Budget Reconciliation Act (COBRA) of 1985. COBRA requires employers of 20 or more workers to provide those employees who leave the firm the opportunity to purchase continued health insurance coverage for 18 months (Fronstin, 1999). Although COBRA has prevented many workers from becoming totally uninsured, often on short notice, it leaves many problems unsolved. Policies purchased under these conditions are often quite expensive, especially for unemployed workers. COBRA also does not cover workers in smaller firms, who can still lose their health insurance altogether if they lose their jobs. And of course, when 18 months have passed, even workers eligible under COBRA are on their own again.

Bridge Jobs

Older workers who do not make crisp transitions to retirement often are employed in what economists call **bridge jobs,** which span the period between full-time employment in a career job and permanent retirement (Quinn and Kozy, 1996). Bridge jobs are clustered in a smaller set of industries and occupations than are regular jobs occupied by younger workers (Shapiro and Sandell, 1985; Hutchens, 1988, 1993). They not only differ in occupation and industry from career jobs but also often involve part-time employment or self-employment. Whether they are full- or part-time, bridge jobs usually pay significantly lower wages and represent a slide down the occupational ladder (Barth, McNaught, and Rizzi, 1995; Couch, 1998). For example, one 53-year-old man with only 10 years of education had worked his way up from a laborer to an engineering technician. He lost that job and remained unemployed for 13 months before finding a job as a delivery person at much lower wages. Another 50-year-old man lost his managerial position and after 44 weeks of unemployment found a job as a shoe salesman (Parnes, Gagen, and King, 1981).

Part-time employment—defined as working less than 35 hours a week—is highest among very young workers (under 24) and older workers (over 65). In 1993, fewer than 7 percent of men younger than age 60 worked part-time, but 42 percent aged 65 to 69 and well over half aged 70 or older worked part-time (Quadagno and Quinn, 1996). The U.S. Department of Labor makes a distinction between **voluntary part-time work** and **economic part-time work.** Voluntary part-timers do not wish to work full-time. Economic part-time workers are unable to find full-time jobs. Among male workers aged 65 to 69, approximately 5 percent were working part-time for economic reasons, but nearly 40 percent were voluntary part-timers. Among male workers older than 70, more than half chose part-time work voluntarily. At all ages, women are more likely than men to work part-time and to work part-time voluntarily. Thus, many people who work in bridge jobs have chosen this type of employment.

Among those who have not chosen bridge jobs, the experience of downward mobility can be costly and painful. A multiracial study of 29 older women workers documented the harsh life that can accompany a bridge job. Two Chinese women who lost their jobs in a garment factory described their present work conditions:

I stand eight hours a day serving food, not allowed to sit down except for one 10-minute break in the A.M., the other in P.M., and one half-hour lunch. There are no other Chinese, and the younger black and Hispanic workers in the kitchen do not speak to me.

I work eight hours a day cleaning and folding sheets in a badly ventilated room. I am not allowed to sit on a stool while I fold, although I have said it would help me, and I could still do a good job. I get two 15-minute breaks a day, and no paid lunch time. . . . I travel almost one hour to work each way on public transportation that sometimes doesn't work. (Rayman, Allshouse, and Allen, 1993:148)

Phased Retirement

How would you like a job working four hours a day, three days a week? That's a choice many older people would love to have. During the 1990s some employers adopted **phased retirement** programs as a way to encourage older workers to remain on the job. Phased retirement is any arrangement that allows older workers to scale back their work responsibilities for the purpose of easing into full retirement (Townsend, 2001). Options for phased retirement include working fewer hours each day, working fewer days a week, job sharing between two employees, or rehiring former employees on as consultants (Clark and Quinn, 2002). Phased retirement gives employers the benefit of older workers' experience and allows older people who want to work the chance to make a contribution without having to work full-time.

Contingent Work

The 1980s and 1990s witnessed an expansion of **contingent work,** an arrangement under which workers do not become a part of a firm's permanent workforce but are hired only to do a specific job on a part-time or temporary basis (Herz and Rones, 1989). Contingent workers cost employers less because most do not receive benefits such as pensions or health insurance. They can also be laid off more easily during economic downturns (Cohen and Zysman, 1987; Belous, 1990).

Theoretically, contingent work provides an ideal opportunity for older workers to ease into retirement (Hall and Mirvis, 1993). Some firms whose scheduling requires flexibility (such as banks) and others that experience peak seasons (such as the insurance industry) have hired older workers on this basis. However, most of the increase in contingent work among older workers has occurred at the bottom of the labor market, among child care workers, supermarket checkers, and fast-food employees, rather than in big firms seeking to take advantage of older workers' special skills (Appelbaum and Gregory, 1990; Sum and Fogg, 1990b).

Employment among Older Women

Older women workers face a different set of issues than men. Many of today's older women (55 or older) have worked intermittently. Researchers have identified three patterns of labor force participation among this cohort of women, each representing a different family–work pathway over the life course. One path is equivalent to the male model, with women having worked continuously until retirement, although they may have differed from their male counterparts by delaying entry into the labor force. In a second path, women were generally work oriented but experienced brief spells out of the labor market. The third path is characterized by extended spells out of the labor market. These women were primarily family oriented but worked during at least one stage of the life course (Pienta, Burr, and Mutchler, 1994). Some of these women stayed home for 10 or 15 years; others had several shorter spells out of the labor force (Shaw, 1996). In addition, a small proportion of women in this cohort, approximately 7 percent, never worked outside the home for wages.

Women who reenter the labor force in middle age often face numerous obstacles. Their biggest problem is that most of the jobs open to them pay low wages. Another is that these jobs lack pension coverage and other benefits such as health insurance. Thus, what may be defined as a bridge job for a male who has been continuously employed full-time may be the only career job open to a woman (Shaw, 1996).

Job opportunities have improved for women, but most of these better-paying jobs have benefited younger women who have recently entered the labor force. Younger women are more likely to work as professional, managerial, and technical employees and less likely to be employed in clerical positions (Doeringer, 1991). Between 1960 and 1990, the percentage of female lawyers increased from 2 to 25 and of female physicians from 5 to 33. Women in their 30s now represent 14 percent of all engineers, compared to less than 1 percent of their mothers' generation (Farley, Bianchi, and Voss, 1997). Although the future will be brighter for younger women, thousands of middle-aged women face old age with few marketable skills, little earning capacity, and no pension coverage.

CAUSES OF LABOR FORCE WITHDRAWAL

The transition from work to retirement can be strongly influenced by social and economic forces beyond an individual's control. In this section, we analyze the roles played by employer pensions and public benefits such as Social Security and Disability Insurance in stabilizing the economy, reducing unemployment, and encouraging early retirement.

Social Security Benefits

One factor that has encouraged early retirement of workers between the ages of 62 and 65 is the early retirement option in Social Security benefits. Beginning in 1962, men were allowed to retire at age 62 with reduced benefits (women already had that privilege; see Chapter 11). By 1970, the number of workers retiring at age 62 had increased significantly; by 1990, men were *more* likely to retire at age 62 than at 65 (Hurd, 1990; Leonesio, 1993b).

Improvements in Social Security benefits have also encouraged older workers to retire. Until 1968 Social Security benefits were quite low; as late as 1960, poverty rates among people over age 65 were higher than 35 percent (U.S. Bureau of the Census, 1998c). Between 1968 and 1972, Congress increased Social Security benefits more than 30 percent and in 1972 added automatic **cost-of-living adjustments (COLAs)** (Derthick, 1979). Now Social Security benefits increase each year to keep up with inflation. COLAs encouraged workers to retire to an even greater extent than other improvements (Myles, 1988b).

In 2000 President Clinton signed into law a bill eliminating the earnings test for Social Security recipients aged 65 to 69 (see Chapter 11). Now workers in this age group can earn as much as they can and keep all their Social Security benefits. The elimination of the earnings test is likely to increase labor force participation among older workers. "An Issue for Public Policy" on page 294 explains why Congress decided to eliminate the earnings test.

Some evidence suggests that women are less responsive than men to the incentives inherent in Social Security benefits. Rather, their decisions about employment in later life are associated with their familial responsibilities; unlike men, they leave work to care for ill or aging family members (Flippen and Tienda, 2000). Married women's retirement decisions are also influenced by their husbands' pension income, because even women who work full-time often have not worked long enough

to qualify for a pension (Reitzes, Mutran, and Fernandez, 1996; Flippen and Tienda, 2000). As more women qualify for pensions based on their own work records, women should begin to make more independent decisions.

Disability Insurance

Disability Insurance is part of the Social Security system (see Chapter 11). It pays a monthly benefit to disabled workers younger than age 65. To be eligible for DI, a worker must be insured by Social Security by having worked 10 years and be unable to engage in any substantial gainful activity because of a mental or physical impairment. Although the goal of DI is to provide income for people who are unable to work, the program acts as a de facto pension plan. In 1992, the average age of former workers receiving DI was just over 50 (Koitz, Kollman, and Neisner, 1992). Half of the DI recipients were aged 50 to 64 (National Academy of Social Insurance, 1994).

How is eligibility for DI determined? This is a complex question because *impairment* and *disability* are not synonymous. Impairment is an organic condition that can be diagnosed by a physician. Disability is the effect of an impairment on an individual's ability to work. Thus, disability is a social, not a medical concept; it is defined by the relationship between the individual's actual performance and societal expectations for people of similar age, gender, and education.

Economic Trends

Although Social Security benefits and Disability Insurance have provided incentives for workers in their 60s to retire, economic trends have also influenced their rates of labor force participation. Most research on this topic has focused on how the economy has affected older male workers. It shows that during the 1970s and 1980s, a sluggish economy reduced rates of labor force participation among older workers. Simply put, low economic growth and high unemployment meant fewer job opportunities for older Americans.

The job shortage was especially acute in manufacturing industries, which employed many older

An Issue for Public Policy

ELIMINATION OF THE EARNINGS TEST FOR SOCIAL SECURITY RECIPIENTS

Suzanne Somerset runs a thriving real estate business in Apalachicola, Florida. She works out of a cottage in this tiny village, where oystermen still ply their trade, scooping up oysters with long wooden tongs while standing in their boats. The vacation home business has boomed in the past several years, and so has Suzanne's business. She sells cottages and beach houses to tourists, who come for a visit and fall in love with the charming town and its nearby beaches.

Even though her business is prospering, Suzanne almost sold it in 1998, when she turned 65 and found that she either had to give it up or surrender her Social Security benefits. At that time anyone who worked past the normal retirement age of 65 lost $1 in Social Security benefits for every $3 earned over the cap of $17,000. But on April 7, 2000, President Clinton signed into law a bill passed unanimously by both houses of Congress, which eliminated the restrictions on earnings. Now people aged 65 to 69 can work as much as they want without losing any Social Security benefits. In signing the historic measure, President Clinton noted that the income restrictions "made some sense in the Great Depression, when the nation was desperate to find jobs for young workers with families," but did not make sense at a time when unemployment was at a 30-year low.

Why did Congress take years to eliminate the earnings test? One reason was cost. The old law would have saved the Social Security trust fund over $8 billion annually by withholding some benefits from people aged 65 to 69 who earned more than the income cap. Another reason was that the elimination of the earnings test would benefit mostly those people with relatively high incomes. People who work at minimum wage jobs in fast-food restaurants or as greeters at Wal-Mart will receive no benefit from the new legislation, but a corporate executive can earn $100,000 or more a year and still receive full Social Security benefits.

A positive effect of the new law is that it will encourage people to work longer. More older workers will continue to pay payroll taxes, helping to defray some of the cost of the program. But the elimination of the earnings test will have a much more profound effect that cannot be measured in dollars and cents. The new law has permanently changed the nature of Social Security. It is no longer a retirement program but a benefit granted automatically to any qualified worker aged 65 or older.

What Do You Think?

1. Has anyone in your family benefited from the elimination of the earnings test? If so, did the change in the law increase your relative's willingness to continue working?
2. Do you think it is fair for a corporate executive to earn $100,000 a year and still draw Social Security benefits? Why do you think Congress wrote the law this way?

workers. In the auto industry, production began to decline after the oil shortage of 1973 caused the price of gas to soar. As gas prices rose, Americans abandoned their gas-guzzling domestic vehicles and began buying smaller, fuel-efficient autos produced in Japan (Piore and Sabel, 1984). In 1950, the United States had produced 80 percent of the world's cars; by 1988 the figure was just 14.6 percent (Feldman and Betzold, 1990). The textile, agriculture, steel, and shoe industries experienced similar declines.

As manufacturing plants shut down, many workers were laid off or lost their jobs forever (Sum and Fogg, 1990a; Doeringer, 1991). At first, older workers were protected from these losses because their trade unions had negotiated contracts that granted preference to those with seniority (Hardy, Hazelrigg, and Quadagno, 1996). But when an entire plant shut down, the seniority system offered them no protection (Tomasko, 1987).

During the 1980s many firms encouraged older workers to retire by offering them **early retirement incentive programs (ERIPs).** Under these programs the usual rules for receiving pensions were waived, and employees might also be offered a financial bonus. In 1986, when oil prices were declining, Exxon Corporation, the nation's largest oil company, offered immediate retirement to those employees aged 50 and over with more than 15 years of service (Meier, 1986). And in 1987, when auto prices plummeted, General Motors offered some of its workers special incentives to retire early. More than 14,000 GM workers retired the next year, compared to just 7,000 three years earlier (Hardy, Hazelrigg, and Quadagno, 1996). By 1991 early retirement incentives were included in 97 percent of the pension plans of medium and large companies (Barth, McNaught, and Rizzi, 1995).

In the early 1990s, the combined effects of a recession and a wave of mergers forced many older white-collar workers out of the labor market. A 1995 survey of displaced workers found that manufacturing workers accounted for only one-third of the 4.5 million workers who lost their jobs in the early 1990s (U.S. Bureau of Labor Statistics, 1995). The rest were white-collar workers, including many college-educated middle managers (Gordon, 1996).

The Shift from Defined Benefit to Defined Contribution Plans

The downward trend in labor force participation among older workers was brought to a halt partly by a shift from defined benefit to defined contribution pension plans (see Chapter 15). A **defined benefit (DB)** plan pays a specified amount when a worker reaches a given age. Under DB plans, there is no advantage in continuing to work beyond retirement age because a worker's pension does not increase with additional years (Clark and McDermed, 1990). In fact, DB plans typically impose stiff financial penalties on workers who do not retire "on time" (Fields and Mitchell, 1984).

Since the 1970s, a different kind of pension plan has become increasingly popular. This newer plan, called a **defined contribution (DC)** plan, is basically a savings plan with some tax advantages (Reno, 1993b). The employer contributes a given percentage of a worker's annual earnings to a pension account, or the worker makes direct contributions. The longer a worker pays into a DC plan, the higher his or her retirement income.

Between 1981 and 2001 the number of workers covered by a defined benefit plan only declined from 58 to 12 percent while the number with a defined contribution plan only rose from 20 to 58 percent. Because defined contribution plans reduce the incentive to retire, workers in these plans retire later than workers with defined benefit plans. One study found that workers with defined benefit pensions planned to retire at 63.9 while those with defined contribution plans expected to retire at 65.2 (Munnell, Cahill, and Jivan, 2003).

International Trends in Labor Force Participation

The decline in labor force participation among older men that occurred between the 1960s and 1980s was not limited to the United States; it occurred in most industrialized countries (Kohli et al., 1991). During the 1980s unemployment rates skyrocketed in many European countries. To ease unemployment and open jobs to younger workers, many European governments tried to induce older workers to retire (Guillemard, 1991a). In some countries officials loosened the eligibility requirements for disability insurance; in others they turned unemployment compensation programs into de facto old age pensions.

France is an extreme example of the international trend toward early retirement. In 1988, as the result of changes in the French pension system and an expansion of unemployment benefits, only 67 percent of men aged 55 to 59 remained in the French labor force (Jacobs, Kohli, and Rein, 1991). Until 1970 the French pension system gave citizens an incentive to work into old age. The legal age for full retirement was 65, and those who worked past that age received a bonus of 5 percent a year. A worker who retired at age 60, in contrast, would receive only a half pension.

But in the 1970s the French government lowered the retirement age from 65 to 60 and in 1972 extended unemployment benefits to unemployed workers over age 60. In 1983 the government expanded the program further to include workers who had resigned from their jobs (Guillemard, 1991b). Since unemployment benefits were higher than pension benefits, older workers had a strong incentive to quit their jobs and leave the labor force permanently. Not surprisingly, labor force participation among men aged 55 to 59 dropped dramatically. The unemployment program had become a de facto old-age fund (Guillemard, 1991b).

A different set of incentives produced a similar outcome in Germany, where approximately one-fourth of men aged 55 to 59 were out of the labor force; most retired on disability benefits (Jacobs et al., 1991). Initially, the German government defined a disability in strictly medical terms. Any individual who was capable of working even part-time was deemed ineligible for a disability pension. But when unemployment rates rose in the 1970s, German courts allowed part-time workers to receive a full disability pension, regardless of their health.

The German government has also encouraged early retirement. In the past, a male worker had to be 65 to receive a pension, but recently, any 60-year-old male who has worked at least 15 years and been unemployed at least 52 weeks in the past year

and a half has received a pension. This provision has no effect on women, because they are allowed to retire at age 60 (Jacobs et al., 1991). German citizens are now beginning to wonder if these generous pension and unemployment benefits have become a drain on their economy. They worry that their government has created a two-tier state—one composed of workers and the other of nonworkers—and that the cost of supporting so many nonworkers is slowing their economy (Esping-Anderson, 1995).

In Japan, workers retire later than in any other country. Until recently Japanese employees could expect to glide smoothly into a low-stress, largely ceremonial job as they aged. But as Japan struggles to pull its economy out of the doldrums and reduce the costs associated with an aging population, the traditional practice of "lifetime employment" is eroding.

Although the labor force participation rates of older workers vary from one nation to another, most nations use some form of public welfare to encourage retirement, from pension programs to disability and unemployment benefits. Even though they offer different incentives, the average age of retirement is remarkably similar, as Table 12–3 shows. While the decline in labor force participation

Table 12-3	International Variations in Average Age of Retirement, 1995	
	Men	*Women*
Australia	61.8	57.2
Austria	58.6	56.5
Canada	62.3	58.8
France	59.2	58.3
Germany	60.5	58.4
Italy	60.6	57.2
Japan	66.5	63.7
Norway	63.8	62.0
Switzerland	64.6	60.6
United States	63.6	61.6

Source: Organization for Economic Cooperation and Development (1998:53).

rates of older workers has recently leveled off, the increase in retirement rates is straining European economies. Many countries have begun to revise their pension systems to halt the trend toward early retirement (Myles and Quadagno, 2000).

RETIREMENT AS AN INDIVIDUAL DECISION

From the previous discussion, it should be apparent that broader economic forces, beyond the control of the individual, play a large role in retirement. But the decisions people make are not solely determined by external forces. Within the constraints imposed by the labor market and the welfare state, people time their retirement on the basis of their own desire to trade work for leisure.

Although 75 percent of all men and 78 percent of all women are no longer in the labor force by age 65, there is considerable variation in the timing of retirement. Some retire well before they reach 60; others continue working past 70. How do people decide when to retire? Research indicates that five factors play a role: the rules of the job, the meaning of work, health, income, and familial responsibilities.

The Rules of the Job

The first generation of research on retirement typically contrasted *voluntary* with *involuntary* retirement. Voluntary retirees were people who said they wanted to retire; involuntary retirees were forced out, because they had lost their jobs or were in poor health (Henretta, Chan, and O'Rand, 1992).

These early research findings showed that in the postwar period, many workers were forced out of their jobs by **mandatory retirement** rules. As we saw earlier, such rules once covered nearly half of all American workers. That mandatory retirement has been abolished does not mean that involuntary retirement has been eliminated (Quinn and Burkhauser, 1990).

Among blue-collar workers, the choice may be to retire or to continue working with the threat of a plant closing hanging over one's head. White-collar managers may stay on at lower wages but know that next week a merger or buyout could cost them their jobs. Faced with these options and uncertainties, many workers leave their jobs when they are eligible for a pension. Many then also leave the labor force. Is their departure voluntary? Yes, in that they choose to take their pension and leave the firm. No, in that preferable options like staying on the job at the same salary may have disappeared (Hardy and Quadagno, 1995).

The Meaning of Work

How people feel about their jobs affects how they feel about leaving those jobs. Professionals who receive intrinsic rewards from work often delay retirement. Dr. Fred Snyder, the 70-year-old chairman of pediatrics at a large medical center, had no plans to retire. He didn't think he was "cut out for sitting on [his] hands and doing nothing" (Quadagno, 1978:69).

By contrast, people who have worked at routine and unchallenging jobs all their lives are often eager to retire. For them, the purpose of work is to earn money to do other things. Listen to Lorenzo Sharpe, a native-born Cuban who began working for Ford in 1965. He would love to retire: "If they raised retirement benefits and let me retire now, I wouldn't work a day more. For what? The earlier I leave, the more I can enjoy life. I don't want to retire and die within two or three years like a lot of people do" (Feldman and Betzold, 1990:35). The only thing stopping him is insufficient income.

Health

Poor health has always been a factor in the timing of the retirement decision. In self-reports where interviewers ask people to rate their health, men who say they have poor health retire earlier than those who say their health is good. The same holds true for women, except that inadequate income often prevents unhealthy women from being able to retire (Iams, 1986). In one study, unemployed men aged 55 to 69 were found to be less likely to reenter the labor force if they had health insurance (Mutchler et al., 1999).

The effect of health on the likelihood of retirement can be seen by comparing the health status

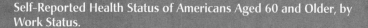

Figure 12-4   Self-Reported Health Status of Americans Aged 60 and Older, by Work Status.

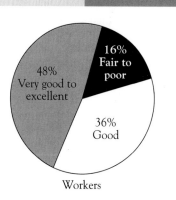

Workers

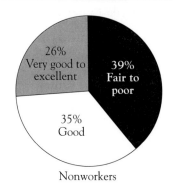

Nonworkers

Source: National Academy on an Aging Society (2000).

of workers to retirees. As Figure 12–4 shows, among people aged 60 and older, workers are almost twice as likely as retirees to report having very good or excellent health, and half as likely as their nonworking counterparts to report they have fair or poor health (National Academy on an Aging Society, 2000).

There are also racial differences in the timing of retirement due to poor health. As previously noted, on average African American men retire sooner than whites, mainly because of poor health. Disability benefits provide the income that allows them to leave the labor force (Hayward, Friedman, and Chen, 1996).

In the past 20 years, the proportion of people listing poor health as a reason for retiring has declined. It may be that in the past poor health was a "respectable" reason for retiring. Today, fewer jobs require strenuous physical effort, and more jobs require only light or moderate physical exertion. Thus, workers who in the past may have been forced to retire for health reasons may be able to continue working longer (Burtless and Quinn, 2002).

Income

Throughout this chapter, we have emphasized the ways income affects the timing of retirement (Schulz, 1995). Most people need income from a combination of sources, including Social Security

and a pension, to be able to retire. Without sufficient income, they will continue working. As we saw earlier, people aged 65 to 69 may now continue working and still receive full Social Security benefits. One study of women who were receiving Social Security benefits found that they were two to three times more likely to continue working if they did not also have income from a private pension (Iams, 1986). Unmarried women retire later than married women, because married people have considerably higher total incomes than unmarried people (Iams, 1986; Ruhm, 1996).

A survey of 12,000 Americans between the ages of 51 and 60 indicated that 40 percent would have no pension income other than Social Security, 20 percent had no assets, and 14 percent had no health insurance (Sterns and Sterns, 1995). All these people will feel pressure to delay retirement. Another study of people approaching retirement age found that a substantial number who had a pension did not even know what age they would be eligible to receive benefits or how much their monthly pension income would be when they retired (Ekerdt and Hackney, 2002).

Family Responsibilities

Much early research on the timing of retirement treated it as an isolated experience, unconnected to an individual's other life spheres (Szinovacz, Ekerdt, and Vinick, 1992). The basic assumption behind this research was that work was central to men's lives and that the worlds of work and family constituted separate spheres (Calasanti, 1996). This separation between work and family was presumed to extend into the retirement years. As the labor force participation rates of women have increased, social gerontologists have discovered numerous links between the family and the retirement experience. For example, women who have had continuous work histories are more likely to delay retirement than women who have been more family-oriented and thus employed more intermittently (Pienta et al., 1994). Another recent discovery is that the timing of retirement is becoming a couple experience. Husbands and wives take each other into account when planning to retire, and retirement becomes a joint decision (Szinovacz, 1989). Given that couples negotiate responsibilities for child rearing and the division of household tasks in their younger years, it should not be surprising that they also jointly plan when to retire. Retirement planning is not simply an individual event but rather a household decision (Pienta and Hayward, 2002).

Dual-worker couples can retire at the same time, a choice called **joint retirement;** or they can retire in sequence, with either the husband or the wife retiring first while the other continues to work, a pattern called **sequential retirement** (O'Rand, Henretta, and Krecker, 1992). The most common pattern is for women to retire when their husbands do, as evidenced by a sharp drop in female labor force participation at age 60 (Hurd, 1990). Part of that decline may occur because 60 is the age at which women first become eligible for widow's Social Security benefits, but it also suggests that women are coordinating their own retirement with that of their husbands.

Some wives do continue to work after their husbands retire. Compared to women who retire, those who continue working tend to live in larger households, have children younger than age 21, and have husbands who retired because of health problems. When the husband continues to work after the wife retires, there likely is a dependent child still in the home. Some of these men have older wives (Ruhm, 1996).

Joint retirement seems to be the pattern of choice when a couple can afford to do so. It is also more common among couples who shared both work and family roles early in their marriage (Henretta, O'Rand, and Chan, 1993). Sequential retirement is common in families of lower socioeconomic status who have inadequate income and thus a need for the continued employment of either the husband or the wife (O'Rand et al., 1992).

The retirement decisions of single women are also affected by family matters. The probability of an unmarried woman retiring rises dramatically if she has an elderly parent in the household and even more so if there are two elderly parents in the household (Hatch and Thompson, 1992; Weaver, 1994). Yet caring for an elderly parent often involves additional financial expenses, and many single caregivers must keep working, even while providing care, to pay these extra costs (Ruhm, 1996).

The consensus now is that retirement from work is not a single event. Rather, work in later life represents a dynamic process that may involve new kinds of jobs and reductions in time worked (Elder and Pavalko, 1993). The simple organization of the modern life course into three periods—education (or labor force preparation), economic activity, and retirement—no longer fits the later-life pattern of many workers (Kohli, 1986). Instead of asking questions about what is meant by retirement, it is more relevant to explore how people make the transition from work to retirement.

SATISFACTION WITH RETIREMENT

Given the importance of work for most people in middle age, the transition to retirement can involve an abrupt adjustment that transforms an individual's social world, relationships, and daily routines. On the positive side, retirees have more freedom and independence than they may have had since they were children. But retirees may find that they miss a more structured existence with clear goals, and they may also feel a loss of the social status that comes with a job (Kim and Moen, 2001).

Two theories have been used to explain how well people adjust to retirement: crisis theory and continuity theory. **Crisis theory** views the occupational role as the major source of personal validation, at least for men (Friedmann and Havighurst, 1954). According to crisis theory, the loss of the work role is a wrenching experience that deprives men of a job, status, and a meaningful role in society (Cavan et al., 1949). Many early studies supported this view. Retirees often had poorer health and lower morale than people who were still working (George and Maddox, 1977; Blau, 1981; Palmore, 1981).

Other studies from the same era contradicted this picture of retirement. Many men neither viewed work as their central life experience nor experienced retirement as a crisis (Atchley, 1971; Friedman and Orbach, 1974). These findings were more in line with **continuity theory,** which stresses the persistence of personal identity through the expansion of other roles (see Chapter 2). According to continuity theory, retirement has become acceptable in contemporary society, and most people base their identity on a number of roles. Retirees are likely to experience retirement in a positive way if they substitute new roles to fill the gap created by retirement (Atchley, 1971).

Recent research supports continuity theory. One longitudinal study of 300 men and women aged 58 to 64 found continuity in self-assessment in the transition to retirement. Those who had high self-esteem before they retired continued to have high self-esteem after retirement. Preretirement roles and identities had a positive influence on the postretirement assessment of self (Reitzes, Mutran, and Fernandez, 1996). However, men and women who obtained their sense of identity from work were less satisfied in retirement and less likely to report that their retirement years were better than their working years (Quick and Moen, 1998).

Although the ability to substitute new activities for work is related to satisfaction with retirement, the best predictors of positive attitudes toward retirement are the material conditions of retirement, or what are called the *status aspects* of the retirement experience. The status aspects of retirement refer to the resources that determine what people can do (physically) and what they can afford to do (financially).

The most consistent finding is that happiness in retirement is associated with good health (George and Maddox, 1977; Gratton and Haug, 1983; Reitzes, Mutran, and Pope, 1991). Adequate income is also an important predictor of life satisfaction in retirement. Advanced planning contributes to satisfaction in retirement. Voluntary retirees report high satisfaction with retirement, while involuntary retirees experience the most negative transitions (Quick and Moen, 1998).

There are also significant effects of family status on retirement satisfaction. People who are married have more positive attitudes in retirement, higher satisfaction with retirement, and better adaptation to retirement than unmarried people. Social and emotional support from wives is particularly important for married men (Szinovacz and Washo, 1992). Despite the positive effect of marriage on retirement satisfaction, marital quality drops for most couples when only one spouse retires while the other remains employed. When husband and wife retire at the same time, men in particular are much happier with their marriages. As the couple settles into retirement, marital conflict declines and marital satisfaction increases again (Moen, Kim, and Hofmeister, 2001). Clearly, retirement, like any other significant role transition, involves major adjustments.

Unmarried people, especially men, often lack close relationships with kin because it is women who maintain familial ties. Unmarried men are also more likely than married men to feel the loss of social contact with colleagues at work. Men who maintain their friendships after they retire have higher levels of satisfaction than those who do not (Szinovacz and Ekerdt, 1995).

Finally, satisfaction with retirement is associated with preretirement planning. One recent survey found that 76 percent of middle-aged workers had done some financial planning for retirement, but only a few also engaged in lifestyle planning. Yet planning was the strongest predictor of positive attitudes toward retirement. Retirement planning

In Their Own Words

The Transition to Retirement

*W*hen Zoe Levin retired from her job as a lab technician, she embarked on an era of self-discovery.

> What particularly excited me about retirement was when I began to see it as a new chapter with empty pages, ones that I was free to fill in any way I wanted to. And I didn't realize how stressful the work was until I left it—like you don't know how tight your shoes are until you take them off.... Oren and I went off camping for three weeks after I retired. I took a pile of novels, worked through my insecurities, the nostalgia, the blues, doubts, mourning for people. I saw that happiness was a route, not a destination. My last day at work I slipped off my watch and I haven't put one on since. And since then, I've been able to do what I want to *when* I want to. I see weeds in the daisy patch and I just get right down there and pull them out—now, not later. I had to get out of the mind-set that you can't do the things you really enjoy until the evening or the weekend. It's the people who make the most of the time they live in now who are timeless.

Source: Savishinsky (2000).

may reduce the tensions that accompany an exit from the labor force, and it may help people adjust afterward (Kim and Moen, 2001).

In sum, men and women who have adequate income and good health, reside in a suitable environment, and have access to a satisfactory social support system are more likely to be satisfied with retirement than those who do not (Streib and Schneider, 1971; Mutran and Reitzes, 1981; Beck, 1982; Seccombe and Lee, 1986; Reitzes et al., 1991). The relationship between status factors and retirement satisfaction is straightforward: A lifestyle that is both more financially secure and more enjoyable is a source of satisfaction. Zoe Levin, a retired lab technician, describes her satisfaction with her retirement in "In Their Own Words."

Retirement refers not only to a change in status, however, but also to a process, a transition from employment to nonemployment. Some research suggests that the degree of satisfaction depends on how that process is experienced. Early studies on the retirement process emphasized how involuntary retirement created dissatisfaction in old age. Given that voluntary retirement has no absolute meaning, which aspects of the preretirement experience are most likely to affect postretirement satisfaction? One factor is being able to choose when to retire. As Matthews and Brown (1988) reported, "having wanted to retire when they did was the strongest predictor of retirement having affected individuals in a positive way" (p. 563). Another predictor of retirement satisfaction is having a favorable attitude and an accurate preconception of retirement (Thompson, 1958).

A more subtle explanation of how the preretirement process can affect postretirement experiences has been posited by Ekerdt and DeViney (1993), who argued "that time left at work organizes the experience of older workers" (p. 535). Their research showed that the closer men came to retirement, the more they regarded their jobs as burdensome. Thus, the literature on the transition to retirement suggests that experiences regarding whether the choice is voluntary or involuntary and the temporal dimension of the preretirement cycle shape postretirement satisfaction.

Daily Activities and Health

Although early characterizations of retirement as a "roleless role" may have been accurate at one time, that is no longer the case. Most retirees sustain busy and active lives and play a productive part in their families and their own communities. Some engage in leisure activities for self-fulfillment—shopping, playing golf or cards, traveling, and socializing. Others care for their grandchildren or other family members or participate in organizations. Using this broad definition of productive activity as leisure activity and organizational and care work, 39 percent of people aged 60 or older report engaging in at least 1,500 hours of productive activity a year; 41 percent, in 500 to 1,499 hours; and 18 percent, in 1 to 499 hours.

Not surprisingly, the nature of leisure-time pursuits changes over the life course. The young–old are more likely to play tennis or go bicycling, while the old–old take nature walks, play golf, or sightsee. Frequent participation in leisure-time activities as a young person is associated with continued involvement in later life. The most important constraints on participation in leisure-time activities and organizations are a lack of economic resources and poor health. The low-income elderly must spend all their money on basic necessities; they lack the discretionary income to pursue leisure involvements. A lack of transportation, which is a particular problem for the aged poor, is another barrier to involvement in activities (Cutler and Hendricks, 1990).

People who are in poor health tend to engage in more passive activities than those who are in good health; those in the poorest health are least active (Cutler and Hendricks, 1990). Many of the old–old, people who are 85 or older, are limited in their mobility and must organize their activities around their health problems. For these people, managing the basic activities of daily living can be time-consuming. An elderly woman describes her typical day:

I'm a good half hour in the bathroom before I can start my day. Then I have breakfast and read the paper. By then, much of the morning is taken up, and then lunch takes me two hours to prepare and eat. Everything is scheduled. After lunch I must take a nap, or I'll fall asleep before dinner. In the evening, I eat dinner, watch the news, and then go to bed. There are no evenings for us old folks. We never go out at night. (Johnson and Barer, 1997:135)

Although elderly people may keep up with the activities they enjoyed when they were younger, they usually make some compromises. An 88-year-old former vaudeville performer describes how he continues with activities he has always enjoyed, even though he has had to adapt to declining health:

Yesterday I was up on the roof cleaning out the gutters. That was awful—I had to hail a neighbor to help me get down. I have had a slight stroke and have fallen twice, so I can't do what I used to do. Despite everything though, I feel pretty good. Now I swim only three laps. My memory is worse, so I can't learn new songs like I used to. I got tired of all the time it takes me to clean this place, so I threw out all my rugs. (Johnson and Barer, 1997:141)

An interesting finding is that older people's activities are similar in diverse settings. For a description of the daily activities of the elderly in Germany, see "Aging around the World."

Overall, most elderly people find ways to cope with hassles that might seem daunting to much younger individuals, conducting their daily business with a sense of accomplishment and good spirits. In the future, as disabilities decline even among the oldest–old, the aged may be able to remain active through most of their retirement years.

Volunteering

Since the 1970s Americans have worked on fewer and fewer community projects. In 1975 more than two of every five adults surveyed said they had worked on some community project over the past

Aging around the World

EVERYDAY ACTIVITIES AMONG GERMAN ELDERS

*H*ow do you spend a typical day? Make a list of everything you do from the minute you wake up until you go to sleep. Then count the number of minutes you spend in each activity. You might be surprised at how you spend your time. Do you watch more television than you realized? Study less than you should?

A group of German researchers wondered how older people spend their time during a typical day. Their Berlin Aging Study involved 516 men and women between the ages of 70 and 105. Using a measure called the Yesterday Interview, the researchers asked the participants to keep track of the type, duration, and frequency of their activities the day before researchers interviewed them. The activities were divided into eight main categories: basic personal care (eating, bathing, tooth brushing), instrumental activities of daily living (housework, bill paying, shopping), paid work, socializing with others, watching television, reading, other leisure activities, and resting. Figure 12–5 shows how much of the day participants spent on each activity on a daily basis. They spent the most time on IADLs, followed by resting, television watching, and personal care. Participants over age 90 spent considerably more time on basic personal care and resting than people in their 70s and 80s.

Figure 12–6 shows the social and physical context in which these daily activities occurred. Participants spent more than two-thirds (64.4 percent) of their day alone and 80 percent of their day in their own homes (Horgas, Wilms, and Baltes, 1998).

Are the German aged unique in the way they spend their time? The answer is *no;* the responses to the Yesterday Interview were much the same when it was used with American subjects (Moss and Lawton, 1982).

What Do you Think?

1. How do your aged relatives spend their time? Would they respond to the Yesterday Interview in the same way as the subjects of the Berlin Aging Study did?
2. What are the social policy implications of Figures 12–5 and 12–6? How could public officials use this type of information?

Figure 12-5   How German Elders Spend Their Day.

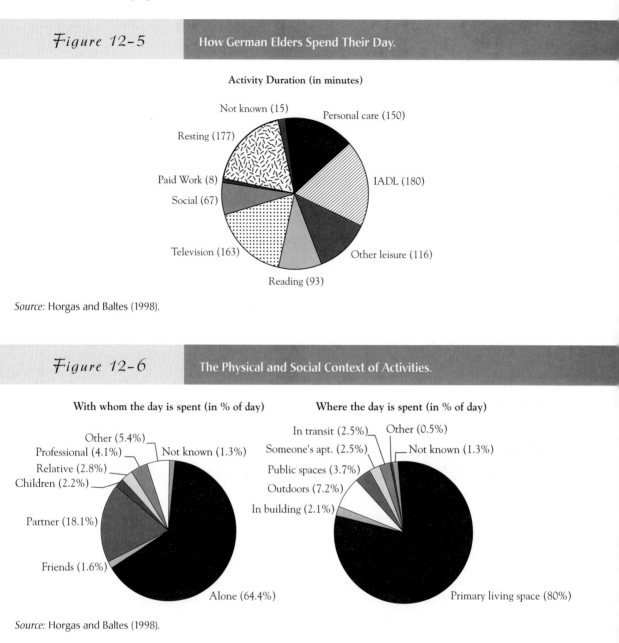

Activity Duration (in minutes)

Not known (15)
Personal care (150)
Resting (177)
Paid Work (8)
IADL (180)
Social (67)
Television (163)
Other leisure (116)
Reading (93)

Source: Horgas and Baltes (1998).

Figure 12-6   The Physical and Social Context of Activities.

With whom the day is spent (in % of day)

Other (5.4%)
Professional (4.1%)
Relative (2.8%)
Children (2.2%)
Not known (1.3%)
Partner (18.1%)
Friends (1.6%)
Alone (64.4%)

Where the day is spent (in % of day)

In transit (2.5%)
Other (0.5%)
Someone's apt. (2.5%)
Not known (1.3%)
Public spaces (3.7%)
Outdoors (7.2%)
In building (2.1%)
Primary living space (80%)

Source: Horgas and Baltes (1998).

year. By 1999 fewer than one in three made that claim. However, one-on-one volunteering has increased since 1975. People volunteer in schools, in Big Brother and Big Sister programs, and as foster grandparents.

Who are these new volunteers who provide personal service to others? Virtually the entire increase in volunteering is concentrated among people aged 60 and over. In the last quarter of the twentieth century, volunteer work among older people nearly doubled, from an average of 6 times a year to 12 times a year. Among people over age 75, volunteering increased 140 percent (Putnam, 2000). A recent survey of adults 60 and older found that

This retired woman spends 10 hours each week volunteering at a local school. Here she helps children with their reading.

35 percent volunteered. The average amount of time spent volunteering was 30 hours a year, but 25 percent of the volunteers donated more than 160 hours (Morrow-Howell et al., 2003). Volunteering among older adults not only benefits their communities but also enhances their own sense of well-being.

Nearly half the volunteer work done by older people is for churches, synagogues, or church-related organizations; hospitals, nursing homes, and hospices rank second. Among the responsibilities older people undertake are tutoring, advising, or coaching others (29 percent), working with their hands (27 percent), fund-raising (16 percent), serving on boards and committees (11 percent), working in an office (10 percent), or driving a car or van (8 percent) (Caro and Bass, 1995). Many others would like to volunteer but cannot because of employment or family obligations, poor health, or a lack of knowledge of volunteer opportunities.

What accounts for this rise in volunteer work among older people? Several factors are responsible. Older people today are in better health, more highly educated, and more financially secure than any previous generation. They enjoy longer and more active postretirement lives than their predecessors. Time diaries show a significant increase in free time among people over 60 in the last two or three decades. Not surprisingly, people who have

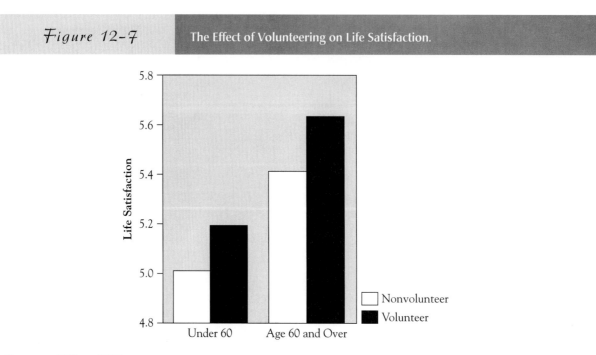

Figure 12-7   The Effect of Volunteering on Life Satisfaction.

Source: van Willigen (2000).

personal and financial resources are more likely to volunteer their time than people who are in poor health and must struggle to make ends meet. But sociologists have also identified a cohort effect. Men and women who were born before World War II have been engaged in civic affairs their entire lives—more so than either their predecessors or their successors. Now in retirement, they continue a lifelong pattern of good citizenship.

While volunteering benefits others, it also benefits the volunteers themselves (van Willigen, 2000). Figure 12–7 shows that while volunteering improves life satisfaction for people of all ages, older volunteers reap the most benefit. Volunteering also appears to have a positive effect on one's health. Although younger people's self-rated health is higher than older people's, older volunteers rate their health more positively than older nonvolunteers (see Figure 12–8). Of course, poor health may prevent some older people from engaging in volunteer work. There is even some evidence that a moderate amount of volunteer work reduces mortality (Musick, Herzog, and House, 1999). Evidence on

the connection between volunteering and well-being provides support for the activity theory of aging—that older people who remain productive and maintain their social networks have higher levels of life satisfaction than those who disengage from their activities. (Morrow-Howell et al., 2003). Mrs. Hauge, 86 years old, lives independently and visits the nearby YWCA and the Norwegian Club, a short bus ride away. She also has a large friendship network and many interests:

I practically live at the Y. I go there three times a week, play bridge, do the exercises, and see many friends. On Tuesdays, after the Y, I go out with my friend. She is like me—always wants to be on the go. On Wednesday I have another friend who still drives. She picks me up and we go out shopping and for lunch. On Thursday, it is Golden Age Day at the Norwegian Club. The Noriega 17 bus goes by my house and then straight there. On Friday afternoon there is bingo at the center. There is a man there who is interested in me and wants to take me out, but I am too busy for that. On weekends, my younger son

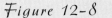

The Effect of Volunteering on Self-Rated Health.

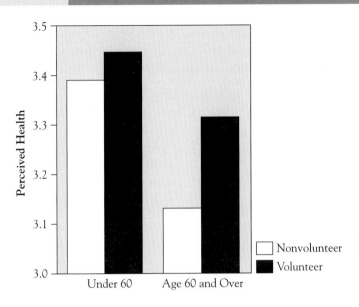

Source: van Willigen (2000).

comes and I cook dinner. Then every few weeks I stay home and clean the house. I love people, I love to play bridge and bingo, and I love to sit with my friends for lunch. I go out so much. I do a lot of dancing at the Norwegian Club. I love to be around people my age, particularly if they are Norwegian. (Johnson and Barer, 1997:116)

What will happen to civic life when this cohort dies? Thus far, the baby boomers have shown less inclination to participate in civic and community affairs, much less than their parents' generation. In the past, the rate of volunteering has increased with age, and people in their 50s and 60s have been most likely to be active in clubs and civic groups. The same increase in civic participation has not yet occurred among the baby boomers. Indeed, all forms of civic involvement have declined, largely because a highly civic-minded generation is being replaced by one that is less so. Young Americans now in their 20s, however, are the most civic-minded generation to come along in decades. They have demonstrated a commitment to volunteerism that

suggests the United States may be entering an era of civic renewal (Putnam, 2000).

Religious Participation

As we have seen, the most common form of volunteering among older adults is participation in a religious organization. Nearly 65 percent of older volunteers donate time to their church, synagogue, or mosque (van Willigen, 2000).

Religious involvement is related to a variety of demographic and social characteristics. Women tend to be more involved than men in religious organizations and to state that prayer is important to them. In general, religiosity tends to increase with age, though not on all measures. For example, among respondents to the National Survey of Black Americans aged 18 and over, the subjective sense of religiosity was stronger among older respondents. But older people were no different from younger people in their organizational activities and religious involvement (Chatters, Levin, and Taylor, 1992).

People express their faith in numerous ways, from public experiences such as attending services to private activities such as praying or watching religious programs on television. Although attendance at services is a commonly used measure of religiosity, the nonorganizational features of religion—faith and spirituality—are equally important.

Racial differences in religious activity

Most research has documented distinct racial differences in religious activity. Older African Americans are more likely than whites to be involved in a variety of religious activities. They have higher rates of church attendance, are more likely to define themselves as religious-minded, are more likely to receive religious instruction, and are more likely to talk with clergy about their problems (Levin, Taylor, and Chatters, 1994). Older African Americans may receive instrumental support as well as emotional support from their church affiliations. For example, one childless elderly black widower receives a great deal of help from his church deacon:

He takes me to church, takes me to the clinic, runs errands for me when I need him to. He's doing things for me all the time. Sometimes a little thing go wrong with the car, he'll fix that. (Ball and Whittington, 1995:101)

Participation in a religious community provides members with a framework for deriving meaning from their life experience and provides opportunities to interact with those who share similar values, attitudes, and beliefs. In the African American tradition, religion also provides important personal and institutional resources for overcoming racial and economic discrimination. As Levin, Taylor, and Chatters (1994:137) explain, "The resiliency of African American religious traditions is found in their ability to confront these pernicious life conditions, to provide alternative methods for their amelioration, and to invest diverse meaning in those experiences."

Religious involvement and well-being

Research on the impact of religion on adaptation to aging shows that it can improve health and reduce disability, increase self-esteem, reduce symptoms of depression, and enhance life satisfaction (Levin and Taylor, 1997). One study found that rates of depression were lower among older Catholics and Jews who attended religious services regularly (Kennedy et al., 1996). For many older people, religion gives meaning to life that helps them transcend suffering, loss, and the sure knowledge of death (McFadden, 1996).

Evidence that religion provides comfort and support is substantial. Numerous studies have demonstrated a positive association between religion and various indicators of health, such as hypertension and cancer (McFadden, 1996). Studies of older adults' mental health also suggest that religious beliefs have a positive effect on well-being. One study of Mexican Americans aged 65 to 80 found that those who frequently attended religious services had higher life satisfaction and lower levels of depression than those who did not (Levin, Markides, and Ray, 1996). A note of caution is in order in interpreting the results of such studies, however, for increased disability and poor health may prevent people from participating in religious activities.

Chapter Resources

LOOKING BACK

1. **How has the percentage of Americans who work changed over time, and how do workers' gender, age, and racial or ethnic group affect their employment rate?** *From 1970 until 1990 there was a steady decline in labor force participation among men in the United States. In the past decade this trend has come to a halt, and there is even a slight increase in work among older men. The trends for women are more difficult to discern. Although some older women retire early, others enter the labor force in middle age and continue to work well into old age.*

   Racial and ethnic differences in employment histories over the life course create different patterns of labor force participation in middle and old age. Higher rates of unemployment among minority workers compared to white workers push minority workers toward early retirement. Yet older Hispanic men often continue working because they are ineligible for Social Security benefits.

2. **What are the employment prospects for older workers, and how are they affected by age discrimination?** *Some older workers choose to remain in full-time jobs; others prefer to scale down their work efforts. Bridge jobs span the period between full-time employment in a career job and permanent retirement. The expansion of contingent work provides some opportunities for older workers, but currently most of these jobs are at the bottom of the labor market and do not take advantage of older workers' special skills.*

   Although the Age Discrimination in Employment Act of 1967 banned discrimination against workers aged 40 to 65, it contains many loopholes that allow employers to discriminate against older workers. Employers often prefer to hire younger workers who have lower salaries. Some employers also mistakenly assume that older workers are less productive than younger workers. Yet research shows that older workers are more reliable and more loyal to their employers.

3. **What economic forces cause workers to withdraw from the labor force?** *During the 1970s and 1980s low economic growth and high unemployment rates led to many older workers withdrawing from the labor force. Early retirement was especially common in manufacturing industries, in which many older workers were laid off or lost their jobs. Firms also tried to encourage older workers to retire by offering early retirement incentive programs. Then a recession in the 1990s pushed more college-educated, white-collar workers out of the labor force. By the end of the 1990s, however, these trends were reversed. A booming economy created more job opportunities for older workers, and the result has been a decline in early retirement.*

4. **How do individuals decide when to retire?** *Within the constraints imposed by the economy, people time their retirement on the basis of a desire to trade work for leisure. The timing of the retirement decision is determined by such factors as the rules of the job, the meaning of work, health, expected income, and a spouse's employment plans.*

5. **What personal factors are associated with an individual's relative satisfaction in retirement?** *Satisfaction in retirement partly depends on lifestyle factors. People with adequate income, good health, and a social support system are most likely to be satisfied in retirement. People who retire unwillingly are least likely to be satisfied. Women who retire for family reasons such as caring for an aging parent or ailing spouse are the most dissatisfied.*

THINKING ABOUT AGING

1. Many older women drop out of the labor force to care for ill or aging relatives. In doing so, they forgo Social Security benefits later in life. Should the government give these women credit for the unpaid work

they do? What might be the practical problems in doing so?

2. What can government do to help older workers who have lost their jobs and health insurance but are not yet old enough to retire?

3. What do you think of the trend toward hiring contingent workers who do not receive the same benefits as permanent employees? Does it provide employment opportunities that older workers would not otherwise have, or does it undermine their well-being?

4. Should government be in the business of moving older workers out of the workforce to make room for younger workers? Explain your position.

5. How soon do you yourself hope to retire? Why?

KEY TERMS

Age Discrimination in Employment Act of 1967 (ADEA) 289

bridge jobs 291

contingent work 292

continuity theory 300

cost-of-living adjustments (COLAs) 293

crisis theory 300

defined benefit (DB) 295

defined contribution (DC) 295

early retirement incentive programs (ERIPs) 295

economic part-time work 291

joint retirement 299

mandatory retirement 297

phased retirement 292

sequential retirement 299

voluntary part-time work 291

EXPLORING THE INTERNET

Note: While all the URLs listed were current as of the printing of this book, these sites often change. Please check our website www.mhhe.com/quadagno for updates.

1. Sheldon Steinhauser, an associate professor at The Metropolitan State College of Denver has constructed a website designed to inform students, businesses, and organizations about issues involving the aged and the workforce. Go to the website (http://clem.mscd.edu/~steinhas/), link to "Threat of Costly Age Discrimination and Older Worker Issues Gains National Attention," and answer the following the questions:

a. How much has been spent by corporate America since 1996 on lawsuits involving age discrimination?

b. What percentage of discrimination lawsuits are on the basis of age?

c. Of discrimination lawsuits on the basis of sex, race, disability, and age, which tends to have the largest settlements?

Now go back to the main page, link to "Top Ten list For Reducing, Eliminating Age Discrimination in the workplace," and answer the following questions:

a. What is meant by an organization's "culture," and how does age fit into this?

b. According to the website, what is the main factor contributing to the likely rise in age discrimination lawsuits?

2. The National Council on Aging (http://www.ncoa.org) is one of the nation's oldest associations dedicated to promoting the dignity, self-determination, and well-being of older persons. Go to the council's home page, link to "Press Room," and then "News Archive." Scroll down, link to the article, "Boomers and Retirements Chart Books Reveal New Trends," and answer the following questions:

a. What percentage of boomers think that employer pressure to retire is very or somewhat important?

b. What percent of mature workers are employed full-time by choice?

c. What is the reason for this increasing trend of more mature workers being employed full-time?

d. For older employees, what are the important elements of a job?

Chapter 13

Health and Health Care

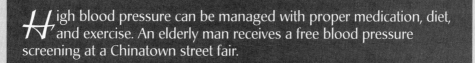

*H*igh blood pressure can be managed with proper medication, diet, and exercise. An elderly man receives a free blood pressure screening at a Chinatown street fair.

Looking Ahead

1. Why has poor health become associated with old age, and how are recent improvements in health care changing that association?
2. How do people's lifestyles and social support systems affect their health in old age?
3. What is the best measure of an elderly person's socioeconomic status, and how is SES connected to a person's health?
4. How do gender, race, and ethnicity affect an older person's health?
5. How have changes in Medicare and the health care industry affected older Americans?

What does it mean to be in good health? Although we often think of health in relation to disease or illness, the definition of health is much broader. The World Health Organization defines health as a state of complete physical, mental, and social well-being, not just the absence of disease (Cockerham, 1995). To some extent, people have control over their health.

Such behaviors as smoking, drinking, and exercise can either enhance prospects for the prevention of disease or promote illness and disability. Thus, people who engage in unhealthy lifestyles when they are young—smoking, drinking too much, never exercising—may pay a price in the form of heart disease, lung cancer, or emphysema when they are old. Other factors that contribute to poor health later in life are beyond a person's control. An individual's resources influence access to health care and the quality of health care available. Social factors also influence the way societies organize their resources to deal with health hazards and deliver medical care. Cultural and political values affect both the organization of the health care system and the levels of funding for health care services.

313

In the first half of this chapter, we analyze the social causes and consequences of health and illness among the aged. We examine what research shows about the relationship between lifestyle factors and health, and we discuss the factors that create inequality in the distribution of good health. In the second half, we examine the social organization of the health care delivery system in the United States, the social behavior of health care personnel, and the effect of changing health care delivery systems on the treatment of the elderly. Finally, we describe the problem of increasing health care costs and discuss the politically charged issues we face in the future regarding the distribution of responsibility for health care between the public and private sectors.

ADDING YEARS TO LIFE OR LIFE TO YEARS?

Stages of the Epidemiologic Transition

In Chapter 2, we described the demographic transition as a process in which a change from high birth and death rates to low birth and death rates results in population aging. The demographic transition is accompanied by an **epidemiologic transition,** signifying a change in the leading causes of death from infectious diseases to chronic diseases. **Health behavior** refers to activity undertaken by an individual to promote good health and prevent health problems. The increased concern with health behavior has arisen out of societal changes caused by the epidemiologic transition.

Three distinct stages of the epidemiologic transition can be identified. The first stage is the age of pestilence and famine. It is characterized by high death rates from chronic malnutrition and periods of epidemics of infectious disease and famine. Bubonic plague swept across western Europe in the fourteenth century, killing an estimated 24 million people. Then from the 1700s to the mid-20th century, millions died from epidemics of smallpox, measles, malaria, diphtheria, scarlet fever, and cholera. In the United States, high mortality rates

from infectious diseases were caused by typhoid fever, typhus, and yellow fever (McLeroy and Crump, 1994).

The second stage of the epidemiologic transition is characterized by a decline in deaths from epidemics and famine. Infectious diseases such as tuberculosis, pneumonia, and influenza become the major cause of death. As knowledge of public health grows, measures are taken to prevent the spread of disease. Modern medicine contributes to a decrease in death rates of young people. Finally, in the third stage, there is a shift in the leading causes of death from infectious disease to *chronic disease*, that is, conditions for which there is no cure (McLeroy and Crump, 1994).

The increase in chronic illness means that poor health becomes associated with old age. As Table 13–1 shows, rates of chronic illness increase steadily with age in most cases. In 1999 arthritis was the most common chronic disease, afflicting 45.3 percent of people aged 65 to

Table 13-1	Prevalence of Chronic Conditions in the U.S. Civilian Noninstitutional Population Aged 65+, 1999		
Chronic Conditions	***Total***	***65–74***	***75+***
Arthritis	48.2%	45.3%	52.4%
Hypertension	40.3	39.2	42.0
Hearing impairment	30.3	25.5	37.0
Heart disease	30.8	26.8	36.4
Vision disease	22.9	19.9	27.1
Visual impairment	8.4	7.0	10.4
Orthopedic impairment	15.8	17.5	13.4
Diabetes	12.6	13.3	11.7
Arteriosclerosis Varicose veins	8.1	7.7	8.7
Cerebrovascular disease	7.1	5.2	9.9
Chronic sinusitis	15.3	15.7	14.9
Emphysema/chronic bronchitis	9.8	10.1	9.3

Source: National Center for Health Statistics (1999).

Recovering from a Stroke

When the poet and novelist May Sarton had a stroke at the age of 74, she kept a diary of her experiences. As a writer she felt a compelling need to record her experiences on paper. As she explained, "It may prove impossible because my head feels so queer and the smallest effort, mental or physical, exhausts, but I feel so deprived of my *self* being unable to write, cut off since January from all that I mean about my life that I think I must try to write a few lines a day" (Sarton, 1988:15).

At first she was very discouraged. "I lie around most of the afternoon, am in bed by eight and there in my bed alone the past rises like a tide, over and over, to swamp me with memories I cannot handle. I am as fragile and naked as a newborn babe" (p. 3).

Gradually, as she began her arduous recovery, Sarton found herself able to take pleasure in small things. "If I have learned something in these months of not being well, it may be to live moment by moment—listening to the tree frogs all night . . . waking late to the insistent coos of the wood pigeon—and at this moment the hush-hushing of the ocean. Being alive as far as I am able to the *instant*" (p. 19).

A year later she was fully recovered. "So this is the anniversary and I am well! It has been a long journey, but now I do not think about the past at all, only rejoice in the present—and dream about the future and a little dachshund puppy who will come here after my last poetry reading tour in California in April and my seventy-fifth birthday on May third. . . . There is much I still hope to do. And I rejoice in the life I have recaptured and in all that still lies ahead" (p. 280).

Source: Sarton (1988).

74, and 52.4 percent of those 75 and older. Next most common were hypertension (high blood pressure), hearing impairment, and heart disease. Not only does the risk of suffering from a chronic disease increase as people age, so does the risk of suffering from multiple chronic ailments. Sixty percent of people 65 or older report having more than one chronic condition (Jette, 1996). Forty percent of the old–old, those 85 or older, are disabled by chronic illnesses (Kane and Kane, 1990; Williams, 1994). But 60 percent are free from disability, so having a chronic illness does not necessarily mean being disabled (unable to perform activities of daily living on one's own). Older people may lead full and active lives despite having health problems. In "In Their Own Words,"

the poet May Sarton describes her gradual recovery after a stroke.

The Compression of Morbidity Thesis

Most young people are quite healthy. Of course, they have the usual bouts of colds and flu each winter, and some—about 13 percent—suffer from asthma. But most of them don't worry about their health because it's not a problem. In fact, only about 4 percent of males and 3 percent of females aged 17 or younger report being in "fair" or "poor" health.

Older people are more likely than young people to worry about their health, and for good reason. The elderly are much more likely than others to suffer from **chronic diseases**—that is, diseases for which there is no cure—and to have health problems that limit their daily activities. Among people aged 75 or older, one-third report that their health is "fair" or "poor" (National Academy on an Aging Society, 1999). Yet some older people remain remarkably healthy until they are well advanced in years.

Over a half century ago, the sociologist Philip Hauser (1953) noted, "We have . . . succeeded in adding years to life; we are only beginning to turn to the task of adding life to years" (p. 162). Hauser's words were prescient, for social scientists seeking to evaluate what the extension of increased life expectancy means have been engaged in a lively debate over two scenarios for the future. One is a utopian vision first suggested by James Fries in 1980. Fries's theory, termed the **compression of morbidity thesis,** is based on two premises. The first is that the human life span, that is, the maximum number of years a human has been known to live, is fixed and finite. Second, improvements in health care and prevention will compress the years that an individual will be disabled into the last few years of the life span. As a result, demand for health care resources will decline, the quality of life for the aged will improve, and increased life expectancy will not bring about increased illness and disability in those additional years in the future.

On the other side of the debate are those who are pessimistic about what the increase in life expectancy portends. They assert that people will gain no active healthy years but simply spend more time ill and disabled (Verbrugge, 1994). Consequently, health care costs will rise and resources may be strained.

For several decades, research bore out the latter view. Gains in life expectancy merely added years in which people were chronically disabled. As new cohorts move into old age, however, the evidence increasingly supports the compression of morbidity thesis. More people today are living longer but maintaining better health until advanced old age than was true in the past (Manton and Stallard, 1996). Although the oldest–old are growing rapidly in number, the prevalence of chronically disabled people has declined steadily (Manton,

Corder, and Stallard, 1993). Advances in medical technology, changing lifestyles, a new cohort entering old age with more resources and years of schooling, better health, and greater access to health care are adding "life to years." Longer life expectancy does foretell better rather than worsening health (Hayward, Crimmins, and Saito, 1997).

Survey data also lend support to the compression of morbidity thesis. For example, in a survey three-fourths (74.3 percent) of people aged 65 to 74 described their health as good, very good, or excellent, compared to others their own age, as did two-thirds (66.8 percent) of those 75 or older (and not in a nursing home) (Hobbs and Damon, 1996). People are likely to view their health in positive terms if their ailments do not limit their daily activities. Therein lies the difference between being diagnosed with a chronic disease and being disabled. The former is a **diagnostic measure;** the latter is a measure of **functional status** (George, 1996).

Functional status refers to the degree of difficulty an individual experiences in performing activities of daily life (Verbrugge and Jette, 1994). More specifically, "a functional disability is the degree to which a chronic health problem, either physical or mental, produces a behavioral change in a person's capacity to perform the necessary tasks for daily living so that the help of another person is required" (Bould et al., 1989:52). These tasks typically include personal activities of daily living, such as bathing, eating, dressing, and toileting, and instrumental activities of daily living, such as shopping, preparing meals, managing money, and getting outside (see Chapter 10 for a fuller discussion of measures of disability). Many people who have multiple chronic diseases are not disabled.

SOCIAL DETERMINANTS OF HEALTH

Health Lifestyles

Although such factors as heredity and biology partially determine whether an individual develops a chronic disease, research also shows that social factors play an important role. The likelihood of developing a chronic disease that produces disability is partly a function of one's **health lifestyle,** defined as a pattern of behavior based on choices and options that are available to people according to their life situations (Cockerham, Abel, and Lueschen, 1993). Health lifestyles include behaviors that directly affect health care, such as having checkups and complying with prescribed treatment, as well as decisions about smoking, food, exercise, personal hygiene, alcohol use, and risky behaviors such as unprotected sex.

The effect of smoking

Smoking contributes to 400,000 deaths from cancer and heart disease each year in the United States. Because nicotine is so addictive and because most lifelong smokers have their first cigarette when they are in their teens, public health efforts to reduce smoking focus on young people. Between 1965 and 1990, there were large reductions in smoking among 18- to 24-year olds, especially among African Americans. Since 1990, however, this decline has stopped. Rates of smoking among young people are higher for whites than for blacks or Hispanics. Smoking rates for Asians are the lowest of all racial groups; smoking rates are highest among American Indians. Among middle-aged people, chronic disease is the most important indicator of health. Heart disease and cancer are the two leading causes of death among people aged 45 to 64, and both diseases are a direct result of smoking (National Center for Health Statistics, 2002).

Smokers 65 or older have probably been smoking for most of their lives. Table 13–2 reports smoking patterns among people 65 or older by race and gender from 1965 to 1992. Older men are more likely to smoke than older women. Black men are much more likely to smoke than white men. Although smoking has been declining among both black and white men, it has been rising among black and white women.

Research has linked smoking to all three major causes of death (heart attack, cancer, and stroke). Smoking also is associated with the condition known as **chronic obstructive pulmonary disease (COPD),** a chronic obstruction of air flow in the lungs. This disorder is more common in men and worse in people over the age of 50 (Spence, 1995). Symptoms include difficulty breathing and loss of energy. Two of the most common COPDs are emphysema and chronic bronchitis, both linked to smoking. In the period leading up to death, people with a history of smoking are more likely than nonsmokers to be disabled. Smoking doesn't just shorten life, it also reduces the quality of life by reducing one's active life expectancy (see Chapter 6) (Hobbs and Damon, 1996).

The effect of exercise

If you look around the mall on your next shopping trip, you are likely to see young people "cruising" and older people "power walking." Modern shopping malls, with their miles of covered corridors, provide an ideal setting for power walkers. Air-conditioned in summer and free of snow

Table 13-2	Persons 65 Years or Older Who Smoked Cigarettes at Time of Survey, by Sex and Race, 1965–92					
	Male			**Female**		
Year	*All Races*	*White*	*Black*	*All Races*	*White*	*Black*
1992	16.1%	14.9%	28.3%	12.4%	12.6%	11.1%
1990	14.6	13.7	21.5	11.5	11.5	11.1
1985	19.6	18.9	27.7	13.5	13.3	14.5
1979	20.9	20.5	26.2	13.2	13.8	8.5
1974	24.8	24.3	29.7	12.0	12.3	8.9
1965	28.5	27.7	36.4	9.6	9.8	7.1

Note: Data are based on household interviews of a sample of the civilian noninstitutionalized population.
Source: National Center for Health Statistics (1994b; table 72).

Smoking contributes to 400,000 deaths each year in the United States. Boxer Laila Ali fights "Craving Man" as part of an anti-smoking campaign.

and slush in winter, they allow older people to take the best preventive medicine of all—exercise.

After smoking, exercise is the next most important lifestyle influence on health in later life. Most young people are so healthy that variations in the amount of exercise they perform probably have little effect on health. With advancing age, people who exercise more are more fit, more able to keep their weight under control, and more likely to have fewer backaches and joint problems than those who are sedentary. The disadvantages of a sedentary lifestyle accumulate with age so that by the time sedentary and active adults reach old age, the differences in well-being are significant (Mirowsky and Ross, 1992).

People who exercise regularly show improved cardiovascular function, better long-term and short-term memory, and less disability than sedentary people (Hill, Storandt, and Malley, 1993). One study found that elderly people who simply walked one mile a week had a lower disability risk than

those who didn't (Lawrence and Jette, 1996). Another study found that sedentary men and women aged 50 to 65 who participated in regular exercise showed significantly improved physical health one year later (Stewart, King, and Haskell, 1993).

One of the most convincing studies on the relationship between exercise and health was conducted by a team of researchers at Stanford University. The researchers compared a group of men and women aged 50 to 72 who belonged to a runners' club with a control group of people from the community. At the start of the study, the runners had lower blood pressure, less arthritis and fewer other medical problems, less joint swelling, and less overall disability. Eight years later, only 63 percent of the runners were still running, but those who had stopped running had switched to other vigorous activities such as swimming, bicycling, brisk walking, aerobic dance, and racquet sports. They reported devoting an average of 262 minutes a week to exercise compared to only 118 minutes per week for the control group. Over the eight years of the study, the mortality rate was only 1.5 percent among members of the runners' club, compared to 7 percent among the control group. The gap in disability levels noted at the beginning of the study between the runners' club members and control group continued to widen. Those who no longer belonged to the runners' club but exercised vigorously maintained the same level of fitness as those who continued to run (Fries et al., 1994).

Even moderate exercise can reduce the risk of disease. Scientists monitored a group of men aged 71 to 93 for two years, recording the number of miles they walked each day. They found that men who walked less than a quarter mile a day had a 50 percent increased risk of coronary heart disease compared to men who walked at least one and a half miles a day. The further the men walked, the less likely they were to develop coronary heart disease (Hakim et al., 1999). The lesson is simple: Leading an active life protects against decline in old age.

The effect of alcohol consumption Alcohol consumption can have both positive and negative effects on health and longevity. Heavy drinkers, defined as people who consume 14 or more drinks per week, are more likely to suffer from cirrhosis of the liver, certain cancers, and hypertension, among other diseases. However, people who drink an occasional glass of wine with dinner actually have a lower risk of mortality than nondrinkers, mainly because moderate alcohol consumption appears to protect against heart disease (Klatsky and Friedman, 1995). In one study, moderate alcohol consumption also decreased the risk of a stroke. Men and women with an average age of 70 who were moderate drinkers or who abstained from alcohol were significantly less likely than heavy drinkers to have a stroke (Sacco et al., 1999).

The effect of diet Being overweight is another factor that increases the risk of disability. People who are obese are at risk of heart disease, diabetes, and joint problems, especially as they get older.

Figure 13–1 shows patterns of weight gain over the life course. The percentage of women who are overweight peaks at ages 55 to 64 and then declines. Menopause may be one factor in the weight gain exhibited by women after 55. Men peak

Figure 13–1   **Percentage of Population Overweight, by Age and Sex, 1994.**

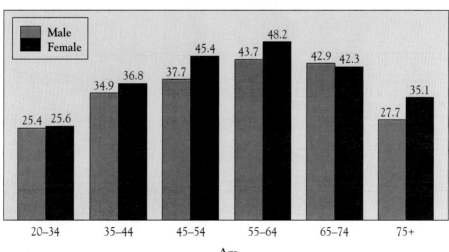

Source: National Center for Health Statistics (1998).

somewhat later, at 65 to 74, and they are more likely than women to be overweight at this point in their lives. The decline in overweight men and women after age 75 may be caused by an attrition factor, as heavier people are likely to die early. It may also be that older people see physicians more frequently than younger people, and their doctors may advise them about eating a healthy, low-fat diet. Very old people sometimes experience a loss of appetite and thus lose weight (Hobbs and Damon, 1996). All of these factors likely explain variations in weight over the life course.

Although healthy lifestyles play a large role in determining the onset, course, and outcome of illness, the emphasis on the individual excuses the larger society from accountability. The benefits of the compression of morbidity are not evenly distributed, for there are significant differences in health and disability by gender, social class, and race and ethnicity (Kaplan and Strawbridge, 1994; George, 1996).

Social Support Systems

As we saw in Chapter 8, a strong social support system can improve morale, reduce depression, and enhance recovery from surgery. Social support has a positive effect on the cardiovascular, endocrine, and immune systems (Uchino, Cacioppo, and Kiecolt-Glaser, 1996). Among older adults, emotional support is associated with better physical functioning and reduced risk of mortality. These results have been found consistently in other countries as well as in the United States.

In Malaysia, for example, most people live in nuclear family households, but household composition is fluid as family members move in and out as their needs change. Approximately three-quarters of elderly people live with younger family members, and more than half rely on their children and grandchildren for material support. Even when adult children do not live with their parents, they often live nearby. Traditionally, the family has provided a strong social support system for the aged.

What effect does this traditional family support system have on the health of the elderly in Malaysia? Can it buffer older people from the unhealthy effects of low socioeconomic status? To answer these questions, researchers turned to the Malaysian Family Life Survey, whose Senior Sample provides a representative group from the older Malaysian population. They found that having daily contact with their children did protect older Malaysians against illness. Children helped their parents by giving them goods and money and providing them with companionship and a sense of respect. These tangible and intangible supports enhanced the health of their aging parents (Wu and Rudkin, 2000).

Socioeconomic Status

On March 23, 1997, Americans were startled to open their morning newspapers and see 76-year-old former president George Bush descending in a parachute from a skydive. What explains why one person is so remarkably fit in old age while another of the same age is disabled? The healthy lifestyles

Former president George H. W. Bush makes a landing from his parachute jump. His remarkable fitness at age 76 was due in part to his healthy lifestyle and his affluence.

described are certainly factors, for George Bush is active, thin, and, except for a dislike of broccoli, a healthy eater. But his ability to engage in healthy behaviors that increase fitness is also a product of his socioeconomic status (SES).

Research over the past 40 years has consistently demonstrated a link between social class and health. Over the life course, there are major differences in health according to socioeconomic status, and the gap between the upper and lower classes widens as people reach their 50s (House, Kessler, and Herzog, 1990; Rogers, Rogers, and Belanger, 1992). People in the upper socioeconomic strata maintain relatively good health and low levels of disability until quite late in life. People at the bottom continue to experience declining health with advancing age.

Measuring SES   The main indicators of SES are occupation, income, and education. One of the difficulties of measuring the relationship between SES, health, and aging is that these indicators don't work very well in sorting out the aged.

Occupation is the key status indicator. One problem with the use of occupation as an indicator of SES is that people without paid employment are typically the most disadvantaged; thus, any sample that includes only workers leaves out those most likely to be at the low end of the continuum. Another problem is that occupation excludes the nonemployed—those who are retired, engage in nonpaid domestic labor, or are unemployed. As people age, the chances that they will be in the labor force decline. Income is also inadequate as a lifelong measure of SES because income usually decreases with age. For these reasons, as we saw in Chapter 4, education is often preferred as a proxy for SES, especially in research about the elderly. Compared to income or occupation, educational attainment is relatively fixed. Although more adults are returning to school, most individuals complete their education in youth or young adulthood. As Ross and Wu (1996) explained, "Education is the key to one's position in the stratification system" (p. 105).

Theory of cumulative disadvantage versus convergence theory   There are two theories about the relationship between education, health, and aging. The first, called the **theory of cumulative disadvantage** (discussed in Chapter 3), is that people who begin life with greater resources continue to have opportunities to accumulate more of them while those who begin with few resources fall further behind (O'Rand, 1996a). According to this perspective, the gap in health status should increase with age. A second theory, **convergence theory,** asserts that old age is a great leveler, reducing inequality that was evident at earlier stages of the life course. This theory would predict that the gap in health between rich and poor narrows with age.

Research supports the theory of cumulative disadvantage (Ross and Wu, 1996). The health gap between the least and most educated continues to increase with age. Although health declines with age among all people, those with high levels of education are typically able to postpone the decline in health until advanced old age. According to Ross and Wu (1996), "people with a college degree feel healthy and function well into their 60s, 70s, and 80s, whereas those with less than a college degree do not" (p. 117). Only in advanced old age does the gap begin to close, probably because many people in poor health have died or moved to nursing homes (House et al., 1994).

How does education affect health? Most social scientists agree that health outcomes are a consequence of psychosocial and environmental factors combined (House et al., 1990). For example, as a group, people with more education engage in behaviors that reduce their risk of illness. They exercise more, drink less, and smoke less than people with fewer years of schooling.

But why do better-educated people exercise more than those who are less educated? One reason is that they have more resources that enable them to do so. People with college degrees are more likely to work for companies that have gyms or that provide time out for exercise. Moreover, because they typically have higher earnings than those who did not attend college, they can afford vacations during which they can ski, play tennis, swim, or climb. They also live in neighborhoods where it is safe to walk or jog and where there are tennis courts and bike paths (Ross, 1993).

Aging around the World

WHY DO THE JAPANESE ELDERLY LIVE SO LONG?

*P*opulation aging has occurred more rapidly in Japan than in the United States. Currently, over 16 percent of the population in Japan is 65 or older. The Japanese have the highest life expectancy at birth of any nation and significantly lower rates of death from cancer and heart disease than Americans. Overall, the Japanese live three to six years longer than Americans. Why do the Japanese live so long?

One reason may be that they are protected by their families. In Japan there is a strong belief that children are responsible for their aging parents. More than half of elderly Japanese live with their children, and a large proportion receive financial assistance from children. Thus, they are likely to experience the advantages that come from a strong social support system. Another factor that might reduce illness and mortality among the Japanese is a relatively low level of income inequality. Japan has a large middle class whose members are quite similar in their attitudes and lifestyles (Liang et al., 2002). Thus, socioeconomic status likely has less effect on health than it does in the United States. Finally, the Japanese have a healthier diet, which may reduce the risk of heart disease and some forms of cancer.

What Do You Think?

1. How healthy is your diet? Do you eat healthy food on a regular basis or snack on junk food?
2. How does your ethnic background influence your lifestyle and food preferences?

Education also affects health because better-educated people may be exposed to fewer hazards and stressors at work (House et al., 1994). They are less likely to engage in hard physical labor that brings a greater risk of injury or exposure to harmful chemicals. Further, a health problem such as arthritis is more likely to interfere with work in a physically demanding job than in a sedentary job (Loprest, Rupp, and Sandell, 1995). An individual in such a job may be forced to retire early and thus have lower income. In summary, high-SES groups have numerous advantages over those in the lower strata.

Nonetheless, among the very old—people over 80—the disability gap diminishes. In part this may be because the less healthy die at younger ages or enter nursing homes and are thus not included in surveys. Government programs such as Medicare and Medicaid, which give the aged access to health care, may also reduce the inequalities experienced earlier in life and cushion their impact. Social support systems and SES have an effect on health in later life among people everywhere. The "Aging around the World" feature explores some of the reasons for the longevity of the Japanese.

Gender

Studies consistently show that women have poorer health and higher levels of disability than men (George, 1996). Women are more likely than men to have musculoskeletal conditions, digestive problems, thyroid diseases, anemia, migraines, urinary disease, and varicose veins. Men have higher rates of heart disease, lung cancer, stroke, and liver disease (Verbrugge, 1990). As a result, although men have lower life expectancy, they have longer active life expectancy, meaning more years with no disabling conditions (see Chapter 6).

Gender differences in health appear not only in the United States but in other developed nations and in developing nations. One study compared the health of adult men and women in the United States, Jamaica, Malaysia, and Bangladesh. Although the countries differed in levels of socioeconomic development, lifestyles, and gender norms, women fared worse than men on a variety of measures of health in all four countries (Rahman et al., 1994).

One theory attributes gender differences in health primarily to biological factors. Although men and women may have different predispositions to illness, social factors also are relevant. One social explanation for gender differences in rates of illness is differences in help-seeking behavior. It is through contact with other people that individuals deal with their illnesses and obtain help with medical problems (Pescosolido, 1992). Women engage in more help-seeking behavior than men; as a result, they have more contact with the health care system at all levels, from having physical exams to being admitted to hospitals. In addition, women generally know more about their health than men and take better care of themselves. More frequent contact with health providers means women are more likely to report ailments (Verbrugge, 1989). The higher levels of disability among women are also due to the fact that they live longer than men and thus experience more years at the ages when people are most vulnerable to illness.

Race and Ethnicity

Race and ethnicity are also consistently linked to health status (Rogers, Rogers, and Belanger, 1992).

Research generally shows that African Americans, Hispanics, and Native Americans have poorer health than whites on a variety of measures and that with age they are more likely to develop a serious illness and to rate their health as "poor" (Ferraro and Farmer, 1996).

For example, African Americans have the highest cancer risk of all ethnic and racial groups and the highest mortality rates among those who get cancer (Baquet, 1988). Rates of hypertension are also significantly higher among blacks, leading to more heart disease and strokes (Anderson, 1988).

Some researchers argue that the black–white disparity in health is due to race per se—that is, that it is caused by genetic and physiological racial differences. But most research suggests that a large share of the black–white health gap can be explained by social factors (Schoenbaum and Waldman, 1997). For a discussion of why rates of hypertension are higher among African Americans, see "Diversity in the Aging Experience."

In levels of disability, African Americans older than 75 appear to have an advantage over whites. However, this is not because the health of blacks improves after age 75. Rather, an **adverse mortality selection process** means that those who are at high risk of contracting life-threatening diseases die earlier, leaving a group of relatively healthy older black men and women in the community (Gibson, 1991).

Poor health in old age among African Americans is partly caused by poor health lifestyles. Compared to whites, black men and women engage in more high-risk behaviors such as smoking and excessive alcohol consumption. Older blacks also tend to have lower levels of physical activity than whites. In addition, they have more nutritional inadequacies in their diets than elderly whites and are more likely to be overweight and to suffer from diseases related to obesity (Jerome, 1988; Clark et al., 1996). It's important to keep in mind, however, that lifestyle factors are linked both directly and indirectly to income and education. Almost all the racial differences in diet, smoking, and activity level can be explained by differences in education (Clark, 1995). Blacks and whites who have similar levels of education exhibit similar health behaviors.

THE PUZZLE OF HYPERTENSION AMONG AFRICAN AMERICANS

*N*early all Americans experience a steady rise in blood pressure as they grow older. About one-quarter suffer from hypertension, the medical term for chronically high blood pressure. High blood pressure must be controlled; otherwise, it can lead to heart attacks, stroke, and kidney failure.

Among African Americans the problem is greater than in the general population: 35 percent have hypertension. The condition accounts for 20 percent of all deaths among blacks—double the figure for whites. One explanation for this racial disparity in mortality rates is that people of African descent have a genetic susceptibility to high blood pressure. Yet race may also be a proxy for other causes, such as socioeconomic status. The problem is how to separate environmental causes from genetic causes.

One ingenious solution to this problem, devised by three researchers, was to compare people of African descent in the United States with people from Nigeria and Jamaica. Many African Americans are descended from Nigerians who were captured by slave traders on the west coast of Africa and forcibly taken to the United States and the Caribbean. The researchers found that just 7 percent of the subjects from Nigeria had high blood pressure, compared to 26 percent of the Jamaicans and 33 percent of the African Americans. Certain risk factors for hypertension, namely obesity and salt intake, were also more prevalent among African Americans than among Nigerians or Jamaicans. The researchers concluded that obesity, lack of exercise, and poor diet explained 40 to 50 percent of the increased hypertension among African Americans (Cooper, Rotimi, and Ward, 1999).

These findings suggest that environmental factors provide a better explanation of the high rates of hypertension among African Americans. They also suggest that all Americans could reduce their blood pressure by controlling their weight, reducing their salt intake, and exercising regularly.

What Do You Think?

1. If poor health habits accounted for 40 or 50 percent of the increased hypertension among African American participants in this study, what might have accounted for the other 50 to 60 percent?
2. Does anyone in your family suffer from hypertension? If so, does excess weight, lack of exercise, or poor diet contribute to the problem? What is your relative's age?

Source: Cooper, Rotimi, and Ward (1999).

Older blacks also have poorer health than whites because they receive less effective treatment from the health care system. African Americans are usually diagnosed at later stages of their illnesses, making full recovery less likely (Gibbs, 1988). This is partly due to differences in help-seeking behavior, since older African Americans are less likely than whites to go to a doctor (Gibbs, 1988). But it's also due to differential treatment by physicians. One study of Medicare beneficiaries found that 26 percent of white women received a mammogram, compared to only 17 percent of black women. Blacks were also less likely than whites to receive flu shots (Gornick et al., 1996).

Hispanics also have poorer health in old age than whites. This is due in part to differences in access to health care. Hispanics of all ages are the least likely of any racial or ethnic group to have health insurance, and older Hispanics are least likely to be eligible for Medicare, a subject discussed in detail in Chapter 17 (Angel and Angel, 1996).

On the whole, the Asian elderly are healthier than people of other ethnic minorities. Their better health is partly a function of higher socioeconomic status, for Asians have the highest level of income and education of all minority groups. SES, in turn, influences health behavior. Asians have a lower risk of death from alcohol and smoking-related illnesses. Even among the poor, the Asian elderly engage in more desirable health practices than white, black, or Hispanic elderly. As Asian Americans have become acculturated to American habits, however, they have shown an increase in certain diseases, such as cardiovascular disease, diabetes, and some cancers (Yee and Weaver, 1994).

The differences in health between whites, Asians, Hispanics, and African Americans can largely be explained by the theory of cumulative disadvantage. Poor health behaviors often are a response to a stressful environment and lack of resources. People with low income have a tendency to purchase filling, inexpensive food, which often is high in fat, and consume alcohol or smoke to reduce stress (Lieberman, 1988). Living in a high-crime area is also associated with high blood pressure (Anderson, 1988). Thus, racial discrimination in education, employment, and housing has

life course consequences reflected in poor health and ultimately in lower life expectancy.

Finally, public efforts to educate people about the dangers of poor health behaviors often do not reach the minority elderly population because they are promoted through the mass media. The minority elderly are more likely to respond to messages about health that are communicated through community institutions, such as churches or social and fraternal clubs, but such messages are rarely conveyed through these channels (Yee and Weaver, 1994).

THE ELDERLY IN THE HEALTH CARE SYSTEM

The U.S. health care system consists of a conglomerate of health practitioners, agencies, and institutions. The treatment that older people receive is partly influenced by their interactions with physicians and other health care providers. The attitudes of doctors toward elderly patients determine how they perform exams and what treatments they recommend. The attitudes of the aged in turn affect whether they will go to a doctor when they have symptoms of illness and whether they will comply with treatment. Access to health care also influences the quality of care received. An individual who lacks health insurance, for example, may postpone visiting a doctor until a disease like cancer has progressed to a fatal stage.

Health Care Providers and the Elderly

Several studies have found that many physicians hold biased or stereotypical views of the aged and express little desire to work with older people. Why would physicians be opposed to treating the elderly? To understand the source of these attitudes, a team of researchers conducted in-depth interviews with 20 practicing physicians. Most of the doctors said that they enjoyed their interactions with older patients, but they also expressed a number of concerns about providing care for them. Several mentioned that elderly patients were more difficult to care for than younger people because they had more complex health problems and were at risk of rapid

In Their Own Words

Physicians' Attitudes toward Elderly Patients

Dr. E: Every time they come in something's aching or hurting or "My back's a little sore" or "I'm a little stiff, I don't have the energy I used to," "Well, maybe I'm a little depressed." Sometimes they get to be those people that you look at the list and go, "Ahhh, doggone, that name again."

Dr. O: You know, there are some patients that they're always going to have the same problems year after year after year. They're not going to be fixed. You know, it's their back pain from osteoporosis and scoliosis, and you can't do anything about it, or they

may be a little depressed, but they won't take any medicine, and they're chronically constipated and you know, sometimes those are the most frustrating.

Dr. L: You wake up in the middle of the night in a cold sweat thinking, "Oh my God! The Office of Inspector General showed up at my office today and wants to go through every file in my charts." So it's sobering to know what Medicare could do to you and your practice if they chose to.

Source: Adams et al. (2002).

---

decline. Medical education is oriented toward curing disease, so physicians find it frustrating to treat older patients with chronic conditions that are incurable. Physicians also found it more difficult to communicate with older patients because of cognitive impairments or hearing problems. Finally, physicians complained about burdensome Medicare regulations that consumed too much of their time. In "In Their Own Words," three physicians recount their experiences with elderly patients.

Medical treatment begins with a dialogue between the doctor and the patient. The effectiveness of the communication depends on their ability to understand each other. Compared to younger people who are likely to ask questions about a diagnosis or seek explanations for why the physician is ordering certain tests, older people are more likely to be passive in their communications with doctors and to accept a physician's diagnosis without question (Haug and Lavin, 1983).

Communication problems are especially likely to occur if the doctor and patient come from

different cultural backgrounds. For this reason many elderly Koreans residing in the United States prefer traditional healers over modern doctors. The healers, who take longer to examine patients and spend more time listening, are particularly effective in treating ill-defined physical problems for which Western medicine has no cure (Pourat et al., 1999).

Because of physician biases and poor communication between doctor and patient, illness in older people is sometimes undertreated (Rubenstein et al., 1994). For example, the standard treatments for cancer—surgery, chemotherapy, and radiation therapy—are pursued less aggressively in the elderly. One reason is that physicians fear older people can't withstand the rigors of the full treatment regime. Yet studies show that very old cancer patients have response and survival rates similar to those of younger people when given chemotherapy (Cassileth, 1994). Older patients are also undertreated in terms of receiving rehabilitative services, preventive services, mental health services, and primary care. One explanation might be the reluctance of the medical profession to prescribe treatment to people who don't have long to live.

Paradoxically, overprovision of some kinds of services is also a problem in the treatment of the elderly. For example, many costly surgical procedures that are covered by Medicare—such as coronary artery bypass surgery—are performed even though their value has not been proved. The dual problem of undertreatment in some areas and overprovision in others is caused partly by physicians' attitudes toward the aged or by poor communications between doctor and patient and partly by misplaced incentives in Medicare, which rewards heroic care and reliance on specialists but not prevention and primary care (Rubenstein et al., 1994).

The Organization of Health Care

Until the 1950s, individual physicians treated most patients in private practices and sent those who needed surgery to small community hospitals. Family physicians played central roles, most people paid for health care in cash, and the primary arrangement for reimbursing physicians for providing care to patients was called **fee-for-service.** Physicians set the fees, and people paid when they visited doctors according to the treatment received. Fee-for-service arrangements granted doctors a great deal of autonomy in determining the course of patient care but also contained numerous financial incentives to perform many services and procedures. The more services physicians performed, the more fees they received.

The passage of Medicare and Medicaid in 1965 created two public health insurance programs for the aged and the poor (see Chapter 11). Since then, public responsibility for health care has grown, making rising health care costs a public issue. Between 1970 and 1995, the proportion of the gross national product devoted to health care increased from 7.4 to 15.2 percent (Cockerham, 1995). Other factors contributing to increased costs include the growth of the aging population, which has had a dramatic effect on the demand for health care, and the increase in expensive, high-tech care.

In recent years, efforts to control costs have led to the growth of new forms of organization for delivering health care to the public. A rapidly expanding form is the **health maintenance organization (HMO),** also referred to as **managed care.** HMOs are health insurance plans run by financial officers. A group of physicians are members of the HMO, and the services offered by the physicians are monitored by administrators to achieve efficiency and control costs. Unlike fee-for-service systems, HMOs do not offer an unrestricted choice of physicians; rather, people must choose among doctors contracted by the HMO. Initially, managed care appeared to be more effective in controlling costs than were fee-for-service arrangements. Much of the cost containment was due to a system called **capitation,** a method of payment in which reimbursements to health care providers are set in advance. Under a capitation arrangement, an HMO receives a flat monthly fee for each patient in the system, regardless of what services are performed. Recently, fees have been rising, casting doubt on the ability of HMOs to contain costs.

Since 1976, enrollments in HMOs have increased nearly tenfold among the nonelderly population. Presently, nearly 75 percent of all younger Americans are under managed care (Ware et al., 1996). As medical care has increasingly come under the jurisdiction of HMOs, physicians have lost much of their autonomy in determining the course of care; they are under financial pressure to do less. Nearly every aspect of the doctor–patient relationship is affected—how many patients a doctor accepts, how much time he or she spends with them, what diagnostic tests the doctor orders, what referrals to specialists the doctor makes, what procedures to perform, what therapies to administer, whether to hospitalize a patient, when to discharge a patient, and when to give up on a severe illness (Stone, 1997). Numerous studies have shown that HMOs reduce hospital admission rates, shorten hospital stays, rely on fewer specialists, and make less use of expensive technologies (Miller and Luft, 1994).

It is still relatively early in this new social experiment to determine whether HMOs compromise patient care. One study compared the physical and mental health outcomes of chronically ill aged people in an HMO with those in fee-for-service arrangements (Ware et al., 1996). The results indicated that people 65 or older who were treated in HMOs showed greater declines in physical health than those who were treated under a fee-for-service arrangement. Another study found that patients in HMOs who had a stroke were less likely to go to a rehabilitation facility than were fee-for-service patients. They also were more likely to be sent to a nursing home. However, survival rates were the same for both groups of patients (Retchin et al., 1997). The frail elderly are potentially most vulnerable to cost-cutting efforts, and HMOs must be monitored to ensure that financial savings don't come at the expense of quality care.

Changing incentives in Medicare   As health care costs have increased in the economy as a whole, Medicare expenditures have also grown rapidly. Each year the government calculates whether the amount of money credited to the Medicare trust fund is adequate to pay the benefits promised. When the baby boom generation reaches 85, Medicare expenditures will soar. In 2031, the first baby boomer will turn 85; by 2040, the average baby boomer will be 85.

Efforts to control the growth of Medicare spending have been under way for some time. In 1983, the **Prospective Payment System (PPS)** was instituted to pay the hospital bills of Medicare recipients. The PPS payment schedule estimates what the cost of an average patient with a specific diagnosis would be and how long that patient would need to remain hospitalized. Since there are so many medical diagnoses, the various diagnoses were grouped into **diagnostic-related groupings (DRGs).** Under the DRG system, a patient who is admitted to a hospital with a particular diagnosis is expected to stay for a specific length of time and consume a fixed amount of resources. Thus, the DRG system contained costs by setting reimbursement rates in advance rather than letting hospitals set their own rates (Wiener, 1996).

Another cost-saving effort was allowing Medicare beneficiaries to choose a managed care plan (Palmer and Chapman, 1997). The plans, which are paid a per capita fee for each enrollee, have a good deal of discretion in determining what services to provide.

Older people are attracted to HMOs because they often pay prescription drug benefits that traditional fee-for-service plans don't cover. On average, people aged 65 and older spend 19 percent of their income on health care, but those who belong to HMOs have much lower out-of-pocket expenses (Crystal et al., 2000). Unfortunately, insuring the aged is expensive, and many HMOs have begun pulling out of Medicare. For a discussion of the Medicare HMO crisis, see "An Issue for Public Policy."

Other options for reducing Medicare costs include requiring older people to pay more of the cost of medical care out of their own pockets; reducing the services they receive; and raising the age of eligibility for Medicare from 65 to 67. The rationale for raising the age of eligibility is that people are now living longer and are receiving Medicare benefits for more years than anticipated when Congress enacted the program. Since the age of eligibility for full Social Security benefits has already been raised to 67, proponents of this proposal contend that Medicare should follow suit. The problem is that although life expectancy has increased, many 65-year-olds are not healthy. Moderately disabled people of that age may have trouble purchasing private insurance and may end up uninsured.

Although the growth of Medicare costs has slowed since DRGs, managed care systems, and other cost-saving measures have been introduced, some analysts believe that the quality of health care has suffered as a result. Critics charge that doctors have incentives either to skimp on care or to make diagnoses that put patients in categories that pay higher rates. The elderly are especially vulnerable, since they are the heaviest users of health care services.

To control the growth of Medicare spending, Congress passed the Balanced Budget Act (BBA) of 1997. The BBA reduced payments for services provided in hospitals, skilled nursing facilities, and home health agencies and established new prospective payment systems. It also created the Medicare+Choice program, which expands beneficiaries' choice of private health plans. Since the BBA was enacted, Medicare spending has increased more slowly, but concerns have arisen about whether the quality of care has been compromised.

The role of the private sector   On August 26, 1996, Pabst Brewing Company announced it

An Issue for Public Policy

THE MEDICARE HMO CRISIS

A few years ago, HMOs seemed to provide a solution to rising Medicare costs, but recent events cast doubt on that possibility. In 1998 and 1999, HMOs withdrew from Medicare programs in more than 400 towns and cities in 33 states, directly affecting over 734,000 beneficiaries. Then in 2000, HMOs dropped another 900,000 elderly and disabled beneficiaries—nearly one-sixth of all Medicare recipients enrolled in HMO programs.

Why are HMOs dropping their elderly clients? According to representatives of the HMOs, the $6,876 a year the government paid HMOs in 1999 was not enough to cover the expense of treating the elderly. Put more simply, HMOs lose money on Medicare.

Medicare beneficiaries who are dropped by an HMO have the option of enrolling in another managed care plan, if one exists in their area, or of turning to a fee-for-service program. For many older people, a fee-for-service program means giving up prescription drug benefits and other services that HMOs typically provide (Health Care Financing Administration, 2000a). Prescription drugs can be enormously expensive, averaging $996 a month in 2003. Some older people don't take the medicines their doctors prescribe because they can't afford to pay for them. Currently, nearly 60 percent of Medicare beneficiaries have prescription drug coverage (Kaiser Family Foundation, 2003).

What Do You Think?

1. Do you have an elderly relative who has trouble paying for prescription drugs? If so, has he or she ever gone without medicine or other necessities as a result of the high cost of drugs?
2. If you were a government policymaker, how would you solve the HMO crisis?

could no longer afford to provide health care benefits for its 750 retirees. Retirees and their families were informed that they would lose their coverage on September 1. For decades Pabst had provided fully paid health insurance benefits and prescription drug coverage to former employees like Roman Makarewicz, a 74-year-old retiree, who had worked for Pabst for 42 years. Plagued by high blood pressure, arthritis in his knees so severe that

he could hardly walk, Roman would have to pay $112 a month for his medications alone. He felt as though he had been stabbed in the back. Eighty-year-old Leon Rubitsky, who had retired after 34 years with Pabst, also worried about the loss of his wife's prescription drugs. Hopelessly, he asked, "What are you going to do when they start changing the rules? A little guy can't do anything" (Causey, 1996:1).

The problem was that beer production in the Milwaukee brewery was down by two-thirds, and 200 out of 600 employees had lost their jobs. According to the company's director of labor relations, Pabst would have to close its aging Milwaukee plant if it didn't cancel the retirees' health benefits. The employees' union filed a lawsuit against the company. Two Milwaukee congressmen asked the U.S. Department of Labor to determine whether the action taken by Pabst violated ERISA. Instead of re-installing the benefits, Pabst made good on its threat to close the Milwaukee plant.

Many employers began offering health insurance to their retired employees in the 1960s, after Congress passed Medicare. Retiree health insurance combined with pensions encouraged older workers to retire. Presently, about half of the aged have **Medigap policies.** Of those who have Medigap policies, half pay the cost of the premiums themselves, and half are covered by their former employers (General Accounting Office, 2001). These policies pay for out-of-pocket expenses not covered by Medicare. Three-quarters of the white elderly have such supplemental private insurance policies, compared to 44 percent of the black elderly and 39 percent of the Hispanic elderly (National Center for Health Statistics, 1998). In recent years, however, employers have come to see retiree health insurance as a liability, and many companies have been reducing this benefit or eliminating it altogether.

There are several reasons employers don't want to pay for retiree health insurance. One is that these policies have become increasingly expensive, as health care costs have increased. Another is the aging of the workforce, which has increased the ratio of retired to active workers (Clark, Ghent, and Headen, 1994). A third reason is that the federal government now requires firms to report all the costs and liabilities associated with retiree health plans. Given the number of workers expected to retire over the next few decades, many firms have very large unfunded liabilities associated with promised retiree health benefits. This means that they have promised to pay for the health insurance of these workers when they retire but have saved no money to pay for this benefit. Corporate leaders fear that having these unfunded liabilities on the books might reduce the market value of their firms' stock (General Accounting Office, 2001).

There has been much discussion of reducing federal spending by turning some of the functions of government over to the private sector; but increasingly, firms have been unwilling to take on additional responsibilities, and some have eliminated benefits they provided in the past. There seems to be no easy answer to the problem of rising health care costs.

Chapter Resources

LOOKING BACK

1. **Why has poor health become associated with old age, and how are recent improvements in health care changing that association?** *Poor health has become associated with old age because of the epidemiologic transition. The epidemiologic transition is defined as a change in the leading cause of death from infectious diseases to chronic diseases. Recent improvements in health care and prevention now mean that most older people will remain in relatively good health and that the years spent being disabled are likely to be compressed into the final years of life. This is termed the compression of morbidity thesis.*

2. **How do people's lifestyles and social support systems affect their health in old age?** *Lifestyles have a large impact on health over the life course. People who don't smoke and who exercise, drink in moderation, and keep their weight in the normal range are less likely to become disabled than those who do not. The increasing significance of healthy lifestyles means that medicine is no longer the sole answer to dealing with threats to health. Social support systems also play a role in health outcomes. Having a strong social support system improves morale, reduces the risk of depression, and even enhances recovery from surgery.*

3. **What is the best measure of an elderly person's socioeconomic status, and how is SES connected to a person's health?** *The best measure of an elderly person's socioeconomic status is education. People of higher SES have better health in old age than people of lower SES. One reason is that they have better access to health care. People of lower SES are more likely to have worked in stressful jobs where they could be injured. People of higher SES also have more resources that give them the opportunity to engage in positive health practices.*

4. **How do gender, race, and ethnicity affect an older person's health?** *Women have poorer health and higher levels of disability than do men.*

This is true not only for the United States but for other countries as well. Both biological and behavioral factors appear to account for the differences. Older minorities have poorer health than whites on several measures. As they age, they are more likely to develop a serious illness and more likely to rate their health as "poor."

5. **How have changes in Medicare and the health care industry affected older Americans?** *Medicare is one of the fastest growing federal programs. Costs will rise sixfold as the baby boom generation approaches retirement age. As political pressures increase to cut Medicare expenditures, more elderly are likely to be treated by physicians affiliated with health maintenance organizations. The danger is that efforts to save costs may reduce the quality of care. And recently many HMOs have pulled out of the Medicare program. One of the main political issues for the future will be determining how best to control the costs of Medicare while maintaining quality health care for the aged.*

THINKING ABOUT AGING

1. A great deal of money has been spent in recent years on antismoking campaigns aimed at persuading young people not to start smoking. Do you think these campaigns are an effective way to prevent health problems in old age? If not, can you think of a better approach?

2. State officials have successfully sued tobacco companies on behalf of consumers whose health was damaged by cigarette smoking. Why not take the same approach to manufacturers of alcoholic beverages?

3. Describe some government programs that promote a healthy lifestyle. Is the government doing enough to encourage people to live healthy lives? What else could be done?

4. If a person's socioeconomic status is a good predictor of health, should the government attempt to promote better health through educational assistance programs?

5. Medicare pays an older person's medical bills regardless of that person's lifestyle. Should people who choose to live an unhealthy lifestyle—who smoke or drink too much, for example—pay higher Medicare premiums than those who don't?

KEY TERMS

adverse mortality selection process 323

capitation 327

chronic disease 316

chronic obstructive pulmonary disease (COPD) 317

compression of morbidity thesis 316

convergence theory 321

diagnostic measure 316

diagnostic-related grouping (DRG) 328

epidemiologic transition 314

fee-for-service 327

functional status 316

health behavior 314

health lifestyle 316

health maintenance organization (HMO) 327

managed care 327

Medicap policy 330

Prospective Payment System (PPS) 328

theory of cumulative disadvantage 321

EXPLORING THE INTERNET

Note: While all the URLs listed were current as of the printing of this book, these sites often change. Please check our website www.mhhe.com/quadagno for updates.

1. One important function of the Centers for Disease Control and the National Center for Health Statistics (http://www.cdc.gov/nchs/) is providing the public with information on citizens' health. To read about the health of elderly Americans, go to the website, link to news releases, and select 1999. Read the article titled "Annual Report on Nation's Health Spotlights Elderly Americans" (October 13 1999) and answer the following questions:

   a. Since 1970, how much have death rates from heart disease been reduced among persons aged 65 to 84?
   b. What disease afflicts a majority of noninstitutionalized persons aged 70 or older?
   c. How many nondisabled persons 65 years of age and older participated in some form of exercise at least once during a recent two-week period?
   d. What group of elder Americans was least likely to have private insurance to supplement Medicare coverage?
   e. About how many of the older Americans who exercise achieve the recommended levels of exercise?

2. The objective of the World Health Organization (www.who.int/hpr/ageing/index.htm) is the attainment of the highest possible level of health by all people. To find out more about the health of older people, go to WHO's website and link to "World Health Day 1999: Active Aging," then to "The Facts." Answer the following questions:

   a. What are the effects of alcohol on older people?
   b. What are the benefits of physical activity in older age?
   c. What is the "Global Embrace"?
   d. What percentage of men and women aged 65 to 74 in developed countries are smokers?

Chapter 14

Dying, Death, and Bereavement

*J*n Mexico death is celebrated once a year in a national fiesta, *El Dia de los Muertos.*

Looking Ahead

1. How have cultural attitudes toward death changed over time?
2. How do people prepare for death?
3. What are the moral and legal issues involved in care of the dying?
4. What is a hospice, and how are hospice patients cared for?
5. How does an aged person's death affect family members?

*J*n her book *On Death and Dying*, Elizabeth Kubler-Ross (1970) described a scene recalled from her childhood:

I remember as a child the death of a farmer. He fell from a tree and was not expected to live. He asked simply to die at home, a wish that was granted without questioning. He called his daughters into the bedroom and spoke with each one of them alone for a few minutes. He arranged his affairs quietly, though he was in great pain. . . . He asked his friends to visit him once more, to bid goodbye to them. . . . When he did die, he was left at home, in his own beloved home, which he had built, and

among his friends and neighbors who went to take a last look at him where he lay in the midst of flowers in the place he had loved so much. (p. 3)

The custom of dying in one's home surrounded by family and friends has largely been abandoned. Now death is more likely to take place in a hospital or nursing home in the presence of complicated machines that monitor brain waves, heart and pulse rates, and blood pressure. A person who would once have expired peacefully might now be kept alive with intravenous antibiotics and a mechanical respirator. The technology that has made it possible to sustain life indefinitely raises complex

335

legal and ethical issues. How long should life be prolonged? Should people suffering from a terminal illness have a right to choose to die? Can physicians legally assist in that process? Who should have priority in obtaining access to costly new technology? In contemporary society, these questions have special relevance for the elderly and their families.

This chapter analyzes dying, death, and bereavement as a social phenomenon. First, we examine beliefs and practices regarding death from historical and cross-cultural perspectives, tracing the developments over the past century that have transformed the way in which death is viewed in the United States. Dying is a major life event experienced by individuals and their families. We describe this process and then analyze how changes in the nature of death have influenced the process of dying. Included here is an analysis of the legal and moral issues raised in the debate about euthanasia and the right to die. Then the chapter turns to a discussion of the main alternative to euthanasia, hospice care. Finally, we consider the process of bereavement, as we examine the impact of a death on a spouse and other family members.

Cross-Cultural and Historical Perspectives on Death

Just as our behavior throughout life is shaped by our culture, so is our view of death influenced by our society's values, beliefs, and institutional arrangements (Marshall and Levy, 1990). Although death is a universal human experience, the societal response to death varies according to prevailing attitudes and beliefs. There is enormous variation across cultures in how death is perceived and how grief is expressed.

Death in Preliterate Societies

The human concern for death predates written history. In Neanderthal burial sites from more than 50,000 years ago, archaeologists have discovered food, ornamental shells, and stone tools buried with the dead, suggesting that these early humans

believed that the deceased would need these items in some afterlife (DeSpelder and Strickland, 1992).

In many preliterate societies, the dead are imbued with special powers and considered potentially harmful to the living. Many customs and funereal rituals surrounding death represent efforts to ensure the well-being of the community. Among some of the aboriginal tribes of Australia, for example, a dead person is never mentioned by name after the burial. Similarly, the ancient Hebrews regarded the corpse as unclean and not to be touched.

Among most traditional Native American tribes, dying was less feared than the ghosts of the dead. Many believed that the spirit of the deceased lingered for days near the site of death before passing on to the next life, and customs reflected a desire to protect the living and to ensure that the deceased moved on to the afterlife. For example, the Ohlone tribe of the California coast adorned the corpse with feathers, flowers, and beads and wrapped it in blankets and skins. All of these items were then placed on the funeral pyre and burned so that the soul of the deceased would have no reason to remain in this world (Margolin, 1978).

In other societies, however, the dead are considered members of the community; they may be valuable allies, perform services for the living, or serve as intermediaries between the worlds of the living and the dead (DeSpelder and Strickland, 1992). Since ancient times, Mexican culture has reflected the themes of life, death, and resurrection. Life and death are viewed not as opposites but rather as part of a continuing process of regeneration, with a person's death mirroring his or her life. Once a year, death is celebrated in a national fiesta, *El Dia de los Muertos,* "the Day of the Dead." The fiesta is an occasion for communion between the living and the dead who return to visit; they are welcomed with food, drink, and even their favorite cigarettes (Moore, 1980).

Death in Non-Western Cultures

Eastern thought seeks to discover the unity that underlies apparently contradictory phenomena. What Westerners identify as the self is insubstantial in

Eastern culture, part of an ever-changing process. One of the distinguishing features of Hinduism is the belief in the transmigration of souls, the passing at death of the soul from one body to another, giving rise to successive rounds of death and rebirth. Death is a reminder that there is no permanent solid self.

One of the practices associated with Hinduism from the fourteenth to the eighteenth centuries was that of burning or burying women alive with their deceased husbands; there are also accounts of widow sacrifice occurring in ancient Scandinavia, Greece, Egypt, China, and Finland. In the most common form of widow sacrifice, or **suttee,** a widow or her eldest son was required to light the fire. On her progression to her funeral pyre, the widow was the object of public attention as she distributed money and jewels to the crowd. No woman who had been unfaithful to her husband could be a *sati,* or sacrificed woman, so suttee was proof of her virtue. A widow who did not choose this prescribed death was doomed to a humiliating life as a penitent sinner.

Suttee was rationalized under Hindu orthodoxy according to the belief that a widow was responsible for her husband's death. His preceding her in death meant that she must have sinned in this or a previous life, for in the normal course of events, a woman would die first. By her burning, a widow and her family would be guaranteed a position in paradise. More pragmatically, the practice of suttee meant that her husband's family was guaranteed undisputed guardianship of her children and that she relinquished claims over her husband's estate.

With the spread of British rule and the expansion of Western influence, there arose vehement opposition to suttee, especially among British missionaries. Suttee was abolished in Madras, British-governed territory, in 1830 and was gradually suppressed throughout India. The last legal burning occurred in 1861, although reports of suttee continue to the present day (Yang, 1989).

The dominant religion in Cambodia is Buddhism. Cambodian Buddhists do not fear death because they believe that dying is an inescapable part of life and that people who lead a good life and perform meritorious deeds for others will be rewarded in their next life. In Cambodia, the bodies of the dead are cremated in the fields because few crematoria exist. The ashes are kept at the temple.

In the 1970s many Cambodians migrated to the United States to escape the communist Khmer Rouge regime, which killed more than one and a half million people. Today these immigrants are elderly and approaching the end of their lives. Many continue to mourn the deaths of loved ones and seek to make sense of the suffering they witnessed. Most express feelings of nostalgia for Cambodia and hope to return there to die, but few have the funds to realize this dream. More likely they will die in the United States, where they still follow their traditional customs.

When someone dies, a close male relative becomes an honorary monk for a day to help carry his loved one's spirit to heaven. A monk comes from the temple each day until the Saturday after the death, when the funeral is held. Each person at the funeral places a flower in the casket and offers a prayer for the deceased. The body is then cremated. One hundred days after the funeral, the monk returns to pray with the family of the deceased and to prevent spirits from causing harm (Becker 2002).

At the end of World War II hundreds of Filipinos immigrated to the United States and established communities in various American cities. Now that they are elderly, many Filipinos, like the Cambodian immigrants, express a desire to return home to die. In "In Their Own Words," a 64-year-old Filipino man explains why he would prefer to be buried in the Philippines. His reasons illustrate the significance of ritual in giving meaning to death.

Death in Western Civilization

The middle ages to the victorian era

Three distinct periods can be identified in regard to the Western cultural outlook toward death: the Middle Ages, the Enlightenment, and the Romantic era. During the Middle Ages from about A.D. 500 to A.D. 1200, the core ideology was that the universe was bound together by divine and natural law and that death was an integral part of human existence. The dying person would confess his or her sins to

In Their Own Words

A Filipino Man Dreams of Returning Home to Die

*W*ell, for me, I think I will go back. That's where my mother, my father, my brother and my sister are buried. When I am really old, like 72 or 73, I will go home to the Philippines. I'll tell you why I don't want to die here. In the Philippines, if I die there, my family will watch me all the time. There are people praying, there is singing, and when they bury you there, if you are rich, they will hire a musical band that will escort you. . . . Here they don't. They put the dead person in the morgue and then at 10:00 people have to go home. That's it. In the Philippines, it's not like that. . . . Overnight in the chapel, there are a lot of people that gamble, a lot of mourners, and a lot of people playing mahjong and cards. They do not leave the body or fall asleep while watching the body.

Source: Becker (2002:S89)

the priest and then wait for death (DeSpelder and Strickland, 1992). Except for a few church notables or royalty, people were buried in churchyards in anonymous graves.

By the twelfth century, innovations in culture, agriculture, and political life opened the way for new intellectual pursuits. As people gained a greater sense of individual identity, death came to have a more personal meaning. There was a growing tendency to preserve the identity of the deceased through grave markers. Another major influence on attitudes toward death was the plague, which arrived in Europe in 1347 and wiped out one-third of the population, more than 25 million people, within three years. The ravages of the plague continued for another 80 years and encouraged the view that death was less a part of the natural order of things and more an abrupt rupture.

By the eighteenth century, social and intellectual life had become more secularized. Challenges to religious beliefs created a more diverse environment, and death became romanticized. The loss of a loved one was expressed by hysterical expressions of grief by the survivors and a desire to memorialize the deceased. Ornate memorials to the dead were constructed.

The transformation of death in the United States Since the nineteenth century, there has been a radical transformation in how death is viewed and how the dying are treated in the United States. One factor in this transformation is changing demographics. In 1900, more than half the reported deaths involved individuals 14 years old or younger. A significant percentage of babies were stillborn. Childhood diseases such as whooping cough, diphtheria, and polio took the lives of many young children. Over time, the average life expectancy increased, and the chance of dying in childhood or young adulthood greatly diminished. Today, fewer than 3 percent of deaths occur among people 14 or younger. Instead, most deaths occur in old age, two-thirds among people 65 or older (National Center for Health Statistics, 1996:23). This shift in the proportion of deaths among the young and the elderly is called an *epidemiologic transition* (see Chapter 13).

In addition to this redistribution of the number of deaths in childhood and old age, this epidemiologic transition was characterized by a shift in the types of disease that were likely to end in death. In the past, acute diseases such as diphtheria, tuberculosis, and pneumonia struck and killed quickly. Today, the two major causes of death are chronic diseases: heart disease and cancer. Although heart attacks may result in sudden death, heart disease and cancer are often progressive in nature, with death occurring only after a prolonged period of illness and decline (National Center for Health Statistics, 1996).

Death has also become less visible. A century ago most people died in their own beds, and most people had an opportunity to witness death firsthand. Now most people die in institutional settings, often surrounded by an array of machinery designed to sustain life. A study that examined the circumstances surrounding the deaths of 1,277 people whose average age at death was 80 found that 45 percent died in a hospital and 25 percent in a nursing home. Only 30 percent died at home (Foley et al., 1995).

Once an accepted part of life, death has become a taboo subject. Now the ritual dimensions of dying have been replaced by technological processes that not only can prolong life but sometimes bring into question the very definition of when life ceases.

Facing Death

Preparing for Death

A large body of research suggests that attitudes toward death vary over the life course. In young adulthood, death may be viewed as inevitable but distant. Most young people know few people who have died and tend to avoid thoughts of death. When they are asked to think about death, they tend to romanticize it and imagine themselves living into old age and then dying at home, quickly, surrounded by loved ones, alert and lucid to the end (Kastenbaum and Norman, 1990). However, Foley and colleagues (1995) found that before the elderly they studied had died, 75 percent had been unable to walk or were fully bedridden, 40 percent had difficulty recognizing family, and 88 percent were in fair or poor health. Yet people rarely died alone; nearly all had close contact with spouses and children in the three days prior to death.

Most people remain oblivious to death until they reach middle age, when a heightened awareness of their mortality triggers increased self-reflection and reminiscence (Marshall, 1986). Middle age is a period of taking stock, as time left to live becomes less than time since birth. People become aware of impending death not as a general conception but as a personal matter. When people grow old, they think and talk more about death, but death becomes less frightening. Yet older people also fear dying in pain and are concerned about the grief their death will cause their loved ones.

According to the noted gerontologist Robert Butler (1963), the tendency to reminisce about one's experiences, a process he called a **life review,** is a universal process that allows the aged to integrate their experiences and images of self into a whole. Marshall (1986) also saw this life review as an attempt by individuals to write the last chapters of their life stories so they could find meaning in past events and acts. According to Marshall, those who engage in social reminiscence—meaning that they discuss their past with others—are more likely to view their lives as having integrity and more able to attain a sense of having lived life as a whole.

A Stage Theory of Dying

According to the physician Elizabeth Kubler-Ross, there is a natural progression to the dying process in which recognition of impending death proceeds through a series of stages. On the basis of her work with dying patients, Kubler-Ross (1970) determined that dying people progress through a series of psychological reactions to their situation. In her model, people experience five **stages of dying:** an early period of denial, followed by anger, then bargaining, depression, and finally acceptance.

When confronted by the prospect of death, a person's initial response is avoidance or denial of the truth. There is a tendency to suppress the information or exclude it from consciousness. This reaction serves as a coping mechanism that helps the person to avoid facing an unwelcome reality. Often, the response is, "Oh no, it can't be me. The test results must be for someone else." Once a person has acknowledged that death is inevitable, the reaction changes to anger, which may be manifested as hostility. Caregivers may become the object of this anger, or the anger might be displayed by complaints about the food or the quality of care.

The next phase, according to Kubler-Ross, is the bargaining stage. At this point, the dying person may try to strike a bargain with God, to enter into an agreement that will postpone the inevitable. Some promise of "good behavior" is offered in the hope that God will grant the person an extension of life. Bargaining appears to be a way to postpone the dreaded outcome: "I'll stop smoking if I can live to see my grandson graduate from high school."

Eventually, according to Kubler-Ross, some patients come to accept their situation. They acknowledge that they are seriously ill, explore dispassionately the issues they are facing, and find productive ways of dealing with the changes in their lives. Acceptance does not mean giving up but rather resolving the crisis and reaching a personally satisfying adjustment.

The idea that dying occurs in stages has been subject to a good deal of criticism. A major criticism of this theory is that these stages do not occur in a fixed sequence. Some people may not move beyond the stage of denial. Others may experience some of the stages but never come to accept the inevitability of death. Some people may experience a variety of emotions—anger, sadness, resentment—simultaneously, or a person who initially accepts the inevitability of death may die raging against the inevitable. How an individual copes with death tends to be similar to how he or she has responded to the other stresses in life (Feifel, 1990).

MANAGING DEATH

The Right to Die

The traditional understanding of the Hippocratic Oath, formulated by the Greek physician Hippocrates in the fifth century B.C. and still taken by physicians today, is that physicians shall do no harm. Implicit in the oath is the notion that physicians need not take extreme measures to prolong life (DeSpelder and Strickland, 1992). In practice, many physicians have traditionally let terminally ill patients expire peacefully without subjecting them to arduous or painful treatment. In recent years, however, doctors have increasingly turned to modern technologies whose function often appears to be to keep the patient alive at all costs.

The ability to prolong life raises ethical questions about the lengthening of the dying process and the preservation of human dignity. It poses far-reaching issues for the dying and their families and also exposes physicians to new ethical questions and legal liabilities. When should care cease? Should a physician assist a terminally ill patient who wants to die? What should be done when a patient's wishes are unknown? How can patients be assured of the highest possible ethical standards in treatment, regardless of their age, race, or income? The "Diversity in the Aging Experience" feature discusses racial differences in attitudes toward end-of-life treatment, which may be rooted to some extent in ethical failures of the past.

The ability of modern medicine to prolong life has changed the nature of public discussion about **euthanasia.** Euthanasia is the act of killing or permitting the death of hopelessly sick or injured individuals in a painless, merciful way. It is sometimes called *mercy killing.* There are two forms of euthanasia: **passive euthanasia** and **active euthanasia.**

Passive euthanasia Passive euthanasia has been recognized for decades. It has been employed in hospitals, nursing homes, and other health care settings. It simply involves withholding or withdrawing medical treatment from the hopelessly ill (Raffin, 1995).

The debate over passive euthanasia first reached public attention in 1975 when a 22-year-old woman named Karen Quinlan entered the intensive care unit of a New Jersey hospital in a coma. She remained unresponsive, in a persistent vegetative state, with no hope of recovery. Her vital processes were sustained by a mechanical respirator. When her parents asked to have the respirator removed so that she could die peacefully, their request was opposed by the medical staff responsible for Karen's care. In a lawsuit to determine who should have the right to act on Karen's behalf, the New Jersey Superior Court ruled in favor of the medical staff. This decision was overturned by the Supreme Court of New Jersey in March 1976. The artificial respirator was turned off, and Karen was transferred to a nursing home. Karen did not die, however, but lived for another nine years. She died in June 1985 at the age of 31 without ever awakening from a coma (Glick, 1992).

Diversity in the Aging Experience

RACIAL DIFFERENCES IN ATTITUDES TOWARD END-OF-LIFE CARE

*D*o people's feelings about the treatment they receive when they are critically ill differ based on race? To find out, researchers interviewed relatives of 540 deceased participants in the Asset and Health Dynamics among the Oldest Old (AHEAD) study, a nationally representative survey of adults aged 70 or older. They asked both black and white respondents about their wishes regarding end-of-life care. The researchers found that white participants were more likely than African American participants to discuss treatment preferences before death, to complete a living will, and to give power of attorney over their affairs to a relative. Among those who made treatment decisions, whites were more likely to want to limit care under certain conditions, and to refuse treatment before death if they were terminally ill. Blacks were more likely to request all possible life-prolonging care (Hopp and Duffy, 2000).

These results indicate that important racial differences exist in advanced care planning and end-of-life decision making. What explains these racial differences? One answer may be lingering distrust of the health care system among African Americans. In the past, black people have not always been treated in an ethical manner by doctors and hospitals. For example, in the Tuskegee Syphilis Study, black men who suffered from syphilis were allowed to go untreated for more than 20 years, even though a cure was available (Thomas and Quinn, 1991). Another explanation for racial differences in end-of-life decision making may lie in religious and cultural differences in attitudes toward death and dying. Regardless of the cause, health professionals need to be sensitive to racial differences in helping patients with end-of-life decisions.

What Do You Think?

1. Has anyone in your family completed a living will or discussed his or her last wishes with relatives? If so, did your relative want to prolong life or withhold treatment under certain circumstances?
2. If you were a hospital social worker, how could you reassure a patient who is hesitant about completing a living will or power of attorney?

In the past, doctors routinely used their professional judgment to decide when to stop treatment and withdraw life-sustaining measures. In recent years, as the number of court cases disputing these decisions has increased, doctors and hospitals have grown increasingly concerned about being sued if they withhold treatment. Consequently, many no longer do so without explicit legal protection (Glick, 1992).

Court cases have revolved around two issues in defining the physician's right to withhold or terminate treatment: (1) the kind of medical care a terminally ill patient desires and (2) the requests of patients who want to die to have treatment withdrawn. Such requests assume that any treatment will only postpone the process of dying. In an effort to address these issues, court decisions have given physicians the right to honor **living wills.**

In a living will, individuals specify their wishes for treatment in advance in case they should become terminally ill. Living wills may include instructions as to whether life-supporting treatments such as mechanical respirators, dialysis machines, tube feeding, or intravenous liquids may be used. They also may state whether not-for-resuscitation orders are desired (Cartwright and Steinberg, 1995). Living wills represent a means of extending self-determination to people no longer capable of participating in decisions about their care.

All states have enacted legislation that provides for legally binding living wills either in the form of an advanced directive from the patient or by the appointment of a proxy who has power of attorney. There is also the federal Patient Self Determination Act, which requires all government-funded health providers to give patients the opportunity to complete a directive when they are admitted to a hospital (Cartwright and Steinberg, 1995). However, the actual use of advance directives is quite low, ranging from 4 to 20 percent. Among the elderly who are most likely to face a life-threatening situation, the use of advance directives is no higher than it is for the population as a whole (High, 1993).

Research in Canada, the United States, and Australia has shown that most people would like the chance to prepare some form of a living will (Cartwright and Steinberg, 1995). The problem with living wills lies in how to interpret their meaning, for it has become increasingly difficult to define what a terminal illness is and exactly what constitutes life-sustaining treatment. Nor is it always clear when such treatment should be withdrawn.

Active euthanasia   The second type of euthanasia, active euthanasia, is also known as *assisted suicide*. Active euthanasia occurs when a physician, close friend, or relative helps an ill or disabled person terminate his or her life. Although there is no legal distinction between active euthanasia and assisted suicide (Wekesser, 1995), the common understanding is that assisted suicide involves more planning and cooperation between the ill person and the individual who will assist. Yet the distinction between active euthanasia and assisted suicide is vague at best; so we will use the terms interchangeably.

Surveys show that public opinion favors physician-assisted suicide for mentally competent patients who choose to die if they face terrible pain, an insensate existence, or a life so diminished that death would be preferable. Older people are more ambivalent. In 1992, the Gallup organization surveyed 802 randomly selected men and women aged 60 or older regarding their attitudes toward suicide and assisted suicide. The majority of respondents opposed suicide and were evenly divided on whether physician-assisted suicide should be legalized. Those most likely to favor legalizing assisted suicide were white males who were less religious, had strained family relationships, and were in failing health (Seidlitz et al., 1995).

Many physicians also support the idea of assisted suicide in certain circumstances. Researchers interviewed fourth-year medical students in Oregon regarding their attitudes toward assisted suicide. Two-thirds favored legalizing physician-assisted suicide, and 55 percent said they "might be willing to write a lethal prescription" if the practice were legal. Nearly one in four students had received a patient request for a lethal prescription in the past year (Mangus, Dipiero, and Hawkins, 1999).

In New York, Dr. Timothy Quill prescribed a lethal dosage of a barbiturate to a terminally ill leukemia patient, knowing that she would use it to kill herself (Quill, 1995). The patient died, but

Dr. Quill was not indicted for this act of euthanasia even though he described his role in an article published in the *New England Journal of Medicine*. In 1994, three physicians joined three patients in a lawsuit asking the courts to strike down a New York state law prohibiting doctors from helping dying patients commit suicide. As one of the physicians in the suit, Dr. Samuel Klagsbrun, explained: "I am one of many doctors who have been practicing quietly, doing our own things out of the limelight. I've been treating people, taking care of their pain, managing it in a traditional medical way. Some have lived. Some have died" (Bruni, 1996).

Assisted suicide remains in legal limbo. In recent years, legislation authorizing doctors to help patients die, under careful control, was narrowly defeated in California and Washington and then adopted by referendum in Oregon. On April 3, 1996, a federal appeals court overturned the New York ban on assisted suicide. The ruling stated:

What interest can the state possibly have in requiring the prolongation of a life that is all but ended? And what business is it of the state to require the continuation of agony when the result is imminent and inevitable? (Bruni, 1996)

Opponents of assisted suicide denounced the decision as a chilling precedent, and New York state's attorney general immediately announced he would file an appeal to the U.S. Supreme Court. In 1997, the Supreme Court ruled that patients did not have the right to assisted suicide, but the ruling left open the possibility that states could legalize assisted suicide in certain cases.

Proponents of active euthanasia contend that prolonging the suffering of the terminally ill who are in constant pain is inhumane. Noting that euthanasia literally means a "good death," they argue that in a caring society euthanasia should be offered to hopelessly sick persons as an act of love (Humphry, 1995). For every argument in favor of assisted suicide, there are counterarguments by those who consider it akin to murder and thus never morally justified (Otremba, 1995). Opponents compare it to programs used by the Nazis to exterminate the medically and mentally handicapped, Jews, homosexuals, and Gypsies. Given the strong feelings on both sides, this issue is unlikely to be resolved soon. "Aging around the World" on page 344 discusses the debate over assisted suicide in other countries.

Suicide among the aged

Although people 65 or older make up less than 13 percent of the population, they commit 17 to 25 percent of all suicides (Brant and Osgood, 1990). Suicide rates are especially high among men 85 and older. Elderly white men are the only group more likely to commit suicide than to die in an auto accident. Table 14–1 shows suicide rates by race, sex, and ethnic origin.

The story of Joseph Wiseman, a 72-year-old retired postal worker, illustrates the circumstances that might lead an older man to commit suicide. Wiseman was going blind and feared he might no longer be able to care for his 69-year-old wife, who had been confined to a wheelchair for 11 years and could not talk or feed or bathe herself. One day he shot and killed his wife and then shot himself (Gottschalk, 1986).

There are many reasons why rates of suicide increase with advancing age. Old age may be accompanied by social isolation, boredom, a sense of uselessness, financial hardship, the multiple losses of loved ones, or chronic illness and pain. Older people may also fear becoming a burden to family members. Despair sometimes occurs in patients with progressive mental degeneration, as in Alzheimer's disease sufferers, who fear becoming a burden to others and losing their dignity as their mental

Table 14–1	**Death Rates from Suicide among People Aged 65+ by Race, Ethnic Origin, and Gender, 1989–1991 (deaths per 100,000)**	

	Male	*Female*
White	43.7%	6.5%
Black	16.0	1.9
Native American	11.4	3.4
Asian and Pacific Islander	18.5	8.9
Hispanic	25.9	2.5

Source: National Center for Health Statistics (1994c: table 37).

Aging around the World

ASSISTED SUICIDE IN THE NETHERLANDS

In 2000 the Dutch parliament approved a bill allowing euthanasia and physician-assisted suicide, making Holland the first country to legalize the practice. Until that legislation was passed, assisted suicide had been a quiet but accepted practice. In one study 49 percent of Dutch physicians acknowledged having practiced euthanasia on very ill patients; 22 percent reported having done so in the past 24 months (Van der Mass, Pijnenborg, and J. van Delden, 1995). The average age of patients who died by euthanasia was 62 for men and 65 for women (Zehetmayr, 1996).

The new legislation includes guidelines that liberalize previous guidelines in place since 1993. Under the earlier guidelines, a patient had to be experiencing unbearable suffering, be aware of all other medical options, and have sought a second opinion. Doctors were not allowed to suggest euthanasia as an option. Rather the request had to be made voluntarily by the patient of sound mind. The new legislation allows patients to leave a written request for euthanasia, giving doctors the right to use their discretion when patients become too ill, mentally or physically, to decide for themselves.

In 1993 the American psychiatrist Herbert Hendlin, a leading expert on suicide, traveled to the Netherlands to study the Dutch system for relieving end-of-life suffering. Hendlin, who has treated numerous suicidal patients in his psychiatric practice, came away convinced that legalizing assisted suicide raises more ethical questions than it answers. In the Netherlands, the law requires a second opinion when a patient asks a doctor for help in ending his or her life. But, according to Hendlin, many doctors simply refer their patients to like-minded doctors, so the second opinion is always yes.

capabilities are destroyed. They believe that the only way they can die with dignity is to leave the world before they lose the ability to make an informed decision.

Depression is the most frequent psychiatric disorder in the elderly, and the reason for most suicides in this age group. The elderly who commit suicide are more likely than younger people to live alone and be socially isolated, to have experienced multiple personal losses, and to have serious physical and mental health problems (Carney, Burke, and Fowler, 1994). One of the more distressing aspects of suicide among older people is that it tends to happen without warning, thus lessening the chances of prevention. One study of suicide victims aged 21 to 92 found that older victims were more likely to plan their deaths, to use less violent methods, and to give fewer warnings of their intentions (Conwell et al., 1998). Another study of attempted suicides found that completion rates were highest among people 85 and older (Purcell, Thrush, and Blanchette, 1999). Whereas younger

Another safeguard is that a patient must ask to die at least twice. Hendlin found abuses of this safeguard as well.

Euthanasia is tolerated in Switzerland, Colombia, and Belgium. In other countries where it is banned, the ban is being challenged. In one case in Canada, a terminally ill woman argued that her constitutional rights were being denied because she was too disabled to commit suicide herself. Although she lost her appeal to the Canadian Supreme Court, the decision was not unanimous. In 1996 Australia's Northern Territory approved euthanasia, but the federal Parliament revoked the law in 1997. It seems that the movement to legalize assisted suicide is unlikely to succeed soon. There are too many ethical questions that cannot be resolved simply and easily.

What Do You Think?

1. Has anyone you know ever expressed a wish to die prematurely rather than suffer through a painful terminal illness? If so, did that person ask a doctor for help?
2. Do you think physicians should be allowed to help terminally ill patients die?

Emilie van Eeghen holds a photo of her father, who died using an "assisted suicide" method in the Netherlands. She is a supporter of assisted suicide.

people may display a cry for help, the elderly just do it (Rosowsky, 1993).

Hospice Care

The two extremes of dying in pain or seeking relief by means of euthanasia do not exhaust the possibilities for the stricken patient. The goal of the **hospice** movement is to allow the terminally ill to die easily and at peace, without pain, in their own homes, special units of hospitals, or hospice facilities (Saunders, 1980).

The hospice movement   The term *hospice* means stranger or host. It originated in medieval Europe, when the term was used to refer to settings that provided shelter for travelers and care for the ill, weary, dying, and abandoned (Siebold, 1992). The first modern hospice was St. Christopher's, which opened in 1967 in London (Saunders, 1980). Hospices recognize the difficulties surrounding death and strive "to make life's journey easier for those who are nearing its end" (Hayslip and Leon, 1992:1). Hospice supporters emphasize the quality over the quantity of life and the importance of both physical and spiritual contact between people as life draws to a close.

Hospice advocates view death with dignity as an alternative to the coldly scientific, medical model of dying. A central component of hospice philosophy is pain management. Terminal pain is considered an illness in itself to be diagnosed and treated according to an individual's needs. Therefore, drugs are adjusted according to need and administered regularly to prevent a vicious spiral of tension, increased pain, and a need for a higher dose of medication. According to the hospice philosophy, the best treatment for terminal pain is prevention.

One tale from St. Christopher's illustrates why hospice supporters are so opposed to any form of euthanasia. One elderly woman arrived at St. Christopher's severely incapacitated from a stroke. She was terribly depressed and had asked first her daughter and then another resident, Mrs. B., if they would get her some pills so she could kill herself. A year later with proper care "she has changed her mind; she can walk . . . and can do crochet. She does not want to die now, her whole outlook has changed" (Saunders, 1980:554).

The hospice movement in the United States was launched in 1974 in Branford, Connecticut. As the idea of a more compassionate attitude toward dying spread, so did the hospice movement. By 1991 there were over 1,700 hospices in the United States.

The structure of hospice care   In the United States, hospices are based on one of five models. The first is home-based care, often provided by groups of professionals and volunteers. Second is home-based care provided by health care agencies or visiting nurses associations. Third are freestanding hospice facilities. A fourth type of hospice is found in special units or wards of hospitals that emphasize the relief of pain and suffering. A fifth, the most recent form of hospice care, is provided in the nursing home. Of the more than 2,000 hospices certified for Medicare payment, nearly 1,000 are freestanding, over 700 are based in home health, and another 500 are hospital based (Parham, 2002). In recent years, however, the nursing home population has become the fastest-growing group of hospice users (Gold, 1995).

The problem with providing hospice care to dying patients in nursing homes is that hospice volunteers are present only a few hours a week. When they are not available, patients experience the same difficulties facing many nursing home residents—overworked staff and inadequate care. As a result, patients do not always receive the pain relief they deserve (Parham, 2002). Advantages and disadvantages of providing hospice care in a nursing home are the subject of "An Issue for Public Policy."

Although hospices vary in terms of which model they follow, the basic services they provide are similar: a medically directed continuum of care and support for terminally ill patients. An aspect of hospice care that distinguishes it from traditional medical care is that family members are also provided care. The family can receive counseling and respite support before the death of a loved one and follow-up bereavement care for up to a year after the death. The services are provided by a team that includes a registered nurse, a social worker, a physician, clergy, and home health aides. Ideally, the services are available 24 hours a day, seven days a week. The care plan is focused on pain management, not treatment of the terminal disease. Each care plan is unique and tailored to meet the physical, emotional, spiritual, and economic needs of the patient and his or her family during the final stages of illness (Pepper Commission on Aging, 1990).

A problem with home hospice care is that it presumes a family caretaker is present and able to assume most of the daily caregiving responsibilities. With an increasing divorce rate, a larger number of families headed by single parents, smaller family size, and more women in the labor force, a family member may not always be available to care for a dying relative.

Paying for hospice care   There are five sources of payment for hospice services: Medicare, Medicaid, private insurance, private pay, and charitable donations (Vladeck, 1995:449). Medicare and Medicaid are the main sources of payment; together the two programs covered 60 percent of the 300,000 patients cared for in hospices in 1994 (Vladeck, 1995:449). If patients outlive their

An Issue for Public Policy

HOSPICE CARE IN NURSING HOMES

Since the mid-1990s the fastest growing group of hospice users in the United States has been nursing home residents. This increase is mainly the result of a new government rule in 1996 that allows Medicare to pay for hospice benefits in nursing homes. The rule resulted from growing recognition that the nursing home is most likely to be the final home for an increasing number of the aged.

At first, some nursing home administrators were suspicious of hospice care, viewing it as an intrusion. They believed that hospice would be reimbursed for care that the nursing home was already providing, and they feared that hospice volunteers might be critical of the care that nursing home staff provided to dying residents. Now most administrators realize that there are advantages to having hospice care provided in their facility. Hospice provides skilled nurses who can evaluate residents' needs, provide the nursing home's aides with training on pain management, and assume responsibility for the care needs of patients in the hospice program (Jones, Nackerud, and Boyle, 1997).

Despite hospice's goal of relieving pain in the final months of life, Parham (2002) found that hospice had little effect on the care of dying patients. One problem was that hospice staff was present in the nursing home only a few times a week and so had little input into the ongoing care of residents. Another problem was lack of communication between hospice staff and the nursing home aides who provided most of the hands-on care. Even when recommendations for pain relief were made by hospice staff or volunteers, there was not always follow-up to ensure that the recommendations were carried out. As a result, many nursing home residents who are supposed to receive pain relief in their final months of life still suffer needlessly.

What Do You Think?

1. Have any of your family members received hospice care?
2. What can be done to improve communication between hospice staff and nursing home aides?

---

insurance coverage, their expenses are paid with privately raised funds and charitable donations. Table 14–2 shows the sources of hospice payments and the percentage that each source pays.

Congress passed legislation in 1982 allowing payment for hospice care through Medicare, the program of health insurance for people aged 65 and older. Although policymakers believed that hospice care would be less costly than hospital-based care, that has turned out to be a false assumption. One study attempted to measure the savings hospice care was expected to yield. The researchers

Table 14-2	Hospice Primary Payment Source, 1995

Source of Payment	Percentage Paid by Source
Medicare	65%
Medicaid	8
Private insurance	12
Indigent care	4
Other	11

Source: National Hospice and Palliative Care Organization (2000).

found that although the number of days terminally ill patients spent in the hospital declined by 8 to 10 percent after 1982, overall hospital admission rates did not change (Gaumer and Stabins, 1992). Nearly two-thirds of all Medicare patients were admitted to a hospital at least once during the last 90 days of their lives.

The same study found that while the number of deaths occurring in a hospital decreased, the number of deaths preceded by home health services increased. Although dying at home instead of a hospital may be preferable from an individual's perspective, the savings are minimal because costs are simply shifted from one part of the Medicare budget (hospital care) to another (physician and home care services). Overall, hospice care saves just over 3 percent of Medicare costs—hardly the billions of dollars predicted when the program was first implemented (Emanuel and Emanuel, 1994). In 1997 Medicare spent just over $2,024 million for hospice care for 374,723 dying patients (Health Care Financing Administration, 2000b).

The real issue concerning hospice care is whether containing costs should be the main objective of public policy or whether other goals are more important. As the researchers point out, "hospice care (was) developed to ensure patients' autonomy and to provide high-quality care at the end of life. Compassion and dignity are sufficient justification for their use" (Emanuel and Emanuel, 1994:540).

Dying is an expensive process. Nearly 30 percent of all Medicare payments go to the 5 to 6 percent of

beneficiaries who die that year (Emanuel and Emanuel, 1994). Forty-six percent of costs in the last year of life occur in the last 60 days (Gaumer and Stabins, 1992). The rising costs of high-tech medical approaches to prolonging life contribute to this great expense.

BEREAVEMENT

Death and the Family

It is rather sobering to realize that every person who marries and remains married will one day be widowed, unless he or she dies first. Among Americans who are 65 or older, almost half of the women and one-fifth of the men have lost their marital partners. With each year that one lives beyond age 65, the risk increases of having one's life partner die. Women have a greater probability of becoming widowed because they typically live longer than men and because they are usually younger than their husbands (O'Bryant, 1990–91).

Widowhood is mentally and physically devastating for most people. The death of a spouse is associated with increased risk of illness and mortality, particularly during the bereavement period (Ferraro, 1985; Silverstein and Bengtson, 1991). How is bereavement linked to illness? No one knows for sure. One theory proposes that the stress of bereavement has a negative influence on the functioning of the immune system, which protects us from harmful microorganisms and strikes down cancerous cells (see Chapter 6 for a discussion of the immune system). But that theory hasn't been proved.

Women as widows   There have been many studies of the process of adjustment to widowhood among women. Research shows that most women go through three stages: preparation, grief and mourning, and adaptation (Heinemann and Evans, 1990).

The amount of preparation for widowhood varies greatly. In some instances, the partner is felled swiftly without warning. In other cases, a person with a terminal illness will live for several weeks or months, giving the spouse a chance to grieve and to prepare for the death. Deaths that follow a lingering illness can place a great burden of physical care and financial strain on the family; thus when they do occur, grief is often tempered with relief. A wife who prepares for widowhood by anticipating the grief and the imminent loss of her husband does not experience less grief than one who does not, but she does adjust better to her circumstances over the long term.

Regardless of the medical circumstances, widowhood is difficult. At two months after the loss of a spouse, widowed older adults, regardless of gender, are extremely depressed, stressed, and lonely. A widow may initially feel that life is not worth living. Although family and friends offer comfort in the first weeks following the loss, eventually she is left to face her grief alone. After two years, the sense of yearning, of missing one's spouse, remains, but the depression has diminished significantly (O'Bryant and Hansson, 1995). When the period of grief and mourning has passed or lessened, some widows find that they enjoy their new independence, the free time, and the reduced load of housework. Widows who adjust best are those who keep busy, take on new roles, and see friends often (Lund, 1993).

A widow's grief may be compounded by her being much poorer than she was before her husband died. A widow may lose rights to her husband's pension benefit, and her Social Security benefit will be cut by one-third (see Chapter 16). One study comparing life satisfaction of widows and married women found that much of the unhappiness and dissatisfaction expressed by widows could be explained by their relative lack of financial resources (Heinemann and Evans, 1990).

In her pioneering research on widows, Helena Lopata (1973) found that women react differently to their husbands' deaths, depending on the nature of the relationships they and their husbands shared. For some, the husband's death means the loss of a unique, deeply loved person with whom they shared a multidimensional companionship. In this case, death brings a crushing sense of personal loneliness. For others, widowhood means a change in status, the loss of a social position and of a couples-oriented lifestyle that cannot be re-created.

A more recent study examined the effect of marital quality on depression and anxiety among widows and widowers. In the Changing Lives of Older Couples study, researchers compared 319 recently widowed men and women aged 65 or older with a matched group of people who were not widowed. Although the widows and widowers were significantly more likely than the control group to be depressed, marital quality had an important effect on their mood. Those who had enjoyed emotionally close marriages and had depended on their spouses for help in handling daily tasks experienced greater difficulty adjusting to widowhood than those who had had conflicted marriages (Carr et al., 2000).

Research shows that older people who lose a close relative survive longer when they have intimate ties to an adult child. Intimate relationships increase the widowed individual's sense of security, and the children attend to the widowed parent's physical needs (Silverstein and Bengtson, 1991). Rates of contact with children and other relatives following widowhood vary by race and ethnicity, with African Americans and Hispanics having more frequent contact than Asians and whites (Pelham and Clark, 1987).

Widowhood reorganizes the social support network in a variety of ways. It may intensify existing family ties. One study of widows found that they talked on the phone more often with their children (Gibbs, 1985). If their children lived in the same community, they saw them more often than before. Widows who had siblings nearby saw them and talked to them often. However, widows were most likely to interact with siblings to whom they felt emotionally close, even if they lived far away.

Widowhood also alters friendship patterns. One study of helping patterns among married and widowed women 60 or older found that wives spent more time helping family members and widows spent more time helping friends (Gallagher and Gerstel, 1993). The authors of this study concluded that "the loss of the wife role has a significant positive effect on help to nonkin" (p. 681).

Many new widows discover that other women share their plight and that membership in a support group of other widows is open to them. Support networks more readily welcome older widows than young widows. Deborah Van den Hoonaard (1994) conducted a longitudinal study of a condominium-type retirement community on the east coast of Florida. When she started her research in 1980, most of the residents were married couples. By 1989, 23 percent of the households contained single people, mostly widows. Although the married couples perceived no change in the community as a result of the increasing number of widows, the widows noticed a striking change in their relationships with the couples. Widows commonly reported being excluded from activities by people whom they had previously considered good friends. After they lost their husbands, they were rarely invited to go out to dinner or to theater outings, and they felt uncomfortable attending community activities like dances that seemed to require a partner. From the perspective of the couples, the widows associated with other widows by choice, but the widows reported being "dropped like a hot potato." Although many formed a new support network comprised of other widows, it took some effort to establish this new connection. Those who failed to do so were isolated and lonely.

Overall, older widows are resilient and adapt well. One study found that at least one-third of widows discovered new strengths and talents, tried new things, and entered into fresh relationships (Lieberman, 1996). Another study compared women who had been widowed for 10 years with married women (McCrae and Costa, 1988). There were no differences on measures of well-being, depression, and health, although widows suffered reductions in income and were more likely to be institutionalized.

Men as widowers

Although there has been much less research on widowers than on widows, what we do know suggests that men experience greater difficulties adjusting to widowhood than women. Many older men are totally unprepared to assume the role of widower, because they do not expect their wives to die first. In addition, most older men have been cared for by their wives for most of their adult lives and so find it difficult to adjust to the practical demands of life on their own. Many, for example, have never prepared a meal. Not knowing how to cook, they tend to eat

Women who are newly widowed find comfort in sharing their feelings with other widows, as in this support group.

out of cans and to skip meals; as a consequence, their health suffers. Widows, by contrast, continue to prepare regular meals and maintain their health.

The decline in health is often accompanied by depression, which may lead to biological changes that make men more vulnerable to heart attacks and other diseases. Men are much more likely than women to die in the first six months to a year after they are widowed (Moyers, 1993). One researcher followed 500 elderly widows and widowers for six years after the death of a spouse (Bowling, 1988–89). She found that widowers older than 75 had higher mortality rates than men of the same age in the general population.

The traditional male role emphasizes independence, which compounds the problems of widowers.

Masculine stereotypes make no provision for men to be old, infirm, and unable to cope. Widowers are less likely than widows to receive financial support from children and more likely to live alone (Berardo, 1970). Support groups, which are common for widows, are rare for widowers. Although young widowers will most likely remarry, older widowers are much less likely to do so. Thus, an older widower may feel, with good reason, that he was one of the unlucky ones.

The Death of a Parent

The death of a parent is a natural part of the life course. Most people lose one of their parents when they are in their 50s. By age 62, 75 percent of adult children have lost both parents (Umberson and Chen, 1994). Because many parents and adult children maintain frequent contact and engage in mutual support and exchanges, parents remain central to the lives of their adult children. The death of an adult child's parent represents the loss of a long-term relationship that is important to psychological well-being.

The loss of a parent also has great symbolic meaning. People often report that the death of a parent changes their outlook on life, spurring them "to examine their lives more closely, to begin to change what they didn't like, to appreciate more the relationships they had" (Douglas, 1990–91:128). Although any death may be a reminder of an individual's own mortality, the death of a parent brings this message home forcefully. When a person's parents are alive, a son or daughter has the knowledge that the parents are usually there for support. The death of one parent may shake that security; this is especially true when both parents die.

Some research suggests that the loss of a mother is more upsetting than the loss of a father. This may be because familial ties are more likely to be maintained by the mother. However, this conclusion may be a statistical artifact—that is, since fathers typically die before mothers, the death of a mother in most cases represents the loss of both parents and thus is more upsetting.

A number of factors affect the amount of grieving that occurs after a parent's death. Some research suggests that children who have had poor relationships with one of their parents suffer the greatest grief when that parent dies, because they harbor feelings of guilt. Other research indicates that children who have had positive relationships with one of their parents are more adversely affected by the parent's death. Negative childhood memories of a parent often correlate with less stress upon the parent's death, suggesting that the death may come as a relief to a child who has had a difficult family history (Umberson and Chen, 1994).

Sons and daughters react differently to a parent's death, which is not surprising given that there are substantial gender differences in relationships between adult children and their parents (Umberson, 1992). Typically, a son reacts to his father's death in ways that parallel how the father dealt with stress. If the father abused alcohol, the son is more likely to increase his own alcohol consumption following the father's death. Similarly, sons who recall their fathers as having mental problems experience more psychological distress. This is not true for daughters (Umberson and Chen, 1994).

The typical response of a daughter to her mother's death also reflects a struggle to deal with the social requirements and dictates of loss. One study examined the responses of 107 married, middle-aged daughters to the death of their mothers. Nearly all the daughters described a process of selectively controlling or managing their feeling of grief. For example, they mentioned protecting their children from the burden of seeing their pain. A few daughters also avoided intense expressions of grief for fear of evoking sibling jealousy that they were more loved.

Anticipatory grief was a common experience among daughters whose mothers had been ill for a long time before dying. One daughter explained the feelings she had when her mother was diagnosed with Alzheimer's disease: "My mother started to die five years ago, and I did my grieving then. I was torn so badly. . . . I mourned when she lived" (Klapper et al., 1994:36). Thus, the daughter's grief reflected her reaction to her mother's incremental losses as much as to her death.

Another type of grief was *selfish grief*. Selfish grief occurred when a daughter wished her mother was still alive but felt that she should suppress her yearning because it would be selfish to extend her mother's suffering. One daughter expressed her conflicting emotions at her mother's funeral, saying she could see her mother "lying there so peacefully that I knew she was at peace. And yet, you know, it all comes back to the same thing, you'll never see her again" (Klapper et al., 1994:36).

We see then that just as customs and practices surrounding death are socially determined, so are the expected reactions of individuals. Gender differences in behavior are apparent across the life course, and these differences extend to the expression of grief.

Modern technology has altered the trajectory of dying and raised ethical issues about when life ends, how to protect terminally ill people from needless, dehumanizing, and demeaning procedures, and how to meet the emotional needs of the dying person and his or her family. Given the trend toward population aging and the fact that most deaths now occur in old age, these issues are likely to become even more pressing in the future.

Chapter Resources

LOOKING BACK

1. **How have cultural attitudes toward death changed over time?** *There are enormous variations across societies and over time in attitudes toward death. Some societies engage in death avoidance while others celebrate the communion between the living and the dead. In the United States there has been an immense change in the process of dying from the nineteenth century to the present. This change is partly due to a shift in the average age of death and the association of dying with old age. It is also caused by a change in the causes of death. At one time most people died from acute illnesses that struck swiftly. Now people are more likely to die from a chronic illness that leads to a slow death. The setting for death has also changed. Most deaths once occurred in the home. Now death typically takes place in an institutional setting such as a hospital or nursing home.*

2. **How do people prepare for death?** *Some people prepare for death by engaging in a life review. A life review is a process of reminiscing over one's experiences and finding meaning in past events. It helps the individual to view his or her life as having integrity.*

3. **What are the moral and legal issues involved in care of the dying?** *Now that modern health technology has made it possible to extend life indefinitely, people face ethical and legal issues regarding the right to die. No issue has raised more controversy than euthanasia. There are two types of euthanasia. The less controversial form is passive euthanasia, the withholding or withdrawal of treatment. Active euthanasia, also known as assisted suicide, remains in legal limbo. Although it is illegal in most of the Western world, public opinion supports it under certain conditions.*

4. **What is a hospice, and how are hospice patients cared for?** *Hospices are dedicated to providing death with dignity, free of pain. Hospices have expanded in the United States since payment for hospice care was allowed under Medicare. Although hospice care saves little in terms of public expenditures, it fulfills another objective, that of providing high-quality care at the end of life. Hospice care may be provided in several different settings including a hospital, a nursing home, or an individual's home.*

5. **How does an aged person's death affect family members?** *Every married person who does not divorce or who does not die before his or her spouse will become widowed one day. The loss of a spouse is a stressful event that is associated with greater risk of illness and mortality. Although the death of a parent is a natural part of middle age and middle-aged people lead independent lives, parental death holds great symbolic meaning and represents a personal loss that also symbolizes one's own aging. Sons and daughters react to parental loss in gender-stereotypical ways. Sons are more likely to mimic their father's ways of dealing with stress. Daughters are more likely to consider the feelings of others and evaluate their own behavior in light of societal expectations for the proper expression of grief.*

THINKING ABOUT AGING

1. Which is better, the traditional way of dying at home or the modern way of dying in a medical institution? What does your answer say about the culture you live in?

2. Many people say they would rather die young than waste away in old age from a degenerative disease. What do you think?

3. What would you say to a terminally ill person who wants to end his or her life?

4. Life-extending medical technology is extremely expensive. Should it be rationed depending on a person's age? Why or why not?

5. If you were dying, what kind of care would you prefer to receive and where? Would you refuse life-prolonging treatments? Would you want help in ending your life?

KEY TERMS

active euthanasia 340

euthanasia 340

hospice 345

life review 339

living will 342

passive euthanasia 340

stages of dying 339

suttee 337

EXPLORING THE INTERNET

Note: While all the URLs listed were current as of the printing of this book, these sites often change. Please check our website www.mhhe.com/quadagno *for updates.*

1. Duke University has researched the elderly's attitudes toward assisted suicide. Go to Duke University's medical news site (http://www.dukemednews.duke.edu/home/index_flash.php) and do a search for "assisted suicide." Scroll down and link to the article, "Frail, Elderly Patients More Opposed to Physician-Assisted Suicide than Younger Relatives." Read the article and answer the questions:

   a. What was the sample size? What percent favored physician-assisted suicide for terminally ill patients?

   b. What percent of the patient's relatives favored the measure under the same circumstances?

   c. What types of patients are most likely to be opposed to the measure?

   d. Were spouses and children of the elderly able to adequately predict what they might think about physician-assisted suicide?

   e. What group felt more favorable toward assisted suicide?

2. The American Association of Retired Persons (http://www.aarp.org) is a nonprofit, nonpartisan organization dedicated to shaping and enriching the experience of aging. To find statistical information on widowhood in the United States, go to the AARP's Web page and type "widowhood" in the search bar. Read the article titled "On Being Alone: A Guide for the Newly Widowed," and answer the following questions:

   a. How do they recommend dealing with emotions?

   b. Is grief something that can be overcome?

   c. How can a new widow reduce stress that might be detrimental to the grieving process?

   d. What kinds of activities are recommended for widows who want to return to a "normal life?"

   e. What is the name of the organization that offers educational opportunities in the U.S. and abroad?"

Part Five

AGING AND SOCIETY

opulation aging raises issues that extend beyond the family and community to a societal level. The three chapters in this section discuss the economic and political aspects of aging.

Chapter 15 first examines generational differences in economic opportunity over the life course. Next, the chapter describes various proposals for reforming the Social Security system and evaluates the advantages and disadvantages of each option. In the last portion of the chapter, trends in private sources of income are discussed. There is great inequality among the aged in the distribution of income and wealth.

Chapter 16 examines the social and political processes that create gender inequality in old age. It also describes the racial and ethnic characteristics of the elderly population in the United States. Finally, the chapter examines how being a minority influences access to income, wealth, and health care. Issues concerning the aged are a central part of public debates.

Chapter 17 presents research on the politics *of* the aged and politics *about* the aged. First, it examines the various methods older people use to express their political preferences and asks whether the aged are really a powerful political force. The chapter also considers in some detail the debates about generational equity and the entitlement crisis and evaluates the accuracy of how the issues associated with aging are portrayed.

Chapter 15

The Economics of Aging

Deborah Perotta lost her all her retirement savings in the collapse of the Enron Corporation.

Looking Ahead

1. How has the economic status of the aged changed over recent decades?
2. What is the present status of the Social Security system, and what is its future?
3. What measures might be taken to ensure the viability of the Social Security system for future generations?
4. What is the difference between a defined benefit plan and a defined contribution plan?
5. How do personal savings contribute to the support of the aged?

I t's been called the largest corporate fraud in the nation's history: the collapse of Enron Corporation, the leading energy trading firm, in the midst of accounting misdeeds and charges of political influence peddling. As the scandal gradually unfolded on the nightly news, the public was outraged to learn that Enron executives had issued false financial statements, ordered the shredding of company documents, and made millions unloading company stock at high prices while preventing Enron employees from selling their shares even as prices spiraled downward. The big losers were Enron's older employees who had most of their life savings in company stock.

As the stock market plummeted, the misery spread. Jim and Jan Pringle had decided to retire in January 2000. After making more than $2 million selling their large advertising agency in Atlanta, they put all their savings into the stock market and began building their dream house on the ocean. When the stock market took a nosedive in the wake of the Enron scandal, the Pringles lost more than 75 percent of their investment. Their only choice was to mortgage their house and go back to

357

work, one of many couples forced to postpone retirement (Zernike, 2002).

How important is it to save for retirement? What is the best strategy for preserving those savings? This chapter provides an introduction to the key economic issues facing older people.

In the first section, we discuss some basic principles of economics and touch on their significance for policies concerning the elderly. We then place the present public debate in a historical context. We examine generational differences in economic well-being over the life course and describe the forces that have wrought significant social change. In the third section of the chapter, we examine proposals for restructuring Social Security in the context of the broader framework of the organization of the welfare state.

Social Security restructuring, should it occur, will not take place in a vacuum. Any decreased role for the public sector in the provision of income support in retirement ultimately means an expanded role for the private sector. In this chapter, we analyze the role of the private sector in providing retirement income and discuss trends in access to benefits. Finally, the chapter examines rates of savings by individuals and considers whether younger generations are preparing adequately for their own retirement.

AGING POLICY AND THE ECONOMY

Although political, social, cultural, and philosophical issues often make the evening news, many of the most compelling problems of the day are primarily economic. Economic problems arise because of the scarcity of available resources. A society's resources consist of gifts of nature such as land, forests, and minerals; human resources, both mental and physical; and resources made by humans, including tools, machinery, and buildings. These resources are used to produce commodities, which can be divided into tangible goods, such as cars or shoes, and services, such as health care and haircuts. Production is the act of making goods and services; consumption is the use of goods and services to satisfy wants and needs.

Because resources are scarce—that is, they are limited in quantity—all societies must decide what to produce and how to divide the output among

their members. One of the ways in which the economy of the United States is different from that of China or Sweden is in the amount of influence the government has over such choices. Some governments, such as ours, lean toward a policy of minimal interference in the economy. Others, such as those in China and to a lesser extent Sweden, exert greater control. The central decision that policymakers and the public must make is determining what government should do and what should be left to the private sector. Some people contend that the United States spends too little for such valuable commodities as health care and education while the economy is saturated with privately produced goods like cars and electric can openers (Eisner, 1994). Others charge that the government does badly what the private sector could do better (Peterson, 1987).

The primary policy tools of government are the power to tax and the power to spend. The main purpose of taxes is to raise money to finance government expenditures on, for instance, the environment, public highways, defense, and Social Security. But taxes have other effects. By taking more from one group than from others, taxes can change the distribution of income. For example, progressive income taxes that tax the rich more heavily than the poor redistribute income across social classes. Payroll taxes, which finance Social Security and Medicare, take income from workers to pay for benefits for retirees. Thus, they redistribute income across generations.

Many of the economic debates now occupying center stage focus on issues regarding how best to distribute societal resources across generations. In the following section, we examine generational differences in economic opportunity.

GENERATIONAL DIFFERENCES IN INCOME AND WEALTH

Why has the economic status of the aged improved? Will the aged be even better off in the future? A simple answer to these questions is that the aged have fared well under the economic conditions of the past quarter century and are likely to do even better. Yet vast disparities among the aged as a group remain.

Figure 15-1

Median Income of People 65 or Older by Marital Status, 1962 and 2001 (in 2001 dollars).

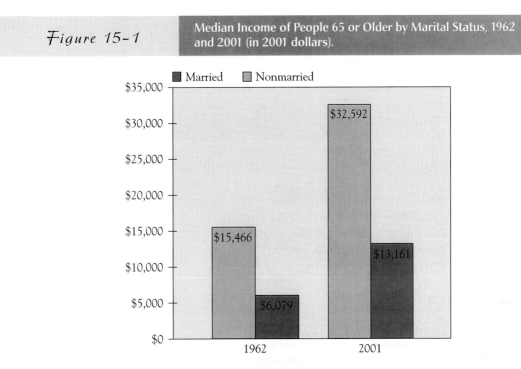

Source: Social Security Administration (2001).

The Improving Economic Status of the Aged

Figure 15–1 compares the median income of married couples and single people in 1962 and 2001. In both years, married couples had significantly higher household income than unmarried individuals. Regardless of their marital status, older people have experienced an increase in income of more than 95 percent in the past few decades, even after adjusting for inflation. The aged of today also have more diverse sources of income compared to the aged of the 1960s. As Figure 15–2 shows, the proportion of older people who receive income from assets grew from a little over one-half in 1962 to 58 percent by 2001. Over the same 40-year period, receipt of private pensions more than tripled while income from earnings shrank. More people can now support themselves in old age without working. What is responsible for these improvements in the economic well-being of the aged?

Today's Older Generation

One answer is that the elderly of today have benefited from the rising tide of prosperity in the post–World War II era. From 1945 to 1973, the average standard of living improved substantially, even for those with little education. Median family income increased by 42 percent between 1949 and 1959 and by 38 percent between 1959 and 1969 (Levy, 1988). The smaller number of people of this generation meant that, in a thriving economy, jobs were plentiful (Easterlin, Schaeffer, and Macunovich, 1993). Economic prosperity also was associated with family stability. The cohort that reached adulthood in the 1950s had high marriage rates, high birth rates, and low divorce rates. More children grew up in two-parent families than at any other time in American history (Cherlin and Furstenberg, 1988). Each year since 1970, those turning 65 have had higher levels of education, more stable job histories, and higher preretirement

Figure 15-2   Source of Income for the Aged, 1962 and 2001.

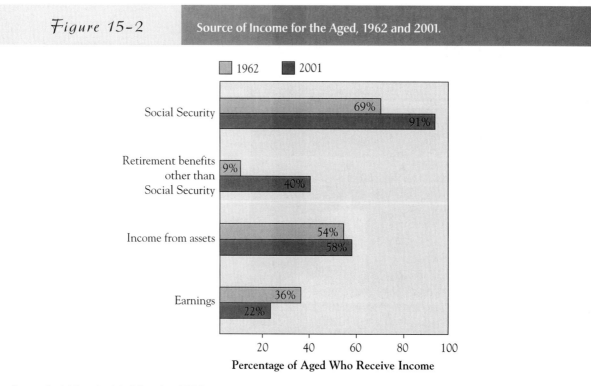

Source: Social Security Administration (2001).

incomes (Quinn and Smeeding, 1993). Thus, as this cohort has grown old, it has benefited from a lifetime of improving opportunity, stable family life, and upward mobility.

Improvements in Social Security benefits during this period have also contributed to the increased economic well-being of the aged. Between 1969 and 1972, benefits rose significantly and were indexed to keep pace with inflation automatically. As the cost of living went up, so did Social Security payments. As a result of improved living standards and Social Security benefits, the postretirement decline in income that accompanied old age in the past has been reduced substantially.

The benefits of age are even clearer in regard to wealth. Wealth is usually measured by net worth. **Median net worth** is the total value of all assets (e.g., a house, other property, personal savings) minus any debts. Net worth increases steadily with

age. For 1993 the median net worth of households of people younger than 35 was $5,786; it was $86,324 for those 65 and older.

Yet net worth is a deceptive measure of the ageds' well-being. The fact is, most of the ageds' net worth is in their homes. By the time most people reach 65, they own their homes outright or have only a small amount left to pay on their mortgages. If home equity is excluded from net worth calculations, the figure drops significantly. Among the least affluent elderly—those in the bottom fifth of the income distribution—median net worth in 1993, including a home, was $30,500. But if the value of the home is excluded from this figure, median net worth was less than $3,000 (U.S. Bureau of the Census, 1993b). Not counting a home, the typical older American has very few resources, enough to get by for only about six months (Smith, 1997).

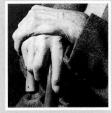

Diversity in the Aging Experience

INCOME INEQUALITY IN LATER LIFE

Although the aged as a group are relatively well-off financially, there is a great disparity between the poorest and the most affluent. Median income in 2001 for people aged 65 and older was $18,965, but 21 percent had incomes below $10,000 and 15 percent had incomes above $50,000 (see Figure 15–3). Some of the income inequality in later life is the cumulative effect of a lifetime of low wages (Social Security Administration, 2003). People who are poor in their younger years are likely to be poor in old age. Sometimes adverse life events such as widowhood or a prolonged illness cause a precipitous drop in income.

What most separates the low-income elderly from the more affluent is assets. For the majority of Americans, assets are the second most important source of income after Social Security (Choudhury, 2001–02). Assets include savings accounts, certificates of deposit, stocks, bonds, individual retirement accounts, such as 401(k)s, and rental property. People who have asset income have the highest incomes; those with no asset income are concentrated in the lowest income group. Stock assets are the most highly skewed. The top 1 percent of people own almost 50 percent of the wealth from stocks.

How do some people accumulate substantial assets in old age? Some people inherit assets from their parents; others save during their working years. Yet people who save at the same rate can still end up with different assets in later life, depending on the investment choices they make. People who have only a small amount to invest prefer relatively safe asserts such as checking accounts or real estate; wealthier households prefer stocks. Although stocks are riskier investments, they provide higher yields over the long term. Thus, income inequality in old age is a result of opportunities people have and of choices they make along the way.

What Do You Think?

1. When do you plan to start saving for retirement?
2. What assets do you currently have? Do you think you will inherit any assets before you retire?

Finally, despite impressive gains in income and wealth, it is important to recognize that the gains have been unevenly distributed across the aged population. The "Diversity in the Aging Experience" feature describes some of the sources of income inequality in later life.

The Aging of the Baby Boomers

Members of the baby boom cohort have had fewer opportunities than their parents did. One reason is sheer competition. As the baby boomers reached working age, the increase in the supply of young

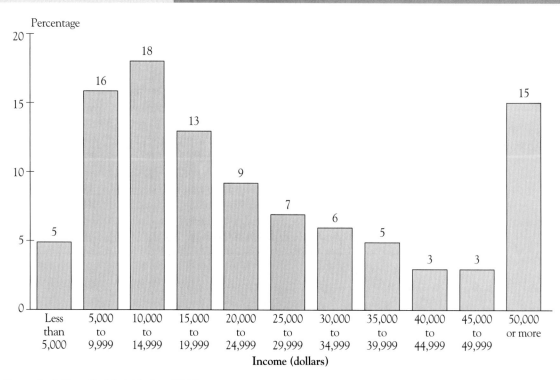

Figure 15-3   Income Inequality in Later Life.

Source: Social Security Administration (2003).

workers had a marked negative effect on wages, rates of employment, and prospects for upward job mobility (Easterlin et al., 1993). Another factor is the economy, which fared poorly from the 1970s until the mid-1990s, when it entered a renewed period of growth. Between 1973 and 1991, while the purchasing power of the aged increased, median family income grew a modest $1,165, and wages stagnated. In fact, among men with a high school education or less, real wages fell 13 percent between 1979 and 1989 (Mishel and Bernstein, 1993).

As a generation, the boomers have made decisions that have mitigated to some degree the adverse effects of these trends. They have married later than their parents, waited longer to have children, and had fewer children. Although there has

been a loss in earning power among men, the impact of this has been offset by the increased labor force participation of married women, which rose continuously between 1968 and 1990, both in the percentage of women who work and in the average number of weeks worked per year (Karoly, 1994). By 1990, more than 60 percent of all families had two earners. The incomes of women became crucial to family security, as the share of family income represented by the wife's earnings rose (Cancian, Danziger, and Gottschalk, 1994). And because female baby boomers on average have substantially higher earnings than their mothers, overall this generation is doing as well as or better than their parents were at the same age (Easterlin et al., 1993).

The baby boomers also have benefited from the considerable amount of sharing that occurs between generations. Middle-aged and elderly parents help their children and grandchildren by loaning money or giving outright gifts and by sharing their homes. These intergenerational transfers have buffered the effect of declining economic opportunity on young families (Easterlin, Macunovich, and Crimmins, 1994).

Although social scientists at one time predicted that the baby boomers would fare poorly in old age, the decisions they have made to delay marriage, have fewer children, and establish households with two earners bode well for the future. Demographers now predict that boomers will enter retirement with more savings, better pension coverage, and greater prospects for inheriting wealth than any generation in the past.

Despite these favorable trends, the picture isn't entirely rosy. A higher divorce rate and an increase in the number of children born out of wedlock created more single-parent households. Because most single-parent families depend on the earning power of women, they are at greater risk of poverty. In 1996, 27.3 percent of households headed by white females, 50.9 percent of those headed by Hispanic females, and 43.7 percent of those headed by black females had incomes below the poverty level (U.S. Bureau of Census, 1993b). As the number of two-parent households has declined, poverty has become decoupled from stages in the life course and more closely associated with household type. The highest poverty rates are found among single women, whether they are 25 or 75. We discuss the causes of poverty among older women in Chapter 16.

RESTRUCTURING THE WELFARE STATE

In Chapter 11, we described three types of social welfare programs, *social assistance, social insurance,* and *fiscal welfare,* each with its own set of rules regarding who pays for the benefit, who is eligible to receive it, and how much beneficiaries receive. Social assistance provides benefits for the poor. People who apply for benefits are subject to a means test, which deems all but the most destitute ineligible for assistance. Social insurance is distinguished from social assistance in that workers contribute to a common pool, which gives them an earned right to benefits. Finally, fiscal welfare provides indirect payments to individuals through the tax system. Debates about Social Security reform are actually about the future structure of the American welfare state—specifically, about the distribution of benefits among those three types of programs.

The Status of Social Security

Social Security has worked remarkably well since 1935 (see Chapter 11). Benefits have always been delivered on time, automatic cost-of-living increases have protected benefits against inflation, and the program has been administered very efficiently. In fact, administrative costs are only about 1 percent of benefits (Schulz, 1995). In broader terms, the program has removed large numbers of older people from poverty and allowed them to live fuller lives in retirement than had formerly been the case. Over its more than 60-year history, Social Security has proved to be the most successful program of the American welfare state.

Because of this exceptional record, public support for Social Security is strong. A 1986 survey by Cook and Barrett (1992) found that 96.7 percent of respondents favored maintaining or increasing Social Security benefits. Similarly, 84 percent of the respondents to a 1994 poll by the American Association of Retired Persons said Social Security benefits were "very important," and 88 percent opposed cutting benefits to reduce the federal deficit (American Association of Retired Persons, 1994b).

Yet in recent years, confidence in Social Security has been declining. In 1993, only 30 percent of the American public felt confident that Social Security benefits would be paid throughout their retirement. Lack of confidence is especially prevalent among young people (Marmor et al., 1990; Friedland, 1994). Two-thirds of Americans aged 25 to 34 believe they will not receive their Social Security benefits when they reach retirement age. The same proportion doubts that the program will even be there when they retire (Reno and Friedland, 1996).

Underlying these fears are concerns about charges that Social Security has increased the federal deficit and that the trust fund will be broke in the future (see Chapter 17) (Marmor, Cook, and Scher, 1997). Let us first examine the relationship of Social Security to the federal budget and then discuss the advantages and disadvantages of various proposals for reforming Social Security.

Social Security and the federal budget   To understand the relationship of Social Security to the federal budget, one must first understand how the trust fund operates. The payroll taxes that fund Social Security benefits are deposited into the government's general treasury, and a corresponding amount of special Treasury bonds are issued to the trust fund (Koitz, 1996a). Benefits are then paid out of the general treasury with corresponding reductions made in the securities held by the trust fund. Thus, the fund's income and outgo are ledger entries; no money actually goes in or out of the fund. Income is recorded by posting federal securities to it, outgo by deleting securities. The trust fund securities represent spending authority for the programs involved, a promise of future funding (Koitz, Falk, and Winters, 1990).

The future of the trust fund   At the present time there is more credit in the trust fund than is required for payment of Social Security benefits. But by 2025 revenue coming into the trust fund will fall below the level of benefits being paid out, and by 2037 the trust fund will be depleted (Social Security Advisory Board, 2001). That means there will not be enough money coming in from payroll taxes to pay all benefits promised.

Several social changes have contributed to the problem. One is the aging of the baby boom generation. Another is that population growth slowed significantly after 1960 as women began having fewer children. A third is that people are living longer in old age. Coupling declining fertility with increased life expectancy means that as the baby boomers begin to retire, a smaller generation of workers will pay for the benefits of a larger number of retirees. In 1960 there were five workers for every single retiree. By 2025 that ratio will fall to 2.2 (see Figure 15–4). The challenge facing policy-makers is determining how to solve the problem. The core issue is whether the solution will preserve the basic framework of Social Security as a program of social insurance or whether the American welfare state will shift the balance toward more social assistance or fiscal welfare.

In the following section, we evaluate the arguments for and against proposals for Social Security reform in the context of how they would alter the structure of the American welfare state. These arguments are summarized in Table 15–1.

Restoring the Trust Fund

As we saw in Chapter 11, Social Security is based on the principle that everyone who has contributed to Social Security in his or her working years has a right to receive benefits in retirement. Generally speaking, solutions that preserve this principle fall into three categories: raising the retirement age, cutting benefits, and increasing revenues.

Raising the retirement age   When Social Security was enacted in 1935, the age of eligibility for benefits, the **normal retirement age,** was set at 65, establishing for the first time a quasi-legal national definition of old age. In 1962, when unemployment was high, amendments to the Social Security Act allowed workers to retire at age 62 but with a 20 percent reduction in benefits (see Chapter 12). The intent of setting the **early retirement age** at 62 was to encourage retirement and in so doing to create job opportunities for younger workers (Kingson and Berkowitz, 1993).

Figure 15–5 illustrates the effect Social Security benefits have had on the labor force participation of men and women. For both men and women there is a sharp decline at age 62 and 65, the ages of eligibility for early and normal Social Security benefits. For men, labor force participation rates drop by 12 points at age 62 and 10 points at 65; for women, they drop by 9 and 7 points, respectively. Clearly, the financial incentives in Social Security influence retirement behavior (Quadagno and Quinn, 1996).

Now, given the projected financing troubles of Social Security, the wisdom of encouraging workers

Figure 15-4	**Number of Workers per Social Security Beneficiary, 1960–2075 (projected).**

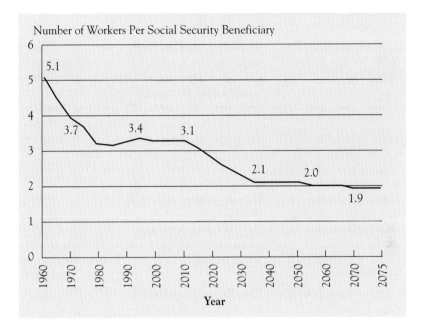

Number of Workers Per Social Security Beneficiary

Source: Social Security Advisory Board (2001).

to retire at 62 is being questioned, and proposals abound for encouraging workers to delay retirement. One way to do so would be to raise the normal retirement age, which has already been raised from 65 to 67 for people retiring in the twenty-first century. Presently, the early retirement age remains 62, but future early retirees will see their benefits cut by 30 percent, not 20 percent. At issue is whether the retirement age should be raised even higher. One proposal would raise the normal retirement age to 70. Another would link the normal retirement age to increases in life expectancy (Myers, 1991). A third proposal would raise the early retirement age from 62 to 65.

The key issue in this proposal is, Who will feel the effect the most? Raising the early retirement age would have a disproportionate impact on racial and ethnic minorities. In general, middle-aged African Americans and Hispanics are in poorer health than middle-aged whites; the gap between the two groups widens with age. Much of the difference in labor force participation among these groups can be explained by these racial and ethnic differences in health (see Chapter 12) (Wray, 1996). Members of minoritys groups are more likely than whites to hold physically demanding jobs, in which poor health can prevent a person from working (Bound, Schoenbaum, and Waidmann, 1996). Thus, while raising the early retirement age might help to resolve the budget problem facing the Social Security Administration, it could worsen racial and ethnic inequality among older Americans.

There are a number of plausible arguments for raising the normal retirement age. When the Social Security Act was passed in 1935, average life expectancy was only 61. By 2000 it had increased to 77. Given that older people today are more affluent, healthier, and better educated than their counterparts for whom the Social Security system was designed, why shouldn't they work longer?

Table 15-1	Options for Social Security Reform		
Issue	**Options**	**Pros**	**Cons**
Restoring the trust fund	Raise the age for full Social Security benefits from 67 to 70.	People today are in better health and are living longer than when Social Security was enacted. Why shouldn't they work longer?	Some older people won't find jobs because of age discrimination. Job competition might increase, causing wages for younger workers to decline. Older minorities would be most affected by any raise in the retirement age since they are most likely to retire early.
	Cut Social Security benefits by decreasing what higher earners receive, or make an across-the-board cut for all retirees.	Cutting benefits would help restore the trust fund's long-range solvency without undermining confidence in Social Security.	High earners already receive a low return on their payroll taxes. The poorest elderly would be most severely affected by any across-the-board cut in benefits.
	Increase revenues by raising payroll taxes.	Payroll taxes in the United States are low relative to other countries. Americans can afford a small hike in the payroll tax.	The cost of raising the payroll tax will fall most heavily on younger workers. Most Americans are opposed to any type of tax increase.
Means testing	Make the affluent elderly ineligible for Social Security benefits.	The standard of living has increased for many older people. People who have high income should not receive resources from the government.	Public support for Social Security might decline if people who had made contributions all their working lives found they were ineligible for benefits when they retired. Means testing also might reduce the incentive to save for old age.
Privatization	Provide retirees a small basic benefit with most retirement income coming from individual contributions to a personal security account.	Workers might receive a better rate of return on their investment than what they receive from making contributions to Social Security.	Inequality in old age would rise because low income workers would have less to invest. Some people might invest poorly and lose all their retirement savings.

One problem is that people who are 65 or older may be unable to find employment. Although age discrimination is illegal, it has not been eliminated. A large segment of today's older workforce (those aged 55 or older) is concentrated in heavy manufacturing, the sector of the economy that has been in decline for more than three decades. In industries such as steel and automobiles, early retirement

Figure 15-5   **Labor Force Participation Rates, by Sex and Age, 2000.**

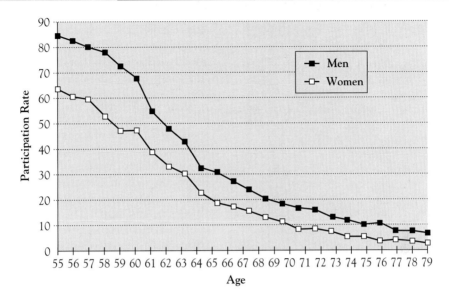

Source: Social Security Advisory Board (2001).

has become a painless way for employers to get rid of older workers (see Chapter 12). Even white-collar workers with college degrees have experienced declining job security.

Another consequence of raising the retirement age is increased competition for jobs among workers of all ages. If the labor market is flooded with older workers looking for jobs, there will be fewer jobs for younger workers. Wages could decline as they did when the baby boom cohort hit the job market. Raising the retirement age won't solve the problem if the unemployment and welfare rolls increase.

Despite these pitfalls, the United States is not alone in thinking about raising the retirement age. Other nations facing similar problems of aging populations and rising public budgets have chosen this solution. Until reforms were passed in 1998, Hungary allowed men to retire with full benefits at age 60, and women to retire at age 55. Now, both men and women must wait until age 62 to receive their full benefits (Global Aging Report, 1998b). Other countries that have raised the retirement age are Argentina, Colombia, Germany, Japan,

New Zealand, Portugal, Sweden, Turkey, and the United Kingdom. Unlike in the United States, however, the existing retirement age was under 65 in these countries (Kollman, 1995). In most countries it has been raised only to 62. Only in Norway is the present age of eligibility for public pensions set at 67 (Wheeler and Kearney, 1996). And it's important to recognize that raising the retirement age is only a partial solution to the predicted financing shortfall in Social Security, one option in a total package of changes.

Reducing benefits   Another option for eliminating the long-term deficit in the Social Security trust fund is to reduce benefits. Benefit reductions can take a variety of forms. (Of course, raising the retirement age is a benefit reduction since people will receive benefits for fewer years, but this option is usually not discussed in these terms.) One way to reduce benefits is to tinker with the formula for calculating what people receive. This can be done by lengthening the years of work needed for full benefits or by decreasing what high earners get back.

Some people argue that the age of eligibility for Social Security benefits should be raised because the elderly of today are healthier and live longer than the elderly of the past.

Many countries have adjusted their benefit calculations. France is gradually reducing benefits in this way; so are Italy, the United Kingdom, Germany, and Sweden (Kollman, 1995).

Another way to reduce benefits is to decouple benefit increases from cost-of-living increases. That way benefits stay the same but gradually are worth less because of inflation. Some countries in Latin American and Eastern Europe have taken this approach (Kollman, 1995).

The problem with any across-the-board reduction in Social Security benefits is that the effects will be felt most by those who can least afford them. That's because Social Security is so much more important to low-income elderly than it is to higher-income elderly. Older people with the lowest income depend on Social Security for 81.2 percent of their income, whereas the most affluent receive only 22.7 percent of their income from Social Security. A fair proposal for benefit reductions should guarantee that the impact on the most disadvantaged be minimized.

Increasing revenues To keep the trust fund solvent, the United States could increase the present payroll tax rate of 15.2 percent (Myers, 1996). Payroll taxes in most European countries already are much higher than that. Figure 15–6 illustrates payroll tax rates in 22 nations; they range from a high of nearly 35 percent in Portugal to less than 10 percent in Canada. The United States is fifth from the bottom at 15.2 percent. (Organization for Economic Cooperation and Development, 1988b). Not only is this a low payroll tax rate by international standards, but these funds also pay for Medicare.

A problem with raising payroll taxes is that the cost will fall most heavily on young workers who already pay more in payroll taxes than they do in income taxes. Any tax increase is likely to be perceived as unfair if it hits hardest those who can least afford it. And public opinion in the United States is against raising taxes of any type. Thus, a solution based on raising payroll taxes is likely to meet with public resistance.

Means Testing

The passage of the Social Security Act in 1935 represented a rejection of the social assistance philosophy and an acceptance of the idea that the nation's primary program of retirement income should be based on the principle of social insurance (Kingson and Schulz, 1997). At that time, means-tested social assistance programs were intentionally harsh and punitive to discourage the poor from applying for benefits and to encourage them to work. In the means-tested programs that did exist, eligibility levels were set very low, so only the very poor qualified for benefits.

The most recent proposals for means testing Social Security differ from traditional social

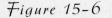

| Figure 15-6 | Combined Employer/Employee Payroll Tax in OECD Countries, 1995. |

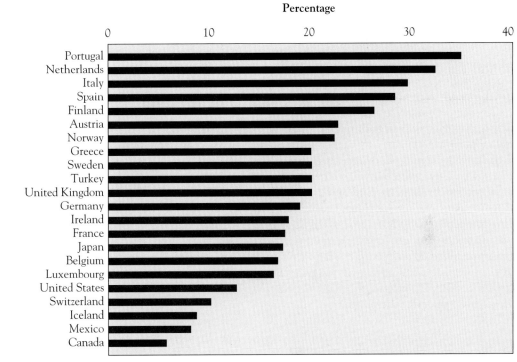

Source: Social Security Administration (1995c).

assistance approaches in two important respects. Traditional social assistance programs sought to restrict benefits to the poor, and financial eligibility was determined by a local social welfare agency. The new *affluence test*, as it is called, would reduce benefits only to higher-income individuals and would be administered through the tax system instead of a welfare bureaucracy (Peterson, 1993).

The idea of reducing the benefits of the high-income elderly appeals to many Americans. One factor contributing to the change in public opinion is the remarkable improvement in the economic well-being of older people since 1960, as noted earlier. Another is the slow growth in living standards for most working Americans.

In the past, critics were able to mobilize some formidable arguments against means testing. They contended that if Social Security was means tested, it would be perceived as welfare and public support would unravel (Kingson, 1994). But such arguments hold less weight when most older Americans would remain eligible for benefits and eligibility for benefits would be administered through the tax system. No one would experience the degrading scrutiny of the welfare bureaucracy.

Should the United States adopt means testing? One major obstacle is that means testing would discourage saving. People who had saved a significant amount of money during their working years would be penalized in old age by being denied benefits or deemed eligible for only modest benefits. Consider what would happen to two individuals who worked for the same company and earned the same salary: Sandy was a big spender. He purchased a large house in a fancy neighborhood, drove a Mercedes, sent his children to private schools, and vacationed in Europe. His buddy, Bernie, by contrast, owned a modest home, drove a Ford Fiesta, sent his children to neighborhood schools, and visited his parents on most of his vacations. Because Bernie lived so modestly, he was able to save a substantial portion of his salary, which he invested in rental property. If Social Security was means tested, Bernie would pay a high price for his lifelong frugality. His savings and income from the rental property would make him ineligible for Social Security, whereas Sandy, the big spender, would have no savings and investments and thus remain eligible for benefits. Such incentives are likely to produce a system fraught with fraud, with nearly everyone finding a way to participate.

Means testing has also been criticized on the grounds that it "would undermine the political support, the legitimacy, and ultimately the financing of Social Security" (Kingson, 1994:740). Critics contend that support for the program would dwindle if workers who had made contributions for 20 or 30 years found they were ineligible for benefits when they retired (Kingson and Schulz, 1997).

The United States can learn much from the experience of Australia, one of the few developed nations that does not have a national social insurance program linked to prior employment (Shaver, 1991). In Australia the means-tested Age Pension program provides the bulk of public retirement income. Eligibility for the Age Pension is based on age, residency, and financial need. Because the level of the means test is set quite high, presently nearly 70 percent of older Australians are eligible for benefits, which are approximately one-fourth of average national wages (Wheeler and Kearney, 1996).

The Australian system has been criticized for being overly complex, unfair, and inefficient. Because both income and assets (i.e., an individual's wealth) are tested in determining eligibility for benefits, complex evaluations of each individual's application for benefits must be made (Shaver, 1991).

The program began in 1983, and each year since then the means-test criteria have been tightened. As a result, each year fewer people are eligible for benefits. That is what could happen should the United States implement a means test.

The greatest risk of means testing, and one confirmed by the Australian experience, is that over time there would be two highly unequal classes of retirees, one that receives a low, means tested benefit and another that receives income primarily from private sources.

Privatization

Privatization of Social Security can be accomplished in many ways, but the basic idea is that individuals should become more responsible for their own retirement income, and the government less so. Thus privatization would shift some of the responsibility for old-age security from the Social Security Administration to individual Americans. Numerous proposals have been made to create personal retirement accounts that would replace or supplement Social Security benefits to future recipients. Some proposals would allow workers to accumulate assets directly, through their own accounts. Others would be designed to soften the impact of cuts in Social Security benefits that may be needed to restore the system's long-range solvency. Much of the debate over these plans is fueled by the belief that accounts that are invested in the private sector are likely to exceed the value of future Social Security benefits (Koitz, 2000). "An Issue for Public Policy" examines the pros and cons of privatizing Social Security.

One country that already has a privatization program in place is Chile, which replaced its social security system with a mandatory savings scheme in 1982. Since then, other Latin American countries, including Argentina, Colombia, Mexico, and Peru, have begun to replace or supplement their public pensions with Chilean-type systems (Kollman, 1995). How well has this system worked in Chile?

Under Chile's mandatory savings scheme, workers must place 10 percent of their monthly earnings in a private pension fund selected from among funds authorized by the government (Bosworth, Dornbusch, and Laban, 1994). Citizens are allowed to transfer their private accounts from one fund to another.

An Issue for Public Policy

EVALUATING PRIVATIZATION PROPOSALS

*W*ould workers get a better "rate of return" on personal retirement accounts than they receive from Social Security? While the stock market has done well in recent years, such has not always been the case. From 1975 to 1980 rates of return were actually negative at 22.0 percent. Critics fear that if Social Security were privatized, a stock market plunge could leave retirees with little income in their old age. Another risk of privatization is that of increased inequality. The current Social Security program pays a better replacement rate to low-income workers than to high-income workers. A privatized system would have no income redistribution built into it. Low-income workers would have less to invest than high-income workers so they would end up with less money in old age even if they made the same investment decisions as wealthier workers. More likely, though, low-income workers would not make the same investment decisions, because they would have less access than others to skilled financial planners, stock brokers, and other investment advisors. Thus, they could lose all their money through bad investments. Even equal savers could end up with very different benefits, depending on when they retired or on how well their investments performed (Quadagno 1999). Finally, there is the risk of a life crisis. Though policymakers hope that workers would save their investment accounts for retirement, some might need to withdraw their savings in the event of an emergency such as a sudden job loss or failing health.

Privatization is at best a long-term approach to strengthening the Social Security program. Even in the most optimistic scenario, baby boomers would not have enough time to build up large personal accounts relative to their Social Security benefits. But private accounts could be helpful to people who retire after 2030, since they would have several decades to build them. Workers who retired in 2050 could accrue substantial savings (Koitz, 2000).

What Do You Think?

1. Which of the potential dangers of privatization of the Social Security system strikes you as the most serious? Why?
2. On balance, do you favor privatization of the Social Security system? Explain your reasoning.

The amount of a person's pension at retirement is based on the value of the contributions made plus whatever earnings the fund has accumulated over the years. However, the Chilean government guarantees that no benefit will be lower than 85 percent of the current minimum wage. It also guarantees a minimum rate of return on contributions, so that even a foolish investor cannot lose everything.

To protect workers from making unwise investments, the Chilean government has imposed strict regulations on companies that manage pension funds. If a fund does not maintain a minimum return on investments, managers must make up the difference from a reserve fund. If the reserve fund goes bankrupt, the government will make up whatever individual investors lost. Since the program began operating, the government has liquidated at least one fund (Kollman, 1995).

How well is the Chilean privatization program working? On the positive side, the first pensions paid out under the plan were at least 50 percent higher than they would have been under the old system. The Chilean economy has grown 3 to 5 percent annually, and personal savings have tripled. On the darker side, one survey found that 60 percent of the population has little confidence in the new system. Indeed, nearly half of all Chilean workers do not pay into the supposedly compulsory scheme. Another problem is that workers switch funds frequently, wasting too much money on sales commissions. And recently some funds have actually had negative returns (Global Aging Report, 1998c). Critics worry that a downturn in the Chilean economy could bankrupt many funds, forcing the government to bail them and their pensioners out.

After Chile adopted its social security system, several other Latin American countries and certain of the countries in central and Eastern Europe implemented similar reforms. "Aging around the World" describes the reforms in the former communist countries and compares them to the Latin American experience.

PRIVATE SOURCES OF INCOME IN OLD AGE

As we saw earlier, Social Security rarely is the sole source of retirement income. People supplement their Social Security income with employer pensions, private savings, and earnings (see Chapter 12). Some of the problems that have occurred in private pension plans are instructive in evaluating proposals for Social Security reform.

Employer Pensions

Defined benefits   The first employer pensions were mostly **defined benefit** plans. These pensions were first negotiated between workers and employers in heavy industries such as steel and automobile manufacturing and subsequently were extended to workers in other industries (see Chapter 12). Defined benefit plans typically pay monthly benefits to a worker at retirement, with the amount based on years of service and prior earnings (Reno, 1993b).

Not every employee is eligible for a pension: only those who remain with a firm for a minimum number of years. The length of time required is specified in the company's **vesting rules.** For example, workers who haven't been with a company at least 10 years may lose all rights to a pension if they leave the firm before reaching retirement age. The original purpose of vesting rules was to reduce labor turnover and encourage worker loyalty to the firm (Clark and McDermed, 1990). Thus, defined benefit pensions served both worker and employer. They provided the worker a guaranteed income in retirement, and they provided employers a stable workforce and a humane way to ease older workers out of that force.

Although defined benefit plans have allowed many workers to retire with a guaranteed income, there are a number of problems with this type of pension. One problem is access. Many workers are employed in jobs that do not have pensions, especially women and Hispanics. Another problem is related to the vesting rules. In the past, employers were free to establish lengthy periods of service, sometimes as long as 30 years, before workers were vested. Workers who lost their jobs or took other jobs lost all pension credits. A third problem is that many defined benefit plans are not indexed to inflation. As the value of the pension declines, people become poorer with advancing age.

The biggest problem, however, is with the funds themselves. In some cases, workers have lost benefits because company pension funds were insufficient to cover those eligible to receive them. This may have occurred because of bad planning, because the funds were invested poorly, or because of

Aging around the World

SOCIAL SECURITY IN CENTRAL AND EASTERN EUROPE

*I*n 1989 the communist governments of central and eastern Europe nations fell. Hungary, Poland, Bulgaria, Croatia, and other countries suddenly were faced with the need to make a transition from the planned economy of a communist state to a free market. Under communist regimes the state provided all of the financing for the social security system and nearly all workers were covered because they worked either in government-owned industries or on collective farms. People received benefits based on the number of years they were employed, not on how much money they paid into the system.

The transition to a market economy ended government ownership of businesses and farms. Some of these businesses became large, private firms. Others were broken up into smaller firms. Many individuals who had formerly been employed by the government became self-employed. A new Social Security fund was set up to pay for retirement benefits for employees, but many employers failed to make regular contributions to the fund. To keep the Social Security system solvent, the government raised the retirement age and increased contribution rates. The government also gave workers the option of contributing to individual retirement accounts similar to the Chilean system. Hungary switched to individual accounts in 1998, and Poland in 1999. Bulgaria and Croatia offered individual accounts beginning in 2002. Although older workers who had grown up under communism expected the state to take care of them in retirement, these accounts proved to be quite popular among younger workers.

Social security systems in both Latin American and eastern and central European countries have some common problems. One problem is that administrative costs are high and consume a portion of the funds that could be used to pay benefits. Another problem is that women receive lower benefits than men because they earn less on average. Finally, in many of these countries a large number of people work in an "underground" economy and therefore are not covered by the social security system. They will have no source of income when they reach old age (Kritzer, 2001–02).

What Do You Think?

1. Should the United States adopt a plan like Chile's and require people to contribute to individual retirement accounts?
2. What would be some of the advantages and disadvantages of mandatory individual retirement accounts?

fraud or embezzlement (Schulz, 1996). Another problem has arisen as a result of mergers and takeovers. In some cases, pension plans have been terminated, and workers have lost benefits they thought were secure. Between 1975 and 1989, over 12,000 defined benefit plans were terminated. Workers often ended up with little or nothing. For example, in 1989 when Random House bought out Crown Books, the Crown pension plan was terminated and several long-term Crown employees were fired. Employees who had worked for the company for as long as 16 years received only a lump sum of $4,000. Similarly, in 1986 Exxon terminated its pension plan, paid off employees with a lump sum, and reverted $1.6 billion of the surplus assets to the corporation's treasury (Ghilarducci, 1992).

To curb some of the problems associated with defined benefit pension plans, in 1974 Congress passed the **Employee Retirement Income Security Act (ERISA).** ERISA required companies to establish minimum vesting standards, set more stringent funding requirements, and establish better methods of reporting plan benefits and finances to workers (Schulz, 1995). To further protect workers, Congress also created the **Pension Benefit Guaranty Corporation (PBGC).** If a terminated pension plan has insufficient funds to meet its obligations to the workers, the PBGC assumes the responsibility for paying the benefits owed. The PBGC is financed partly by premiums paid by the plans or the employers who sponsor these plans. Since the PBGC was established, it has assumed responsibility for more than 2,000 pension plans (Schulz, 1996). The premiums pay only part of the cost of the government's responsibility. Citizens' taxes pick up the rest of the tab. Thus, what appears to be a private sector benefit is partly paid for by public tax revenues.

As government regulation and the costs of contributing to the PBGC have risen, companies have been reluctant to establish new defined benefit pension plans. As a result, the percentage of the workforce with defined benefit plans declined from 39 in 1975 to 26 in 1992. In that same period, the percentage of the workforce with defined contribution plans increased from 14 to 37 (Bassett et al., 1996).

Defined contributions   **Defined contribution** plans represent a different contractual arrangement between worker and employer. The employer, the worker and employer, or the worker alone pays a fixed amount into an account that is invested on behalf of the worker. The most common defined contribution plan is called a 401(k) plan. Benefits at retirement are based on the amount that has accumulated in the account, including contributions and any gains or losses from investments, expenses, or forfeitures (Reno, 1993b). Thus, benefits are determined by the level of employer and employee contributions and the results of the worker's investment decisions (Jeweler, 1993; Schmitt, 1993).

One problem with defined contribution plans is that workers may withdraw the funds before retirement. Although there is a tax penalty for early withdrawal, many people still do so when family resources are pinched, as the following example illustrates. Bob Jones, age 47, lost his job as a vice president of a large bank in California. He was unemployed for six months. With his daughter starting college and mortgage payments to make, he withdrew all the funds in his pension plan to pay his family's expenses until he found another job (Quadagno, 1996a). Now he has nothing for retirement.

Another problem with defined contribution plans is that participation is voluntary. Rates of participation among young workers and lower-paid workers are quite low. Table 15–2 shows rates of participation in pension plans by age and earnings level. Among young Americans (aged 30 to 32) who earn low wages (the first earnings quintile) only 15 percent of the women and 19 percent of the men participate in a pension plan. Those Americans who are most likely to participate in a pension plan are high-earning men between the ages of 43 and 57. Participation goes down with both age and earnings.

A third problem with defined contribution plans is that workers sometimes are encouraged or required to place all their contributions into company stock. Should the company fall on hard times, the stock prices will take a beating. Workers may take huge losses and wind up with little retirement savings. For example, Edith Thomson worked for Carter Hawley for 41 years, wrapping gifts in the

| | Table 15-2 | Pension Plan Participation Rates by Age, Earnings, and Gender, 1997 |

	Earnings Quintile				
Age	*First*	*Second*	*Third*	*Fourth*	*Fifth*
Men					
30–32	19%	34%	51%	62%	68%
33–37	28	45	62	72	78
38–42	35	53	69	78	83
43–47	39	57	73	81	86
48–52	42	60	75	83	87
53–57	41	58	74	82	86
58–62	35	53	69	78	83
Women					
30–32	15%	25%	43%	59%	68%
33–37	22	33	53	68	76
38–42	25	38	57	72	80
43–47	28	41	60	75	82
48–52	26	39	58	73	81
53–57	25	37	56	72	79
58–62	22	33	53	69	77

Source: U.S. Bureau of the Census (2000).

company's Emporium department store. In 1991, Carter Hawley went bankrupt. Mrs. Thompson's nest egg plummeted from $84,000 to $8,000 (Henriques and Johnston, 1996). Paul "P. J." Palombo describes what happened to his retirement savings when the stock market took a tumble. Present law provides no protection for people like Mrs. Thompson.

The decline of defined benefit pensions and the rise of defined contribution plans partially reflects a shift in responsibilities from employers to workers, from employers saying "we'll do our part" to "we'll do what we can" (Paine, 1993). It also reflects declining employer paternalism toward workers and increasing responsibility by the individual for his or her own income security. Because defined contribution plans place more of the decision making and risk on the individual, workers increasingly must take active roles in determining their financial future (Marks, 1994). Yet sometimes those decisions are out of their control.

Personal Savings

Private savings are the third leg of a three-legged stool of income in retirement. People are encouraged to save for retirement because of tax rules that allow them to put money into special retirement accounts. One type of account, called an **Individual Retirement Account (IRA),** allows certain groups of workers and their spouses to contribute a yearly amount without paying taxes on the income or the earnings. Employers may also set up voluntary savings plans for workers (Schulz, 1996). In other cases, people simply save by investing in the stock market, bonds, or real estate.

Many Americans recognize that they need to save for retirement, and two-thirds of all current workers are confident that they will have sufficient income for retirement. Yet of those who are confident, 30 percent have saved nothing to date, and 60 percent have not attempted to calculate what

The Risk of Defined Contribution Plans

Paul "P. J." Palombo will be 62 next month. A long-distance truck driver for Kimball International, he began contributing to a 401 (k) plan in 1982. When he switched jobs, he rolled the money into an individual retirement account and now continues to contribute yearly. "I got in when the getting was good, and it grew from zero to almost $250,000. I said, 'This is great! I can retire at 55.'" When the stock market took a downturn in 2001, it ravaged his portfolio. "I've lost close to $50,000 this year alone. I've got thousands of shares of mutual funds, and if I sell now, I've lost it all." Now Mr. Palombo, who is single, isn't sure when he can retire. He jokingly says he'll have to work until he's 137 years old: "Then I'll have to supplement my retirement by flipping burgers at some interplanetary burger joint 37 light years from the planet, and I'll still be quite poor."

Source: Dugas, 2002.

they will need to fund a comfortable lifestyle (Employee Benefit Research Institute, 1995). Are most workers unrealistically optimistic?

The answer is *yes*. And younger workers are especially unrealistic. Among workers aged 35 to 44 who said they were very confident they would have enough money for retirement, the average expected age of retirement was 57. These same workers won't be eligible to receive full Social Security benefits until age 67 (Employee Benefit Research Institute, 1995).

The advantages of saving early are substantial. Consider the experiences of three colleagues, Mary, Joe, and Rita, who met at their 30-year college reunion. All three had graduated from the same college and taught in the same school district. When Mary was 30, she began saving through her employer's pension plan. By investing $3,000 a year for 25 years, at age 55 she had a nest egg of $236,863. Joe didn't start saving for his retirement until he was 40. His contribution of $3,000 a year for 15 years had grown to $87,973. Rita, whose divorce made her a single mother with three children to raise, wasn't able to begin saving for retirement until she was 50. At 55 her yearly savings of $3,000 added up to only $19,008 (Valic, 1996).

Part of the problem of planning for retirement savings is that no one can predict the future. Many uncertainties exist. Not knowing how long you will live makes it difficult to determine how much money you will need for retirement. Another uncertainty is created by the labor market. Unexpected periods of unemployment can rapidly erode retirement savings (Quadagno, MacPherson, and Keene, 2001). Health status is another uncertainty. Even people with high retirement income can find their resources rapidly depleted because of a chronic illness or a stay in a nursing home. Divorce is also unpredictable and reduces household income for both husbands and wives, especially wives. The age of retirement is yet another uncertainty. People who plan to retire at 65 or later may find themselves out of a job at a younger age. And finally, no one can predict the future rate of inflation. Income that appears adequate can rapidly lose value if inflation is high (Schulz, 1995).

Given all these uncertainties, it is difficult to determine how well people in the United States are

Savings is a life-long habit. Someone who saves as a child is more likely to plan for retirement.

doing in saving for retirement. Generally, however, they are not doing as well as they should. From 1950 to 1969, the savings rate by households was 8.6 percent. By 1993 it had declined to 5.8 percent (Bosworth, 1997). There are many debates among economists about why the national savings rate has declined, but one factor is the leveling off of economic opportunity and the decline in family income growth noted earlier. People who are barely paying their expenses don't have much to save. On a more positive note, 62 percent of current workers save

some money for retirement and 56 percent started saving by age 30 (Employee Benefit Research Institute, 1995). People understand that they must save, but they just are not saving as much as they should.

Savings rates are also low among the elderly because they spend most of their income on basic necessities. Spending on essentials (housing, food, transportation, health care, and clothing) accounts for 93.4 percent of total household spending among the poor elderly and 87.1 percent among the most affluent elderly. Nearly

| *Figure 15-7* | Coverage Rates for Workers Aged 40 to 60, 1980–2000. |

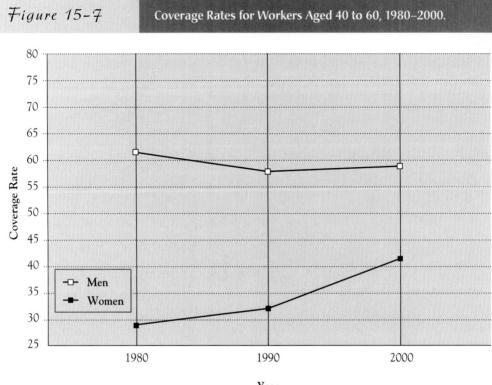

Source: MacPherson (2002).

15 percent of the income of people 65 or older is spent on health care, compared to only 5 percent among those aged 45 to 54 (Cook and Settersten, 1995). That's because they have poorer health and higher out-of-pocket health care costs than people in any other age group (see Chapter 13).

Most countries today follow an approach for providing retirement income that is similar to that of the United States. They combine public programs with employer-provided pensions and private savings. Where they differ is in the nature of the mix. The debate over the future of Social Security really involves deciding how much of the mix of retirement income will come from each of these sources.

Increased life expectancy, the shift from manufacturing to services, and the increase in the number of households where both husband and wife are employed are just a few of the changes that occurred in the twentieth century (Steuerle, 1997). In both the private and the public sectors, forms of income security in old age are in constant transition. A key issue for the twenty-first century is how best to distribute scarce societal resources through the mix of social insurance, social assistance, and fiscal welfare to protect individuals and families over the life course.

Chapter Resources

LOOKING BACK

1. **How has the economic status of the aged changed over recent decades?** *For most of the twentieth century, being old meant facing a high risk of being poor. In the past three decades, however, poverty among the aged has declined faster than it has for other age groups. Today's elderly have benefited from improved living standards in the post–World War II era and are better educated than their parents' generation. These factors, coupled with improvements in Social Security benefits, mean that the postretirement income decline is the lowest ever recorded. Now low income is more closely linked to household type than to phase of the life course.*

2. **What is the present status of the Social Security system, and what is its future?** *Under current projections, the Social Security system will become insolvent in 2037. That means there will be insufficient income coming in from payroll taxes to fully fund the benefits people have been promised. The much-publicized concerns about the long-range solvency of the trust fund have undermined public confidence in the program, and considerable disagreement exists over how to solve the problem.*

3. **What measures might be taken to ensure the viability of the Social Security system for future generations?** *One proposal would restore the trust fund's long-range solvency through a package of modest changes including raising the retirement age, reducing benefits, and raising revenues. Each of these options has advantages and disadvantages, but none is a solution in and of itself. More radical options also are being proposed that would fundamentally alter the nature of Social Security. One proposal is to means-test benefits. Means testing is likely to raise political opposition because it would discourage personal saving and undermine political support for Social Security. Privatizing Social Security has also received a good deal of media attention. Privatization transfers* the risk of income security in retirement from the government to the private sector. One risk of privatization is that some people might invest poorly and have little or nothing when they reach old age. Another problem is that the stock market might be in a slump when people are ready to retire.

4. **What is the difference between a defined benefit plan and a defined contribution plan?** *Many retirees supplement their Social Security benefits with income from pensions. One type of pension is called a defined benefit. Workers receive a monthly benefit based on their years of service to the firm and their prior earnings. Because defined benefit plans have been subject to a number of problems, the government has passed laws regulating them. The Employee Retirement Income Security Act of 1974 required companies to establish minimum vesting standards, set more stringent funding requirements, and establish better methods of reporting plan benefits and finances to workers. An increasing proportion of the labor force is covered by defined contribution plans. Under defined contribution plans, workers or employers make contributions into a fund, which is invested on behalf of the worker. Benefits in retirement are based on the level of contributions and the success of the investment decisions.*

5. **How do personal savings contribute to the support of the aged?** *Personal savings currently pay for only a small proportion of retirement income. In the past two decades, however, Congress passed many tax rules that encourage people to save money for retirement. Although most Americans recognize the need to save, few have saved enough, a problem that is especially apparent among young people.*

THINKING ABOUT AGING

1. Social Security obviously benefits the aged. How might it benefit younger age groups?

2. Of the three ways to restore solvency to the Social Security trust fund—raising the

retirement age, reducing benefits, and increasing revenues—which would you favor? Why?

3. Would you favor means testing of Social Security beneficiaries? Why or why not?

4. Aside from the need to find a solution to the looming Social Security crisis, what other benefits might privatization of the federal pension program bring?

5. Could the federal government do more to encourage people to save for their retirement? Be specific.

KEY TERMS

defined benefit 372

defined contribution 374

early retirement age 364

Employee Retirement Income Security Act (ERISA) 374

Individual Retirement Account (IRA) 375

median net worth 360

normal retirement age 364

Pension Benefit Guaranty Corporation (PBGC) 374

privatization 370

vesting rules 372

EXPLORING THE INTERNET

Note: While all the URLs listed were current as of the printing of this book, these sites often change. Please check our website www.mhhe.com/quadagno for updates.

1. Many are worried about the future of Social Security. They are worried that the Social Security system is broken and there won't be any money left for retirement, especially for the large cohort of baby boomers who are on the verge of retiring. Go to the AARP's website (www.aarp.org)

and link to "legislation and elections." Next, click on "Social Security," and then "About Social Security." Read the article titled, "Four Questions about Social Security," and answer the following questions:

a. How many boomers are currently paying into the Social Security System?

b. Approximately how much money is currently in the Social Security trust fund? Is it growing or being depleted?

c. Without doing anything to the current system, how long will the system be able to make total payments to recipients before we run into problems?

d. How does the Social Security system compare with investing money?

e. Is Social Security a program that only helps individuals after they retire, or does it also assist them while they are working?"

2. The website of the Federal Intra-agency Forum on Age-Related Statistics (http://www.agingstats.gov/) provides much interesting information on older Americans. Go to the website and link to "Older Americans 2000: Key Indicators of Well-Being;" then link to "Economics." Read the information on income distribution, sources of income, and net worth, and answer the following questions:

a. Has the percentage of older Americans living in extreme poverty changed greatly over time?

b. Between 1962 and 1998, what happened to the percentage of Americans aged 65 and older who fell into the low-income group?

c. Has the proportion of income older Americans derive from their earnings increased recently?

d. Explain the major shift that has taken place recently in employer-provided pensions.

e. What percentage of income does Social Security account for among older Americans in the lowest fifth of the nation's income distribution?

Chapter 16

Poverty and Inequality

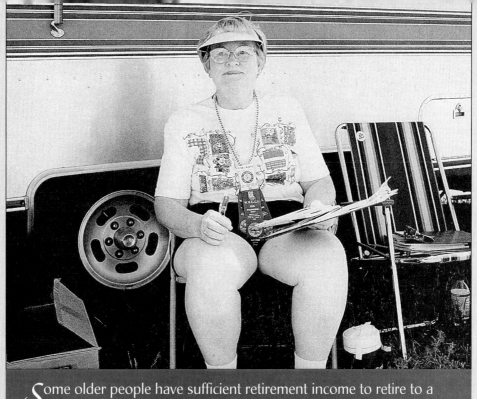

Some older people have sufficient retirement income to retire to a warm climate and enjoy a life of leisure.

Looking Ahead

1. What is the theory of cumulative disadvantage, and how does it explain gender, racial, and ethnic differences in material well-being among the aged?
2. How do gender and marital status affect a person's eligibility for Social Security benefits?
3. How does the Social Security benefit for spouses operate?
4. How do gender and marital status affect a person's eligibility for employer pensions?
5. How do racial and ethnic groups vary in terms of their economic security in old age?

Leah Maynard, a 71-year-old widow, lives with her two dogs, Sassy and Bobo, in a double-wide trailer a block from the county fairgrounds of a southern city. She moved to Florida when she became too disabled to continue working as a dietitian at a midwestern hospital. Leah thought her generous disability pension would allow her to live out her retirement years in comfort. Much to her surprise and dismay, her disability benefits ceased when she turned 65 and became eligible for Social Security benefits. Now she supplements her meager Social Security income of $460 a month with a job as a "hostess" at the local Burger King. Leah is in constant pain from severe arthritis, and her doctor thinks she should have both hips and knees replaced. Leah doesn't know how she will pay for her share of the medical bills, and she fears losing her job if she takes time off from work for the operations.

Nate and Selma Fiske are snowbirds. They spend their winters in Fort Lauderdale, Florida, in a pleasant condominium community, and their summers in their hometown of Springfield, Massachusetts.

Nate is a retired accountant, Selma a retired book-keeper. They live comfortably on Nate's pension, the income from their investments, and their Social Security benefits. The two have a large network of friends, retirees like themselves, with whom they spend time playing golf and bridge, catching the "early bird" specials at local restaurants, and enjoying visits from children and grandchildren.

Emma and Samuel Thompson, an African American couple, have been married 40 years. Both are in their late 60s, and both still work full-time. The couple is raising their two grandchildren, Alisha, age 7, and Martin, age 5. Emma works on the janitorial staff of a large state university. Her shift begins at 5:00 A.M., so she rouses her sleepy grandchildren at 4:00 A.M. to make sure they eat a healthy breakfast and get ready for school. After she leaves, Alisha and Martin do their chores, then watch TV until the alarm on the kitchen clock reminds them to head for the corner, where the school bus picks them up at 7:20. Samuel works at construction sites, doing whatever work he can find. Both Sam and Emma would like to retire, but they can't afford to stop working. They have another generation to raise.

As these three vignettes indicate, people over 65 are no more alike in race, gender, social class, geographic distribution, or living arrangements than are people in their 20s or 30s. Some struggle to make ends meet, others live comfortably, and a very few are wealthy.

In this chapter we will explore inequality among the aged in the distribution of income, wealth, prestige, and power. Throughout this book, we have addressed issues of inequality based on race, gender, and ethnic origin in regard to such topics as work in later life (Chapter 12), health (Chapter 13), and care of the frail elderly (Chapter 15). We have also considered how social class affects family relationships (Chapter 8) and the distribution of income (Chapter 15). In this chapter, we focus primarily on economic stratification among the aged. We first analyze the social and political processes that create gender inequality in old age. Next we examine the racial and ethnic characteristics of the older population, and finally, we describe how minority status affects access to income, wealth, and health care in later life.

AGING AND SOCIAL STRATIFICATION

The basic sociological approach to stratification views inequality as a product of social processes, not innate differences between individuals. All human societies use sex, age, and kinship to assign people to social roles and to rank individuals in a hierarchy. For example, the old are usually given authority over the young, males over females. These rankings create the most basic forms of inequality and thus form the simplest type of social stratification. As societies become more complex in the division of labor, more complex types of social stratification emerge.

Class stratification appears in societies with growing economies, which require the specialized expertise that creates a ranking within the occupational system. The dimensions of social class include economic variables such as income and wealth, prestige variables that refer to a subjective ranking, and power, such as political participation and the distribution of justice (Weber, 1946). When a full system of stratification is in place, "social positions are ranked in terms of importance, rewarded differentially, acquired by individuals (and thus their families) and transmitted over generations" (Rossides, 1997:12). The study of inequality is the study of social stratification systems. The central question in the study of stratification is how social inequality is produced, maintained, and transmitted from one generation to another.

The Theory of Cumulative Disadvantage

The theory of cumulative disadvantage provides a life course framework for analyzing stratification systems among the aged. According to this theory, inequality is not a static outcome but rather is a cumulative process that unfolds over the life course (Dannefer, 1991; O'Rand, 1996a). The central premise of the theory is that although people may move up or down the social ladder, generally those who begin life with greater resources have more opportunities to acquire additional resources, and those who begin life with little fall further and further

Figure 16-1	Poverty Status, by Marital Status, Sex of Nonmarried Persons, Race, and Hispanic Origin, 2001.

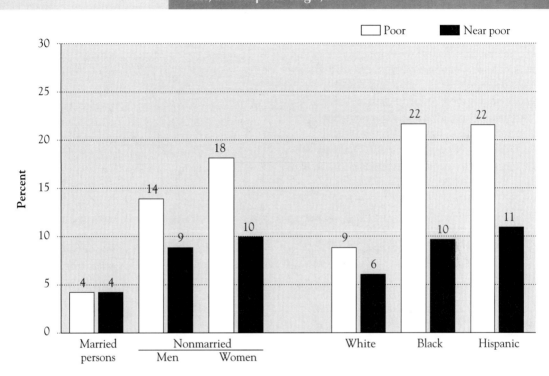

Source: Social Security Administration (2001).

behind. Inequality is not random among the aged; rather, patterns of who is systematically disadvantaged and who is advantaged exist. Thus, the causes of the patterned differences in opportunities over the life course must be sought in historical analyses.

Income and Poverty

Since the 1960s, when more than 30 percent of the elderly were poor, the economic circumstances of people over 65 have improved significantly. But not all older people have shared equally in these gains.

The poverty rate is the percentage of people below the poverty level. Among the older population as a whole, poverty rates are lower than they are for people of other age groups. In 2001, 10.1 percent of Americans aged 65 and older had

incomes below the poverty level—a rate slightly below that for the population as a whole (U.S. Bureau of the Census, 2002). But certain subgroups of the elderly had very high poverty rates. As Figure 16–1 shows, married couples fared better than the single elderly; the Hispanic and black elderly fared worse than whites. Among all racial groups, however, women have higher poverty rates than men (U.S. Bureau of the Census, 2002b). Table 16–1 reports poverty rates among older people by race and gender.

If we use median income (the middle of the income distribution) instead of poverty rates to measure economic well-being, we see that both young and old fare poorly compared to others. As Table 16–2 shows, in 2001 the median incomes for males and females were $29,101 and $16,614, respectively, but the range varied considerably by age. Among 35- to 44-year-olds and 45- to 54-year-olds,

Table 16-1	Poverty Rates of People 65 and Older by Race and Gender, 2001			
	All Races	*White*	*Black*	*Hispanic**
Both Sexes				
65 years and over	10.1%	8.9%	21.9%	21.8%
65 to 74 years	9.2	7.8	20.2	21.6
75 years and over	11.2	10.2	24.8	22.0
Male				
65 years and over	7.0	6.0	15.6	18.1
65 to 74 years	6.8	5.7	14.3	17.5
75 years and over	7.3	6.4	18.1	19.4
Female				
65 years and over	12.4	11.1	26.1	24.5
65 to 74 years	11.2	9.6	24.5	25.0
75 years and over	13.6	12.5	28.3	23.7

Note: Percentages = percentage below poverty level.
*Hispanics may be of any race.
Source: U.S. Bureau of the Census (2002b).

Table 16-2	Median Income in the United States by Age and Sex, 2001	
Age	*Males*	*Females*
	$29,101	$16,614
Under 65 years	30,951	18,876
15–24	9,301	7,467
25–34	30,510	21,473
35–44	38,340	22,471
45–54	41,104	24,135
55–64	35,637	17,823
65 and older	19,688	11,313
65–74	21,695	11,201
75 and older	17,521	11,396

Source: U.S. Bureau of the Census (2002b).

median household income was considerably above the median for all persons; among people over 65, income was well below the median. Very young women and very old women had the lowest incomes. Median household income for women over 75 years and older was only $11,396; for women 15 to 24, only $7,467 (U.S. Bureau of the Census, 2002b). These figures suggest that gender is a better predictor of economic security than is age.

Income disparities by race and ethnic origin are due in part to differences in sources of income. Social Security makes up a larger share of the total income of minorities than it does of whites, who are more likely to have other sources of income. Figure 16–2 shows income sources among people 65 and older by race and ethnicity. The largest source of racial disparity is income from assets—stocks, bonds, and rental property (Hogan, Kim, and Perrucci, 1997). In 2001 only 29 percent of African Americans and 26 percent of Hispanics aged 65 and older received income from assets, compared to 62 percent of whites. Whites were also more likely than either African Americans or Hispanics to receive income from pensions. As a result of these disparities, Social Security benefits are a much more important part of the income of

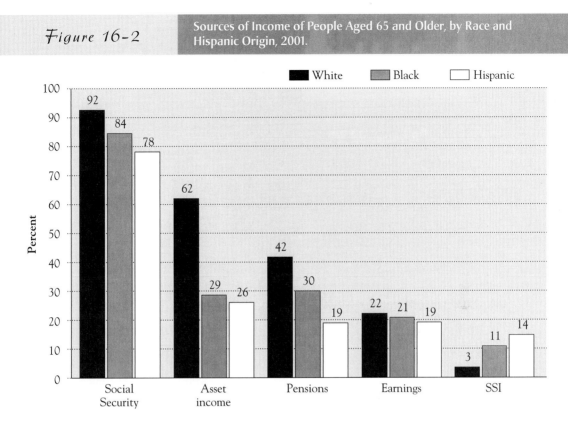

Figure 16-2 **Sources of Income of People Aged 65 and Older, by Race and Hispanic Origin, 2001.**

Source: Social Security Administration (2001).

older minorities than they are for whites. Even though women and minorities depend more on Social Security benefits for income than do white men, the benefits they receive are lower, as Table 16–3 shows.

Women are also less likely than men to receive income from private pensions. Only 28 percent of women receive income from pensions, compared to 45 percent of men (U.S. Bureau of the Census, 2002c). Further, women and minorities who do receive pensions have lower benefits than those of white men. Regardless of race or ethnicity, women are less likely than men to receive pensions, and the amount of pension income they receive is lower.

These figures clearly document that inequality in old age is not random but rather demonstrates a persistent pattern. How, then, can we explain this

Table 16-3 **Average Monthly Social Security Benefit for Retired Workers by Gender and Race, 1999**

	White	*Black*	*Other*
Men	$922	$756	$716
Women	706	626	597

Source: Social Security Administration (2000a).

pattern? The answer lies in a process of cumulative disadvantage associated with employment patterns over the life course. To a large extent, an individual's work history determines his or her income security in old age.

Table 16-4	Percentage of People Aged 65 or Older Receiving Pension Income by Race, Sex, and Hispanic Origin, 1992*

	White	Black	Hispanic Origin
Men	53%	32%	35%
Women	30	19	13

*Pension benefits other than Social Security.
Source: Grad (1994).

GENDER INEQUALITY IN OLD AGE

Patterns of Gender Inequality

Gender inequality in old age reflects the consequences of the gender division of labor in the household and the effect of women's familial responsibilities on their career patterns. Although women have always performed the bulk of the unpaid labor in the home, in the past half century the amount of paid labor they perform has increased dramatically. Between 1960 and 1995, the labor force participation rates of married women rose from 30.5 percent to 61.1 percent. Equally striking is the rise in employment among mothers. In 1950, only 13.6 percent of mothers with children younger than 6 and 32.8 percent of women with children aged 6 to 17 were in the labor force; by 1995, these figures were, respectively, 63.5 percent and 76.2 percent (Howe and Jackson, 1994; U.S. Bureau of the Census, 1996a:400). In the 1960s and 1970s, women who worked outside the home for wages carried the full burden of housework and child care.

Although men now do more around the house than they did 30 years ago, working women still perform nearly as much housework and child care as nonemployed married women (Schor, 1992). And of course, most divorced and unmarried mothers carry all of the burden of household labor. In "In Their Own Words," two women describe their daily schedules as they tried to coordinate work responsibilities with family demands.

Because women shoulder a disproportionate share of household labor, their familial responsibilities frequently disrupt their employment. Today, most women who are 65 or older have moved in and out of the labor force to care for children and aging parents. Although younger women are considerably more likely than older women to have continuous labor force participation, women of all ages are still twice as likely as men to be out of the labor force (U.S. Department of Labor, 1991).

The costs of a disorderly work history can be high, for women who move in and out of the labor force to care for their families are penalized by rules that determine levels of Social Security benefits and access to private pensions. Thus, women's familial responsibilities over the life course are reflected in the distribution of economic resources in old age.

Inequality in Social Security Income

Women obtain access to Social Security benefits in two ways. The first is through their history of paid work; the second is through their unpaid household labor, as dependents of male breadwinners (Williamson and Rix, 2000).

Paid work and eligibility for Social Security   Social Security benefits reward high earners. As we saw in Chapter 11, people who have the highest lifetime earnings receive the highest benefits. For example, the monthly Social Security benefit for a high earner retiring at age 65 in 2001 was $1,367, for an average earner, $1,051, and for a low earner, $640. Historically, women have earned lower wages than men. In 2002, women who were full-time workers earned an average of $30,203 per year compared to $39,429 for men (U.S. Bureau of the Census, 2003). The gender disparity is greater among older women. Women aged 55 to 64 earn 53 percent of what men earn. Because their earnings are less, women's Social Security benefits are lower than those of men.

Social Security also rewards people who have stable work histories. Benefits are based on what a worker has earned over 40 years, excluding the 5 years of lowest earnings or 5 years of zero earnings. A person who worked continuously with no

The Gendered Division of Household Labor

$\mathcal{M}$any married women work two jobs, one that involves paid employment, the other as nonpaid domestic labor caring for their families. Cecile and Annie describe their years of working full-time outside the home and having primary responsibility for most household duties.

Cecile: And I found that . . . I was just so tired when I came home I couldn't do anything. And of course, I'd worked for 25 years and raised five children, you know. And I worked all day long, and of course when the children was younger, I used to come home, even at lunch and put a roast or something in the oven and fix something for supper where I could just stick it in when I came in before the girls got larger, you know, where they could do it. . . . And it was just when I came home, it was just go go go right on 'til the end, you know, to go to bed.

Annie: It was important that we do our jobs and so that had to come first and everything else was built around it. . . . Like bright and early every morning you're up and you get the kids off to school and get your husband off to work and then you get ready to go to work, and you put in your day and stop off on the way home getting groceries, come in, fix supper, do dishes, do a couple of loads of laundry, run the sweeper and whatever has to be done. . . . It was wild. I don't know how I ever did it.

Source: Calasanti and Slevin (2001:128–29).

Many women work two jobs, one that involves paid employment, the other in nonpaid domestic work caring for their families.

break receives higher benefits than someone who had periods out of the labor force (Harrington Meyer, 1990). Because of their familial responsibilities, relatively few older women have contributed to Social Security the full 35 years. Among people currently receiving Social Security benefits, men on average have zero earnings for only one year out of 35; women average zero earnings for 12 years (Harrington Meyer, 1996).

Although the reward for stable employment—higher Social Security benefits—is built into the rules, on occasion the government has made exceptions to the rules. Wage credits toward Social Security have been given to members of the armed services and to Japanese Americans who were interned during World War II. Such credits have never been given to women who leave the labor force to care for children or aging parents (Greenberg, 1978).

There have been numerous options proposed for calculating Social Security benefits to take women's work histories into account. The main approach is based on a strategy of **gender recognition.** This approach presumes that gender equality can be achieved only by taking into account the differences between men and women and taking measures to compensate the disadvantaged sex (Sainsbury, 1996). One proposal based on this approach would eliminate the penalty mothers pay for taking time out of the labor force to care for their children by removing periods of child care from the computation of Social Security benefit levels. Another proposal would provide child care credit under a special minimum benefit (O'Rand, 1996b).

Although the idea of crediting parents for child care responsibilities has been criticized for being too complicated to administer, other countries manage to do so. In Germany, for example, the Pension Reform of 1986 credited a mother (or father) with 75 percent of average earnings for one year for each child raised. In 1992, the number of child care years credited rose to three per child. In France, a parent who has stayed home to care for a child is credited with two years of paid labor force participation for each child. In Canada, the years in which a person stays home to care for a child under age 7 are dropped from the calculation of the final pension benefit. In these countries, family

caregivers won't have years of zero contributions added into their total contributions as they would in the United States (O'Grady-LeShane, 1993).

Because younger women today work more continuously than women of older generations, the gender disparity in Social Security benefits may decline in the future. Yet even by 2030 it is estimated that only 40 percent of women will have contributed to Social Security the full 35 years. The remaining 60 percent will continue to have periods of zero earnings entered into their benefit calculations (U.S. House of Representatives, 1992).

Gender differences may also decrease because job stability among men appears to be declining. Since the 1980s, the likelihood of a man, especially a less-educated man, remaining permanently employed has dropped, and job turnover, which used to be highest among blue-collar workers, has hit workers in white-collar industries as well (Farber, 1996). As these men age, they will be more likely to have had periods of unemployment over their lives and thus more years of zero earnings in their benefit calculations. A final factor that may reduce the gender disparity in Social Security benefits is greater earnings equality. The pay gap between men and women has been closing, albeit gradually, and women aged 25 to 34 now earn 79 percent of men's earnings (U.S. Bureau of the Census, 1996a:471).

Unpaid work and eligibility for Social Security Women also obtain access to Social Security benefits through their unpaid labor as dependents of male breadwinners. When Congress passed the Social Security Act in 1935, no provisions for wives and widows were included. Consequently, married retired men had insufficient benefits to support two people, and if a retired man died, his widow had nothing. To redress these problems, Congress amended the Social Security Act in 1939, adding a spouse benefit and a widow's benefit (Harrington Meyer, 1996).

Originally, only wives were eligible for a spouse or widow's benefit, but recent reforms in the Social Security system have emphasized **gender neutrality,** which means reformulating laws in gender-neutral terms (Sainsbury, 1996). Since 1972, a man has been eligible for a spouse benefit when his wife retires or for a survivor's benefit if his wife dies first. In practice,

Table 16-5	Calculation of Social Security Benefits for Retired Workers, Spouses, and Widow(er)s

Type of Recipient	Social Security Benefit	Average Monthly Benefit, 1999
Retired worker	*Receives higher of:* own benefit as a worker, or 50 percent of spouse's benefit (i.e., "dually entitled")	$804
Spouse ineligible for retired worker benefit (i.e., did not work sufficiently in covered employment)	*Receives:* 50 percent of spouse's benefit	$412
Widow(er)	*Receives higher of:* deceased spouse's retired-worker benefit, or own benefit as a worker	$775

Source: Social Security Administration (2000a, table 5.A1).

Table 16-6	Benefits for Three Couples with the Same Combined Monthly Earnings

Couple	Husband's Monthly Earnings		Wife's Monthly Earnings		Combined Monthly Earnings	Combined Couple's Benefit	Survivor's Monthly Benefit (Under Current Law)
Allen	$1,000	+	$ 0	=	$1,000	$919	$613
Bono	$ 750	+	$250	=	$1,000	$800	$533
Wong	$ 500	+	$500	=	$1,000	$900	$450

however, 99 percent of those receiving spouse and survivor's benefits are women (Harrington Meyer, 1996).

Under the law today, a woman (or man) who has been married for at least a year to a worker who retires at 65 can receive a **spouse benefit** at age 62. The spouse benefit is equal to 50 percent of the worker's benefit.

Women (or men) who have worked outside the home for wages and who are also eligible for benefits as spouses are considered dually entitled. Under the rules for **dual entitlement,** an individual receives a benefit as a worker plus an additional amount if the worker benefit is less than the spouse benefit (Harrington Meyer, 1996). If a retired worker dies, his or her survivor loses the spouse benefit but

receives a **survivor's benefit.** The survivor's benefit is equal to 100 percent of the worker benefit. Table 16–5 shows how Social Security benefits are calculated for spouses and widows of retired workers.

Current law favors the traditional family in which the husband is the sole earner. Table 16–6 presents the benefits for three hypothetical couples, with the same combined monthly earnings ($1,000). Each couple receives a different Social Security benefit, depending on how their income is divided between husband and wife (Fitzpatrick and Entmacher, 2000). Mr. Allen earns $1,000 a month and is the sole breadwinner in his household; Mrs. Allen has never worked outside the home for wages. When Mr. Allen retires, the couple's monthly Social Security benefit will be $919. Should Mr. Allen die,

An Issue for Public Policy

SOCIAL SECURITY AND DIVORCE

*W*hen the Social Security system was designed in 1935, divorce was uncommon. Thus when Congress added benefits for the wives and widows of retired workers in 1939, legislators paid little attention to the needs of divorced women. By the 1960s divorce had become more common. At retirement, many women found they had no right to their former husbands' Social Security benefits. To protect divorced spouses, in 1965 policymakers added a provision allowing the lower earner in a divorced couple to keep the spouse benefit (one-half of the primary worker's benefit), provided the marriage had lasted at least 20 years.

The problem with this provision was that a low-earning spouse—nearly always the wife—was ineligible for spouse benefit even if she had been married for 18 or 19 years. Thus many divorced women still had little or no income in old age. In 1977 Congress, acknowledging that older divorced women were still at risk of extreme poverty, extended eligibility for the spouse benefit to women who had been married for only 10 years. If the primary worker remarried, the divorced spouse would still get the spouse benefit. But if the divorced spouse remarried, she forfeited her claim to the benefit (Stanfield, 2000). (Although both divorced men and women were eligible for the benefit, in practice few men received it; most recipients were women.)

Today many more people are affected by the divorce provision than policymakers ever expected. Four out of every 10 couples who marry are likely to divorce, and fewer divorced people

Mrs. Allen will receive a widow's benefit of $613, two-thirds of the couples benefit.

Mr. and Mrs. Bono have the same combined monthly income as the Allens—$1,000. However, Mr. Bono earns less than Mr. Allen—only $750 a month—and Mrs. Bono earns just $250 a month. The Bonos will receive only $800 a month from Social Security, and Mrs. Bono's survivor's benefit will be $533 a month. Thus, even though Mrs. Bono worked outside the home, she will receive less from Social Security than Mrs. Allen because she was not married to a high earner. Finally, Mr. and Mrs. Wong also have combined monthly earnings of $1,000; each earns $500 a month. The Wongs' combined couples benefit will be $900 a month, but Mrs. Wong will receive only $450 when Mr. Wong dies. Her own benefit as a retired worker pays more than she would receive from a spouse benefit.

These three examples demonstrate some problems with the way the spouse benefit is distributed. Compared to a one-earner couple, a two-earner couple pays more in taxes and receives lower benefits. The relative difference in benefits tends to increase after the husband's death (Burkhauser and now remarry. In 1970 divorcees who hadn't remarried totaled 4.3 million people—just 3 percent of adults. In 1996 there were 18.3 million unmarried divorcees—10 percent of all adults.

The criteria for awarding Social Security benefits after a divorce have produced some strange results. Consider these quirks:

- The death of a former spouse can provide a payoff, because the spouse benefit becomes a survivor's benefit (100 percent of the primary worker's benefit) when a former spouse dies.
- A high earner with multiple marriages leaves the public with a large bill. If one worker has four marriages, each lasting 10 years, four former spouses are eligible for the spouse benefit.
- Protecting divorced women doesn't necessarily protect the neediest women. A divorced woman who never worked outside the home but was married to a high earner may receive higher Social Security benefits than a low-income single mother who worked and contributed to Social Security while raising her children.

Few proposals for Social Security reform have addressed the perverse incentives created by the extension of benefits to divorced people. Should the eligibility criteria be revised to reflect changes in the family? One proposal under consideration would establish a universal minimum benefit to ensure that no older person falls into poverty. Although divorced women do need protection, policymakers should be able to establish better criteria than those currently in place (Steurele and Spiro, 1999).

What Do You Think?

1. Has divorce limited the amount of Social Security income someone you know receives? If so, explain.
2. Would you favor reforming Social Security to eliminate inequities in the distribution of spouse benefits? If so, what kind of solution would you propose?

Smeeding, 1994). Many people rightly argue that spousal benefits should not consistently favor the spouses of high-income males.

The loss of the spouse benefit is one reason the income of a married woman drops when she becomes a widow. She loses one-third of the Social Security income she and her husband enjoyed as a couple. A woman's risk of poverty increases even more if she gets a divorce. Under Social Security rules, an ex-spouse is eligible for a spouse benefit if she (or he) is at least 60 years old, had been married at least 10 years, and is not currently married.

Here's how the spouse benefit works in the case of a divorce. Consider another average couple, Mr. and Mrs. Savich. Should they divorce, Mrs. Savich would receive only the spouse benefit of $432, while Mr. Savich would receive his retired worker benefit of $864. If Mrs. Savich happened to be only 57 when her former husband retired, she would be ineligible for any benefits from Social Security until she turned 60, even if Mr. Savich had been her sole source of support their entire marriage. For some criticisms of the divorced spouse benefit, see "An Issue for Public Policy."

As these examples make clear, Social Security was designed to correspond to a particular family type—the traditional family in which the husband was the sole breadwinner, the wife was a family caretaker, and the marriage was permanent. That model fit the typical family in 1935, when only 22 percent of women were in the labor force and divorce rates were much lower than they are today. The spouse benefit provided a modest supplement to retirees in two-person households, and the widow's benefit granted a minimal income for nonworking wives.

By 1996, the typical family no longer consisted of a male breadwinner and a female caretaker. The majority of married women were in the labor force, which means that more women are becoming eligible for Social Security benefits on the basis of their own earnings history, rather than their spouses'. Yet many working women receive no more in benefits—indeed they often are eligible for less—than married women who have not worked outside the home for wages. This disparity has led to accusations that Social Security is unfair to working women and has prompted some critics to question the value of the spouse benefit (Burkhauser and Holden, 1982).

One solution to this problem is to eliminate the spouse benefit. Critics argue that it rewards most those women who never worked outside the home. (Fitzpatrick and Entmacher, 2000). But those who favor retaining the spouse benefit argue that it has served an important function in providing income for older women; that it recognizes women's nonmarket contribution to national productivity; and that it allows women to stay home and care for their children (Flowers, 1979). In the absence of spouse and widow benefits, many older women would be destitute. An alternative solution would be to increase the survivor's benefit for low-income, two-earner families like the Wongs from one-half to two-thirds—the same as for a one-earner household. In light of changing female labor patterns and family composition, some reevaluation of how these benefits are distributed seems justified. The precise solution remains a subject of debate (Fitzpatrick and Entmacher, 2000).

Inequality in Supplemental Security Income

A program already exists for alleviating poverty in old age; but it succeeds only in theory. As we saw in Chapter 11, Supplemental Security Income, or SSI, provides income for the aged, blind, and disabled poor. To qualify, an individual must be 65 or older, blind, or disabled and have an income below a certain level.

Nearly 74 percent of the aged who receive SSI benefits are women, and more than one-third are very old, over age 80 (U.S. House of Representatives, 1994). The problem with the SSI benefit is that the average monthly SSI payment is only about 72 percent of poverty level. In 2003, this came to $646 (Social Security Administration, 2003). If you think for a moment about just the cost of rent, utilities, and food, you can see that it would be very difficult to live on $466. And of course, everyone has other expenses, such as for clothing, transportation, and medical care. The low level of SSI benefits explains why an older, single woman in the United States is at such a high risk for poverty. The safety net has a big hole in it.

Poverty among older women is less of a problem in other Western nations. The United States is the only country where single elderly women have higher rates of poverty than older couples (Quinn and Smeeding, 1993). The reasons for this situation lie in the way the safety net is constructed. In the United States, the safety net for the aged poor consists of SSI, Social Security, and food stamps. An elderly person eligible for all three benefits would still have an income below the poverty level. By contrast, there are virtually no poor among the Swedish elderly, and the elderly in the Netherlands experience only a small risk of poverty (Sainsbury, 1996). These countries manage to keep older women out of poverty by providing a universal basic pension available to all older people, which is set sufficiently above the poverty level.

Given the high proportion of older women on SSI, a simple way to eliminate poverty would be to raise the SSI benefit above the poverty line. Although a few states increase the federal SSI benefit with a supplementary payment, most do not. Thus, most SSI recipients remain desperately poor.

Inequality in Employer Pension Coverage

Social Security provides a modest floor of protection in old age, but it was never designed to provide full income security in retirement. Rather it is one leg of a three-legged stool that also includes personal savings and pensions provided by employers. Most people are able to maintain their previous living standards in retirement only if they have employer pensions, personal savings, and some investments.

Pension benefits   Many of the same factors that penalize women in terms of Social Security benefits also operate with employer pensions. The primary factor that determines access to a pension is the individual's job, and historically, women have worked in jobs that lack pension coverage. Employer pensions are most likely to be offered by large firms, especially those in the unionized manufacturing sector, whereas women typically work in smaller, nonunionized firms in the service sector of the economy (Beck, Horan, and Tolbert, 1980). One-fourth of all American women work in retail and service industries, which have the lowest pension coverage (Reskin and Hartmann, 1986).

Women's interrupted work histories also reduce their pension eligibility. Most pension plans require a certain number of years of service before a worker is eligible, or vested. Because women take time out for family responsibilities, many never become vested. Even if a woman has worked for an employer for many years, she may still not qualify for a pension because of interruptions in employment (Quadagno, 1988b). Fewer years of total employment and more intermittent employment reduce pension benefits. That is the penalty women pay for performing most of the unpaid household labor. In 2003 the average pension benefit for a woman was $4,161 a year, compared to $7,678 for a man (U.S. Bureau of Labor Statistics, 2003).

The fastest growing defined contribution plans are 401(k)s. Currently, many employees hold a significant portion of their 401(k) funds in their companies' stock. Investing in one stock increases risk. Most participants are not sophisticated investors and underestimate the risk of holding company stock (Munnell and Sunden, 2002). The most recent high-profile example is the failure of Enron Corporation. Many former Enron employees lost their entire life savings, which they had invested in Enron stock (Zernike, 2002). The challenge is to educate people to help them choose diversified portfolios.

These issues will become even more important in the future for both men and women. In the past decade there has been a dip in private pension coverage among men aged 40 to 60 but a significant rise among women. "Diversity in the Aging Experience" examines issues of gender equality in 401(k) plans.

Survivor's benefits   Unlike Social Security, which pays a spouse benefit while the retiree is still alive, private pension plans pay benefits only to the worker. When the worker dies, the survivor may receive a survivor's pension, but not necessarily. Until 1984, a husband could waive his wife's right to a survivor's benefit without her knowledge. In many cases, widows were surprised to find that they had no survivor's benefits because their husbands had signed them away. Divorced women also found that they had no legal right to a share of their spouse's private pension. The following quote illustrates the dilemma many older women unexpectedly face as widows:

Recently, my husband passed away, leaving me with what he thought was half of the payments on his pension. A few weeks later I received a letter claiming nothing was left as a pension for me to draw on as his survivor. (American Association of Retired Persons, 1994a:3)

The **Retirement Equity Act of 1984 (REA)** protected spouses in the event of a death or divorce. Pensions for married employees now must be **joint and survivor annuities.** This means that the worker must take a reduced pension for life and the spouse must get a 50 percent survivor's pension unless both husband and wife agree, in writing, to waive the survivor's pension (American Association of Retired Persons, 1995). A husband can no longer sign away his wife's right to survivor's benefits without her knowledge.

Diversity in the Aging Experience

SEX AND 401(K) PLANS

In the past decade private pension coverage has shifted from defined benefit plans to defined contributions plans. Most are in the form of 401(k)s, which provide a lump-sum benefit at retirement. Retirees who want to have a monthly income from their 401(k)s typically purchase an **annuity** from an insurance company. The insurance company takes the funds in the 401(k) and provides the retiree with a benefit for life.

Because women live longer on average than men, insurance companies in some states provide women a lower monthly stipend. For example, a 65-year-old woman who purchased a $100,000 lifetime annuity could expect to receive $695 a month, but a man of the same age would get $740 a month. Lifetime benefits would be the same, given average differences in life expectancy. Thus, the total amount an insurance company would pay out should be equal for men and women. The problem with this logic is that women do not have lower monthly expenses than men. Further, there is considerable overlap in life expectancy between men and women. Some women live fewer years than the average male, and some men live much longer than the average female.

Current practices by insurance companies of providing different benefit levels to men and women raise important questions about proposals to create individual accounts for Social Security. Currently, Social Security provides unisex benefits. Men and women of the same age who made the same contributions will receive the same benefits when they retire. If people are allowed to purchase individual annuities with the funds in their individual accounts, then some decision will have to be made about whether to allow sex-distinct pricing.

What Do You Think?

1. Should men and women receive different monthly benefits because women live longer than men?
2. Do you know anyone who has purchased an annuity?

Usually the decision to waive survivor's benefits is economically motivated; couples who choose to receive them get lower benefits while the husband is alive. For example, a 65-year-old man with a 62-year-old wife might be entitled to a pension benefit of $1,000 a month for life. If he and his wife waive the survivor's benefit, his wife receives nothing when he dies. If they take the benefit, they will receive only $890 a month, but his widow would receive a survivor's benefit of $445 after his death (American Association of Retired Persons, 1994a).

The Retirement Equity Act also allowed **pension-splitting** to become part of a divorce decree. Now the pension is considered part of the property settlement.

Following a divorce, a wife might be entitled to half her husband's pension benefit, or vice versa.

A gap in protection for many widows and former wives remains in effect, however, for the Retirement Equity Act applies only to private sector workers. Because state pension plans are excluded from federal law, not all state and local government workers are regulated by the REA. Presently, only 11 states have provisions requiring spousal consent to waive survivor pensions. Thus, some widows still find to their dismay that they have no pension rights to their deceased husbands' benefit. Although in the future, women will be somewhat more likely to have pension coverage in their own names, thousands of wives of state and local government workers will remain vulnerable to old-age poverty until states extend the protection of the Retirement Equity Act to them.

As the preceding discussion makes clear, the unequal risk of falling into poverty is not merely an accident of fate. Rather, it is a consequence of political decisions about eligibility rules that create institutionalized mechanisms that penalize women for earlier life choices and restricted labor market opportunities.

RACE, ETHNICITY, AND INEQUALITY

In the United States social classes do not form a clearly defined set of strata; rather, there are multiple dimensions of inequality. People's life chances and opportunities are partly conditioned by their racial and ethnic backgrounds.

The Social Construction of Race and Ethnicity

Although race and ethnicity are salient social categories, the determination of who belongs to what category is highly unscientific and socially constructed. Most of the statistical data we have about racial and ethnic minorities in the United States comes from the Census Bureau. Since 1970, race has been self-reported. Each person writes down his or her own racial identity. Race in national statistics is whatever people choose.

Until 1970, Hispanic was not listed as a separate category. Then leaders of the Hispanic community demanded that people of Spanish origin be allowed to identify themselves as Hispanic so that politicians would recognize them as a large, politically powerful group. In 1970, in response to these demands, the Census Bureau added a new category to reporting forms, allowing Hispanics to identify themselves by origin. They may also identify with a racial group.

In 2000, Americans were offered 16 racial categories. Table 16–7 shows the three questions used by the Census Bureau to ascertain race and ethnic origin. A cursory look at the race categories in item 6 shows that along with the familiar categories of black and white are another 14 choices that distinguish people on the basis of race *and* place of origin. They include Native American or Alaska Native, 11 varieties of Asian and Pacific Islander, and "other."

One item of contention has been that respondents must select only one category for item 6. As a result, individuals who are biracial had to choose one race or mark "other," even though they were allowed to report multiple ancestries in item 10. The lack of a multiracial category once again embroiled the Census Bureau in intense political debate. Because of increasing rates of intermarriage between people defined as members of different races, some people now advocate adding a multiracial category. However, the government decided that a multiracial category would not be included in the 2000 Census, although Americans of mixed ancestry were allowed to check as many categories as applied. Although we use the standard racial and ethnic designations in this chapter, it's important to keep in mind that they are arbitrary and subject to political manipulation.

Racial and Ethnic Variations among the Aged

In 1998 there were 32.4 million people in the United States aged 65 or older. As we have seen, there are significant differences in economic security in old age between minority groups and also between individuals within minority groups. In the following

Table 16-7	Race and Ancestry Items in the U.S. Census, 2000

Item 5   **Is this person Spanish/Hispanic/Latino?** Mark ⊗ the "**No**" box if not Spanish/Hispanic/Latino.

○ No, not Spanish/Hispanic/Latino
○ Yes, Mexican, Mexican Am., Chicano
○ Yes, Puerto Rican
○ Yes, Cuban
○ Yes, other Spanish/Hispanic/Latino—*Print group.*

Item 6   **What is the person's race?** **Mark ⊗ one or or more races** to indicate what this person considers himself/herself to be.

○ White
○ Black, African Am., or Negro
○ American Indian or Alaska Native—*Print name of enrolled or principal tribe.*

○ Asian Indian   ○ Native Hawaiian
○ Chinese   ○ Guamanian or Chamorro
○ Filipino   ○ Samoan
○ Japanese   ○ Other Pacific Islander
○ Korean
○ Vietnamese
○ Other Asian—*Print race.*

○ Some other races—*Print race.*

Item 10   **What is this person's ancestry or ethic origin?**

(For example: Italian, Jamaican, African Am., Cambodian, Cape Verdean, Norwegian, Dominican, French Canadian, Haitian, Korean, Lebanese, Polish, Nigerian, Mexican, Taiwanese, Ukrainian, and so on.)

Source: U.S. Bureau of the Census (2000).

sections, we analyze the distinctive historical patterns among various minority groups that have created similar outcomes for their elderly members.

The African American elderly
African Americans are the largest minority group in the United States. The economic position of older blacks today can be understood only from a life course perspective of cumulative disadvantage. Because of racial discrimination, African Americans have always experienced higher rates of unemployment than whites, more sporadic employment, and lower wages. In 1960, black men earned only 58 percent of what white men earned, and most black women were employed as domestic servants (see Chapter 12). African Americans seldom worked side by side with whites in the same job and seldom received the same pay if they did (Farley, 1996). Lower earnings during

| Table 16-8 | Home Ownership Rates by Race and Ethnic Origin, 1999 | | |

White	*Black*	*Hispanic*	*Asian/Pacific Islander*
69.1%	44.1%	42.5%	50.8%

Source: U.S. Bureau of the Census (1999).

their working years means lower Social Security benefits in retirement. Sporadic employment also means less opportunity to become vested in private pension systems and less opportunity to accumulate pension savings.

Racial discrimination has also impeded the accumulation of wealth by blacks. Among people aged 70 or older, the average net worth of white families is almost four times that of black families (Smith and Jawer, 1997). Part of the racial disparity in wealth is due to differences in home ownership. The home is the single most important asset of most Americans, yet as Table 16–8 shows, in 1999 only 44.1 percent of African Americans owned their own homes, compared to 69 percent of whites (U.S. Bureau of the Census, 1996a:24). The value of homes owned by blacks is also lower. The Health and Retirement Survey (HRS) is a nationally representative study of employment, income, assets, health, and retirement plans of individuals who were aged 51 to 61 in 1992. According to the HRS survey, the value of home equity in that year was $36,658 for blacks, compared to $78,708 for whites (Angel and Angel, 1996).

Why is housing wealth so much lower for African Americans? The answer lies in a legacy of racial discrimination by real estate agents, white neighborhoods, and the federal government. For most of the twentieth century, African Americans were relegated to racially segregated neighborhoods. Racial segregation became part of official federal housing policy in 1934, when Congress established the Federal Housing Authority (FHA) to enable people to buy homes by insuring banks against defaults on mortgage loans. FHA policy encouraged **redlining:** Red lines were literally drawn on maps around areas of cities where loans were considered

risky for economic or racial reasons. Redlining meant that most black families were ineligible for federally insured loans. Until 1949, the FHA also encouraged the use of **restrictive covenants** banning African Americans, Asians, Hispanics, and in some cases, Jews and Catholics from white Protestant neighborhoods; the FHA also refused to insure mortgages in integrated neighborhoods (Quadagno, 1994). Many blacks and other minorities who are now old were victims of these practices.

Although now illegal, racial discrimination in access to housing remains embedded in the practices of private lenders (Myers and Chung, 1996). A 1991 study by the Federal Reserve found widespread institutional discrimination in the nation's banking system. Nationwide, commercial banks rejected black applicants for home mortgages twice as often as they rejected white applicants. In some cities, such as Chicago, Boston, and Philadelphia, the rejection rate was three times higher: The poorest white applicant was three times more likely than a black person in the highest income bracket to get a loan approved. The Federal Reserve study concluded that mortgage refusal rates have little, if any, relationship to neighborhood or income (Oliver and Shapiro, 1995).

FHA policy and continuing racial discrimination in lending practices have had a lasting impact on the asset accumulation of African Americans. One consequence, already noted, is that fewer blacks own their own homes. Another consequence is that because of housing segregation, most blacks who purchased homes did so in central cities. Instead of benefiting from the housing boom of the 1980s, when real estate prices rose dramatically, their investments often declined in value (Oliver and Shapiro, 1995).

The unequal distribution of wealth perpetuates cumulative disadvantage. Because older African Americans have less wealth than whites, most have less income security for their own old age and no fail-safe system if an emergency depletes their resources. They also have less to pass on to their children. As a result, racial inequality in wealth accumulation is transmitted to the next generation.

Since 1965, there has been significant progress in the economic and social status of African Americans on many fronts. As civil rights laws ended segregation, the number of blacks and whites attending college reached near parity, the number of black elected officials increased, there was a sizable increase in the number of black men and women holding professional positions, and the income gap between blacks and whites declined (Wilson, 1978, 1987). Despite these gains, the median income of black elders relative to white elders actually fell in the past decades, from 70 percent in 1967 to only 60 percent today (Hudson, 2002). Although the economic status of the African American elderly should be much better in the future, continuing inequality of opportunity over the life course means continuing inequality in old age.

The Hispanic elderly   The term *Hispanic* refers to individuals who identify themselves as Spanish in origin. Hispanics have migrated to the United States from Mexico, Cuba, Puerto Rico (a U.S. territory), Central and South America, and Europe. The three largest groups of Hispanics are Mexican, Puerto Rican, and Cuban. Of the 27,521,000 people of Hispanic origin, 63 percent are from Mexico, 10 percent from Puerto Rico, and 3 percent from Cuba. Thus, it's important to recognize that the term *Hispanic* includes people who differ significantly in cultural beliefs, race, education level, and income.

Many people of Mexican origin have lived in the United States for centuries. Their ancestors lived on land that belonged to Mexico until it was annexed by the United States in 1850. Others came during and after World War II under the bracero program (see Chapter 12). The most recent Mexican immigrants are relatively young and heavily concentrated in a few states, especially California and Texas. Many Mexican Americans have worked as migrant laborers, toiling in the fields, moving from job to job, and receiving no benefits.

Cuban Americans immigrated to the United States in two waves. The first, during the 1960s, was a political migration of people fleeing Fidel Castro's communist government. Most of these early migrants were drawn from the Cuban upper and middle classes, and they arrived with high levels of education, skills, and capital. These Cubans formed tight-knit ethnic enclaves in the cities where they landed, especially in Miami. They used the wealth they brought with them to build businesses, and many have prospered. A second wave of Cubans arrived in 1980 when Fidel Castro allowed a flotilla of small boats to depart from the port of Mariel. The Mariel Cubans were less educated than the first wave, came from lower social classes, and have not fared as well.

Of all groups of Hispanic origin, Puerto Rican families are the most disadvantaged. Many who left Puerto Rico for the mainland dwell in segregated enclaves in large urban areas. They left the island because they were very poor but found few opportunities for good jobs and adequate housing when they arrived. Among all Hispanic groups, they have the lowest rates of labor force participation and the lowest levels of education (Sandefur and Tienda, 1988).

The differences among the Hispanic-origin groups are reflected in income. Cubans as a group have higher income than others classified as Hispanic. In 1995, the median income for Cubans was $39,584, compared to $23,606 for Mexican Americans and $20,929 for Puerto Ricans.

Hispanics are a relatively young population; only 5.2 percent were 65 or older in 1995. The main reason why there are relatively few older people among Hispanics is the high birth rate. However, this rate varies by country of origin. Only 4.4 percent of Mexicans and 6.5 percent of Puerto Ricans are 65 or older, compared to 17.7 percent of Cubans. The Cuban percentage reflects the fact that many Cuban immigrants were middle-aged when they came to the United States (U.S. Bureau of the Census, 1999a).

Poverty rates among the Hispanic aged follow the income patterns for the three groups. In 1995, the poverty rate was highest for Puerto Ricans (31.7 percent); it was relatively high for Mexicans (23.1 percent); and for Cubans it was just slightly more than that for whites (12.1 percent) (U.S. Bureau of the Census, 1996b:51).

Because many Mexicans worked as migrant laborers, they have the lowest rates of health insurance coverage of any group. In 1990, approximately 32 percent of Hispanics of all ages had no health insurance, compared to 20 percent of blacks and 13 percent of whites (Angel and Angel, 1996). Among people in their 50s, 40.8 percent of Mexican Americans had no health insurance, compared to 17.9 percent of blacks and 9.3 percent of whites (Angel and Angel, 1996).

Because many older Hispanics worked in occupations not covered by Social Security, they are also ineligible for Medicare. In 1990, 20 percent of Hispanics were ineligible for Medicare, compared to 12 percent of blacks and 7 percent of whites (National Council de la Raza, 1992). Another barrier that prevents many Mexican Americans from participating in Social Security is that they never became legal residents of the United States, even though they may have lived and worked in this country for decades (Angel and Angel, 1996).

Older Hispanics and African Americans have had irregular patterns of work because they typically worked in sectors of the labor force where layoffs are common or work is seasonal. A lifetime of work in low-status jobs characterized by sporadic work patterns, high turnover, and low earnings has cost older minorities pension income. Unstable, poorly paid work translates directly into less access to private pensions for older African Americans and Hispanics (Gibson, 1995; Hardy and Hazelrigg, 1995). This helps to explain why a higher percentage of their income is from earnings than is the case for whites. The lack of pension benefits often forces minority group members to continue working even after they reach age 65.

The Asian elderly In 1995 there were 8,715,000 people in the United States classified as Asian or Pacific Islanders; 7.6 percent were 65 or older (U.S. Bureau of the Census, 1996b:48). Like Hispanics, they represent a diverse people; their origins are in Vietnam, China, Japan, the Philippines, Korea, Hawaii, and the Pacific Islands.

Among elderly Asians there are a small number of surviving Chinese men who immigrated to the West Coast early in the twentieth century to build the railroads. Because there were so few women immigrants, many of these men never married. As a result, they faced old age with no family support system. Some of today's Asian elderly are the children of these first immigrants. They tend to be less educated and more economically deprived than later Asian immigrants. When the Chinese immigrants arrived in the United States, whites who lived on the West Coast feared their culture and lobbied to ban more Chinese from entering. In 1917, the United States closed its borders to Asian immigrants.

Many of the Japanese who are now old lost all their property during World War II when they were placed in prison camps. More numerous are Asians who began arriving in the United States in 1952 after the long-standing prohibition on immigration from Asia ended with token quotas of 100 a year from China and Japan. These immigrants were subject to laws that prevented them from buying property or holding public jobs. In 1965, in the wake of the civil rights movement, Congress allowed 290,000 immigrants to enter the United States each year, although no more than 20,000 were allowed from any one country. Following this loosening of immigration restrictions on Asian immigrants, a new wave began arriving. Many from Vietnam and Cambodia came to the United States in the 1970s as political refugees. More recently, immigrants have come from China, Japan, and Korea to obtain educations. Many receive advanced degrees (Farley, 1996).

Despite a history of discrimination against them, many Asian Americans have transcended the barriers placed before them. Asian Americans are the most prosperous group of immigrants. In 2002, median family income for Asian Americans was $50,312, and rates of home ownership were 54 percent. (U.S. Bureau of the Census 2003). Their prosperity can be explained in part by the high value many place on education. Asians remain in school the longest among minorities and are most overrepresented among those getting college and professional degrees; 38 percent have completed four years of college (U.S. Bureau of the Census, 1996a:48). The prosperity of Asians as a whole is reflected by their having the lowest rates of poverty in old age of any minority group. Indeed, older Asian women have lower poverty rates than older white women.

The native American elderly In 1990 there were 1,931,000 people classified as American Indians or Eskimos in the United States, a figure that

Aging around the World

INEQUALITY IN PENSION INCOME IN EUROPE

Most European nations developed their national pension programs before World War II, when most immigrants were white Europeans from neighboring countries. At that time, immigrants who settled permanently in these European nations were thoroughly assimilated. After World War II, Europe experienced an influx of temporary immigrants, admitted on work permits, from Third World nations (Ireland, 1995). These "guest worker" immigrants congregated in countries to which they had ex-colonial or other historical ties—Algerians in France, Turks in Germany, West Indians and South Asians in Britain (Gordon, 1995). Eventually, many of these "guest workers" stayed on, creating resident ethnic communities. As a general rule, these later immigrants to Europe have higher rates of poverty than the native born population (Gordon, 1995).

The causes of higher poverty among immigrants are complex. Many face exclusion and marginalization because of their racial or ethnic origin. A Eurobarometer opinion survey conducted in 1989 asked citizens if they believed there were "too many residents of another race" in their countries. Thirty-seven percent of Germans, 44 percent of British, and 43 percent of French respondents said "yes" (Gordon, 1995:535). Many immigrants also face language barriers. Their educational credentials may be incompatible with those of the host country, their job skills may be nontransferable, and they may not belong to job-hunting networks (Halli and Kazemipur, 1999). Finally, non-European immigrants may bring their poverty with them from their country of origin.

In some cases, permanent immigrants have been granted citizenship privileges that guarantee them residency rights, political participation, and social benefits, including the right to old-age pensions (Ireland, 1995). But groups that were admitted on limited work permits often do not receive

had increased since 1980 because of a rise in the number of people identifying themselves on the U.S. census as Indian. The largest Native American groups, in descending order are the Cherokee, Navajo, Chippewa, and Lakota. In 1990, 54.1 percent lived on reservations or tribal lands; the others lived in rural and urban areas (U.S. Bureau of the Census, 1996a:50).

American Indians are an indigenous people. There are nearly 500 federally recognized tribes and more than 300 languages, although fewer than 3 percent speak no English. Because of high rates of intermarriage, the number of American Indians reporting their race as Indian was considerably higher than the number reporting Indian ancestry.

American Indians have the highest unemployment rates and the highest mortality rates of any minority. In 1990, 31.6 percent of Indians lived below the poverty level, and median household income was just $19,886 (American Association of Retired Persons, 1996b). The high levels of poverty among elderly American Indians reflect the outcome of these rights (Gordon, 1995). In Germany, Austria, and Switzerland, for example, guest workers initially had no citizenship rights, although restrictions were loosened a bit in the 1980s.

In Great Britain, waves of immigration occurred at different times and under different circumstances for each ethnic group. The decade of greate immigration was the 1950s; thus, an increasing number of ethnic minorities are now British-born. The early 1960s brought an influx from the Caribbean; the early 1970s, one from India and Pakistan; and the 1980s, another from Bangladesh and Hong Kong. The income of older men and women in these minority ethnic groups reflects their employment and earnings history since their arrival in Britain. Their main sources of income are government pensions, earnings, private pensions, and interest on savings and investments. Minority elders are more likely than white elders to depend on means-tested benefits for their income, and less likely than whites to receive income from private pensions. Although income from pensions varies by ethnic group, all racial and ethnic minorities in Great Britain have less pension coverage and receive lower pension income than their white counterparts (Ginn and Arber, 2000).

Young blacks and Asians currently entering the British labor market are better prepared to compete than their parents' generation. Yet their returns to education are still lower than for whites, because "job opportunities for blacks and Asians have been limited by entrenched inequality and by racial discrimination" (Brown, 1995:590). In one study researchers found that one-third of private employers discriminated against Asian and Afro-Caribbean job applicants (Brown, 1995). Thus, although these workers should enjoy higher pension income than their parents' generation, continuing discrimination in employment suggests that inequality based on race and ethnicity will persist in the future.

What Do You Think?

1. Does an older person you know lack a pension because of ethnic or racial discrimination in employment? If so, explain the circumstances.
2. Should government attempt to compensate elderly people who have been deprived of pensions because of ethnic or racial discrimination? If so, how?

more than a century of federal policy toward indigenous people. In the late nineteenth century, the federal government created the reservation system in remote and often destitute settings, where tribes languished in isolation with little prospect for development or economic growth. Indian education has been the responsibility of the federal government, which operated day schools on the reservations in the nineteenth century and then established boarding schools for Indian youth in the twentieth century to acculturate Indians to the dominant society

(Nagel, 1996). Many of these schools were poorly equipped and poorly run. As a result, American Indians are the most poorly educated of all minority groups. According to the 1990 Census, only 5 percent of all Native Americans had college degrees.

During World War II, many American Indians left the reservations and many never returned to live permanently. Federal Indian employment and urban relocation programs established in the 1950s and 1960s were designed to end the era of reservation life, train Indians for wage labor jobs, and relocate trainees to urban areas. Between 1952 and 1972, more than 100,000 American Indians were relocated to urban areas. Some returned to the reservations, but many stayed in the cities. As a result of the outflow of young people, many Indian elderly were left isolated on reservations.

In the 1970s and 1980s, the federal government settled hundreds of claims for land that had been confiscated a century earlier. Some tribes received as much as $40 billion. The new resources created a resurgence of people claiming their Indian heritage (Nagel, 1996). Although land-claim settlements and legalized gambling have made some tribes prosperous, the benefits have not been evenly distributed. On many reservations, the elderly remain impoverished.

In 1990, only a small number of American Indians, 5.6 percent, were 65 or older (U.S. Bureau of the Census, 1996a:50). High mortality has reduced life expectancy and decreased the number of Native Americans who survive to old age. The federal government has the responsibility for providing health care for all American Indians who align with or are members of tribal organizations. The legal foundation of the Indian Health Service (IHS) is defined in federal treaty obligations, stipulating that health care be provided American Indians at no cost as reparation for tribal lands stolen from them. Since health care became the responsibility of the federal government, the general health of the majority of American Indians has improved, life expectancy has increased, and mortality rates have dropped (American Association of Retired Persons, 1996b). On the negative side, IHS-funded services for the Indian elderly provide few chronic and long-term-care services. Another problem is that of American Indians 55 or older living on or near reservations, 50 percent live more than 30 minutes from any source of health care; 20 percent live more than an hour away. Thus, many health care needs of the Native American elderly remain unfulfilled.

Minorities in Canada and Europe   Inequality in old age because of race or ethnicity is not unique to the United States. Minorities elsewhere also suffer the consequences of cumulative disadvantage. In Canada, for example, poverty rates among immigrants are high. Poverty stands at 41 percent among those from Latin America and West Asia, and at 39.4 percent among those of Arab origin (Kazemipur and Halli, 1997). Among the Canadian elderly, immigrants from Asia, Africa, and Latin America are more likely to be employed in their later years and less likely to receive pensions of any kind (Street, 1996). The same holds true in Great Britain. Lifelong patterns of high unemployment, low wages, and employment in jobs that lack pension coverage mean that minorities in these countries, regardless of ethnic origin, have less access to private pensions and lower income from public pensions when they grow old.

In analyzing systems of stratification, the object of study is the social institutions that penalize certain groups for having a fixed range of options and restricted opportunities. Inequality in outcomes is not random or accidental. Rather, it is the result of political decisions made by some people who have the power to limit opportunities for other people.

"Aging around the World" describes some of the factors associated with old age inequality among immigrant populations in Great Britain and other European countries.

Chapter Resources

LOOKING BACK

1. **What is the theory of cumulative disadvantage, and how does it explain gender, racial, and ethnic differences in material well-being among the aged?** *The basic sociological approach to stratification views inequality as a product of social processes, not innate differences between individuals. The central question in the study of stratification is how social inequality is produced, maintained, and transmitted from one generation to another. According to the theory of cumulative disadvantage, inequality is not a static outcome but rather is a cumulative process that unfolds over the life course. Women and members of racial and ethnic minorities have lower incomes and higher rates of poverty in old age than white males because of earlier experiences and opportunities.*

2. **How do gender and marital status affect a person's eligibility for Social Security benefits?** *Social Security is an important source of income for nearly all older people. Those at the lower end of the income distribution—women and minorities—depend most on this program, yet their average benefits are lower than those of white men. Women and minorities receive lower Social Security benefits than white males because the eligibility rules reward workers who have had continuous work histories and high-paying jobs. Women and minorities have more sporadic records of labor force participation and receive lower wages than white men. As a result, their benefits tend to be lower. The gender disparity in Social Security benefits may diminish in the future. One reason is that women are working more steadily than in the past; so when they reach retirement age, they will have had more continuous work histories. Another reason is that the job stability of white males has declined. Also, the pay gap between younger men and women has declined.*

3. **How does the Social Security benefit for spouses operate?** *The spouse benefit supplements the retirement income of a married couple by providing one-half of the retired worker's benefit. When the worker dies, the widow or widower loses the spouse benefit but retains a survivor's benefit equal to 100 percent of the worker' benefit. A former spouse is eligible for one-half of the worker' benefit but not until she or he reaches age 60.*

4. **How do gender and marital status affect a person's eligibility for employer pensions?** *The same factors that reduce Social Security benefits for women and minorities also affect their access to employer pensions. Low wages and discontinuous work histories make many people ineligible for these pensions. The advantage of Social Security, however, is that nearly 99 percent of older people (as mentioned in Chapter 11) receive some income from it. By contrast, less than half of retirees receive income from employer pensions.*

5. **How do racial and ethnic groups vary in terms of their economic security in old age?** *Compared to whites, African Americans have had higher rates of unemployment, more sporadic employment, and lower wages. Lower earnings during their working years mean lower Social Security benefits in retirement. Sporadic employment also means less opportunity to become vested in private pension systems and less opportunity to accumulate pension savings. Because of past and continuing discrimination in the sale of housing, older blacks and Hispanics are less likely than whites to own a home. Further, because of segregated housing patterns, the homes owned by blacks are less valuable than those of whites.*

   Among the Hispanic aged, poverty rates vary by country of origin. They are highest among Puerto Ricans, relatively high among Mexicans, and just slightly higher than whites' rates among Cubans. The Asian American aged are the most prosperous group of immigrants. They have the highest median family income, lowest poverty rates, and highest rates of home ownership. American Indians have the highest unemployment rates and the highest mortality rates of any minority. The high levels of poverty among elderly American Indians reflect the results of more than a century of federal policy toward indigenous peoples. The federal government has the responsibility for providing health care for American Indians.

THINKING ABOUT AGING

1. Which do you think has a more powerful effect on an aged person's economic well-being: gender or race and ethnicity?
2. From a purely economic point of view, would a young woman be better off in old age by marrying or by staying single and working?
3. Why haven't women's organizations or retired people's associations made the problem of poverty among elderly women a priority? Should they be doing more to solve it?
4. What can government do to increase the economic security of minority group members in their old age?
5. Can you think of a way to increase the well-being of minority groups in their old age that does *not* involve the government?

KEY TERMS

annuity 396	redlining 399
dual entitlement 391	restrictive covenant 399
gender neutrality 390	
gender recognition 390	Retirement Equity Act of 1984 (REA) 395
joint and survivor annuity 395	spouse benefit 391
pension-splitting 396	survivor's benefit 391

EXPLORING THE INTERNET

Note: While all the URLs listed were current as of the printing of this book, these sites often change. Please check our website www.mhhe.com/quadagno for updates.

1. The American Association of Retired Persons (http://research.aarp.org/general) provides statistical information on older minorities. In the search bar, type "A Profile of Older Americans" and click on "AARP Research/ A Profile of Older Americans: 2002." Pay particular attention to the education, employment, income status, and poverty of the older Americans described in the article. Then answer the following questions:

   a. How does the average educational level of blacks compare to that of whites, Hispanics, and Native Americans?
   b. Compare the employment of Native Americans over age 65 to that of blacks, whites, and Asian/Pacific Islanders over age 65.
   c. Compare the median income of elderly Hispanics to that of elderly whites, blacks, and Asian/Pacific Islanders.
   d. What percentage of Asian/Pacific Islanders live below the poverty level?
   e. In terms of poverty, how do Asian/Pacific Islander women age 65 and over compare to white women age 65 and over?
   f. What percentage of the Native American population is over age 65? What percentage is over age 75?

2. The National Academy of Social Insurance (http://www.nasi.org/) contributes to the debate over the future of Social Security by presenting information and briefs on the retirement program. Go to the Academy's website and click on Search by Subject. Check the box next to Social Security and click the "Search on Documents in Interest Area" button. Scroll down and click on "Fact Sheet: Social Security Questions and Answers" and answer the first three questions below; then go back to the Social Security page and click on "Widows, Poverty, and Social Security" to answer the final question.

   a. About how many Americans receive monthly Social Security benefits?
   b. How are Social Security benefits paid for?
   c. Why are Social Security benefits projected to cost more in the future?
   d. Summarize in your own words what the brief says about poverty among elderly widows.

Chapter 17

The Politics of Aging

Senator Robert Byrd and Senator Ted Kennedy are senior statesman who have both been in the Senate for more than 30 years.

Looking Ahead

1. What are the voting patterns and preferences of older Americans?
2. What are the major interest groups that represent older Americans, and what have they accomplished?
3. What social movements have older Americans participated in?
4. What concepts have been used in debates about government spending on the aged?

On August 19, 1989, outraged demonstrators accosted Representative Dan Rostenkowski, then chairman of the House Ways and Means Committee, as he attempted to drive away from a meeting. Shouting "Coward!" "Recall!" and "Impeach!" the angry mob surrounded Rostenkowski's car, beating it with picket signs and pounding on its windows. The shaken congressman abandoned his car and fled the scene on foot (Himelfarb, 1995:74). Who were the rabble-rousers? Environmentalists? Animal rights activists? No. They were middle-class senior citizens, enraged over new legislation that would increase their taxes to pay for benefits many didn't need.

The scene, which was replayed many times on the nightly news, drew much attention because it was so unusual. Of all age groups, people 65 or older are the least likely to engage in political protest, least likely to demonstrate, and most likely to state that they don't believe in demonstrations (MacManus, 1996).

What went wrong? Congress had just given older people a new benefit that extended Medicare coverage, and yet it seemed they didn't want it. Some observers suggest that the demonstration in question represented a turning point in politicians' willingness to support programs for the elderly

(Day, 1990). If that is true, then it seems clear that the exercise of politics *by* the elderly may have consequences for politics *about* the elderly.

These two subjects are the focus of this chapter. In the first part, the ways in which older people express their political preferences are discussed. We examine voting behavior, the impact of interest groups on politics, the participation of older people in social movements, and the role played by older political leaders. The second part of the chapter addresses contemporary political issues and debates affecting the elderly. In this section, we consider the so-called generational equity debate and the entitlement crisis against the backdrop of society's changing perceptions of the elderly.

POLITICAL ACTIVISM AMONG THE ELDERLY

The preamble to the Constitution starts with the statement, "We, the people of the United States." More than any other country, the United States invests its governing authority in its citizens. The public has insisted on the right to elect officials at every level of government from the president, to the Congress, to judges and even sheriffs. Compared to any other modern nation, the United States has more legal offices open for election and more frequent elections. American state and local governments also submit many proposed laws, bond issues, and constitutional amendments to popular votes, something other democratic polities rarely do. And the citizenry may propose legislation through initiative petition, a right that hardly exists elsewhere (Lipset, 1996). To a degree that is unique in the Western world, American citizens have numerous opportunities to influence politics. They can participate in politics directly by becoming involved in local organizations, they can run for higher office, they can take to the streets and demonstrate, or they can vote.

Voting

Voting, the basic right of a democratic polity, is the most common form of political participation. People vote for many reasons. Partly they do so because they want to be good citizens. They also use their votes to reward politicians or parties that have behaved in ways they agree with or to punish parties or individual candidates with whom they disagree.

The influence of class, race, and gender

Although voting is the most direct link between citizens and the government, not all citizens utilize their right to vote. As Table 17–1 shows, **voter turnout** is influenced by race, class, educational level, gender, and age. More affluent, better-educated people are more likely to vote than poorer, less-educated people. People in professional and white-collar jobs are more likely to vote than manual workers. And whites vote more often than African Americans, Hispanics, or Asians, although in recent years black voter turnout in big cities has exceeded that of whites (Straits, 1990).

One factor that may explain the class and race bias in voting patterns is that middle- and upper-class people may perceive that they have a greater stake in society than those who are less well off. Better-educated citizens are also more likely to view voting as an important responsibility.

Another factor is restrictive state laws that, until recently, made registering to vote cumbersome and impeded voting among poor people. Many such laws were passed in the twentieth century by the southern states to prevent African Americans from voting. Although such requirements as poll taxes and literacy tests are now illegal, registering remained difficult until 1993, when the National Voter Registration Act, popularly known as the **Motor Voter Bill,** was passed (Piven and Cloward, 1988). The Motor Voter Bill requires all states to allow people to register to vote when they apply for driver's licenses and at any number of other designated government agencies. As soon as the bill became effective in January 1995, voter registration rates increased (MacManus, 1996).

Among younger people, political activity increases with income. More affluent people tend to be more politically involved. When the issue is Social Security, however, this pattern is reversed among senior citizens. Lower-income elders are more likely to write letters to their elected officials

Table 17-1	Self-Reported Voter Turnout (as a Percentage of Voting-Age Population, 1972–96)						
	Percentage Reporting They Voted in Presidential Election Years						
	1972	*1976*	*1980*	*1984*	*1988*	*1992*	*1996*
Age							
18–24	50%	42%	40%	41%	36%	43%	32%
25–44	63	59	59	58	54	58	49
45–64	71	69	69	70	68	70	64
65+	64	62	65	68	69	70	68
Race/Ethnicity							
White	64	61	61	61	59	64	62
Black	52	49	51	56	52	54	53
Hispanic origin	37	32	30	33	29	29	30
Sex							
Male	64	60	59	59	56	60	59
Female	62	59	59	61	58	62	61
Education							
8 years or less	47	44	43	43	37	35	34
1–3 years high school	52	47	46	44	41	41	40
4 years high school	65	59	59	59	55	58	57
1–3 years college	74	68	67	68	65	69	68
4 or more years college	83	80	80	79	78	81	80

Source: U.S. Bureau of the Census (1998b); Binstock (2000).

urging support for Social Security and more likely to vote for candidates who support Social Security and to send them campaign contributions. The most likely explanation for this behavior is that lower-income elderly are especially dependent on Social Security and likely to be affected by any cut in benefits (Campbell, 2002).

Men and women turn out to vote in approximately equal numbers, but throughout the 1980s and 1990s they distributed their votes differently. Women of all ages supported Democratic candidates more strongly than men, because Republicans are perceived by women as being less sympathetic to social programs that disproportionately benefit women and because Democrats are pro choice on abortion. In the 1996 election the gender gap was particularly sharp; President Clinton received the highest percentage of votes among women of reproductive age (Binstock, 1997).

Age and cohort differences in voter turnout
Washington politicians and the media view the elderly as a political powerhouse (Street, 1996). How accurate is that perception? Do older people wield undue political influence? If so, how do they exert such power over elected officials? Is it by their votes?

Table 17–2 shows that age has been a consistent predictor of voter registration. Several points are noteworthy. First, between 1972 and 1996 the percentage of people reporting they had registered to vote declined for all age groups except for people 65 or older. Second, the largest decline occurred among the youngest voters, those 18 to 24. And third, by

Table 17-2	Percentage of Voting-Age Persons Who Registered to Vote, by Age Groups, in U.S. Presidential Elections, 1972–96						
Age Group	1972	1976	1980	1984	1988	1992	1996
18–24	60%	51%	50%	51%	48%	53%	49%
25–44	71	66	66	67	63	65	62
45–64	80	76	76	77	76	75	74
65+	76	71	75	77	78	78	77

Source: Binstock (2000).

1996 there was a distinct and steady increase in voter registration with advancing age. Whereas only 48 percent of people 18 to 24 were registered to vote, 77 percent of people 65 or older were registered. These figures suggest that the aged are a potential political force to be reckoned with.

Yet being registered to vote is not the same as actually voting. Although the voter turnout pattern is similar to the voter registration pattern, there is one important difference. Younger people who are registered to vote are less likely to actually vote than older people. Table 17–2 shows that in 1996, 49 percent of 18- to 24-year-olds were registered to vote, yet according to Table 17–1, only 32 percent of that age group voted—a 17 point gap. By contrast, registered voters 65 or older were much more likely to vote.

Because older people are most likely to register and most likely to vote, they represent a disproportionate share of the electorate. Even though they make up only about 12 percent of the population, in recent years they have constituted over 20 percent of those who actually voted (Binstock, 1997). This pattern holds true in other countries as well. Although Canadians of all ages are more likely to vote than Americans (perhaps because unwieldy impediments to registering have never existed in Canada), voter turnout in Canada increases steadily with age (Street, 1996). Similarly, voter turnout in Germany is high among all age groups compared to the United States, but senior citizens are most likely to vote. In the 1994 elections, 86 percent of Germans aged 60 to 70 voted, compared to 76 percent of Germans younger than 60. In all, more than 30 percent of those who voted were over 60 (Naegele, 1999). In the Netherlands, 91 percent of citizens over age 71 voted in 1994, compared to 65 percent of those 18 to 26 (Schuyt, Garcia, and Knipscheer, 1999).

Voting patterns by age represent a classic example of the difficulty of separating age, period, and cohort effects, described in Chapter 1. If an *age* effect is operating, one might conclude that people are more likely to vote as they grow older. However, it may be that increased voting among older people is due to a *cohort* effect. In this case, the conclusion might be that people who are older now have always been inclined to exercise their right to vote. One might also conclude that the decline in voter registration among people 18 to 64 is due to a *period* effect—that over time, Americans have become more cynical about politics and politicians and thus less inclined to vote. But voter turnout is consistently high among older people for all election years, and voting increases with age in any single election year, suggesting that an aging effect is operating. People do seem to become more politically aware as they grow older. Perhaps, however, a cohort effect is operating, too. The young people who seem disaffected by politics may never become more active.

Age and voting preferences   Although a high percentage of the elderly vote, older people have the potential to swing elections and thus to influence the behavior of politicians only if they vote as a bloc. **Bloc voting,** in turn, can be used either prospectively or retrospectively. **Prospective voting** is the giving of votes to candidates based on promises made;

During the contested 2000 presidential election, turnout was heavy among older voters in the Wynmoor Village condominium development in Broward County, Florida.

retrospective voting is the withholding of votes based on a judgment of past performance (Street, 1996). An old-age voting bloc exists only if people vote on the basis of age for a candidate who makes certain promises, such as protecting Social Security benefits from cuts, or if they vote against a candidate who has taken certain actions, such as cutting benefits.

Like most other Americans, older people don't engage in bloc voting. Indeed, most older people can't vote as a bloc because, like most Americans, they don't know how their representatives vote on most issues. What they hear from the mass media is obscured by confusing talk of conference committees, floor votes, presidential vetoes, and administrative rulings (Walker, 1991). Also, like people of all ages, older people are quite diverse in income, social class, education, health, and almost any other criterion one might name. Because they are such a heterogeneous group, their electoral choices are rarely based on age-group interests (Binstock and Day, 1996). And doesn't this make sense? Why should someone who is female, Catholic, Hispanic, and college-educated vote the same way as a white,

Protestant male with a high school diploma simply because they both happen to be 70 years old?

There is evidence that health in combination with age influences the likelihood of voting. One survey of 1,240 people, which included 700 people with disabilities, found that voter turnout was 20 percentage points lower among people with disabilities than among people without disabilities who were otherwise similar. There was great variation among the disabled subjects. Lower turnout was concentrated among people with disabilities who were not employed or who were 65 or older, and who had difficulty going outside alone even though absentee ballots were available. The authors concluded that disability has social and psychological effects that decrease voter turnout through decreased identification with mainstream society, particularly among senior citizens (Schur, Shields, and Kruse, 2002).

Even on the seemingly crucial matter of how candidates stand on programs for the elderly, older voters have shown little inclination to vote on this basis. In 1981, for example, President Reagan proposed large cuts in Social Security benefits. In the subsequent midterm election in 1982, Republicans lost the Senate, a loss that many journalists attributed to the retribution of elderly voters. But in the 1984 presidential election, people 65 or older were most likely to have voted for Reagan (Jacobs, 1990). We find the same pattern in other countries. Even after politicians cut old-age programs, older voters in Canada and Great Britain did not punish them at the polls (Street, 1996).

That the aged are similar to other voters can also be measured by looking at their opinions on given issues. There are two theories that attempt to explain political preferences: **rational choice theory** and **symbolic politics theory.** According to rational choice theory, individual behavior and attitudes are rationally calculated to further one's self-interest. If older people are more likely than others to support programs that benefit them, we would say they are acting on the basis of self-interest. Symbolic politics theory presumes that behavior and attitudes are more strongly linked to personal beliefs than to material interests. According to this approach, an individual's party identification or self-description as liberal or conservative would be a better predictor of his or her voting preferences (Cook and Barrett, 1992).

Evidence from opinion surveys mostly supports the symbolic politics perspective with regard to age. On most policy issues, including those pertaining to the elderly, older people are nearly indistinguishable from young adults. For example, there are only minimal differences by age in support for Social Security or Medicare. Among people younger than age 30, 54.4 percent favored increasing Social Security benefits in a 1986 survey, compared to 56 percent of people 60 or older (Cook and Barrett, 1992). In the same survey, support for increasing Medicare was even higher (70.7 percent) among young people than it was among older people (64.2 percent). Over a decade later, a telephone survey of 403 Americans aged 18 to 34 showed support for Social Security was still strong among young people. In this 1999 survey, 81 percent of young adults said they supported Social Security and only 16 percent opposed it (Hart, 2000). Research does show, however, that senior citizens are much more interested

in news about Social Security compared to younger people (Campbell, 2003).

Most surveys also show that people of all ages think that Social Security taxes are about right (MacManus, 1996). Similarly, in regard to local issues, there are no age differences in the willingness to raise taxes for education. One study found that 47 percent of people younger than 55 and 49 percent of people 55 or older would vote to raise taxes for public schools (Rosenbaum and Button, 1993). In Florida, where older voters make up nearly 40 percent of the electorate, the elderly did play a role in defeating a series of school tax referenda in several counties (MacManus, 1998). But on the whole, research disputes the claim that the elderly are more likely than others to be motivated by self-interest in their political preferences.

What matters much more than age in predicting support for Social Security and Medicare is gender, race, income, and educational level. Women, African Americans, and Hispanics, low-income people, and people with less than a high school education are most likely to say the government doesn't spend enough on the elderly. These are also the people who depend most on government programs (Day, 1990).

Given that age has little influence on political beliefs, it is not surprising that voting preferences do not differ much by age. Table 17–3 shows the distribution of votes by age for six presidential elections. Overall, there are few age differences. The exception was the 1992 election, in which voters aged 60 or older favored Clinton but were unlikely to vote for Perot. Their low levels of support for Perot may reflect their reluctance to accept him as a serious candidate. In the 1980 election, voters 60 or older were also unlikely to vote for Anderson, another third-party candidate. Research consistently shows that older people are more firmly attached to traditional political institutions than to third-party platforms and their candidates. Moreover, as Binstock (1997:16) argued, "the accumulated life course experiences of years of participating in the political process tends to make them more skeptical of the value of voting for an independent."

Despite the lack of evidence that people vote their age, in politics perceptions often matter more

Table 17-3 — Nationwide Vote Distribution, by Age Groups and Gender in U.S. Presidential Elections (1980, 1984, 1988, 1992, 1996, 2000)

	1980			1984		1988		1992			1996			2000		
	Reagan	Carter	Anderson	Reagan	Mondale	Bush	Dukakis	Clinton	Bush	Perot	Clinton	Dole	Perot	Gore	Bush	Nader
All voters																
All ages	51%	41%	7%	59%	40%	53%	45%	43%	38%	19%	49%	41%	8%	48%	46%	5%
18–29	43	44	11	59	40	52	47	44	34	22	53	34	10	48	49	2
30–44	55	36	8	57	42	54	45	41	38	21	48	41	9	48	49	2
44–59	55	39	5	60	40	57	42	41	40	19	48	41	9	51	47	2
60 years or older	54	41	4	60	39	50	49	50	38	12	48	44	7			
Men																
All ages	55	36	7	62	37	57	41	41	38	21	43	44	10			
18–29	47	39	11	63	36	55	43	38	36	25	47	38	12			
30–44	59	31	8	61	38	58	40	39	38	23	41	46	10			
44–59	60	34	5	62	36	62	36	40	40	20	44	43	10			
60 years or older	56	40	3	62	37	53	46	49	36	15	43	48	8			
Women																
All ages	47	45	7	56	44	50	49	45	37	17	54	38	7			
18–29	39	49	10	55	45	49	50	48	33	19	58	31	9			
30–44	50	41	8	54	45	50	49	44	38	18	54	37	7			
44–59	50	44	5	57	42	52	48	42	40	18	52	40	7			
60 years or older	52	43	4	58	42	48	52	50	40	10	53	41	5			

Sources: Binstock (1997).

than reality. If politicians believe that older people carry clout at the ballot box, old-age advocacy groups will take advantage of this perception by employing the "electoral bluff," convincing politicians that they ignore the interests of the elderly at their peril (Binstock and Day, 1996). In recent years, this threat of retribution at the polls by older voters has diminished. "An Issue for Public Policy" describes how the presidential candidates tackled the issue of Social Security reform in the 2000 election.

Interest Group Politics

Because the U.S. government is divided into three branches—executive, legislative, and judicial—special interest and lobbying organizations exert a greater influence than they do in nations that have unified parliamentary governments. In the United States, congressional candidates are largely on their own. Parties have little to do with nominating or electing them. Because candidates finance their own campaigns through their own efforts, they are dependent on and vulnerable to influence from individuals and organizations that can produce money and campaign workers for them. As a result, American politicians are particularly susceptible to special interests (Lipset, 1996). The constitutional structure provides citizens with numerous opportunities to bring their special interests to the attention of public officials, and the need of politicians for funds and support makes them willing to bargain and make compromises.

Interest groups are organizations that represent individuals by lobbying politicians to take certain actions and by suggesting alternative proposals. Interest groups can also support candidates by informing their members that a certain candidate favors or opposes an issue of importance to them and urging members to vote accordingly (Street, 1996). Legislation proposed by interest groups does not automatically get enacted. Nor are interest groups always able to block legislation contrary to the interests of members. For example, the American Medical Association has wielded considerable influence, but Medicare was passed over the organization's heated objections (Marmor, 1973). Similarly, although the National Rifle

Association (NRA) has impeded gun control legislation for decades, assault weapons were banned over the NRA's vehement opposition. On any given issue, there are always competing interest groups lobbying actively. Who wins and who loses generally depends on such factors as who has the most money to contribute to a candidate's campaign, who has the most access to politicians who are in office, and what the American public will support.

The rise of interest group politics   Although interest groups have been a part of the American political landscape from the country's origins, they did not play a central role in politics until relatively late in the twentieth century. The rise of interest group politics is associated with the decline of political parties. The American party system reached its peak in the late nineteenth century when powerful party organizations, known as *machines*, were run by *bosses* who doled out patronage to their supporters in the form of jobs and special access to contracts for road-building or construction projects. Party organizations controlled nominations and kept their members loyal to the central party platform. Patronage politics, the machine, and the boss ruled (Walker, 1991).

During the twentieth century, other powerful interests, such as large corporations, emerged to challenge the dominance of parties. The exodus to the suburbs that began after World War II further weakened urban political machines, as suburbanites began to question the traditional distribution of power and argue that they were underrepresented in state governments and the House of Representatives. In 1964, a Supreme Count ruling gave more seats to the suburbs and shifted the balance of party power away from the cities (Walker, 1991).

Another challenge to party dominance originated in the civil rights and anti–Vietnam War movements of the 1960s when people protesting against the establishment found they had no voice in their own parties. Many Democratic party organizations in several cities became the target of protest over the Vietnam War. As antiwar protesters turned against the party leadership, they further fractured party loyalty (Ware, 1985).

An Issue for Public Policy

THE CANDIDATES' POSITIONS ON SOCIAL SECURITY IN THE 2000 PRESIDENTIAL ELECTION

*U*ntil the 2000 election, most presidential candidates took vague positions on Social Security reform, promising to "save" the program but never explaining how they would do it. They feared voters would retaliate if they even hinted at cuts in Social Security benefits. Thus nearly everyone was surprised when, early in the 2000 campaign, presidential candidate George W. Bush introduced a plan to "privatize" Social Security. Equally surprising was the lack of controversy following Bush's announcement. Even four years earlier, reaction to the plan would have been more critical.

Bush's plan would leave Social Security as is for those who were retired or nearing retirement but would allow younger workers to put a small part of their Social Security taxes, perhaps 2 percent, into a private fund invested in stocks and bonds. By putting less money into the Social Security trust fund, workers who chose private investment accounts would agree to accept lower Social Security benefits. Over a lifetime, however, a worker could accumulate thousands of dollars in investments to replace the lost Social Security income (Duka, 2000). In fact, Bush argued, many workers would be better off under his plan.

Bush's opponent, Al Gore, took what appeared to be a more traditional approach. Gore advocated using some of the federal budget surplus to shore up the Social Security program over the long term. A close look, however, revealed that Gore's plan was as radical as Bush's. For the first time, Social Security benefits would have been paid out of federal income tax dollars rather than payroll taxes.

Although both Bush and Gore proposed innovative solutions to the problem of Social Security reform, more important was the fact that both candidates talked openly about changing the system. That was a first in American politics. Subsequent analysis of the results of the 2000 election showed that Bush's support for allowing workers to invest part of their Social Security contributions in the stock market helped him win support from voters (Miller and Klobucar, 2003).

What Do You Think?

1. Are you worried about the future of the Social Security program? If so, what is your major concern—the availability of benefits when you retire or taxpayers' ability to pay for the program?
2. Does the Bush or the Gore proposal make more sense to you? Why?

Protestors march to protest the privatization of Medicare in 2003.

By the 1970s, with the old party machines fading in influence, parties had devised new ways of operating. The new model of party organization was built around the latest techniques of mass communication, professional fund-raisers, and campaign consultants. Although appeals to ethnic and racial loyalties remained a part of campaigns, candidate- rather than party-centered politics meant there was more room for individuals and organizations to make direct appeals to the public. As the potential for interest groups to intervene directly has increased, so has the number of such organizations. The growth of organizations representing the elderly thus must be evaluated in this context of expanding interest group politics overall.

The growth of the gray lobby   Until the 1960s, there were few organizations representing the interests of the aged. Beginning in the 1970s and expanding in the 1980s, there was an extraordinary organizational wave on a scale that probably exceeded that of any previous time in American history, a phenomenon that gave rise to what has been described as the **gray lobby** (Pratt, 1993).

What contributed to this phenomenal growth of old-age interest groups? One factor was the battle over health insurance for the aged. In the early 1960s, the AFL-CIO created the **National Council of Senior Citizens (NCSC)**, an organization of retired trade union members, to lobby for health insurance legislation. In 1965, 1,400 NCSC members attended the opening session of Congress, and that year Medicare was passed over the vehement objections of the American Medical Association, which spent over $20 million lobbying to prevent it (Marmor, 1973).

Another factor contributing to the expansion of the gray lobby was the convening of the **White House Conference on Aging.** Held for the first time in 1961, the conferences have taken place about every 10 years since then. The first White House Conference on Aging brought old-age advocates inside the government, which meant that grievances and proposals could be presented to the president at an officially recognized forum (Pratt, 1976). Automatic cost-of-living increases in Social Security benefits were one of the resolutions adopted at the 1971 conference. When Congress approved them the following year, the old-age organizations gained legitimacy as a viable political force.

Then in 1977, national attention was again drawn to the presence of the gray lobby when President Carter considered cutting Social Security benefits as a solution to declining reserves in the program's trust fund. Save Our Security (SOS), a coalition of senior citizen organizations, was formed to protect Social Security benefits from being cut. SOS members lobbied Congress and helped prevent any cuts in Social Security benefits.

When in 1981 President Reagan proposed a 10 percent cut in future Social Security benefits, a 31 percent cut in early retirement benefits, and a tightening of the eligibility criteria for disability benefits, his public approval rating dropped 16 points, and he immediately dropped his package of cuts (Light, 1985). However, the attack on Social Security stimulated another wave of organizing by senior citizen groups. SOS, which had been dormant for several years, was reinvigorated. SOS members wrote thousands of letters to Congress protesting the proposed cuts. New organizations were formed, and by 1994 there were 61 national organizations representing the interests of the elderly. There now exists a national network of organizations representing the interests of older people, coupled with thousands of others that are regional or local in focus.

The major senior organizations The largest senior organization, indeed, the largest voluntary organization in the United States, is the **American Association of Retired Persons (AARP)** (see Table 17–4). Founded in 1958

Table 17–4	Organizations Representing Older People
American Association of Retired Persons	The largest senior citizen organization, AARP had more than 33 million members in 1995. Publishes *Modern Maturity*. Lobbies on issues relevant to the elderly.
National Council of Senior Citizens	Created by the AFL-CIO to lobby for Medicare. Has approximately four-and-a-half million members, primarily blue-collar workers and trade unionists. Retains a liberal Democratic bias.
National Committee to Preserve Social Security and Medicare	Founded in 1982. Has more than 5 million members. Played a key role in killing the Medicare Catastrophic Coverage Act of 1988.
National Association of Retired Federal Employees	Has a membership of approximately half a million members. Primarily concerned with issues of interest to retired federal employees, especially protecting federal employees' pensions.

mainly to offer health and life insurance to retirees, AARP had more than 33 million members by 1995. AARP lobbies actively on behalf of senior issues and scored a big success in lobbying for the elimination of mandatory retirement. It has a paid staff of 1,300 and an annual budget of approximately a quarter of a billion dollars. Its magazine, The AARP Magazine, has the highest circulation of any magazine in the United States (Quadagno, 1991). *Modern Maturity* publishes voters' guides on candidates' positions, runs a wire service that provides newspaper reports on issues pertaining to the elderly, and sponsors a weekly television series. During the 1988 presidential election, in New Hampshire alone AARP mailed out 250,000 pieces of literature detailing the candidates' positions on Social Security, long-term health care, and other issues of relevance to older people. Although AARP appears powerful because it is so large, its size is also a constraint. With so diverse a membership, AARP can rarely take a position without angering at least some members. Thus, on most issues AARP takes a middle-of-the-road stance.

Other organizations are not hamstrung by these constraints. The National Council of Senior Citizens has approximately 4.5 million members, primarily blue-collar workers and trade unionists, and it retains a liberal Democratic bias. Organized around 4,000 active local clubs, NCSC has access to the full lobbying power of the AFL-CIO. Moreover, its smaller size and the shared background of its members make it more capable of taking a stance on particular issues than the unwieldy AARP (Light, 1985).

The **National Committee to Preserve Social Security and Medicare** was founded in 1982 and has more than 5 million members, a budget of $40 million, and a well-funded political action committee. It played a key role in killing the Medicare Catastrophic Coverage Act of 1988, described later in this chapter. Finally, the **National Association of Retired Federal Employees** has a membership of approximately half a million members and is concerned primarily with issues of interest to retired federal employees. It has an annual budget of $5 million and a large political action committee. This list of organizations that comprise the old-age lobby, while not exhaustive, gives some sense of those that are the most active and influential.

How effective is the gray lobby? Interestingly, although there have been a few exceptional cases where age-based interest groups have been very effective, most legislation for older people has actually been proposed by others. More often the main role of the old-age interest groups has been that of protecting existing benefits, not winning new ones. Thus, while it would be misleading to say that these groups are a political powerhouse, it would be equally misleading to say that the gray lobby has not had some influence at key moments.

Until recently, older Europeans were less politically active than older Americans. This trend is changing rapidly, however. "Aging around the World" describes the political mobilization of the aged in Europe.

Social Movement Politics

If you pick up a newspaper on any given day, you are likely to see some protest activity occurring over such diverse issues as abortion, animal rights, civil rights, gender equality, gun control, or gay marriage. These are conspicuous social happenings called **social movements.** Like interest groups, social movements are collectivities of people organized to promote or resist change. However, interest groups are embedded within the mainstream political environment and are typically regarded as legitimate actors within that environment. By contrast, social movements are "typically outside the polity or overlap with it in a precarious fashion" (McAdam and Snow, 1997:xxi). Another difference is that interest groups pursue their collective objectives through institutionalized methods such as lobbying or soliciting campaign contributions, whereas social movements resort to noninstitutional methods such as demonstrations or sit-ins.

In general, older people are least likely of all age groups to be adherents to a social movement. Because they have the strongest investment in traditional political activities such as voting, they rarely express their political beliefs by participating in

Aging around the World

POLITICAL INVOLVEMENT AMONG OLDER EUROPEANS

For much of the post–World War II period, older Europeans were excluded from many political institutions, including trade unions and political parties (Walker, 1999). From the 1950s to the 1970s, numerous pensioner organizations did form, but most represented older people's interests in the policy arena, rather than mobilizing them to participate directly in politics.

The 1990s saw an upsurge of direct political involvement by older Europeans. Two countries, the Netherlands and the Czech Republic, have "gray" parties that have won some seats in the national parliaments (Kohli, 2000). In Portugal the Party of National Solidarity, which supports candidates whose views are favorable to the aged, has helped to swing the outcomes of several elections (Walker, 1999).

In other European countries, senior citizens have organized protective associations. In Germany the Senior Protection Association, formed in 1975, has 200 local chapters. Also known as the Gray Panthers, the association is nevertheless a small organization, with only about 15,000 members. In the United Kingdom the Pensioner Protection Party, started in 1991, has more than 2 million members. In Denmark the "C" Team, a group of organizations representing older people, coordinates mass demonstrations aimed at preventing cuts in health care and social services. The C Team also advocates measures aimed at improving programs for the frail elderly.

What has created this rise in senior citizens' political involvement? The major cause has been the cuts in pension programs European governments have been making. Another factor is the encouragement of policymakers, who have invited the aged to participate more actively in the political process. In many cases, local governments have established senior citizen boards to advise them on policy issues (Walker and Naegele, 1999). Despite the upsurge in political participation, however, the majority of older Europeans do not participate in political organizations, and those who do have only minimal influence.

What Do You Think?

1. Compare the political activities of older Europeans to those of older Americans. How do they differ?
2. Relate what you have learned about the demographics and social welfare systems of European countries (see Chapters 4 and 11) to the relative lack of participation of the elderly in European politics.

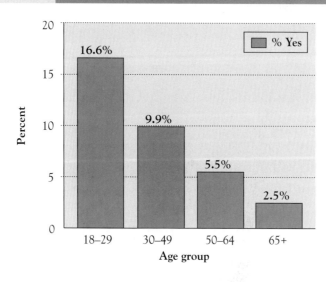

Figure 17-1   Percentage of People Who Took Part in a Public Demonstration.

Source: MacManus (1996).

protest rallies or demonstrations. As Figure 17–1 shows, 16.6 percent of people between the ages of 18 and 29 said they took part in a political demonstration in the past year, compared to only 2.5 percent of those 65 or older. Moreover, only 28.5 percent of people 65 or older believe that staging protests is an effective way to influence government, compared to 56.7 percent of young people (MacManus, 1996). It takes an issue of great magnitude to trigger protest among the elderly. Indeed, only twice in the twentieth century were older people sufficiently disturbed about an issue to be drawn to a social movement or to participate widely in social movement activity.

The Townsend movement   The first major social movement attracting primarily older people was the **Townsend movement,** founded in 1933. Named after its founder, Dr. Francis Townsend, the movement was dedicated to enacting the Townsend plan, a proposal to give all people 65 or older a pension of $150 a month (Holtzman, 1963). A retired physician, Townsend traversed the country, giving inspirational speeches on the plight of the elderly. A network of Townsend clubs was formed across the nation, and members bombarded members of

Congress with letters and postcards pleading for the enactment of a national old-age pension. At its peak, the Townsend movement claimed more than a million members. When Townsend-backed candidates won elections, incumbent elected officials across the nation sat up and took notice. The Townsend movement has been credited with hastening passage of the Social Security Act of 1935 (Amenta and Zylan, 1991).

Medicare Catastrophic Coverage Act of 1988   Not until 1988, when Congress passed the **Medicare Catastrophic Coverage Act,** did the elderly again rise up in protest. On July 1, 1988, the act was signed into law. It increased coverage of long-term hospital stays and added a prescription drug benefit, mammography screenings, hospice care, and caregiver support. But the new legislation provided no help with the burdensome cost of nursing home care, the major worry of most elderly (Street, 1993). Furthermore, the new benefits were financed by a surtax of up to $800 a year, to be paid by middle- and upper-income aged, many of whom already were covered by private supplemental health insurance policies.

The Catastrophic Coverage Act triggered an explosive reaction from the aged—the first major protest since the Townsend movement. Congressional offices were flooded with letters and phone calls from incensed constituents, who demanded that Congress repeal the legislation, reduce the tax, or give them the right to opt out of the program (Binstock, 1997). On October 4, 1989, members of the House voted to repeal the program they had approved just 16 months earlier. Two days later the Senate voted to repeal the surtax and eliminate all but the long-term hospital benefits (Day, 1993). The lesson of this experience was that Americans are unwilling to pay for a program that is not going to benefit them.

The Aged as Political Office Holders

Few Americans ever run for political office, even at the local level. Some think they would have no chance of winning. Others think they don't know enough about the issues. Many believe that a life in politics takes too great a personal toll. Holding office means giving up privacy and time with one's family and perhaps even entails a move to Washington or to a state capital. Add to that lots of travel and the cost of maintaining a second home, and it's easy to see why most Americans have no interest in a political career.

Given such sacrifices, why does anyone run at all? Some people run for office because they are committed to a cause and believe they can make a difference. Others are interested in a career in politics and see each office held as a step toward a higher office. A local city council member may decide to run for a vacant seat in the state senate. A member of the House of Representatives may decide to run for governor. A governor may run for the presidency. That's what Jimmy Carter, Ronald Reagan, Bill Clinton, and George W. Bush did.

In general, the higher the office, the older is the age of the officeholder. In part, this reflects minimum age requirements for certain offices. The U.S. Constitution requires that an individual be at least 25 years old to be a member of the House of Representatives, 30 to be in the Senate, and 35 to become

president. Many state constitutions also have minimum age requirements for state and local government positions. The older age of officeholders in high-government positions also reflects career patterns in politics as people move to more prestigious positions (MacManus, 1996).

Age sometimes arises as an issue when someone of advanced age runs for political office. In the twentieth century, only three presidents were 65 or older when they were inaugurated (Stanley and Niemi, 1994). Ronald Reagan was the oldest person to become president, and during his campaign people wondered if he was too old to be president, and especially whether he would remain healthy. Despite these concerns, he won the election. In the 1996 presidential election, Bob Dole's age was sometimes an issue. The press had a field day when Dole confused the pop star Michael Jackson with the basketball player Michael Jordon. And public opinion polls found that two out of five Americans thought Dole was too old for the White House (Thomma, 1996). Still, it seems that the outcome of elections is determined more by issues than by the candidate's age.

Does it matter whether there are older people in politics? The issue of who is represented raises a fundamental question about the meaning of democracy. What really is being asked is, Should political leaders mirror the people they represent? Women and minorities, always underrepresented in politics, respond, *yes*, it does matter. After all, women were not granted the right to vote in national elections until 1920, and most African Americans living in the South could not vote until 1965, when the Voting Rights Act was passed. For most of the twentieth century, both women and minorities sought political office and made slow and modest gains. The real issue is whether female officeholders are likely to take different positions from males—positions that better represent women—and whether minorities bring a different perspective to political debates. Do voters prefer to have people in office who share their views, regardless of age, race, or gender, or to have women or African Americans in office regardless of the positions they might hold on given issues (Phillips, 1991)?

There are no simple answers to these questions. When the elderly President Reagan proclaimed to elderly delegates to a White House conference, "We are of the same generation," a cartoon mocked his position, comparing his income of $515,878 to that of a Social Security recipient living on the minimum benefit of $2,043 per year (Powell, Branco, and Williamson, 1996). Yet older people might also be more sensitive to issues that a younger person might overlook.

Other Forms of Political Involvement

Older people are involved in politics in many other ways besides holding office. They are more likely than younger people to follow primary contests from beginning to end, more likely to watch party conventions on television, and more likely to become involved in political party activities. They work in voter registration drives, help recruit local candidates to run for office, and get involved in party organizations. The next time you vote, notice who is helping at the polls (MacManus, 1998). You will see many older people handing out ballots. Older people may also get involved in local community politics. In California, a group of senior citizens from the Laguna Woods retirement community successfully fought a plan to build an airport near their homes (Andel and Liebig, 2002).

Joseph Dimow, a retired machine shop worker, has been a lifelong political activist since he got out of the Army. In "In their Own Words," he describes some of his many activities.

POLITICAL DEBATES ABOUT THE AGED

The core social insurance programs of the American welfare state are Social Security and Medicare (see Chapter 11). These programs are **entitlements.** In budgetary terms, what distinguishes entitlements from other programs is that entitlements are governed by formulas set in law and not subject to annual appropriations by Congress (Congressional Budget Office, 1994). In other words, entitlement

programs are on automatic pilot: If people meet the eligibility criteria, they automatically receive the benefits. Entitlements stand in distinction to two other federal budget categories, discretionary spending, which includes domestic and defense spending, and net interest on the debt.

In considering the nature of politics about the aged, it is important to understand that much of what appears to be a political debate about the elderly is, in reality, a struggle over the future of Social Security and Medicare. Struggles over policies are struggles not only over concrete options but also over meaning and interpretation. The outcome of these struggles organizes the political terrain and places limits on what options might be considered. For example, Theda Skocpol (1995) noted that "universalistic programs have sustained moral imageries that allow the programs to redistribute income and deliver special services to disadvantaged Americans without risking public disaffection and political backlash" (p. 21). Similarly, Carroll Estes (1996) explained, when definitions of reality become widely shared, they "take on the character of objective reality, regardless of inherent validity, because people act as if they are connected to concrete realities" (p. 446). These definitions of reality "influence opinions and shape the public policies that flow from them." These struggles have become embedded in the American political scene because public support for social programs is not determined solely by economic considerations but is mediated by political discourse (Quadagno, 1996b).

In the following sections, we describe the changing status of the aged and discuss how these changes have influenced public debates about the proper distribution of resources between generations.

The Deserving Elderly

In fewer than three decades, a dramatic transformation in the perception of the aged occurred. For most of the twentieth century, the elderly were viewed as deserving and needy, and it was comparatively easy to garner public support for income and health care benefits for older people. As we saw in Chapter 11, the Social Security Act of 1935 was passed during the Great Depression in response

In Their Own Words

Reminiscences of a Lifelong Activist

Joseph Dimow describes his lifelong political activities this way:

> In all this time, all the decades that I worked in shops, my other activities in the evenings and weekends . . . they were always as important or more important to me. I worked in electoral campaigns, I worked in community groups ranging from neighborhood improvement associations to tenants groups to ethnic groups . . . I was a member of an advisory committee to the community school, the citywide president of that for several years . . . I was involved in several minor party efforts to get on the ballot–the Progressive Party, the Citizens Party, the Peace and Freedom Party. I was also a member of an advisory committee to the police department on community relations. We worked on getting more minorities on the police department, changing some of the rules and regulations, attitudes of police toward women . . . and all that sort of thing. (Shuldiner, 1995:48)

Now that he is no longer working, Dimow is still a political activist:

> I write a monthly column for *Jewish Currents* magazine. And I'm involved with an organization, World Fellowship, that runs a summer camp with educational programs. . . . There are other organizations that I meet with too, like Veterans for Peace. I helped organize a chapter of that. (Shuldiner, 1995:60)

Dimow is also branching out, exploring new interests. He always regretted that he never received a college education. Now he is taking classes at a university, learning about music, art history, and philosophy.

Source: Shuldiner (1995).

---

to reports of high unemployment and poverty among older people. Despite those benefits, in 1960 poverty rates for people 65 or older hovered around 30 percent (Duncan and Smith, 1989). Old-age poverty remained high because of rising retirement rates among older men, inadequate Social Security benefits, and high health care costs. Over the next two decades, several factors improved the economic security of older people. Among them were the passage of Medicare and Medicaid in 1965, substantial increases in Social Security benefits between 1968 and 1972, and automatic cost-of-living increases added to Social Security in 1972 (Derthick, 1979). As the economic status of the aged improved, rates of poverty among children increased. Figure 17–2 shows the trajectory of poverty levels in the United States among children and people 65 or older. The reversal of fortune for children and the elderly fueled debates about equity between generations.

The Generational Equity Debate

In the past two decades discussions of programs for the aged have been couched in terms of a "crisis" (Estes, Linkins, and Binney, 1996). The themes in these discussions have been those of **generational equity** (Thurow, 1999) and an **entitlement crisis** (Quadagno, 1989; Quadagno, 1996b). The argument is that the elderly have been the beneficiaries of an unfair distribution of public resources that has left them as a group financially better off than the nonaged population (Peterson, 1993; Lamm, 1999). Because the flow of resources to the elderly seems "intergenerationally

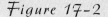

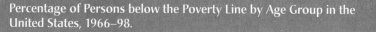

Percentage of Persons below the Poverty Line by Age Group in the United States, 1966–98.

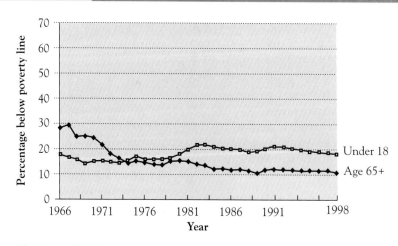

Source: U.S. Bureau of the Census (1999a).

inequitable," it will eventually create intergenerational conflict (Kingson, Hirshorn, and Cornman, 1986:130). Thus there is a political trade-off between meeting the needs of the young and the old.

This argument first gained credence in 1984, when the distinguished demographer Samuel Preston published an article in a leading scholarly journal decrying the rise in child poverty. Preston noted that public expenditures on children had been declining even as expenditures on older people rose. According to Preston, in the public sphere, gains for one group come partly at the expense of another. In his view, income transfers from workers to the elderly also represented transfers away from children (Preston, 1984). This argument was then repeated in more sensational terms by generational equity proponents such as the writer Phillip Longman (1982), who argued that we should not be "squandering the nation's limited wealth on an unproductive segment of the population" (p. 24) but rather should do more for children.

Social scientists who have evaluated the merits of the generational equity argument have responded that claims of crisis are frequently made in American politics. Compelling illustrations can always be found to dramatize a problem and support a proposed solution (Marmor, Cook, and Scher,

1997). Too often these are used to simplify a complex social problem and justify a single policy response. As Munnell (1999) points out, Social Security and Medicare costs are often lumped together and treated as a single "crisis," when in fact the two are separate programs that are financed separately and face different problems. Furthermore, public opinion polls show that the American public supports spending on Social Security, although between 1986 and 1997 there was a slight increase in the percentage who favored reducing Social Security benefits, particularly among young adults (Silverstein, Angelelli, and Parrott 2001).

A central issue in the generational equity debate is whether there is a trade-off between spending on the elderly and spending on children. Pampel (1994) analyzed international trends in spending on children and the elderly in 18 Western nations and found that high spending for the elderly was *not* associated with low spending for children. To the contrary, nations with high levels of spending on the elderly also spent highly on children. In other words, it's possible to provide adequately for children *and* the elderly.

Defining child poverty as an issue of generational equity misses the real issue: Poor children live in households run by parents with low income. Rising poverty among children is partly a result of declines in family income over time, as real wages and family incomes stagnated since the 1970s (Gottschalk and Danziger, 1993). Child poverty has also increased because of a substantial rise in female-headed households. In just 10 years, from 1979 to 1989, the proportion of never-married mothers grew by 84 percent, and these families have the highest rates of poverty, at about 36 percent (Mishel and Bernstein, 1993:293). Families headed by women are poor because women still earn lower wages than men, because the majority of fathers still pay no child support, and because many women with young children are unable to work given problems with transportation and finding affordable child care.

Generational equity in comparative perspective

The notion of generational equity is not exclusively American. Following reforms to the Dutch early-retirement scheme to encourage older workers to work longer, there was a sudden increase in concern about generational equity. Whereas previously people had favored preserving jobs for young workers and encouraging older workers to leave the labor force, during the 1990s support for age equality in job opportunities for both young and old workers in the labor market increased significantly (Dalen and Henkins, 2002). In New Zealand and Great Britain, similar issues have been raised (Thomson, 1996; Walker, 1996). The issue has also been raised in Canada, in the context of public policy discussions, though it is rarely discussed in the media (Cook et al., 1994; Marmor, Cook and Scher, 1997). One study compared how often the term *generational equity* was used in Canadian and U.S. newspapers and magazines. Between 1980 and 1992, there were many articles in Canadian newspapers dealing with the old and the young, but they usually emphasized cooperation and positive communication. Common titles were "Young and Young at Heart Give Education a New Twist: Children, Seniors, Learning from Each Other"; "Age Barriers Knocked Down as Youngsters Mix with Elderly" (Cook et al., 1994:97–98). The term *generational equity* appeared in only one article in Canada over the entire period studied.

In the United States during the same period, 39 references to generational equity appeared; the number peaked at 13 in 1987. Headlines like the following were common: "U.S. Coddles Elderly but Ignores Plight of Children"; "America Is at War with Its Children"; "Robbing Baby Peter to Pay Aging Paul" (Cook et al., 1994). One newspaper, the *Kansas City Star*, ran a year-long editorial campaign that argued repeatedly for cuts in Social Security and Medicare. Generational inequity was a strong theme of the series, which contained shrill and unflattering portrayals of age-group interests but did little to advance civic understanding of policy issues (Ekerdt, 1998).

Why are generational relations portrayed so differently in Canada and the United States? One reason is that, compared to Canada, the United States spends more for health care on the elderly than it spends on children. That's because the United States only provides Medicare to the elderly and Medicaid to the poor, whereas Canada has national health insurance for all people, regardless of age and income. Until 1992, Canada also had a program of family allowances, a small payment out of federal funds for all families with children younger than 18. The United States has no equivalent program (Quadagno, 1991). Another reason is that Canada has no senior citizen organizations equivalent to the gray lobby that has been so visible in the United States. The perception that gray organizations are powerful contributes to a sense of generational inequity (Cook et al., 1994). Finally, generational equity may have become a more acceptable framework for discussions of public policy in the United States because the U.S. poverty levels among children and the elderly have not converged as they have in Canada. In 1991, about 20 percent of people aged 65 or older and 20 percent of children younger than 18 in Canada were living in poor households with low income (Cook et al., 1994).

Is generational conflict likely in the future?

For the past two decades, political commentators have been predicting a generational war that has yet to materialize. Are apprehensions of generational antagonisms ill founded?

As we saw earlier, most research shows no difference by age in regard to public policy issues (Jacobs, 1990). Nonetheless, the results of one study of generational differences in public opinion suggest that sufficient cleavages exist in attitudes toward certain issues to raise concern (Rosenbaum and Button, 1993).

In this study, a representative sample of Florida residents was asked about attitudes toward the aging. The researchers selected Florida because its high proportion of older residents puts it on "the leading edge of a profound urban demographic transformation in which the aging will become an increasingly large proportion . . . of many communities and political constituencies" (Rosenbaum and Button, 1993:488). They found that substantial

proportions of younger Floridians (from one-third to one-half) agreed that older residents in their city or county were "an economic burden, an economically selfish voting bloc, a generationally divisive influence, or an unconstructive community element" (p. 488). They also found that people with the most critical attitudes toward the aged came from counties with a high proportion of older residents. The researchers concluded that antipathy toward the aged is likely to grow as the size of the local aged population increases.

This example notwithstanding, although the theme of generational equity has appeared frequently in the media, few Americans have bought the depiction of the elderly as greedy, selfish, and unproductive. Unlike the poor, hidden from sight

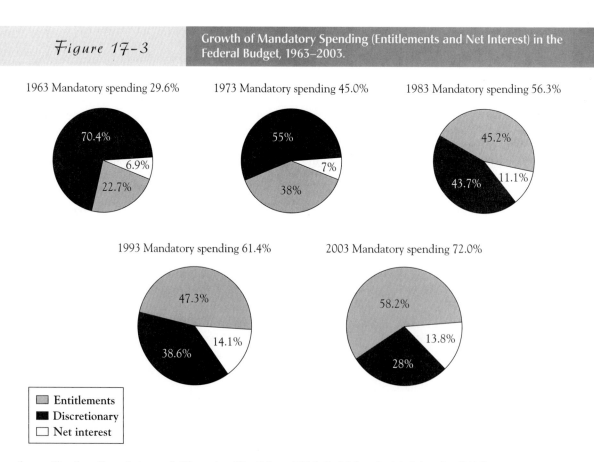

Figure 17-3 **Growth of Mandatory Spending (Entitlements and Net Interest) in the Federal Budget, 1963–2003.**

Source: Bipartisan Commission on Entitlement and Tax Reform (1996); Social Security Administration (2003).

in bleak inner cities, the elderly are highly visible, present in every American family. People have only to look at their own parents and grandparents to know that most older people are living comfortably but not grandly and that if the federal government stopped providing income security and health care, they—their children and grandchildren—would have to bear the burden. As discussions of generational equity waned, political discourse became focused on a new theme: the impending *entitlement crisis* (Quadagno, 1989; 1996b).

The Entitlement Crisis

The notion of an entitlement crisis is centered on two themes: (1) approximately one-third of the federal budget has been devoted to programs for older people, and (2) spending on the elderly will increase as the baby boom generation reaches retirement age (Congressional Budget Office, 1995a). The large amount of expenditures devoted to the aged has supported stereotypes depicting older people as prosperous, hedonistic, selfish, and politically powerful (Binstock and Day, 1996).

The core thesis of believers in an entitlement crisis is that entitlement spending is consuming a disproportionate share of the federal budget, crowding out other social needs (Penny and Schier, 1996; Quadagno, 1996b, 1999). According to this scenario, entitlement spending cannot be sustained at current levels. The "graying of the welfare state is likely to have catastrophic consequences for the living standards of most working-age Americans" because taxes will have to be raised to astronomical levels to pay older Americans the benefits that they have been promised (Howe, 1997:36).

How valid are these concerns? Figure 17–3 shows that there *was* an increase in entitlement spending from 22.7 to 47.3 percent of the federal budget, between 1965 and 1993, a result of start-up costs associated with Medicare, which was passed in 1965. However, entitlement spending only grew slowly after 1975. In the 10-year period from 1993 to 2003, entitlement spending increased by less than one percent, from 47.3 to 47.9 percent of federal expenditures. Spending on the three largest programs—Social Security, Medicare, and Medicaid—has been stable for more than a decade. There is no current entitlement crisis (Congression Budget Office, 2003).

What's important to recognize is that public policies are constantly undergoing revision. The Social Security trust fund does have a long-term financing problem that must be resolved (Kingson and Quadagno, 1996). In doing so, it may be necessary to make other changes, a subject we considered in more detail in Chapter 15. Medicare has experienced numerous cuts in the past two decades, and it is likely to experience more in the future. Combining all entitlement spending in one category doesn't help solve these pressing policy dilemmas. The problem with crisis scenarios such as generational equity and the entitlement crisis is that the substance of the issues becomes obscured in heated rhetoric.

Chapter Resources

LOOKING BACK

1. **What are the voting patterns and preferences of older Americans?** *Older people have the potential to exert a significant influence on any election since they comprise a disproportionate share of the electorate. However, there is no evidence that they engage in bloc voting. Often older people have supported candidates or parties that enacted proposals against their interests. In general, there are few age differences in political preferences. Young and old have similar attitudes toward public spending and similar preferences for presidential candidates. An exception was the 1992 presidential election, in which older voters were less likely to vote for Ross Perot, a reflection of the skepticism older people have regarding the effectiveness of third-party candidates.*

2. **What are the major interest groups that represent older Americans, and what have they accomplished?** *The American Association of Retired Persons is the largest organization of older people in the United States. Other important organizations include the National Council of Senior Citizens, the National Committee to Preserve Social Security and Medicare, and the National Association of Retired Federal Employees. Despite the presence of many large organizations representing the interests of older people, it is important not to overestimate their political power. Very large organizations, such as AARP, find it difficult to take a position on any issue because their membership is so diverse. Often the old-age organizations disagree with each other. The greatest accomplishment of these interest groups has been in protecting Social Security and Medicare.*

3. **What social movements have older Americans participated in?** *Although older people are the least likely age group to participate in a political demonstration, on two occasions in the twentieth century they felt strongly enough about an issue to become involved in a social movement. The first social movement composed primarily of older people was the Townsend movement. Supporters lobbied Congress for a national old-age pension. Many observers believe that their influence hastened passage of the Social Security Act of 1935. The Medicare Catastrophic Coverage Act of 1988 generated an exceptional kind of protest politics by the elderly because they felt they were being taxed unfairly and because the legislation did not provide the one benefit they needed most—help with the costs of nursing home care.*

4. **What concepts have been used in debates about government spending on the aged?** *Until recently the aged have been considered deserving recipients of social benefits. As improvements in Social Security benefits raised the living standards of the retired, some people began to claim that the elderly were receiving an unfair share of societal resources, especially compared to what children receive. This is the central idea behind the notion of generational equity. Generational equity is primarily an American idea that has had little influence in other countries in debates about government spending. Another concept that is widely used is that there is an entitlement crisis. The notion of an entitlement crisis consists of two themes. The first is that expenditures on the aged are usurping an unfair share of federal resources. The second is that current trends cannot be sustained in the future when the baby boom generation begins to retire.*

THINKING ABOUT AGING

1. What do you think is the single most pressing political issue for older Americans?

2. The "gray lobby" has been advocating prescription drug coverage for the aged for some time. What interest groups

might oppose such legislation? Would some older Americans belong to those interest groups?

3. Today's older Americans tend to engage in the same kind of political activity they engaged in when they were younger. When members of the baby boom generation retire, what kind of political activity can we expect to see from them? Be specific.

4. Now that Americans are living longer, should there be an upper limit on the age of candidates for high public office? Why or why not?

5. Do you think children in the United States deserve the same degree of support from their government as the aged? Explain your reasoning in sociological terms.

KEY TERMS

American Association of Retired Persons (AARP) 419

bloc voting 412

entitlement crisis 425

entitlements 424

generational equity 425

gray lobby 418

interest groups 416

Medicare Catastrophic Coverage Act of 1988 422

Motor Voter Bill 410

National Association of Retired Federal Employees 420

National Committee to Preserve Social Security and Medicare 420

National Council of Senior Citizens (NCSC) 419

prospective voting 412

rational choice theory 414

retrospective voting 413

social movements 420

symbolic politics theory 414

Townsend movement 422

voter turnout 410

White House Conference on Aging 419

EXPLORING THE INTERNET

Note: While all the URLs listed were current as of the printing of this book, these sites often change. Please check our website www.mhhe.com/quadagno for updates.

1. The Senior Caucus is a website devoted to senior citizens and those concerned about the well-being of senior citizens within the Democratic Party. To find out more about which candidates National Organizations endorse, go to the Senior Caucus website (www.seniorcaucus.com) and link to "Archive." Link to the article, "National Council of Senior Citizens Endorses Al Gore For President," and answer the following questions:

   a. Why did the NCSC endorse Gore?
   b. Why did the NCSC describe the 2000 election as the "most significant crossroads for America's seniors in many years"?
   c. How did presidential candidates Al Gore and George Bush differ in their stances on seniors' income and health security?
   d. What would be the impact of Bush's privatization plan for the Social Security program?

2. The Gray Panthers (http://www.graypanthers.org/) is a group of activists dedicated to working for elders' social and economic interests. Go to the Panthers' website and link to Campaigns to answer the following questions.

   a. What is the Panthers' stance on the Medicare program?
   b. Summarize at least three of the seven principles that the Gray Panthers assert must guide Medicare reform.
   c. After reading the Jobs Position Statement, explain what MAI means.
   d. Do the Gray Panthers think the Social Security program is in crisis? Explain.
   e. What is the Gray Panthers' three-part proposal for strengthening the Social Security program?

Glossary

A

active euthanasia *Also known as assisted suicide, occurs when a physician, close friend, or relative helps an ill or disabled person terminate his or her life.*

active life expectancy *Measure of the number of years a person can expect to live without a disability.*

activities of daily living (ADL) *Measure of need for help with basic functions such as eating, bathing, dressing, getting to and from the bathroom, getting in and out of bed, and walking.*

activity theory *A theory of aging which states that the psychological and social needs of the elderly are no different from those of the middle-aged and that it is neither normal nor natural for older people to become isolated and withdrawn; also called the implicit theory of aging.*

adaptation *A range of behaviors to meet demands; includes developing habits to confront problems and manage frustration and anxiety.*

adverse mortality selection process *Those who are at high risk of contracting life-threatening diseases die earlier, leaving a group of relatively healthy survivors.*

age cohort *Refers to people who were born at the same time and thus share similar life experiences.*

age discrimination *Negative behavior toward older people; acting on the basis of stereotypes.*

Age Discrimination in Employment Act of 1967 (ADEA) *Banned discrimination against workers aged 40 to 65; made it illegal for employers to fire, demote, or reduce the salary of older workers without showing good cause.*

age effect *A difference due to chronological age or life course stage.*

age grade *Use of age as a social category to group people by status—the expectations for when the transition from one role to another should occur.*

age integration theory *a theory that recognizes that societies have both age-segregated and age-integrated institutions that can either impede or enhance the participation of the aged.*

ageism *A systematic stereotyping of and discrimination against people because they are old.*

age norm *Informal rules, which specify age-appropriate roles and behavior.*

age stratification theory *Underlying proposition is that all societies group people into social categories and that these groupings provide people with social identities; age is one principle of ranking, along with wealth, gender, and race.*

age structure *The distribution of people across various age cohorts.*

age 30 transition *One of Levinson's developmental periods of adulthood; major tasks in this period are establishing a niche in society and developing competence in a chosen craft and then working at succeeding.*

age timetable *Similar to age norms but looser and more flexible; informal rules, which specify age-appropriate roles and behavior.*

aging in place *The natural aging of an area as the members of the population grow old; often accompanied by the out-migration of young adults; also refers to when elderly people live at home or in a community setting rather than in a nursing home.*

almshouse *An institution for the poor.*

Alzheimer's disease *Severe organic deterioration of the brain that affects memory, cognitive functions, and personality to a degree sufficient to interfere with normal activities and social functioning; symptoms include impairment of memory, intellect, judgment, and orientation and excessive or shallow emotions; the most common type of dementia.*

American Association of Retired Persons (AARP) *The largest senior organization and the largest voluntary organization in the United States; lobbies actively on behalf of senior issues.*

angina *Chest pain that may precede a heart attack.*

aphasia *Involves damage to the speech and language centers in the brain; one of the consequences of a stroke; occurs when the brain is deprived of oxygen; patients may be unable to produce meaningful speech or to understand spoken or written language.*

arthritis *A chronic disease that causes joint inflammation and its consequences of pain, swelling, and deformity.*

assisted living facility *A type of housing that includes assistance with daily activities and 24-hour oversight; caters to a more affluent clientele than board and care homes; usually provides private rooms and baths or small apartments, social and recreational facilities, and individualized care.*

B

basal cell carcinoma *Common type of skin cancer; easily cured.*

bean pole family structure *The phenomenon of four or five generations of a family surviving at one time.*

bloc voting *When individuals vote as a group on the basis of some characteristic such as age.*

board and care home *A facility that provides meals and assistance in basic activities of daily living; ranges from small, unlicensed rooms in a residential setting to hotel-like arrangements housing 200 or more residents.*

bridge jobs *Jobs that span the period between full-time employment in a career job and permanent retirement.*

C

capitation *A payment system in which a health maintenance organization receives a flat monthly fee for each patient in the system regardless of what services are performed.*

caregiver burden *Difficulty in managing the specific tasks to be performed in caring for the frail elderly.*

caregiver stress *The subjective appraisal of the strain on the caregiver.*

cataract *A condition in which the lens of the eye becomes cloudy, and light cannot penetrate.*

central nervous system *The brain and spinal cord.*

cerebellum *A brain structure involved in body movements and, to some degree, balance; located at the back and base of the brain; essential in the fine-tuning of voluntary and involuntary muscular movements.*

child dependency ratio *The number of persons younger than 18 relative to those of working age.*

chronic disease *Condition for which there is no cure.*

chronological age *Number of years a person has lived.*

classic aging pattern *Age-related declines in verbal and performance intelligence among people 60 or older.*

climacteric *The syndrome of physical and psychological changes that occur in midlife.*

clinical depression *A set of symptoms that includes depressed mood, loss of interest in pleasurable activities, loss of appetite, sleep disturbance, fatigue, feelings of worthlessness and guilt, difficulties in thinking and concentration, psychomotor disturbances, and suicidal notions.*

cognitive psychology *The study of mental processes.*

cohort *The aggregate of individuals who experienced the same event within the same time interval.*

cohort aging *The continuous advancement of a cohort from one age category to another over its life span.*

cohort effect *A difference due to the experiences or characteristics of the particular cohort to which an individual belongs.*

companionate grandparenting *Grandparents who focus on emotionally satisfying, leisure-time activities and report an easygoing, friendly style of interaction with their grandchildren.*

compression of morbidity thesis *The theory that improvements in health care and prevention will compress the years that an individual will be disabled into the last few years of the life span.*

contingent work *An arrangement where workers are not a part of the firm's permanent workforce but are hired only to do a specific job on a temporary basis.*

continuing care retirement community (CCRC) *A planned retirement community that provides a continuum of housing arrangements and services ranging from independent living to assisted living to skilled nursing care.*

continuity theory *A more formal elaboration of activity theory; uses a life course perspective to define normal aging and to distinguish it from pathological aging.*

convergence theory   A theory of aging that views old age as a great leveler, which reduces inequality that was evident at earlier stages of the life course.

convoy model of social relations   A theoretical model stating that each person moves through life surrounded by a group of people to whom he or she is related through the exchange of social support; dynamic and lifelong in nature.

coping   A state of compatibility between the individual and the environment so that the individual maintains a sense of well-being or satisfaction with quality of life.

coronary bypass surgery   A procedure to reduce blockage of the blood vessels supplying the heart.

cost-of-living adjustment   Automatic yearly increase in Social Security that is linked to inflation.

countertransition   A life course transition produced by the role changes of others.

creativity   A measure of divergent thinking; the production of alternative solutions to a problem or situation; most elusive mental process to define and measure.

crisis theory   A theory that views the occupational role as the major source of personal validation; perceives the loss of the work role as a wrenching experience that deprives the individual of a job, status, and a meaningful role in society.

cross-linkage theory of aging   A theory of biological aging; states that the accumulation of cross-linked collagen is responsible for many changes associated with aging such as the loss of elasticity of the skin, hardening of the arteries of the circulatory system, and stiffness of joints throughout the body.

cross-sectional research   Research comparing people of different age cohorts at a single point in time.

crowded nest   The trend of young adults returning to the parental home.

crystallized intelligence   Intelligence based on the information, skills, and strategies that people have learned through experience; reflects accumulated past experience and socialization.

D

deeds of gift   Contracts specifying obligations owed to parents by children in return for inheritance of family property; found in colonial New England.

deferred exchange strategies   Exchanges between individuals over the life course.

defined benefit   A pension plan in which the benefit level is based on years of service and prior earnings; a specified amount that is guaranteed when a worker reaches a given age.

defined contribution   A pension benefit based on the amount that has accumulated in the account, including contributions plus any gains or losses from investments, expenses, or forfeitures; a savings account with certain tax advantages.

dementia   A form of mental illness that mainly occurs in old age.

demographic transition   The shift from high mortality and fertility to low mortality and fertility that causes population aging; occurs in three stages.

demography   The study of the basic population processes of fertility, mortality, and migration.

diagnostic measure   A medical diagnosis of a disease.

diagnostic-related groups   A cost-control measure in Medicare; sets a rate for a patient who is admitted to the hospital with a particular diagnosis; contains costs by setting reimbursement rates in advance rather than letting doctors and hospitals set their own rates and fees.

Disability Insurance   A monthly benefit provided to disabled workers younger than age 65; to be eligible for DI, a worker must be insured by Social Security by having worked 10 years and be unable to engage in any substantial gainful activity because of a mental or physical impairment.

disengagement theory   The first formal theory of aging; the view that normal aging involves a natural and inevitable mutual withdrawal or disengagement, resulting in decreasing interaction between an aging person and others.

dual entitlement   A term that describes the benefits of an individual who is eligible for a Social Security benefit as a worker and an additional benefit as a spouse.

E

early adulthood   One of Levinson's developmental periods of adulthood; ages 17 to 45.

early adult transition   One of Levinson's developmental stages; the era when childhood draws to a close; the developmental tasks are to begin forming an adult identity and to separate from one's family of origin.

early retirement age   The age of eligibility for reduced Social Security benefits, presently set at 62.

early retirement incentive program (ERIP) *Special pension provisions that allow workers to retire early even if they are ineligible for benefits under regular eligibility rules.*

earnings test *A limit on earnings for workers 62 to 65 that determines the amount of Social Security benefits received.*

echo boomers *The generation of Americans born between 1977 and 1994.*

economic part-time work *Part-time workers who are unable to find full-time jobs.*

EET regime *Refers to the tax treatment of contributions to pension funds; pension funds are exempt (E) from taxation, the pension savings are exempt (E) from taxation, and benefits are taxed (T) as they are withdrawn in retirement.*

elderly dependency ratio *The number of persons aged 65 or older per 100 persons of working age.*

Elizabethan poor laws *A system of local government and local responsibility for the poor; established criteria for local welfare programs.*

Employee Retirement Income Security Act (ERISA) *A law passed by Congress in 1974 to regulate private pensions; required companies to establish minimum vesting standards, to set stringent funding requirements, and to establish methods for reporting plan benefits and finances to workers.*

empty nest *Period when a couple is alone together following the departure of children from the home.*

encoding *A stage of memory when information that is learned is stored for later use.*

entitlement crisis *The perception that entitlement spending is causing the federal deficit, consuming a disproportionate share of the federal budget, and crowding out funds for other social needs.*

entitlements *Benefits governed by formulas set in law and not subject to annual appropriations by Congress; people who meet the eligibility criteria automatically receive the benefits.*

epidemiologic transition *A shift in the proportion of deaths among the young and the elderly; accompanies the demographic transition; signifies a change in the leading causes of death from infectious diseases to chronic diseases.*

erectile dysfunction *The inability to maintain an erection sufficient for penetration or sexual intercourse.*

euthanasia *The act of killing or permitting the death of a hopelessly sick or injured individual in a painless way as an act of mercy.*

exchange theory *A theory that social interaction between individuals is based on rational calculations and that people seek to maximize their rewards from these exchanges and minimize their costs; exchange theorists argue that interaction between the old and the young decreases, because older people have fewer resources to bring to the exchange.*

expansive women *One of Apter's types of midlife women; these women sought fundamental change in their lives in midlife.*

extended family *The network of familial relationships, including grandparents, aunts, uncles, cousins, nieces, and nephews outside the nuclear family.*

extended family household *Household consisting of several generations, usually parents, their adult children, and their grandchildren.*

eye blink classical conditioning *The reflex that makes an individual blink when air is blown into the eye.*

F

family life cycle *The life course stages of the nuclear family.*

fee-for-service *A system of reimbursement for health care costs in which physicians set the fees and payments are based on the treatment received; patients have an unrestricted choice of physicians.*

feminist theory *The central purpose is to illuminate the gendered nature of society; gender relations are the main subject matter; notions of masculinity and femininity are seen as socially constructed; emphasis is on the different ways aging is experienced by men and women.*

fertility rate *A measure of the incidence of births or the inflow of new lives into a population.*

filial piety *The Japanese tradition of respect and reverence for the elderly.*

financial assets *Total wealth minus the value of a home and other real estate assets.*

fiscal welfare *Indirect payments to individuals through the tax system.*

flexible employment *A type of employment where workers do not become a part of a firm's permanent workforce but rather are hired to do a specific job on a part-time or temporary basis.*

fluid intelligence *Refers to reasoning, memory, and information-processing skills; involves the ability to devise novel solutions to unforseen problems;*

required to identify relationships and to draw inferences on the basis of that understanding.

frail elderly   Older people who depend on others for carrying out their daily activities; they show some mental or physical deterioration and need care from family members.

free radical theory of aging   A theory of biological aging; the view that free radicals contribute to the aging process by forming age pigment and by producing cross-links.

functional age   A definition of age based on how people look and what they can do; in functional terms, a person becomes old when he or she can no longer perform the major roles of adulthood.

functional status   A measure of the extent to which a chronic health problem, either physical or mental, produces a behavioral change in a person's capacity to perform the necessary tasks for daily living so that the help of another person is required.

G

gender neutrality   An approach that emphasizes reformulating laws in gender-neutral terms.

gender recognition   An approach that presumes that gender equality can only be achieved by taking into account the differences between men and women and taking measures to compensate the disadvantaged sex.

gender splitting   A term used by Levinson to characterize women's life course transitions; takes one of four forms, including the splitting of the domestic sphere and the public sphere as domains for men and women, the presence of the traditional marriage enterprise and the split it creates between the female homemaker and the male provider, the splitting of women's work and men's work, and the splitting of masculine and feminine in the individual psyche.

generation   A term applied to studies of family processes; refers to kinship links.

generational equity   The view that there is a political trade-off between meeting the needs of the young and the old, that the flow of resources to the elderly has been inequitable, and that this issue will create intergenerational conflict.

genetic control theory of aging   A theory of biological aging; the view that the life span is programmed into the genes.

gerontocracy   A community ruled by the aged.

gerontology   The scientific study of the biological, psychological, and social aspects of aging.

glaucoma   A serious condition that can lead to blindness; occurs when fluid cannot leave the anterior cavity of the eye through the normal channels; pressure builds up within the eye, gradually destroying vision.

grandparent career   The life course pattern to grandparent-grandchild relationships.

gray lobby   The organizations that represent the interests of the aged.

H

health behavior   Activity undertaken by an individual to promote good health and prevent illness.

health lifestyle   A pattern of behavior based on choices and options that are available to people according to their life situations; includes behaviors that directly affect health care, such as having checkups and complying with prescribed treatment as well as decisions about smoking, food, exercise, personal hygiene, alcohol use, and risky behaviors like unprotected sex.

health maintenance organization (HMO)   A health insurance plan run by a financial officer; a group of physicians belong to the HMO and the services provided are monitored by administrators to achieve efficiency and control costs; individuals who are insured through an HMO do not have an unrestricted choice of physicians but rather must choose among doctors contracted by the HMO.

home and community-based services (HCBS)   A range of services provided to the aged in the home; includes personal care such as bathing, dressing, feeding, and grooming, housekeeping, grocery shopping, transportation, medical services, bill paying, and case management.

Home and Community-Based Waiver Services Program (HCBS)   An alternative to nursing home care; a program that allows states to provide the poor and the disabled with a variety of services, including homemaker services, respite care, day care, meals-on-wheels, physical therapy, and help with chores.

hormone replacement therapy   A treatment to eliminate the physical symptoms of menopause and to provide protection against heart disease and osteoporosis.

hospice   A place where the terminally ill are allowed to die easily and at peace; an alternative to the medical, scientific model of dying; central component of hospice philosophy is pain management.

hypertension   High blood pressure.

hypertensive cardiovascular disease   *Hypertension leading to a heart attack.*

I

immediate exchange strategies   *Exchanges between individuals in goods and services at one point in time.*

immune function theory of aging   *A biological theory of aging based on two discoveries: (1) protective immune reactions decline with age, with the body becoming less capable of producing sufficient quantities and kinds of antibodies, and (2) the aging immune system mistakenly produces antibodies against normal body proteins, leading to a loss of self-recognition; as the immune system becomes less efficient, normal aging occurs.*

independent living   *Living in one's own home; the main living arrangement of older people in the United States.*

independent living community   *A new type of continuing care retirement community that is geared toward a younger, healthier clientele.*

Individual Retirement Account (IRA)   *Way of using the tax code to encourage people to save for retirement; individuals are allowed to put money into special retirement accounts without paying taxes on the income or the earnings.*

industrialization   *Process of transforming an agricultural economy into an industrial one; predominant characteristics include production by machine rather than by hand, involvement of an increasing proportion of the workforce in manufacturing, the concentration of production in large factories, rapid population increase, and urbanization.*

innovative women   *One of Apter's types of midlife women; women who were pioneers in a men's world.*

instrumental activities of daily living (IADL)   *Measure of need for help with such activities as keeping track of money, doing light housework, taking medicine, and running errands.*

intelligence   *A measure of intellectual ability.*

interest groups   *Organizations that lobby politicians to take certain actions; may support candidates running for office by informing their members that a certain candidate favors or opposes an issue of importance to them and urging members to vote accordingly.*

intergenerational solidarity   *A measure of family closeness that includes the frequency of interaction,* the amount of interaction, the amount of positive sentiment about family members, the level of agreement about values and beliefs, the degree to which services are exchanged, and the amount of geographical proximity.

involved grandparenting style   *Grandparents who take an active role in rearing their grandchildren; frequently they behave more like parents than grandparents; see grandchildren daily, often because they are living with them.*

J

joint and survivor annuities   *Type of pension arrangement for married employees in which the worker takes a reduced pension for life and the spouse receives a 50 percent survivor's pension; both husband and wife may agree, in writing, to waive the survivor pension.*

joint retirement   *A husband and wife retire at the same time.*

K

Kansas City Study of Adult Life   *A series of studies designed to identify how people adjusted to normal aging processes; the studies coupled an emphasis on adjustment with measures of social role performance across the life span.*

Keys Amendment   *First attempt to regulate board and care homes; required states to establish and enforce standards for homes serving residents who receive SSI.*

L

learning   *The process of acquiring knowledge and skills.*

lentigo   *The discoloration or spotting that commonly appears on the face, back of hands, and forearms of people 50 or older.*

life course   *The interaction between historical events, personal decisions, and individual opportunities; experiences early in life affect subsequent outcomes.*

life course framework   *An approach to the study of aging that combines the study of the changing age structure with the aging experiences of individuals.*

life expectancy   *The average number of years people in a given population can expect to live; the mean age at death; a measure of the combined outcome of* many births and deaths calculated by taking the sum of the ages of death of all individuals in a given population and dividing it by the number of people in that population.

life review   The process of reminiscing about one's experiences.

life span   The longest number of years any member of a species has been known to survive.

living will   Document in which an individual can specify his or her wishes for treatment in advance in case he or she should become terminally ill.

longitudinal research   Process of sorting complex-methodological issues involved in distinguishing between age effects, cohort effects, and period effects.

long-term care   The range of services and supportive living environments that help the elderly and disabled live independently; also refers to institutional care for those who need more extensive help.

long-term memory   The permanent storage site for past experiences; involves the ability to recall distant people and events; helps people make meaningful connections between the past and the present.

M

malignant melanoma   Dangerous skin cancer, which can metastasize and send cancerous cells to other parts of the body.

managed care   A form of health care organization; decisions are made by a financial officer.

mandatory retirement   The practice of forcing workers to retire at a given age.

means-test   Eligibility requirement for social benefits that is usually set quite low and accompanied by social stigma; only the very poor are able to qualify for benefits.

median net worth   The total value of all assets (e.g., a house, other property, personal savings) minus any debts.

Medicaid   Enacted in 1965; a program of health insurance for the poor; pays a large share of nursing home costs.

Medicare   Enacted in 1965; a national health insurance program for all people 65 or older who are eligible for Social Security; granted as an automatic right to all qualified workers and their spouses.

Medicare Catastrophic Coverage Act of 1988   Would have provided extensive benefits; represented the largest expansion of the Medicare program since 1965; repealed three months after it was enacted.

Medicare Part A   Hospital insurance paid for through payroll taxes.

Medicare Part B   An optional program that pays for 80 percent of the cost of physician office visits.

Medigap policies   Insurance policies that pay for health care expenses not covered by Medicare.

memory   The retention or storage of knowledge.

menopause   The permanent cessation of the menstrual cycle.

middle adulthood   One of Levinson's developmental stages; lasts from age 40 to 65 following midlife transition.

middle-old   People aged 75 to 84.

midlife transition   One of Levinson's developmental stages; terminates the era of early adulthood.

migration   The movement of people across borders.

migratory stream   The migration of people from one region to another, such as the movement of older people to the Sun Belt.

modernization theory   The view that nations can be placed on a continuum from least developed to most developed, according to such indicators as the level of industrialization or the degree of urbanization, with those exhibiting certain qualities of social structure termed modern; basic premise is that the aged were revered in the past and that modernization has caused the status of the aged to decline.

mortality rate   The incidence of death in a population.

motor nerves   They carry outgoing information from the central nervous system to muscles and glands throughout the body.

Motor Voter Bill   Requires all states to allow people to register to vote when they apply for driver's licenses or at any number of other designated government agencies.

N

National Association of Retired Federal Employees   An organization concerned primarily with issues of interest to retired federal employees.

National Committee to Preserve Social Security and Medicare   A senior organization founded in 1982; has diverse membership of more than five million members; played a key role in killing the Medicare Catastrophic Coverage Act of 1988.

National Council of Senior Citizens (NCSC)   An organization of retired trade union members; has a liberal Democratic bias.

neurons *Brain cells that carry information throughout the body in the form of electrical signals.*

new ageism *A tendency to patronize and be overly solicitous to the elderly.*

normal retirement age *The age of eligibility for full Social Security benefits, presently 65; will rise to 67 in the twenty-first century.*

nuclear family *The family unit consisting of husband, wife, and children.*

nuclear family household *Household composed solely of parents and their children.*

nursing home *An institutional setting where long-term care to the frail and disabled elderly is provided.*

O

Old Age Assistance *Part of the Social Security Act of 1935; jointly funded and administered by the states and the federal government; converted to SSI in 1972; provided income for the aged poor who had not earned the right to Social Security benefits.*

Older Americans Act *Passed in 1965; provides a number of services intended to enhance independent living, including congregate meals, personal care and nursing services, day care, chore services, and meals-on-wheels.*

oldest–old *People 85 or older.*

ombudsmen program *Watchdogs that monitor the quality of care in nursing homes by investigating complaints by families and residents against facilities, reporting complaints to other regulatory agencies, gathering information, and meeting with those involved in disputes.*

osteoporosis *Disease that causes the outside walls of the bone to become thinner and the inner part of the bone to become spongy; in the later stages, symptoms include a loss of height, back pain, and a curving of the upper back or spine, sometimes called a dowager's hump where spinal bones weaken and slowly collapse under the weight of the upper bones.*

out-relief *Direct grants of aid to the poor.*

P

Parkinson's disease *A chronic brain disorder that may occur as early as age 30 but is more commonly diagnosed among people 60 or older; signs include a slowing of movement, a stooped posture with the head forward, elbows flexed, a shuffling gait, slurred speech, and a noticeable tremor.*

passive euthanasia *Involves withholding or withdrawing medical treatment to the hopelessly ill.*

payroll tax *A tax levied on workers and employers to fund social insurance programs; also defined as a contribution to a social insurance pool.*

Pension Benefit Guaranty Corporation (PBGC) *The federal agency that assumes responsibility for paying the promised pension benefits owed by firms if a terminated pension plan has insufficient funds to meet its obligations to the workers.*

pension-splitting *A practice in which a pension becomes part of a divorce decree.*

performance anxiety *A psychological syndrome in which a man becomes anxious about his ability to achieve an erection.*

period effect *The impact of a historical event on the people who live through it.*

peripheral nervous system *All parts of the nervous system except the brain and the spinal cord; includes the spinal nerves that arise from the spinal cord.*

personality traits *The attributes used to measure all facets of personality–who we are and how we react to events in our environment.*

plateau phase *Second stage of sexual response cycle, in which maximum level of sexual arousal is attained.*

political economy theory *A theory that old age is socially constructed and created through power struggles; highlights the structural influences on aging and emphasizes the relevance of power relationships for understanding how the aged are defined and treated.*

population aging *Occurs when the proportion of older people relative to younger generations increases; a term that refers to an increase in the proportion of people 65 or older.*

population pyramid *A bar chart that reflects the distribution of a population by age and sex.*

postfall syndrome *The fear of falling in the elderly who have had a prior fall.*

presbycusis *Normal loss of hearing with age.*

presbyopia *An inability of the eye to focus on near objects.*

primary caregiver *Person who takes basic responsibility for caring for elderly; tends to be a daughter.*

primogeniture *The inheritance practice in which a father passes his property on to one child, usually the eldest son.*

privatization   *The reduction of government responsibility and an increase in the responsibility of individuals for their own welfare; the taking over of government functions by the private sector.*

progressive taxes   *A method for calculating tax liabilities based on the premise that the higher one's income, the higher the tax rate.*

prospective payment system   *Instituted a schedule to determine payments for hospital bills of Medicare recipients; estimates what the cost of an average patient with a specific diagnosis would be and how long that patient would need to remain hospitalized.*

prospective voting   *Voting for a candidate on the basis of promises made during a campaign.*

protestors   *One of Apter's types of midlife women; had faced early responsibilities that constrained their first years of adulthood; sought ways to develop the spontaneity they had missed earlier.*

psychologic fatigue   *Monotony in sexual activity that becomes patterned and routine.*

Q

qualitative research   *Based on open-ended interviews and observation of behavior.*

quantitative research   *Relies on numerical summaries of the responses of many people and reports the results in statistical form.*

R

race crossover   *Among the oldest-old, the mortality rate for African Americans falls below that of whites.*

rational choice theory   *The theory that individual behavior and attitudes are rationally calculated to further an individual's self-interest.*

reality orientation   *A form of therapy often used in nursing homes with Alzheimer's patients; patients are continuously reminded of their names, the date, and current events.*

regressive taxes   *A method for calculating tax liabilities where lower-income people are taxed at the same or a higher rate than affluent people.*

remote grandparenting   *Grandparents who see their grandchildren infrequently and have a relationship that is mainly ritualistic and symbolic.*

replacement rate   *The portion of preretirement pay that is replaced by the Social Security benefit.*

restrictive covenants   *The practice of banning people from neighborhoods on the basis of race, religion, or ethnic origin.*

retirement contracts   *Detailed contracts between parents and children regarding the parents' rights and the children's responsibilities; found in agricultural societies.*

Retirement Equity Act of 1984 (REA)   *Protected the pension rights of a spouse in the event of the death of the worker or of divorce.*

retrospective voting   *The withholding of votes from a candidate on the basis of a judgment of past performance.*

reverse mortgages   *Plans to pay for long-term care or other needs in old age by selling the individual's home equity back to a bank in exchange for a monthly stipend.*

rheumatoid arthritis   *Inflammation of the synovial membranes, which line the joint capsule and the cartilage that covers the bones.*

role   *The expected behaviors associated with a given status; also a status and the behaviors associated with it.*

role allocation   *The processes by which roles are assigned to individuals and the dynamics of role entry and exit.*

role conflict   *An inability to meet competing demands of two or more roles; occurs when two or more roles are partially or wholly incompatible.*

role reversal   *Reversal of parent-child role, with the child becoming the decision maker.*

role transition   *Refers to the role changes individuals make as they leave school, take a job, get married, have children, or retire.*

S

self-concept   *The organized and integrated perception of self; consists of such aspects as self-esteem, self-image, beliefs, and personality traits.*

senescence   *The study of the biological processes that cause mental and physical decline in old age.*

senile purpura   *Purple bruises; sites where fragile blood vessels have ruptured.*

senior centers   *Community-based facilities that provide meals and offer social activities for older people.*

sensory nerves   *Peripheral nerves that carry incoming messages from the environment to the central nervous system.*

sequential retirement   *A husband and wife retire in sequence, with either the husband or the wife retiring first while the other continues to work.*

sex ratio   *The ratio of males to females; determined by the number of males relative to females at birth and by different survival rates over the life course.*

sexual response cycle   *Four phases of sexual arousal.*

shared housing   *Program to place elderly homeowners with younger individuals who perform services in exchange for housing.*

short-term memory   *Working memory; a limited capacity system that keeps memory in consciousness; only lasts a few seconds.*

single room occupancy hotel (SRO)   *Apartment dwellings or old hotels, often in dilapidated inner city neighborhoods.*

social assistance   *A type of social benefit; contains eligibility criteria designed to encourage the able-bodied poor to work; derived from the sixteenth-century British system of poor relief.*

social clock   *The age norms that provide a prescriptive timetable, which orders major life events.*

social constructionism   *Sociological tradition that places individual intentions, motivations, and actions at the center of social theory; view that human beings are active creators of their own social reality.*

social gerontology   *The study of the social aspects of aging.*

social insurance   *Basic purpose of social insurance is to provide economic security over the life course and to prevent people from falling into destitution; distinguished from social assistance in that people contribute to a common pool and share risks; contributors earn the right to benefits.*

social movements   *Collectivities of people organized to promote or resist change; typically they operate outside the political mainstream.*

social role   *A set of expectations or guidelines for people who occupy a given position or status, such as widow, grandfather, or retiree.*

Social Security   *Old-age insurance; public pension system for retired workers who have made payroll tax contributions; also includes benefits for the disabled, widows, and spouses.*

Social Security Act of 1935   *The first federal welfare legislation for workers; initiated the American welfare state; included programs for retired workers, the unemployed, and dependent children.*

Social Services Block Grant   *Grants provided by the federal government to the states for a range of social services.*

social support system   *The network of relatives, friends, and organizations that provide both emotional support, such as making the individual feel loved or comforted, and instrumental support, which refers to help in managing activities of daily living.*

somatic mutation theory of aging   *A biological theory of aging that genetic damage causes aging of cells and tissues.*

somewhat impaired elderly   *People who are beginning to experience chronic ailments and need some assistance from family or community service agencies.*

spouse benefit   *A Social Security benefit paid to the spouse of a retired worker that is equal to 50 percent of the worker's benefit.*

stages of dying   *Elizabeth Kubler-Ross's five stages include denial, anger, bargaining, depression, and acceptance.*

stem family   *An arrangement whereby parents live with one of their married children, usually the oldest son, who then inherits the family property.*

stereotypes   *A composite of ideas and beliefs attributed to people as a group or social category.*

stroke   *A rupture or obstruction of a blood vessel to the brain that damages brain tissue; symptoms include memory deficits, emotional liability, and depression.*

structural lag   *A perspective that asserts that there is a mismatch between societal needs and individual opportunities; occurs because of age-differentiated structures dictating that education is for youth, work for people in middle age, and leisure for the old.*

subculture theory   *A theory that people who share similar interests, problems, and concerns will form a subculture; the aged are believed to have a positive affinity for each other.*

subjective age identity   *How people subjectively define their age; most important factors in determining subjective age identity are activity level and health.*

successful aging   *The attainment of peak physical and psychological functioning and participation in rewarding social activities.*

Supplemental Security Income (SSI)   *A federal means-tested, social assistance program for the aged, blind, and disabled poor.*

support bank   *The exchanges made between members of the social support network over the life course.*

supportive housing   *A variety of group-housing options that include assistance with activities of daily living; designed to help residents stay in one place and avoid or delay the need for institutional care.*

suttee   *A form of widow sacrifice.*

survivor's benefit   *A Social Security benefit payable to the widow or widower of a deceased worker; equal to 100 percent of the worker's benefit.*

symbolic politics theory   *Presumes that behavior and attitudes are more strongly linked to personal beliefs than to material interests.*

T

tax expenditure   *Special income tax provisions that are implemented through the tax code; designed to accomplish some social or economic goal.*

temperament   *A person's characteristic, biologically based, emotional style of approaching and reacting to people and situations.*

theory of cumulative disadvantage   *A theory that people who begin life with greater resources continue to have opportunities to accumulate more of them while those who begin with few resources fall further behind.*

theory of intergenerational solidarity   *A theory that geographic arrangements will be adjusted over time to reflect the changing needs and resources of different generations.*

total dependency ratio   *The combined ratio of children and older people to workers.*

total institution   *Central features are a breakdown of the normal barriers that separate the main spheres of life—sleep, work, and play—and the handling of many human needs by a bureaucratic organization.*

Townsend movement   *The first major social movement consisting primarily of older people; founded in 1933; named after its founder, Dr. Francis Townsend; dedicated to enacting the Townsend plan, a proposal to give all people aged 65 or older a pension of $150 a month.*

traditional women   *One of Apter's types of midlife women; stayed within the conventional feminine framework and defined themselves in terms of their family roles.*

trait theory   *A theory that everyone has most personality traits to some degree, but that everyone also has a core group of traits that define his or her personality; defining traits include five major factors: neuroticism, extroversion, openness, agreeableness, and conscientiousness.*

transition   *Refers to the shifts in roles that occur over the life course.*

trajectory   *A series of transitions such as education, work, and retirement.*

V

vascular dementia   *A common form of dementia; results from the cumulative effect of a number of small strokes, which eventually impair brain functioning; symptoms include blackouts, heart problems, kidney failure, and hypertension.*

veneration   *An attitude toward the aged that emphasizes respect, honor, obligation, and deference; also, a feeling of religious awe and reverence that approaches a form of worship.*

verticalization   *The increase in family linkages between preceding and subsequent generations because of increased life expectancy coupled with reduced fertility.*

vested   *State of having enough years of service to qualify for a pension benefit.*

vesting rules   *These specify a minimum number of years a worker is required to be employed by a firm to be eligible for a pension.*

voluntary part-time work   *Part-timer workers who do not wish to work full-time.*

voter turnout   *The number of registered voters who actually vote in a given election.*

W

wealth   *All financial assets including a home and other real estate.*

wear and tear theory of aging   *A theory of biological aging; views the body as similar to a machine, like an old car or truck, that simply wears out.*

welfare state   *The combination of social programs that protect people from the risks of loss of income due to unemployment, disability, divorce, poor health, or retirement.*

well elderly   *People who are healthy and active, involved in social and leisure activities, often employed or busy with volunteer work, still carrying out family responsibilities, and fully engaged in the life of the community.*

White House Conference on Aging   *Conferences held every 10 years to present grievances and proposals on issues of interest to older people; way to present issues to the president at an officially recognized forum.*

wisdom   *The acquisition of practical expertise in everyday life.*

Y

young-old   *People 65 to 74.*

References

Abel, E. K. 1986. "Adult Daughters and Care for the Elderly." *Feminist Studies* 12:479–97.

Achenbaum, W. Andrew. 1978. *Old Age in the New Land.* Baltimore, MD: Johns Hopkins University Press.

———. 1996. *Crossing Frontiers: Gerontology Emerges as a Science.* New York: Cambridge University Press.

Adams, Wendy, Helen McIlvain, Naomi Lacy, Homa Magsi, Benjamin Crabtree, Sharon Yenny, and Michael Sitorius. 2002. "Primary Care for Elderly People: Why Do Doctors Find It So Hard?" *The Gerontologist* 42(6):835–42.

Aday, Ronald, Cyndee Rice Sims, and Emilie Evans. 1991. "Youth's Attitudes toward the Elderly: The Impact of Intergenerational Partners." *Journal of Applied Gerontology* 10:372–84.

Ade-Ridder, Linda. 1990. "Sexuality and Marital Quality among Older Couples." Pp. 48–67 in *Family Relationships in Later Life,* edited by T. Brubaker. Beverly Hills, CA: Sage.

Adlersberg, M., and S. Thorne. 1990. "Emerging from the Chrysalis: Older Widows in Transition." *Journal of Gerontological Nursing* 16:4–8.

Advisory Council on Social Security. 1997. *Report of the 1994–1996 Advisory Council on Social Security: Findings and Recommendations.* Washington, DC: Advisory Council on Social Security.

Aldrich, Jonathan. 1982. "Earnings Replacement Rates of Old-Age Benefits in 12 Countries, 1969–80." *Social Security Bulletin* 45(11):3–11.

Alford, Elissa. 1997. "Piano Lessons." Unpublished manuscript.

Alford-Cooper, Finnegan. 1998. *For Keeps: Marriages That Last a Lifetime.* Armonk, NY: M. E. Sharpe.

Allen, Katherine, and Victoria Chin-Sang. 1990. "The Context and Meanings of Leisure for Aging Black Women." *The Gerontologist* 30:6.

Allen, Susan. 1994. "Gender Differences in Spousal Caregiving and Unmet Need for Care." *Journal of Gerontology* 49:S187–95.

Alter, George, Lisa Cliggett, and Alex Urbiel. 1996. "Household Patterns of the Elderly and the Proximity of Children in a Nineteenth Century City: Verivews, Belgium, 1831–1846." Pp. 30–52 in *Aging and Generational Relations over the Life Course,* edited by T. Hareven. Berlin: Aldine de Gruyter.

Amato, Paul, and Juliana Sobolewski. 2001. "The Effects of Divorce and Marital Discord on Adult Children's Psychological Well-Being." *American Sociological Review* 66:900–21.

Amenta, Ewin, and Yvonne Zylan. 1991. "It Happened Here: Political Opportunity, the New Institutionalism, and the Townsend Movement." *American Sociological Review* 56:250–65.

American Association of Retired Persons. 1990. "Understanding Senior Housing for the 1990s." Washington, DC: American Association of Retired Persons.

———. 1994a. "Falling Short." Washington, DC: American Association of Retired Persons.

———. 1994b. "Public Opinion on Entitlement Programs." Research report from AARP Research Division. Unpublished typescript.

———. 1994c. *Coming Up Short: Increasing Out-of-Pocket Health Spending by Older Americans.* Washington, DC: American Association of Retired Persons.

———. 1995. "Transportation: The Older Persons' Interest." Public Policy Institute Fact Sheet No. 44, Washington, DC.

———. 1996a. "Older Drivers." Public Policy Institute Fact Sheet No. 51, Washington, DC.

———. 1996b. "Native Americans and the U.S. Health Care System." Public Policy Institute Fact Sheet No. 55, Washington, DC.

———. 2000. "Out-of-Pocket Spending on Health Care by Medicare Beneficiaries Age 65 and Older: 1999 Projections." Washington, DC: American Association of Retired Persons.

American Psychiatric Association. 1994. *Diagnostic and Statistical Manual of Mental Disorders.* 4th ed. Washington, DC: American Psychiatric Association.

Amoss, Pamela, and Stevan Harrell. 1981. *Other Ways of Growing Old.* Stanford, CA: Stanford University Press.

Anastas, Jeane, Janice Gibeau, and Pamela Larson. 1990. "Working Families and Eldercare: A National Perspective in an Aging America." *Social Work* 35:405–11.

Andel, Ross, and Phoebe Liebig. 2002. "The City of Laguna Woods: A Case of Senior Power in Local Politics." *Research on Aging* 24(1):87–105.

Anders, T. R., J. L. Fozard, and T. D. Lillyquist. 1972. "Effects of Age upon Retrieval from Short-Term Memory." *Developmental Psychology* 6:214–17.

Anderson, Michael. 1972. "Household Structure and the Industrial Revolution: Mid-Nineteenth Century Preston in Comparative Perspective." Pp. 215–35 in *Household and Family in Past Time,* edited by P. Laslett. Cambridge: Cambridge University Press.

———. 1977. "The Impact on the Family Relationships of the Elderly of Changes since Victorian Times in Governmental Income-Maintenance." Pp. 36–59 in *Family, Bureaucracy and the Elderly,* edited by E. Shanas and M. Sussman. Durham, NC: Duke University Press.

Anderson, Norman. 1988. "Aging and Hypertension among Blacks: A Multidimensional Perspective." Pp. 190–214 in *The Black American Elderly,* edited by J. S. Jackson. New York: Springer.

Anderson, R., and J. F. Newman. 1973. "Societal and Individual Determinants of Medical Care Utilization in the United States." *Milbank Memorial Fund Quarterly* 51:95–124.

Angel, Jacqueline. 2001. "Challenges of Caring for Hispanic Elders." *Public Policy and Aging Research Brief.* Washington, DC: National Academy on an Aging Society.

Angel, Jacqueline Lowe, and Dennis Hogan. 1994. "The Demography of Minority Aging Populations." Pp. 9–21 in *Minority Elders: Five Goals toward Building a Public Policy Base,* edited by Task Force on Minority Issues in Gerontology. Washington, DC: Gerontological Society of America.

Angel, Ronald, and Jacqueline Angel. 1996. "The Extent of Private and Public Health Insurance Coverage among Adult Hispanics." *The Gerontologist* 36:332–40.

———. 1997. "Health Service Use and Long-Term Care among Hispanics." Pp. 343–59 in *Minorities, Aging and Health,* edited by Kyriakos Markides and Manual Miranda. Thousand Oaks, CA: Sage.

Antonucci, Toni. 1985. "Personal Characteristics, Social Support, and Social Behavior." Pp. 94–128 in *Handbook of Aging and the Social Sciences,* edited by R. Binstock and E. Shanas. New York: Van Nostrand Reinhold.

———. 1990. "Social Support and Social Relationships." Pp. 205–26 in *Handbook of Aging and the Social Sciences,* edited by R. Binstock and L. George. San Diego, CA: Academic Press.

Antonucci, Toni, and Hiroko Akiyama. 1987. "Social Networks in Adult Life and a Preliminary Examination of the Convoy Model." *Journal of Gerontology* 42:519–27.

———. 1995. "Convoys of Social Relations: Family and Friendships within a Life Span Context." Pp. 355–71 in *Handbook of Aging and the Family,* edited by R. Blieszner and V. Hilkevitch Bedford. Westport, CT: Greenwood Press.

Applebaum, Eileen, and Judith Gregory. 1990. "Flexible Employment: Union Perspectives." Pp. 130–45 in *Bridges to Retirement: Older Workers in a Changing Labor Market,* edited by P. Doeringer. Ithaca, NY: ILR Press.

Apter, Terri. 1995. *Secret Paths: Women in the New Midlife.* New York: Norton.

Aquilino, W., and K. Supple. 1991. "Parent–Child Relations and Parents' Satisfaction With Living Arrangements When Adult Children Live at Home." *Journal of Marriage and the Family* 53:13–27.

Arber, Sara, and Jay Ginn. 1991. *Gender and Later Life.* London: Sage.

Ardelt, Monika. 1997. "Wisdom and Life Satisfaction in Old Age." *Journal of Gerontology* 52B:P15–27.

Armstrong, M. Jocelyn, and Karen Goldsteen. 1990. "Friendship Support Patterns of Older American Women." *Journal of Aging Studies* 4:391–404.

Armstrong, Orlan Kay. [1931]. *Old Massa's People: The Old Slaves Tell Their Story.* Indianapolis, IN: Bobbs-Merrill.

Association for Gerontology in Higher Education. 1996. *Careers in Aging: Opportunities and Options.* Washington, DC: Association for Gerontology in Higher Education.

Atchley, Robert. 1971. "Retirement and Leisure Participation: Continuity or Crisis?" *The Gerontologist* 11:13–17.

———. 1989. "A Continuity Theory of Normal Aging." *The Gerontologist* 29:183–90.

———. 1997. "The Subjective Importance of Being Religious and Its Effect on Health and Morale 14 Years Later." *Journal of Aging Studies* 11(2):131–42.

Attias-Donfut, Claudine. 2000. "Cultural and Economic Transfers between Generations: One Aspect of Age Integration." *The Gerontologist* 40(3):270–71.

Azarnoff, Roy, and Andrew Scharlach. 1988. "Can Employees Carry the Eldercare Burden?" *Personnel Journal* 67:67–69.

Bagby, Meredith. 1994. *The First Annual Report of the United States of America.* New York: HarperCollins.

Bailey, John. 1999. *Elegy for Iris.* New York: St. Martin's Press.

Baker, Dorothy, and Phyllis Pallett-Hehn. 1995. "Care of Control: Barriers to Service Use by Elderly People." *Journal of Applied Gerontology* 14:261–74.

Ball, Mary, and Frank Whittington. 1995. *Surviving Dependence: Voices of African American Elders.* Amityville, NY: Baywood.

Ball, Robert. 1994. "Social Security: Where Are We Going?" Working Paper No. PI-94-27, Pepper Institute on Aging and Public Policy, Florida State University, Tallahassee, FL.

Ball, Robert, and Thomas Bethell. 1997. "Bridging the Centuries: The Case for Traditional Social Security." Pp. 259–94 in *Social Security in the 21st Century,* edited by E. Kingson and J. Schulz. New York: Oxford University Press.

Baltes, P., and J. Smith. 1990. "Towards a Psychology of Wisdom and Its Ontogenesis." Pp. 17–42 in

Wisdom: Its Nature, Origins and Development, edited by R. J. Sternberg. Cambridge: Cambridge University Press.

Baltes, P., J. Smith, and U. Staudinger. 1992. "Wisdom and Successful Aging." Pp. 103–21 in *Nebraska Symposium on Motivation*, edited by T. Sonderegger. Lincoln, NE: University of Nebraska Press.

Baltes, P., U. Staudinger, A. Maercker, and J. Smith. 1995. "People Nominated as Wise: A Comparative Study of Wisdom-Related Knowledge." *Psychology and Aging* 10:155–66.

Baquet, Claudia. 1988. "Cancer Prevention and Control in the Black Population: Epidemiology and Aging Implications." Pp. 50–68 in *The Black American Elderly*, edited by J. S. Jackson. New York: Springer.

Barbagli, Marzio. 1996. "Asymmetry in Intergenerational Family Relationships in Italy." Pp. 191–207 in *Aging and Generational Relations over the Life Course*, edited by T. Hareven. Berlin: Aldine de Gruyter.

Barber, Janet. 1983. "Old Age and the Life Course of Slaves." Unpublished doctoral dissertation, Department of Sociology, University of Kansas, Lawrence, KS.

Bardwick, Judith. 1971. *The Psychology of Women*. New York: Harper & Row.

Barrett, Anne. 2003. "Socioeconomic Status and Age Identity: The Role of Dimensions of Health in the Subjective Construction of Age Identity." *Journal of Gerontology* 58B(2):S101–10.

Barth, Michael, William McNaught, and Philip Rizzi. 1995. "Older Americans as Workers." Pp. 35–70 in *Older and Active: How Americans over 55 Are Contributing to Society*, edited by S. A. Bass. New Haven, CT: Yale University Press.

Bass, Scott. 1995. "Older and Active." Pp. 1–9 in *Older and Active: How Americans over 55 Are Contributing to Society*, edited by S. A. Bass. New Haven, CT: Yale University Press.

Bassett, William, Michael Fleming, and Anthony Rodriquez. 1996. "How Workers Use 401(k) Plans: The Participation, Contribution and Withdrawal Decisions." Brown University and the Federal Reserve Bank of New York. Unpublished manuscript.

Baum, Joel A. 1999. "The Rise of Chain Nursing Homes in Ontario, 1971–1996." *Social Forces* 78(2):543–85.

Bazargan, Mohsen, and Verneda Hamm-Baugh. 1995. "The Relationship between Chronic Illness and Depression in a Community of Urban Black Elderly Persons." *Journal of Gerontology* 50B:S119–27.

Beach, Diane. 1997. "Family Caregiving: The Positive Impact on Adolescent Relationships." *The Gerontologist* 37:233–38.

Bean, Frank, George Myers, Jacqueline Angel, and Omer Galle. 1994. "Geographic Concentration, Migration, and Population Redistribution among the Elderly." Pp. 319–54 in *Demography of Aging*, edited by L. G. Martin and S. H. Preston. Washington, DC: National Academy Press.

Beck, E. M., Patrick Horan, and Charles Tolbert. 1980. "Industrial Segregation and Labor Market Discrimination." *Social Problems* 28(2):113–30.

Beck, Scott. 1982. "Adjustment to and Satisfaction with Retirement." *Journal of Gerontology* 37:616–24.

Becker, Gay. 1993. "Continuity after a Stroke: Implications of Life-Course Disruption in Old Age." *The Gerontologist* 33:148–58.

———. 2002. "Dying away from Home: Quandries of Migration for Elders in Two Ethnic Groups." *Journal of Gerontology* 57B(2):S79–95.

Bedford, Victoria. 1995. "Sibling Relationships in Middle and Old Age." Pp. 201–22 in *Handbook of Aging and the Family*, edited by R. Blieszner and V. Hilkevitch Bedford. Westport, CT: Greenwood Press.

Belgrave, L. 1988. "The Effect of Race Differences in Work History, Work Attitudes, Economic Resources, and Health on Women's Retirement." *Research on Aging* 10:383–98.

Bell, Daniel. 1973. *The Coming of Post-Industrial Society*. New York: Basic Books.

Bell, John. 1992. "In Search of a Discourse on Aging: The Elderly on Television." *The Gerontologist* 32:305–11.

Belous, Richard. 1990. "Flexible Employment: The Employer's Point of View." Pp. 111–29 in *Bridges to Retirement: Older Workers in a Changing Labor Market*, edited by P. Doeringer. Ithaca, NY: ILR Press.

Bengtson, Vern, and James Dowd. 1981. "Sociological Functionalism, Exchange Theory and Life Cycle Analysis: A Call for More Explicit Theoretical Bridges." *International Journal of Aging and Human Development* 12:55–73.

Bengtson, Vern, Tonya Parrott, and Elisabeth Burgess. 1996. "Progress and Pitfalls in Gerontological Theorizing." *The Gerontologist* 36:768–72.

———. 1997. "Theory, Explanation, and a Third Generation of Theoretical Developments in Social Gerontology." *Journal of Gerontology* 52B:S72–88.

Bengtson, Vern, Carolyn Rosenthal, and Linda Burton. 1990. "Families and Aging: Diversity and Heterogeneity." Pp. 263–81 in *Handbook of Aging and the Social Sciences*, edited by R. Binstock and L. George. San Diego, CA: Academic Press.

———. 1996. "Paradoxes of Families and Aging." Pp. 253–82 in *Handbook of Aging and the Social Sciences*, edited by R. Binstock and L. George. San Diego, CA: Academic Press.

Berardo, Felix. 1970. "Survivorship and Social Isolation: The Case of the Aged Widower." *The Family Coordinator* 1:11–25.

Berger, R. 1982. *Gay and Gray: The Older Homosexual Man.* Urbana, IL: University of Illinois Press.

Berkner, Lutz. 1972. "The Stem Family and the Developmental Cycle of the Peasant Household: An Eighteenth Century Austrian Example." *American Historical Review* 77:398–418.

Bernard, Miriam, and Judith Phillips. 2000. "The Challenge of Ageing in Tomorrow's Britain." *Ageing and Society* 20:33–54.

Bernheim, B. D., A. Shleifer, and L. H. Summers. 1985. "The Strategic Bequest Motive." *Journal of Political Economy* 93:1045–76.

Bernstein, M. 1991. "No, Changing Retirement Age Is a Blunt Instrument." Pp. 231–44 in *Retirement and Public Policy,* edited by A. Munnell. Washington, DC: National Academy of Social Insurance.

Bessey, Barbara, and Srijati Ananda. 1991. "Age Discrimination in Employment: An Interdisciplinary Review of the ADEA." *Research on Aging* 13:413–57.

Bianchi, Suzanne. 1995. "Changing Economic Roles of Women and Men." Pp. 17–23 in *State of the Union: American in the 1990s,* edited by R. Farley. New York: Russell Sage Foundation.

Biggar, Jean. 1980. "Who Moved among the Elderly?" *Research on Aging* 2:73–91.

Binstock, Robert. 1994a. "Changing Criteria in Old-Age Programs: The Introduction of Economic Status and Need for Services." *The Gerontologist* 34:726–30.

——. 1994b. "Transcending Intergenerational Equity." Pp. 155–85 in *Economic Security and Intergenerational Justice,* edited by T. Marmor, T. Smeeding, and V. Greene. Washington, DC: Urban Institute Press.

——. 1996. "Continuities and Discontinuities in Public Policy and Aging." Pp. 308–24 in *Adulthood and Aging,* edited by V. Bengtson. New York: Springer.

——. 1997. "The 1996 Election: Older Voters and Implications for Policies on Aging." *The Gerontologist* 37:15–19.

——. 1999. "Scapegoating the Old: Intergenerational Equity and Age-Based Health Care Rationing." Pp. 157–184 in *The Generational Equity Debate,* edited by J. Williamson and R. Kingson. New York: Columbia University Press.

——. 2000. "Older People and Voting Participation: Past and Future." *The Gerontologist* 40:18–31.

Binstock, Robert, and Christine Day. 1996. "Aging and Politics." Pp. 362–82 in *Handbook of Aging and the Social Sciences,* edited by R. Binstock and L. George. San Diego, CA: Academic Press.

Bipartisan Commission on Entitlement and Tax Reform. 1994. *Interim Report to the President.* Washington, DC: Superintendent of Documents.

Birmingham, Jacqueline J. 1993. "Discharge Planning and Home Health Care in the United States." *Journal of Cross-Cultural Gerontology* 8:417–29.

Birren, James, and Johannes Schroots. 1996. "History, Concepts and Theory in the Psychology of Aging." Pp. 3–23 in *Handbook of the Psychology of Aging,* edited by J. Birren and K. Warner Schaie. New York: Academic Press.

Blanc, E. S., C. M. Viscoli, and J. B. Henrich. 1999. "Postmenopausal Estrogen Replacement Therapy Is Associated with Adverse Breast Cancer Prognostic Indices." *Journal of Women's Health* 8(6):815–23.

Blanchette, Katherine. 1997. *New Directions for State Long-Term Care Systems: Volume III: Supportive Housing.* Washington, DC: American Association of Retired Persons.

Blau, Peter, and Otis Duncan. 1967. *The American Occupational Structure.* New York: Wiley.

Blau, Zena. 1981. *Aging in a Changing Society.* New York: Franklin Watts.

Blazer, D., B. Burchett, C. Service, and L. George. 1991. "The Association of Age and Depression among the Elderly: An Epidemiological Exploration." *Journal of Gerontology* 46:M210–15.

Blom, Ida. 1991. "The History of Widowhood: A Bibliographic Overview." *Journal of Family History* 16:191–220.

Blumstein, Philip, and Pepper Schwartz. 1983. *American Couples: Money, Work and Sex.* New York: Morrow.

Blustein, J. 1995. "Medicare Coverage, Supplemental Insurance, and the Use of Mammography by Older Women." *New England Journal of Medicine* 332(17):1138–43.

Board of Trustees. 1994. *Annual Report of the Board of Trustees of the Federal Old-Age and Survivors Insurance and Disability Insurance Trust Funds.* Washington, DC: U.S. Government Printing Office.

——. 1996. *Annual Report of the Board of Trustees of the Federal Old-Age and Survivors Insurance and Disability Insurance Trust Funds.* Washington, DC: U.S. Government Printing Office.

Bolland, J., and N. Maxwell. 1990. "Stochastic Modeling as an Approach to Policy Analysis: Application to Elder Abuse." *Journal of Human and Human Resources Administration* 13(1):25–51.

Bongaarts, John, and Zachary Zimmer. 2002. "Living Arrangements of Older Adults in the Developing World: An Analysis of Demographic and Health Survey Household Surveys." *Journal of Gerontology* 57B(2):S145–57.

Bootzin, R., and J. Acocella. 1988. *Abnormal Psychology.* New York: Random House.

Bosworth, Barry. 1997. "What Economic Role for the Trust Funds?" Pp. 156–77 in *Social Security in the 21st Century,* edited by E. Kingson and J. Schulz. New York: Oxford University Press.

Bosworth, Barry, Rudiger Dornbusch, and Raul Laban. 1994. *The Chilean Economy: Policy Lessons and Challenges.* Washington, DC: The Brookings Institution.

Bould, Sally, Beverly Sanborn, and Laura Reif. 1989. *Eighty-Five Plus: The Oldest Old.* Belmont, CA: Wadsworth.

Bound, John, Michael Schoenbaum, and Timothy Waidmann. 1995. "Race and Education Differences in Disability Status and Labor Force Attachment in the Health and Retirement Survey." *Journal of Human Resources* 30:226–67.

——. 1996. "Race Differences in Labor Force Attachment and Disability Status." *The Gerontologist* 36:311–21.

Bowling, Ann. 1988–89. "Who Dies after Widow(er)hood? A Discriminate Analysis." *Omega* 19:135–53.

Boyd, Sandra, and Judith Treas. 1989. "Family Care of the Frail Elderly: A New Look at Women in the Middle." *Women's Studies Quarterly* 112:66–73.

Branch, Lawrence G. 2002. "The Epidemiology of Elder Abuse and Neglect." *The Public Policy and Aging Report* 12(2):19–23.

Branch, L., A. Horowitz, and C. Carr. 1989. "The Implications for Everyday Life of Incident Self-Reported Visual Decline among People over Age 65 Living in the Community." *The Gerontologist* 29:359–65.

Brant, Barbara, and Nancy Osgood. 1990. "The Suicidal Patient in Long-Term Care Institutions." *Journal of Gerontological Nursing* 16:15–18.

Braun, Rudolf. 1966. "The Impact of Cottage Industry." Pp. 53–64 in *The Rise of Capitalism,* edited by D. S. Landes. New York: Macmillan.

Brecher, Edward. 1984. *Love, Sex and Aging.* Boston: Little, Brown.

Breiter, J., B. A. Gau, K. A. Welsh, B. L. Plassman, W. M. McDonald, M. J. Helms, and C. J. Anthony. 1990. "Alzheimer's Disease in the National Academy of Sciences Registry of Aging Twin Veterans." *Dementia* 1:297–303.

——. 1993. "Use of Twin Cohorts for Research in Alzheimer's Disease." *Neurology* 43:261–67.

Bretschneider, J., and N. McCoy. 1988. "Sexual Interest in Healthy 80–102 Year Olds." *Archives of Sexual Behavior* 17:109–130.

Brody, Elaine. 1985. "Parent Care as a Normative Family Stress." *The Gerontologist* 25:19–29.

——. 1989. "The Family at Risk." Pp. 191–208 in *Alzheimer's Disease Treatment and Family Stress,* edited by E. Light and B. Lebowitz. Washington, DC: National Institute of Mental Health.

——. 1990. *Women in the Middle: Their Parent Care Years.* New York: Springer.

Brokaw, Tom. 1999. *The Greatest Generation Speaks.* New York: Random House.

Brown, Charles C. 1996. "Income and Wealth." *The Gerontologist* 36:336–41.

Brown, Colin. 1995. "Poverty, Immigration and Minority Groups: Policies toward Minorities in Great Britain."

Pp. 585–606 in *Poverty, Inequality and the Future of Social Policy,* edited by Katherine McFate, Roger Lawson, and William Julius Wilson. New York: Russell Sage Foundation.

Brown, G. W., and T. O. Harris. 1978. *Social Origins of Depression: A Study of Psychiatric Disorders in Women.* London: Tavistock.

Brown, Robert L. 1994. "A Demographer's Review of the Assumptions Underlying the OASDI Trustees Report." Presented at the annual meeting of the National Academy of Social Insurance, January 26, Washington, DC.

Browning, Christopher, and Edward O. Laumann. 1997. "Sexual Contact between Children and Adults: A Life Course Perspective." *American Sociological Review* 62:540–60.

Brubaker, Timothy. 1985. "Responsibility for Household Tasks: A Look at Golden Anniversary Couples." Pp. 27–36 in *Social Bonds in Later Life,* edited by W. Peterson and J. Quadagno. Beverly Hills, CA: Sage.

Bruce, Juliet. 1994. "To Drive or Not to Drive." *Aging* 366:49–51.

Bruni, Frank. 1996. "Federal Ruling Allows Doctors to Prescribe Drugs to End Life." *New York Times,* April 3, p. 1A.

Bulcroft, Kris, and Richard Bulcroft. 1985. "Dating and Courtship in Late Life: An Exploratory Study." Pp. 115–28 in *Social Bonds in Later Life: Aging and Interdependence,* edited by W. A. Peterson and J. Quadagno. Beverly Hills, CA: Sage.

Burgess, Ernest. 1960. *Aging in Western Societies.* Chicago, IL: University of Chicago Press.

Burkhauser, Richard. 1993. "Introduction." Pp. 1–4 in *Pensions in a Changing Economy,* edited by R. Burkhauser and D. Salisbury. Washington, DC: Employee Benefit Research Institute.

Burkhauser, Richard, Kenneth Couch, and John Phillips. 1996. "Who Takes Early Social Security Benefits? The Economic and Health Characteristics of Early Beneficiaries." *The Gerontologist* 36:789–99.

Burkhauser, Richard, and Karen Holden. 1982. *A Challenge to Social Security: The Changing Roles of Men and Women in American Society.* New York: Academic Press.

Burkhauser, Richard, and Timothy Smeeding. 1994. "Social Security Reform: A Budget Neutral Approach to Reducing Older Women's Disproportionate Risk of Poverty." Policy Brief No. 2, Center for Policy Research, Maxwell School of Citizenship and Public Affairs, Syracuse, NY.

Burnette, Denise. 1999. "Social Relationships of Latino Grandparent Caregivers: A Role Theory Perspective." *The Gerontologist* 39(1):49–58.

Burr, J. A., and J. E. Mutchler. 1999. "Race and Ethnic Variation in Norms of Filial Responsibility among Older Persons." *Journal of Marriage and the Family* 61(3):674–87.

Burtless, Gary, and Joseph Quinn. 2002. "Is Working Longer the Answer for an Aging Workforce?" Issue Brief Number 11. Boston: Center for Retirement Research.

Burton, Linda. 1993. "Families and the Aged: Issues of Complexity and Diversity." Pp. 1–6 in *Families and Aging*, edited by L. Burton. San Francisco: Baywood Press.

Burton, Linda, and Cynthia deVries. 1993. "Challenges and Rewards: African American Grandparents as Surrogate Parents." Pp. 101–8 in *Families and Aging*, edited by L. Burton. San Francisco: Baywood Press.

Butler, Robert. 1963. "The Life Review: An Interpretation of Reminiscence in the Aged." *Psychiatry* 26:65–76.

———. 1969. "Ageism: Another Form of Bigotry." *The Gerontologist* 9:243–46.

———. 1989. "Dispelling Ageism: The Cross-Cutting Intervention." *Annals of the American Academy of Political and Social Sciences* 503:138–47.

———. 2002. *Preparing for an Aging Nation: The Need for Academic Geriatricians.* Issue Brief. New York: International Longevity Center.

Butler, Robert, and M. Lewis. 1986. *Love and Sex after 40.* New York: Harper & Row.

Byer, Curtis, and Louis Shainberg. 1994. *Dimensions of Human Sexuality.* Madison, WI: W. C. Brown.

Calasanti, Toni M. 1993. "Bringing in Diversity: Toward an Inclusive Theory of Retirement." *Journal of Aging Studies* 7:133–50.

———. 1996. "Gender and Life Satisfaction in Retirement: An Assessment of the Male Model." *Journal of Gerontology* 51B:S18–29.

Calasanti, Toni, and Kathleen Slevin. 2001. *Gender, Social Inequalities and Aging.* Walnut Creek, CA: AltaMira Press.

Calasanti, Toni M., and Anna M. Zajicek. 1993. "A Socialist Feminist Approach to Aging: Embracing Diversity." *Journal of Aging Studies* 7:117–31.

California Department of Aging. 1994. "Taking Care of Tomorrow: Consumer's Guide to Long-Term Care." Publication No. 21356RWJCA (694), Sacramento, CA.

Callahan, Daniel. 1987. *Setting Limits.* New York: Simon & Schuster.

———. 1996. "Health Care for the Elderly Should Be Limited." Pp. 150–54 in *An Aging Population: Opposing Viewpoints*, edited by C. Cozic. San Diego, CA: Greenhaven Press.

———. 1997. "Living to Be 100: Good or Bad?" *Journal of Applied Gerontology* 16(3):267–69.

Callahan, L. F., J. Rao, and M. Boutaugh. 1996. "Arthritis and Women's Health: Prevalence, Impact, and Prevention." *American Journal of Preventative Medicine* 12:401–9.

Campbell, Andrea. 2002. "Self-Interest, Social Security and the Distinctive Participation Patterns of Senior Citizens." *American Political Science Review* 96(3):565–74.

Campbell, Andrea L. 2003. *How Policies Make Citizens.* Princeton, NJ: Princeton University Press.

Campbell, John Creighton, and Naoki Ikegami. 2000. "Long-Term Care Insurance Comes to Japan." *Health Affairs* 19:26–39.

Campbell, Richard, and Duane Alwin. 1996. "Quantitative Approaches: Toward an Integrated Science of Aging and Human Development." Pp. 31–51 in *Handbook of Aging and the Social Sciences*, edited by R. Binstock and L. George. San Diego, CA: Academic Press.

Campbell, Sheila, and Alicia Munnell. 2002. "Sex and 401(k) Plans." Center for Retirement Research. Boston: Boston College.

Cancian, Maria, Sheldon Danziger, and Peter Gottschalk. 1994. "Working Wives and Family Income Inequality among Married Couples." Pp. 195–222 in *Uneven Tides: Rising Inequality in America*, edited by S. Danziger and P. Gottschalk. New York: Russell Sage Foundation.

Carney, Suzanne, Patricia Burke, and Richard Fowler. 1994. "Suicide over 60: The San Diego Study." *Journal of the American Geriatrics Society* 42:174–80.

Caro, Francis, and Scott Bass. 1995. "Increasing Volunteering among Older People." Pp. 71–96 in *Older and Active: How Americans over 55 Are Contributing to Society*, edited by S. A. Bass. New Haven, CT: Yale University Press.

Carp, Frances. 2001. "Retirement and Women." Pp. 112–28 in *Handbook on Women and Aging*, edited by J. Coyle. Westport, CT: Praeger.

Carr, Deborah, James S. House, Ronald C. Kessler, Randolph Nesse, John Sonnega, and Camille Wortman. 2000. "Marital Quality and Psychological Adjustment to Widowhood among Older Adults: A Longitudinal Analysis." *Journal of Gerontology* 55B(4):S197–207.

Carroll, J., K. Volk, and J. Hyde. 1985. "Differences between Males and Females in Motives for Engaging in Sexual Intercourse." *Archives of Sexual Behavior* 14:131–39.

Cartwright, Colleen, and Margaret Steinberg. 1995. "Decision-Making in Terminal Care: Older People Seek More Involvement." *Social Alternatives* 14(2):7–10.

Cassileth, Barrie. 1994. "Psychosocial Status in Cancer Patients." Pp. 133–44 in *Aging and the Quality of Life*, edited by R. Abeles, H. Gift, and M. Ory. New York: Springer.

Causey, James. 1996. "Retiree Benefit at Risk as Firms Try to Pare Costs." *Milwaukee Journal Sentinel*, August 1:1–2.

Cavan, Ruth, Ernest W. Burgess, Robert J. Havighurst, and Herbert Goldhamer. 1949. *Personal Adjustment in Old Age.* Chicago, IL: Social Science Research Associates.

Centers For Medicare and Medicaid Services. 2003. *State Waiver and Demonstration Programs.* Baltimore, MD: CMS.

Chafe, William. 1986. *The Unfinished Journey: Americans since World War II.* New York: Oxford University Press.

Chang, Cyril, and Shelley White-Means. 1991. "The Men Who Care: An Analysis of Male Primary Caregivers Who Care for Frail Elderly at Home." *Journal of Applied Gerontology* 10:343–58.

Chapin, R., and D. Dobbs-Kepper. 2001. "Aging in Place in Assisted Living: Philosophy versus Policy." *The Gerontologist* 41(1):43–50.

Chapleski, Elizabeth. 1997. "Long-Term Care among American Indians." Pp. 367–77 in *Minorities, Aging and Health,* edited by Kyriakos Markides and Manual Miranda. Thousand Oaks, CA: Sage.

Chapuy, M. C., and P. J. Meunier. 1995. "Prevention and Treatment of Osteoporosis." *Aging* 7:164–73.

Chatters, Linda, Jeffrey Levin, and Robert Joseph Taylor. 1992. "Antecedents and Dimensions of Religious Involvement among Older Black Adults." *Journal of Gerontology* 47:S269–78.

Chatters, Linda, and Robert J. Taylor. 1993. "Intergenerational Support: The Provision of Assistance to Parents by Adult Children." Pp. 69–83 in *Aging in Black America,* edited by J. S. Jackson, L. M. Chatters, and R. J. Taylor. Newbury Park, CA: Sage.

Chen, Young-Ping. 1994. "Improving the Economic Security of Minority Persons as They Enter Old Age." Pp. 22–31 in *Minority Elders: Five Goals toward Building a Public Policy Base,* edited by Task Force on Minority Issues in Gerontology. Washington, DC: Gerontological Society of America.

Cherlin, Andrew J. 1996. *Public and Private Families.* New York: McGraw-Hill.

Cherlin, Andrew, and Frank Furstenberg, Jr. 1988. "The Changing European Family: Lessons for the American Reader." *Journal of Family Issues* 9:291–97.

——. 1992. *The New American Grandparent.* Cambridge, MA: Harvard University Press.

Cherry, Ralph. 1993. "Community Presence and Nursing Home Quality of Care: The Ombudsman as a Complementary Role." *Journal of Health and Social Behavior* 34:336–45.

Cho, Pill Jay. 1998. "Awareness and Utilization: A Comment." *The Gerontologist* 38(3):317–19.

Choi, N. G., and Mayer, J. 2000. "Elder Abuse, Neglect, and Exploitation: Risk Factors and Prevention Strategies." *Journal of Gerontological Social Work* 33(2):2–25.

Choudhury, Chandra. 2001–02. "Racial and Ethnic Differences in Wealth and Asset Choices." *Social Security Bulletin* 64(4):1–15.

Chudacoff, Howard, and Tamara Hareven. 1978. "Family Transitions into Old Age." Pp. 217–41 in *Transitions: The Family and the Life Course in Historical Perspective,* edited by T. Hareven. New York: Academic Press.

Clark, D. O. 1995. "Racial and Educational Differences in Physical Activity among Older Adults." *The Gerontologist* 35:472–80.

Clark, Daniel, Christopher Callahan, Simon Mungai, and Fredric Wolinsky. 1996. "Physical Function among Retirement-Aged African American Men and Women." *The Gerontologist* 36:322–31.

Clark, Robert. 1990. "Income Maintenance Policies in the United States." Pp. 382–97 in *Handbook of Aging and the Social Sciences,* edited by R. Binstock and L. George. New York: Academic Press.

——. 1993. "Population Aging and Work Rates of Older Persons: An International Comparison." Pp. 57–77 in *As the Workforce Ages: Costs, Benefits and Policy Challenges,* edited by O. Mitchell. Ithaca, NY: ILR Press.

——. 1994. "Employment Costs and the Older Worker." Pp. 1–26 in *Older Workers: How Do They Measure Up?* edited by S. Rix. Washington, DC: American Association of Retired Persons.

Clark, Robert, Linda Schumaker Ghent, and Alvin Headen, Jr. 1994. "Retiree Health Insurance and Pension Coverage: Variations by Firm Characteristics." *Journal of Gerontology* 49:S53–61.

Clark, Robert, and Juanita Kreps. 1989. "Employer-Provided Health Care Plans for Retirees." *Research on Aging* 11:206–24.

Clark, Robert, and Ann McDermed. 1990. *The Choice of Pension Plans in a Changing Regulatory Environment.* Washington, DC: AEI Press.

Clark, Robert, and Joseph Quinn. 2002. "Patterns of Work and Retirement for a New Century." *Generations,* Summer:17–30.

Clarke, Edward J., Mar Preston, Jo Raksin, and Vern L. Bengtson. 1999. "Types of Conflict and Tensions between Older Parents and Adult Children." *The Gerontologist* 39(3):261–70.

Clausen, John. 1993. *American Lives: Looking Back at the Children of the Great Depression.* New York: Free Press.

Clement, Priscilla Ferguson. 1985. *Welfare and the Poor in a Nineteenth Century City, Philadelphia, 1800–1854.* Rutherford, NJ: Fairleigh Dickinson University Press.

Cleveland, W., and D. Gianturco. 1976. "Remarriage Probability after Widowhood: A Retrospective Method." *Journal of Gerontology* 31:99–103.

Cockerham, William. 1995. *Medical Sociology.* Englewood Cliffs, NJ: Prentice Hall.

Cockerham, William, Thomas Abel, and Gunther Lueschen. 1993. "Max Weber, Formal Rationality and Health Lifestyles." *Sociological Quarterly* 34:413–25.

Cohen, Carl, Jeanne Teresi, Douglas Holmes, and Eric Roth. 1997. "Survival Strategies of Older Homeless Men." Pp. 118–31 in *Worlds of Difference,* edited by E. Palo Stoller and R. Campbell Gibson. Thousand Oaks, CA: Pine Forge Press.

Cohen, S., and J. Zysman. 1987. *Manufacturing Matters: The Myth of the Post-Industrial Economy.* New York: Basic Books.

Colditz, G. A. 1999. "Hormones and Breast Cancer: Evidence and Implications for Consideration of Risks and Benefits of Hormone Replacement Therapy." *Journal of Women's Health* 8(3):347–57.

Cole, Thomas. 1992. *The Journey of Life: A Cultural History of Aging in America.* Cambridge: Cambridge University Press.

Coleman, Barbara. 2000. "Assuring the Quality of Home Care: The Challenge Involving the Consumer." *AARP Issue Brief*, No. 43. Washington, DC: AARP.

Colman, Hila. 1998. "Just Desserts." *New York Times Sunday Magazine,* May 23, p. 84.

Comijs, H., C. Jonker, W. van Tilburg, and J. Smit. 1999. "Hostility and Coping Capacity as Risk Factors of Elder Mistreatment." *Social Psychiatry* 34(January):48–52.

Comijs, H., A. Pot, J. Smit, L. Bouter, and C. Jonker. 1998. "Elder Abuse in the Community: Prevalence and Consequences." *Journal of the American Geriatrics Society* 46(7):885–88.

Committee on Economic Security. 1937. *Social Security in America.* Washington, DC: U.S. Government Printing Office.

Commonwealth Fund. 1987. *Medicare's Poor.* Washington, DC: Commission on Elderly People Living Alone.

Congressional Budget Office. 1993. *Baby Boomers in Retirement: An Early Perspective.* Washington, DC: U.S. Government Printing Office.

——. 1994. *The Economic and Budget Outlook: Fiscal Years 1995–1999.* Washington, DC: U.S. Government Printing Office.

——. 1995a. *The Economic and Budget Outlook: Fiscal Years 1996–2000.* Washington, DC: U.S. Government Printing Office.

——. 1995b. *Immigration and Welfare Reform.* Washington, DC: U.S. Government Printing Office.

Congressional Budget Office. 2003. *The Budget and Economic Outlook: Fiscal Years 2004–2013.* Washington, DC: Government Printing Office.

Connidis, Ingrid Arnet. 1994. "Sibling Support in Old Age." *Journal of Gerontology* 49:309–17.

Conwell, Y., P. R. Duberstein, C. Cox, J. Herrman, N. Forbes, and E. Caine. 1998. "Age Differences in Behaviors Leading to Completed Suicide." *American Journal of Geriatric Psychiatry* 6(2):122–26.

Coogle, Constance, Edward Ansello, Joan Wood, and J. James Cotter. 1995. "Partners II–Serving Persons with Developmental Disabilities: Obstacles and Inducements to Collaboration among Agencies." *Journal of Applied Gerontology* 14:275–88.

Cook, Faye Lomax. 1992. "Ageism: Rhetoric and Reality." *The Gerontologist* 32:292–95.

Cook, Faye Lomax, and Edith Barrett. 1992. *Support for the American Welfare State: The Views of Congress and the Public.* New York: Columbia University Press.

Cook, Faye Lomax, Victor Marshall, Joanne Gard Marshall, and Julie Kaufman. 1994. "The Salience of Intergenerational Equity in Canada and the United States." Pp. 91–132 in *Economic Security and Intergenerational Justice,* edited by T. Marmor, T. Smeeding, and W. Greene. Washington, DC: Urban Institute Press.

Cook, Faye Lomax, and Richard Settersten, Jr. 1995. "Expenditure Patterns by Age and Income among Mature Adults: Does Age Matter?" *The Gerontologist* 35:10–23.

Cooney, Teresa, and Lori Ann Smith. 1996. "Young Adults' Relations with Grandparents following Recent Parental Divorce." *Journal of Gerontology* 51B:S91–95.

Cooney, Teresa, and Peter Uhlenberg. 1990. "The Role of Divorce in Men's Relations with Their Adult Children after Midlife." *Journal of Marriage and the Family* 52:677–88.

Coontz, Stephanie. 1992. *The Way We Never Were: American Families and the Nostalgia Trap.* New York: HarperCollins.

——. 1997. *The Way We Really Are.* New York: Basic Books.

Cooper, Richard, Charles Rotimi, and Ryk Ward. 1999. "The Puzzle of Hypertension in African Americans." *Scientific America* (February):1–8.

Cornelius, S. W., and A. Caspi. 1987. "Everyday Problem Solving in Adulthood and Old Age." *Psychology and Aging* 2:144–53.

Costa, Dora. 1998. *The Evolution of Retirement.* Chicago: University of Chicago Press.

Costa, Paul, and Robert McCrae. 1988. "Personality in Adulthood: A Six-Year Longitudinal Study of Self-Reports and Spouse Ratings on the NEO Personality Inventory." *Journal of Personality and Social Psychology* 54:853–63.

——. 1989. "Personality Continuity and the Changes of Adult Life." *APA Master Lectures.* Washington, DC: American Psychological Association.

Cottrell, Fred. 1942 "The Adjustment of the Individual to His Age and Sex Roles." *American Sociological Review* 7:617–20.

Couch, Kenneth. 1998. "Later Life Job Displacement." *The Gerontologist* 38:7–17.

Coughlin, J. 2001. "Beyond Health and Retirement: Placing Transportation on the Aging Policy Agenda." *The Public Policy and Aging Report* 11(4):20–23.

Cowart, Marie, and Jill Quadagno. 1995. *Crucial Decisions in Long-Term Care.* Tallahassee, FL: Mildred and Claude Pepper Foundation.

Cowgill, Donald. 1974. "The Aging of Populations and Societies." *Annals of the American Academy of Political and Social Science* 415(29):1–18.

Cowgill, Donald, and Lowell Holmes. 1972. *Aging and Modernization.* New York: Appleton-Century-Crofts.

Cowley, Malcolm. 1980. *The View from 80.* New York: Viking Press.

Craik, F. I. M., and J. M. Jennings. 1992. "Human Memory." Pp. 51–110 in *Handbook of Aging and Cognition*, edited by F. Craik and T. A. Salthouse. Hillsdale, NJ: Erlbaum.

Cristofalo, Vincent. 1988. "An Overview of the Theories of Biological Aging." Pp. 118–28 in *Emergent Theories of Aging*, edited by J. Birren and V. Bengtson. New York: Springer.

———. 1996. "Ten Years Later: What Have We Learned about Human Aging from Studies of Cell Cultures?" *The Gerontologist* 36:737–41.

Cristofalo, Vincent, Maria Tresini, Mary Kay Francis, and Craig Volker. 1999. "Biological Theories of Senescence." Pp. 98–112 in *Handbook of Theories of Aging*, edited by Vern Bengtson and K. Warner Schaie. New York: Springer.

Crystal, Stephen. 1996. "Economic Status of the Elderly." Pp. 388–409 in *Handbook of Aging and the Social Sciences*, edited by R. Binstock and L. George. San Diego, CA: Academic Press.

Crystal, Stephen, Richard Johnson, Jeffrey Harman, Usha Sambamoorthi, and Rizie Kumar. 2000. "Out-of-Pocket Health Care Costs among Older Americans." *Journal of Gerontology* 55B(1):S51–62.

Cuellar, Alison Evans, and Joshua M. Wiener. 2000. "Can Social Insurance for Long-Term Care Work? The Experience of Germany." *Health Affairs* 19:8–25.

Cumming, Elaine, and William Henry. 1961. *Growing Old: The Process of Disengagement*. New York: Basic Books.

Cutler, Stephen, and Jon Hendricks. 1990. "Leisure and Time Use across the Life Course." Pp. 169–85 in *Handbook of Aging and the Social Sciences*, edited by R. Binstock and L. George. San Diego, CA: Academic Press.

Cutler, Winiford, Celso Garcia, and Norma McCoy. 1987. "Perimenopausal Sexuality." *Archives of Sexual Behavior* 16:225–34.

Cutler, Winiford, Celso Garcia, Gerald Huggins, and George Preti. 1986. "Sexual Behavior and Steroid Levels among Gynecological Mature Premenopausal Women." *Fertility and Sterility* 45:496–502.

Czaja, Sara, and C. C. Lee. 2001. "The Internet and Older Adults: Design Challenges and Opportunities." Pp. 60–81 in *Aging and Communication*, edited by Neil Charness. New York: Springer.

Dalen, Hendrik P. Van, and Kene Henkins. 2002. "Early Retirement Reform: Can It and Will It Work?" *Ageing and Society* 22(March):209–31.

Daly, Mary, and John Bound. 1996. "Worker Adaptation and Employer Accommodation Following the Onset of a Health Impairment." *Journal of Gerontology* 51B(2): S53–60.

Damush, Theresa M., and Joseph G. Damush. 1999. "The Effect of Strength Training on Strength and Health-Related Quality of Life in Older Adult Women." *The Gerontologist* 36(6):705–10.

Dannefer, Dale. 1984. "Adult Development and Social Theory: A Paradigmatic Appraisal." *American Sociological Review* 49:100–16.

———. 1991. "The Race Is to the Swift: Images of Collective Aging." Pp. 155–72 in *Metaphors of Aging in Science and Humanities*, edited by G. M. Kenyon, J. E. Birren and J. F. Schroots. New York: Springer.

———. 2003. "Whose Life Course Is It Anyway? Diversity and Linked Lives in Global Perspective." Pp. 259–68 in *Invitation to the Life Course*, edited by Richard Settersten, Jr. Amityville, NY: Baywood.

DaVanzo, Julie, and Frances Kobrin Goldscheider. 1990. "Coming Home Again: Returns to the Parental Home of Young Adults." *Population Studies* 44:241–55.

Davis, R. H., and J. A. Davis. 1986. *TV's Image of the Elderly*. Lexington, MA: Lexington.

Day, Christine. 1990. *What Older Americans Think*. Princeton, NJ: Princeton University Press.

———. 1993. "Public Opinion toward the Costs and Benefits of Social Security and Medicare." *Research on Aging* 15:279–98.

Dean, A., B. Kolodny, and P. Wood. 1990. "Effects of Social Support from Various Sources on Depression in Elderly Persons." *Journal of Health and Social Behavior* 31:148–61.

DeBaggio, Thomas. 2000. "Loss of Memory, Loss of Hope." *New York Times*, Sunday, June 25. p. D–1.

DeMallie, Diane, Carol North, and Elizabeth Smith. 1997. "Psychiatric Disorders among the Homeless: A Comparison of Older and Younger Groups." *The Gerontologist* 37(1):61–66.

Demos, John. 1978. "Old Age in Early New England." Pp. 220–56 in *The American Family in Socio-Historical Perspective*, edited by M. Gordon. New York: St. Martin's Press.

Denney, Nancy, Jeffrey Field, and David Quadagno. 1986. "Sex Differences in Sexual Needs and Desires." *Archives of Sexual Behavior* 13:233–46.

Dennis, Helen. 2002. "The Retirement Planning Specialty." *Generations*, Summer:55–60.

Derthick, Martha. 1979. *Policymaking for Social Security*. Washington, DC: The Brookings Institution.

DeSpelder, Lynne, and Albert Strickland. 1992. *The Last Dance: Encountering Death and Dying*. 3d ed. Mountain View, CA: Mayfield.

Dharma-Wardene, M., C. deGara, H. Au, J. Hanson, and J. Hatcher, 2002. "Ageism in Rectal Carcinoma? Treatment and Outcome Variations." *International Journal of Gastrointestinal Cancer* 32(2–3):129–38.

Diamond, Timothy. 1992. *Making Gray Gold: Narratives of Nursing Home Care*. Chicago: University of Chicago Press.

Dittmar, N. 1989. "Facility and Resident Characteristics of Board and Care Homes for the Elderly." Pp. 1–26 in

Preserving Independence, Supporting Needs: The Role of Board and Care Homes, edited by M. Moon, G. Gaberlavage, and S. Newman. Washington, DC: American Association of Retired Persons.

Doeringer, Peter. 1991. *Turbulence in the American Workplace.* New York: Oxford University Press.

Douglas, Joan Delaney. 1990–91. "Patterns of Change following Parent Death in Midlife Adults." *Omega* 22:123–37.

Douglass, Frederick. 1960. *Narrative of the Life of Frederick Douglass: An American Slave.* Cambridge, MA: Belknap Press.

Dowd, James. 1975. "Aging as Exchange: A Preface to Theory." *Journal of Gerontology* 30:584–94.

——. 1987. "The Reification of Age: Age Stratification Theory and the Passing of the Autonomous Subject." *Journal of Aging Studies* 1:317–35.

Dugas, Christine. 2002. "Retirement Crisis Looms as Many Come Up Short." *USA Today,* July 19: 1A.

Duka, Walt. 2000. "Voters Face Clear Choice on Social Security Plans." *AARP Bulletin* (July–August):6–7.

Duncan, Greg, and Ken Smith. 1989. "The Rising Affluence of the Elderly: How Far, How Fair and How Frail?" *Annual Review of Sociology* 15:261–89.

Durkheim, Emile. [1893] 1964. *The Division of Labor in Society.* Reprint. New York: Free Press.

Duster, Troy. 1995. "Postindustrialism and Youth Unemployment: African Americans as Harbingers." Pp. 461–87 in *Poverty, Inequality and the Future of Social Policy,* edited by K. McFate, R. Lawson, and W. J. Wilson. New York: Russell Sage Foundation.

Duvall, E. M. 1962. *Family Development.* New York: Lippincott.

Easterlin, Richard. 1996. "Economic and Social Implications of Demographic Patterns." Pp. 73–93 in *Handbook of Aging and the Social Sciences,* edited by R. Binstock and L. George. San Diego, CA: Academic Press.

Easterlin, Richard A., Diane J. Macunovich, and Eileen M. Crimmins. 1994. "Economic Status of the Young and Old in the Working Age Population, 1964 and 1987." Pp. 67–86 in *The Changing Contract across Generations,* edited by V. Bengtson and W. A. Achenbaum. New York: Aldine de Gruyter.

Easterlin, Richard, C. M. Schaeffer, and Diane Macunovich. 1993. "Will Baby Boomers Be Less Well Off than Their Parents? Income, Wealth, and Family Circumstances over the Life Cycle in the United States." *Population and Development Review* 19:497–522.

Eckert, J. Kevin, and Stephanie Lyon. 1991. "Regulation of Board-and-Care Homes: Research to Guide Policy." *Journal of Aging and Social Policy* 3(1/2):147–62.

Eckert, Kevin. 1980. *The Unseen Elderly.* San Diego, CA: Campanile Press.

Eisenstadt, S. 1956. *From Generation to Generation.* Glencoe, IL: Free Press.

Eisner, Robert. 1994. *The Misunderstood Economy.* Boston: Harvard Business School Press.

Ekerdt, David. 1998. "Entitlements, Generational Equity and Public Opinion Manipulation in Kansas City." *The Gerontologist* 38:525–36.

Ekerdt, David J., and Stanley DeViney. 1990. "On Defining Persons as Retired." *Journal of Aging Studies* 4:211–30.

——. 1993. "Evidence for a Preretirement Process among Older Male Workers." *Journal of Gerontology* 48:S35–43.

Ekerdt, David, and Jennifer Hackney. 2002. "Workers' Ignorance of Retirement Benefits." *The Gerontologist* 42(4):543–51.

Elder, Glen. 1974. *Children of the Great Depression.* Chicago: University of Chicago Press.

——. 1985. *Life Course Dynamics: Trajectories and Transitions, 1968–1980.* Ithaca, NY: Cornell University Press.

——. 1994. "Time, Human Agency and Social Change: Perspectives on the Life Course." *Social Psychology Quarterly* 57:4–15.

Elder, Glen, and Eliza Pavalko. 1993. "Work Careers in Men's Later Years: Transition, Trajectories and Historical Change." *Journal of Gerontology* 48:80–191.

Ellwood, Paul, and George Lundberg. 1996. "Managed Care: A Work in Progress." *Journal of the American Medical Association* 276:1083–86.

Elman, C. and P. Uhlenberg. 1995. "Co-residence in the Early Twentieth Century: Elderly Women in the United States and their Children." *Population Studies* 49, 3 (November):501–11.

Elstad, Jon Ivar. 1997. *Recent Developments in the Norwegian Health Care System: Pointing in What Direction?* Oslo: Norsk Institute for Forskning om Oppvekst.

Emanuel, Ezekiel, and Linda Emanuel. 1994. "The Economics of Dying: The Illusion of Savings at the End of Life." *New England Journal of Medicine* 330:540–44.

Emery, V., and T. Oxman. 1994. *Dementia Presentations, Differential Diagnosis, and Nosology.* Baltimore, MD: Johns Hopkins University Press.

Employee Benefit Research Institute. 1995. "Are Workers Kidding Themselves? Results of the 1995 Retirement Confidence Survey." EBRI Issue Brief No. 168, Washington, DC.

Enriquez, Priscilla. 1996. "Precious Moments: A Granddaughter's Account." *Parenting Grandchildren: A Voice for Grandparents* 2(2):6–7.

Erikson, Erik. 1950. *Childhood and Society.* New York: W. W. Norton.

——. 1959. "Identity and the Life Cycle: Selected Papers." *Psychological Issues* 1: Monograph No. 1.

——. 1964. "Inner and Outer Space: Reflections on Womanhood." *Daedalus* 93(Spring):582–606.

Erikson, Erik, Joan Erikson, and Helen Kivnick. 1986. *Vital Involvement in Old Age.* New York: W. W. Norton.

Esping-Anderson, Gosta. 1990. *The Three Worlds of Welfare Capitalism.* Cambridge: Polity Press.

———. 1995. "Welfare States without Work: The Impasse of Labor Shedding and Familism in Continental European Social Policy." Presented to Research Group 19, Pavia, Italy, Sept. 17.

Espino, David. 1993. "Hispanic Elderly and Long-Term Care: Implications for Ethnically Sensitive Services." Pp. 101–12 in *Ethnic Elderly and Long-Term Care,* edited by C. Barresi and D. Stull. New York: Springer.

Esselstyn, Caldwell. 1965. *Oral History.* New York: Columbia University Oral History Collection.

Estes, Carroll. 1979. *The Aging Enterprise.* San Francisco: Jossey-Bass.

———. 1991. "The New Political Economy of Aging: Introduction and Critique." Pp. 19–36 in *Critical Perspectives on Aging,* edited by M. Minkler and C. Estes. Amityville, NY: Baywood.

———. 1996. "The Political Economy of Aging." Pp. 346–59 in *Handbook of Aging and the Social Sciences,* edited by R. Binstock and L. George. San Diego, CA: Academic Press.

Estes, Carroll, Lenore Gerard, Jane Sprague Zones, and James Swan. 1984. *Political Economy, Health and Aging.* Boston: Little, Brown.

Estes, Carroll, Karen Linkins, and Elizabeth Binney. 1996. "The Political Economy of Aging." Pp. 346–60 in *Handbook of Aging and the Social Sciences,* edited by R. Binstock and L. George. San Diego, CA: Academic Press.

Etzioni, Amitai. 1996. "Health Care for the Elderly Should Not Be Limited." Pp. 155–60 in *An Aging Population: Opposing Viewpoints,* edited by C. Cozic. San Diego, CA: Greenhaven Press.

Ewertz, M. 1996. "Hormone Therapy in the Menopause and Breast Cancer Risk—A Review." *Maturitas* 23:241–46.

Fairlie, Henry. 1988. "Talkin' bout My Generation." *The New Republic* (March 28):17–20.

Farber, Henry. 1993. "The Incidence and Costs of Job Loss: 1982–1991." Working Paper No. 309, Industrial Relations Section, Princeton University, Princeton, NJ.

———. 1996. "The Changing Face of Job Loss in the United States, 1981–1993." Working Paper No. 360, Industrial Relations Section, Princeton University, Princeton, NJ.

Farley, Reynolds. 1984. *Blacks and Whites, Narrowing the Gap?* Cambridge, MA: Harvard University Press.

———. 1996. *The New American Reality.* New York: Russell Sage.

Farley, Reynolds, and Walter Allen. 1987. *The Color Line and the Quality of Life in America.* New York: Russell Sage Foundation.

Farley, Reynolds, Suzanne Bianchi, and Paul Voss. 1997. "Using the Census: What It Tells Us about America's People, Workforce and Small Communities." Transcript of proceedings, Congressional Breakfast Seminar, Consortium of Social Science Associations, May 2, Washington, DC.

Farmer, M. E., L. R. White, J. A. Brody, and K. Bailey. 1984. "Race and Sex Differences in Hip Fracture Incidence." *American Journal of Public Health* 74:1374–80.

Featherman, David. 1983. "Life-Span Perspectives in Social Science Research." Pp. 1–57 in *Life-Span Development and Behavior,* edited by P. Baltes and O. Brim. New York: Academic Press.

Feifel, Herman. 1990. "Psychology and Death: Meaningful Rediscovery." *American Psychologist* 45:537–43.

Feinson, Marjorie. 1991. "Reexamining Some Common Beliefs about Mental Health and Aging." Pp. 125–36 in *Growing Old in America,* edited by B. Hess and E. Markson. New Brunswick, NJ: Transaction.

Feldman, H., I. Goldstein, D. Hatzichristou, R. Krane, and J. McKinlay. 1994. "Impotence and Its Medical and Psychosocial Correlates: Results of the Massachusetts Male Aging Study." *Journal of Urology* 151:54–61.

Feldman, Jacob. 1991. "Life Expectancy and Work Capacity." Pp. 151–58 in *Retirement and Public Policy,* edited by A. Munnell. Washington, DC: National Academy of Social Insurance.

Feldman, Richard, and Michael Betzold. 1990. *End of the Line: Autoworkers and the American Dream.* Urbana, IL: University of Illinois Press.

Ferrante, Lynn, and Diana Woodruff-Pak. 1995. "Longitudinal Investigation of Eye Blink Classical Conditioning in Elderly Human Subjects." *Journal of Gerontology* 50B:P42–50.

Ferraro, Kenneth. 1985. "The Effect of Widowhood on the Health Status of Older Persons." *International Journal of Aging and Human Development* 21:9–25.

———. 1992. "Cohort Changes in Images of Older Adults, 1974–1981." *The Gerontologist* 32:296–304.

Ferraro, Kenneth, and C. Cobb. 1987. "Participation in Multipurpose Senior Centers." *Journal of Applied Gerontology* 6:429–47.

Ferraro, Kenneth, and Melissa Farmer. 1996. "Double Jeopardy to Health Hypothesis for African Americans: Critique and Analysis." *Journal of Health and Social Behavior* 37:27–43.

Ferraro, Kenneth, Roland Thorpe, and Jody Wilkinson. 2003. "The Life Course of Severe Obesity: Does Childhood Overweight Matter?" *Journal of Gerontology* 58B(2):S110–19.

Ferree, Myra Marx, and Patricia Yancey Martin. 1995. *Feminist Organizations.* Philadelphia: Temple University Press.

Fessman, N., and D. Lester. 2000. "Loneliness and Depression among Elderly Nursing Home Patients." *International Journal of Aging and Human Development* 51(2):137–41.

Field, Dorothy, Meredith Minkler, R. Frank Falk, and E. Victor Leino. 1993. "The Influence of Health on Family Contacts and Family Feelings in Advanced Old Age: A Longitudinal Study." *Journal of Gerontology* 48:P18–28.

Fielding, R. A. 1995. "The Role of Progressive Resistance Training and Nutrition in the Preservation of Lean Body Mass in the Elderly." *Journal of the American College of Nutrition* 14(December):87–94.

Fields, Gary S., and Olivia Mitchell. 1984. *Retirement, Pensions and Social Security.* Cambridge, MA: MIT Press.

Fillenbaum, Gerda, Linda K. George, and Erdman Palmore. 1985. "Determinants and Consequences of Retirement among Men of Different Races and Economic Levels." *Journal of Gerontology* 40:85–94.

Finne-Soveri, U. 1998. "How Accurate Is the Terminal Diagnosis in the Minimum Data Set?" *American Geriatrics* 46(August):1023–24.

Fischer, David Hackett. 1977. *Growing Old in America.* New York: Oxford University Press.

Fischer, Lucy Rose. 1985. "Elderly Parents and the Caregiving Role: An Asymmetrical Transition." Pp. 105–14 in *Social Bonds in Later Life: Aging and Interdependence,* edited by W. Peterson and J. Quadagno. Beverly Hills, CA: Sage.

Fitzpatrick, Sharon, and Debra Entmacher. 2000. "Retirement Security for Older Women." Occasional Paper Number 6. Washington, DC: The Urban Institute.

Flint, William, and Robert Applebaum. 1993. "The Impact of Ideology on Regulation: The Case of Board and Care Homes." *Journal of Aging Studies* 7:395–408.

Flippen, Chenoa, and Marta Tienda. 2000. "Pathways to Retirement: Patterns of Labor Force Participation and Labor Market Exit among the Pre-Retirement Population by Race, Hispanic Origin, and Sex. *Journal of Gerontology* 55B(1):S14–27.

Flowers, Marilyn. 1979. "Supplemental Benefits for Spouses under Social Security: A Public Choice Explanation." *Economic Inquiry* 17:125–30.

Fogel, Robert, and Stanley Engerman. 1974. *Time on a Cross.* Boston: Little, Brown.

Foley, Daniel, Toni Miles, Dwight Brock, and Caroline Phillips. 1995. "Recounts of Elderly Deaths: Endorsements for the Patients, Self-Determination Act." *The Gerontologist* 35:119–21.

Folkemer, Donna. 1994. "State Use of Home and Community-Based Services for the Aged under Medicaid: Waiver Programs, Personal Care, Frail Elderly Services and Home Health Services." No. 9405, American Association of Retired Persons Public Policy Institute, Washington, DC.

Foner, Anne, and David Kertzer. 1978. "Age Stratification and the Changing Family." *American Journal of Sociology* 84:340–65.

Foner, Nancy. 1994. *The Caregiving Dilemma: Work in an American Nursing Home.* Berkeley, CA: University of California Press.

Foner, Philip. 1981. *Organized Labor and the Black Worker, 1619–1981.* New York: International Publishers.

Fowlkes, Martha. 1994. "Single Worlds and Homosexual Lifestyles: Patterns of Sexuality and Intimacy." Pp. 151–84 in *Sexuality across the Life Course,* edited by A. Rossi. Chicago: University of Chicago Press.

Francis, Doris. 1990. "The Significance of Work Friends in Later Life." *Journal of Aging Studies* 4:405–26.

Fratiglioni, L., A. Ahlbom, M. Viitanen, and B. Winblad. 1993. "Risk Factors for Late Onset Alzheimer's Disease: A Population-Based Case-Control Study." *Annals of Neurology* 33:258–66.

Freud, Sigmund. 1905. *Three Essays on the Theory of Sexuality.* London: Hogarth Press.

Friedland, Robert. 1994. *When Support and Confidence Are at Odds: The Public's Understanding of the Social Security Program.* Washington, DC: National Academy of Social Insurance.

——. 2001. "Expenditures for Long-Term Care." Paper prepared for the Citizens for Long Term Care. Washington, DC: Citizens for Long Term Care.

Friedland, Robert B., and Laura Summer. 1999. *Demography Is Not Destiny.* Washington, DC: National Academy on an Aging Society.

Friedmann, Eugene, and Robert Havighurst. 1954. *The Meaning of Work and Retirement.* Chicago: University of Chicago Press.

Friedmann, Eugene, and Harold Orbach. 1974. "Adjustment to Retirement." Pp. 97–111 in *American Handbook of Psychiatry,* edited by Silvano Arieti. New York: Basic Books.

Fries, James. 1980. "Aging, Natural Death and the Compression of Morbidity." *New England Journal of Medicine* 303:130–35.

Fries, James, Gurkirpal Singh, Dianne Morfeld, Helen Hubert, Nancy Lane, and Byron Brown, Jr. 1994. "Running and the Development of Disability with Age." *Annals of Internal Medicine* 121:502–9.

Fronstin, Paul. 1999. "Retirement Patterns and Employee Benefits: Do Benefits Matter?" *The Gerontologist* 39(1):37–48.

Fry, Christine. 1999. "Anthropological Theories of Age and Aging." Pp. 271–86 in *Handbook of Theories of Aging*, edited by Vern Bengtson and K. W. Schaie. New York: Springer.

Fuguitt, Glenn, and Calvin Beale. 1993. "The Changing Concentration of the Older Metropolitan Population, 1960–90." *Journal of Gerontology* 48:S278–88.

Furstenberg, Frank. 1987. "The New Extended Family: The Experience of Parents and Children after Remarriage." Pp. 42–61 in *Remarriage and Stepparenting*, edited by K. Pasley and M. Ihinger-Tallman. New York: Guilford Press.

Gallagher, Sally, and Naomi Gerstel. 1993. "Kinkeeping and Friend Keeping among Older Women: The Effect of Marriage." *The Gerontologist* 33:675–81.

Gallup, G., Jr., and S. Jones. 1989. *One Hundred Questions and Answers: Religion in America*. Princeton, NJ: Princeton Research Center.

Ganong, Lawrence H., and Marilyn Coleman. 1998. "Attitudes Regarding Filial Responsibilities to Help Elderly Divorced Parents and Stepparents." *Journal of Aging Studies* 12(3):271–90.

Gatz, M., and M. Hurwicz. 1990. "Are Old People More Depressed? Cross-Sectional Data on CES-D Factors." *Psychology and Aging* 5:284–90.

Gatz, M., J. Kasl-Godby, and M. Karel. 1996. "Aging and Mental Disorders." Pp. 365–82 in *Handbook of the Psychology of Aging*, edited by J. Birren and K. Warner Schaie. New York: Academic Press.

Gaumer, G. L., and J. Stabins. 1992. "Medicare Use in the Last 90 Days of Life." *Health Services Research* 26:725–42.

Gaunt, David. 1979. "The Retired Farmer: His Property and His Family Relations since the Middle Ages: Northern and Central Europe." Presented to the Cambridge Group for the History of Population and Social Structure, October 14, Cambridge, England.

Genazzani, A. R., and M. Gambacciani. 1999. "Hormone Replacement Therapy: The Perspectives for the 21st Century." *Maturitas* 31(1):11–17.

General Accounting Office. 1990. "Extent of Companies' Retiree Health Coverage." GAO/HRD-90-92, Washington, DC.

———. 1995. *Long-Term Care: Current Issues and Future Directions*. Washington, DC: General Accounting Office.

———. 1999. *Staff Shortages in Nursing Homes*. Washington, DC: U.S. Government Printing Office.

———. 2001. *Retiree Health Benefits*. Washington, DC: U.S. Government Printing Office.

George, Linda. 1980. *Role Transitions in Later Life*. Belmont, CA: Wadsworth.

———. 1993. "Sociological Perspectives on Life Transitions." *Annual Review of Sociology*, 19:353–73.

———. 1996. "Social Factors and Illness." Pp. 229–68 in *Handbook of Aging and the Social Sciences*, edited by R. Binstock and L. George. San Diego, CA: Academic Press.

George, Linda, and Deborah Gold. 1991. "Life Course Perspectives on Intergenerational and Generational Connections." *Marriage and Family Review* 16:67–88.

George, Linda, and George Maddox. 1977. "Subjective Adaptation to Loss of the Work Role: A Longitudinal Study." *Journal of Gerontology* 32:456–62.

George, Linda, and I. Siegler. 1982. "Stress and Coping in Later Life." *Educational Horizons* 60:147–54.

Gerike, Ann. 1990. "On Gray Hair and Oppressed Brains." *Journal of Women and Aging* 2:14–29.

Ghilarducci, Teresa. 1992. *Labor's Capital: The Economics and Politics of Private Pensions*. Cambridge, MA: MIT Press.

Gibbs, Jeanne. 1985. "Family Relations of the Older Widow: Their Location and Importance for Her Social Life." Pp. 91–114 in *Social Bonds in Later Life*, edited by W. Peterson and J. Quadagno. Beverly Hills, CA: Sage.

Gibbs, Tyson. 1988. "Health-Seeking Behavior of Elderly Blacks." Pp. 282–91 in *The Black American Elderly*, edited by J. Jackson. New York: Springer.

Gibson, Rose. 1991. "Age-by-Race Differences in the Health and Functioning of Elderly Persons." *Journal of Aging and Health* 3:335–51.

———. 1994a. "The Age-by-Race Gap in Health and Mortality in the Older Population: A Social Science Research Agenda." *The Gerontologist* 34:454–62.

———. 1994b. "Reconceptualizing Retirement for Black Americans." Pp. 120–27 in *Worlds of Difference: Inequality in the Aging Experience*, edited by E. Palo Stoller and R. Gibson. Thousand Oaks, CA: Pine Forge Press.

———. 1995. "The Black American Retirement Experience." Pp. 309–26 in *Aging for the Twenty-First Century*, edited by J. Quadagno and D. Street. New York: St. Martin's Press.

Gilbert, T., and J. Hirdes. 2000. "Stress, Social Engagement and Psychological Well-Being in Institutional Settings: Evidence Based on the Minimum Data Set 2.0." *La Revue Canadienne du Vielillissement* 19(2):50–66.

Ginn, Jay, and Sara Arber. 2000. "Ethnic Inequality in Later Life: Variation in Financial Circumstances by Gender and Ethnic Group." *Education and Aging* 15(1):65–83.

Glick, Henry. 1992. *The Right to Die: Policy Innovation and Its Consequences*. New York: Columbia University Press.

Global Aging Report. 1998a. "A Global View of Aging and Productivity." May/June (3):3.

———. 1998b. "Private Savings Bolsters Future Retirement Funds." May/June (3):4.

——. 1998c. "Report Card from Chile." May/June (3):4.

Goffman, Erving. 1961. *Asylums.* Garden City, NY: Anchor Books.

Golant, Stephen. 1996. "Homeownership." Pp. 265–72. in Lois A. Vitt and J. Siegenthaler (Eds.), *Encyclopedia of Financial Gerontology.* Westport, CT: Greenwood Press.

Golant, Stephen, and Anthony La Greca. 1994. "Housing Quality of U.S. Elderly Households: Does Aging In Place Matter?" *The Gerontologist* 34:803–14.

Gold, Deborah. 1996. "Continuities and Discontinuities in Sibling Relationships across the Life Span." Pp. 228–45 in *Adulthood and Aging,* edited by V. Bengtson. New York: Springer.

Gold, Deborah, and Marc Drezner. 1995. "Quality of Life." Pp. 475–86 in *Osteoporosis: Etiology, Diagnosis and Management,* edited by B. Lawrence Riggs and L. Joseph Melton. Philadelphia: Lippincott-Raven.

Gold, Deborah, Kimberly Stegmaier, Connie Bales, Kenneth Lyles, Ronald Westlund, and Marc Drezner. 1993. "Psychosocial Functioning and Osteoporosis in Late Life: Results of a Multidisciplinary Intervention." *Journal of Women's Health* 2:149–55.

Gold, Marthe. 1995. "Hospice Care Allows Death with Dignity." *Provider* (Summer):84–86.

Goldman, J., and L. Cote. 1991. "Aging of the Brain: Dementia of the Alzheimer's Type." Pp. 974–83 in *Principles of Neural Science,* edited by E. Kandel, J. Schwartz, and T. Jessell. New York: Elsevier.

Goldscheider, Frances Kobrin, and Julie DaVanzo. 1985. "Living Arrangements and the Transition to Adulthood." *Demography* 22:545–63.

Goldscheider, Frances Kobrin, and Calvin Goldscheider. 1993. *Leaving Home before Marriage.* Madison, WI: University of Wisconsin Press.

Goldsmith, Elizabeth, and Ronald Goldsmith. 1995. "Full-Time Employees as Caregivers to the Elderly." *Journal of Social Behavior and Personality* 10:719–30.

Goldstein, Samuel. 1971. "The Biology of Aging." *New England Journal of Medicine* 285:1120–29.

Goldstein, Samuel, Joseph Gallo, and William Reichel. 1989. "Biologic Theories of Aging." *American Family Physician* 40:195–200.

Goodfellow, Gordon, and Sylvester Schieber. 1993. "The Role of Tax Expenditures in the Provision of Retirement Income Security." Pp. 79–94 in *Pensions in a Changing Economy,* edited by R. Burkhauser and D. Salisbury. Washington, DC: Employee Benefit Research Institute.

Goodman, Ellen. 1995. "Women Are Caught in the Middle of the Estrogen Debate." *Boston Globe,* June 20, p. 9A.

Gordon, David. 1996. *Fat and Mean.* New York: Free Press.

Gordon, Ian. 1995. "The Impact of Economic Change on Minorities and Migrants in Western Europe." Pp. 489–520 in *Poverty, Inequality and the Future of Social Policy,* edited by Katherine McFate, Roger Lawson, and William Julius Wilson. New York: Russell Sage Foundation.

Gordon, R., and D. Brill. 2001. "The Abuse and Neglect of the Elderly." *International Journal of Law and Psychiatry* 24:183–97.

Gordus, J. P. 1980. *Leaving Early: Perspectives and Problems in Current Retirement Practice and Policy.* Kalamazoo, MI: W. E. Upjohn Institute for Employment Research.

Gornick, M. E., P. W. Eggers, T. W. Reilly, R. M. Mentnech, L. K. Fitterman, L. E. Kucken, and B. C. Vladeck. 1996. "Effects of Race and Income on Mortality and Use of Services among Medicare Beneficiaries." *New England Journal of Medicine* 335:791–99.

Gorshe, N. 2000. "Supporting Aging in Place and Assisted Living through Home Care." *Caring* (June):20–22.

Gottlieb, Benjamin, E. Kevin Kelloway, and Maryann Fraboni. 1994. "Aspects of Eldercare That Place Employees at Risk." *The Gerontologist* 34:815–21.

Gottschalk, E. C., Jr. 1986. "After Years of Decline, Suicide Rate Is Rising among Elderly in U.S." *Wall Street Journal,* July 30, p. 16.

Gottschalk, Peter, and Sheldon Danziger. 1993. "Family Structure, Family Size and Family Income." Pp. 165–94 in *Uneven Tides: Rising Inequality in America,* edited by S. Danziger and P. Gottschalk. New York: Russell Sage Foundation.

Grad, Susan. 1994. "Income of the Population 55 or Older, 1992." Publication No. 13–11871, Social Security Administration, Office of Research and Statistics, Washington, DC.

Graebner, William. 1980. *A History of Retirement: The Meaning and Function of an American Institution.* New Haven, CT: Yale University Press.

Gratton, Brian, and Marie Haug. 1983. "Decision and Adaptation: Research on Female Retirement." *Research on Aging* 5:59–76.

Green, V., M. Lovely, M. Miller, and J. Ondrich. 1993. "The Cost Effectiveness of Community Services in a Frail Elderly Population." *The Gerontologist* 33:177–89.

Greenberg, Joel. 1978. "The Old Age Survivors and Disability Insurance (OASDI) System: A General Overview of the Social Problem." HS 7094, U.S. Report No. 78–200 EPW, Health Care Financing Administration, Washington, DC.

Greene, Vernon, and Deborah Monahan. 1989. "The Effect of a Support and Education Program on Stress and Burden among Family Caregivers to the Frail Elderly." *The Gerontologist* 29:472–77.

Greenwell, Lisa, and Vern Bengtson. 1997. "Geographic Distance and Contact between Middle-Aged Children and Their Parents: The Effects of Social Class over 20 Years." *Journal of Gerontology* 52B:S13–26.

Greenwood, S. 1992. *Menopause Naturally: Preparing for the Second Half of Life.* Volcano, CA: Volcano Press.

Gregory, Steven. 2001. *The Nursing Home Workforce: Certified Nurse Assistants.* Washington, DC: AARP.

Greven, Philip. 1970. *Four Generations: Population, Land and Family in Colonial America.* New York: Cornell University Press.

Grigsby, Jill S. 1991. "Paths of Future Population Aging." *The Gerontologist* 31:195–203.

Grogan, Colleen, and Eric Patashnik. 2003. "Between Welfare Medicine and Mainstream Entitlement: Medicaid at the Political Crossroads." *Journal of Health Politics, Policy and Law* 28(4):201–42.

Gronfein, W. 1985. "Incentives and Intentions in Mental Health Policy: A Comparison of the Medicaid and Community Mental Health Programs." *Journal of Health and Social Behavior* 26:192–206.

Groove, Andy. 1996. "Taking on Prostate Cancer." *Fortune,* May 13, pp. 55–72.

Grossman, Arnold, Anthony D'Augelli, and Scott Hershberger. 2000. "Social Support Networks of Lesbian, Gay and Bisexual Adults 60 Years of Age and Older." *Journal of Gerontology* 55B(3):P171–79.

Guarente, L. 2002. *Ageless Quest: One Scientists Search for Genes that Prolong Youth.* Cold Spring Harbor Press. Cold Spring Harbor, New York.

Gubrium, Jaber. 1975. *Living and Dying at Murray Manor.* New York: St. Martin's Press.

Gubrium, Jaber, and D. R. Buckholdt. 1977. *Toward Maturity.* San Francisco: Jossey-Bass.

Gubrium, Jaber, and Robert Lynott. 1983. "Rethinking Life Satisfaction." *Human Organization* 42:30–38.

Gubrium, Jaber, and Andrea Sankar. 1994. *Qualitative Methods in Aging Research,* edited by J. Gubrium. Thousand Oaks, CA: Sage.

Guemple, L. 1983. "Growing Old in Inuit Society." Pp. 138–51 in *Growing Old in Different Societies,* edited by J. Sokolovsky. Belmont, CA: Wadsworth.

Guillemard, Anne-Marie. 1991a. "International Perspectives on Early Withdrawal from the Labor Force." Pp. 209–26 in *States, Labor Markets and the Future of Old Age Policy,* edited by J. Myles and J. Quadagno. Philadelphia: Temple University Press.

———. 1991b. "France: Massive Exit through Unemployment Compensation." Pp. 127–80 in *Time for Retirement,* edited by Martin Kohli, Martin Rein, Anne-Marie Guillemard, and Herman van Gunsteren. New York: Cambridge University Press.

Guillemard, Anne-Marie, and M. Rein. 1993. "Comparative Patterns of Retirement: Recent Trends in Developed Societies." *Annual Review of Sociology* 19:469–503.

Guinnane, Timothy. 1996. "The Family, State Support and Generational Relations in Rural Ireland at the Turn of the Twentieth Century." Pp. 100–19 in *Aging and Generational Relations over the Life Course,* edited by T. Hareven. Berlin: Aldine de Gruyter.

Gutmann, D. 1980. "Observations on Culture and Mental Health in Later Life." Pp. 429–47 in *Handbook of Mental Health and Aging,* edited by J. E. Birren and R. B. Sloane. Englewood Cliffs, NJ: Prentice Hall.

Haber, Carole. 1983. *Beyond Sixty-Five: The Dilemma of Old Age in America's Past.* New York: Cambridge University Press.

———. 1994. "And the Fear of the Poorhouse: Perceptions of Old Age Impoverishment in Elderly Twentieth-Century America." Pp. 75–84 in *Changing Perceptions of Aging and the Aged,* edited by D. Shenk and W. A. Achenbaum. New York: Springer.

Haber, Carole, and Brian Gratton. 1989. "Old Age, Public Welfare and Race: The Case of Charleston, South Carolina, 1800–1949." *Journal of Social History* 21:261–69.

———. 1994. *Old Age and the Search for Security.* Bloomington: Indiana University Press.

Hagestad, Gunhild. 1986. "Dimensions of Time and the Family." *American Behavioral Scientist* 29:679–94.

———. 1987. "Parent–Child Relations in Later Life: Trends and Gaps in Past Research." Pp. 405–32 in *Parenting across the Life Span,* edited by J. Lancaster, J. Altman, A. Rossi, and L. Sherrod. New York: Aldine de Gruyter.

———. 1988. "Demographic Change and the Life Course: Some Emerging Trends in the Family Realm." *Family Relations* 37:405–10.

———. 1990. "Social Perspectives on the Life Course." Pp. 151–68 in *Handbook of Aging and the Social Sciences,* edited by R. Binstock and L. George. San Diego, CA: Academic Press.

Hagestad, Gunhild, and Dale Dannefer. 2001. "Concept and Theories of Aging: Beyond Microfication in Social Science Approaches." Pp. 3–21 in *Handbook of Aging and the Social Sciences,* edited by R. Binstock and L. George. San Diego, CA: Academic Press.

Haines, Michael. 1996. "Long-Term Marriage Patterns in the United States from Colonial Times to the Present." *The History of the Family* 1:15–40.

Hakamies-Blomqvist, Liisa. 1994. "Aging and Fatal Accidents in Male and Female Drivers." *Journal of Gerontology* 49:S286–90.

Hakim, A., D. Curb, H. Petrovitch, B. Rodriguez, K. Yano, G. Ross, L. White, and R. Abbott. 1999. "Effects of Walking on Coronary Heart Disease in Elderly Men: The Honolulu Heart Program." *Circulation* 100(1):9–13.

Hall, D., and P. Mirvis. 1993. "How to Overcome 'Barriers' to New Older Worker Roles." *Perspectives on Aging* (Oct.–Dec.):15–17.

Halli, S., and A. Kazemipur. 1999. "A Study of Poverty of Immigrants in Canada." Paper presented at the Metropolis Conference, Vancouver, Canada, January 15.

Halper, Thomas. 1978. "Paternalism and the Elderly." Pp. 321–39 in *Aging and the Ederly*, edited by Stuart F. Spicker, Kathleen Woodward, and David Van Tassel. Atlantic Highlands, NJ: Humanities Press.

Han, Lein, Charles Barrilleaux, and Jill Quadagno. 1996. "The Distribution of Medicaid: Race and Gender Differences in Access to Home and Community-Based Services." *Journal of Aging and Social Policy* 7(3/4):93–108.

Hardwick, Susan, P. Jennifer Pack, Elizabeth Ann Donohoe, and Kristen Aleksa. 1994. *Across the States 1994: Profiles of Long-Term Care Systems.* Washington, DC: American Association of Retired Persons.

Hardy, Melissa, and Lawrence Hazelrigg. 1995. "Gender, Race/Ethnicity and Poverty in Later Life." *Journal of Aging Studies* 9:43–63.

Hardy, Melissa, Lawrence Hazelrigg, and Jill Quadagno. 1996. *Ending a Career in the Auto Industry: 30 and Out.* Orlando, FL: Plenum.

Hardy, Melissa, and Jill Quadagno. 1995. "Satisfaction with the Early Retirement Decision: Making Choices in the Auto Industry." *Journal of Gerontology* 50:S217–28.

Hareven, Tamara. 2001. "Historical Perspectives on Aging." Pp. 102–22 in *Handbook of Aging and the Social Sciences*, edited by R. Binstock and L. George. San Diego, CA: Academic Press.

Hareven, Tamara, and Andrejs Plakans. 1987. *Family History at the Crossroads.* Princeton, NJ: Princeton University Press.

Harrington, Charlene. 1991. "The Nursing Home Industry: A Structural Analysis." Pp. 153–64 in *Critical Perspectives on Aging: The Political and Moral Economy of Growing Old*, edited by M. Minkler and C. Estes. Amityville, NY: Baywood.

Harrington, C., J. O'Meara, J. Angelelli, D. Gifford, J. Morris, and T. Moore. 2003. "Designing a Report Card for Nursing Facilities: What Information Is Needed and Why." *The Gerontologist* 43(II):47–57.

Harrington Meyer, Madonna. 1990. "Family Status and Poverty among Older Women: The Gendered Distribution of Retirement Income in the United States." *Social Problems* 37:1101–113.

——. 1991. "Universalism vs. Targeting as the Basis of Social Distribution: Gender, Race and Long-Term Care in the U.S." Ph.D dissertation, Tallahassee, FL: Florida State University.

——. 1994. "Gender, Race and the Distribution of Social Assistance: Medicaid Use Among the Frail Elderly." *Gender and Society* 8:8–28.

——. 1996. "Making Claims as Workers or Wives: The Distribution of Social Security Benefits." *American Sociological Review* 61:449–65.

Harrington Meyer, Madonna, and Michelle Kesterke-Storbakken. 2000. "Shifting the Burden Back to Families?" Pp. 217–28 in *Care Work*, edited by Madonna Harrington Meyer. New York: Routledge.

Harris, Mary. 1994. "Growing Old Gracefully: Age Concealment and Gender." *Journal of Gerontology* 49:P149–58.

Harris, Phyllis. 1993. "The Misunderstood Caregiver? A Qualitative Study of the Male Caregiver of Alzheimer's Disease Victims." *The Gerontologist* 33:551–56.

——. 2000. "Listening to Caregiving Sons: Misunderstood Realities." *The Gerontologist* 38(3):342–52.

Hart, Peter D. 2000. *Survey of Young Americans.* Washington, DC: Peter D. Hart Research Association.

Hartung, Beth, and Kim Sweeney. 1991. "Why Adult Children Return Home." *Social Science Journal* 28:467–80.

Hasher L, C. Chung, C. P. May, N. Foong. 2002. "Age, time of Testing, and Proactive Interference." *Canadian Journal of Experimental Psychology* 56(3):200–07.

Hatch, Laurie Russell, and Aaron Thompson. 1992. "Family Responsibilities and Women's Retirement." Pp. 99–113 in *Families and Retirement*, edited by M. Szinovacz, D. Ekerdt, and B. Vinick. Newbury Park, CA: Sage.

Haug, Marie, and Bebe Lavin. 1983. "Practitioner or Patient—Who's in Charge?" *Journal of Health and Social Behavior* 22:212–29.

Hauser, Philip M. 1953. "Facing the Implications of an Aging Population." *Social Review* 26:162–76.

Havighurst, Robert. 1957. "The Social Competence of Middle-Aged People." *Genetic Psychological Monographs* 56:297–375.

Havighurst, Robert J., Bernice L. Neugarten, and Sheldon S. Tobin. 1968. "Disengagement and Patterns of Aging." Pp. 161–72 in *Middle Age and Aging: A Reader in Social Psychology*, edited by B. Neugarten. Chicago: University of Chicago Press.

Hayflick, L. 1996. *How and Why We Age.* New York: Ballantine Books.

Hayslip, Bert, Jr., and Joel Leon. 1992. *Hospice Care.* Newbury Park, CA: Sage.

Hayslip, Bert, Jerald Shore, Craig Henderson, and Paul Lambert. 1998. "Custodial Grandparenting and the Impact of Grandchildren with Problems on Role Satisfaction and Role Meaning." *Journal of Gerontology* 53B(3):S164–73.

Hayward, Mark D., Eileen M. Crimmins, and Yasuhiko Saito. 1998. "Cause of Death and Active Life Expectancy in the Older Population in the United States." *Journal of Aging and Health*, 10:192–213.

Hayward, Mark D., Eileen M. Crimmins, and Linda Wray. 1994. "The Relationship between Retirement Life Cycle Changes and Older Men's Labor Force Participation Rates." *Journal of Gerontology* 49:5219–31.

Hayward, Mark D., Samantha Friedman, and Hsinmu Chen. 1996. "Race Inequities in Men's Retirement." *Journal of Gerontology* 51B:S1–10.

Hayward, Mark, and Melonie Heron. 1999. "Racial Inequality and Active Life among Adult Americans." *Demography*, 36:77–91.

Health Care Financing Administration. 2000a. *Medicare Health Maintenance Organizations.* Washington, DC: U.S. Government Printing Office.

——. 2000b. *Medicare 2000: 35 Years of Improving Americans' Health and Security.* Washington, DC: U.S. Government Printing Office.

Heclo, Hugh. 1974. *Modern Social Politics in Britain and Sweden.* New Haven, CT: Yale University Press.

Heinemann, A., A. Colorez, S. Frank, and D. Taylor. 1988. "Leisure Activity Participation of Elderly Individuals with Low Vision." *Journal of Gerontology* 28:181–84.

Heinemann, Gloria, and Patricia Evans. 1990. "Widowhood: Loss, Change and Adaptation." Pp. 142–67 in *Family Relationships in Later Life,* edited by T. Brubaker. Beverly Hills, CA: Sage.

Helmuth L. 2003. "Aging: The wisdom of the Wizened." *Science* 299(5611): 1300–02.

Hendley, Alexa. 1996. "Gender Differences in Private Pension Coverage." Unpublished master's paper, Department of Sociology, Florida State University, Tallahassee, FL.

Hendlin, Herbert. 1997. *Seduced by Death.* New York: Norton.

Hendricks, Jon. 1992. "Generations and the Generation of Theory in Social Gerontology." *International Journal of Aging and Human Development* 35:31–47.

——. 1994. "Revisiting the Kansas City Study of Adult Life: Roots of the Disengagement Model in Social Gerontology." *The Gerontologist* 34:753–55.

——. 1996. "Qualitative Research: Contributions and Advances." Pp. 52–72 in *Handbook of Aging and the Social Sciences,* edited by R. Binstock and L. George. San Diego, CA: Academic Press.

Henretta, John. 2000. "The Future of Age Integration in Employment." *The Gerontologist* 40(3):286–91.

Henretta, John C., Christopher G. Chan, and Angela M. O'Rand. 1992. "Retirement Reason versus Retirement Process: Examining the Reasons for Retirement Typology." *Journal of Gerontology* 47:S1–7.

Henretta, John, Angela O'Rand, and Christopher G. Chan. 1993. "Joint Role Investments and Synchronization of Retirement: A Sequential Approach to Couples' Retirement Timing." *Social Forces* 71:981–1000.

Henriques, Diana, and David Cay Johnston. 1996. "Managers Staying Dry as Corporations Sink." *New York Times,* October 14, pp. A1, A8–9.

Herz, Diane. 1988. "Employment Characteristics of Older Women, 1987." *Monthly Labor Review* 9:3–12.

Herz, Diane, and Philip L. Rones. 1989. "Institutional Barriers to Employment of Older Workers." *Monthly Labor Review* 11:14–21.

Herzog, A. Regula, and Hael Markus. 1999. "The Self-Concept in Life Span and Aging Research." Pp. 227–52 in *Handbook of Theories of Aging,* edited by Vern Bengtson and K. Warner Schaie. New York: Springer.

Hess T. M., and C. Auman. 2001. "Aging and Social Expertise: The Impact of Trait-Diagnostic Information on Impressions of Others." *Psychology and Aging* 16(3):497–510.

High, Dallas. 1993. "Advance Directives and to the Elderly: A Study of Intervention Strategies to Increase Use." *The Gerontologist* 33(3):342–49.

Hill, Gretchen J. 1994. "Age, Labor Force Participation, and Income Patterns for Working-Class Households in the United States and England, 1889–1890." *Mid-American Review of Sociology* 17:1–21.

Hill, Richard, and Cynthia Negry. 1989. "Deindustrialization and Racial Minorities in the Great Lakes Region, USA." Pp. 168–78 in *Reshaping of America: Social Consequences of the Changing Economy,* edited by D. S. Eitzen and M. Baca Zinn. Englewood Cliffs, NJ: Prentice Hall.

Hill, Robert, Martha Storandt, and Mary Malley. 1993. "The Impact of Long-Term Exercise Training on Psychological Function in Older Adults." *Journal of Gerontology* 48:P12–17.

Himelfarb, Richard. 1995. *Catastrophic Politics: The Rise and Fall of the Medicare Catastrophic Coverage Act of 1988.* University Park, PA: Pennsylvania State University Press.

Himes, Christine. 1992. "Future Caregivers: Projected Family Structures of Older Persons." *Journal of Gerontology* 47:S17–26.

Himes, Christine, Dennis Hogan, and David Eggebeen. 1996. "Living Arrangements of Minority Elders." *Journal of Gerontology* 51B:S42–48.

Himmelstein, D., J. Lewontin, and S. Woolhandler. 1996. "Medical Care Employment in the United States, 1968–1993." *American Journal of Public Health* 86(4):525–28.

Hobbs, Frank, and Bonnie Damon. 1996. *65+ in the United States.* Washington, DC: U.S. Bureau of the Census.

Hobbs, Frank, and Nicole Stoops. 2002. *Demographic Trends in the 20th Century.* Washington, DC: U.S. Bureau of the Census.

Hochschild, Arlie. 1975. "Disengagement Theory: A Critique and Proposal." *American Sociological Review* 40:553–69.

——. 1978. *The Unexpected Community.* Berkeley: University of California Press.

Hodgson, Lynne Gershenson. 1992. "Adult Grandchildren and Their Grandparents: The Enduring Bond." *International Journal of Aging and Human Development* 34:209–25.

Hodson, Diane, and Patsy Skeen. 1994. "Sexuality and Aging: The Hammerlock of Myths." *Journal of Applied Gerontology* 13:219–35.

Hofferth, S. L. 1984. Long-Term Economic Consequences for Women of Delayed Childbearing and Reduced Family Size." *Demography* 21:140–49.

Hogan, Dennis P., and Nan Marie Astone. 1986. "The Transition to Adulthood." *Annual Review of Sociology* 12:109–30.

Hogan, Dennis, David Eggebeen, and Sean Snaith. 1996. "The Well-Being of Aging Americans with Very Old Parents." Pp. 327–46 in *Aging and Generational Relations over the Life Course,* edited by T. Hareven. Berlin: Aldine de Gruyter.

Hogan, Dennis, Lingxin Hao, and William Parish. 1990. "Race, Kin Networks, and Assistance to Mother-Headed Families." *Social Forces* 68:797–812.

Hogan, Richard, Meesook Kim, and Carolyn Perrucci. 1997. "Racial Inequality in Men's Employment and Retirement Earnings." *The Sociological Quarterly* 38(3):431–38.

Holahan, C., and J. Chapman. 2002. "Longitudinal Predictors of Proactive Goals and Activity Participation at Age 80." *Journal of Gerontology* 57B(5):P418–25.

Holahan, C. K., and R. H. Moos. 1987. "Personal and Contextual Determinants of Coping Strategies." *Journal of Personality and Social Psychology* 52:946–55.

Holden, Karen. 1996. "Social Security and the Economic Security of Women: Is It Fair?" Pp. 91–104 in *Social Security in the 21st Century,* edited by E. Kingson and J. Schulz. New York: Oxford University Press.

Holden, Karen, and Daphne Kuo Hsiang-Hui. 1996. "Complex Marital Histories and Economic Well-Being: The Continuing Legacy of Divorce and Widowhood as the HRS Cohort Approaches Retirement." *The Gerontologist* 36:383–90.

Holtzman, Abraham. 1963. *The Townsend Movement.* New York: Bookman Associates.

Hopp, F., and S. Duffy. 2000. "Racial Variations in End-of-Life Care." *Journal of the American Geriatrics Society* 48(6):658–63.

Horgas, Wilms, and Paul Baltes. 1998. "Daily Life in Very Old Age: Everyday Activities as Expression of Successful Living." *The Gerontologist* 38(5):556–68.

Horwitz, Amy. 1985. "Sons and Daughters as Caregivers to Older Parents: Differences in Role Performance and Consequences." *The Gerontologist* 25:612–17.

Hospice Association of America. 1997. *Hospice Facts and Statistics.* Washington, DC: Hospice Association of America.

House, James, Ronald Kessler, and A. Regula Herzog. 1990. "Age, Socioeconomic Status, and Health." *Milbank Quarterly* 68(3):383–411.

House, James, James Lepkowski, Ann Kinney, Richard Mero, Ronald Kessler, and A. Regula Herzog. 1994. "The Social Stratification of Aging and Health." *Journal of Health and Social Behavior* 35:213–34.

Howard, Christopher. 1993. "The Hidden Side of the American Welfare State." *Political Science Quarterly* 108:403–36.

Howe, Anna L. 2000. "Rearranging the Compartments: The Financing and Delivery of Care for Australia's Elderly." *Health Affairs* 19:57–71.

Howe, Neil. 1997. "Why the Graying of the Welfare State Threatens to Flatten the American Dream—or Worse." Pp. 36–45 in *The Future of Age-Based Policy,* edited by R. B. Hudson. Baltimore: Johns Hopkins University Press.

Howe, Neil, and Richard Jackson. 1994. *Entitlements and the Aging of America.* Washington, DC: National Taxpayers Union Foundation.

Howell, Cicely. 1976. "Peasant Inheritance Customs in the Midlands, 1280–1700." Pp. 112–55 in *Family and Inheritance,* edited by J. Goody, J. Thirsk, and E. P. Thompson. Cambridge: Cambridge University Press.

Hudson, Robert. 1978. "The 'Graying' of the Federal Budget and Its Consequences for Old Age Policy." *The Gerontologist* 18:428–40.

———. 1994. "A Contingency-Based Approach for Assessing Policies on Aging." *The Gerontologist* 34:743–48.

———. 1996. "Social Protection and Services." Pp. 446–66 in *Handbook of Aging and the Social Sciences,* edited by R. Binstock and L. George. San Diego, CA: Academic Press.

———. 2002. "People of Color and the Challenge of Retirement Security." *Public Policy and Aging Research Brief.* Washington, DC: National Academy on an Aging Society.

Hughes, Everett. 1971. *The Sociological Eye.* Chicago: Aldine.

Hultsch, D. F., and R. A. Dixon. 1990. "Learning and Memory and Aging." Pp. 258–74 in *Handbook of the Psychology of Aging,* edited by J. E. Birren and K. W. Schaie. San Diego, CA: Academic Press.

Hummert, Mary Lee, Teri Garstka, Jaye Shaner, and Sharon Strahm. 1994. "Stereotypes of the Elderly Held by Young, Middle-Aged and Elderly Adults." *Journal of Gerontology* 49:P240–49.

Humphry, Derek. 1995. "Euthanasia Is Ethical." Pp. 17–20 in *Euthanasia: Opposing Viewpoints,* edited by C. Wekesser. San Diego, CA: Greenhaven Press.

Hungerford, Thomas, Matthew Rassette, Howard Iams, and Melissa Keonig. 2003. "Trends in the Economic Status of the Elderly, 1976–2000." http://www.ssa.gov/policy/docs/ssb/v64n3p12.html.

Hunt, M. 1974. *Sexual Behavior in the 1970s.* Chicago: Playboy Press.

Hurd, Michael. 1990. "Research on the Elderly: Economic Status, Retirement, and Consumption and Saving." *Journal of Economic Literature* 28:565–637.

Hutchens, R. M. 1988. "Do Job Opportunities Decline with Age?" *Industrial and Labor Relations Review* 42:89–99.

———. 1993. "Restricted Job Opportunities and the Older Worker." Pp. 81–102 in *As the Workforce Ages: Costs, Benefits and Policy Challenges,* edited by O. S. Mitchell. Ithaca, NY: ILR Press.

Huyck, Margaret Helli. 1995. "Marriage and Close Relationships of the Marital Kind." Pp. 181–200 in *Handbook of Aging and the Family,* edited by R. Blieszner and V. Hilkevitch Bedford. Westport, CT: Greenwood Press.

Iams, Howard M. 1986. "Employment of Retired Workers: Women." *Social Security Bulletin* 49(3):5–13.

Insurance Institute for Highway Safety. 1992. "A Report on Older Drivers." Washington, DC: Insurance Institute for Highway Safety.

Ireland, Patrick R. 1995. "Migration, Free Movement and Immigrant Integration in the EU: A Bifurcated Policy Response." Pp. 231–66 in *European Social Policy,* edited by Stephan Liebfried and Paul Pierson. Washington, DC: The Brookings Institution.

Israel, D., and G. McConnell. 1991. "New Law Protects Older Workers." *HR Magazine* (September):77–78.

Jacobs, Bruce. 1990. "Aging and Politics." Pp. 349–59 in *Handbook of Aging and the Social Sciences,* edited by R. Binstock and L. George. San Diego, CA: Academic Press.

Jacobs, Klaus, Martin Kohli, and Martin Rein. 1991. "Germany: The Diversity of Pathways." Pp. 181–221 in *Time for Retirement,* edited by Martin Kohli, Martin Rein, Anne Marie Guillemard, and Herman van Gunsteren. New York: Cambridge University Press.

Jaffe, Dale. 1989. *Shared Housing for the Elderly.* New York: Greenwood Press.

Jaffe, Dale, and Elizabeth Howe. 1988. "Agency-Assisted Shared Housing: The Nature of Programs and Matches." *The Gerontologist* 28:318–24.

James, Estelle. 1994. *Averting the Old-Age Crisis: Policies to Protect the Old and Promote Growth.* Washington, DC: The World Bank.

Jenkins, Virginia, and Martha Perkins. 1991. "Portrayals of Persons in Television Commercials Age 50 and Over." *Psychology* 28:30–37.

Jerome, Norge. 1988. "Dietary Intake and Nutritional Status of Older U.S. Blacks: An Overview." Pp. 129–49 in *The Black American Elderly,* edited by J. S. Jackson. New York: Springer.

Jette, Alan. 1996. "Disability Trends and Transitions." Pp. 94–117 in *Handbook of Aging and the Social Sciences,* edited by R. Binstock and L. George. San Diego, CA: Academic Press.

Jeweler, Robin. 1993. "Retiree Employment Benefits in Bankruptcy." Congressional Research Service Report No. 94–367, August 25, Washington, DC.

Johannes, C., and N. Avis. 1997. "Gender Differences in Sexual Activity among Mid-Aged Adults in Massachusetts." *Maturitas* 26(3):175–84.

Johnson, Christopher J., and Roxanna H. Johnson. 2000. "Alzheimer's Disease as a 'Trip Back in Time.'" *American Journal of Alzheimer's Disease* 15, 2:87–92.

Johnson, Colleen L. 1993. "Divorced and Reconstituted Families: Effects on the Older Generation." Pp. 33–41 in *Families and Aging,* edited by L. Burton. San Francisco: Baywood Press.

Johnson, Colleen, and Barbara Barer. 1992. "Patterns of Engagement and Disengagement among the Oldest–Old." *Journal of Aging Studies* 6:351–64.

———. 1997. *Life beyond 85 Years.* New York: Springer.

———. 2002. "Life Course Effects of Early Parental Loss among Very Old African Americans." *Journal of Gerontology* 57B(2):S108–16.

Johnson, R. J., and Stephen Crystal. 1997. Health Insurance Coverage at Midlife: Characteristics, Costs and Dynamics." *Health Care Financing Review* 18:123–48.

Joint Committee on Taxation. 1993. *Estimates of Federal Tax Expenditures for Fiscal Years 1994–1998.* Washington, DC: U.S. Government Printing Office.

Jones, Brent, Larry Nackerud, and David Boyle. 1997. "Differential Utilization of Hospice Services in Nursing Homes." *The Hospice Journal* 12(3):41–57.

Kahana, Eva, and Boaz Kahana. 1996. "Conceptual and Empirical Advances in Understanding Aging Well through Proactive Adaptation." Pp. 18–40 in *Adulthood and Aging,* edited by V. Bengtson. New York: Springer.

Kahn, Robert, and Toni Antonucci. 1980. "Convoys over the Life Course: Attachment, Roles and Social Support." Pp. 253–86 in *Lifespan Development and Behavior,* edited by P. Baltes and O. Brim. New York: Academic Press.

Kaiser Family Foundation. 2003. *Medicare at a Glance.* Fact Sheet, February 2003. Menlo Park, CA: Henry J. Kaiser Family Foundation.

Kane, Robert, and Rosalie Kane. 1990. "Health Care for Older People: Organizational and Policy Issues." Pp. 415–37 in *Handbook of Aging and the Social Sciences,* edited by R. Binstock and L. George. Beverly Hills, CA: Sage.

Kanter, Rosabeth Moss. 1977. *Men and Women of the Corporation.* New York: Basic Books.

Kaplan, George, and William Strawbridge. 1994. "Behavioral and Social Factors in Health Aging." Pp. 57–78 in *Aging and the Quality of Life,* edited by R. Abeles, H. Gift, and M. Ory. New York: Springer.

Karoly, Lynn. 1994. "The Trend in Inequality among Families, Individuals and Workers in the United States: A Twenty-Five Year Perspective." Pp. 19–97 in *Uneven Tides: Rising Inequality in America,* edited by S. Danziger and P. Gottschalk. New York: Russell Sage Foundation.

Karp, David. 1991. "A Decade of Reminders: Changing Age Consciousness between Fifty and Sixty Years Old." Pp. 67–92 in *Growing Old in America,* edited by B. Hess and E. Markson. New Brunswick, NJ: Transaction.

Kassner, Enid. 2003. *Long Term Care Insurance, Fact Sheet.* Washington, DC: AARP.

Kastenbaum, Robert, and Claude Norman. 1990. "Deathbed Scenes as Imagined by the Young and Experienced by the Old." *Death Studies* 14:201–17.

Katz, Michael. 1989. *The Undeserving Poor.* New York: Pantheon.

Katzman, R. 1986. "Alzheimer's Disease." *Trends in Neuroscience* 42:522–25.

Kaufman, Sharon. 1994. "In-Depth Interviewing." Pp. 123–36 in *Qualitative Methods in Aging Research,* edited by J. Gubrium and A. Sankar. Thousand Oaks, CA: Sage.

Kazemipur, A., and S. S. Halli. 1997. "Plight of Immigrants: The Spatial Concentration of Poverty." *Canadian Journal of Regional Science* 20:11–28.

Keith, Jennie. 1982. *Old People as People.* Boston: Little, Brown.

——. 1985. "Age in Anthropological Research." Pp. 231–62 in *Handbook of Aging and the Social Sciences,* edited by R. Binstock and E. Shanas. San Diego, CA: Academic Press.

——. 1990. "Age in Social and Cultural Context." Pp. 91–111 in *Handbook of Aging and the Social Sciences,* edited by R. Binstock and E. Shanas. San Diego, CA: Academic Press.

Keith, Pat M. 1989. *The Unmarried in Later Life.* New York: Praeger.

Keith, Verna, and Carol Long. 1997. "Health Care Use and Long-Term Care among African Americans." Pp. 319–41 in *Minorities, Aging and Health,* edited by Kyrialos Markids and Manual Miranda. Thousand Oaks, CA: Sage.

Kelly, D. A. 1991a. "Sleep and Dreaming." Pp. 792–804 in *Principles of Neural Science,* edited by E. Kandel, J. Schwartz, and T. Jessell. New York: Elsevier.

——. 1991b. "Disorders of Sleep and Consciousness." Pp. 803–19 in *Principles of Neural Science,* edited by E. Kandel, J. Schwartz, and T. Jessell. New York: Elsevier.

Kendig, Hal. 1990. "Comparative Perspectives on Housing, Aging and Social Structure." Pp. 288–306 in *Handbook of Aging and the Social Sciences,* edited by R. Binstock and L. George. San Diego, CA: Academic Press.

Kennedy, Gary, Howard Kelman, Cynthia Thomas, and Jiming Chen. 1996. "The Relation of Religious Preference and Practice to Depressive Systems among 1,855 Older Adults." *Journal of Gerontology* 51B:P301–08.

Kerns, V. 1980. "Aging and Mutual Support among the Black Carib." Pp. 163–186 in *Aging in Culture and Society,* edited by Christine Fry. New York: Praeger.

Kijakazi, Kilolo. 2002. "Impact of Unreported Social Security Earnings on People of Color and Women." *Public Policy and Aging Report* 12(3):9–12.

Kim, Cheong-Seok, and Ka-Oak Rhee. 2000. "Living Arrangements in Old Age: Views of Elderly and Middle-Aged Adults in Korea." *Hallym International Journal of Aging* 1(2):94–111.

Kim, Jungmeen, and Phyllis Moen. 2001. "Moving into Retirement: Preparation and Transitions in Late Midlife." Pp. 487–527 in *Handbook of Midlife Development,* edited by Margie Lachman. New York: John Wiley and Sons.

Kimmel, Douglas. 1992. "The Families of Older Gay Men and Lesbians." *Generations* 16:37–38.

Kingsberg, S. A. 2002. "The Impact of Aging on Sexual Function in Women and Their Partners." *Archives of Sexual Behavior* 31(5):431–37.

Kingson, Eric. 1992. *The Diversity of the Baby Boom Generation.* Washington, DC: American Association of Retired Persons.

——. 1994. "Testing the Boundaries of Universality: What's Mean? What's Not?" *The Gerontologist* 34: 733–40.

——. 1996. "Ways of Thinking about the Long-Term Care of the Baby Boom Cohorts." *Journal of Aging and Social Policy* 7:3–24.

Kingson, Eric, and Edward Berkowitz. 1993. *Social Security and Medicare: A Policy Primer.* Westport, CT: Auburn House.

Kingson, Eric, Jack Cornman, and Judith Leavitt. 1996. "Strengthening the Social Compact: An Intergenerational Strategy." Proceedings of the Wingspread Conference, Generations United, October 22–24, Racine, WI.

Kingson, Eric, Barbara Hirshorn, and John Cornman. 1986. *Ties That Bind: The Interdependence of Generations.* Washington, DC: Seven Locks Press.

Kingson, Eric, and Jill Quadagno. 1996. "Social Security: Marketing Radical Reform." *Generations* 19(3):43–49.

Kingson, Eric, and James Schulz. 1997. "Should Social Security Be Means-Tested?" Pp. 41–61 in *Social Security in the 21st Century,* edited by E. Kingson and J. Schulz. New York: Oxford University Press.

Kinsella, Kevin, and Yvonne J. Gist. 1998. *International Brief: Mortality and Health.* U.S. Department of Commerce, Economic and Statistics administration. Washington, DC: Bureau of the Census.

Kinsey, A., W. Pomeroy, and C. Martin. 1948. *Sexual Behavior in the Human Male.* Philadelphia: W. B. Saunders.

Kinsey, A., W. Pomeroy, C. Martin, and P. Gebhard. 1953. *Sexual Behavior in the Human Female.* Philadelphia: W. B. Saunders.

Kivett, Vera. 1985. "Grandfathers and Grandchildren: Patterns of Associations, Helping and Psychological Closeness." *Family Relations* 34:565–71.

Klapper, Jennifer, Sidney Moss, Miriam Moss, and Robert L. Rubinstein. 1994. "The Social Context of Grief among Adult Daughters Who Have Lost a Parent." *Journal of Aging Studies* 8:29–44.

Klatsky, Arthur, and Gary Friedman. 1995. "Annotation: Alcohol and Longevity." *American Journal of Public Health* 85:16–17.

Kline, D., and C. Scialfa. 1996. "Visual and Auditory Aging." Pp. 181–93 in *Handbook of the Psychology of Aging,* edited by J. Birren and K. W. Schaie. New York: Academic Press.

Knodel, John, Napaporn Chayovan, and Siriwan Siriboon. 1996. "Familial Support and the Life Course of Thai Elderly and Their Children." Pp. 338–461 in *Aging and Generational Relations over the Life Course,* edited by T. Hareven. Berlin: Aldine de Gruyter.

Knottnerus, J. David. 1987. "Status Attainment Research and Its Image of Society." *American Sociological Review* 52:113–21.

Knox, Sarah. 1996. "Psychosocial Profiles of Men and Women with Angina-Like Chest Pain before and after Retirement." *Journal of Gender, Culture and Health* 1:111–24.

Kohli, Martin. 1985. "The World We Forgot: A Historical Overview of the Life Course." Pp. 271–303 in *Later Life: The Social Psychology of Aging,* edited by V. Marshall. Beverly Hills, CA: Sage.

———. 1986. "Social Organization and Subjective Construction of the Life Course." Pp. 271–92 in *Human Development and the Life Course,* edited by A. Sorensen, F. Weinert, and L. Sherrod. Hillsdale, NJ: Lawrence Erlbaum.

———. 2000. "Age Integration through Interest Mediation: Political Parties and Unions." *The Gerontologist* 40(3):279–81.

Kohli, Martin, Martin Rein, Anne Marie Guillemard, and Herman van Gunsteren, eds. 1991. *Time for Retirement.* New York: Cambridge University Press.

Koitz, David. 1994a. "The Financial Outlook for Social Security and Medicare." Congressional Research Service, July 17, Washington, DC.

———. 1994b. "Social Security Disability Issues: Fact Sheet." Congressional Research Service, May 9, Washington, DC.

———. 1996a. "Social Security: Its Funding Outlook and Significance for Government Finance." Congressional Research Service, June 1, Washington, DC.

———. 1996b. "The Entitlements Debate." Congressional Research Service, December 27. Washington, DC.

———. 2000. *Social Security Reform: How Much of a Role Could Personal Retirement Accounts Play?* Congressional Research Service. Washington, DC: Library of Congress.

Koitz, David, Gene Falk, and Philip Winters. 1990. "Trust Funds and the Federal Deficit." Congressional Research Service, February 26, Washington, DC.

Koitz, David, Geoffrey Kollman, and Jennifer Neisner. 1992. "Status of the Disability Programs of the Social Security Administration." Congressional Research Service, September 8, Washington, DC.

Kollman, Geoffrey. 1993a. "Means-Testing Social Security Benefits: An Issue Summary." Congressional Research Service Report, September 10, Washington, DC.

———. 1993b. "Social Security: Raising the Retirement Age: An Issue Summary." Congressional Research Service Report, January 12, Washington, DC.

———. 1994. "Social Security: Raising the Retirement Age: Background and Issues." Congressional Research Service Report September 18, Washington, DC.

———. 1995. "Social Security: Worldwide Trends." Congressional Research Service Report, December 20, Washington, DC.

Konik, Michael. 1995. "Manifest Destiny." *Sky Magazine* (September):17–20.

Kopetz, S., C. D. Steele, J. Brandt, A. Baker, M. Kronberg, E. Galik, M. Steinberg, A. Warren, and C. G. Lyketso. 2000. "Characteristics and Outcomes of Dementia Residents in an Assisted Living Facility." *International Journal of Geriatric Psychiatry* 15:586–93.

Korczyk, Sophie. 1993. "Gender Issues in Employer Pensions." Pp. 59–65 in *Pensions in a Changing Economy,* edited by R. Burkhauser and D. Salisbury. Washington, DC: Employee Benefit Research Institute.

Korpi, W. 1989. "Power, Politics, and State Autonomy in the Development of Social Citizenship." *American Sociological Review* 54:309–28.

Kosnik, W. D., R. Sekuler, and D. W. Kline. 1990. "Self-Reported Problems of Older Drivers." *Human Factors* 32:597–608.

Kotlikoff, Lawrence J., and David Wise. 1989. *The Wage Carrot and the Pension Stick: Retirement Benefits and Labor Force Participation.* Kalamazoo, MI: W. E. Upjohn Institute.

Krause, Neil. 1996. "Neighborhood Deterioration and Self-Rated Health in Later Life." *Psychology and Aging* 11:342–52.

———. 1998. "Neighborhood Deterioration, Religious Coping and Changes in Health during Late Life." *The Gerontologist* 38(6):653–64.

———. 2003. "Religious Meaning and Subjective Well-Being in Late Life." *Journal of Gerontology* 58B(5):S294–307.

Kritzer, Barbara. 2001–02. "Social Security Reform in Central and Eastern Europe: Variations on a Latin American Theme." *Social Security Bulletin* 64(4):16–32.

Krout, J., Stephen Cutler, and R. Coward. 1990. "Correlates of Senior Center Participation: A National Analysis." *The Gerontologist* 30:72–79.

Krugman, Paul. 1996. "The Spiral of Inequality." *Mother Jones* (November/December): 44–49.

Kubler-Ross, Elizabeth. 1970. *On Death and Dying.* New York: Macmillan.

Kunkel, Suzanne, and Robert Applebaum. 1992. "Estimating the Prevalence of Long-Term Disability for an Aging Society." *Journal of Gerontology* 47:S253–60.

Kuller L. H. 2003. Hormone Replacement Therapy and Risk of Cardiovascular Disease–Implications of the Results of the Women's Health Initiative. *Arteriosclerosis Thrombosis and Vascular Biology* 23(1):11–16.

Kutza, Elizabeth. 1997. "Rejoinder to Skinner." Pp. 62–64 in *Controversial Issues in Aging,* edited by A. Scharlach and L. Skinner. Boston: Allyn and Bacon.

Lacayo, Carmela. 1993. "Hispanic Elderly: Policy Issues in Long-Term Care." Pp. 223–34 in *Ethnic Elderly and Long-Term Care,* edited by C. Barresi and D. Stull. New York: Springer.

Lamm, Richard. 1999. "Care for the Elderly: What about Our Children?" Pp. 87–100 in *The Generational Equity Debate,* J. Williamson and R. Kingson, eds. New York: Columbia University Press.

Langer, Nieli. 1990. "Grandparents and Adult Grandchildren: What Do They Do for One Another?" *International Journal of Aging and Human Development* 31:101–10.

Laslett, Peter. 1976. "Societal Development and Aging." Pp. 87–116 in *Handbook of Aging and the Social Sciences,* edited by R. Binstock and E. Shanas. New York: Van Nostrand Reinhold.

Lassey, William R., and Marie L. Lassey. 2001. *Quality of Life for Older People: An International Perspective.* Englewood Cliffs, NJ: Prentice Hall.

Lauer, Robert, Jeanette Lauer, and Sarah Kerr. 1995. "Husbands' and Wives' Perceptions of Marital Fairness across the Family Life Cycle." Pp. 35–42 in *The Ties of Later Life,* edited by J. Hendricks. Amityville, NY: Baywood Press.

Laumann, E., J. Gagnon, R. Michael, and S. Michaels. 1994. *The Social Organization of Sexuality: Sexual Practices in the United States.* Chicago: University of Chicago Press.

Lawrence, Renee H., and Alan Jette. 1996. "Disentangling the Disablement Process." *Journal of Gerontology* 51B(4):S173–82.

Lawton, M. Powell. 1990. "Knowledge Resources and Gaps in Housing the Aged." Pp. 287–309 in *Aging in Place,* edited by D. Tilson. Glenview, IL: Scott, Foresman.

Lechner, Viola. 1991. "Predicting Future Commitment to Care for Frail Parents among Employed Caregivers." *Journal of Gerontological Social Work* 18:69–84.

Lee, G. R., C. Peek, and R. Coward. 1998. "Race Differences in Filial Responsibility Expectations among Older Parents." *Journal of Marriage and the Family* 60(2):402–12.

Leiblum, Sandra. 1990. "Sexuality and the Midlife Woman." *Psychology of Women Quarterly* 14:495–508.

Lemert, Charles. 1995. *Sociology after the Crisis.* Boulder, CO: Westview Press.

Lemon, Bruce, Vern Bengtson, and James Peterson. 1972. "An Exploration of the Activity Theory of Aging: Activity Types and Life Satisfaction among In-Movers to a Retirement Community." *Journal of Gerontology* 27:511–23.

Lennartsson, C., and Merrill Silverstein. 2001. "Does Engagement with Life Enhance Survival of Elderly People in Sweden? The Role of Social and Leisure Activities." *Journal of Gerontology* 56(6):S335–42.

Leonesio, Michael. 1993a. "Social Security and Older Workers." *Social Security Bulletin* 56:47–57.

———. 1993b. "Social Security and Older Workers." Pp. 183–204 in *As the Workforce Ages: Costs Benefits and Policy Challenges,* edited by Olivia Mitchell. Ithaca, NY: ILR Press.

Leventhal, H., E. Leventhal, and P. Schaefer. 1992. "Vigilant Coping and Health Behavior." Pp. 109–40 in *Aging, Health and Behavior,* edited by M. Ory, R. Abeles, and P. Lipman. Newbury Park, CA: Sage.

Leviatan, Uriel. 1999. "Contribution of Social Arrangements to the Attainment of Successful Aging–The Experience of the Israeli Kibbutz." *Journal of Gerontology* 54B(4):P 205–13.

Levin, Jeffrey, Kyriakos Markides, and Laura Ray. 1996. "Religious Attendance and Psychological Well-Being in Mexican Americans: A Panel Analysis of Three-Generation Data." *The Gerontologist* 36(4):454–63.

Levin, Jeffrey, and Robert Joseph Taylor. 1997. "Age Differences in Patterns and Correlates of the Frequency of Prayer." *The Gerontologist* 37:75–88.

Levin, Jeffrey, Robert Joseph Taylor, and Linda Chatters. 1994. "Race and Gender Differences in Religiosity in Older Adults: Findings from Four National Surveys." *The Gerontologist* 49(3):S136–45.

Levinson, Daniel. 1978. *The Season's of a Man's Life.* New York: Alfred A. Knopf.

———. 1996. *The Seasons of a Woman's Life.* New York: Alfred A. Knopf.

Levy, Frank. 1988. *Dollars and Dreams: The Changing American Income Distribution.* New York: W. W. Norton.

Levy, Frank, and Richard Michel. 1991. *The Economic Future of American Families: Income and Wealth Trends.* Washington, DC: The Urban Institute.

Levy, Judith. 1994. "Sex and Sexuality in Later Life Stages." Pp. 287–309 in *Sexuality across the Life Course,* edited by A. Rossi. Chicago: University of Chicago Press.

Lewis, Robert. 1990. "The Adult Child and Older Parents." Pp. 68–85 in *Family Relationships in Later Life,* edited by T. Brubaker. Beverly Hills, CA: Sage.

Liang, Jersey, Joan Bennett, Neil Krause, Erika Kobayashi, Hyekyung Kim, J. Winchester Brown, Hiroko Akiyama, Hidehiro Sugisawa, and Arvind Jain. 2002. "Old Age Mortality in Japan: Does the Socioeconomic Gradient Interact with Gender and Age?" *Journal of Gerontology* 57B(5):S294–307.

Libman, Eva. 1989. "Sociocultural and Cognitive Factors in Aging and Sexual Expression: Conceptual and Research Issues." *Canadian Psychology* 30:560–67.

Licht, M. R. 1999. "Use of Oral Sildenafil (Viagra) in the Treatment of Erectile Dysfunction." *Comprehensive Therapy* 25(2):90–94.

Lieberman, Sue. 1988. "Diabetes and Obesity in Elderly Black Americans." Pp. 150–89 in *The Black American Elderly,* edited by James S. Jackson. New York: Springer.

Lieberman, Morton. 1996. "Perspective on Adult Life Crises." Pp. 146–67 in *Aging and Adulthood,* edited by Vern Bengtson. New York: Springer.

Liebig, Phoebe. 1998. "Housing and Supportive Services for the Elderly: Intergenerational Perspectives and Options." Pp. 51–74 in *New Directions in Old Age Policies,* edited by J. Steckenrider and T. Parrott. Albany, NY: State University of New York Press.

Light, Donald. 1992. "The Practice and Ethics of Risk-Related Health Insurance." *Journal of the American Medical Association* 267(18):2501–10.

Light, Paul. 1985. *Artful Work: The Politics of Social Security Reform.* New York: Random House.

——. 1988. *Baby Boomers.* New York: W. W. Norton.

Lighthouse Research Institute. 1995. *The Lighthouse National Survey on Vision Loss.* New York: The Lighthouse Inc.

Limacher, M. C. 1994. "Aging and Cardiac Function: Influence of Exercise." *Southern Medical Journal* 87:13–16.

Lindenberger, U., and P. Baltes. 1994. "Sensory Functioning and Intelligence in Old Age." *Psychology and Aging* 9:339–55.

Linton, Ralph. 1936. *The Study of Man.* New York: Appleton-Century-Crofts.

Lipset, Seymour Martin. 1990. *The Continental Divide: The Values and Institutions of the United States and Canada.* London: Routledge.

——. 1996. *American Exceptionalism: A Double-Edged Sword.* New York: Norton.

Litchfield, R. Burr. 1978. "The Family and the Mill: Cotton Mill Work, Family Work Patterns and Fertility in Mid-Victorian Stockport." Pp. 180–96 in *The Victorian Family,* edited by Anthony S. Wohn. London: Croon Helm.

Litwak, Eugene, and Charles Longino. 1987. "Migration among the Elderly: A Developmental Perspective." *The Gerontologist* 27:266–72.

Liu, Korbin, Kenneth Manton, and Barbara M. Liu. 1985. "Home Care Expenses for the Disabled Elderly." *Health Care Financing Review* 7(2):51–58.

Liu, K., T. McBride, and T. Coughlin. 1990. "Costs of Community Care for Disabled Elderly Persons: The Policy Implications." *Inquiry* 27:61–72.

Loeser, John, and Mark Sullivan. 1997. "Doctors, Diagnosis and Disability: A Disastrous Diversion." *Clinical Orthopaedics and Related Research* 336:61–66.

Longino, Charles. 1990. "Geographical Distribution and Migration." Pp. 45–63 in *Handbook of Aging and the Social Sciences,* edited by R. Binstock and L. George. San Diego, CA: Academic Press.

——. 1994. "Myths of an Aging America." *American Demographics* (August): 36–42.

Longino, Charles F., Jr., David J. Jackson, Rick S. Zimmerman, and Julia E. Bradsher. 1991. "The Second Move: Health and Geographic Mobility." *Journal of Gerontology* 46:218–24.

Longino, Charles, and Cary Kart. 1982. "Explicating Activity Theory: A Formal Replication." *Journal of Gerontology* 17:713–22.

Longman, Philip. 1982. "Taking America to the Cleaners." *Washington Monthly* (November): 24.

——. 1979. *Women as Widows.* New York: Elsevier.

——. 1995. "Feminist Perspectives on Social Gerontology." Pp. 114–31 in *Handbook of Aging and the Family,* edited by R. Blieszner and V. Hilkevitch Bedford. Westport, CT: Greenwood Press.

Lopata, Helena. 1973. *Widowhood in an American City.* Cambridge, MA: Schenkman.

Loprest, Pamela, Kalmann Rupp, and Steven Sandell. 1995. "Gender, Disabilities and Employment in the Health and Retirement Survey." *Journal of Human Resources* 30:293–318.

Love, Roger, and Susan Poulin. 1991. "Family Income Inequality in the 1980s." *Canadian Economic Observer,* September:4.1–4.13.

Lund, D. A. 1993. "Widowhood: The Coping Response." Pp. 537–41 in *Encyclopedia of Adult Development,* edited by R. Kastenbaum. Phoenix: Oryx.

Lyman, Karen. 1994. "Fieldwork in Groups and Institutions." Pp. 155–72 in *Qualitative Methods in Aging Research,* edited by J. Gubrium and A. Sankar. Thousand Oaks, CA: Sage.

Lynott, Robert, and Patricia Passuth Lynott. 1996. "Tracing the Course of Theoretical Development in the Sociology of Aging." *The Gerontologist* 36:749–60.

Maas, Ineke, and Richard Settersten. 1999. "Military Service during Wartime: Effects on Men's Occupational Trajectories and Later Economic Well-Being." *European Sociological Review* 15(2):213–32.

Macey, Susan, and Dona Schneider. 1993. "Deaths from Excessive Heat and Excessive Cold among the Elderly." *The Gerontologist* 33:497–500.

MacManus, Susan A. 1996. *Young v. Old: Generational Combat in the 21st Century.* Boulder, CO: Westview Press.

——. 1998. " The Changing Political Activism of Older Americans." Pp. 111–30 in *New Directions for Old-Age Policies,* edited by Janie Steckenrider and Tonya Parrott. Albany: State University of New York Press.

MacPherson, David. 2002. "Sex Differences in Retirement Income: Recent Trends and Future Prospects." *Pepper Institute on Aging and Public Policy Working Paper.* Tallahassee, FL: Pepper Institute on Aging and Public Policy.

Macunovich, Diane J. 1995. "Booms and Busts: Can We Ignore Them in Making Long-Term Projections?" Presented at the annual meetings of the National Academy of Social Insurance, January 26, Washington, DC.

Maddox, George. 1964. "Disengagement Theory: A Critical Evaluation." *The Gerontologist* 4:80–82.

——. 1965. "Fact and Artifact: Evidence Bearing on Disengagement Theory from the Duke Geriatrics Projects." *Human Development* 8:117–30.

Magaziner, Jay, and Doris Cadigan. 1989. "Community Resources and Mental Health of Older Women Living Alone." *Journal of Aging and Health* 1:35–49.

Maioni, Antonia. 1998. *Parting at the Crossroads: The Emergence of Health Insurance in the United States and Canada.* Princeton, NJ: Princeton University Press.

Malatesta, V., D. Chambless, M. Pollack, and A. Cantor. 1988. "Widowhood, Sexuality and Aging: A Life Span Analysis." *Journal of Sex and Marital Therapy* 14:49–62.

Mangus, R., A. Dipiero, and C. Hawkins. 1999. "Medical Students Attitudes toward Physician-Assisted Suicide." *Journal of the American Medical Association* 282(21):2080–81.

Manton, Kenneth, Larry Corder, and Eric Stallard. 1993. "Estimates of Change in Chronic Disability and Institutional Evidence and Prevalence Rates in the U.S. Elderly Population from the 1982, 1984 and 1989 National Long-Term Care Survey." *Journal of Gerontology* 48:S153–66.

Manton, K., and E. Stallard. 1996. "Changes in Health, Mortality, and Disability and Their Impact on Long-Term Care Needs." *Journal of Aging and Social Policy* 7(3/4):25–51.

Margolin, Leslie, and Lynn White. 1987. "The Continuing Role of Physical Attractiveness in Marriage." *Journal of Marriage and the Family* 49:21–27.

Margolin, Malcolm. 1978. *The Ohlone Way.* Berkeley, CA: Heyday Books.

Margolis, Richard. 1990. *Risking Old Age in America.* Boulder, CO: Westview Press.

Marjama-Lyons, J. M., and W. C. Koller. 2001. "Parkinson's Disease. Update in Diagnosis and Symptom Management." *Geriatrics* 56(8):24–25, 29–30, 33–35.

Markides, Kyriakos, and Charles Mindel. 1987. *Aging and Ethnicity.* Newbury Park, CA: Sage.

Marks, Mitchell Lee. 1994. *From Turmoil to Triumph: New Life after Mergers, Acquisitions, and Downsizing.* New York: Lexington Books.

Markson, Elizabeth. 1991. "Physiological Changes, Illness and Health Care in Later Life." Pp. 173–86 in *Growing Old in America,* 4th ed., edited by B. Hess and E. Markson. New Brunswick, NJ: Transactional.

Marmor, Theodore. 1973. *The Politics of Medicare.* Chicago: Aldine.

Marmor, Theodore, Fay Lomax Cook, and Stephen Scher. 1997. "Social Security Politics and the Conflict between Generations: Are We Asking the Right Questions?" Pp. 195–207 in *Social Security in the 21st Century,* edited by E. Kingson and J. Schulz. New York: Oxford University Press.

Marmor, Theodore, Jerry L. Mashaw, and Philip Harvey. 1990. *America's Misunderstood Welfare State.* New York: Basic Books.

Marottoli, Richard, Adrian Ostfeld, Susan Merrill, Gary Perlman, Daniel Foley, and Leo Cooney. 1993. "Driving Cessation and Changes in Mileage Driven among Elderly Individuals." *Journal of Gerontology* 48:S255–60.

Marshall, T. H. 1964. *Class, Citizenship and Social Development.* Chicago: University of Chicago Press.

Marshall, Victor. 1986. "A Sociological Perspective on Death and Dying." Pp. 125–46 in *Later Life: The Social Psychology of Aging,* edited by V. Marshall. Beverly Hills, CA: Sage.

——. 1994. "Sociology, Psychology, and the Theoretical Legacy of the Kansas City Studies." *The Gerontologist* 34:768–74.

——. 1996. "The State of Theory in Aging and the Social Sciences." Pp. 12–30 in *Handbook of Aging and the Social Sciences,* edited by R. Binstock and L. George. San Diego, CA: Academic Press.

Marshall, Victor, and Judith Levy. 1990. "Aging and Dying." Pp. 245–69 in *Handbook of Aging and the Social Sciences,* edited by R. Binstock and L. George. New York: Academic Press.

Marsiglio, William, and Denise Donnelly. 1991. "Sexual Relations in Later Life: A National Study of Married Persons." *Journal of Gerontology* 46:S338–44.

Martin, Clyde. 1981. "Factors Affecting Sexual Functioning in 60–79 Year Old Married Males." *Archives of Sexual Behavior* 10:399–420.

Martin, Linda, and Kevin Kinsella. 1994. "Research on the Demography in Developing Countries." Pp. 356–404 in *Demography of Aging,* edited by L. Martin and S. Preston. Washington, DC: National Academy Press.

Masoro, Edward. 1991. "Biology of Disease, Biology of Aging: Facts, Thoughts, and Experimental Approaches." *Laboratory Investigation* 65:500–10.

Massie, Dawn, Kenneth Campbell, and Allan Williams. 1995. "Traffic Accident Involvement Rates by Driver Age and Gender." *Accident Analysis and Prevention* 27:73–87.

Masters, William, and Virginia Johnson. 1966. *Human Sexual Response.* Boston: Little Brown.

——. 1970. *Human Sexual Inadequacy.* Boston: Little Brown.

Mathias, Ruth, James Lubben, Kathryn Atchison, and Stuart Schweitzer. 1997. "Sexual Activity and Satisfaction among Very Old Adults: Results from a Community-Dwelling Medicare Population Survey." *The Gerontologist* 37:6–14.

Matsumoto, David, K. K. Pun, Mihoko Nakatani, Dai Kadowaki, Michelle Weissman, Loren McCarter, Deboa Fletcher, and Sachiko Takeuchi. 1996. "Osteoporosis Risk Factors in First- and Second-Generation Japanese American Women." *Journal of Gender, Culture and Health* 1:135–49.

Matthews, Anne Martin, and Kathleen Brown. 1987. "Retirement as a Critical Life Event." *Research on Aging* 9:548–71.

Matthews, Sarah. 1994. "Men's Ties to Siblings in Old Age: Contributing Factors to Availability and Quality." Pp. 178–96 in *Older Men's Lives,* edited by E. Thompson. Newbury Park, CA: Sage.

Mayer, Karl U. 1988. "German Survivors of World War II: The Impact on the Life Course of the Collective Experience of Birth Cohorts." Pp. 229–46 in *Social Structures and Human Lives,* edited by M. W. Riley. Newbury Park, CA: Sage.

Mayer, Karl, and Walter Muller. 1986. "The State and the Structure of the Life Course." Pp. 217–45 in *Human Development and the Life Course,* edited by A. Sorensen, F. Weinert, and L. Sherrod. Hillsdale, NJ: Lawrence Erlbaum.

Mayer, Karl Ulrich, and Urs Schoepflin. 1989. "The State and the Life Course." *Annual Review of Sociology* 15:187–209.

McAdam, Doug, and David Snow. 1997. *Social Movements.* Los Angeles: Roxbury.

McClearn, Gerald E., Boo Johansson, Stig Berg, Nancy Pedersen, Frank Ahern, Stephen Petrill, and Robert Plomin. 1997. "Substantial Genetic Influence on Cognitive Abilities in Twins 80+ Years Old." *Science* 276:1560–63.

McCoy, J., and R. Conley. 1990. "Surveying Board and Care Homes: Issues and Data Collection Problems." *The Gerontologist* 30:147–53.

McCrae, Robert, and Paul Costa. 1984. *Emerging Lives, Enduring Dispositions.* Boston: Little Brown.

——. 1988. "Psychological Resilience among Widowed Men and Women: A 10-year Follow-Up of a National Sample." *Journal of Social Issues* 44:129–42.

McDaniel, Susan. 1997. "Health Care Policy in an Aging Canada: The Alberta Experiment." *Journal of Aging Studies* 11(3):211–28.

McFadden, Susan. 1996. "Religion, Spirituality and Aging." Pp. 162–77 in *Handbook of the Psychology of Aging,* edited by James Birren and K. Warner Schaie. San Diego, CA: Academic Press.

McGarry, Kathleen, and Robert Schoeni. 1997. "Transfer Behavior within the Family: Results from the Asset and Health Dynamics Study." *Journal of Gerontology* 52B(May):82–92.

McGee, Jeanne, and Kathleen Wells. 1982. "Gender Typing and Androgyny in Later Life: New Directions for Theory and Research." *Human Development* 25:116–39.

McKinlay, John. 1996. "Some Contributions from the Social System to Gender Inequalities in Heart Disease." *Journal of Health and Social Behavior* 37:1–26.

McKinlay, J., and H. Feldman. 1994. "Age-Related Variation in Sexual Activity and Interest in Normal Men: Results from the Massachusetts Male Aging Study." Pp. 261–86 in *Sexuality across the Life Course,* edited by A. Rossi. Chicago: University of Chicago Press.

McKinnon, Mary. 2000. "Lifestyle Choice." *Assisted Living Today* 7:169–70.

McLeroy, Kenneth, and Carolyn Crump. 1994. "Health Promotion and Disease Prevention: A Historical Perspective." *Generations* (Spring):9–17.

McNaught, W., M. C. Barth, and P. H. Henderson. 1991. "Older Americans: Willing and Able to Work." Pp. 101–15 in *Retirement and Public Policy,* edited by A. Munnell. Washington, DC: National Academy of Social Insurance.

Meier, E. L. 1986. "Employment Experience and Income of Older Women." American Association of Retired Persons, No. 8609, Washington, DC.

Mellor, Jennifer. 2000. "Filling In the Gaps in Long-Term Care Insurance." Pp. 202–16 in *Care Work,* edited by Madonna Harrington Meyer. New York: Routledge.

Mendelson, Michael. 1991a. "Assuring Quality of Care: Nursing Home Resident Councils." *Journal of Applied Gerontology* 10:103–16.

——. 1991b. "Universalism vs. Targeting as the Basis of Social Distribution: Gender, Race, and Long-Term Care in the U.S." Ph.D. dissertation, Department of Sociology, Florida State University, Tallahassee, FL.

——. 1993. *Social Policy in Real Time.* Ottawa, Canada: Caledon Institute of Social Policy.

——. 1994. "Institutional Bias and Medicaid Use in Nursing Homes." *Journal of Aging Studies* 8:179–94.

Merlis, Mark. 2000. "Caring for the Frail Elderly: An International Perspective." *Health Affairs* 19:141–49.

Miech R. A., J. C. Breitner, P. P. Zandi, A. S. Khachaturian, J. C. Anthony, L. Mayer. 2002. "Incidence of AD May Decline in the Early 90s for Men, Later for Women—The Cache County Study." *Neurology* 58(2):209–18.

Mijatovic, V., M. J. Van der Mooren, and C. D. Stehouwer. 1999. "Postmenopausal Hormone Replacement, Risk Estimators for Coronary Artery Disease and Cardiovascular Protection." *Gynecology and Endocrinology* 13(2):130–44.

Miller, Arthur, and Thomas Klobucar. 2003. "The Role of Issues in the 2000 U.S. Presidential Election." *Presidential Studies Quarterly* 33(March):101–24.

Miller, M. A. 1994. "The Biology of Aging and Longevity." Pp. 3–18 in *Principles of Geriatric Medicine and Gerontology*, edited by W. R. Hazzard, E. L. Bierman, J. P. Blass, W. H. Ettinger Jr., and J. B. Halter. New York: McGraw-Hill.

Miller, Richard A. 1990. "Aging and the Immune Response." Pp. 157–72 in *Handbook of the Biology of Aging*, edited by E. Schneider and J. Rowe. San Diego, CA: Academic Press.

Miller, R. H., and H. S. Luft. 1994. "Managed Care Plan Performance since 1980: A Literature Analysis." *Journal of the American Medical Association* 271:1512–19.

Miller, Sue. 1995. *The Distinguished Guest.* New York: HarperCollins.

——. 2003. *The Story of My Father.* New York: Alfred A. Knopf.

Mills, E. M. 1994. "The Effect of Low-Intensity Aerobic Exercise on Muscle Strength, Flexibility and Balance among Sedentary Elderly Persons." *Nursing Research* 43:207–11.

Miner, Sonia, John Logan, and Glenna Spitze. 1993. "Predicting the Frequency of Senior Center Attendance." *The Gerontologist* 33:650–57.

Minicuci, Nadia, Stefania Maggi, Mara Paven, Giuliano Enzi, and Gaetano Crepaldi. 2002. "Prevalence Rate and Correlates of Depressive Symptoms of Older Individuals: The Veneto Study." *Journal of Gerontology* 57:M155–61.

Minkler, Meredith. 1989. "Gold in Gray: Reflections on Business' Discovery of the Elderly Market." *The Gerontologist* 29:17–23.

Mirowsky, John. 1996. "Age and the Gender Gap in Depression." *Journal of Health and Social Behavior* 37:362–80.

Mirowsky, John, and Catherine Ross. 1992. "Age and Depression." *Journal of Health and Social Behavior* 33:187–205.

Mishel, Lawrence, and Jared Bernstein. 1993. *The State of Working America.* Washington, DC: Economic Policy Institute.

Mitchell, Olivia, ed. 1993. *As the Workforce Ages: Costs Benefits and Policy Challenges.* Ithaca, NY: ILR Press.

Mitchell, Olivia, and Joseph Quinn. 1995. *Final Report of the Technical Panel on Trends and Issues in Retirement Savings.* Washington, DC: Advisory Council on Social Security.

Mittelstaedt, H. F., W. D. Nichols, and P. R. Reiger. 1994. "Factors Underlying the Decision to Reduce Coverage in Employer-Sponsored Retiree Health Care Plans." Pp. 27–40 in *Proceedings from The Center for Pension and Retirement Research Conference.* Oxford, OH: Miami University.

Moen, Phyllis, J. Kim, and H. Hofmeister. 2001. "Couples Work/Retirement Transition, Gender and Marital Quality." *Social Psychology Quarterly* (March):55–71.

Moen, Phyllis, Julie Robison, and Vivian Fields. 1994. "Women's Work and Caregiving Roles: A Life Course Approach." *Journal of Gerontology* 49:S176–86.

Moen, Phyllis, Vandana Plassman, and Stephen Sweet. 2001. *The Cornell Midcareer Paths and Passages Study.* Ithaca, NY: Cornell University.

Moen, Phyllis, and Elaine Wethington. 1999. *Life in the Middle.* New York: Academic Press.

Moody, Harry. 1994. *Aging: Concepts and Controversies.* Thousand Oaks, CA: Pine Forge Press.

Moon, Ailee, James Lubben, and Valentine Villa. 1998. "Awareness and Utilization of Community Long-Term Care Services by Elderly Korean and Non-Hispanic White Americans." *The Gerontologist* 38(2):309–16.

Moon, Marilyn. 1989. "Introduction." Pp. vii–x in *Preserving Independence, Supporting Needs: The Role of Board and Care Homes*, edited by M. Moon, G. Gaberlavage, and S. Newman. Washington, DC: American Association of Retired Persons.

——. 1993. *Medicare Now and in the Future.* Washington, DC: The Urban Institute Press.

——. 1997. "Are Social Security Benefits Too High or Too Low?" Pp. 62–75 in *Social Security in the 21st Century*, edited by J. Schulz and E. Kingson. New York: Oxford University Press.

Mooney, Elizabeth. 1981. "A Widow's World: Growing Up Alone in Middle Age." *Washington Post*, July 26, p. 1B.

Moore, Joan. 1980. "The Death Culture of Mexico and Mexican Americans." Pp. 73–89 in *Death and Dying*, edited by R. Kalish. New York: Baywood.

Mor-Barak, Michal, and Leonard Miller. 1991. "A Longitudinal Study of the Causal Relationship between Social Networks and Health of the Poor Frail Elderly." *Journal of Applied Gerontology* 10:293–310.

Morgan, Leslie, J. Kevin Eckert, and Stephanie Lyon. 1993. "Social Marginality: The Case of Small Board and Care Homes." *Journal of Aging Studies* 7:383–94.

Morioka, Kiyomi. 1996. "Generational Relations and Their Changes as They Affect the Status of Older People in Japan." Pp. 511–25 in *Aging and Generational Relations over the Life Course,* edited by T. Hareven. Berlin: Aldine de Gruyter.

Morrow-Howell, Nancy, Jim Hinterlong, Philip Rozario, and Fengyan Tang. 2003. "Effects of Volunteering on the Well-Being of Older Adults." *Journal of Gerontology* 58B(3):S137–45.

Moss, M., and M. Powell Lawton. 1982. "Time Budgets of Older People: A Window on Four Lifestyles." *Journal of Gerontology* 35:576–82.

Moss, Miriam, and Sidney Moss. 1992. "Themes in Parent–Child Relationships when Elderly Parents Move Nearby." *Journal of Aging Studies* 6:259–71.

Moyer, Martha Sebastian. 1993. "Sibling Relationships among Older Adults." Pp. 109–19 in *Families and Aging,* edited by L. Burton. San Francisco: Baywood Press.

Moyers, Bill. 1993. *Healing and the Mind.* New York: Doubleday.

Mui, Ada. 1992. "Caregiver Strain among Black and White Daughter Caregivers: A Role Theory Perspective." *The Gerontologist* 32:203–12.

Mulligan, Thomas, and Robert Palguta. 1991. "Sexual Interest and Satisfaction among Male Nursing Home Residents." *Archives of Sexual Behavior* 20:199–204.

Munnell, A. H. 1999. "America Can Afford to Grow Old." Pp. 117–39 in *The Generational Equity Debate,* edited by B. Williamson, D. M. Watts-Roy, and E. R. Kingson. New York: Columbia University Press.

Munnell, Alicia, and Annika Sunden. 2002. "401(k)s and Company Stock: How Can We Encourage Diversification?" Issue Brief No. 9. Center for Retirement Research. Boston: Boston College.

Munnell, Alicia, Kevin Cahill, and Natalia Jivan. 2003. "How Has the Shift to 401(K)s Affected the Retirement Age?" Issue Brief No. 13. Center for Retirement Research. Boston, MA: Boston College.

Murphy, J., and B. Isaacs. 1982. "The Postfall Syndrome: A Study of 36 Elderly Patients." *Gerontology* 28:265–70.

Musick, Mark A., A. Regula Herzog, and James S. House. 1999. "Volunteering and Mortality among Older Adults: Findings from a National Sample." *Journal of Gerontology* 54B(3):S173–80.

Mutchler, Jan, Jeffrey Burr, Michale Massagli, and Amy Pienta. 1999. "Work Transitions and Health in Later Life." *Journal of Gerontology* 54B(5):S252–61.

Mutchler, Jan, Jeffrey Burr, Amy Pienta, and Michael Massagli. 1997. "Pathways to Labor Force Exit: Work Transition and Work Instability." *Journal of Gerontology* 52B:S4–12.

Mutran, Elizabeth, and Donald Reitzes. 1981. "Retirement, Identity and Well-Being: Realignment of Role Relationships." *Journal of Gerontology* 36:733–40.

Mydans, Seth. 1997. "Legal Euthanasia: Australia Faces a Grim Reality." *New York Times,* February 2, p. 3.

Myers, A. H., Y. Young, and J. A. Langlois. 1996. "Prevention of Falls in the Elderly." *Bone* 18:87–101.

Myers, George. 1990. "Demography of Aging." Pp. 19–44 in *Handbook of Aging and the Social Sciences,* edited by R. Binstock and L. George. San Diego, CA: Academic Press.

———. 1996. "Aging and the Social Sciences: Research Directions and Unresolved Issues." Pp. 1–11 in *Handbook of Aging and the Social Sciences,* edited by R. Binstock and L. George. San Diego, CA: Academic Press.

Myers, Jane, and Guy Perrin. 1993. "Grandparents Affected by Parental Divorce: A Population at Risk?" *Journal of Counseling and Development* 72:62–72.

Myers, Robert. 1991. "Yes, Changes Are Needed." Pp. 223–30 in *Retirement and Public Policy,* edited by A. Munnell. Washington, DC: National Academy of Social Insurance.

———. 1997. "Will Social Security Be There for Me?" Pp. 208–16 in *Social Security in the 21st Century,* edited by E. Kingson and J. Schulz. New York: Oxford University Press.

Myers, Samuel, and Chanjin Chung. 1996. "Racial Differences in Home Ownership and Home Equity among Preretirement-Aged Households." *The Gerontologist* 36:350–60.

Myles, John. 1988a. "Decline or Impasse? The Current State of the Welfare State." *Studies in Political Economy* 26:73–107.

———. 1988b. "Postwar Capitalism and the Extension of Social Security into a Retirement Wage." Pp. 265–91 in *The Politics of Social Policy in the United States,* edited by M. Weir, A. Orloff, and T. Skocpol. Princeton, NJ: Princeton University Press.

———. 1989. *Old Age in the Welfare State.* Lawrence: University Press of Kansas.

———. 1990. "States, Labor Markets and Life Cycles." Pp. 271–98 in *Beyond the Marketplace: Rethinking Economy and Society,* edited by R. Friedland and S. Robertson. New York: Aldine de Gruyter.

———. 1996. "Racial Differences in Home Ownership and Home Equity among Preretirement-Aged Households." *The Gerontologist* 36:350–60.

Myles, John, and Jill Quadagno. 2000. "Envisioning a Third Way?: The Welfare State in the Twenty-First Century." *Contemporary Sociology* 29:156–68.

Myles, John, and Les Teichroew. 1991. "The Politics of Dualism: Pension Policy in Canada." Pp. 84–104 in *States, Labor Markets and the Future of Old Age Policy,* edited by J. Myles and J. Quadagno. Philadelphia: Temple University Press.

Naegele, Gerhard. 1999. "The Politics of Old Age in Germany." Pp. 93–109 in *The Politics of Old Age in Europe.* Buckingham, U.K.: Open University Press.

Nagel, Joan. 1996. *American Indian Ethnic Renewal.* New York: Oxford University Press.

National Academy on Aging. 1994. "Old Age in the 21st Century." Report to the Assistant Secretary for Aging, U.S. Dept. of Health and Human Services, Washington, DC.

National Academy on an Aging Society. 1999. *Chronic Conditions: A Challenge for the 21st Century.* No. 1. November. Washington, DC: National Academy on an Aging Society.

——. 2000. *Who Are Young Retirees and Older Workers?* No. 1. June. Washington, DC: National Academy on an Aging Society.

National Academy of Social Insurance. 1994. "Preliminary Status Report of the Disability Policy Panel." Washington, DC.

National Center for Health Statistics. 1981. "Current Estimates from the National Health Interview Survey, United States, 1979." *Vital and Health Statistics.* Series 10, No. 136.

——. 1991. "Current Estimates from the National Health Interview Survey, 1990." *Vital and Health Statistics.* Series 10, no. 181, Washington, DC.

——. 1992. *Monthly Vital Statistics.* Report 41. Washington, DC: U.S. Government Printing Office.

——. 1994a. *Monthly Vital Statistics.* Report 43, No. 6, Supplement. Washington, DC: U.S. Government Printing Office.

——. 1994b. *Health: United States.* Hyattsville, MD: Public Health Service.

——. 1994c. *Supplement on Aging.* Washington, DC: U.S. Government Printing Office.

——. 1996. "Deaths, by Selected Cause and Selected Characteristics." *Statistical Abstract of the United States.* Washington, DC: U.S. Government Printing Office.

——. 1998. *National Vital Statistics.* Washington, DC: U.S. Government Printing Office.

National Center for Health Statistics. 1999. *National Vital Statistics.* Washington, D.C.: Government Printing Office.

——. 2002. *Changing America: Indicators of Social and Economic Well-Being by Race and Hispanic Origin.* Atlanta, GA: Centers for Disease Control.

——. 2003. *Trends in Vision and Hearing among Older Americans.* Atlanta, GA: Centers for Disease Control.

National Council de la Raza. 1992. *Hispanics and Health Insurance.* Washington, DC: Labor Council for Latin American Advancement.

National Hospice and Palliative Care Organization. 2000. Facts and Figures on Hospice Care in America. Alexandria, VA: National Hospice and Palliative Care Organization.

National Osteoporosis Foundation. 1996. *Evaluate Your Risk of Osteoporosis.* Washington, DC: National Osteoporosis Foundation.

Nelson, M. E., M. A. Fiatarone, C. M. Morganti, I. Trice, R. A. Greenberg, and W. J. Evans. 1994. "Effects of High-Intensity Strength Training on Multiple Risk Factors for Osteoporotic Fractures: A Randomized Controlled Trial." *Journal of the American Medical Association* 272:1909–14.

Netting, F. Ellen, and Cindy Wilson. 1994. "CCRC Oversight: Implications for Public Regulation and Private Accreditation." *Journal of Applied Gerontology* 13:250–66.

Neugarten, Bernice. 1964. *Personality in Middle and Later Life.* New York: Atherton.

——. 1968. *Middle Age and Aging: A Reader in Social Psychology.* Chicago: University of Chicago Press.

——. 1977. "Personality and Aging." Pp. 626–49 in *Handbook of the Psychology of Aging,* edited by J. Birren and K. W. Schaie. New York: Van Nostrand Reinhold.

——. 1979. "Public Policy for the 1980s: Age or Need Entitlement?" Pp. 48–52 in *Aging: Agenda for the Eighties,* edited by J. P. Hubbard. Washington, DC: Government Research Corporation.

——. 1987. "Kansas City Studies of Adult Life." Pp. 372–73 in *The Encyclopedia of Aging,* edited by George Maddox. New York: Springer.

Neugarten, Bernice, Robert Havighurst, and Sheldon Tobin. 1968. "Personality Patterns and Aging." Pp. 173–77 in *Middle Age and Aging,* edited by B. Neugarten. Chicago: University of Chicago Press.

Neugarten, Bernice, Joan Moore, and John Lowe. 1965. "Age Norms, Age Constraints, and Adult Socialization." *American Journal of Sociology* 70(May):710–16.

Neuschler, E. 1987. *Medicaid Eligibility for the Elderly in Need of Long-Term Care.* Washington, DC: National Governor's Association.

Newman, Katherine S. 1988. *Falling from Grace: The Experience of Downward Mobility in the American Middle Class.* New York: Free Press.

Neysmith, Sheila. 1991. "Dependency among Third World Elderly: A Need for New Directions in the Nineties." Pp. 311–21 in *Critical Perspectives on Aging,* edited by M. Minkler and C. Estes. Amityville, NY: Baywood.

Nguyen, T. V., P. J. Kelly, P. N. Sambrook, C. Gilbert, N. A. Pocock, and J. A. Eisman. 1994. "Lifestyle Factors and Bone Density in the Elderly: Implications for Osteoporosis Prevention." *Journal of Bone Mineral Research* 9:1339–46.

Norgard, Theresa, and Willard Rodgers. 1997. "Patterns of In-Home Care among Elderly Black and White Americans." *Journal of Gerontology* 52B (May):93–101.

Norton, Mary Beth, David Katzman, Paul Escott, Howard Chudakoff, Thomas Paterson, and William Tuttle, Jr. 1982. *A People and a Nation.* Boston: Houghton Mifflin.

Norwood, Thomas, James R. Smith, and Gretchen Stein. 1990. "Aging at the Cellular Level: The Human Fibroblastlike Cell

Model." Pp. 131–47 in *Handbook of the Biology of Aging*, edited by E. Schneider and J. Rowe. San Diego, CA: Academic Press.

O'Bryant, S. L. 1990–91. "Forewarning of a Husband's Death: Does It Make a Difference for Older Widows?" *Omega* 22:227–39.

O'Bryant, Shirley, and Robert Hansson. 1995. "Widowhood." Pp. 440–58 in *Handbook of Aging and the Family*, edited by R. Blieszner and V. Hilkevitch Bedford. Westport, CT: Greenwood Press.

Office of Health Technology Assessment. 1994. "The Changing Health Care System." Pp. 279–82 in *Dominant Issues in Medical Sociology*, edited by H. Schwartz. New York: McGraw-Hill.

Office of Management and Budget. 1996. *Budget of the United States, Fiscal Year 1997.* Washington, DC: U.S. Government Printing Office.

O'Grady-LeShane, Regina. 1993. "Changes in the Lives of Women and Their Families: Have Old Age Pensions Kept Place?" *Generations* 17:27–31.

Oliver, Melvin, and Thomas Shapiro. 1995. *Black Wealth/White Wealth: A New Perspective on Racial Inequality.* New York: Routledge.

Olshansky, S. Jay, and A. Brian Ault. 1986. "The Fourth Stage of the Epidemiologic Transition: The Age of Delayed Degenerative Diseases." *The Milbank Memorial Fund Quarterly* 64:355–91.

Olson, Philip. 1988. "Modernization in the People's Republic of China: The Politicization of the Elderly." *Sociological Quarterly* 29:241–62.

Oppenheimer, Valerie. 1970. *The Female Labor Force in the United States.* Berkeley, CA: Institute for International Studies.

O'Rand, Angela. 1990. "Stratification and the Life Course." Pp. 130–48 in *Handbook of Aging and the Social Sciences*, edited by R. Binstock and L. George. San Diego, CA: Academic Press.

———. 1996a. "The Precious and the Precocious: Understanding Cumulative Disadvantage and Cumulative Advantage over the Life Course." *The Gerontologist* 36:230–38.

———. 1996b. *The Vulnerable Majority: Older Women in Transition.* Syracuse, NY: National Academy on Aging.

———. 1996c. "The Cumulative Stratification of the Life Course." Pp. 188–205 in *Handbook of Aging and the Social Sciences*, edited by R. Binstock and L. George. San Diego, CA: Academic Press.

O'Rand, Angela, John Henretta, and Margaret Krecker. 1992. "Family Pathways to Retirement." Pp. 81–98 in *Families and Retirement*, edited by M. Szinovacz, D. Ekerdt, and B. Vinick. Newbury Park, CA: Sage.

Orbach, Harold. 1974. "The Disengagement Theory of Aging, 1960–1970." Doctoral dissertation, Department of Sociology, University of Michigan, Ann Arbor, MI.

Organization for Economic Cooperation and Development. 1988a. *The Future of Social Protection.* Paris: OECD.

———. 1988b. *Reforming Public Pensions.* Paris: OECD.

———. 1993. *Private Pensions in OECD Countries: The United States.* Paris: OECD.

———. 1994. *New Orientations for Social Policy.* Paris: OECD.

———. 1998. *Maintaining Prosperity in an Aging Society.* Working Paper 14.

Orloff, Ann. 1993. "Gender and Social Rights of Citzenship: The Comparative Analysis of Gender Relations and Welfare States." *American Sociological Review* 58:303–28.

Otremba, Ronald. 1995. "Euthanasia Is Unethical." Pp. 21–23 in *Euthanasia: Opposing Viewpoints*, edited by Carol Wekesser. San Diego, CA: Greenhaven Press.

Oxman, Thomas, and Jay Hull. 1997. "Social Support, Depression, and Activities of Daily Living in Older Heart Surgery Patients." *Journal of Gerontology* 52B:P1–14.

Ozcan, Yasar, and J. James Cotter. 1994. "An Assessment of Efficiency of Area Agencies on Aging in Virginia through Data Development Analysis." *The Gerontologist* 34:363–70.

Paillat, Paul. 1977. "Bureaucratization of Old Age: Determinants of the Process." Pp. 60–74 in *Family, Bureaucracy and the Elderly*, edited by Ethel Shanas and Marvin Sussman. Durham, NC: Duke University Press.

Paine, Thomas. 1993. "The Changing Character of Pensions: Where Employers Are Headed." Pp. 33–40 in *Pensions in a Changing Economy*, edited by R. Burkhauser and D. Salisbury. Washington, DC: National Academy on Aging.

Palmer, Heather, and Richard Chapman. 1997. "Quality of Care for Medicare Beneficiaries: Implications of Changing Health Care Financing Mechanisms." No. 9703. Washington, DC: AARP.

Palmer, Heather, and Keith Dobson. 1994. "Self-Medication and Memory in an Elderly Canadian Sample." *The Gerontologist* 34:658–64.

Palmore, Erdman. 1975. *The Honorable Elders: A Cross-Cultural Analysis of Aging in Japan.* Durham, NC: Duke University Press.

———. 1981. *Social Patterns in Normal Aging.* Durham, NC: Duke University Press.

Palmore, Erdman, Bruce Burchett, Gerda Fillenbaum, Linda George, and Laurence Wallman. 1985. *Retirement, Causes and Consequences.* New York: Springer.

Palmore, Erdman, and Kenneth Manton. 1974. "Modernization and the Status of the Aged: International Correlations." *Journal of Gerontology* 29:205–10.

Pampel, Fred. 1986. "Cross-National Patterns and Determinants of Female Retirement." *American Journal of Sociology* 91:932–55.

——. 1994. "Population Aging, Class Context and Age Inequality in Public Spending." *American Journal of Sociology* 100:53–95.

——. 1998. *Aging, Social Inequality and Public Policy.* Beverly Hills, CA: Pine Forge Press.

Pampel, Fred, and Jane Weiss. 1983. "Economic Development, Pension Policies and the Labor Force Participation of Aged Males: A Cross-National Longitudinal Analysis." *American Journal of Sociology* 89:350–72.

Panish, Jacqueline, and George Stryker. 2001. "Parental Marital Conflict in Childhood and Influence on Adult Sibling Relationships." *Journal of Psychotherapy in Independent Practice* 51:791–803.

Papadopoulos, C. 1991. "Sex and the Cardiac Patient." *Medical Aspects of Human Sexuality* 25:18–26.

Papalia, Diane, Cameron Camp, and Ruth Duskin Feldman. 1996. *Adult Development and Aging.* New York: McGraw-Hill.

Papalia, D., and S. Olds. 1998. *Human Development.* New York: McGraw-Hill.

Paplau, L., and S. Cochran. 1990. "A Relational Perspective on Homosexuality." Pp. 321–49 in *Homosexuality/ Heterosexuality: Concepts of Sexual Orientation,* vol. 2, Kinsey Institute Series, edited by P. McWhirter, S. Sanders, and J. Reinisch. New York: Oxford University Press.

Parham, Lori. 2002. "Contrasts in Care Work: Hospice Care in Nursing Homes." Ph.D. dissertation, Tallahassee, FL: Florida State University.

Parnes, Herbert, Joan Crowley, R. Jean Haurin, Lawrence Less, William Morgan, Frank Mott, and Gilbert Nestel. 1985. *Retirement among American Men.* Lexington, MA: D. C. Heath.

Parnes, Herbert, Mary Gagen, and Randall King. 1981. "Job Loss among Long-Service Workers." Pp. 66–93 in *Work and Retirement: A Longitudinal Study of Men,* edited by H. Parnes. Cambridge, MA: MIT Press.

Parnes, Herbert, and D. Sommers. 1994. "Shunning Retirement: Work Experience of Men in Their Seventies and Early Eighties." *Journal of Gerontology* 49:S117–24.

Parsons, Talcott. 1942. "Age and Sex in the Social Structure of the United States." *American Sociological Review* 7:604–16.

——. 1951. *The Social System.* New York: Free Press.

Passuth, Patricia M., and Vern L. Bengtson. 1988. "Sociological Theories of Aging: Current Perspectives and Future Directions." Pp. 333–55 in *Emergent Theories of Aging,* edited by J. Birren and V. Bengtson. New York: Springer.

Paykel, E. S. 1994. "Incidence of Dementia in a Population Older than 75 in the United Kingdom." *Archives of General Psychiatry* 51:325–32.

Pear, Robert. 1997. "GOP Lawmakers Want $16 Billion for Health Plan." *New York Times,* June 9, p. A1.

Pearlin, Leonard, Carol Aneshensel, Joseph Mullan, and Carol Whitlatch. 1996. "Caregiving and Its Social Support." Pp. 283–302 in *Handbook of Aging and the Social Sciences,* edited by R. Binstock and L. George. San Diego, CA: Academic Press.

Pearson, C., Fugh-Berman, A., Allina, A., Massion, C., Whatley, M., Worcester, N., and Zones, J. 2002. *The Truth About Hormone Replacement Therapy.* Prima Publishing Co. Roseville, CA.

Pelham, A., and W. Clark. 1987. "Widowhood among Low-Income Racial and Ethnic Groups in California." Pp. 162–84 in *Widows: North America,* edited by H. Lopata. Durham, NC: Duke University Press.

Penny, Timothy, and Steven Schier. 1996. *Payment Due: A Nation in Debt, A Generation in Trouble.* Boulder, CO: Westview Press.

Penrod, Joan, Rosalie Kane, Robert Kane, and Michael Finch. 1995. "Who Cares? The Size, Scope, and Composition of the Caregiver Support System." *The Gerontologist* 35:489–97.

Peplau, L. A. 1991. "Lesbians and Gay Relationships." Pp. 128–42 in *Homosexuality: Implications for Social Policy,* edited by J. C. Gonsiorek and J. D. Weinrich. Newbury Park, CA: Sage.

Pepper Commission on Aging. 1990. *A Call for Action.* Washington, DC: U.S. Bipartisan Commission on Comprehensive Health Care.

Perkins, Kathleen. 1993. "Working-Class Women and Retirement." *Journal of Gerontological Social Work* 20(3/4):129–46.

Perkinson, Margaret, and David Rockemann. 1996. "Older Women Living in a Continuing Care Retirement Community: Marital Status and Friendship Formation." *Journal of Women and Aging* 8(3/4):159–77.

Perlmutter, Marion, and Elizabeth Hall. 1992. *Adult Development and Aging.* New York: John Wiley and Sons.

Pescosolido, Bernice. 1992. "Beyond Rational Choice: The Social Dynamics of How People Seek Help." *American Journal of Sociology* 97:1096–138.

Peterson, Paul. 1993. "An Immodest Proposal: Let's Give Children the Vote." *Brookings Review* (Winter):19–23.

Peterson, Peter. 1987. "The Morning After." *Atlantic Monthly,* October: 41–49.

——. 1994. *Facing Up: How to Rescue the Economy from Crushing Debt and Restore the American Dream.* New York: Simon and Schuster.

Pfeiffer, E. 1977. "Sexual Behavior in Old Age." Pp. 130–41 in *Behavior and Adaptation in Late Life,* 2d ed., edited by E. Busse and E. Pfeiffer. Boston: Little, Brown.

Phillips, Anne. 1991. *Engendering Democracy.* University Park, PA: Pennsylvania State University Press.

Physician's Desk Reference. 2003. Medical Economics Company Publisher. Montvale, New Jersey.

Pienta, Amy, Jeffrey Burr, and Jan Mutchler. 1994. "Women's Labor Force Participation in Later Life: The Effects of Early Work and Family Experiences." *Journal of Gerontology* 49:S231–39.

Pienta, Amy, and Mark Hayward. 2002. "Who Expects to Continue Working after Age 62? The Retirement Plans of Couples." *Journal of Gerontology* 57B(4):S199–208.

Pierson, Paul, and Miriam Smith. 1994. "Shifting Fortunes of the Elderly: The Comparative Politics of Retrenchment." Pp. 21–59 in *Economic Security and Intergenerational Justice,* edited by T. Marmor, T. Smeeding, and V. Greene. Washington, DC: Urban Institute Press.

Pillemer, C., J. Suitor, C. Henderson, R. Meador, L. Schultz, J. Robison, and C. Hegeman. 2003. "A Cooperative Communication Intervention for Nursing Home Staff and Family Members of Residents." *The Gerontologist* 43(II):96–106.

Pina, Darlene, and Vern Bengtson. 1995. "Division of Household Labor and the Well-Being of Retirement-Aged Wives." *The Gerontologist* 35:308–17.

Piore, Michael J., and Charles F. Sabel. 1984. *The Second Industrial Divide: Possibilities for Prosperity.* New York: Basic Books.

Piven, Frances Fox, and Richard Cloward. 1988. *Why Americans Don't Vote.* New York: Pantheon.

Plakans, Andrejs. 1996. "Retirement, Inheritance and Generational Relations." Pp. 140–57 in *Aging and Generational Relations over the Life Course,* edited by T. Hareven. Berlin: Aldine de Gruyter.

Plovsing, Jan. 1992. *Home Care in Denmark.* Copenhagen: Danish Institute of Social Research.

Pollitz, Karen. 2001. "Extending Health Insurance Coverage for Older Workers and Early Retirees." Pp. 233–54 in *Ensuring Health and Income Security for an Aging Workforce,* edited by P. Budetti, R. Burkhauser, J. Gregory, and A. Hunt. Kalamazod, MI: W. E. Upjohn Institute for Employment Research.

Poloma, M., and G. Gallup, Jr. 1991. *Varieties of Prayer.* Philadelphia: Trinity Press International.

Popenoe, David. 1993. "American Family Decline, 1960–1990: A Review and Appraisal." *Journal of Marriage and the Family* 55:527–55.

Pourat, N., J. Lubben, S. Wallace, and A. Moon. 1999. "Predictors of Use of Traditional Healers among Elderly Koreans in Los Angeles." *The Gerontologist* 39(6):711–19.

Powell, Lawrence, Kenneth Branco, and John Williamson. 1996. *The Senior Rights Movement: Framing the Policy Debate in America.* New York: Twayne.

Pratt, Henry. 1976. *The Gray Lobby.* Chicago: University of Chicago Press.

——. 1993. *Gray Agendas: Interest Groups and Public Pensions in Canada, Britain and the United States.* Ann Arbor: University of Michigan Press.

Premo, Terri. 1990. *Winter Friends: Women Growing Old in the New Republic, 1785–1835.* Urbana: University of Illinois Press.

President's Bipartisan Commission on Entitlement and Tax Reform. 1994. *Interim Report.* Washington, DC: U.S. Government Printing Office.

Preston, Samuel. 1984. "Children and the Elderly: Divergent Paths for America's Dependents." *Demography* 21(4):435–57.

——. 1992. "Cohort Succession and the Future of the Oldest Old." Pp. 50–57 in *The Oldest Old,* edited by R. Suzman, D. Willis, and K. Manton. New York: Oxford University Press.

Preston, Samuel, and Linda Martin. 1994. "Introduction." Pp. 1–7 in *Demography of Aging,* edited by L. Martin and S. Preston. Washington, DC: National Academy Press.

Preston, Samuel H., and Paul Taubman. 1994. "Socioeconomic Differences in Adult Mortality and Health Status." Pp. 279–318 in *Demography of Aging,* edited by L. G. Martin and S. H. Preston. Washington, DC: National Academy Press.

Pruchno, Rachel. 1999. "Raising Grandchildren: The Experiences of Black and White Grandmothers." *The Gerontologist* 39(2):209–21.

Pruchno, R. A., and M. S. Rose. 2000. "The Effect of Long-Term Care Environments on Health Outcomes." *The Gerontologist* 40(4):422–28.

Prudham, D., and J. Evans. 1981. "Factors Associated with Falls in the Elderly: A Community Study." *Age and Ageing* 10:141–46.

"Public Opinion on Entitlement Programs." 1994. Research Report from American Association of Retired Persons Research Division. Unpublished typescript.

Purcell, D., C. R. Thrush, and P. L. Blanchette. 1999. "Suicide among the Elderly in Honolulu County: A Multiethnic Comparative Study." *International Psychogeriatrics* 11(1):57–66.

Purdy, Matthew. 1995. "A Sexual Revolution for the Elderly." *New York Times,* November 6, p. A14.

Putnam, Robert. 2000. *Bowling Alone.* New York: Simon and Schuster.

Pynoos, Jon, and Stephen Golant. 1996. "Housing and Living Arrangements for the Elderly." Pp. 303–24 in *Handbook of Aging and the Social Sciences,* edited by R. Binstock and L. George. San Diego, CA: Academic Press.

Pynoos, Jon, and Tonya Parrott. 1996. "The Politics of Mixing Older Persons and Younger Persons with Disabilities in Federally Assisted Housing." *The Gerontologist* 36:518–29.

Pynoos, Jon, and D. L. Redfoot. 1995. "Housing Frail Elders in the United States." Pp. 187–210 in *Housing Frail Elders: International Policies Perspectives and Prospects,* edited by J. Pynoos and P. Liebig. Baltimore: Johns Hopkins University Press.

Quadagno, Jill. 1978."Career Continuity and Retirement Plans of Men and Women Physicians: The Meaning of Disorderly Careers." *Sociology of Work and Occupations* 5:55–74.

———. 1982. *Aging in Early Industrial Society: Work, Family and Social Policy in Nineteenth Century England.* New York: Academic Press.

———. 1988a. *The Transformation of Old Age Security: Class and Politics in the American Welfare State.* Chicago: University of Chicago Press.

———. 1988b. "Women's Access to Pensions and the Structure of Eligibility Rules: Systems of Production and Reproduction." *Sociological Quarterly* 29:541–58.

———. 1989. "Generational Equity and the Politics of the Welfare State." *Politics and Society* 17:353–76.

———. 1991. "Interest Group Politics and the Future of U.S. Social Security." Pp. 36–58 in *States, Labor Markets and the Future of Old Age Policy,* edited by J. Myles and J. Quadagno. Philadelphia: Temple University Press.

———. 1992. "Social Movements and State Transformation: Labor Unions and Racial Conflict in the War on Poverty." *American Sociological Review* 57:616–34.

———. 1994. *The Color of Welfare: How Racism Undermined the War on Poverty.* New York: Oxford University Press.

———. 1996a. "Downsizing and the Risks of Privatization." Presented to the Gerontological Society of America, November 1996, Washington, DC.

———. 1996b. "Social Security and the Myth of the Entitlement Crisis." *The Gerontologist* 36:391–99.

Quadagno, Jill. 1999. "Creating the Capital Investment Welfare State: The New American Exceptionalism." *American Sociological Review* 64:1–11.

———. 2003. "Why the U.S. Has No National Health Insurance: Stakeholder Mobilization against the Welfare State." Paper presented to the American Sociological Association, August, Atlanta, GA.

Quadagno, Jill, and Melissa Hardy. 1995. "Work and Retirement." Pp. 325–45 in *Handbook of Aging and the Social Sciences,* edited by R. Binstock and L. George. New York: Academic Press.

———. 1996. "Private Pensions, State Regulations and Income Security for Older Workers: The Case of the Auto Industry." Pp. 136–58 in *The Privatization of Social Policy? Occupational Welfare and the Welfare State in America, Scandinavia and Japan,* edited by Michael Shalev. London: Macmillan.

Quadagno, Jill, Madonna Harrington Meyer, and Blake Turner. 1991. "Falling through the Medicaid Gap: The Hidden Long-Term Care Dilemma." *The Gerontologist* 31:521–26.

Quadagno, Jill, and J. M. Janzen. 1987. "Old Age Security and the Family Life Course: A Case Study of Nineteenth Century Mennonite Immigrants to Kansas." *Journal of Aging Studies* 1:33–49.

Quadagno, Jill, David MacPherson, and Jennifer Reid Keene. 2001. "The Effect of a Job Loss on the Employment Experience, Health Insurance and Retirement Benefits of Workers in the Banking Industry." Pp. 199–219 in *Ensuring Health and Income Security for an Aging Workforce,* edited by P. Budetti, R. Burkhauser, J. Gregory, and A. Hunt. Kalamazoo, MI: W. E. Upjohn Institute for Employment Research.

Quadagno, Jill, and Joseph Quinn. 1996. "Does Social Security Discourage Work?" Pp. 127–46 in *Social Security in the 21st Century,* edited by E. Kingson and J. Schulz. New York: Oxford University Press.

Queen, Stuart, Robert Habenstein, and Jill Quadagno. 1985. *The Family in Various Cultures.* New York: Harper and Row.

Quick, Heather E., and Phyllis Moen. 1998. "Gender, Employment and Retirement Quality: A Life Course Approach to the Differential Experiences of Men and Women." *Journal of Occupational Health Psychology* 3(1):44–64.

Quill, Timothy. 1995. "Physicians Should Assist in Euthanasia." Pp. 101–4 in *Euthanasia: Opposing Viewpoints,* edited by Carol Wekesser. San Diego, CA: Greenhaven Press.

Quinn, Jane Bryant. 1997. "Social Security in Better Shape than Many Say." *Washington Post,* May 3, p. 1C.

Quinn, Joseph. 1991. "The Nature of Retirement: Survey and Econometric Evidence." Pp. 115–38 in *Retirement and Public Policy,* edited by A. Munnell. Washington, DC: National Academy of Social Insurance.

———. 1997. "Retirement Trends and Patterns in the 1990s: The End of an Era?" *Public Policy and Aging Report* 8(3):10–19.

Quinn, Joseph, and Richard Burkhauser. 1990. "Work and Retirement." Pp. 307–27 in *Handbook of Aging and the Social Sciences,* edited by R. Binstock and L. George. New York: Academic Press.

Quinn, Joseph, Richard V. Burkhauser, and D. Myers. 1990. *Passing the Torch: The Influence of Economic Incentives on Work and Retirement.* Kalamazoo, MI: W. E. Upjohn Institute for Employment Search.

Quinn, Joseph, and Michael Kozy. 1996. "The Role of Bridge Jobs in the Retirement Transition: Gender, Race and Ethnicity." *The Gerontologist* 36:363–72.

Quinn, Joseph, and Timothy Smeeding. 1993. "The Present and Future Economic Well-Being of the Aged." Pp. 5–18 in *Pensions in a Changing Economy*, edited by R. Burkhauser and D. Salisbury. Washington, DC: Employee Benefit Research Institute.

Quirouette, Cecile, and Dolores Pushkar Gold. 1995. "Spousal Characteristics as Predictors of Well-Being in Older Couples." Pp. 21–34 in *The Ties of Later Life*, edited by J. Hendricks. Amityville, NY: Baywood Press.

Raffin, T. 1995. "Withdrawing Life Support: How Is the Decision Made?" *Journal of the American Medical Association* 273:738–39.

Rahman, Omar, John Strauss, Paul Gertler, Deanna Askley, and Kristin Fox. 1994. "Gender Differences in Adult Health: An International Comparison." *The Gerontologist* 34:463–69.

Ralston, Penny. 1991. "Senior Centers and Minority Elders: A Critical Review." *The Gerontologist* 31:325–31.

Raphael, Bette-Jane. 1995. "September's Child." *Family Circle*, August 8, p. 130.

Rasmussen, David, Isaac Megbolugbe, and Barbara Morgan. 1995. "The Potential Demand for Reverse Mortgage Products." Washington, DC: Fannie Mae Office of Housing Research.

Rayman, Paula, Kimberly Allshouse, and Jessie Allen. 1993. "Resiliency amidst Inequity: Older Women Workers in an Aging United States." Pp. 133–66 in *Women on the Front Lines: Meeting the Challenge of an Aging America*, edited by J. Allen and A. Pifer. Washington, DC: Urban Institute Press.

Reay, A., and Browne, K. 2001. "Risk Factor Characteristics in Carers Who Physically Abuse or Neglect Their Elderly Dependants." *Aging and Mental Health* 5(1):56–62.

Rein, Martin, and Harold Salzman. 1995. "Social Integration, Participation and Exchange in Five Industrial Countries." Pp. 238–63 in *Older and Active*, edited by S. Bass. New Haven, CT: Yale University Press.

Reinhardt, Joann. 1996. "The Importance of Friendship and Family Support in Adaptation to Chronic Vision Impairment." *Journal of Gerontology* 51B:P268–78.

Reiss, Ira. 1995. "Is This the Definitive Sexual Survey?" *Journal of Sex Research* 32:77–85.

Reitzes, Donald, Elizabeth Mutran, and Maria Fernandez. 1996. "Does Retirement Hurt Well-Being? Factors Influencing Self-Esteem and Depression among Retirees and Workers." *The Gerontologist* 36:649–56.

Reitzes, Donald C., Elizabeth Mutran, and Hallowell Pope. 1991. "Location and Well-Being among Retired Men." *Journal of Gerontology* 46:195–203.

Rempel, David. 1973–74. "The Mennonite Commonwealth in Russia: A Sketch of Its Founding and Endurance, 1989–1919." *Mennonite Quarterly Review* 47–48:5–54.

Reno, Virginia. 1993a. "The Role of Pensions in Retirement Income: Trends and Questions." *Social Security Bulletin* 56:29–43.

———. 1993b. "The Role of Pensions in Retirement Income." Pp. 19–32 in *Pensions in a Changing Economy*, edited by R. Burkhauser and D. Salisbury. Washington, DC: Employee Benefit Research Institute.

Reno, Virginia, and Robert B. Friedland. 1996. "Strong Support but Low Confidence: What Explains the Contradiction?" Pp. 178–94 in *Social Security in the 21st Century*, edited by E. Kingson and J. Schulz. New York: Oxford University Press.

Reskin, Barbara, and Heidi Hartmann. 1986. *Women's Work and Men's Work: Sex Segregation on the Job*. Washington, DC: National Academy of Sciences.

Resnick, Helaine, Brant Fries, and Lois Verbrugge. 1997. "Windows to their World: The Effect of Sensory Impairments on Social Engagement and Activity Time in Nursing Home Residents." *Journal of Gerontology*, 52(3):S135–45.

Retchin, Sheldon, Randall Brown, Jennifer Shu-Chuan, Dexter Chu, and Lorenzo Moreno. 1997. "Outcomes of Stroke Patients in Medicare Fee-for-Service and Managed Care." *Journal of the American Medical Association* 278:119–24.

Revicki, Dennis, and John Mitchell. 1990. "Strain, Social Support and Mental Health in Rural Elderly Individuals." *Journal of Gerontology* 45:S267–74.

Rich, Spencer. 2002. "The Policy Dilemma." *National Journal* (March):840–44.

Riley, Matilda White. 1971. "Social Gerontology and the Age Stratification of Society." *American Sociological Review* 52:1–14.

———. 1976. "Age Strata in Social Systems." Pp. 189–217 in *Handbook of Aging and the Social Sciences*, edited by R. Binstock and E. Shanas. New York: Van Nostrand Reinhold.

———. 1994. "Aging and Society: Past, Present and Future." *The Gerontologist* 34:436–46.

———. 1995. "Age Stratification." *Age Stratification and Cohort Studies: As Components of the Aging and Society Paradigm*. Washington, DC: National Institute on Aging.

———. 1996. "Age Stratification." *Encyclopedia of Gerontology* 1:81–92.

Riley, Matilda White, and Ann Foner. 1968. *Aging and Society*. New York: Russell Sage.

Riley, Matilda White, Anne Foner, and Joan Waring. 1988. "Sociology of Age." Pp. 243–90 in *Handbook of Aging and the Social Sciences*, edited by N. Smelser. Newbury Park, CA: Sage.

Riley, Matilda White, and Karen Loscocco. 1994. "The Changing Structure of Work Opportunities: Toward an Age-Integrated Society." Pp. 235–52 in *Aging and the Quality of Life*, edited by R. Abeles, H. Gift, and M. Ory. New York: Springer.

Riley, Matilda White, and John W. Riley. 1994. "On the Sociology of Age: Autobiographical Notes." *The Annals of* the *American Academy of Political and Social Sciences* 4:217–38.

———. 2000. "Age Integration: Conceptual and Historical Background." *The Gerontologist* 40(3):266–70.

Rindfuss, Ronald, C. Gray Swicegood, and Rachel Rosenfeld. 1987. "Disorder in the Life Course: How Common and Does It Matter?" *American Sociological Review* 52:785–801.

Risteen Hasselkus, Betty. 1992. "Physician and Family Caregiver in the Medical Setting: Negotiation of Care?" *Journal of Aging Studies* 6:67–80.

Ritchie, K., D. Kildea, and J. M. Robine. 1992. "The Relationship between Age and the Prevalence of Senile Dementia: A Meta-Analysis of Recent Data." *International Journal of Epidemiology* 21:763–69.

Rivlin, Alice, and Joshua M. Wiener. 1988. *Caring for the Disabled Elderly: Who Will Pay?* Washington, DC: Brookings Institution.

Rix, Sara. 1994. *Older Workers: How Do They Measure Up?* Washington, DC: American Association of Retired Persons.

Robb, C., H. Chen, and W. E. Haley. 2002. Ageism in Mental Health Care: A Critical Review. *Journal of Clinical Geropsychology* 8(1):1–12.

Roberto, Karen, and Johanna Stroes. 1992. "Grandchildren and Grandparents: Roles, Influences and Relationships." *International Journal of Aging and Human Development* 34:227–39.

Roberts, Pearl. 1974. "Human Warehouse: A Boarding Home Study." *American Journal of Public Health* 64:277–82.

Roberts, Robert E., and Vern Bengtson. 1993. "Relationships with Parents, Self-Esteem and Psychological Well-Being in Young Adulthood." *Social Psychology Quarterly* 56:263–315.

Roberts, Robert E., Leslie Richards, and Vern Bengtson. 1991. "Intergenerational Solidarity in Families: Untangling the Ties That Bind." *Marriage and Family Review* 16:11–46.

Robertson, A. 1991. "The Politics of Alzheimer's Disease: A Case Study in Apocalyptic Demography." Pp. 135–50 in *Critical Perspectives on Aging,* edited by M. Minkler and C. Estes. Amityville, NY: Baywood.

Robison, Julie, Phyllis Moen, and Donna Dempster-McClain. 1995. "Women's Caregiving: Changing Profiles and Pathways." *Journal of Gerontology,* 50B:S362–73.

Roebuck, Janet. 1983. "Grandma as Revolutionary: Elderly Women and Some Modern Patterns of Change." *International Journal of Aging and Human Development* 17:249–66.

Rogers, Richard, Andrei Rogers, and Alain Belanger. 1992. "Disability-Free Life among the Elderly in the United States." *Journal of Aging and Health* 4:19–42.

Rogers, Stacy, and Paul Amato. 1997. "Is Marital Quality Declining? The Evidence of Two Recent Marriage Cohorts." *Social Forces* 75:1089–1100.

Rollinson, Paul. 1990. "The Story of Edward: The Everyday Geography of Elderly Single Room Occupancy (SRO) Hotel Tenants." *Journal of Contemporary Ethnography* 19(2):188–206.

Rosano, G. M., and G. Panina. 1999. "Cardiovascular Pharmacology of Hormone Replacement Therapy." *Drugs and Aging* 15(3):219–34.

Rose, Arnold. 1962. "The Subculture of the Aging: A Framework for Research in Social Gerontology." *Gerontology* 2:123–27.

———. 1964. "A Current Theoretical Issue in Social Gerontology." *The Gerontologist* 4:46–50.

Rose, Madeleine Kornfeld, and Harriet Hailparn Soares. 1993. "Sexual Adaptations of the Frail Elderly: A Realistic Approach." *Journal of Gerontological Social Work* 19:167–78.

Rosen, Raymond, John Kostis, and Albert Jekelis. 1988. "Beta-Blocker Effects on Sexual Function in Normal Males." *Archives of Sexual Behavior* 17:241–55.

Rosen, Raymond, John Kostis, Albert Jekelis, and Lynn Taska. 1994. "Sexual Sequelae of Antihypertensive Drugs: Treatment Effects on Self-Report and Physiological Measures in Middle-Aged Male Hypertensives." *Archives of Sexual Behavior* 23:135–52.

Rosenbaum, Walter, and James Button. 1993. "The Unquiet Future of Intergenerational Politics." *The Gerontologist* 33:481–90.

Rosenberg, Charles. 1987. *The Care of Strangers: The Rise of America's Hospital System.* New York: Basic Books.

Rosenberg, Roger, and Ralph Ricther. 1996. "Low Rates of Alzheimer's Disease Found in Cherokee Indians." *Archives of Neurology* 63:997–1000.

Rosenthal, Carolyn, Sarah Matthews, and Victor Marshall. 1989. "Is Parent Care Normative? The Experience of a Sample of Middle-Aged Women." *Research on Aging* 11:244–60.

Rosowsky, Erlene. 1993. "Suicidal Behavior in the Nursing Home and a Postsuicide Intervention." *American Journal of Psychotherapy* 47:127–42.

Ross, Catherine. 1993. "Fear of Victimization and Health." *Journal of Qualitative Criminology* 9:159–75.

Ross, Catherine, and Chia-Ling Wu. 1996. "Education, Age and the Cumulative Advantage in Health." *Journal of Health and Social Behavior* 37:104–20.

Rossi, Alice. 1980. "Life Span Theories and Women's Lives." *Signs* 6:4–32.

Rossi, Alice, and Peter Rossi. 1990. *Of Human Bonding: Parent-Child Relations across the Life Course.* New York: Aldine de Gruyter.

Rossides, Daniel. 1997. *Social Stratification.* Upper Saddle River, NJ: Prentice Hall.

Roth, Philip. 1991. *Patrimony.* New York: Simon and Schuster.

Rothman, David. 1971. *The Discovery of the Asylum.* Boston: Little, Brown.

Rowe, John W., and Robert L. Kahn. 1997. "Successful Aging." *The Gerontologist* 37(4):433–40.

———. 1998. *Successful Aging.* New York: Pantheon Books.

Rubenstein, Laurence, Theodore Marmor, Robyn Stone, Marilyn Moon, and Linda Harootyan. 1994. "Medicare: Challenges and Future Directions in a Changing Health Care Environment." *The Gerontologist* 35:620–27.

Rubin, Lillian. 1976. *Worlds of Pain.* New York: Basic Books.

———. 1979. *Women of a Certain Age.* New York: Harper and Row.

Rubin, Rose, and Kenneth Keolln. 1993. "Out-of-Pocket Health Expenditure Differentials between Elderly and Non-Elderly Households." *The Gerontologist* 33:595–602.

Rubin-Terrado, M. 1994. "Social Support and Life Satisfaction of Older Mothers and Childless Women Living in Nursing Homes." Unpublished doctoral dissertation, Department of Sociology, Northwestern University, Evanston, IL.

Ruchlin, H. S., and J. N. Morris. 1987. "The Congregate Housing Services Program: An Analysis of Service Utilization and Cost." *The Gerontologist* 27:87–91.

Ruggie, Mary. 1996. *Realignments in the Welfare State: Health Policy in the United States, Britain and Canada.* New York: Columbia University Press.

Ruggles, Steven. 1987. *Prolonged Connections: The Rise of the Extended Family in Nineteenth Century England and America.* Madison, WI: University of Wisconsin Press.

Ruhm, Christopher. 1989. "Why Older Americans Stop Working." *The Gerontologist* 29:294–300.

———. 1996. "Gender Differences in Employment Behavior during Late Middle Age." *Journal of Gerontology* 51B:S11–17.

Rumack, R. 1992. "Assessing the OWBPA, an Amendment to ADEA." *Pension World* (April):38–40.

Ruth, Jan-Erik, and Peter Coleman. 1996. "Personality and Aging: Coping and Management of the Self in Later Life." Pp. 308–22 in *Handbook of the Psychology of Aging,* edited by J. Birren and K. W. Schaie. San Diego, CA: Academic Press.

Ryan, Ellen, Sherrie Bieman-Copland, Sheree Kwong See, Carolyn Ellis, and Ann Anas. 2002. "Age Excuses: Conversational Management of Memory Failure in Older Adults." *Journal of Gerontology* 57B(3):P256–67.

Ryder, Norman. 1965. "The Cohort as a Concept in the Study of Social Change." *American Sociological Review* 30:843–61.

Sabean, David. 1976. "Aspects of Kinship Behavior and Property in Rural Western Europe before 1800." Pp. 96–111 in *Family and Inheritance,* edited by J. Goody, J. Thirsk, and E. P. Thompson. Cambridge: Cambridge University Press.

Sacco, R., M. Elkind, B. Boden-Albala, I. L. Kargman, W. Hauser, S. Shea, and M. Paik. 1999. "The Protective Effect of Moderate Alcohol Consumption on Ischemic Stroke." *Journal of the American Medical Association* 281:53–59.

Sainsbury, Diane. 1996. *Gender, Equality, and Welfare States.* Cambridge: Cambridge University Press.

Salisbury, Dallas. 1993. "Policy Implications of Changes in Employer Benefit Protection." Pp. 41–58 in *Pensions in a Changing Economy,* edited by R. Burkhauser and D. Salisbury. Washington, DC: National Academy on Aging.

———. 1994. "Baby Boomers in Retirement: What Are Their Prospects?" Employee Benefit Research Institute Special Report No. 151, Washington, DC.

Salthouse, Timothy. 1999. "Theories of Cognition." Pp. 196–208 in *Handbook of Theories of Aging,* edited by Vern Bengtson and K. Warner Schaie. New York: Springer.

Saluter, Arlene. 1997. "Marital Status and Living Arrangements." Washington, DC: U.S. Bureau of the Census.

Sandefur, Gary, and Marta Tienda. 1988. *Divided Opportunities: Poverty, Minorities and Social Policy.* New York: Plenum Press.

Sankar, Andrea, and Jaber Gubrium. 1994. "Introduction." Pp. vii–xvii in *Qualitative Methods in Aging Research,* edited by J. Gubrium and A. Sankar. Thousand Oaks, CA: Sage.

Sarton, May. 1988. *After the Stroke.* New York: W. W. Norton.

Saunders, Cicely. 1980. "Dying They Live: St. Christopher's Hospice." Pp. 554–68 in *Aging, the Individual and Society,* edited by J. Quadagno. New York: St. Martin's Press.

Savishinsky, Joel S. 2000. *Breaking the Watch: The Meanings of Retirement in America.* Ithaca, NY: Cornell University Press.

Savitt, Todd L. 1978. *Medicine and Slavery.* Chicago: University of Illinois Press.

Schaffer, C. L. 1993. *Journal of Cross-Cultural Gerontology* 8:161–73.

Schaie, K. W. 1994. "The Course of Adult Intellectual Development." *American Psychologist* 49:304–13.

———. 1996. "Intellectual Development in Adulthood." Pp. 266–86 in *Handbook of the Psychology of Aging,* edited by J. Birren and K. W. Schaie. New York: Academic Press.

Schaie, K. W., and S. L. Willis. 1991. "Adult Personality and Psycho-Motor Performance: Cross-Sectional and Longitudinal Analyses." *Journal of Gerontology* 46:P275–84.

Scharlach, Andrew. 1994. "Caregiving and Employment: Competing or Complementary Roles." *The Gerontologist* 34:378–85.

Scharlach, Andrew, and Sandra Boyd. 1989. "Caregiving and Employment: Results of an Employee Survey." *The Gerontologist* 29:382–87.

Scharlach, Andrew, and Lenard Kaye. 1997. *Controversial Issues in Aging.* Boston: Allyn and Bacon.

Scheibel, A. 1996. "Structural and Functional Changes in the Aging Brain." Pp. 105–23 in *Handbook of the Psychology of Aging,* edited by J. Birren and K. W. Schaie. New York: Academic Press.

Schein, P., S. West, B. Munoz, S. Vitale, M. Maguire, H. Tayler, and N. Bressler. 1994. "Cortical Lenticular Opacification: Distribution and Location in a Longitudinal Study." *Investigative Ophthalmology and Visual Science* 35:363–66.

Schiavi, R. C., J. Mandeli, and P. Schreiner-Engel. 1994. "Sexual Satisfaction in Healthy Aging Men." *Journal of Sex and Marital Therapy* 20:3–13.

Schlumbohm, Jurgen. 1996. "Micro-History and the Macro-Models of the European Demographic System: Life Course Patterns in the Parish of Belm, Germany—Seventeenth to the Nineteenth Centuries." *The History of the Family* 1:81–96.

Schmitt, Ray. 1993. *Pension Issues: Challenges to Retirement Income Security.* Congressional Research Service Report, June 22, Washington, DC.

Schnaiberg, Alan, and Sheldon Goldenberg. 1989. "From Empty Nest to Crowded Nest: The Dynamics of Incompletely Launched Young Adults." *Social Problems* 36:251–69.

Schneider, E. L. 1983. "Aging, Natural Death and the Compression of Morbidity: Another View." *New England Journal of Medicine* 309:854–56.

Schoenbaum, Micahel, and Timothy Waldman. 1997. "Race, Socioeconomic Status and Health: Accounting for Race Differences in Health." *Journal of Gerontology* 52B(May):61–73.

Schor, Juliet. 1992. *The Overworked American.* New York: Basic Books.

Schulz, James. 1985. *The Economics of Aging.* New York: Van Nostrand Reinhold.

——. 1995. *The Economics of Aging.* Westport, CT: Greenwood Press.

——. 1996. "Economic Security Policies." Pp. 410–26 in *Handbook of Aging and the Social Sciences,* edited by R. Binstock and L. George. San Diego, CA: Academic Press.

Schulz, James, and John Myles. 1990. "Old Age Pensions: A Comparative Perspective." Pp. 398–414 in *Handbook of Aging and the Social Sciences,* edited by R. Binstock and L. George. New York: Academic Press.

Schuman, Howard, Charlotte Steeh, Lawrence Bobo, and Maria Krysan. 1997. *Racial Attitudes in America.* Cambridge, MA: Harvard University Press.

Schunk, Michaela, and Carroll Estes. 2001. "Is German Long-Term Care Insurance a Model for the United States?" *International Journal of Health Services* 31:617–34.

Schur, Lisa, Todd Shields, and Douglas Kruse. 2002. "Enabling Democracy: Disability and Voter Turnout." *Political Research Quarterly* 55(March):167–90.

Schuyt, Theo, Lucia Garcia, and Kees Knipscheer. 1999. "The Politics of Old Age in the Netherlands." Pp. 123–35 in *The Politics of Old Age in Europe.* Buckingham, U.K.: Open University Press.

Scott, Jean Pearson. 1990. "Sibling Interaction in Later Life." Pp. 86–99 in *Family Relationships in Later Life,* edited by T. Brubaker. Beverly Hills, CA: Sage.

Scrutton, Steve. 1990. *Age: The Unrecognized Discrimination.* London: Age Concern.

Seccombe, Karen, and Gary R. Lee. 1986. "Gender Differences in Retirement Satisfaction and Its Antecedents." *Research on Aging* 8:426–40.

Seidlitz, Larry, Paul Duberstein, Christopher Cox, and Yeates Conwell. 1995. "Attitudes of Older People toward Suicide and Assisted Suicide: An Analysis of Gallup Poll Findings." *Journal of the American Geriatrics Society* 43(9):993–98.

Selkoe, D. 1992. "Aging Brain, Aging Mind." *Scientific American* (September):135–42.

Semple, Shirley. 1992. "Conflict in Alzheimer's Caregiving Families: Its Dimensions and Consequences." *The Gerontologist* 32:648–55.

Serow, William J., David F. Sly, and J. Michael Wrigley. 1990. *Population Aging in the United States.* New York: Greenwood Press.

Settersten, Richard. 1999. *Lives in Time and Place.* Amityville, NY: Baywood.

Settersten, Richard, and Gunhild Hagestad. 1996a. "What's the Latest? Cultural Age Deadlines for Family Transitions." *The Gerontologist* 36:178–88.

——. 1996b. "What's the Latest? II. Cultural Age Deadlines for Family Transitions." *The Gerontologist* 36:602–13.

Sewell, William, and Robert Hauser. 1975. *Education, Occupation and Earnings: Achievements in the Early Career.* New York: Academic Press.

Shah, Nasra, Kathryn Yount, Makhdoom Shah, and Indu Menon. 2003. "Living Arrangements of Older Women and Men in Kuwait." *Journal of Cross-Cultural Gerontology* 17:337–55.

Shahrani, M. Nazif. 1981. "Growing in Respect: Aging among the Kirghiz of Afghanistan." Pp. 175–92 in *Other Ways of Growing Old,* edited by P. Amoss and S. Harrell. Stanford, CA: Stanford University Press.

Shalev, Michael. 1996. *The Privatization of Social Policy?* London: Macmillan.

Shammus, Carole, Marylynn Salmon, and Michel Dahlin. 1987. *Inheritance in America: From Colonial Times to the Present.* New Brunswick, NJ: Rutgers University Press.

Shanahan, Michael, Glen Elder, and Richard Miech. 1997. "History and Agency in Men's Lives: Pathways to

Achievement in Cohort Perspective." *Sociology of Education* 70:54–67.

Shanas, E., P. Townsend, D. Wedderburn, H. Friis, P. Milhoj, and J. Stenhouwer. 1968. *Old People in Three Industrial Societies.* London: Routledge and Kegan Paul.

Shapiro, D., and S. Sandell. 1985. "Age Discrimination in Wages and Displaced Older Men." *Southern Economic Journal* 52:90–102.

Shaver, Sheila. 1991. "Considerations of Mere Logic: The Australian Age Pension and the Politics of Means-Testing." Pp. 105–26 in *States, Labor Markets and the Future of Old Age Policy,* edited by J. Myles and J. Quadagno. Philadelphia: Temple University Press.

Shaw, Lois. 1996. "Special Problems of Older Women Workers." Pp. 327–50 in *Aging for the Twenty-First Century,* edited by J. Quadagno and D. Street. New York: St. Martin's Press.

Shea, Dennis, Toni Miles, and Mark Hayward. 1996. "The Health-Wealth Connection: Racial Differences." *The Gerontologist* 36:342–49.

Sheehy, Gail. 1995. *New Passages: Mapping Your Life across Time.* New York: Random House.

Shorter, Edward. 1975. *The Making of the Modern Family.* New York: Basic Books.

Shoupe, D. 1999. "Hormone Replacement Therapy: Reassessing the Risks and Benefits." *Hospital Practice* 34(8):97–103.

Shuldiner, David P. 1995. *Aging Political Activists: Personal Narratives from the Old Left.* Westport, CT: Praeger.

Shumaker S. A., C. Legault, S. R. Rapp, L. Thal, R. B. Wallace, J. K. Ockene, S. L. Hendrix, B. N. Jones, A. R. Assaf, R. D. Jackson, J. M. Kotchen, S. Wassertheil-Smoller, and J. Wactawski-Wende. 2003. "Estrogen Plus Progestin and the Incidence of Dementia and Mild Cognitive Impairment in Postmenopausal Women—The Women's Health Initiative Memory Study: A Randomized Controlled Trial." *Journal of the American Medical Association* 289(20):2651–62.

Siebold, Cathy. 1992. *The Hospice Movement: Easing Death's Pains.* New York: Twayne.

Siegel, Jacob S. 1993. *A Generation of Change: A Profile of America's Older Population.* New York: Russell Sage Foundation.

Sikorska, Elzbieta. 1999. "Organizational Determinants of Resident Satisfaction with Assisted Living." *The Gerontologist* 39(4):450–56.

Sit, R. A., and A. D. Fisk. 1999. "Age-Related Performance in a Multiple Task Environment." *Human Factors* 41(1):26–34.

Silver, J. J., and T. A. Einhorn. 1995. "Osteoporosis and Aging: Current Update." *Clinical Orthopedics* 316:10–20.

Silverstein, Merril. 1995. "Stability and Change in Temporal Distance between the Elderly and Their Children." *Demography* 32:29–45.

Silverstein, Merril, Joseph J. Angelelli, and Tonya Parrott. 2001. "Changing Attitudes toward Aging Policy in the United States during the 1980s and 1990s: A Cohort Analysis." *Journal of Gerontology* 56B(1):S36–43.

Silverstein, Merril, and Vern Bengtson. 1991. "Do Close Parent-Child Relations Reduce the Mortality Risk of Older Parents?" *Journal of Health and Social Behavior* 32:382–95.

———. 1997. "Intergenerational Solidarity and the Structure of Adult Child-Parent Relationships in American Families." *American Journal of Sociology* 103:429–60.

Silverstein, Merril, and E. Litwak. 1993. "A Task-Specific Typology of Intergenerational Family Structure in Later Life." *The Gerontologist* 33:258–64.

Simmons, Leo. 1945. *The Role of the Aged in Primitive Society.* New Haven, CT: Yale University Press.

Simoneau, G., and H. Leibowitz. 1996. "Posture, Gait and Falls." Pp. 204–17 in *Handbook of the Psychology of Aging,* edited by J. Birren and K. W. Schaie. New York: Academic Press.

Simonton, D. 1990. "Creativity and Wisdom in Aging." Pp. 320–29 in *Handbook of the Psychology of Aging,* edited by J. Birren and K. W. Schaie. New York: Academic Press.

Sinnott, Jan Dynda. 1984. "Older Men, Older Women: Are Their Perceived Sex Roles Similar?" *Sex Roles* 10:847–56.

Skinner, John. 1997. "Should Age Be Abandoned as a Basis for Program and Service Eligibility?" Pp. 58–62 in *Controversial Issues in Aging,* edited by A. Scharlach and L. Skinner. Boston: Allyn and Bacon.

Skocpol, Theda. 1990. "Sustainable Social Policy: Fighting Poverty without Poverty Programs." *American Prospect* (Summer):61–70.

———. 1995. "Why It Happened: The Rise and Resounding Demise of the Clinton Health Security Plan." Presented at the Brookings Institution conference on "The Past and Future of Health Reform," January 24, Washington, DC.

Skodol, A., and R. Spitzer. 1983. "Depression in the Elderly: Clinical Criteria." Pp. 242–51 in *Depression and Aging,* edited by L. Breslau and M. Haug. New York: Springer.

Skolnick, Arlene. 1991. *Embattled Paradise.* New York: Basic Books.

Slessarev, Helen. 1988. "Racial Tensions and Institutional Support: Social Programs during a Period of Retrenchment." Pp. 357–80 in *The Politics of Social Policy in the United States,* edited by M. Weir, A. Orloff, and T. Skocpol. Princeton, NJ: Princeton University Press.

Sloan, Frank, May Shayne, and Christopher Conover. 1995. "Continuing Care Retirement Communities: Prospects for Reducing Institutional Long Term Care." *Journal of Health Politics, Policy and Law* 20(1):75–96.

Smeeding, Timothy. 1990. "Economic Status of the Elderly." In *Handbook of Aging and the Social Sciences,* edited by R. Binstock and L. George. New York: Academic Press.

Smeeding, Timothy, Barbara Torrey, and Lee Rainwater. 1993. "Going to Extremes: An International Perspective on the Economic Status of the U.S. Aged." Working Paper No. 87, Luxembourg Income Study. Syracuse, NY.

Smelser, Neil. 1988. "Social Structure." Pp. 103–30 in *Handbook of Sociology*, edited by N. Smelser. Newbury Park, CA: Sage.

Smith, A. 1996. "Memory." Pp. 236–50 in *Handbook of the Psychology of Aging*, edited by J. Birren and K. W. Schaie. New York: Academic Press.

Smith, Adam. [1776] 1937. *An Inquiry into the Nature and Causes of the Wealth of Nations.* Reprint. New York: Modern Library.

Smith, Gregory, Mary F. Smith, and Ronald Toseland. 1992. "Problems Identified by Family Caregivers in Counseling." *The Gerontologist* 31:15–22.

Smith, James. 1997. "The Changing Economic Circumstances of the Elderly: Income, Wealth and Social Security." Policy Brief, Center for Policy Research. No. 8/1997. Syracuse, NY: Maxwell School of Citizenship and Public Affairs.

Smith, James P. 1997. "Wealth Inequality among Older Americans." *Journal of Gerontology* 52B:74–81.

Smith, J., and P. Baltes. 1990. "Wisdom-Related Knowledge: Age/Cohort Differences in Response to Life-Planning Problems." *Developmental Psychology* 26:494–505.

Smith, L. 1992. "The Tyranny of America's Old." *Fortune*, January 13, pp. 68–72.

Smyer, M. A., S. Zarit, and S. H. Qualls. 1990. "Psychological Intervention with the Aging Individual." Pp. 150–59 in *Handbook of the Psychology of Aging*, edited by J. Birren and K. W. Schaie. San Diego, CA: Academic Press.

Snyder, Donald. 1993. "The Economic Well-Being of Retired Workers by Race and Hispanic Origin." Pp. 67–78 in *Pensions in a Changing Economy*, edited by R. Burkhauser and D. Salisbury. Washington, DC: Employee Benefit Research Institute.

Social Security Administration. 1995a. *Research and Statistics: Fast Facts and Figures about Social Security.* Washington, DC: U.S. Government Printing Office.

——. 1995b. *Basic Facts about Social Security.* Washington, DC: U.S. Government Printing Office.

——. 1995c. *Social Security Programs throughout the World. 1995.* Washington, DC: U.S. Government Printing Office.

——. 1998. *Income of the Population 55 or Older.* Washington, DC: U.S. Government Printing Office.

——. 1999. "Annual Statistical Supplement." *Social Security Bulletin.* Washington, DC: U.S. Government Printing Office.

——. 2000a. *Income of the Aged Chartbook.* Washington, DC: U.S. Government Printing Office.

——. 2000b. *Income of the Population 55 or Older.* Washington, DC: U.S. Government Printing Office.

Social Security Administration. 2001. *Income of the Population 55 or Older.* Washington, DC: Government Printing Office.

Social Security Administration. 2003. *Income of the Aged Chartbook, 2001.* Washington, DC: Social Security Administration.

Social Security Advisory Board. 2001. Agenda for Social Security:Challenges for the New Congress and the New Administration. Washington, DC: Social Security Advisory Board.

Social Security Advisory Board. 2001. *Social Security: Why Action Should Be Taken Soon.* Washington, DC: Social Security Advisory Board.

Soldo, Beth, Michael Hurd, Willard Rodgers, and Robert Wallace. 1997. "Asset and Health Dynamics among the Oldest Old: An Overview of the AHEAD Study." *Journal of Gerontology* 52B(May):1–20.

Solomon, David H. 1999. "The Role of Aging Processes in Aging-Dependent Diseases." Pp. 133–50 in *Handbook of Theories of Aging*, edited by Vern Bengtson and K. W. Schaie. New York: Springer.

Solomon, Paul, Marisa Brett, Mary Ellen Groccia-Ellison, Catherine Oyler, Marie Tomasi, and William Pendlebury. 1995. "Classical Conditioning in Patients with Alzheimer's Disease: A Multiday Study." *Psychology and Aging* 10:248–54.

Solomon, Paul, Elizabeth Levine, Thomas Bein, and William Pendlebury. 1991. "Disruption of Classical Conditioning in Patients with Alzheimer's Disease." *Neurobiology of Aging* 12:283–87.

Sorokin, P. 1941. *Social and Cultural Dynamics.* New York: American Books.

Spence, Alexander. 1995. *Biology of Human Aging.* Englewood Cliffs, NJ: Prentice Hall.

Spitze, Glenna, and John Logan. 1990a. "More Evidence on Women (and Men) in the Middle." *Research on Aging* 12:182–98.

——. 1990b. "Sons, Daughters and Intergenerational Support." *Journal of Marriage and the Family* 52:420–30.

——. 1992. "Helping as a Component of Parent-Adult Child Relations." *Research on Aging* 14:291–312.

Sprague, Joey, and David Quadagno. 1989. "Gender and Sexual Motivation: An Exploration of Two Assumptions." *Journal of Psychology and Human Sexuality* 2:57–76.

Stanfield, Rochelle. 2000. *Social Security: Out of Step with the Modern Family.* Washington, DC: Urban Institute.

Stanley, Harold, and Richard Niemi. 1994. *Vital Statistics on American Politics.* Washington, DC: CQ Press.

Stannard, Charles. 1973. "Old Folks and Dirty Work: The Social Conditions for Patient Abuse in a Nursing Home." *Social Problems* 20:329–42.

Stearns, Harvey, and Anthony Stearns. 1995. "Health and Employment Capability of Older Americans." Pp. 10–34 in *Older and Active: How Americans over 55 Are Contributing to Society,* edited by S. A. Bass. New Haven, CT: Yale University Press.

Stearns, Peter. 1977. *Old Age in European Society.* London: Croon Helm.

Steckenrider, Janie, and Tonya Parrott. 1998. *New Directions in Old Age Policies.* Albany, NY: State University of New York Press.

Steinback, Ulrike. 1992. "Social Networks, Institutionalization and Mortality among Elderly People in the United States." *Journal of Gerontology* 47:S183–90.

Stephens, Mary Ann Parris, and Melissa Franks. 1995. "Spillover between Daughters' Roles as Caregiver and Wife: Interference or Enhancement?" *Journal of Gerontology* 50:B9–17.

Stephens, Mary Ann Parris, Paula Ogrocki, and Jennifer Kinney. 1991. "Sources of Stress for Family Caregivers of Institutionalized Dementia Patients." *Journal of Applied Gerontology* 10:328–42.

Sternberg, 1990. "Wisdom and Its Relations to Intelligence and Creativity." Pp. 142–59 in *Wisdom,* edited by R. Sternberg. Cambridge: Cambridge University Press.

Sterns, Harvey, and Anthony Sterns. 1995. "Health and the Employment Capability of Older Americans." Pp. 10–34 in *Older and Active: How Americans over 55 Are Contributing to Society,* edited by S. Bass. New Haven, CT: Yale University Press.

Steuerle, C. Eugene. 1997. "Social Security in the Twenty-First Century: The Need for Change." Pp. 241–58 in *Social Security in the 21st Century,* edited by E. Kingson and J. Schulz. New York: Oxford University Press.

Steuerle, C. E., and J. Bakija. 1994. *Retooling Social Security for the 21st Century: Right and Wrong Approaches to Reform.* Washington, DC: Urban Institute Press.

Steuerle, Eugene, and Christopher Spiro. 1999. "Divorce and Social Security: A Rocky Marriage." *The Retirement Project.* No. 14. Washington, DC: Urban Institute.

Stewart, Anita, Abby King, and William Haskell. 1993. "Endurance Exercise and Health-Related Quality of Life in 50–65-Year-Old Adults." *The Gerontologist* 33:782–89.

Stoller, Eleanor Palo. 1994. "Why Women Care: Gender and the Organization of Lay Care." Pp. 187–93 in *Worlds of Difference: Inequality in the Aging Experience,* edited by E. Stoller and R. Gibson. Thousand Oaks, CA: Pine Forge Press.

Stoller, Eleanor Palo, and Rose Gibson. 1997. *Worlds of Difference.* Thousand Oaks, CA: Pine Forge Press.

Stoller, Eleanor Palo, and Karen Pugliesi. 1989. "Other Roles of Caregivers: Competing Responsibilities or Supportive Resources?" *Journal of Gerontology* 44:S231–38.

Stone, Deborah. 1997. "The Doctor as Businessman: Changing Politics of a Cultural Icon." *Journal of Health Politics, Policy and Law* 22:78–93.

Stone, Robyn. 2000. *Long Term Care for the Elderly with Disabilities.* New York: Milbank Memorial Fund.

Stone, Robyn, Gail Lee Cafferata, and Judith Sangl. 1987. "Caregivers of the Frail Elderly: A National Profile." *The Gerontologist* 27:616–26.

Stone, Robyn, and Peter Kemper. 1990. "Spouses and Children of Disabled Elders? How Large a Constituency for Long-Term Care Reform?" *Milbank Memorial Fund Quarterly* 67:485–506.

Stone, Robyn, with Joshua Wiener. 2001. *Who Will Care for Us? Addressing the Long-Term Care Workforce Crisis.* Washington, DC: Urban Institute/American Association of Homes and Services for the Aged.

Straits, Bruce. 1990. "The Social Context of Voter Turnout." *Public Opinion Quarterly* 54:64–73.

Strawbridge, William, and Margaret Wallhagen. 1991. "Impact of Family Conflict on Adult Child Caregivers." *The Gerontologist* 31:770–77.

Strawbridge, William, Margaret Wallhagen, and Richard Cohen. 2002. "Successful Aging and Well-Being: Self-Rated Compared with Rowe and Kahn." *The Gerontologist* 42(6):727–33.

Strawbridge, William, Margaret Walhagen, Sarah Shema, and George Kaplan. 2000. "Negative Consequences of Hearing Impairment in Old Age: A Longitudinal Analysis." *The Gerontologist* 40(3):320–26.

Street, Debra. 1993. "Maintaining the Status Quo: The Impact of Old Age Interest Groups on the Medicare Catastrophic Coverage Act of 1988." *Social Problems* 40:431–44.

——. 1996. *The Politics of Pensions.* Unpublished doctoral dissertation, Department of Sociology, Florida State University, Tallahassee, FL.

Street, Debra, Jill Quadagno, Lori Parham, and Steve McDonald. 2003. "Reinventing Long-Term Care: The Effect of Policy Changes on Trends in Nursing Home Reimbursement and Resident Characteristics: Florida, 1989–1997." *The Gerontologist* 43(II):66–79.

Streib, Gordon, and C. F. Bourg. 1984. "Age Stratification Theory, Inequality, and Social Change." Pp. 104–19 in *Comparative Social Research,* edited by R. F. Thompson. Greenwich, CT: JAI Press.

Streib, Gordon, and C. J. Schneider. 1971. *Retirement in American Society.* Ithaca, NY: Cornell University Press.

Struyk, R. J., and H. Katsura. 1987. "Aging at Home: How the Elderly Adjust Their Housing without Moving." *Journal of Housing for the Elderly* 4:1–19.

Stump, Timothy, Daniel Clark, Robert Johnson, and Fredric Wolinsky. 1997. "The Structure of Health Status among Hispanic, African American, and White Older Adults." *Journal of Gerontology* 52B(May):49–60.

Sugisawa, Hidehiro, Jersey Liang, and Xian Liu. 1994. "Social Networks, Social Support and Mortality among Older People in Japan." *Journal of Gerontology* 49:S3–13.

Suitor, J. Jill, and Karl Pillemer. 1988. "Explaining Intergenerational Conflict: When Adult Children and Elderly Parents Live Together." *Journal of Marriage and the Family* 50:1037–47.

——. 1993. "Support and Interpersonal Stress in the Social Networks of Married Daughters Caring for Parents with Dementia." *Journal of Gerontology* 48:S1–8.

Suitor, J. Jill, Karl Pillemer, Shirley Keeton, and Julie Robison. 1995. "Aged Parents and Aging Children: Determinants of Relationship Quality." Pp. 223–42 in *Handbook of Aging and the Family,* edited by R. Blieszner and V. Hilkevitch Bedford. Westport, CT: Greenwood Press.

Sum, Andrew, and W. Neil Fogg. 1990a. "Labor Market and Poverty Problems of Older Workers and Their Families." Pp. 64–91 in *Bridges to Retirement: Older Workers in a Changing Labor Market,* edited by P. Doeringer. Ithaca, NY: ILR Press.

——. 1990b. "Profile of the Labor Market for Older Workers." Pp. 33–63 in *Bridges to Retirement: Older Workers in a Changing Labor Market,* edited by P. Doeringer. Ithaca, NY: ILR Press.

Suzman, Richard, David Willis, and Kenneth Manton. 1992. *The Oldest Old.* New York: Oxford University Press.

Sweet, J., and L. Bumpass. 1987. *American Families and Households.* New York: Russell Sage Foundation.

Swenson, C., R. Esker, and K. Kohlkepp. 1984. "Five Factors in Long-Term Marriages." *Lifestyles* 7:94–106.

Sylvester, David, and Richard Schiff. 1994. *William de Kooning Paintings.* New Haven, CT: Yale University Press.

Szinovacz, Maximiliane. 1989. "Decision-Making on Retirement Timing." Pp. 286–310 in *Dyadic Decision-Making,* edited by D. Brinberg and J. Jaccard. New York: Springer-Verlag.

——. 1998. "Grandparents Today: A Demographic Profile." *The Gerontologist* 38:37–52.

Szinovacz, Maximiliane, and Stanley DeViney. 1999. "The Retiree Identity: Gender and Race Differences." *Journal of Gerontology* 54B(4):S207–18.

Szinovacz, Maximiliane, Stanley DeViney, and Maxine Atkinson. 1999. "Effects of Surrogate Parenting on Grandparents' Well-Being." *Journal of Gerontology* 54B(6):S376–89.

Szinovacz, Maximiliane, and David Ekerdt. 1995. "Families and Retirement." Pp. 375–400 in *Handbook of Aging and the Family,* edited by R. Bleiesner and V. Hilkevitch Bedford. Westport, CT: Greenwood Press.

Szinovacz, Maximiliane, David Ekerdt, and Barbara Vinick. 1992. *Families and Retirement.* Newbury Park, CA: Sage.

Szinovacz, Maximiliane, and Christine Washo. 1992. "Gender Differences in Exposure to Life Events and Adaptation to Retirement." *Journal of Gerontology* 47:191–96.

Taueber, C., and J. Allen. 1990. "Women in our Aging Society: The Demographic Outlook." Pp. 11–46 in *Women on the Front Lines,* edited by J. Allen and A. Pifer. Washington, DC: Urban Institute.

Taylor, Robert Joseph, Verna Keith, and M. Belinda Tucker. 1993. "Gender, Marital, Familial and Friendship Roles." Pp. 49–68 in *Black Families in America,* edited by J. Jackson, L. Chatters, and R. J. Tayler. Newbury Park, CA: Sage.

Terkel, Studs. 1995. *Coming of Age: The Story of Our Century by Those Who've Lived It.* New York: New Press.

Thienhaus, Ole. 1988. "Practical Overview of Sexual Function and Advancing Age." *Geriatrics* 43:63–67.

Thomas, Jeanne. 1986. "Gender Differences in Satisfaction with Grandparenting." *Psychology and Aging* 1:215–19.

Thomas, Keith. 1976. "Age and Authority in Early Modern England." *Proceedings of the British Academy* 62:205–48.

Thomas, L. Eugene, Matvey Sokolovsky, and Richard Feinberg. 1996. "Ideology, Narrative, and Identity: The Case of Elderly Jewish Immigrants from the Former USSR." *Journal of Aging and Identity* 1:51–72.

Thomas, S., and S. Quinn. 1991. "The Tuskegee Syphilis Study, 1932–1972: Implications for HIV Education and AIDS Risk Education Programs in the Black Community." *American Journal of Public Health* 81(11):163–79.

Thomma, Steven. 1996. "Piece of Cake? Dole's Birthday Hard to Swallow." *Tallahassee Democrat,* June 23, 1996, p. 1A.

Thompson, L., and A. J. Walker. 1987. "Mothers as Mediators of Intimacy between Grandmothers and Their Young Adult Grandchildren." *Family Relations* 36:72–77.

Thompson, Ross, Barbara Tinsley, Mario Scalora, and Ross Parke. 1989. "Grandparents' Visitation Rights: Legalizing the Ties That Bind." *American Psychologist* 44:1217–22.

Thompson, Wayne. 1958. "Pre-Retirement Anticipation and Adjustment in Retirement." *Journal of Social Issues* 14:35–45.

Thomson, David. 1996. *Selfish Generations? How Welfare States Grow Old.* Wellington, New Zealand: White Horse Press.

Thurow, Lester. 1999. "Generational Equity and the Birth of a Revolutionary Class." Pp. 58–74 in *The Generational Equity Debate,* edited by B. Williamson, D. M. Watts-Roy, and E. R. Kingson. New York: Columbia University Press.

Tichenor, John. 1995. *New Federalism and Social Policy: A Case Study of Board and Care Home Regulations.* Unpublished doctoral dissertation, Department of Sociology. Florida State University, Tallahassee, FL.

Tigges, Leann, and Deborah Tootle. 1993. "Underemployment and Racial Competition in Local Labor Markets." *Sociological Quarterly* 34:279–98.

Tilly, Louise, and Joan Scott. 1978. *Women, Work and Family.* New York: Holt, Reinhart and Winston.

Tomasko, R. M. 1987. *Reshaping the Corporation for the Future.* New York: Amacom.

Topp, Robert, Alan Mikesky, Janet Wigglesworth, Worthe Holt, Jr., and Jeffrey Edwards. 1993. "The Effect of a 12-Week Dynamic Resistance Strength Training Program on Gait Velocity and Balance of Older Adults." *The Gerontologist* 33:501–6.

Torres-Gil, Fernando. 1992. *The New Aging: Politics and Change in America.* New York: Auburn House.

Torres-Gil, Fernando, and J. C. Hyde. 1990. "The Impact of Minorities on Long-Term Care Policy in California." Pp. 31–52 in *California Policy Choices for Long-Term Care,* edited by P. Liebig and W. Lammers. Los Angeles: University of Southern California Press.

Townsend, Aloen, and Linda Noelker. 1987. "The Impact of Family Relationships on Perceived Caregiver Effectiveness." Pp. 80–99 in *Aging, Health and Family: Long-Term Care,* edited by T. Brubaker. Beverly Hills, CA: Sage.

Townsend, Bickley. 2001. "Phased Retirement: From Promise to Practice." Issue Brief, Vol. 2, Issue 2. Ithaca, NY: Cornell Employment and Family Careers Institute.

Treas, Judith. 1995a. "Older Americans in the 1990s and Beyond." *Population Bulletin* 50:1–47.

———. 1995b. "Older Immigrants and Supplemental Security Income." Unpublished manuscript, Department of Sociology, University of California, Irvine, CA.

Trien, Susan Flamholtz. 1986. *The Menopause Handbook.* New York: Ballantine Books.

Turner, Barbara, and Castellano Turner. 1991. "Through a Glass Darkly: Gender Stereotypes for Men and Women Varying in Age and Race." Pp. 137–50 in *Growing Old in America,* edited by Beth B. Hess and Elizabeth W. Markson. New Brunswick, NJ: Transaction Publishers.

Tuttle, William M., Jr. 1993. *Daddy's Gone to War: The Second World War in the Lives of American Children.* New York: Oxford University Press.

Twentieth Century Fund. 1996. *Social Security Reform: A Twentieth Century Fund Guide to the Issues.* New York: Twentieth Century Fund.

Uchino, B., J. Cacioppo, and J. Kiecolt-Glaser. 1996. "The Relationship between Social Support and Physiological Processes." *American Journal of Public Health* 83:1443–50.

Uhlenberg, Peter. 1993. "Demographic Change and Kin Relationships in Later Life." *Annual Review of Gerontology and Geriatrics* 13:219–38.

———. 1996a. "The Burden of Aging: A Theoretical Framework for Understanding the Shifting Balance of Caregiving and Care Receiving as Cohorts Age." *The Gerontologist* 36:761–67.

———. 1996b. "Mortality Decline in the Twentieth Century and Supply of Kin over the Life Course." *The Gerontologist* 36:681–85.

———. 1996c. "Mutual Attraction: Demography and Life-Course Analysis." *The Gerontologist* 36:226–29.

———. 1997. "Replacing the Nursing Home." *The Public Interest* 182:73–80.

———. 2000. "Introduction: Why Study Age Integration?" *The Gerontologist* 40(3):261–66.

Uhlenberg, Peter, and Sonia Miner. 1996. "Life Course and Aging: A Cohort Perspective." Pp. 208–28 in *Handbook of Aging and the Social Sciences,* edited by R. Binstock and L. George. San Diego, CA: Academic Press.

Uhlenberg, Peter, and Matilda White Riley. 1995. "Cohort Studies. Age Stratification and Cohort Studies: As Components of the Aging and Society Paradigm." Presented at Program on Age and Structural Change, National Institute on Aging, Washington, DC.

Ulfarsson, J., and B. E. Robinson. 1994. "Preventing Falls and Fractures." *Journal of the Florida Medical Association* 81:763–67.

Umberson, Debra. 1987. "Family Status and Health Behaviors: Social Control as a Dimension of Social Integration." *Journal of Health and Social Behavior* 28:306–19.

———. 1992. "Relationships between Adult Children and Their Parents: Psychological Consequences for Both Generations." *Journal of Marriage and the Family* 54:664–74.

Umberson, Debra, and Meichu D. Chen. 1994. "Effects of a Parent's Death on Adult Children: Relationship Salience and Reaction to Loss." *American Sociological Review* 59:152–68.

Ungerson, Clare. 2000. "Cash in Care." Pp. 68–88 in *Care Work,* edited by Madonna Harrington Meyer. New York: Routledge.

U.S. Bureau of the Census. 1975. *Historical Statistics of the United States: Colonial Times to 1970.* Washington, DC: U.S. Government Printing Office.

———. 1980. *Census of Population, Subject Reports, Characteristics of American Indians by Tribes and Selected Areas.* Vol. 2. Washington, DC: U.S. Government Printing Office.

———. 1988. *Aging in the Third World.* Washington, DC: U.S. Government Printing Office.

———. 1989. *Census of Population, Subject Reports, Characteristics of Indians by Tribes and Selected Areas.* Vol. 2, Secs. 1 and 2. Washington, DC: U.S. Government Printing Office.

———. 1990a. *Statistical Abstract of the United States.* Washington, DC: U.S. Government Printing Office.

———. 1990b. *1990 Census of Population.* Washington, DC: U.S. Government Printing Office.

———. 1991. *Statistical Abstract of the United States* Washington, DC: U.S. Government Printing Office.

———. 1992. *Current Population Survey.* Washington, DC: U.S. Government Printing Office.

——. 1993a. "Poverty in the United States: 1992." *Current Population Reports.* Washington, DC: U.S. Government Printing Office.

——. 1993b. "Money Income of Households, Families and Persons in the United States: 1992." *Current Population Reports.* Washington, DC: U.S. Government Printing Office.

——. 1993c. *Historical Statistics of the United States.* Washington, DC: U.S. Government Printing Office.

——. 1993d. *Asset Ownership of Households.* Washington, DC: U.S. Government Printing Office.

——. 1994a. "School Enrollment, Social and Economic Characteristics of Students: October 1993." *Current Population Reports.* Washington, DC: U.S. Government Printing Office.

——. 1994b. *Current Population Survey.* Washington, DC: U.S. Government Printing Office.

——. 1995a. *Current Population Survey.* Washington DC: U.S. Government Printing Office.

——. 1995b. *Employment, Hours and Earnings.* Washington, DC: U.S. Government Printing Office.

——. 1996a. *Statistical Abstracts of the United States.* Washington, DC: U.S. Government Printing Office.

——. 1996b. *Persons and Families in Poverty by Selected Characteristics, 1995 and 1996.* Washington, DC: U.S. Government Printing Office.

——. 1997a. *Current Population Survey.* Washington, DC: U.S. Government Printing Office.

——. 1997b. *Statistical Abstract of the United States, 1997.* Washington, DC: Government Printing Office.

——. 1998a. "International Data Base." Population Division, International Programs Center. Washington, DC: U.S. Government Printing Office.

——. 1998b. *Current Population Reports.* P20–513. Washington, DC: U.S. Government Printing Office.

——. 1998c. *Money Income in the U.S. Current Population Reports: Consumer Income.* Washington, DC: U.S. Government Printing Office.

——. 1999a. *Annual Demographic Survey.* Washington, DC: U.S. Government Printing Office.

——. 1999b. *Statistical Abstract of the United States: 1999.* Washington, DC: U.S. Government Printing Office.

——. 2000. *Current Population Reports.* Washington, DC: U.S. Government Printing Office.

——. 2002a. *Living Arrangements.* Washington, DC: U.S. Government Printing Office.

——. 2002b. *Current Population Survey.* Washington, DC: U.S. Government Printing Office.

——. 2002c. *Money Income in the United States: 2001.* Washington, DC: U.S. Government Printing Office.

——. 2003. *Homeownership Trends.* Washington, DC: U.S. Government Printing Office.

——. 2003. *Income in the United States: 2002.* Washington, DC: U.S. Government Printing Office.

U.S. Bureau of Labor Statistics. 1995. *Employment, Hours and Earnings.* Washington, DC: U.S. Government Printing Office.

——. 1996. *Employment, Hours and Earnings.* Washington, DC: U.S. Government Printing Office.

——. 2000. *Employment, Hours and Earnings.* Washington, DC: U.S. Government Printing Office.

——. 2003. *Employment, Hours and Earnings.* Washington, DC: U.S. Government Printing Office.

U.S. Department of Commerce. 1991. *Poverty in the United States: 1991.* Washington, DC: U.S. Government Printing Office.

U.S. Department of Housing and Urban Development. 1999. *Housing Our Elders.* Washington, DC: U.S. Department of Housing and Urban Development.

U.S. Department of Labor. 1991. *Working Women: A Chartbook.* Bulletin No.2385. Washington, DC.

U.S. House of Representatives, Subcommittee on Health and Long-Term Care. 1989a. *Board and Care Homes in America: A National Tragedy.* Washington, DC: U.S. Government Printing Office.

——. 1989b. *Private Long-Term Care Insurance: Unfit for Sale?* A Report by the Chairman of the Subcommittee on Health and Long-Term Care of the Select Committee on Aging, 101st Congress, 1st Sess., May 1989. Washington, DC: U.S. Government Printing Office.

——. 1991. *Abuses in the Sale of Health Insurance to the Elderly in Supplementation of Medicare.* Select Committee on Aging. Washington, DC: U.S. Government Printing Office.

——. 1992. *How Well Do Women Fare under the Nation's Retirement Policies?* Subcommittee on Retirement Income. Washington, DC: U.S. Government Printing Office.

——. 1993. *Long-Term Care Insurance: High Percentage of Policyholders Drop Policies.* Subcommittee on Regulation, Business Opportunities and Technology. Washington, DC: U.S. Government Printing Office.

——. 1994. *Green Book: Overview of Entitlement Programs.* Committee on Ways and Means. Washington, DC: U.S. Government Printing Office.

——. 1995. *Board and Care Homes in America: A National Tragedy.* Subcommittee on Health and Long-Term Care. Washington, DC: U.S. Government Printing Office.

U.S. Senate. 1995. *Long-Term Care: Current Issues and Future Directions.* Report to the Chairman, U.S. Senate Special Committee on Aging. Washington, DC: General Accounting Office.

Useem, Michael. 1993. "The Impact of American Business Restructuring on Older Workers." *Perspective on Aging* (October–December):12–14.

Utz, Rebecca, Deborah Carr, Randolph Ness, and Camille Wortman. 2002. "The Effect of Widowhood on Older Adults' Social Participation." *The Gerontologist* 42:522–533.

Vaillant, George. 1977. *Adaptation to Life.* Boston: Little, Brown.

Valic. 1996. "View on Retirement Planning." *Viewpoints* (Winter):1–4.

Van den Hoonaard, Deborah Kestin. 1994. "Paradise Lost: Widowhood in a Florida Retirement Community." *Journal of Aging Studies* 8:121–32.

Van der Mass, P., L. Pijnenborg, and J. van Delden. 1995. "Changes in Dutch Opinions on Active Euthanasia, 1966 through 1991." *Journal of the American Medical Association* 273:1411–14.

Van Hook, Jennifer, and Frank Bean. 1999. "The Growth of Noncitizen SSI Caseloads 1979–1996: Aging versus New Immigrant Effects." *Journal of Gerontology* 54B(1):S16–23.

Van Kleunen, Andy, and Mary Ann Wilner. 2000. "Who Will Care for Mother Tomorrow?" *Journal of Aging and Social Policy* 11(2/3):12–16.

van Willigen, Marieke. 2000. "Differential Benefits of Volunteering across the Life Course." *Journal of Gerontology* 55B(5):S308–18.

Vasil, Latika, and Hannelore Wass. 1993. "Portrayal of the Elderly in the Media: A Literature Review and Implications for Educational Gerontologists." *Educational Gerontology* 19:71–85.

Velkoff, Victoria A., and Valerie A. Lawson. 1998. *International Brief: Caregiving.* U.S. Department of Commerce, Economic and Statistics Administration. Washington, DC: U.S. Bureau of the Census.

Ventrell-Monsees, C. 1991. "Enforce the Age Discrimination Laws." Pp. 193–95 in *Retirement and Public Policy,* edited by A. Munnell. Washington, DC: National Academy of Social Insurance.

Verbrugge, Lois M. 1989. "The Twain Meet: Empirical Explanations of Sex Differences in Health and Mortality." *Journal of Health and Social Behavior* 30:282–304.

———. 1990. "Pathways of Health and Death." Pp. 41–79 in *Women, Health and Medicine in America,* edited by R. D. Apple. New York: Garland.

———. 1994. "Disability in Late Life." Pp. 79–98 in *Aging and the Quality of Life,* edited by R. Abeles, H. Gift, and M. Ory. New York: Springer.

Verbrugge, Lois, and Alan M. Jette. 1994. "The Disablement Process." *Social Science and Medicine* 38:1–14.

Verwoerdt, A., E. Pfeiffer, and H. Wang. 1969a. "Sexual Behavior in Senescence: Changes in Sexual Activity and Interest of Aging Men and Women." *Journal of Geriatric Psychiatry* 2:163–80.

———. 1969b. "Sexual Behavior in Senescence II: Patterns of Sexual Activity and Interest." *Geriatrics* 24:137–54.

Vinton, Linda. 1992. "Services Planned in Abusive Elder Care Situations." *Journal of Elder Abuse and Neglect* 4(3):85–99.

Vladeck, Bruce C. 1995. "End of Life Care." *Journal of the American Medical Association* 274:449.

Von Sydow, Kirsten. 1995. "Unconventional Sexual Relationships: Data about German Women Ages 50 to 91." *Archives of Sexual Behavior* 24:271–90.

Walbroehl, Gordon. 1988. "Effects of Medical Problems on Sexuality in the Elderly." *Medical Aspects of Human Sexuality* (October):154–58.

Walker, Alan. 1996. *The New Generational Contract: Intergenerational Relations, Old Age and Welfare.* Taylor and Francis.

———. 1999. "Public Policy and Theories of Aging: Constructing and Reconstructing Old Age." Pp. 361–78 in *Handbook of Theories of Aging,* edited by Vern Bengtson and K. W. Schaie. New York: Springer.

Walker, Alan, and G. Naegele. 1999. *The Politics of Old Age in Europe.* Buckingham, U.K.: Open University Press.

Walker, Alexis, and Katherine Allen. 1991. "Relationships between Caregiving Daughters and Their Elderly Mothers." *The Gerontologist* 31:389–96.

Walker, Jack L., Jr. 1991. *Mobilizing Interest Groups in America.* Ann Arbor: University of Michigan Press.

Wallace, Meredith. 1992. "Management of Sexual Relationships among Elderly Residents of Long-Term Care Facilities." *Geriatric Nursing* (November/December):308–10.

Wallace, Steven, and Carroll Estes. 1989. "Health Policy for the Elderly." *Society* (September/October):66–75.

Walling, M., B. L. Andersen, and S. R. Johnson. 1990. "Hormonal Replacement Therapy for Postmenopausal Women: A Review of Sexual Outcomes and Related Gynecologic Effects." *Archives of Sexual Behavior* 19:119–27.

Walsh, P., and J. Worthington. 1995. *The Prostate.* Baltimore: Johns Hopkins University Press.

Walz, Thomas, and Nancy Blum. 1987. *Sexual Health in Later Life.* Lexington, MA: D. C. Heath.

Ware, Alan. 1985. *The Townsend Movement.* New York: Bookman Associates.

Ware, John, Martha Bayliss, William Rogers, Mark Kosinski, and Alvin Tarlov. 1996. "Differences in 4-Year Health Outcomes for Elderly and Poor, Chronically Ill Patients

Treated in HMO and Fee-for-Service Systems." *Journal of the American Medical Association* 276:1039–47.

Wasserman, Ira. 1989. "Age, Period, and Cohort Effects in Suicide Behavior in the United States and Canada in the 20th Century." *Journal of Aging Studies* 3:295–311.

Watkins, Susan Cotts, Jane Menken, and John Bongaarts. 1987. "Demographic Foundations of Family Change." *American Sociological Review* 52:346–58.

Wayne, Leslie. 1994. "Pension Shift Raises Concerns." *New York Times,* August 29, Pp. A1, D3.

Wax, J. 1975. "Sex and the Single Grandparent." *New York Times,* September 6, p. 3B.

Weaver, David. 1994. "The Work and Retirement Decisions of Older Women: A Literature Review." *Social Security Bulletin* 57:3–24.

Weaver, K. 1985. "Controlling Entitlements." Pp. 83–92 in *The New Direction in American Politics,* edited by J. Chubb and P. E. Peterson. Washington, DC: The Brookings Institution.

Webber, Thomas. 1978. *Deep Like the Rivers: Education in the Slave Quarter Communities.* New York: W. W. Norton.

Weber, Max. 1946. "Class, Status, Party." Chapter 7 in *From Max Weber,* edited and translated by H. Gerth and C. Wright Mills. New York: Oxford University Press.

Webster, Pamela, and A. Regula Herzog. 1995. "Effects of Parental Divorce and Memories of Family Problems on Relationships between Adult Children and Their Parents." *Journal of Gerontology* 50B:S24–34.

Weibel-Orlando, Joan. 1994. "Grandparenting Styles: Native American Perspectives." Pp. 195–97 in *Worlds of Difference: Inequality in the Aging Experience,* edited by E. Palo Stoller and R. Campbell Bigson. Thousand Oaks, CA: Pine Forge Press.

Weinberg, M., and C. Williams. 1974. *Male Homosexuals: Their Problems and Adaptations.* New York: Oxford University Press.

Wekesser, C. 1995. "Introduction." Pp. 12–14 in *Euthanasia: Opposing Viewpoints,* edited by C. Wekesser. San Diego, CA: Greenhaven Press.

Wenger, G. Clare. 1990. "Change and Adaptation: Informal Support Networks of Elderly People in Wales, 1979–1987." *Journal of Aging Studies* 4:375–90.

Wenger, N. K. 1999. "Postmenopausal Hormone Use for Cardioprotection: What We Know and What We Must Learn." *Current Opinions in Cardiology* 14(4):292–97.

West, H. L., and W. J. Levy. 1985. "Knowledge of Aging in the Medical Profession." *Gerontology and Geriatrics Education* 4:97–105.

Weston, K. 1991. *Families We Chose: Lesbian, Gays and Kinship.* New York: Columbia University Press.

Wheeler, Peter, and John Kearney. 1996. "Income Protection for the Aged in the 21st Century: A Framework to Help Inform the Debate." *Social Security Bulletin* 59(2):3–19.

Whitbeck, Les, Danny Hoyt, and Shirley Huck. 1993. "Family Relationship History, Contemporary Parent-Grandparent Relationship Quality, and the Grandparent-Grandchild Relationship." *Journal of Marriage and the Family* 55:1025–35.

——. 1994. "Early Family Relationships, Intergenerational Solidarity, and Support Provided to Parents by Their Adult Children." *Journal of Gerontology* 49:S85–94.

Whitlach, Carol, Steven Zarit, and Alexander von Eye. 1991. "Efficacy of Interventions with Caregivers." *The Gerontologist* 31:9–14.

Wiener, Joshua. 1996. "Can Medicaid Long-Term Care Expenditures for the Elderly Be Reduced?" *The Gerontologist* 36:800–11.

Wiener, Joshua M., and Raymond J. Hanley. 1992. "Caring for the Disabled Elderly: There's No Place Like Home." Pp. 75–109 in *Improving Health Policy and Management,* edited by S. M. Shortell and U. Reinhart. Ann Arbor, MI: Health Administration Press.

Wiener, Joshua, and Laurel Hixon Illston. 1994. "How to Share the Burden: Long-Term Care Reform in the 1990s." *The Brookings Review* 12:17–21.

——. 1996. "The Financing and Organization of Health Care for Older Americans." Pp. 427–45 in *Handbook of Aging and the Social Sciences,* edited by R. Binstock and L. George. San Diego, CA: Academic Press.

Wiener, Joshua, Jane Tilly, and Susan Goldenson. 2000. "Federal and State Initiatives to Jump Start the Market for Private Long-Term Care Insurance." *The Elder Law Journal* 8(1):57–102.

Wilber, Kathleen. 2000. "Future Shock: The Effects of Demographic Imperative for Jobs in Aging." www.asaging.org/am/cia2/jobs.html

Wilber, K. H., and Nielsen, E. 2002. "Elder Abuse: New Approaches to an Age-old Problem." *The Public Policy and Aging Report* 12(2):24–27.

Wilkinson, Margaret. 1993. "British Tax Policy 1979–90: Equity and Efficiency." *Policy and Politics* 21:207–17.

Williams, B. O. 2000. Ageism Helps to Ration Medical Treatment. *Health Bulletin* 58(3):198–202.

Williams, T. Franklin. 1994. "Rehabilitation in Old Age." Pp. 121–32 in *Aging and the Quality of Life,* edited by R. Abeles, H. Gift, and M. Ory. New York: Springer.

Williamson, John, and Fred Pampel. 1993. *Old Age Security in Comparative Perspective.* New York: Oxford University Press.

Williamson, John, and Sara Rix. 2000. "Social Security Reform: Implications for Women." *Journal of Aging and Social Policy* 11:41–53.

Willis, Sherry. 1996. "Everyday Problem Solving." Pp. 287–307 in *Handbook of the Psychology of Aging,* edited by J. Birren and K. W. Schaie. New York: Academic Press.

Willis, Sherry, and K. Warner Schaie. 1986. "Training the Elderly on the Ability Factors of Spatial Orientation and Inductive Reasoning." *Psychology and Aging* 1:239–47.

Wilmoth, Janet. 1998. "Living Arrangement Transitions among America's Older Adults." *The Gerontologist* 38(4):434–44.

Wilmoth, John, Axel Skytthe, Diana Friou, and Bernard Jeune. 1996. "The Oldest Man Ever? A Case Study of Exceptional Longevity." *The Gerontologist* 36:783–88.

Wilson, William Julius. 1978. *The Declining Significance of Race: Blacks and Changing American's Institutions.* Chicago: University of Chicago Press.

———. 1987. *The Truly Disadvantaged.* Chicago: University of Chicago Press.

———. 1996. *When Work Disappears: The World of the New Urban Poor.* New York: Alfred A. Knopf.

———. 1998. *The Bridge over the Racial Divide.* Berkeley, CA: University of California Press.

Wink, P., and R. Helson. 1993. "Personality Change in Women and Their Partners." *Journal of Personality and Social Psychology* 65:597–605.

Wolf, R. S. 1998. "Domestic Elder Abuse and Neglect." Pp. 161–65 in *Clinical Geropsychology,* edited by I. Nordhus and G. VandenBos. Washington, DC: American Psychological Association.

Wolfson, Christina, Richard Handfield-Jones, Kathleen Cranley Glass, Jacqueline McClaran, and Edward Keyserling. 1993. "Adult Children's Perceptions of Their Responsibility to Provide Care for Dependent Elderly Parents." *The Gerontologist* 33:308–14.

World Bank. 1994. *Averting the Old Age Crisis.* Washington, DC: The World Bank.

———. 2003a. *World Development Indicators Database: Afghanistan Data Profile.* Washington, DC: The World Bank.

———. 2003b. *World Development Indicators Database: African Development Indicators.* Washington, DC: The World Bank.

Wray, Linda. 1996. "The Role of Ethnicity in the Disability and Work Experience of Preretirement Age Americans." *The Gerontologist* 36:287–98.

Wright, Lore. 1991. "The Impact of Alzheimer's Disease on the Marital Relationship." *The Gerontologist* 31:224–37.

Wrigley, E. A. 1977. "Reflections on the History of the Family." *Daedalus* 106:71–85.

Wu, Zheng, and Michael S. Pollard. 1998. "Social Support among Unmarried Childless Elderly Persons." *Journal of Gerontology* 53B(6):S324–35.

Wu, Zheng Helen, and Laura Rudkin. 2000. "Social Contact, Socioeconomic Status, and the Health Status of Older Malaysians." *The Gerontologist* 40(2):228–34.

Yahnke, Robert. 1994. "Representations of Aging in Contemporary Literary Works." Pp. 155–61 in *Changing Perceptions of Aging and the Aged,* edited by D. Shenk and W. A. Achenbaum. New York: Springer.

———. 1999. "Aging, Intergeneration and Community: Waking Ned Devine and Tea with Mussolini." *The Gerontologist* 39(4):504–8.

Yang, Anand. 1989. "Whose Sati? Widow Burning in Early 19th Century India." *Journal of Women's History* 1:8–33.

Yee, Barbara. 1994. "Elders in Southeast Asian Families." Pp. 198–200 in *Worlds of Difference: Inequality in the Aging Experience,* edited by E. Palo Stoller and R. Campbell Gibson. Thousand Oaks, CA: Pine Forge Press.

Yee, Barbara, and Gayle Weaver. 1994. "Ethnic Minorities and Health Promotion: Developing a 'Culturally Competent' Agenda." *Generations* (Spring):39–44.

Yeo, Gwen. 1993. "Ethnicity and Nursing Homes: Factors Affecting Use and Successful Components for Culturally Sensitive Care." Pp. 161–77 in *Ethnic Elderly and Long-Term Care,* edited by Charles Barresi and Donald Stull. New York: Springer.

Young, Heather. 1998. "Moving to Congregate Housing: The Last Chosen Home." *Journal of Aging Studies* 12(2):149–65.

Zedlewski, Sheila, and Timothy D. McBride. 1992. "The Changing Profile of the Elderly: Effects on Future Long-Term Care Needs and Financing." *Milbank Memorial Fund Quarterly* 70:247–75.

Zehetmayr, Berta. 1996. "Surely Euthanasia Is OK . . . Sometimes? . . . Isn't It?" *Generations* 6(1):13–14.

Zernike, Kate. 2002. "Stocks Slide Is Playing Havoc with Older Americans' Dreams." *New York Times,* July 14:1, 16.

Zhou, Xueguang, and Liren Hou. 1999. "Children of the Cultural Revolution: The State and the Life Course in the People's Republic of China." *American Sociological Review* 64:12–36.

Zick, Cathleen, and Ken Smith. 1991. "Patterns of Economic Change Surrounding the Death of a Spouse." *Journal of Gerontology* 46:S310–20.

Acknowledgments

Chapter 2

p. 27 Reprinted from Joel S. Savishinsky, *Breaking the Watch: The Meanings of Retirement in America.* Copyright © 2000 by Joel S. Savishinsky. Used by permission of the publisher, Cornell University Press.

p. 29 Table 2–1 From Charles Longino and Cary Kart, "Explicating Activity Theory: A Formal Replication," *Journal of Gerontology* 17 (1982). Reprinted with the permission of the Gerontological Society of America via Copyright Clearance Center.

p. 36 Figure 2–1 From Donald Cowgill, "The Aging of Populations and Societies" from *Annals of the American Academy of Political and Social Science* 415, 29 (1974). Copyright © 1974 by The American Academy of Political and Social Science. Reprinted with the permission of Sage Publications, Inc.

p. 39 Figure 2–2 From Matilda White Riley, "Age Strata in Social Systems," in *Handbook of Aging and the Social Sciences,* edited by R. Binstock and E. Shanas. Reprinted with the permission of the author.

p. 40 Figure 2–3 From Matilda White Riley and John W. Riley, "Age Integration: Conceptual and Historical Background," *The Gerontologist* 40, 3 (2000). Reprinted with the permission of the Gerontological Society of America via Copyright Clearance Center.

Chapter 3

p. 56 Table 3–1 from Richard Settersten and Gunhild Hagestad, "What's the Latest? Cultural Age Deadlines for Family Transitions," *The Gerontologist* 36 (1996a, 1996b). Reprinted with the permission of the Gerontological Society of America via Copyright Clearance Center.

p. 57 From Hila Colman, "Just Desserts," *New York Times* Sunday Magazine, May 3, 1998, p. 84. Copyright © 1998 Hila Colman. Reprinted by permission from The New York Times.

p. 59 Table 3–2 From Sandra Boyd and Judith Treas, "Family Care of the Frail Elderly: A New Look at Women in the Middle," *Women's Studies Quarterly* 112 (1989).

Copyright © 1989 by Sandra L. Boyd and Judith Treas. Reprinted with the permission of The Feminist Press at the City University of New York.

Chapter 4

p. 74 From "The Centenarians: Joseph Goldstein," *U.S. News and World Report,* August 28/September 4, 1995, p. 96. Copyright © 1995 U.S. News and World Report, L. P. Reprinted with permission.

Chapter 5

p. 99 Reprinted by permission of the publisher from *The Narrative of the Life of Frederick Douglass: An American Slave, Written By Himself,* edited by Benjamin Quarles, 76–77, Cambridge, Mass.: The Belknap Press of Harvard University Press. Copyright © 1960, 1988 by the President and Fellows of Harvard College.

Chapter 6

p. 136 From Susan Flamholtz Trien, *The Menopause Handbook,* Ballantine Books, 1986, pp. 238–239. Reprinted with permission from the publisher via Copyright Clearance Center.

p. 137 Table 6–1 From National Osteoporosis Foundation (1996). Reprinted with the permission of the National Osteoporosis Foundation, Washington, DC 20037.

Chapter 7

p. 150 Figure 7–1 From K. W. Schaie, "The Course of Adult Intellectual Development," *American Psychologist* 49 (1994). Copyright © 1994 by the American Psychological Association. Reprinted with the permission of the author and the American Psychological Association.

p. 152 Figure 7–2 From Timothy Salthouse, "Theories of Cognition" in *Handbook of Theories of Aging,* edited by Vern Bengtson and K. Warner Schaie. Used by permission of Springer Publishing Company, New York 10012.

p. 156 Table 7–1 From K. Ritchie, D. Kildea, and J. M. Robine, "The Relationship between Age and the

Prevalence of Senile Dementia: A Meta-Analysis of Recent Data," *International Journal of Epidemiology* 21 (1992). Reprinted with the permission of Oxford University Press, Ltd.

p. 159 From Sue Miller, *The Story of My Father,* Alfred A. Knopf, 2003, pp. 10, 12–13, 121–123, 128–129. Reprinted with permission from Alfred A. Knopf, a division of Random House, Inc.

p. 160 Figure 7–3 From John Mirowsky and Catherine Ross, "Age and Depression ," *Journal of Health and Social Behavior* 33 (1992). Copyright © 1992 by the American Sociological Association. Reprinted with the permission of the authors and the American Sociological Association.

p. 163 Figure 7–4 from John Mirowsky, "Age and the Gender Gap in Depression," *Journal of Health and Social Behavior* 37 (1996). Copyright © 1996 by the American Sociological Association. Reprinted with the permission of the author and the American Sociological Association.

p. 166 Table 7–2 From D. Papalia and S. Olds, *Human Development.* Copyright © 1998 by McGraw-Hill, Inc. Reprinted with the permission of The McGraw-Hill Companies, Inc. Based on Erik H. Erikson, *Childhood and Society.* Copyright © 1950, 1963 by W. W. Norton & Company, Inc., renewed © 1978, 1991 by Erik H. Erikson. Reprinted with the permission of W. W. Norton & Company, Inc. and The Hogarth Press/The Random House Group, Ltd.

p. 167 Figure 7–5 From Daniel Levinson, *The Seasons of a Man's Life.* Copyright © 1996 by Daniel Levinson. Reprinted with the permission of Alfred A. Knopf, a division of Random House, Inc. and Sterling Lord Literistic, Inc.

p. 169 Table 7–3 From Terri Apter, *Secret Paths: Women in the New Midlife.* Copyright © 1995 by Terri Apter. Reprinted with the permission of W. W. Norton & Company, Inc. and the Jane Rotrosen Agency.

Chapter 8

p. 183 From Finnegan Alford-Cooper, *For Keeps: Marriages That Last a Lifetime,* M.E. Sharpe Press, 1998, pp. 160, 163. Reprinted with permission from the publisher.

p. 188 Table 8–2: From Glenna Spitze and John Logan, "More Evidence on Women (and Men) in the Middle," *Research on Aging* 12 (1992). Copyright ©

1992 by Sage Publications, Inc. Reprinted with the permission of Sage Publications, Inc.

p. 201 Table 8–3 From Colleen Johnson and Barbara Barer, *Life Beyond 85 Years.* Copyright © 1997. Used by permission of Springer Publishing Company, New York 10012.

Chapter 9

p. 222 From Heather Young, "Moving to Congregate Housing: The Last Chosen Home," *Journal of Aging Studies,* 12 (2): 149–165, p. 157. Reprinted with permission from Elsevier Science.

Chapter 10

p. 229 Figure 10–1 From Jacqueline Angel, "Challenges of Caring for Hispanic Elders," *Public Policy and Aging Report.* Reprinted with the permission of the National Academy on an Aging Society.

p. 231 Figure 10–2 From Cyril Chang and Shelley White-Means, "The Men Who Care: An Analysis of Male Primary Caregivers Who Care for Frail Elderly at Home," *Journal of Applied Gerontology* 10 (1991). Copyright © 1991 by The Southern Gerontological Society. Reprinted with the permission of Sage Publications, Inc.

p. 230 Table 10–2 From Martin Rein and Harold Salzman, "Social Integration, Participation and Exchange in Five Industrial Countries," *Older and Active,* edited by S. Bass. Copyright © 1995. Reprinted with the permission of Yale University Press.

p. 236 From John Bayley, *Elegy for Iris,* St. Martin's Press, 1999, pp. 237–238. Reprinted with permission.

Chapter 11

p. 265 From Caldwell Esselstyn, *Oral History,* Columbia University Press, 1965, pp. 3–4. Reprinted with permission.

p. 270 Figure 11–4 From Spencer Rich, "The Policy Dilemma," *National Journal* (March 2002). Copyright © 2002 by National Journal Group, Inc. All rights reserved. Reprinted by permission.

p. 271 Figure 11–5 From Organization for Economic Cooperation and Development (1998). Reprinted with the permission of the OECD.

Chapter 12

p. 285 Figure 12–1: From National Academy on an Aging Society (2000). Reprinted with the permission of the National Academy on an Aging Society.

p. 287 Table 12–1 From Chenoa Flippen and Marta Tienda, "Pathways to Retirement: Patterns of Labor Force Participation and Labor Market Exit among the Pre-Retirement Population by Race, Hispanic Origin, and Sex," *Journal of Gerontology* 55B, 1 (2000). Copyright © 2000 by the Gerontological Society of America. Reprinted with the permission of the Gerontological Society of America via Copyright Clearance Center.

p. 296 Table 12–3 From *Organization for Economic Co-operation and Development, Working Paper 14*, "Maintaining Prosperity in an Aging Society" (1998): 53. Reprinted with the permission of the OECD.

p. 298 Figure 12–4 From National Academy on an Aging Society (2000). Reprinted with the permission of the National Academy on an Aging Society.

p. 301 Reprinted from Joel S. Savishinsky, *Breaking the Watch: The Meanings of Retirement in America*. Copyright © 2000 by Joel S. Savishinsky. Used by permission of the publisher, Cornell University Press.

p. 304 Figures 12–5 and 12–6 From Wilms Horgas and Paul Baltes, "Daily Life in Very Old Age: Everyday Activities as an Expression of Successful Living," *The Gerontologist* 38, 5 (1998). Copyright © 1998 by the Gerontological Society of America. Reproduced with permission of the Gerontological Society of America via Copyright Clearance Center.

p. 306 Figure 12–7 and p. 307 Figure 12–8 From Marieke Van Willigen, "Differential Benefits of Volunteering across the Life Course," *Journal of Gerontology* 55B, 5 (2000). Copyright © 2000 by the Gerontological Society of America. Reproduced with permission of the Gerontological Society of America via Copyright Clearance Center.

Chapter 13

p. 315 From *After the Stroke: A Journal by May Sarton*. Copyright © 1988 by May Sarton. Used by permission of W. W. Norton & Company, Inc.

p. 326 From Wendy Adams, Helen McIlvain, Naomi Lacy, Homa Magsi, Benjamin Crabtree, Sharon Yenny, and Michael Sitorius, "Primary Care for Elderly People: Why Do Doctors Find It So Hard?" *The Gerontologist* 42(6): 835–842. Reprinted with permission.

Chapter 14

p. 338 From Gay Becker, "Dying Away From Home: Quandaries of Migration for Elders in Two Ethnic Minorities," *Journal of Gerontology* 57B(2): S79–95. Reprinted with permission.

Chapter 15

p. 378 Figure 15–7 From David MacPherson, "Sex Differences in Retirement Income: Recent Trends and Future Prospects," *Pepper Institute on Aging and Public Policy Working Paper*. Reprinted with the permission of the Pepper Institute on Aging and Public Policy.

Chapter 16

p. 398 From Toni Calasanti and Kathleen Slevin, *Gender, Social Inequality and Aging*, AltaMira Press, 2001, pp. 128–129. Reprinted with permission from the publisher.

Chapter 17

p. 412 Table 17–2: From Robert Binstock, "Older People and Voting Participation: Past and Future," *The Gerontologist* 40 (1) (February 2000). Copyright © 2000 by the Gerontological Society of America. Reprinted with the permission of the Gerontological Society of America via Copyright Clearance Center.

p. 415 Table 17–3 From Robert Binstock, "The 1996 Election: Older Voters and Implications for Policies on Aging," *The Gerontologist* 37 (1997). Copyright © 1997 by the Gerontological Society of America. Reprinted with the permission of the Gerontological Society of America via Copyright Clearance Center.

p. 422 Figure 17–1 From Susan MacManus, *Young v. Old: Generational Combat in the 21st Century*. Copyright © 1996 by Westview Press. Reprinted with the permission of Westview Press, a member of Perseus Books, LLC.

p. 425 From David Shuldiner, *Aging Political Activists: Personal Narratives from the Old Left*, Greenwood Publishing Group, 1995, pp. 48, 60.

Photo Credits

Chapter 1

Page 3 © John Henley/CORBIS *7* © Dan Budnik/Woodfin Camp & Associates; *p. 17* Volume 66, PhotoDisc/Getty.

Chapter 2

Page 23 © Elizabeth Crews/Stock, Boston; *p. 32* © Amy Etra/PhotoEdit; *p. 41* © Hulton-Deutsch Collection/CORBIS.

Chapter 3

Page 49 © Photo Disc/Getty Images; *p. 55* PhotoLink/Volume 24 Education, PhotoDisc/Getty; *p. 64* © Sovfoto/Eastfoto.

Chapter 4

Page 71 © Norbert von der Groeben/The Image Works; *p. 78* © Chet Gordon/The Image Works; *p. 86* © Patrick Ward/CORBIS.

Chapter 5

Page 95 Tomas van Houtryve/AP/Wide World Photos; *p. 101* Timothy H. O'Sullivan/Library of Congress; *p. 112* CORBIS.

Chapter 6

Page 121 © Sondra Dawes/The Image Works; *p. 131* National Eye Institute; *p. 139* © Michael Siluk/The Image Works.

Chapter 7

Page 147 Pete Souza/AP/Wide World Photos; *p. 154* © Tiffany M. Hermon/Journal-Courier/The Image Works; *p. 165* Photodisc Red/Getty Images; *p. 170* Photodisc Blue, Parenting Today CD/Getty Images.

Chapter 8

Page 177 © Ariel Skelley/CORBIS; *p. 182* © Joel Gordon; *p. 187* © Tony Freeman/PhotoEdit; *p. 189* © Ulrike Welsch/Photo Researchers; *p. 200* © Bill Aron/PhotoEdit.

Chapter 9

Page 207 © David Young-Wolff/PhotoEdit; *p. 210* Bettmann/CORBIS; *p. 216* © Lester Sloan/Woodfin Camp & Associates; *p. 220* Todd Dudek/AP/Wide World Photos.

Chapter 10

Page 227 © Michael Newman/PhotoEdit; *p. 237* © Joel Gordon; *p. 246* © Jim Harrison/Stock, Boston.

Chapter 11

Page 255 AP/Wide World Photos; *p. 259* © Bettmann/CORBIS; *p. 266* © Tim Boyle/Getty Images; *p. 274* © Jeff Lowenthal/Woodfin Camp & Associates.

Chapter 12

Page 283 Ed Reinke/AP/Wide World Photos; *p. 290* © Syracuse Newspapers/Suzanne Dunn/The Image Works; *p. 305* © Mike Greenlar/The Image Works.

Chapter 13

Page 313 Comstock/Getty Images; *p. 318* © Robert Mora/Getty Images; *p. 320* Mike Nelson/AP/Wide World Photos.

Chapter 14

Page 335 © Mark Godfrey/The Image Works; *p. 345* © Bob Daemmrich/The Image Works; *p. 350* Carl D. Walsh/AP/Wide World Photos.

Chapter 15

Page 357 Jacqueline Roggenbrodt/AP Wide World Photos; *p. 368* © Joel Gordon; *p. 377* Keith Brofsky/PhotodiscGreen/Getty Images.

Chapter 16

Page 383 © Jenny Nordquist/CORBIS; *p. 389* Photodisc Green/Getty Images.

Chapter 17

Page 409 Susan Walsh/AP/Wide World Photos; *p. 413* © Marty Katz/The Image Works; *p. 418* Donnell Collins/AP/Wide World Photos.

Author Index

Note: *f* indicates an additional figure; *t* indicates an additional table.

Subject Index

Note: *f* indicates an additional figure; *t* indicates and additional table.